Dutch-English Dictionary

Engels-Nederlands Woordenboek

Berlitz Dictionaries

Dansk	Engelsk, Fransk, Italiensk, Spansk, Tysk
Deutsch	Dänisch, Englisch, Finnisch, Französisch, Italienisch, Niederländisch, Norwegisch, Portugiesisch, Schwedisch, Spanisch
English	Danish, Dutch, Finnish, French, German, Italian, Norwegian, Portuguese, Spanish, Swedish
Español	Alemán, Danés, Finlandés, Francés, Holandés, Inglés, Noruego, Sueco
Français	Allemand, Anglais, Danois, Espagnol, Finnois, Italien, Néerlandais, Norvégien, Portugais, Suédois
Italiano	Danese, Finlandese, Francese, Inglese, Norvegese, Olandese, Svedese, Tedesco
Nederlands	Duits, Engels, Frans, Italiaans, Portugees, Spaans
Norsk	Engelsk, Fransk, Italiensk, Spansk, Tysk
Português	Alemão, Francês, Holandês, Inglês, Sueco
Suomi	Englanti, Espanja, Italia, Ranska, Ruotsi, Saksa
Svenska	Engelska, Finska, Franska, Italienska, Portugisiska, Spanska, Tyska

Dutch-English Dictionary

Engels-Nederlands Woordenboek

Berlitz Publishing /
APA Publications GmbH & Co. Verlag KG,
Singapore Branch, Singapore

CONTACTING THE EDITORS

Every effort has been made to provide accurate information in this publication, but changes are inevitable. The publisher cannot be responsible for any resulting loss, inconvenience, or injury. We would appreciate it if readers would call our attention to any errors or outdated information by contacting Berlitz Publishing, 95 Progress Street, Union, NJ 07083, USA. Fax: 1-908-206-1103. email: comments@berlitzbooks.com

Inhoud

Contents

Voorwoord

Bij het selecteren van de 12 500 woordbegrippen in beide talen voor dit woordenboek stond de redactie in de allereerste plaats de behoeften van de reiziger voor ogen. Dit boekje zal van grote waarde blijken te zijn voor de vele reizigers, toeristen en zakenmensen die het waarderen zich verzekerd te weten van een klein en praktisch woordenboek. Het biedt hen – evenals aan beginners en gevorderden – de benodigde woordenschat, alsook sleutelwoorden en uitdrukkingen voor dagelijks gebruik.

Zoals onze succesvolle taal- en reisgidsen, zijn deze woordenboekjes – tot stand gekomen met behulp van een computer data bank – speciaal ontworpen om in jaszak of handtas gestoken te worden.

Behalve wat u normaliter in woordenboeken vindt, biedt Berlitz nog de volgende extra's:

● een transcriptie van elk grondwoord in het internationale fonetische alfabet (IPA), hetgeen het uitspreken van woorden waarvan de spelling moeilijk lijkt vergemakkelijkt

● een unieke, praktische woordenlijst van culinaire begrippen om het lezen van een menu in een buitenlands restaurant te vereenvoudigen en de mysteries te ontrafelen van bijzondere gerechten

● nuttige informatie over tijdsaanduiding, getallen, de vervoeging van onregelmatige werkwoorden, veel gebruikte afkortingen en een lijst van veel voorkomende uitdrukkingen.

Hoewel geen enkel woordenboek van dit formaat kan pretenderen volledig te zijn, verwachten wij toch dat de gebruiker van dit boek zich goed uitgerust zal voelen om buitenlandse reizen met vertrouwen te ondernemen. Wij zouden het evenwel op prijs stellen opmerkingen, kritiek of suggesties te ontvangen, die mogelijkerwijs kunnen helpen bij het voorbereiden van toekomstige uitgaven.

Preface

In selecting the 12.500 word-concepts in each language for this dictionary, the editors have had the traveller's needs foremost in mind. This book will prove invaluable to all the millions of travellers, tourists and business people who appreciate the reassurance a small and practical dictionary can provide. It offers them—as it does beginners and students—all the basic vocabulary they are going to encounter and to have to use, giving the key words and expressions to allow them to cope in everyday situations.

Like our successful phrase books and travel guides, these dictionaries—created with the help of a computer data bank—are designed to slip into pocket or purse, and thus have a role as handy companions at all times.

Besides just about everything you normally find in dictionaries, there are these Berlitz bonuses:

- imitated pronunciation next to each foreign-word entry, making it easy to read and enunciate words whose spelling may look forbidding

- a unique, practical glossary to simplify reading a foreign restaurant menu and to take the mystery out of complicated dishes and indecipherable names on bills of fare

- useful information on how to tell the time and how to count, on conjugating irregular verbs, commonly seen abbreviations and converting to the metric system, in addition to basic phrases.

While no dictionary of this size can pretend to completeness, we expect the user of this book will feel well armed to affront foreign travel with confidence. We should, however, be very pleased to receive comments, criticism and suggestions that you think may be of help in preparing future editions.

dutch-english

nederlands-engels

Afkortingen

adj	bijvoeglijk naamwoord	*p*	verleden tijd
adv	bijwoord	*pl*	meervoud
Am	Amerikaans	*plAm*	meervoud (Amerikaans)
art	lidwoord	*pp*	voltooid deelwoord
c	gemeenslachtig	*pr*	tegenwoordige tijd
conj	voegwoord	*pref*	voorvoegsel
n	zelfstandig naamwoord	*prep*	voorzetsel
nAm	zelfstandig naamwoord	*pron*	voornaamwoord
	(Amerikaans)	*v*	werkwoord
nt	onzijdig	*vAm*	werkwoord
num	telwoord		(Amerikaans)

Inleiding

Het woordenboek is zodanig opgezet, dat het zoveel mogelijk beantwoordt aan de eisen van de praktijk. Onnodige taalkundige aanduidingen zijn achterwege gelaten. De volgorde van de woorden is strikt alfabetisch, ook als het samengestelde woorden of woorden met een koppelteken betreft. Als enige uitzondering op deze regel zijn enkele idiomatische uitdrukkingen opgenomen als een afzonderlijk artikel, waarbij het meest toonaangevende woord van de uitdrukking bepalend is voor de alfabetische rangschikking. Wanneer bij een grondwoord nog daarvan afgeleide samenstellingen of uitdrukkingen zijn gegeven, staan ook deze weer in alfabetische volgorde.

Achter elk grondwoord vindt u een fonetische transcriptie (zie de Gids voor de uitspraak) en vervolgens, wanneer van toepassing, de woordsoort. Wanneer bij hetzelfde grondwoord meerdere woordsoorten behoren, zijn de vertalingen telkens naar de woordsoort gegroepeerd.

Het meervoud van zelfstandige naamwoorden is altijd opgenomen, wanneer dat onregelmatig is; tevens is het meervoud gegeven van bepaalde woorden waarover de gebruiker in twijfel zou kunnen verkeren.

Wanneer in onregelmatige meervoudsvormen of in afgeleide samenstellingen en uitdrukkingen het teken ~ wordt gebruikt, duidt dit een herhaling aan van het grondwoord als geheel.

In onregelmatige meervoudsvormen van samengestelde woorden wordt alleen het gedeelte, dat verandert, voluit geschreven en het onveranderde deel aangegeven door een liggend streepje (-).

Een sterretje (*) voor een werkwoord geeft aan, dat dit werkwoord onregelmatig is. Voor nadere bijzonderheden kunt u de lijst van onregelmatige werkwoorden raadplegen.

Dit woordenboek is gebaseerd op de Britse spelling. Alle woorden en woordbetekenissen die overwegend Amerikaans zijn, zijn als zodanig aangegeven (zie lijst van gebezigde afkortingen).

Uitspraak

Elk trefwoord in dit deel van het woordenboek wordt gevolgd door een transcriptie in het internationale fonetische alfabet (IPA). In dit alfabet vertegenwoordigt elk teken altijd dezelfde klank. Letters die hieronder niet beschreven zijn worden min of meer op dezelfde wijze uitgesproken als in het Nederlands.

Medeklinkers

b	nooit scherp zoals in he**b**
d	nooit scherp zoals in raa**d**
ð	als de **z** in **z**ee, maar lispend uitgesproken
g	als een zachte **k**, zoals in het Franse **g**arçon
ŋ	als de **ng** in ba**ng**
r	plaats de tong eerst als voor de ʒ (zie beneden), open dan de mond enigszins en beweeg de tong daarbij naar beneden
ʃ	als de **sj** in **sj**ofel
θ	als de **s** in **s**amen, maar lispend uitgesproken
v	als de **w** in **w**aar
w	een korte, zwakke **oe**-klank
ʒ	als de **g** in eta**g**e

N.B. De lettergroep **sj** moet worden uitgesproken als een **s** gevolgd door een **j**-klank, maar *niet* als in **sj**ofel.

Klinkers

ɑː	als de **aa** in m**aa**t
æ	een klank tussen de **a** in **a**ls en de **e** in b**e**st
ʌ	min of meer als de **a** in **a**ls
e	als in b**e**st
ɛ	als de **e** in b**e**st, maar met de tong wat lager
ə	als de **e** in acht**e**r
ɔ	min of meer als de **o** in p**o**t
u	als de **oe** in g**oe**d, maar korter

1) Een dubbele punt (:) geeft aan dat de voorafgaande klinker lang is.

2) Enkele aan het Frans ontleende Engelse woorden bevatten neusklanken, die aangegeven worden d.m.v. een tilde boven de klinker (b.v. ã). Deze worden door de neus en de mond tegelijkertijd uitgesproken.

Tweeklanken

Een tweeklank bestaat uit twee klinkers, waarvan er één sterk is (beklemtoond) en de andere zwak (niet beklemtoond) en die samen als één klinker worden uitgesproken, zoals **ei** in het Nederlands. In het Engels is de tweede klinker altijd zwak. Een tweeklank kan soms gevolgd worden door een [ə]. In dergelijke gevallen heeft de tweede klinker van de tweeklank de neiging zeer zwak te worden.

Klemtoon

Het teken (') geeft aan dat de klemtoon op de volgende lettergreep valt. Als in een woord meer dan één lettergreep wordt beklemtoond, wordt het teken (ı) geplaatst vóór de lettergreep, waarop de bijklemtoon valt.

Amerikaanse uitspraak

Onze transcriptie geeft de gebruikelijke Engelse uitspraak aan. De Amerikaanse uitspraak verschilt in enkele opzichten van het Britse Engels en kent daarbij nog belangrijke regionale verschillen. Hier volgen enkele van de meest opvallende afwijkingen:

1) In tegenstelling tot in het Britse Engels wordt de **r** ook uitgesproken voor een medeklinker en aan het einde van een woord.

2) In vele woorden (b.v. *ask*, *castle*, *laugh* enz.) wordt [ɑ:] uitgesproken als [æ:].

3) De [ɔ]-klank wordt in het Amerikaans uitgesproken als [ɑ], vaak ook als [ɔ:].

4) In woorden als *duty*, *tune*, *new* enz. valt in het Amerikaans de [j]-klank voor de [u:] vaak weg.

5) Bovendien wordt bij een aantal woorden in het Amerikaans de klemtoon anders gelegd.

A

a [ei,ə] *art* (an) een *art*

abbey ['æbi] *n* abdij *c*

abbreviation [ə,bri:vi'eiʃən] *n* afkorting *c*

aberration [,æbə'reiʃən] *n* afwijking *c*

ability [ə'biləti] *n* bekwaamheid *c*; vermogen *nt*

able ['eibəl] *adj* in staat; capabel, bekwaam; *be ~ to* in staat *zijn om*; *kunnen*

abnormal [æb'nɔ:məl] *adj* abnormaal

aboard [ə'bɔ:d] *adv* aan boord

abolish [ə'bɔliʃ] *v* afschaffen

abortion [ə'bɔ:ʃən] *n* abortus *c*

about [ə'baut] *prep* over; betreffende, omtrent; om; *adv* omstreeks, ongeveer; omheen

above [ə'bʌv] *prep* boven; *adv* boven

abroad [ə'brɔ:d] *adv* naar het buitenland, in het buitenland

abscess ['æbses] *n* abces *nt*

absence ['æbsəns] *n* afwezigheid *c*

absent ['æbsənt] *adj* afwezig

absolutely ['æbsəlu:tli] *adv* absoluut

abstain from [əb'stein] zich *onthouden van*

abstract ['æbstrækt] *adj* abstract

absurd [əb'sə:d] *adj* absurd, ongerijmd

abundance [ə'bʌndəns] *n* overvloed *c*

abundant [ə'bʌndənt] *adj* overvloedig

abuse [ə'bju:s] *n* misbruik *nt*

abyss [ə'bis] *n* afgrond *c*

academy [ə'kædəmi] *n* academie *c*

accelerate [ək'seləreit] *v* versnellen

accelerator [ək'seləreitə] *n* gaspedaal *nt*

accent ['æksənt] *n* accent *nt*; nadruk *c*

accept [ək'sept] *v* aanvaarden, *aannemen*; accepteren

access ['ækses] *n* toegang *c*

accessary [ək'sesəri] *n* medeplichtige *c*

accessible [ək'sesəbəl] *adj* toegankelijk

accessories [ək'sesəriz] *pl* toebehoren *pl*, accessoires *pl*

accident ['æksidənt] *n* ongeluk *nt*, ongeval *nt*

accidental [,æksi'dentəl] *adj* toevallig

accommodate [ə'kɔmədeit] *v* *onderbrengen*

accommodation [ə,kɔmə'deiʃən] *n* accommodatie *c*, logies *nt*, onderdak *nt*

accompany [ə'kʌmpəni] *v* vergezellen; begeleiden

accomplish [ə'kʌmpliʃ] *v* *volbrengen*; bereiken

in accordance with [in ə'kɔ:dəns wið] ingevolge

according to [ə'kɔ:diŋ tu:] volgens; overeenkomstig

account [ə'kaunt] *n* rekening *c*; ver-

slag *nt*; ~ **for** verantwoorden; **on** ~
of vanwege

accountable [ə'kauntəbəl] *adj* verklaarbaar

accurate ['ækjurət] *adj* nauwkeurig

accuse [ə'kju:z] *v* beschuldigen; aanklagen

accused [ə'kju:zd] *n* verdachte *c*

accustom [ə'kʌstəm] *v* wennen; **accustomed** gewoon, gewend

ache [eik] *v* pijn *doen; *n* pijn *c*

achieve [ə'tʃi:v] *v* bereiken; presteren

achievement [ə'tʃi:vmənt] *n* prestatie
c

acid ['æsid] *n* zuur *nt*

acknowledge [ək'nɔlidʒ] *v* erkennen;
*toegeven; bevestigen

acne ['ækni] *n* acne *c*

acorn ['eikɔ:n] *n* eikel *c*

acquaintance [ə'kweintəns] *n* bekende
c, kennis *c*

acquire [ə'kwaiə] *v* *verwerven

acquisition [,ækwi'ziʃən] *n* acquisitie *c*

acquittal [ə'kwitəl] *n* vrijspraak *c*

across [ə'krɔs] *prep* over; aan de andere kant van; *adv* aan de overkant

act [ækt] *n* daad *c*; bedrijf *nt*, akte *c*;
nummer *nt*; *v *optreden, hande-
len; zich *gedragen; toneelspelen

action ['ækʃən] *n* actie *c*, handeling *c*

active ['æktiv] *adj* actief; bedrijvig

activity [æk'tivəti] *n* activiteit *c*

actor ['æktə] *n* acteur *c*, toneelspeler *c*

actress ['æktris] *n* actrice *c*, toneelspeelster *c*

actual ['æktʃuəl] *adj* eigenlijk, werkelijk

actually ['æktʃuəli] *adv* feitelijk

acute [ə'kju:t] *adj* acuut

adapt [ə'dæpt] *v* aanpassen

adaptor [ə'dæptə] *n* verbindingsstuk
nt

add [æd] *v* optellen; toevoegen

addition [ə'diʃən] *n* optelling *c*; toe-

additional [ə'diʃənəl] *adj* extra; bijkomend; bijkomstig

address [ə'dres] *n* adres *nt*; *v* adresseren; *aanspreken

addressee [,ædre'si:] *n* geadresseerde
c

adequate ['ædikwət] *adj* toereikend;
adequaat, passend

adjective ['ædʒiktiv] *n* bijvoeglijk
naamwoord

adjourn [ə'dʒə:n] *v* uitstellen

adjust [ə'dʒʌst] *v* afstellen; aanpassen

administer [əd'ministə] *v* toedienen

administration [əd,mini'streiʃən] *n* administratie *c*; beheer *nt*

administrative [əd'ministrətiv] *adj* administratief; bestuurlijk; ~ **law** bestuursrecht *nt*

admiral ['ædmərəl] *n* admiraal *c*

admiration [,ædmə'reiʃən] *n* bewondering *c*

admire [əd'maiə] *v* bewonderen

admission [əd'miʃən] *n* toegang *c*;
toelating *c*

admit [əd'mit] *v* *toelaten; *toegeven,
bekennen

admittance [əd'mitəns] *n* toegang *c*;
no ~ verboden toegang

adopt [ə'dɔpt] *v* adopteren; *aannemen

adult ['ædʌlt] *n* volwassene *c*; *adj* volwassen

advance [əd'va:ns] *n* vooruitgang *c*;
voorschot *nt*; *v *vooruitgaan;
*voorschieten; **in** ~ vooruit, van tevoren

advanced [əd'va:nst] *adj* gevorderd

advantage [əd'va:ntidʒ] *n* voordeel *nt*

advantageous [,ædvən'teidʒəs] *adj*
voordelig

adventure [əd'ventʃə] *n* avontuur *nt*

adverb ['ædvə:b] *n* bijwoord *nt*

advertisement [əd'və:tismənt] *n* advertentie c; annonce c

advertising ['ædvətaiziŋ] n reclame c

advice [əd'vais] n advies nt, raad c

advise [əd'vaiz] v adviseren, *aanraden

advocate ['ædvəkət] n voorstander c

aerial ['ɛəriəl] n antenne c

aeroplane ['ɛərəplein] n vliegtuig nt

affair [ə'fɛə] n aangelegenheid c; verhouding c, affaire c

affect [ə'fekt] v beïnvloeden; *betreffen

affected [ə'fektid] adj geaffecteerd

affection [ə'fekʃən] n aandoening c; genegenheid c

affectionate [ə'fekʃənit] adj lief, aanhankelijk

affiliated [ə'filieitid] adj aangesloten

affirmative [ə'fə:mətiv] adj bevestigend

affliction [ə'flikʃən] n leed nt

afford [ə'fɔ:d] v zich veroorloven

afraid [ə'freid] adj angstig, bang; *be ~ bang *zijn

Africa ['æfrikə] Afrika

African ['æfrikən] adj Afrikaans; n Afrikaan c

after ['ɑ:ftə] prep na; achter; conj nadat

afternoon [,ɑ:ftə'nu:n] n middag c, namiddag c; this ~ vanmiddag

afterwards ['ɑ:ftəwədz] adv later; nadien, naderhand

again [ə'gen] adv weer; opnieuw; ~ and again telkens

against [ə'genst] prep tegen

age [eidʒ] n leeftijd c; ouderdom c; of ~ meerderjarig; under ~ minderjarig

aged ['eidʒid] adj bejaard; oud

agency ['eidʒənsi] n agentschap nt; bureau nt; vertegenwoordiging c

agenda [ə'dʒendə] n agenda c

agent ['eidʒənt] n vertegenwoordiger

c, agent c

aggressive [ə'gresiv] adj agressief

ago [ə'gou] adv geleden

agrarian [ə'grɛəriən] adj agrarisch, landbouw-

agree [ə'gri:] v het eens *zijn; toestemmen; *overeenkomen

agreeable [ə'gri:əbəl] adj aangenaam

agreement [ə'gri:mənt] n contract nt; akkoord nt, overeenkomst c

agriculture ['ægrikʌltʃə] n landbouw c

ahead [ə'hed] adv vooruit; ~ of voor; *go ~ *doorgaan; straight ~ rechtuit

aid [eid] n hulp c; v *bijstaan, *helpen

AIDS [eidz] n AIDS

ailment ['eilmənt] n kwaal c; ziekte c

aim [eim] n doel nt; ~ at richten op, mikken op; beogen, nastreven

air [ɛə] n lucht c; v luchten

air-conditioning ['ɛəkən,diʃəniŋ] n luchtverversing c; **air-conditioned** adj air conditioned

aircraft ['ɛəkrɑ:ft] n (pl ~) vliegtuig nt; toestel nt

airfield ['ɛəfi:ld] n vliegveld nt

air-filter ['ɛə,filtə] n luchtfilter nt

airline ['ɛəlain] n luchtvaartmaatschappij c

airmail ['ɛəmeil] n luchtpost c

airplane ['ɛəplein] nAm vliegtuig nt

airport ['ɛəpɔ:t] n luchthaven c

air-sickness ['ɛə,siknəs] n luchtziekte c

airtight ['ɛətait] adj luchtdicht

airy ['ɛəri] adj luchtig

aisle [ail] n zijbeuk c; gangpad nt

alarm [ə'lɑ:m] n alarm nt; v alarmeren

alarm-clock [ə'lɑ:mklɔk] n wekker c

album ['ælbəm] n album nt

alcohol ['ælkəhɔl] n alcohol c

alcoholic [,ælkə'hɔlik] adj alcoholisch

ale [eil] n bier nt

algebra ['ældʒibrə] *n* algebra *c*
Algeria [æl'dʒiəriə] Algerije
Algerian [æl'dʒiəriən] *adj* Algerijns; *n* Algerijn *c*
alien ['eiliən] *n* buitenlander *c*; vreemdeling *c*; *adj* buitenlands
alike [ə'laik] *adj* eender, gelijk
alimony ['æliməni] *n* alimentatie *c*
alive [ə'laiv] *adj* in leven, levend
all [ɔ:l] *adj* al; ~ **in** alles inbegrepen; ~ **right!** goed!; **at** ~ helemaal
allergic [ə'lədʒik] *adj* allergisch
allergy ['ælədʒi] *n* allergie *c*
alley ['æli] *n* steeg *c*
alliance [ə'laiəns] *n* bondgenootschap *nt*
allot [ə'lɔt] *v* *toewijzen
allow [ə'lau] *v* veroorloven, *toestaan; ~ **to** *laten; *be allowed *mogen; *be allowed to *mogen
allowance [ə'lauəns] *n* toelage *c*
all-round [,ɔ:l'raund] *adj* veelzijdig
almanac ['ɔ:lmənæk] *n* almanak *c*
almond ['ɑ:mənd] *n* amandel *c*
almost ['ɔ:lmoust] *adv* bijna; haast
alone [ə'loun] *adv* alleen
along [ə'lɔŋ] *prep* langs
aloud [ə'laud] *adv* hardop
alphabet ['ælfəbet] *n* alfabet *nt*
already [ɔ:l'redi] *adv* reeds, al
also ['ɔ:lsou] *adv* ook; tevens, eveneens
altar ['ɔ:ltə] *n* altaar *nt*
alter ['ɔ:ltə] *v* wijzigen, veranderen
alteration [,ɔ:ltə'reiʃən] *n* wijziging *c*, verandering *c*
alternate [ɔ:l'tə:nət] *adj* afwisselend
alternative [ɔ:l'tə:nətiv] *n* alternatief *nt*
although [ɔ:l'ðou] *conj* ofschoon, hoewel
altitude ['æltitju:d] *n* hoogte *c*
alto ['æltou] *n* (pl ~s) alt *c*
altogether [,ɔ:ltə'geðə] *adv* helemaal; in totaal
always ['ɔ:lweiz] *adv* altijd
am [æm] *v* (pr be)
amaze [ə'meiz] *v* verwonderen, verbazen
amazement [ə'meizmənt] *n* verbazing *c*
ambassador [æm'bæsədə] *n* ambassadeur *c*
amber ['æmbə] *n* barnsteen *nt*
ambiguous [æm'bigjuəs] *adj* dubbelzinnig; onduidelijk
ambitious [æm'biʃəs] *adj* ambitieus; eerzuchtig
ambulance ['æmbjuləns] *n* ziekenauto *c*, ambulance *c*
ambush ['æmbuʃ] *n* hinderlaag *c*
America [ə'merikə] Amerika
American [ə'merikən] *adj* Amerikaans; *n* Amerikaan *c*
amethyst ['æmiθist] *n* amethist *c*
amid [ə'mid] *prep* onder; tussen, midden in, te midden van
ammonia [ə'mouniə] *n* ammonia *c*
amnesty ['æmnisti] *n* amnestie *c*
among [ə'mʌŋ] *prep* te midden van; tussen, onder; ~ **other things** onder andere
amount [ə'maunt] *n* hoeveelheid *c*; som *c*, bedrag *nt*; ~ **to** *bedragen
amuse [ə'mju:z] *v* amuseren, vermaken
amusement [ə'mju:zmənt] *n* amusement *nt*, vermaak *nt*
amusing [ə'mju:ziŋ] *adj* amusant
anaemia [ə'ni:miə] *n* bloedarmoede *c*
anaesthesia [,ænis'θi:ziə] *n* verdoving *c*
anaesthetic [,ænis'θetik] *n* pijnstillend middel
analyse ['ænəlaiz] *v* ontleden, analyseren
analysis [ə'næləsis] *n* (pl -ses) analyse *c*

analyst ['ænəlist] *n* analist *c*; analyticus *c*

anarchy ['ænəki] *n* anarchie *c*

anatomy [ə'nætəmi] *n* anatomie *c*

ancestor ['ænsestə] *n* voorvader *c*

anchor ['æŋkə] *n* anker *nt*

anchovy ['æntʃəvi] *n* ansjovis *c*

ancient ['einʃənt] *adj* oud; ouderwets, verouderd; oeroud

and [ænd, ənd] *conj* en

angel ['eindʒəl] *n* engel *c*

anger ['æŋgə] *n* toorn *c*, boosheid *c*; woede *c*

angle ['æŋgəl] *v* hengelen; *n* hoek *c*

angry ['æŋgri] *adj* kwaad

animal ['æniməl] *n* dier *nt*

ankle ['æŋkəl] *n* enkel *c*

annex¹ ['æneks] *n* bijgebouw *nt*; bijlage *c*

annex² [ə'neks] *v* annexeren

anniversary [,æni'və:səri] *n* verjaardag *c*

announce [ə'nauns] *v* bekendmaken, aankondigen

announcement [ə'naunsmənt] *n* aankondiging *c*, bekendmaking *c*

annoy [ə'nɔi] *v* irriteren, ergeren

annoyance [ə'nɔiəns] *n* ergernis *c*

annoying [ə'nɔiiŋ] *adj* vervelend, hinderlijk

annual ['ænjuəl] *adj* jaarlijks; *n* jaarboek *nt*

per annum [pər 'ænəm] jaarlijks

anonymous [ə'nɔniməs] *adj* anoniem

another [ə'nʌðə] *adj* nog een; een ander

answer ['ɑːnsə] *v* antwoorden; beantwoorden; *n* antwoord *nt*

ant [ænt] *n* mier *c*

anthology [æn'θɔlədʒi] *n* bloemlezing *c*

antibiotic [,æntibai'ɔtik] *n* antibioticum *nt*

anticipate [æn'tisipeit] *v* verwachten, *voorzien; *voorkomen

antifreeze ['æntifri:z] *n* antivries *c*

antipathy [æn'tipəθi] *n* afkeer *c*

antique [æn'ti:k] *adj* antiek; *n* antiquiteit *c*; ~ **dealer** antiquair *c*

antiquity [æn'tikwəti] *n* Oudheid *c*; **antiquities** *pl* oudheden *pl*

antiseptic [,ænti'septik] *n* antiseptisch middel

antlers ['æntləz] *pl* gewei *nt*

anxiety [æŋ'zaiəti] *n* bezorgdheid *c*

anxious ['æŋkʃəs] *adj* verlangend; bezorgd

any ['eni] *adj* enig

anybody ['enibɔdi] *pron* wie dan ook

anyhow ['enihau] *adv* hoe dan ook

anyone ['eniwʌn] *pron* iedereen

anything ['eniθiŋ] *pron* wat dan ook

anyway ['eniwei] *adv* in elk geval

anywhere ['eniweə] *adv* waar dan ook; overal

apart [ə'pɑːt] *adv* apart, afzonderlijk; ~ **from** afgezien van

apartment [ə'pɑːtmənt] *nAm* appartement *nt*, flat *c*; etage *c*; ~ **house** *Am* flatgebouw *nt*

aperitif [ə'perətiv] *n* aperitief *nt/c*

apologize [ə'pɔlədʒaiz] *v* zich verontschuldigen

apology [ə'pɔlədʒi] *n* excuus *nt*, verontschuldiging *c*

apparatus [,æpə'reitəs] *n* apparaat *nt*, toestel *nt*

apparent [ə'pærənt] *adj* schijnbaar; duidelijk

apparently [ə'pærəntli] *adv* blijkbaar; klaarblijkelijk

apparition [,æpə'riʃən] *n* verschijning *c*

appeal [ə'pi:l] *n* beroep *nt*

appear [ə'piə] *v* *lijken, *schijnen; *blijken; *verschijnen; *optreden

appearance [ə'piərəns] *n* voorkomen *nt*; aanblik *c*; optreden *nt*

appendicitis [ə,pendi'saitis] n blinde-darmontsteking c

appendix [ə'pendiks] n (pl -dices, -dixes) blindedarm c

appetite ['æpətait] n trek c, eetlust c

appetizer ['æpətaizə] n borrelhapje nt

appetizing ['æpətaizin] adj smakelijk

applause [ə'plɔ:z] n applaus nt

apple ['æpəl] n appel c

appliance [ə'plaiəns] n toestel nt, apparaat nt

application [,æpli'keiʃən] n toepassing c; aanvraag c; sollicitatie c

apply [ə'plai] v toepassen; gebruiken; solliciteren; *gelden

appoint [ə'pɔint] v aanstellen, benoemen

appointment [ə'pɔintmənt] n afspraak c; benoeming c

appreciate [ə'pri:ʃieit] v schatten; waarderen, op prijs stellen

appreciation [ə,pri:ʃi'eiʃən] n schatting c; waardering c

approach [ə'prɔutʃ] v naderen; n aanpak c; toegang c

appropriate [ə'prɔupriət] adj juist, geschikt, passend

approval [ə'pru:vəl] n goedkeuring c; instemming c; **on ~** op zicht

approve [ə'pru:v] v goedkeuren; **~ of** instemmen met

approximate [ə'prɔksimət] adj bij benadering

approximately [ə'prɔksimətli] adv circa, ongeveer

apricot ['eiprikɔt] n abrikoos c

April ['eiprəl] april

apron ['eiprən] n schort c

Arab ['ærəb] adj Arabisch; n Arabier c

arbitrary ['a:bitrəri] adj willekeurig

arcade [a:'keid] n zuilengang c, galerij c

arch [a:tʃ] n boog c; gewelf nt

archaeologist [,a:ki'ɔlədʒist] n archeoloog c

archaeology [,a:ki'ɔlədʒi] n oudheidkunde c, archeologie c

archbishop [,a:tʃ'biʃəp] n aartsbisschop c

arched [a:tʃt] adj boogvormig

architect ['a:kitekt] n architect c

architecture ['a:kitektʃə] n bouwkunde c, architectuur c

archives ['a:kaivz] pl archief nt

are [a:] v (pr be)

area ['ɛəriə] n streek c; gebied nt; oppervlakte c; **~ code** netnummer nt

Argentina [,a:dʒən'ti:nə] Argentinië

Argentinian [,a:dʒən'tiniən] adj Argentijns; n Argentijn c

argue ['a:gju:] v argumenteren, debatteren, discussiëren; redetwisten

argument ['a:gjumənt] n argument nt; discussie c; woordenwisseling c

arid ['ærid] adj dor

***arise** [ə'raiz] v *oprijzen, *ontstaan

arithmetic [ə'riθmətik] n rekenkunde c

arm [a:m] n arm c; wapen nt; leuning c; v bewapenen

armchair ['a:mtʃɛə] n fauteuil c, leunstoel c

armed [a:md] adj gewapend; **~ forces** strijdkrachten pl

armour ['a:mə] n harnas c

army ['a:mi] n leger nt

aroma [ə'roumə] n aroma nt

around [ə'raund] prep om, rond; adv rondom

arrange [ə'reindʒ] v rangschikken, ordenen; regelen

arrangement [ə'reindʒmənt] n regeling c

arrest [ə'rest] v arresteren; n aanhouding c, arrestatie c

arrival [ə'raivəl] n aankomst c; komst c

arrive [ə'raiv] v *aankomen

arrow ['ærou] *n* pijl *c*

art [ɑ:t] *n* kunst *c*; vaardigheid *c*; ~ **collection** kunstverzameling *c*; ~ **exhibition** kunsttentoonstelling *c*; ~ **gallery** kunstgalerij *c*; ~ **history** kunstgeschiedenis *c*; **arts and crafts** kunstnijverheid *c*; ~ **school** kunstacademie *c*

artery ['ɑːtəri] *n* slagader *c*

artichoke ['ɑːtitʃouk] *n* artisjok *c*

article ['ɑːtikəl] *n* artikel *nt*; lidwoord *nt*

artifice ['ɑːtifis] *n* list *c*

artificial [,ɑːti'fiʃəl] *adj* kunstmatig

artist ['ɑːtist] *n* kunstenaar *c*; kunstenares *c*

artistic [ɑː'tistik] *adj* artistiek, kunstzinnig

as [æz] *conj* als, zoals; even; aangezien, omdat; ~ **from** vanaf; met ingang van; ~ **if** alsof

asbestos [æz'bestɔs] *n* asbest *nt*

ascend [ə'send] *v* omhoog *gaan; *opstijgen; *beklimmen

ascent [ə'sent] *n* stijging *c*; beklimming *c*

ascertain [,æsə'tein] *v* constateren; zich vergewissen van, zich vergewissen van

ash [æʃ] *n* as *c*

ashamed [ə'feimd] *adj* beschaamd; *be ~ zich schamen

ashore [ə'ʃɔː] *adv* aan land

ashtray ['æʃtrei] *n* asbak *c*

Asia ['eiʃə] Azië

Asian ['eiʃən] *adj* Aziatisch; *n* Aziaat *c*

aside [ə'said] *adv* opzij, terzijde

ask [ɑːsk] *v* *vragen; *verzoeken; uitnodigen

asleep [ə'sliːp] *adj* in slaap

asparagus [ə'spærəgəs] *n* asperge *c*

aspect ['æspekt] *n* aspect *nt*

asphalt ['æsfælt] *n* asfalt *nt*

aspire [ə'spaiə] *v* streven

aspirin ['æspərin] *n* aspirine *c*

ass [æs] *n* ezel *c*

assassination [ə,sæsi'neiʃən] *n* moord *c*

assault [ə'sɔːlt] *v* *aanvallen; aanranden

assemble [ə'sembəl] *v* *bijeenbrengen; in elkaar zetten, monteren

assembly [ə'sembli] *n* vergadering *c*, bijeenkomst *c*

assignment [ə'sainmənt] *n* opdracht *c*

assign to [ə'sain] *opdragen aan; *toeschrijven aan

assist [ə'sist] *v* *bijstaan, *helpen; ~ **at** bijwonen

assistance [ə'sistəns] *n* hulp *c*; steun *c*, bijstand *c*

assistant [ə'sistənt] *n* assistent *c*

associate [ə'souʃiət] *n* partner *c*, vennoot *c*; bondgenoot *c*; lid *nt*; *v* associëren; ~ **with** *omgaan met

association [ə,sousi'eiʃən] *n* genootschap *nt*, vereniging *c*

assort [ə'sɔːt] *v* sorteren

assortment [ə'sɔːtmənt] *n* assortiment *nt*, sortering *c*

assume [ə'sjuːm] *v* *aannemen, veronderstellen

assure [ə'ʃuə] *v* verzekeren

asthma ['æsmə] *n* astma *nt*

astonish [ə'stɔniʃ] *v* verbazen

astonishing [ə'stɔniʃiŋ] *adj* verbazend

astonishment [ə'stɔniʃmənt] *n* verbazing *c*

astronomy [ə'strɔnəmi] *n* sterrenkunde *c*

asylum [ə'sailəm] *n* asiel *nt*; gesticht *nt*, tehuis *nt*

at [æt] *prep* in, bij, op; naar

ate [et] *v* (p eat)

atheist ['eiθiist] *n* atheïst *c*

athlete ['æθliːt] *n* atleet *c*

athletics [æθ'letiks] *pl* atletiek *c*

Atlantic [ət'læntik] Atlantische Oceaan

atmosphere ['ætməsfiə] n atmosfeer c; sfeer c, stemming c

atom ['ætəm] n atoom nt

atomic [ə'tɔmik] adj atomisch; atoom-

atomizer ['ætəmaizə] n sproeier c; spuitbus c, verstuiver c

attach [ə'tætʃ] v hechten, vastmaken; aanhechten; bijvoegen; **attached to** gehecht aan

attack [ə'tæk] v *aanvallen; n aanval c

attain [ə'tein] v bereiken

attainable [ə'teinəbəl] adj haalbaar; bereikbaar

attempt [ə'tempt] v proberen, trachten; beproeven; n poging c

attend [ə'tend] v bijwonen; ~ **on** bedienen; ~ **to** passen op, zich *bezighouden met; letten op, aandacht besteden aan

attendance [ə'tendəns] n opkomst c

attendant [ə'tendənt] n oppasser c

attention [ə'tenʃən] n aandacht c; *pay ~ opletten

attentive [ə'tentiv] adj oplettend

attic ['ætik] n zolder c

attitude ['ætitjuːd] n houding c

attorney [ə'təːni] n advocaat c

attract [ə'trækt] v *aantrekken

attraction [ə'trækʃən] n attractie c; aantrekking c, bekoring c

attractive [ə'træktiv] adj aantrekkelijk

auburn ['ɔːbən] adj kastanjebruin

auction ['ɔːkʃən] n veiling c

audible ['ɔːdibəl] adj hoorbaar

audience ['ɔːdiəns] n publiek nt

auditor ['ɔːditə] n toehoorder c

auditorium [,ɔːdi'tɔːriəm] n aula c

August ['ɔːgəst] augustus

aunt [ɑːnt] n tante c

Australia [ɔ'streiliə] Australië

Australian [ɔ'streiliən] adj Australisch; n Australiër c

Austria ['ɔstriə] Oostenrijk

Austrian ['ɔstriən] adj Oostenrijks; n Oostenrijker c

authentic [ɔ'θentik] adj authentiek; echt

author ['ɔːθə] n auteur c, schrijver c

authoritarian [ɔ,θɔri'tɛəriən] adj autoritair

authority [ɔ'θɔrəti] n gezag nt; macht c; **authorities** pl autoriteiten pl, overheid c

authorization [,ɔːθərai'zeiʃən] n machtiging c; toestemming c

automatic [,ɔːtə'mætik] adj automatisch; ~ **teller** geldautomaat

automation [,ɔːtə'meiʃən] n automatisering c

automobile ['ɔːtəməbiːl] n auto c; ~ **club** automobielclub c

autonomous [ɔ'tɔnəməs] adj autonoom

autopsy ['ɔːtɔpsi] n autopsie c

autumn ['ɔːtəm] n najaar nt, herfst c

available [ə'veiləbəl] adj verkrijgbaar, voorhanden, beschikbaar

avalanche ['ævəlɑːnʃ] n lawine c

avaricious [,ævə'riʃəs] adj gierig

avenue ['ævənjuː] n laan c

average ['ævəridʒ] adj gemiddeld; n gemiddelde nt; **on the** ~ gemiddeld

averse [ə'vəːs] adj afkerig

aversion [ə'vəːʃən] n tegenzin c

avert [ə'vəːt] v afwenden

avoid [ə'vɔid] v *vermijden; *ontwijken

await [ə'weit] v wachten op, afwachten

awake [ə'weik] adj wakker

*awake [ə'weik] v wekken

award [ə'wɔːd] n prijs c; v toekennen

aware [ə'wɛə] adj bewust

away [ə'wei] adv weg; *go ~ *weggaan

awful ['ɔːfəl] adj afschuwelijk, ver-

schrikkelijk
awkward ['ɔ:kwəd] *adj* pijnlijk; onhandig
awning ['ɔ:niŋ] *n* zonnescherm *nt*
axe [æks] *n* bijl *c*
axle ['æksəl] *n* as *c*

B

baby ['beibi] *n* baby *c*; ~ **carriage**
Am kinderwagen *c*
babysitter ['beibi,sitə] *n* babysitter *c*
bachelor ['bætʃələ] *n* vrijgezel *c*
back [bæk] *n* rug *c*; *adv* terug; *go ~
*teruggaan
backache ['bækeik] *n* rugpijn *c*
backbone ['bækboun] *n* ruggegraat *c*
background ['bækgraund] *n* achtergrond *c*; vorming *c*
backwards ['bækwədz] *adv* achteruit
bacon ['beikən] *n* spek *nt*
bacterium [bæk'ti:riəm] *n* (pl -ria) bacterie *c*
bad [bæd] *adj* slecht; ernstig, erg;
stout
bag [bæg] *n* zak *c*; tas *c*, handtas *c*;
koffer *c*
baggage ['bægidʒ] *n* bagage *c*; ~ **deposit office** *Am* bagagedepot *nt*;
hand ~ *Am* handbagage *c*
bail [beil] *n* borgsom *c*
bailiff ['beilif] *n* deurwaarder *c*
bait [beit] *n* aas *nt*
bake [beik] *v* *bakken
baker ['beikə] *n* bakker *c*
bakery ['beikəri] *n* bakkerij *c*
balance ['bæləns] *n* evenwicht *nt*; balans *c*; saldo *nt*
balcony ['bælkəni] *n* balkon *nt*
bald [bɔ:ld] *adj* kaal
ball [bɔ:l] *n* bal *c*; bal *nt*
ballet ['bælei] *n* ballet *nt*

balloon [bə'lu:n] *n* ballon *c*
ballpoint-pen ['bɔ:lpɔintpen] *n* ballpoint *c*
ballroom ['bɔ:lru:m] *n* danszaal *c*
bamboo [bæm'bu:] *n* (pl ~s) bamboe
nt
banana [bə'nɑ:nə] *n* banaan *c*
band [bænd] *n* orkest *nt*; band *c*
bandage ['bændidʒ] *n* verband *nt*
bandit ['bændit] *n* bandiet *c*
bangle ['bæŋgəl] *n* armband *c*
banisters ['bænistəz] *pl* trapleuning *c*
bank [bæŋk] *n* oever *c*; bank *c*; *v* deponeren; ~ **account** bankrekening
c
banknote ['bæŋknout] *n* bankbiljet *nt*
bank-rate ['bæŋkreit] *n* disconto *nt*
bankrupt ['bæŋkrʌpt] *adj* failliet,
bankroet
banner ['bænə] *n* vaandel *nt*
banquet ['bæŋkwit] *n* banket *nt*
banqueting-hall ['bæŋkwitiŋhɔ:l] *n*
banketzaal *c*
baptism ['bæptizəm] *n* doopsel *nt*,
doop *c*
baptize [bæp'taiz] *v* dopen
bar [bɑ:] *n* bar *c*; stang *c*; tralie *c*
barber ['bɑ:bə] *n* kapper *c*
bare [beə] *adj* naakt, bloot; kaal
barely ['beəli] *adv* nauwelijks
bargain ['bɑ:gin] *n* koopje *nt*; *v* *afdingen
baritone ['bæritoun] *n* bariton *c*
bark [bɑ:k] *n* bast *c*; *v* blaffen
barley ['bɑ:li] *n* gerst *c*
barmaid ['bɑ:meid] *n* barjuffrouw *c*
barman ['bɑ:mən] *n* (pl -men) barman
c
barn [bɑ:n] *n* schuur *c*
barometer [bə'rɔmitə] *n* barometer *c*
baroque [bə'rɔk] *adj* barok
barracks ['bærəks] *pl* kazerne *c*
barrel ['bærəl] *n* ton *c*, vat *nt*
barrier ['bæriə] *n* barrière *c*; slagboom

c

barrister ['bæristə] n advocaat c

bartender ['ba:,tendə] n barman c

base [beis] n basis c; grondslag c; v baseren

baseball ['beisbɔ:l] n honkbal nt

basement ['beismənt] n souterrain nt

basic ['beisik] adj fundamenteel

basilica [bə'zilikə] n basiliek c

basin ['beisən] n kom c, bekken nt

basis ['beisis] n (pl bases) grondslag c, basis c

basket ['ba:skit] n mand c

bass¹ [beis] n bas c

bass² [bæs] n (pl ~) baars c

bastard ['ba:stəd] n bastaard c; schoft c

batch [bætʃ] n partij c

bath [ba:θ] n bad nt; ~ salts badzout nt; ~ towel badhanddoek c

bathe [beið] v baden, een bad *nemen

bathing-cap ['beiðiŋkæp] n badmuts c

bathing-suit ['beiðiŋsu:t] n badpak nt; zwembroek c

bathing-trunks ['beiðiŋtrʌŋks] n zwembroek c

bathrobe ['ba:θroub] n badjas c

bathroom ['ba:θru:m] n badkamer c; toilet nt

batter ['bætə] n beslag nt

battery ['bætəri] n batterij c; accu c

battle ['bætəl] n slag c; strijd c, gevecht nt; v *vechten

bay [bei] n baai c; v blaffen

*be [bi:] v *zijn

beach [bi:tʃ] n strand nt; **nudist ~** naaktstrand nt

bead [bi:d] n kraal c; **beads** pl kralensnoer nt; rozenkrans c

beak [bi:k] n snavel c; bek c

beam [bi:m] n straal c; balk c

bean [bi:n] n boon c

bear [beə] n beer c

*bear [beə] v *dragen; dulden; *ver-

dragen

beard [biəd] n baard c

bearer ['beərə] n drager c

beast [bi:st] n beest nt; ~ of prey roofdier nt

*beat [bi:t] v *slaan; *verslaan

beautiful ['bju:tifəl] adj mooi

beauty ['bju:ti] n schoonheid c; ~ parlour schoonheidssalon c; ~ salon schoonheidssalon c; ~ treatment schoonheidsbehandeling c

beaver ['bi:və] n bever c

because [bi'kɔz] conj omdat; aangezien; ~ of vanwege, wegens

*become [bi'kʌm] v *worden; goed *staan

bed [bed] n bed nt; ~ and board vol pension, kost en inwoning; ~ and breakfast logies en ontbijt

bedding ['bediŋ] n beddegoed nt

bedroom ['bedru:m] n slaapkamer c

bee [bi:] n bij c

beech [bi:tʃ] n beuk c

beef [bi:f] n rundvlees nt

beehive ['bi:haiv] n bijenkorf c

been [bi:n] v (pp be)

beer [biə] n bier nt; pils nt

beet [bi:t] n biet c

beetle ['bi:təl] n kever c

beetroot ['bi:tru:t] n beetwortel c

before [bi'fɔ:] prep voor; conj voordat; adv van tevoren; eerder, tevoren

beg [beg] v bedelen; smeken; *vragen

beggar ['begə] n bedelaar c

*begin [bi'gin] v *beginnen; *aanvangen

beginner [bi'ginə] n beginneling c

beginning [bi'giniŋ] n begin nt; aanvang c

on behalf of [ɔn bi'ha:f ɔv] namens, in naam van; ten behoeve van

behave [bi'heiv] v zich *gedragen

behaviour [bi'heivjə] n gedrag nt

behind [bi'haind] *prep* achter; *adv* achteraan

beige [beiʒ] *adj* beige

being [ˈbiːiŋ] *n* wezen *nt*

Belgian [ˈbeldʒən] *adj* Belgisch; *n* Belg *c*

Belgium [ˈbeldʒəm] België

belief [bi'liːf] *n* geloof *nt*

believe [bi'liːv] *v* geloven

bell [bel] *n* klok *c*; bel *c*

bellboy [ˈbelbɔi] *n* piccolo *c*

belly [ˈbeli] *n* buik *c*

belong [bi'lɔŋ] *v* toebehoren

belongings [bi'lɔŋiŋz] *pl* bezittingen *pl*

beloved [bi'lʌvd] *adj* bemind

below [bi'lou] *prep* onder; beneden; *adv* onderaan, beneden

belt [belt] *n* riem *c*; **garter ~** *Am* jarretelgordel *c*

bench [bentʃ] *n* bank *c*

bend [bend] *n* bocht *c*; kromming *c*

***bend** [bend] *v* *buigen; **~ down** zich bukken

beneath [bi'niːθ] *prep* onder; *adv* beneden

benefit [ˈbenifit] *n* winst *c*, baat *c*; voordeel *nt*; *v* profiteren

bent [bent] *adj* (pp bend) krom

beret [ˈberei] *n* baret *c*

berry [ˈberi] *n* bes *c*

berth [bəːθ] *n* couchette *c*; kooi *c*

beside [bi'said] *prep* naast

besides [bi'saidz] *adv* bovendien; trouwens; *prep* behalve

best [best] *adj* best

bet [bet] *n* weddenschap *c*; inzet *c*

***bet** [bet] *v* wedden

betray [bi'trei] *v* *verraden

better [ˈbetə] *adj* beter

between [bi'twiːn] *prep* tussen

beverage [ˈbevəridʒ] *n* drank *c*

beware [bi'weə] *v* zich hoeden, oppassen

bewitch [bi'witʃ] *v* beheksen, betoveren

beyond [bi'jɔnd] *prep* verder dan; voorbij; behalve; *adv* verder

bible [ˈbaibəl] *n* bijbel *c*

bicycle [ˈbaisikəl] *n* fiets *c*; rijwiel *nt*

big [big] *adj* groot; omvangrijk; dik; gewichtig

bile [bail] *n* gal *c*

bilingual [bai'liŋgwəl] *adj* tweetalig

bill [bil] *n* rekening *c*; nota *c*; *v* factureren

billiards [ˈbiljədz] *pl* biljart *nt*

***bind** [baind] *v* *binden

binoculars [bi'nɔkjələz] *pl* verrekijker *c*; toneelkijker *c*

biology [bai'ɔlədʒi] *n* biologie *c*

birch [bəːtʃ] *n* berk *c*

bird [bəːd] *n* vogel *c*

Biro [ˈbairou] *n* ballpoint *c*

birth [bəːθ] *n* geboorte *c*

birthday [ˈbəːθdei] *n* verjaardag *c*

biscuit [ˈbiskit] *n* koekje *nt*

bishop [ˈbiʃəp] *n* bisschop *c*

bit [bit] *n* stukje *nt*; beetje *nt*

bitch [bitʃ] *n* teef *c*

bite [bait] *n* hap *c*; beet *c*; steek *c*

***bite** [bait] *v* *bijten

bitter [ˈbitə] *adj* bitter

black [blæk] *adj* zwart; **~ market** zwarte markt

blackberry [ˈblækbəri] *n* braam *c*

blackbird [ˈblækbəːd] *n* merel *c*

blackboard [ˈblækbɔːd] *n* schoolbord *nt*

black-currant [ˌblæk'kʌrənt] *n* zwarte bes

blackmail [ˈblækmeil] *n* chantage *c*; *v* chanteren

blacksmith [ˈblæksmiθ] *n* smid *c*

bladder [ˈblædə] *n* blaas *c*

blade [bleid] *n* lemmet *nt*; **~ of grass** grasspriet *c*

blame [bleim] *n* schuld *c*; verwijt *nt*; *v* de schuld *geven aan, beschuldigen

blank [blæŋk] *adj* blanco

blanket ['blæŋkit] *n* deken *c*

blast [blɑ:st] *n* explosie *c*

blazer ['bleizə] *n* sportjasje *nt*, blazer *c*

bleach [bli:tʃ] *v* bleken

bleak [bli:k] *adj* guur

*****bleed** [bli:d] *v* bloeden; *uitzuigen

bless [bles] *v* zegenen

blessing ['blesiŋ] *n* zegen *c*

blind [blaind] *n* rolgordijn *nt*, jaloezie *c*; *adj* blind; *v* verblinden

blister ['blistə] *n* blaar *c*, blaas *c*

blizzard ['blizəd] *n* sneeuwstorm *c*

block [blɔk] *v* versperren, blokkeren; *n* blok *nt*; ~ **of flats** flatgebouw *nt*

blonde [blɔnd] *n* blondine *c*

blood [blʌd] *n* bloed *nt*; ~ **pressure** bloeddruk *c*

blood-poisoning ['blʌd,pɔizəniŋ] *n* bloedvergiftiging *c*

blood-vessel ['blʌd,vesəl] *n* bloedvat *nt*

blot [blɔt] *n* vlek *c*; smet *c*; **blotting paper** vloeipapier *nt*

blouse [blauz] *n* blouse *c*

blow [blou] *n* klap *c*, slag *c*; windvlaag *c*

*****blow** [blou] *v* *blazen; *waaien

blow-out ['blouaut] *n* bandepech *c*

blue [blu:] *adj* blauw; neerslachtig

blunt [blʌnt] *adj* bot; stomp

blush [blʌʃ] *v* blozen

board [bɔ:d] *n* plank *c*; bord *nt*; pension *nt*; bestuur *nt*; ~ **and lodging** vol pension, kost en inwoning

boarder ['bɔ:də] *n* kostganger *c*

boarding-house ['bɔ:diŋhaus] *n* pension *nt*

boarding-school ['bɔ:diŋsku:l] *n* internaat *nt*

boast [boust] *v* opscheppen

boat [bout] *n* schip *nt*, boot *c*

body ['bɔdi] *n* lichaam *nt*; lijf *nt*

bodyguard ['bɔdigɑ:d] *n* lijfwacht *c*

bog [bɔg] *n* moeras *nt*

boil [bɔil] *v* koken; *n* steenpuist *c*

bold [bould] *adj* stoutmoedig; vrijpostig, brutaal

Bolivia [bə'liviə] Bolivië

Bolivian [bə'liviən] *adj* Boliviaans; *n* Boliviaan *c*

bolt [boult] *n* grendel *c*; bout *c*

bomb [bɔm] *n* bom *c*; *v* bombarderen

bond [bɔnd] *n* obligatie *c*

bone [boun] *n* been *nt*, bot *nt*; graat *c*; *v* uitbenen

bonnet ['bɔnit] *n* motorkap *c*

book [buk] *n* boek *nt*; *v* reserveren, boeken; *inschrijven

booking ['bukiŋ] *n* reservering *c*, bespreking *c*

bookseller ['buk,selə] *n* boekhandelaar *c*

bookstand ['bukstænd] *n* boekenstalletje *nt*

bookstore ['bukstɔ:] *n* boekwinkel *c*, boekhandel *c*

boot [bu:t] *n* laars *c*; bagageruimte *c*

booth [bu:ð] *n* kraam *c*; hokje *nt*

border ['bɔ:də] *n* grens *c*; rand *c*

bore¹ [bɔ:] *v* vervelen; boren; *n* zeurpiet *c*

bore² [bɔ:] *v* (p bear)

boring ['bɔ:riŋ] *adj* vervelend, saai

born [bɔ:n] *adj* geboren

borrow ['bɔrou] *v* lenen; ontlenen

bosom ['buzəm] *n* borst *c*

boss [bɔs] *n* chef *c*, baas *c*

botany ['bɔtəni] *n* plantkunde *c*

both [bouθ] *adj* beide; **both ... and** zowel ... als

bother ['bɔðə] *v* vervelen, hinderen; moeite *doen; *n* last *c*

bottle ['bɔtəl] *n* fles *c*; ~ **opener** flesopener *c*; **hot-water** ~ warmwaterkruik *c*

bottleneck ['bɔtəlnek] *n* flessehals *c*

bottom ['bɔtəm] n bodem c; achterwerk nt, zitvlak nt; adj onderst

bough [bau] n tak c

bought [bɔːt] v (p, pp buy)

boulder ['bouldə] n rotsblok nt

bound [baund] n grens c; *be ~ to
*moeten; ~ for op weg naar

boundary ['baundəri] n grens c; landsgrens c

bouquet [bu'kei] n boeket nt

bourgeois ['buəʒwaː] adj burgerlijk

boutique [bu'tiːk] n boutique c

bow¹ [bau] v *buigen

bow² [bou] n boog c; ~ tie vlinderdasje nt, strikje nt

bowels [bauəlz] pl darmen, ingewanden pl

bowl [boul] n schaal c

bowling ['boulɪŋ] n bowling c, kegelspel nt; ~ alley kegelbaan c

box¹ [bɔks] v boksen; **boxing match**
bokswedstrijd c

box² [bɔks] n doos c

box-office ['bɔks,ɔfis] n plaatskaartenbureau nt, kassa c

boy [bɔi] n jongen c; joch nt, knaap
c; bediende c; ~ scout padvinder
c

bra [braː] n beha c, bustehouder c

bracelet ['breislit] n armband c

braces ['breisiz] pl bretels pl

brain [brein] n hersenen pl; verstand
nt

brain-wave ['breinweiv] n inval c

brake [breik] n rem c; ~ drum remtrommel c; ~ lights remlichten pl

branch [braːntʃ] n tak c; filiaal nt

brand [brænd] n merk nt; brandmerk
nt

brand-new [,brænd'njuː] adj splinternieuw

brass [braːs] n messing nt; koper nt,
geelkoper nt; ~ band n fanfarekorps nt

brassiere ['bræziə] n bustehouder c,
beha c

brassware ['braːsweə] n koperwerk nt

brave [breiv] adj moedig, dapper;
flink

Brazil [brə'zil] Brazilië

Brazilian [brə'ziljən] adj Braziliaans; n
Braziliaan c

breach [briːtʃ] n bres c

bread [bred] n brood nt; **wholemeal**
~ volkorenbrood nt

breadth [bredθ] n breedte c

break [breik] n breuk c; pauze c

*break** [breik] v *breken; ~ down
stuk *gaan; ontleden

breakdown ['breikdaun] n panne c,
motorpech c

breakfast ['brekfəst] n ontbijt nt

bream [briːm] n (pl ~) brasem c

breast [brest] n borst c

breaststroke ['breststrouk] n schoolslag c

breath [breθ] n adem c; lucht c

breathe [briːð] v ademen

breathing ['briːðiŋ] n ademhaling c

breed [briːd] n ras nt; soort c/nt

*breed** [briːd] v fokken

breeze [briːz] n bries c

brew [bruː] v brouwen

brewery ['bruːəri] n brouwerij c

bribe [braib] v *omkopen

bribery ['braibəri] n omkoping c

brick [brik] n steen c, baksteen c

bricklayer ['brikleiə] n metselaar c

bride [braid] n bruid c

bridegroom ['braidgruːm] n bruidegom
c

bridge [bridʒ] n brug c; bridge nt

brief [briːf] adj kort; beknopt

briefcase ['briːfkeis] n aktentas c

briefs [briːfs] pl slip c, onderbroek c

bright [brait] adj helder; blinkend;
snugger, pienter

brill [bril] n griet c

brilliant ['briljənt] *adj* schitterend; briljant

brim [brim] *n* rand *c*

*****bring** [briŋ] *v* *brengen; *meebrengen; ~ **back** *terugbrengen; ~ **up** opvoeden; *grootbrengen; ter sprake *brengen

brisk [brisk] *adj* levendig

Britain ['britən] Engeland

British ['britiʃ] *adj* Brits; Engels

Briton ['britən] *n* Brit *c*; Engelsman *c*

broad [brɔːd] *adj* breed; ruim, wijd; globaal

broadcast ['brɔːdkɑːst] *n* uitzending *c*

*****broadcast** ['brɔːdkɑːst] *v* *uitzenden

brochure ['brouʃuə] *n* brochure *c*

broke¹ [brouk] *v* (p break)

broke² [brouk] *adj* platzak

broken ['broukən] *adj* (pp break) stuk, kapot

broker ['broukə] *n* makelaar *c*

bronchitis [brɔŋ'kaitis] *n* bronchitis *c*

bronze [brɔnz] *n* brons *nt*; *adj* bronzen

brooch [broutʃ] *n* broche *c*

brook [bruk] *n* beek *c*

broom [bruːm] *n* bezem *c*

brothel ['brɔθəl] *n* bordeel *nt*

brother ['brʌðə] *n* broer *c*; broeder *c*

brother-in-law ['brʌðərinlɔː] *n* (pl brothers-) zwager *c*

brought [brɔːt] *v* (p, pp bring)

brown [braun] *adj* bruin

bruise [bruːz] *n* blauwe plek, kneuzing *c*; *v* kneuzen

brunette [bruːˈnet] *n* brunette *c*

brush [brʌʃ] *n* borstel *c*; kwast *c*; *v* poetsen, borstelen

brutal ['bruːtəl] *adj* beestachtig

bubble ['bʌbəl] *n* bel *c*

bucket ['bʌkit] *n* emmer *c*

buckle ['bʌkəl] *n* gesp *c*

bud [bʌd] *n* knop *c*

budget ['bʌdʒit] *n* begroting *c*, budget *nt*

buffet ['bufei] *n* buffet *nt*

bug [bʌg] *n* wandluis *c*; kever *c*; *nAm* insekt *nt*

*****build** [bild] *v* bouwen

building ['bildiŋ] *n* gebouw *nt*

bulb [bʌlb] *n* bol *c*; bloembol *c*; **light** ~ gloeilamp *c*

Bulgaria [bʌlˈgeəriə] Bulgarije

Bulgarian [bʌlˈgeəriən] *adj* Bulgaars; *n* Bulgaar *c*

bulk [bʌlk] *n* omvang *c*; massa *c*; meerderheid *c*

bulky ['bʌlki] *adj* lijvig, omvangrijk

bull [bul] *n* stier *c*

bullet ['bulit] *n* kogel *c*

bullfight ['bulfait] *n* stierengevecht *nt*

bullring ['bulriŋ] *n* arena *c*

bump [bʌmp] *v* *stoten; botsen; bonzen; *n* stoot *c*, bons *c*

bumper ['bʌmpə] *n* bumper *c*

bumpy ['bʌmpi] *adj* hobbelig

bun [bʌn] *n* broodje *c*

bunch [bʌntʃ] *n* bos *c*; groep *c*

bundle ['bʌndəl] *n* bundel *c*; *v* *samenbinden, bundelen

bunk [bʌŋk] *n* kooi *c*

buoy [bɔi] *n* boei *c*

burden ['bəːdən] *n* last *c*

bureau ['bjuərou] *n* (pl ~x, ~s) bureau *nt*, schrijftafel *c*; *nAm* commode *c*

bureaucracy [bjuəˈrɔkrəsi] *n* bureaucratie *c*

burglar ['bəːglə] *n* inbreker *c*

burgle ['bəːgəl] *v* *inbreken

burial ['beriəl] *n* teraardebestelling *c*, begrafenis *c*

burn [bəːn] *n* brandwond *c*

*****burn** [bəːn] *v* branden; verbranden; aanbranden

*****burst** [bəːst] *v* *barsten; *breken

bury ['beri] *v* *begraven; *bedelven

bus [bʌs] *n* bus *c*

bush [buʃ] *n* struik *c*

business ['biznəs] n zaken pl, handel c; bedrijf nt, zaak c; werk nt; aan-gelegenheid c; ~ **hours** openingstij-den pl, kantooruren pl; ~ **trip** za-kenreis c; **on** ~ voor zaken

business-like ['biznislaik] adj zakelijk

businessman ['biznəsmən] n (pl -men) zakenman c

bust [bʌst] n buste c

bustle ['bʌsəl] n drukte c

busy ['bizi] adj bezig; druk

but [bʌt] conj maar; doch; prep be-halve

butcher ['butʃə] n slager c

butter ['bʌtə] n boter c

butterfly ['bʌtəflai] n vlinder c; ~ **stroke** vlinderslag c

buttock ['bʌtək] n bil c

button ['bʌtən] n knoop c; v knopen

buttonhole ['bʌtənhoul] n knoopsgat nt

***buy** [bai] v *kopen; aanschaffen

buyer ['baiə] n koper c

by [bai] prep door; met, per; bij

by-pass ['baipɑ:s] n ringweg c; v pas-seren

C

cab [kæb] n taxi c

cabaret ['kæbərei] n cabaret nt; nachtclub c

cabbage ['kæbidʒ] n kool c

cab-driver ['kæb,draivə] n taxichauf-feur c

cabin ['kæbin] n cabine c; hut c; kleedhokje nt; kajuit c

cabinet ['kæbinət] n kabinet nt

cable ['keibəl] n kabel c; telegram nt; v telegraferen

cadre ['kɑ:də] n kader nt

café ['kæfei] n café nt

cafeteria [,kæfə'tiəriə] n cafetaria c

caffeine ['kæfi:n] n coffeïne c

cage [keidʒ] n kooi c

cake [keik] n cake c; gebak nt, taart c, koek c

calamity [kə'læməti] n onheil nt, ramp c

calcium ['kælsiəm] n calcium nt

calculate ['kælkjuleit] v uitrekenen, be-rekenen

calculation [,kælkju'leiʃən] n bereke-ning c

calculator ['kælkju'leitə] n reken-machine c

calendar ['kæləndə] n kalender c

calf [kɑ:f] n (pl calves) kalf nt; kuit c; ~ **skin** kalfsleer nt

call [kɔ:l] v *roepen; noemen; opbel-len; n roep c; visite c, bezoek nt; telefoontje nt; *be called *heten; ~ **names** *uitschelden; ~ **on** *be-zoeken; ~ **up** Am opbellen

callus ['kæləs] n eelt nt

calm [kɑ:m] adj rustig, kalm; ~ **down** kalmeren; bedaren

calorie ['kæləri] n calorie c

came [keim] v (p come)

camel ['kæməl] n kameel c

cameo ['kæmiou] n (pl ~s) camee c

camera ['kæmərə] n fototoestel nt; filmcamera c; ~ **shop** fotowinkel c

camp [kæmp] n kamp nt; v kamperen

campaign [kæm'pein] n campagne c

camp-bed [,kæmp'bed] n veldbed nt, stretcher c

camper ['kæmpə] n kampeerder c

camping ['kæmpiŋ] n camping c; ~ **site** camping c, kampeerterrein nt

camshaft ['kæmʃɑ:ft] n nokkenas c

can [kæn] n blik nt; ~ **opener** blik-opener c

***can** [kæn] v *kunnen

Canada ['kænədə] Canada

Canadian [kə'neidiən] adj Canadees;

n Canadees *c*

canal [kə'næl] *n* kanaal *nt*; gracht *c*, singel *c*

canary [kə'neəri] *n* kanarie *c*

cancel ['kænsəl] *v* annuleren; *afzeggen

cancellation [,kænsə'leiʃən] *n* annulering *c*

cancer ['kænsə] *n* kanker *c*

candelabrum [,kændə'la:brəm] *n* (pl -bra) kandelaber *c*

candidate ['kændidət] *n* kandidaat *c*, gegadigde *c*

candle ['kændəl] *n* kaars *c*

candy ['kændi] *nAm* snoepje *nt*; snoep *nt*, snoepgoed *nt*; ~ **store** *Am* snoepwinkel *c*

cane [kein] *n* riet *nt*; stok *c*

canister ['kænistə] *n* trommel *c*, bus *c*

canoe [kə'nu:] *n* kano *c*

canteen [kæn'ti:n] *n* kantine *c*

canvas ['kænvəs] *n* tentdoek *nt*

cap [kæp] *n* pet *c*, muts *c*

capable ['keipəbəl] *adj* kundig, bekwaam

capacity [kə'pæsəti] *n* capaciteit *c*; vermogen *nt*; bekwaamheid *c*

cape [keip] *n* cape *c*; kaap *c*

capital ['kæpitəl] *n* hoofdstad *c*; kapitaal *nt*; *adj* belangrijk, hoofd-; ~ **letter** hoofdletter *c*

capitalism ['kæpitəlizəm] *n* kapitalisme *nt*

capitulation [kə,pitju'leiʃən] *n* capitulatie *c*

capsule ['kæpsju:l] *n* capsule *c*

captain ['kæptin] *n* kapitein *c*; gezagvoerder *c*

capture ['kæptʃə] *v* gevangen *nemen, *vangen; *innemen; *n* vangst *c*; inneming *c*

car [ka:] *n* auto *c*; ~ **hire** autoverhuur *c*; ~ **park** parkeerplaats *c*; ~ **rental** *Am* autoverhuur *c*

carafe [kə'ræf] *n* karaf *c*

caramel ['kærəməl] *n* karamel *c*

carat ['kærət] *n* karaat *nt*

caravan ['kærəvæn] *n* caravan *c*; woonwagen *c*

carburettor [,ka:bju'retə] *n* carburateur *c*

card [ka:d] *n* kaart *c*; briefkaart *c*

cardboard ['ka:dbɔ:d] *n* karton *nt*; *adj* kartonnen

cardigan ['ka:digən] *n* vest *nt*

cardinal ['ka:dinəl] *n* kardinaal *c*; *adj* kardinaal, hoofd-

care [keə] *n* verzorging *c*; zorg *c*; ~ **about** zich bekommeren om; ~ **for** *houden van; *take ~ **of** zorgen voor, verzorgen

career [kə'riə] *n* loopbaan *c*, carrière *c*

carefree ['keəfri:] *adj* onbezorgd

careful ['keəfəl] *adj* voorzichtig; zorgvuldig, nauwkeurig

careless ['keələs] *adj* achteloos, slordig

caretaker ['keə,teikə] *n* concierge *c*

cargo ['ka:gou] *n* (pl ~es) lading *c*, vracht *c*

carnival ['ka:nivəl] *n* carnaval *nt*

carp [ka:p] *n* (pl ~) karper *c*

carpenter ['ka:pintə] *n* timmerman *c*

carpet ['ka:pit] *n* vloerkleed *nt*, tapijt *nt*

carriage ['kæridʒ] *n* wagon *c*; koets *c*, rijtuig *nt*

carriageway ['kæridʒwei] *n* rijbaan *c*

carrot ['kærət] *n* peen *c*, wortel *c*

carry ['kæri] *v* *dragen; voeren; ~ **on** voortzetten; *doorgaan; ~ **out** uitvoeren

carry-cot ['kærikɔt] *n* reiswieg *c*

cart [ka:t] *n* kar *c*, wagen *c*

cartilage ['ka:tilidʒ] *n* kraakbeen *nt*

carton ['ka:tən] *n* kartonnen doos; slof *c*

cartoon [ka:'tu:n] *n* tekenfilm *c*

cartridge ['ka:tridʒ] *n* patroon *c*

carve [kɑ:v] v *snijden; kerven, *houtsnijden

carving ['kɑ:viŋ] n houtsnijwerk nt

case [keis] n geval nt; zaak c; koffer c; etui nt; **attaché ~** aktentas c; **in ~** indien; **in ~ of** in geval van

cash [kæʃ] n contanten pl, contant geld; v verzilveren, incasseren, innen; **~ dispenser** geldautomaat

cashier [kæ'ʃiə] n kassier c; caissière c

cashmere ['kæʃmiə] n kasjmier nt

casino [kə'si:nou] n (pl ~s) casino nt

cask [kɑ:sk] n ton c, vat nt

cast [kɑ:st] n worp c

*cast [kɑ:st] v gooien, *werpen; **cast iron** gietijzer nt

castle ['kɑ:səl] n slot nt, kasteel nt

casual ['kæʒuəl] adj ongedwongen; terloops, toevallig

casualty ['kæʒuəlti] n slachtoffer nt

cat [kæt] n kat c

catacomb ['kætəkoum] n catacombe c

catalogue ['kætələg] n catalogus c

catarrh [kə'tɑ:] n catarre c

catastrophe [kə'tæstrəfi] n catastrofe c

*catch [kætʃ] v *vangen; *grijpen; betrappen; *nemen, halen

category ['kætigəri] n categorie c

cathedral [kə'θi:drəl] n dom c, kathedraal c

catholic ['kæθəlik] adj katholiek

cattle ['kætəl] pl vee nt

caught [kɔ:t] v (p, pp catch)

cauliflower ['kɔliflauə] n bloemkool c

cause [kɔ:z] v veroorzaken; aanrichten; n oorzaak c; beweegreden c, aanleiding c; zaak c; **~ to** *doen

causeway ['kɔ:zwei] n straatweg c

caution ['kɔ:ʃən] n voorzichtigheid c; v waarschuwen

cautious ['kɔ:ʃəs] adj bedachtzaam

cave [keiv] n grot c; spelonk c

cavern ['kævən] n hol nt

caviar ['kævia:] n kaviaar c

cavity ['kævəti] n holte c

cease [si:s] v *ophouden

ceiling ['si:liŋ] n plafond c

celebrate ['selibreit] v vieren

celebration [,seli'breiʃən] n viering c

celebrity [si'lebrəti] n roem c

celery ['seləri] n selderij c

celibacy ['selibəsi] n celibaat nt

cell [sel] n cel c

cellar ['selə] n kelder c

cellophane ['seləfein] n cellofaan nt

cement [si'ment] n cement nt

cemetery ['semitri] n begraafplaats c, kerkhof nt

censorship ['sensəʃip] n censuur c

centigrade ['sentigreid] adj celsius

centimetre ['senti:tə] n centimeter c

central ['sentrəl] adj centraal; **~ heating** centrale verwarming; **~ station** centraal station

centralize ['sentrəlaiz] v centraliseren

centre ['sentə] n centrum nt; middelpunt nt

century ['sentʃəri] n eeuw c

ceramics [si'ræmiks] pl aardewerk nt, ceramiek c

ceremony ['serəməni] n ceremonie c

certain ['sə:tən] adj zeker; bepaald

certificate [sə'tifikət] n certificaat nt; attest nt, akte c, diploma nt, getuigschrift nt

chain [tʃein] n keten c, ketting c

chair [tʃeə] n stoel c; zetel c

chairman ['tʃeəmən] n (pl -men) voorzitter c

chalet ['ʃælei] n chalet nt

chalk [tʃɔ:k] n krijt nt

challenge ['tʃæləndʒ] v uitdagen; n uitdaging c

chamber ['tʃeimbə] n kamer c

chambermaid ['tʃeimbəmeid] n kamermeisje nt

champagne [ʃæm'pein] n champagne

c

champion ['tʃæmpjən] n kampioen c;
voorvechter c

chance [tʃɑːns] n toeval nt; kans c,
gelegenheid c; risico nt; gok c; **by
~** toevallig

change [tʃeindʒ] v wijzigen, veranderen; wisselen; zich verkleden; overstappen; n wijziging c, verandering
c; wisselgeld nt, kleingeld nt

channel ['tʃænəl] n kanaal nt; **English
Channel** het Kanaal

chaos ['keiɔs] n chaos c

chaotic [kei'ɔtik] adj chaotisch

chap [tʃæp] n vent c

chapel ['tʃæpəl] n kerk c, kapel c

chaplain ['tʃæplin] n kapelaan c

character ['kærəktə] n karakter nt

characteristic [,kærəktə'ristik] adj kenmerkend, karakteristiek; n kenmerk
nt; karaktertrek c

characterize ['kærəktəraiz] v kenmerken

charcoal ['tʃɑːkoul] n houtskool c

charge [tʃɑːdʒ] v berekenen; belasten; aanklagen; *laden; n prijs c;
belasting c, lading c, last c; aanklacht c; **~ plate** Am credit card;
free of ~ kosteloos; **in ~ of** belast
met; *take ~ of op zich *nemen

charity ['tʃærəti] n liefdadigheid c

charm [tʃɑːm] n bekoring c, charme
c; amulet c

charming ['tʃɑːmiŋ] adj charmant

chart [tʃɑːt] n tabel c; grafiek c; zeekaart c; **conversion ~** omrekentabel c

chase [tʃeis] v *najagen; *verdrijven,
*verjagen; n jacht c

chasm ['kæzəm] n kloof c

chassis ['ʃæsi] n (pl ~) chassis nt

chaste [tʃeist] adj kuis

chat [tʃæt] v kletsen, babbelen; n
babbeltje nt, praatje nt, geklets nt

chatterbox ['tʃætəbɔks] n babbelkous
c

chauffeur ['ʃoufə] n chauffeur c

cheap [tʃiːp] adj goedkoop; voordelig

cheat [tʃiːt] v *bedriegen; oplichten

check [tʃek] v controleren, *nakijken;
n ruit c; nAm rekening c; cheque
c; **check!** schaak!; **~ in** zich *inschrijven

check-book ['tʃekbuk] nAm chequeboekje nt

checkerboard ['tʃekəbɔːd] nAm
schaakbord nt

checkers ['tʃekəz] plAm damspel nt

checkroom ['tʃekruːm] nAm garderobe c

check-up ['tʃekʌp] n onderzoek nt

cheek [tʃiːk] n wang c

cheek-bone ['tʃiːkboun] n jukbeen nt

cheer [tʃiə] v juichen; **~ up** opvrolijken

cheerful ['tʃiəfəl] adj opgewekt, vrolijk

cheese [tʃiːz] n kaas c

chef [ʃef] n chef-kok c

chemical ['kemikəl] adj scheikundig,
chemisch

chemist ['kemist] n apotheker c;
chemist's apotheek c; drogisterij c

chemistry ['kemistri] n scheikunde c,
chemie c

cheque [tʃek] n cheque c

cheque-book ['tʃekbuk] n chequeboekje nt

chequered ['tʃekəd] adj geruit, geblokt

cherry ['tʃeri] n kers c

chess [tʃes] n schaakspel nt

chest [tʃest] n borst c; borstkas c;
kist c; **~ of drawers** ladenkast c

chestnut ['tʃesnʌt] n kastanje c

chew [tʃuː] v kauwen

chewing-gum ['tʃuːiŋʌm] n kauwgom
c/nt

chicken ['tʃikin] n kip c; kuiken nt

chickenpox ['tʃikinpɔks] n waterpokken *pl*

chief [tʃiːf] *n* chef *c*; *adj* hoofd-, voornaamst

chieftain ['tʃiːftən] *n* opperhoofd *nt*

child [tʃaild] *n* (pl children) kind *nt*

childbirth ['tʃaildbəːθ] *n* bevalling *c*

childhood ['tʃaildhud] *n* jeugd *c*

Chile ['tʃili] Chili

Chilean ['tʃiliən] *adj* Chileens; *n* Chileen *c*

chill [tʃil] *n* rilling *c*

chilly ['tʃili] *adj* kil

chimes [tʃaimz] *pl* carillon *nt*

chimney ['tʃimni] *n* schoorsteen *c*

chin [tʃin] *n* kin *c*

China ['tʃainə] China

china ['tʃainə] *n* porselein *nt*

Chinese [tʃaiˈniːz] *adj* Chinees; *n* Chinees *c*

chink [tʃiŋk] *n* kier *c*

chip [tʃip] *n* schilfer *c*; fiche *c*; *v* *afsnijden, *afbreken; **chips** frites *pl*

chiropodist [kiˈrɔpədist] *n* pedicure *c*

chisel ['tʃizəl] *n* beitel *c*

chives [tʃaivz] *pl* bieslook *nt*

chlorine ['klɔːriːn] *n* chloor *nt*

chock-full [tʃɔkˈful] *adj* afgeladen, stampvol

chocolate ['tʃɔklət] *n* chocola *c*; bonbon *c*; chocolademelk *c*

choice [tʃɔis] *n* keuze *c*; keus *c*

choir [kwaiə] *n* koor *c*

choke [tʃouk] *v* stikken; wurgen; *n* choke *c*

***choose** [tʃuːz] *v* *kiezen

chop [tʃɔp] *n* kotelet *c*, karbonade *c*; *v* hakken

Christ [kraist] Christus

christen ['krisən] *v* dopen

christening ['krisəniŋ] *n* doop *c*

Christian ['kristʃən] *adj* christelijk; *n* christen *c*; ~ **name** voornaam *c*

Christmas ['krisməs] Kerstmis

chromium ['kroumiəm] *n* chroom *nt*

chronic ['krɔnik] *adj* chronisch

chronological [ˌkrɔnəˈlɔdʒikəl] *adj* chronologisch

chuckle ['tʃʌkəl] *v* grinniken

chunk [tʃʌŋk] *n* stuk *nt*

church [tʃəːtʃ] *n* kerk *c*

churchyard ['tʃəːtʃjɑːd] *n* kerkhof *nt*

cigar [siˈgɑː] *n* sigaar *c*; ~ **shop** sigarenwinkel *c*

cigarette [ˌsigəˈret] *n* sigaret *c*; ~ **tobacco** shag *c*

cigarette-case [ˌsigəˈretkeis] *n* sigarettenkoker *c*

cigarette-holder [ˌsigəˈretˌhouldə] *n* sigarettepijpje *nt*

cigarette-lighter [ˌsigəˈretˌlaitə] *n* aansteker *c*

cinema ['sinəmə] *n* bioscoop *c*

cinnamon ['sinəmən] *n* kaneel *c*

circle ['səːkəl] *n* cirkel *c*; kring *c*; balkon *nt*; *v* omringen, *omgeven

circulation [ˌsəːkjuˈleiʃən] *n* circulatie *c*; bloedsomloop *c*; omloop *c*

circumstance ['səːkəmstæns] *n* omstandigheid *c*

circus ['səːkəs] *n* circus *nt*

citizen ['sitizən] *n* burger *c*

citizenship ['sitizənʃip] *n* staatsburgerschap *nt*

city ['siti] *n* stad *c*

civic ['sivik] *adj* burger-

civil ['sivəl] *adj* civiel; beleefd; ~ **law** burgerlijk recht; ~ **servant** ambtenaar *c*

civilian [siˈviljən] *adj* burger-; *n* burger *c*

civilization [ˌsivəlaiˈzeiʃən] *n* beschaving *c*

civilized ['sivəlaizd] *adj* beschaafd

claim [kleim] *v* vorderen, opeisen; beweren; *n* eis *c*, aanspraak *c*

clamp [klæmp] *n* klem *c*; klemschroef *c*

clap [klæp] *v* applaudisseren, klappen

clarify ['klærifai] v ophelderen, verduidelijken

class [klɑ:s] n rang c, klasse c; klas c

classical ['klæsikəl] adj klassiek

classify ['klæsifai] v indelen

class-mate ['klɑ:smeit] n klasgenoot c

classroom ['klɑ:sru:m] n leslokaal nt

clause [klɔ:z] n clausule c

claw [klɔ:] n klauw c

clay [klei] n klei c

clean [kli:n] adj zuiver, schoon; v schoonmaken, reinigen

cleaning ['kli:niŋ] n schoonmaak c, reiniging c; ~ **fluid** reinigingsmiddel nt

clear [kliə] adj helder; duidelijk; v opruimen

clearing ['kliəriŋ] n open plaats

cleft [kleft] n kloof c

clergyman ['klə:dʒimən] n (pl -men) dominee c, predikant c; geestelijke c

clerk [klɑ:k] n kantoorbediende c, beambte c; klerk c; secretaris c

clever ['klevə] adj intelligent; slim, pienter, knap

client ['klaiənt] n klant c; cliënt c

cliff [klif] n rots c, klip c

climate ['klaimit] n klimaat nt

climb [klaim] v *klimmen; *stijgen; n stijging c

clinic ['klinik] n kliniek c

cloak [klouk] n mantel c

cloakroom ['kloukru:m] n garderobe c

clock [klɔk] n klok c; **at ... o'clock** om ... uur

cloister ['klɔistə] n klooster nt

close¹ [klouz] v *sluiten; **closed** adj toe, dicht, gesloten

close² [klous] adj nabij

closet ['klɔzit] n kast c; nAm kleerkast c

cloth [klɔθ] n stof c; doek c

clothes [klouðz] pl kleding c, kleren pl

clothes-brush ['klouðzbrʌʃ] n kleerborstel c

clothing ['klouðiŋ] n kleding c

cloud [klaud] n wolk c; **clouds** bewolking c

cloud-burst ['klaudbə:st] n wolkbreuk c

cloudy ['klaudi] adj betrokken, bewolkt

clover ['klouvə] n klaver c

clown [klaun] n clown c

club [klʌb] n club c; sociëteit c, vereniging c; knots c, knuppel c

clumsy ['klʌmzi] adj onhandig

clutch [klʌtʃ] n koppeling c; greep c

coach [koutʃ] n bus c; rijtuig nt; koets c; trainer c

coachwork ['koutʃwə:k] n carrosserie c

coagulate [kou'ægjuleit] v stollen

coal [koul] n kolen pl

coarse [kɔ:s] adj grof

coast [koust] n kust c

coat [kout] n mantel c, jas c

coat-hanger ['kout,hæŋə] n kleerhanger c

cobweb ['kɔbweb] n spinneweb nt

cocaine [kou'kein] n cocaïne c

cock [kɔk] n haan c

cocktail ['kɔkteil] n cocktail c

coconut ['koukənʌt] n kokosnoot c

cod [kɔd] n (pl ~) kabeljauw c

code [koud] n code c

coffee ['kɔfi] n koffie c

cognac ['kɔnjæk] n cognac c

coherence [kou'hiərəns] n samenhang c

coin [kɔin] n munt c; geldstuk nt, muntstuk nt

coincide [,kouin'said] v *samenvallen

cold [kould] adj koud; n kou c; verkoudheid c; **catch a** ~ kou vatten

collapse [kə'læps] v *bezwijken, instorten

collar ['kɔlə] n halsband c; boord nt/c, kraag c; ~ **stud** boordeknoopje nt

collarbone ['kɔləboun] n sleutelbeen nt

colleague ['kɔli:g] n collega c

collect [kə'lekt] v verzamelen; ophalen, afhalen; collecteren

collection [kə'lekʃən] n collectie c, verzameling c; lichting c

collective [kə'lektiv] adj collectief

collector [kə'lektə] n verzamelaar c; collectant c

college ['kɔlidʒ] n instelling voor hoger onderwijs; school c

collide [kə'laid] v botsen

collision [kə'liʒən] n aanrijding c, botsing c; aanvaring c

Colombia [kə'lɔmbiə] Colombia

Colombian [kə'lɔmbiən] adj Colombiaans; n Colombiaan c

colonel ['kɔ:nəl] n kolonel c

colony ['kɔləni] n kolonie c

colour ['kʌlə] n kleur c; v kleuren; ~ **film** kleurenfilm c

colourant ['kʌlərənt] n kleurstof c

colour-blind ['kʌləblaind] adj kleurenblind

coloured ['kʌləd] adj gekleurd

colourful ['kʌləfəl] adj bont, kleurrijk

column ['kɔləm] n pilaar c, zuil c; kolom c; rubriek c; kolonne c

coma ['koumə] n coma nt

comb [koum] v kammen; n kam c

combat ['kɔmbæt] n strijd c, gevecht nt; v *bestrijden, *vechten

combination [,kɔmbi'neiʃən] n combinatie c

combine [kəm'bain] v combineren; *samenbrengen

* come [kʌm] v *komen; ~ **across** *tegenkomen; *vinden

comedian [kə'mi:diən] n toneelspeler c; komiek c

comedy ['kɔmədi] n blijspel nt, komedie c; **musical** ~ musical c

comfort ['kʌmfət] n gemak nt, komfort nt, gerief nt; troost c; v troosten

comfortable ['kʌmfətəbəl] adj geriefelijk, comfortabel

comic ['kɔmik] adj komisch

comics ['kɔmiks] pl stripverhaal nt

coming ['kʌmiŋ] n komst c

comma ['kɔmə] n komma c

command [kə'mɑ:nd] v *bevelen; n bevel nt

commander [kə'mɑ:ndə] n bevelhebber c

commemoration [kə,memə'reiʃən] n herdenking c

commence [kə'mens] v *beginnen

comment ['kɔment] n commentaar nt; v aanmerken

commerce ['kɔmə:s] n handel c

commercial [kə'mə:ʃəl] adj handels-, commercieel; n reclamespot c; ~ **law** handelsrecht nt

commission [kə'miʃən] n commissie c

commit [kə'mit] v toevertrouwen; plegen, *begaan

committee [kə'miti] n commissie c, comité nt

common ['kɔmən] adj gemeenschappelijk; gebruikelijk, gewoon; ordinair

commune ['kɔmju:n] n commune c

communicate [kə'mju:nikeit] v meedelen, mededelen

communication [kə,mju:ni'keiʃən] n communicatie c; mededeling c

communiqué [kə'mju:nikei] n communiqué nt

communism ['kɔmjunizəm] n communisme nt

communist ['kɔmjunist] n communist c

community [kə'mju:nəti] n samenleving c, gemeenschap c

commuter [kə'mju:tə] *n* forens *c*

compact ['kɔmpækt] *adj* compact

compact disc ['kɔmpækt disk] *n* compact disk *c*; ~ **player** compact disk speler

companion [kəm'pænjən] *n* metgezel *c*

company ['kʌmpəni] *n* gezelschap *nt*; maatschappij *c*; firma *c*

comparative [kəm'pærətiv] *adj* relatief

compare [kəm'peə] *v* *vergelijken

comparison [kəm'pærisən] *n* vergelijking *c*

compartment [kəm'pɑ:tmənt] *n* coupé *c*

compass ['kʌmpəs] *n* kompas *nt*

compel [kəm'pel] *v* *dwingen

compensate ['kɔmpənseit] *v* compenseren

compensation [,kɔmpən'seifən] *n* compensatie *c*; schadevergoeding *c*

compete [kəm'pi:t] *v* wedijveren

competition [,kɔmpə'tifən] *n* wedstrijd *c*; concurrentie *c*

competitor [kəm'petitər] *n* concurrent *c*

compile [kəm'pail] *v* samenstellen

complain [kəm'plein] *v* klagen

complaint [kəm'pleint] *n* klacht *c*

complete [kəm'pli:t] *adj* compleet, volledig; *v* voltooien

completely [kəm'pli:tli] *adv* helemaal, volkomen, geheel

complex ['kɔmpleks] *adj* ingewikkeld

complexion [kəm'plekfən] *n* teint *c*

complicated ['kɔmplikeitid] *adj* gecompliceerd, ingewikkeld

compliment ['kɔmplimənt] *n* compliment *nt*; *v* gelukwensen, feliciteren

compose [kəm'pouz] *v* samenstellen

composer [kəm'pouzə] *n* componist *c*

composition [,kɔmpə'zifən] *n* compositie *c*; samenstelling *c*

comprehensive [,kɔmpri'hensiv] *adj* uitgebreid

comprise [kəm'praiz] *v* omvatten

compromise ['kɔmprəmaiz] *n* compromis *nt*

compulsory [kəm'pʌlsəri] *adj* verplicht

computer [kəm'pju:tə] *n* computer

comrade ['kɔmreid] *n* kameraad *c*

conceal [kən'si:l] *v* *verbergen

conceited [kən'si:tid] *adj* verwaand

conceive [kən'si:v] *v* opvatten

concentrate ['kɔnsəntreit] *v* concentreren

concentration [,kɔnsən'treifən] *n* concentratie *c*

conception [kən'sepfən] *n* begrip *nt*; conceptie *c*

concern [kən'sə:n] *v* *aangaan, *betreffen; *n* zorg *c*; aangelegenheid *c*; bedrijf *nt*, onderneming *c*

concerned [kən'sə:nd] *adj* bezorgd; betrokken

concerning [kən'sə:niŋ] *prep* omtrent, betreffende

concert ['kɔnsət] *n* concert *nt*; ~ **hall** concertzaal *c*

concession [kən'sefən] *n* concessie *c*

concise [kən'sais] *adj* beknopt, summier

conclusion [kəŋ'klu:ʒən] *n* gevolgtrekking *c*, conclusie *c*

concrete ['kɔŋkri:t] *adj* concreet; *n* beton *nt*

concurrence [kəŋ'kʌrəns] *n* samenloop *c*

concussion [kəŋ'kʌfən] *n* hersenschudding *c*

condition [kən'difən] *n* voorwaarde *c*; toestand *c*; omstandigheid *c*

conditional [kən'difənəl] *adj* voorwaardelijk

conditioner [kən'difənə] *n* conditioner

condom ['kɔndəm] *n* condoom *nt*

conduct¹ ['kɔndʌkt] *n* gedrag *nt*

conduct² [kən'dʌkt] *v* leiden; begeleiden; dirigeren

conductor [kən'dʌktə] n conducteur c; dirigent c

confectioner [kən'fekʃənə] n banketbakker c

conference ['kɔnfərəns] n conferentie c

confess [kən'fes] v bekennen; biechten; *belijden

confession [kən'feʃən] n bekentenis c; biecht c

confidence ['kɔnfidəns] n vertrouwen nt

confident ['kɔnfidənt] adj gerust

confidential [,kɔnfi'denʃəl] adj vertrouwelijk

confirm [kən'fə:m] v bevestigen

confirmation [,kɔnfə'meiʃən] n bevestiging c

confiscate ['kɔnfiskeit] v vorderen, beslag leggen op

conflict ['kɔnflikt] n conflict nt

confuse [kən'fju:z] v verwarren

confusion [kən'fju:ʒən] n verwarring c

congratulate [kən'grætʃuleit] v feliciteren, gelukwensen

congratulation [kən,grætʃu'leiʃən] n felicitatie c, gelukwens c

congregation [,kɔngri'geiʃən] n gemeente c; orde c, congregatie c

congress ['kɔngres] n congres nt; bijeenkomst c

connect [kə'nekt] v *verbinden; *aansluiten

connection [kə'nekʃən] n relatie c; verband nt; aansluiting c, verbinding c

connoisseur [,kɔnə'sə:] n kenner c

connotation [,kɔnə'teiʃən] n bijbetekenis c

conquer ['kɔnkə] v veroveren; *overwinnen

conqueror ['kɔnkərə] n veroveraar c

conquest ['kɔnkwest] n verovering c

conscience ['kɔnʃəns] n geweten nt

conscious ['kɔnʃəs] adj bewust

consciousness ['kɔnʃəsnəs] n bewustzijn nt

conscript ['kɔnskript] n dienstplichtige c

consent [kən'sent] v toestemmen; instemmen; n instemming c, toestemming c

consequence ['kɔnsikwəns] n consequentie c, gevolg nt

consequently ['kɔnsikwəntli] adv bijgevolg

conservative [kən'sə:vətiv] adj behoudend, conservatief

consider [kən'sidə] v beschouwen; *overwegen; menen, *vinden

considerable [kən'sidərəbəl] adj aanzienlijk; flink, aanmerkelijk

considerate [kən'sidərət] adj attent

consideration [kən,sidə'reiʃən] n overweging c; consideratie c, aandacht c

considering [kən'sidəriŋ] prep gezien

consignment [kən'sainmənt] n zending c

consist of [kən'sist] *bestaan uit

conspire [kən'spaiə] v *samenzweren

constant ['kɔnstənt] adj aanhoudend

constipation [,kɔnsti'peiʃən] n obstipatie c, constipatie c

constituency [kən'stitʃuənsi] n kiesdistrict nt

constitution [,kɔnsti'tju:ʃən] n grondwet c

construct [kən'strʌkt] v bouwen; opbouwen, construeren

construction [kən'strʌkʃən] n constructie c; opbouw c; gebouw nt, bouw c

consul ['kɔnsəl] n consul c

consulate ['kɔnsjulət] n consulaat nt

consult [kən'sʌlt] v raadplegen

consultation [,kɔnsəl'teiʃən] n raadpleging *c*; consult *nt*; ~ **hours** *n* spreekuur *nt*

consumer [kən'sjuː'mə] *n* verbruiker *c*, consument *c*

contact ['kɔntækt] *n* contact *nt*; aanraking *c*; *v* zich in verbinding stellen met; ~ **lenses** contactlenzen *pl*

contagious [kən'teidʒəs] *adj* aanstekelijk, besmettelijk

contain [kən'tein] *v* bevatten; *inhouden

container [kən'teinə] *n* reservoir *nt*; container *c*

contemporary [kən'tempərəri] *adj* eigentijds; toenmalig; hedendaags; *n* tijdgenoot *c*

contempt [kən'tempt] *n* verachting *c*, minachting *c*

content [kən'tent] *adj* tevreden

contents ['kɔntents] *pl* inhoud *c*

contest ['kɔntest] *n* strijd *c*; wedstrijd *c*

continent ['kɔntinənt] *n* continent *nt*, werelddeel *nt*; vasteland *nt*

continental [,kɔnti'nentəl] *adj* continentaal

continual [kən'tinjuəl] *adj* voortdurend; **continually** *adv* steeds

continue [kən'tinju:] *v* voortzetten, vervolgen; *voortgaan, *doorgaan

continuous [kən'tinjuəs] *adj* voortdurend, doorlopend, onafgebroken

contour ['kɔntuə] *n* omtrek *c*

contraceptive [,kɔntrə'septiv] *n* voorbehoedmiddel *nt*

contract[1] ['kɔntrækt] *n* contract *nt*

contract[2] [kən'trækt] *v* *oplopen

contractor [kən'træktə] *n* aannemer *c*

contradict [,kɔntrə'dikt] *v* *tegenspreken

contradictory [,kɔntrə'diktəri] *adj* tegenstrijdig

contrary ['kɔntrəri] *n* tegendeel *nt*; *adj* tegengesteld; **on the** ~ integen-

deel

contrast ['kɔntraːst] *n* contrast *nt*; verschil *nt*, tegenstelling *c*

contribution [,kɔntri'bjuː'ʃən] *n* bijdrage *c*

control [kən'troul] *n* controle *c*; *v* controleren

controversial [,kɔntrə'vəːʃəl] *adj* controversieel, omstreden

convenience [kən'viːnjəns] *n* gemak *nt*

convenient [kən'viːnjənt] *adj* geriefelijk; geschikt, passend, gemakkelijk

convent ['kɔnvənt] *n* klooster *nt*

conversation [,kɔnvə'seiʃən] *n* conversatie *c*, gesprek *nt*

convert [kən'vəːt] *v* bekeren; omrekenen

convict[1] [kən'vikt] *v* schuldig *bevinden

convict[2] ['kɔnvikt] *n* veroordeelde *c*

conviction [kən'vikʃən] *n* overtuiging *c*; veroordeling *c*

convince [kən'vins] *v* overtuigen

convulsion [kən'vʌlʃən] *n* kramp *c*

cook [kuk] *n* kok *c*; *v* koken; bereiden, klaarmaken

cookbook ['kukbuk] *nAm* kookboek *nt*

cooker ['kukə] *n* fornuis *nt*; **gas** ~ gasfornuis *nt*

cookery-book ['kukəribuk] *n* kookboek *nt*

cookie ['kuki] *nAm* biscuit *nt*

cool [kuːl] *adj* koel; **cooling system** koelsysteem *nt*

co-operation [kou,ɔpə'reiʃən] *n* samenwerking *c*; medewerking *c*

co-operative [kou'ɔpərətiv] *adj* coöperatief; gewillig, bereidwillig; *n* coöperatie *c*

co-ordinate [kou'ɔːdineit] *v* coördineren

co-ordination [kou,ɔːdi'neiʃən] *n* coördinatie *c*

copper ['kɔpə] n roodkoper nt, koper nt

copy ['kɔpi] n kopie c; afschrift nt; exemplaar nt; v kopiëren; namaken; **carbon ~** doorslag c

coral ['kɔrəl] n koraal c

cord [kɔ:d] n koord nt; snoer nt

cordial ['kɔ:diəl] adj hartelijk

corduroy ['kɔ:dərɔi] n ribfluweel nt

core [kɔ:] n kern c; klokhuis nt

cork [kɔ:k] n kurk c; stop c

corkscrew ['kɔ:kskru:] n kurketrekker c

corn [kɔ:n] n korrel c; graan nt, koren nt; eksteroog nt, likdoorn c; **~ on the cob** maïskolf c

corner ['kɔ:nə] n hoek c

cornfield ['kɔ:nfi:ld] n korenveld nt

corpse [kɔ:ps] n lijk nt

corpulent ['kɔ:pjulənt] adj corpulent; gezet, dik

correct [kə'rekt] adj goed, correct, juist; v corrigeren, verbeteren

correction [kə'rekʃən] n correctie c; verbetering c

correctness [kə'rektnəs] n juistheid c

correspond [,kɔri'spɔnd] v corresponderen; *overeenkomen

correspondence [,kɔri'spɔndəns] n briefwisseling c, correspondentie c

correspondent [,kɔri'spɔndənt] n correspondent c

corridor ['kɔridɔ:] n gang c

corrupt [kə'rʌpt] adj corrupt; v *omkopen

corruption [kə'rʌpʃən] n omkoping c

corset ['kɔ:sit] n korset nt

cosmetics [kɔz'metiks] pl kosmetica pl, schoonheidsmiddelen pl

cost [kɔst] n kosten pl; prijs c

***cost** [kɔst] v kosten

cosy ['kouzi] adj knus, gezellig

cot [kɔt] nAm stretcher c

cottage ['kɔtidʒ] n buitenhuis nt

cotton ['kɔtən] n katoen nt/c; katoenen

cotton-wool ['kɔtənwul] n watten pl

couch [kautʃ] n divan c

cough [kɔf] n hoest c; v hoesten

could [kud] v (p can)

council ['kaunsəl] n raad c

councillor ['kaunsələ] n raadslid nt

counsel ['kaunsəl] n raad c

counsellor ['kaunsələ] n raadsman c

count [kaunt] v tellen; optellen; meetellen; achten; n graaf c

counter ['kauntə] n toonbank c; balie c

counterfeit ['kauntəfi:t] v vervalsen

counterfoil ['kauntəfɔil] n controlestrook c

counterpane ['kauntəpein] n sprei c

countess ['kauntis] n gravin c

country ['kʌntri] n land nt; platteland nt; streek c; **~ house** landhuis nt

countryman ['kʌntrimən] n (pl -men) landgenoot c

countryside ['kʌntrisaid] n platteland nt

county ['kaunti] n graafschap nt

couple ['kʌpəl] n paar nt

coupon ['ku:pɔn] n coupon c, bon c

courage ['kʌridʒ] n dapperheid c, moed c

courageous [kə'reidʒəs] adj dapper, moedig

course [kɔ:s] n koers c; gang c; loop c; cursus c; **intensive ~** spoedcursus c; **of ~** uiteraard, natuurlijk

court [kɔ:t] n rechtbank c; hof nt

courteous ['kə:tiəs] adj hoffelijk

cousin ['kʌzən] n nicht c, neef c

cover ['kʌvə] v bedekken; n schuilplaats c, beschutting c; deksel nt; omslag c/nt

cow [kau] n koe c

coward ['kauəd] n lafaard c

cowardly ['kauədli] adj laf

cow-hide ['kauhaid] *n* koeiehuid *c*

crab [kræb] *n* krab *c*

crack [kræk] *n* gekraak *nt*; barst *c*; *v* kraken; *breken, barsten

cracker ['krækə] *nAm* koekje *nt*

cradle ['kreidəl] *n* wieg *c*; bakermat *c*

cramp [kræmp] *n* kramp *c*

crane [krein] *n* hijskraan *c*

crankcase ['kræŋkkeis] *n* carter *nt*

crankshaft ['kræŋkʃɑ:ft] *n* krukas *c*

crash [kræʃ] *n* botsing *c*; *v* botsen; neerstorten; ~ **barrier** vangrail *c*

crate [kreit] *n* krat *nt*

crater ['kreitə] *n* krater *c*

crawl [krɔ:l] *v* *kruipen; *n* crawl *c*

craze [kreiz] *n* rage *c*

crazy ['kreizi] *adj* gek; dwaas, krankzinnig

creak [kri:k] *v* kraken

cream [kri:m] *n* crème *c*; room *c*; *adj* roomkleurig

creamy ['kri:mi] *adj* romig

crease [kri:s] *v* kreuken; *n* vouw *c*; plooi *c*

create [kri'eit] *v* *scheppen; creëren

creature ['kri:tʃə] *n* schepsel *nt*; wezen *nt*

credible ['kredibəl] *adj* geloofwaardig

credit ['kredit] *n* krediet *nt*; *v* crediteren; ~ **card** credit card

creditor ['kreditə] *n* schuldeiser *c*

credulous ['kredjuləs] *adj* goedgelovig

creek [kri:k] *n* inham *c*, kreek *c*

***creep** [kri:p] *v* *kruipen

creepy ['kri:pi] *adj* eng, griezelig

cremate [kri'meit] *v* cremeren

cremation [kri'meiʃən] *n* crematie *c*

crew [kru:] *n* bemanning *c*

cricket ['krikit] *n* cricket *nt*; krekel *c*

crime [kraim] *n* misdaad *c*

criminal ['kriminəl] *n* delinquent *c*, misdadiger *c*; *adj* crimineel, misdadig; ~ **law** strafrecht *nt*

criminality [,krimi'næləti] *n* criminaliteit *c*

crimson ['krimzən] *adj* vuurrood

crippled ['kripəld] *adj* kreupel

crisis ['kraisis] *n* (pl crises) crisis *c*

crisp [krisp] *adj* croquant, knappend

critic ['kritik] *n* criticus *c*

critical ['kritikəl] *adj* kritisch; kritiek, hachelijk, zorgwekkend

criticism ['kritisizəm] *n* kritiek *c*

criticize ['kritisaiz] *v* bekritiseren

crochet ['krouʃei] *v* haken

crockery ['krɔkəri] *n* aardewerk *nt*, vaatwerk *nt*

crocodile ['krɔkədail] *n* krokodil *c*

crooked ['krukid] *adj* verdraaid, krom; oneerlijk

crop [krɔp] *n* oogst *c*

cross [krɔs] *v* *oversteken; *adj* kwaad, boos; *n* kruis *nt*

cross-eyed ['krɔsaid] *adj* scheel

crossing ['krɔsiŋ] *n* overtocht *c*; kruising *c*; oversteekplaats *c*; overweg *c*

crossroads ['krɔsroudz] *n* kruispunt *nt*

crosswalk ['krɔswɔ:k] *nAm* zebrapad *nt*

crow [krou] *n* kraai *c*

crowbar ['kroubɑ:] *n* breekijzer *nt*

crowd [kraud] *n* massa *c*, menigte *c*

crowded ['kraudid] *adj* druk; overvol

crown [kraun] *n* kroon *c*; *v* kronen; bekronen

crucifix ['kru:sifiks] *n* kruisbeeld *nt*

crucifixion [,kru:si'fikʃən] *n* kruisiging *c*

crucify ['kru:sifai] *v* kruisigen

cruel [kruəl] *adj* wreed

cruise [kru:z] *n* boottocht *c*, cruise *c*

crumb [krʌm] *n* kruimel *c*

crusade [kru:'seid] *n* kruistocht *c*

crust [krʌst] *n* korst *c*

crutch [krʌtʃ] *n* kruk *c*

cry [krai] *v* huilen; schreeuwen; *roepen; *n* kreet *c*, schreeuw *c*; roep *c*

crystal ['kristəl] n kristal nt; adj kristallen

Cuba ['kju:bə] Cuba

Cuban ['kju:bən] adj Cubaans; n Cubaan c

cube [kju:b] n kubus c; blokje nt

cuckoo ['kuku:] n koekoek c

cucumber ['kju:kəmbə] n komkommer c

cuddle ['kʌdəl] v knuffelen

cudgel ['kʌdʒəl] n knuppel c

cuff [kʌf] n manchet c

cuff-links ['kʌfliŋks] pl manchetknopen pl

cul-de-sac ['kʌldəsæk] n doodlopende weg

cultivate ['kʌltiveit] v bebouwen; verbouwen, kweken

culture ['kʌltʃə] n cultuur c; beschaving c

cultured ['kʌltʃəd] adj beschaafd

cunning ['kʌnin] adj sluw

cup [kʌp] n kopje nt; beker c

cupboard ['kʌbəd] n kast c

curb [kə:b] n trottoirband c; v beteugelen

cure [kjuə] v *genezen; n kuur c; genezing c

curio ['kjuəriou] n (pl ~s) rariteit c

curiosity [,kjuəri'ɔsəti] n nieuwsgierigheid c

curious ['kjuəriəs] adj benieuwd, nieuwsgierig; raar

curl [kə:l] v krullen; n krul c

curler ['kə:lə] n krulspeld c

curling-tongs ['kə:liŋtɔŋz] pl krultang c

curly ['kə:li] adj krullend

currant ['kʌrənt] n krent c; bes c

currency ['kʌrənsi] n valuta c; **foreign ~** buitenlands geld

current ['kʌrənt] n stroming c; stroom c; adj gangbaar, huidig; **alternating ~** wisselstroom c; **direct ~** gelijkstroom c

curry ['kʌri] n kerrie c

curse [kə:s] v vloeken; vervloeken; n vloek c

curtain ['kə:tən] n gordijn nt; doek nt

curve [kə:v] n kromming c; bocht c

curved [kə:vd] adj krom, gebogen

cushion ['kuʃən] n kussen nt

custodian [kʌ'stoudiən] n suppoost c

custody ['kʌstədi] n hechtenis c; hoede c; voogdij c

custom ['kʌstəm] n gewoonte c; gebruik nt

customary ['kʌstəməri] adj gebruikelijk, gewoon, gewoonlijk

customer ['kʌstəmə] n klant c; cliënt c

Customs ['kʌstəmz] pl douane c; ~ **duty** accijns c; ~ **officer** douanebeambte c

cut [kʌt] n snee c; snijwond c

*** cut** [kʌt] v *snijden; knippen; verlagen; ~ **off** *afsnijden; afknippen; *afsluiten; ~ **class** mengen

cutlery ['kʌtləri] n bestek nt

cutlet ['kʌtlət] n karbonade c

cycle ['saikəl] n fiets c; rijwiel nt; kringloop c, cyclus c

cyclist ['saiklist] n fietser c; wielrijder c

cylinder ['silində] n cilinder c; ~ **head** cilinderkop c

cynical ['sinikəl] adj cynisch

cystitis [si'staitis] n blaasontsteking c

Czech [tʃek] adj Tsjechisch; n Tsjech c

D

dad [dæd] n vader c

daddy ['dædi] n papa c

daffodil ['dæfədil] n narcis c

daily ['deili] adj dagelijks; n dagblad nt

dairy ['dɛəri] n zuivelwinkel c

dam [dæm] n dam c; dijk c

damage ['dæmidʒ] n schade c; v beschadigen

damp [dæmp] adj vochtig; nat; n vocht nt; v bevochtigen

dance [dɑ:ns] v dansen; n dans c

dandelion ['dændilaiən] n paardebloem c

dandruff ['dændrəf] n roos c

Dane [dein] n Deen c

danger ['deindʒə] n gevaar nt

dangerous ['deindʒərəs] adj gevaarlijk

Danish ['deiniʃ] adj Deens

dare [dɛə] v wagen, durven; uitdagen

daring ['dɛəriŋ] adj gedurfd

dark [dɑ:k] adj duister, donker; n duisternis c

darling ['dɑ:liŋ] n schat c, lieveling c

darn [dɑ:n] v stoppen

dash [dæʃ] v snellen; n gedachtenstreepje nt

dashboard ['dæʃbɔ:d] n dashboard nt

data ['deitə] pl gegeven nt

date¹ [deit] n datum c; afspraak c; v dateren; out of ~ ouderwets

date² [deit] n dadel c

daughter ['dɔ:tə] n dochter c

dawn [dɔ:n] n ochtendschemering; dageraad c

day [dei] n dag c; by ~ overdag; ~ trip excursie c; per ~ per dag; the ~ before yesterday eergisteren

daybreak ['deibreik] n dageraad c

daylight ['deilait] n daglicht nt

dead [ded] adj dood; gestorven

deaf [def] adj doof

deal [di:l] n transactie c, affaire c

*deal [di:l] v uitdelen; ~ with v te maken *hebben met; zaken *doen met

dealer ['di:lə] n koopman c, handelaar c

dear [diə] adj lief; duur; dierbaar

death [deθ] n dood c; ~ penalty doodstraf c

debate [di'beit] n debat nt

debit ['debit] n debet nt

debt [det] n schuld c

decaffeinated [di:'kæfineitid] adj coffeïnevrij

deceit [di'si:t] n bedrog nt

deceive [di'si:v] v *bedriegen

December [di'sembə] december

decency ['di:sənsi] n fatsoen nt

decent ['di:sənt] adj fatsoenlijk

decide [di'said] v beslissen, *besluiten

decision [di'siʒən] n beslissing c, besluit nt

deck [dek] n dek nt; ~ cabin dekhut c; ~ chair ligstoel c

declaration [,deklə'reiʃən] n verklaring c; aangifte c

declare [di'klɛə] v verklaren; *opgeven; *aangeven

decoration [,dekə'reiʃən] n versiering c

decrease [di:'kri:s] v verminderen; *afnemen; n vermindering c

dedicate ['dedikeit] v toewijden

deduce [di'dju:s] v afleiden

deduct [di'dʌkt] v *aftrekken

deed [di:d] n handeling c, daad c

deep [di:p] adj diep

deep-freeze [,di:p'fri:z] n diepvrieskast c

deer [diə] n (pl ~) hert nt

defeat [di'fi:t] v *verslaan; n nederlaag c

defective [di'fektiv] adj gebrekkig, defect

defence [di'fens] n verdediging c; defensie c

defend [di'fend] v verdedigen

deficiency [di'fiʃənsi] n gebrek nt

deficit ['defisit] n tekort nt

define [di'fain] v *omschrijven, bepalen, definiëren

definite ['definit] adj bepaald; vastomlijnd

definition [,defi'niʃən] n bepaling c, definitie c

deformed [di'fɔ:md] adj misvormd, mismaakt

degree [di'gri:] n graad c; titel c

delay [di'lei] v vertragen; uitstellen; n oponthoud nt, vertraging c; uitstel nt

delegate ['deligət] n gedelegeerde c

delegation [,deli'geiʃən] n delegatie c, afvaardiging c

deliberate[1] [di'libəreit] v beraadslagen, overleggen

deliberate[2] [di'libərət] adj opzettelijk

deliberation [di,libə'reiʃən] n beraad nt, overleg nt

delicacy ['delikəsi] n lekkernij c

delicate ['delikət] adj fijn; teder; delikaat

delicatessen [,delikə'tesən] n delicatessen pl; delicatessenwinkel c

delicious [di'liʃəs] adj lekker, heerlijk

delight [di'lait] n genot nt, verrukking c; v in verrukking *brengen; **delighted** opgetogen

delightful [di'laitfəl] adj heerlijk, verrukkelijk

deliver [di'livə] v afleveren, bezorgen; verlossen

delivery [di'livəri] n levering c, bezorging c; bevalling c; verlossing c; ~ **van** bestelauto c

demand [di'mɑ:nd] v vereisen, eisen; n eis c; navraag c

democracy [di'mɔkrəsi] n democratie c

democratic [,demə'krætik] adj democratisch

demolish [di'mɔliʃ] v slopen

demolition [,demə'liʃən] n afbraak c

demonstrate ['demənstreit] v aantonen; demonstreren, betogen

demonstration [,demən'streiʃən] n demonstratie c; betoging c

den [den] n hol nt

Denmark ['denmɑ:k] Denemarken

denomination [di,nɔmi'neiʃən] n benaming c

dense [dens] adj dicht

dent [dent] n deuk c

dentist ['dentist] n tandarts c

denture ['dentʃə] n kunstgebit nt

deny [di'nai] v ontkennen; *onthouden, weigeren, *ontzeggen

deodorant [di:'oudərənt] n deodorant c

depart [di'pɑ:t] v *heengaan, *vertrekken; *overlijden

department [di'pɑ:tmənt] n departement nt, afdeling c; ~ **store** warenhuis nt

departure [di'pɑ:tʃə] n vertrek nt

dependant [di'pendənt] adj afhankelijk

depend on [di'pend] *afhangen van

deposit [di'pɔzit] n storting c; statiegeld nt; bezinksel nt, afzetting c; v storten

depository [di'pɔzitəri] n bergplaats c

depot ['depou] n opslagplaats c; nAm station nt

depress [di'pres] v deprimeren

depressed [di'prest] adj neerslachtig

depressing [di'presiŋ] adj triest

depression [di'preʃən] n neerslachtigheid c; depressie c; teruggang c

deprive of [di'praiv] *ontnemen

depth [depθ] n diepte c

deputy ['depjuti] n afgevaardigde c; plaatsvervanger c

descend [di'send] v dalen

descendant [di'sendənt] n afstammeling c

descent [di'sent] n afdaling c

describe [di'skraib] v *beschrijven

description [di'skripʃən] n beschrijving

c; signalement nt

desert[1] ['dezət] n woestijn c; adj woest, verlaten

desert[2] [di'zə:t] v deserteren; *verlaten

deserve [di'zə:v] v verdienen

design [di'zain] v *ontwerpen; n ontwerp nt; doel nt

designate ['dezigneit] v *aanwijzen

desirable [di'zaiərəbəl] adj begeerlijk, wenselijk

desire [di'zaiə] n wens c; zin c, begeerte c; v begeren, verlangen, wensen

desk [desk] n bureau nt; lessenaar c; schoolbank c

despair [di'spεə] n wanhoop c; v wanhopen

despatch [di'spætʃ] v *verzenden

desperate ['despərət] adj wanhopig

despise [di'spaiz] v verachten

despite [di'spait] prep ondanks

dessert [di'zə:t] n dessert nt

destination [,desti'neiʃən] n bestemming c

destine ['destin] v bestemmen

destiny ['destini] n noodlot nt, lot nt

destroy [di'strɔi] v vernielen, vernietigen

destruction [di'strʌkʃən] n vernietiging c; ondergang c

detach [di'tætʃ] v losmaken

detail ['di:teil] n bijzonderheid c, detail nt

detailed ['di:teild] adj uitvoerig, gedetailleerd

detect [di'tekt] v ontdekken

detective [di'tektiv] n detective c; ~ story detectiveroman c

detergent [di'tə:dʒənt] n wasmiddel nt

determine [di'tə:min] v vaststellen, bepalen

determined [di'tə:mind] adj vastbesloten

detour ['di:tuə] n omweg c; omleiding c

devaluation [,di:vælju'eiʃən] n devaluatie c

devalue [,di:'vælju:] v devalueren

develop [di'veləp] v ontwikkelen

development [di'veləpmənt] n ontwikkeling c

deviate ['di:vieit] v *afwijken

devil ['devəl] n duivel c

devise [di'vaiz] v beramen

devote [di'vout] v wijden

dew [dju:] n dauw c

diabetes [,daiə'bi:ti:z] n diabetes c, suikerziekte c

diabetic [,daiə'betik] n suikerzieke c, diabeticus c

diagnose [,daiəg'nouz] v een diagnose stellen; constateren

diagnosis [,daiəg'nousis] n (pl -ses) diagnose c

diagonal [dai'ægənəl] n diagonaal c; adj diagonaal

diagram ['daiəgræm] n schema nt; figuur c, grafiek c

dialect ['daiəlekt] n dialect nt

diamond ['daiəmənd] n diamant c

diaper ['daiəpə] nAm luier c

diaphragm ['daiəfræm] n tussenschot nt

diarrhoea [daiə'riə] n diarree c

diary ['daiəri] n agenda c; dagboek nt

dictaphone ['diktəfoun] n dictafoon c

dictate [dik'teit] v dicteren

dictation [dik'teiʃən] n dictaat nt; dictee nt

dictator [dik'teitə] n dictator c

dictionary ['dikʃənəri] n woordenboek nt

did [did] v (p do)

die [dai] v *sterven; *overlijden

diesel ['di:zəl] n diesel c

diet ['daiət] n dieet nt

differ ['difə] v verschillen

difference ['difərəns] n verschil nt; onderscheid nt

different ['difərənt] adj verschillend; ander

difficult ['difikəlt] adj moeilijk; lastig

difficulty ['difikəlti] n moeilijkheid c; moeite c

*dig [dig] v *graven; *delven

digest [di'dʒest] v verteren

digestible [di'dʒestəbəl] adj verteerbaar

digestion [di'dʒestʃən] n spijsvertering c

digit ['didʒit] n cijfer nt

digital [didʒitəl] adj digitaal

dignified ['dignifaid] adj waardig

dike [daik] n dijk c; dam c

dilapidated [di'læpideitid] adj bouwvallig

diligence ['dilidʒəns] n vlijt c, ijver c

diligent ['dilidʒənt] adj vlijtig, ijverig

dilute [dai'lju:t] v aanlengen, verdunnen

dim [dim] adj dof, mat; donker, zwak

dine [dain] v warm *eten

dinghy ['dingi] n bootje nt

dining-car ['daininka:] n restauratiewagen c

dining-room ['dainiŋru:m] n eetkamer c; eetzaal c

dinner ['dinə] n warme maaltijd; avondeten nt, middageten nt

dinner-jacket ['dinə,dʒækit] n smoking c

dinner-service ['dinə,sə:vis] n eetservies nt

diphtheria [dif'θiəriə] n difterie c

diploma [di'ploumə] n diploma nt

diplomat ['dipləmæt] n diplomaat c

direct [di'rekt] adj rechtstreeks, direct; v richten; *wijzen; leiden; regisseren

direction [di'rekʃən] n richting c; instructie c; regie c; bestuur nt; di-

rectional signal Am richtingaanwijzer c; **directions for use** gebruiksaanwijzing c

directive [di'rektiv] n richtlijn c

director [di'rektə] n directeur c; regisseur c

dirt [də:t] n vuil nt

dirty ['də:ti] adj smerig, vies, vuil

disabled [di'seibəld] adj gehandicapt, invalide

disadvantage [,disəd'va:ntidʒ] n nadeel nt

disagree [,disə'gri:] v het oneens *zijn, van mening verschillen

disagreeable [,disə'gri:əbəl] adj onaangenaam

disappear [,disə'piə] v *verdwijnen

disappoint [,disə'point] v teleurstellen; *be disappointing *tegenvallen

disappointment [,disə'pointmənt] n teleurstelling c

disapprove [,disə'pru:v] v afkeuren

disaster [di'za:stə] n ramp c; catastrofe c, onheil nt

disastrous [di'za:strəs] adj rampzalig

disc [disk] n schijf c; grammofoonplaat c; **slipped ~** hernia c

discard [di'ska:d] v afdanken

discharge [dis'tʃa:dʒ] v lossen, *uitladen; **~ of** *ontheffen van

discipline ['disiplin] n discipline c

discolour [di'skʌlə] v verkleuren

disconnect [,diskə'nekt] v ontkoppelen; uitschakelen

discontented [,diskən'tentid] adj ontevreden

discontinue [,diskən'tinju:] v *opheffen, staken

discount ['diskaunt] n korting c, reductie c

discover [di'skʌvə] v ontdekken

discovery [di'skʌvəri] n ontdekking c

discuss [di'skʌs] v *bespreken; discussiëren

discussion [di'skʌʃən] n discussie c; gesprek nt, bespreking c, debat nt
disease [di'zi:z] n ziekte c
disembark [,disim'ba:k] v van boord *gaan, ontschepen
disgrace [dis'greis] n schande c
disguise [dis'gaiz] v zich vermommen; n vermomming c
disgusting [dis'gʌstiŋ] adj misselijk, walgelijk
dish [diʃ] n bord nt; schotel c, schaal c; gerecht nt
dishonest [di'sɔnist] adj oneerlijk
disinfect [,disin'fekt] v ontsmetten
disinfectant [,disin'fektənt] n ontsmettingsmiddel nt
dislike [di'slaik] v een hekel *hebben aan, niet *houden van; n afkeer c, hekel c, antipathie c
dislocated ['disləkeitid] adj ontwricht
dismiss [dis'mis] v *wegzenden; *ontslaan
disorder [di'sɔ:də] n wanorde c
dispatch [di'spætʃ] v versturen, *verzenden
display [di'splei] v vertonen; tonen; n tentoonstelling c, expositie c
displease [di'spli:z] v ontstemmen, mishagen
disposable [di'spouzəbəl] adj wegwerp-
disposal [di'spouzəl] n beschikking c
dispose of [di'spouz] beschikken over
dispute [di'spju:t] n onenigheid c; ruzie c, geschil nt; v twisten, betwisten
dissatisfied [di'sætisfaid] adj ontevreden
dissolve [di'zɔlv] v oplossen; *ontbinden
dissuade from [di'sweid] *afraden
distance ['distəns] n afstand c; ~ in kilometres kilometertal nt
distant ['distənt] adj ver
distinct [di'stiŋkt] adj duidelijk; verschillend
distinction [di'stiŋkʃən] n onderscheid nt, verschil nt
distinguish [di'stiŋgwiʃ] v onderscheid maken, *onderscheiden
distinguished [di'stiŋgwiʃt] adj voornaam
distress [di'stres] n nood c; ~ signal noodsein nt
distribute [di'stribju:t] v uitdelen
distributor [di'stribjutə] n agent c; stroomverdeler c
district ['distrikt] n district nt; streek c; wijk c
disturb [di'stə:b] v storen, verstoren
disturbance [di'stə:bəns] n storing c; verwarring c
ditch [ditʃ] n greppel c, sloot c
dive [daiv] v *duiken
diversion [dai'və:ʃən] n wegomlegging c; afleiding c
divide [di'vaid] v delen; verdelen; *scheiden
divine [di'vain] adj goddelijk
division [di'viʒən] n deling c; scheiding c; afdeling c
divorce [di'vɔ:s] n echtscheiding c; v *scheiden
dizziness ['dizinəs] n duizeligheid c
dizzy ['dizi] adj duizelig
*do [du:] v *doen; voldoende *zijn
dock [dɔk] n dok nt; kade c; v aanleggen
docker ['dɔkə] n havenarbeider c
doctor ['dɔktə] n arts c, dokter c; doctor c
document ['dɔkjumənt] n document nt
dog [dɔg] n hond c
dogged ['dɔgid] adj hardnekkig
doll [dɔl] n pop c
dome [doum] n koepel c
domestic [də'mestik] adj huiselijk; binnenlands; n bediende c
domicile ['dɔmisail] n woonplaats c

domination [,dɔmi'neiʃən] *n* overheersing *c*

dominion [də'minjən] *n* heerschappij *c*

donate [dou'neit] *v* *schenken

donation [dou'neiʃən] *n* schenking *c*, gift *c*

done [dʌn] *v* (pp do)

donkey ['dɔŋki] *n* ezel *c*

donor ['dounə] *n* donateur *c*

door [dɔ:] *n* deur *c*; **revolving ~** draaideur *c*; **sliding ~** schuifdeur *c*

doorbell ['dɔ:bel] *n* deurbel *c*

door-keeper ['dɔ:,ki:pə] *n* portier *c*

doorman ['dɔ:mən] *n* (pl -men) portier *c*

dormitory ['dɔ:mitri] *n* slaapzaal *c*

dose [dous] *n* dosis *c*

dot [dɔt] *n* punt *c*

double ['dʌbəl] *adj* dubbel

doubt [daut] *v* betwijfelen, twijfelen; *n* twijfel *c*; **without ~** zonder twijfel

doubtful ['dautfəl] *adj* twijfelachtig; onzeker

dough [dou] *n* deeg *nt*

down[1] [daun] *adv* neer; omlaag, naar beneden, omver; *adj* neerslachtig; *prep* langs, van … af; **~ payment** aanbetaling *c*

down[2] [daun] *n* dons *nt*

downpour ['daunpɔ:] *n* stortbui *c*

downstairs [,daun'stɛəz] *adv* naar beneden, beneden

downstream [,daun'stri:m] *adv* stroomafwaarts

down-to-earth [,dauntu'ə:θ] *adj* nuchter

downwards ['daunwədz] *adv* neer, naar beneden

dozen ['dʌzən] *n* (pl ~, ~s) dozijn *nt*

draft [drɑ:ft] *n* wissel *c*

drag [dræg] *v* slepen

dragon ['drægən] *n* draak *c*

drain [drein] *v* droogleggen; afwateren; *n* afvoer *c*

drama ['drɑ:mə] *n* drama *nt*; treurspel *nt*; toneel *nt*

dramatic [drə'mætik] *adj* dramatisch

dramatist ['dræmətist] *n* toneelschrijver *c*

drank [dræŋk] *v* (p drink)

draper ['dreipə] *n* manufacturier *c*

drapery ['dreipəri] *n* stoffen

draught [drɑ:ft] *n* tocht *c*; **draughts** damspel *nt*

draught-board ['drɑ:ftbɔ:d] *n* dambord *nt*

draw [drɔ:] *n* trekking *c*

***draw** [drɔ:] *v* tekenen; *trekken; *opnemen; **~ up** opstellen

drawbridge ['drɔ:bridʒ] *n* ophaalbrug *c*

drawer ['drɔ:ə] *n* la *c*, lade *c*; **drawers** onderbroek *c*

drawing ['drɔ:iŋ] *n* tekening *c*

drawing-pin ['drɔ:iŋpin] *n* punaise *c*

drawing-room ['drɔ:iŋru:m] *n* salon *c*

dread [dred] *v* vrezen; *n* vrees *c*

dreadful ['dredfəl] *adj* vreselijk, ontzettend

dream [dri:m] *n* droom *c*

***dream** [dri:m] *v* dromen

dress [dres] *v* aankleden; zich kleden, zich aankleden; *verbinden; *n* japon *c*, jurk *c*

dressing-gown ['dresiŋgaun] *n* kamerjas *c*

dressing-room ['dresiŋru:m] *n* kleedkamer *c*

dressing-table ['dresiŋ,teibəl] *n* toilettafel *c*

dressmaker ['dres,meikə] *n* naaister *c*

drill [dril] *v* boren; trainen; *n* boor *c*

drink [driŋk] *n* borrel *c*, drank *c*

***drink** [driŋk] *v* *drinken

drinking-water ['driŋkiŋ,wɔ:tə] *n* drinkwater *nt*

drip-dry [,drip'drai] *adj* zelfstrijkend,

nò-iron

drive [draiv] n rijweg c; autorit c

*drive [draiv] v *rijden; besturen

driver ['draivə] n chauffeur c

drizzle ['drizəl] n motregen c

drop [drɔp] v *laten vallen; n druppel c

drought [draut] n droogte c

drown [draun] v *verdrinken; ***be drowned** *verdrinken

drug [drʌg] n verdovend middel; geneesmiddel nt

drugstore ['drʌgstɔ:] nAm drogisterij c, apotheek c; warenhuis nt

drum [drʌm] n trommel c

drunk [drʌŋk] adj (pp drink) dronken

dry [drai] adj droog; v drogen; afdrogen

dry-clean [,drai'kli:n] v chemisch reinigen

dry-cleaner's [,drai'kli:nəz] n stomerij c

dryer ['draiə] n centrifuge c

duchess ['dʌtʃis] n hertogin c

duck [dʌk] n eend c

due [dju:] adj verwacht; verschuldigd; vervallen

dues [dju:z] pl schulden pl

dug [dʌg] v (p, pp dig)

duke [dju:k] n hertog c

dull [dʌl] adj vervelend, saai; flets, mat; bot

dumb [dʌm] adj stom; suf, dom

dune [dju:n] n duin nt

dung [dʌŋ] n mest c

dunghill ['dʌŋhil] n mesthoop c

duration [dju'reiʃən] n duur c

during ['djuəriŋ] prep gedurende, tijdens

dusk [dʌsk] n avondschemering c

dust [dʌst] n stof nt

dustbin ['dʌstbin] n vuilnisbak c

dusty ['dʌsti] adj stoffig

Dutch [dʌtʃ] adj Nederlands, Hollands

Dutchman ['dʌtʃmən] n (pl -men) Nederlander c, Hollander c

dutiable ['dju:tiəbəl] adj belastbaar

duty ['dju:ti] n plicht c; taak c; invoerrecht nt; **Customs ~** accijns c

duty-free [,dju:ti'fri:] adj belastingvrij

dwarf [dwɔ:f] n dwerg c

dye [dai] v verven; n verf c

dynamo ['dainəmou] n (pl ~s) dynamo c

dysentery ['disəntri] n dysenterie c

E

each [i:tʃ] adj elk, ieder; ~ **other** elkaar

eager ['i:gə] adj verlangend, ongeduldig

eagle ['i:gəl] n arend c

ear [iə] n oor nt

earache ['iəreik] n oorpijn c

ear-drum ['iədrʌm] n trommelvlies nt

earl [ə:l] n graaf c

early ['ə:li] adj vroeg

earn [ə:n] v verdienen

earnest ['ə:nist] n ernst c

earnings ['ə:niŋz] pl inkomsten pl, verdiensten pl

earring ['iəriŋ] n oorbel c

earth [ə:θ] n aarde c; grond c

earthenware ['ə:θənwɛə] n aardewerk nt

earthquake ['ə:θkweik] n aardbeving c

ease [i:z] n ongedwongenheid c, gemak nt

east [i:st] n oost c, oosten nt

Easter ['i:stə] Pasen

easterly ['i:stəli] adj oostelijk

eastern ['i:stən] adj oost-, oostelijk

easy ['i:zi] adj gemakkelijk; geriefelijk; ~ **chair** leunstoel c

easy-going ['i:zi,gouiŋ] *adj* ontspannen
* **eat** [i:t] *v* *eten
eavesdrop ['i:vzdrɔp] *v* afluisteren
ebony ['ebəni] *n* ebbehout *nt*
eccentric [ik'sentrik] *adj* excentriek
echo ['ekou] *n* (pl ~es) weerklank *c*,
echo *c*
eclipse [i'klips] *n* verduistering *c*
economic [,i:kə'nɔmik] *adj* economisch
economical [,i:kə'nɔmikəl] *adj* spaarzaam, zuinig
economist [i'kɔnəmist] *n* econoom *c*
economize [i'kɔnəmaiz] *v* sparen
economy [i'kɔnəmi] *n* economie *c*
ecstasy ['ekstəzi] *n* extase *c*
Ecuador ['ekwədɔ:] Ecuador
Ecuadorian [,ekwə'dɔ:riən] *n* Ecuadoriaan *c*
eczema ['eksimə] *n* eczeem *nt*
edge [edʒ] *n* kant *c*, rand *c*
edible ['edibəl] *adj* eetbaar
edition [i'diʃən] *n* editie *c*, uitgave *c*;
morning ~ ochtendeditie *c*
editor ['editə] *n* redakteur *c*
educate ['edʒukeit] *v* opleiden, opvoeden
education [,edʒu'keiʃən] *n* onderwijs
nt; opvoeding *c*
eel [i:l] *n* aal *c*, paling *c*
effect [i'fekt] *n* gevolg *nt*, effect *nt*; *v*
*teweegbrengen; **in** ~ feitelijk
effective [i'fektiv] *adj* doeltreffend, effectief
efficient [i'fiʃənt] *adj* efficiënt, doelmatig
effort ['efət] *n* inspanning *c*; poging *c*
egg [eg] *n* ei *nt*
egg-cup ['egkʌp] *n* eierdopje *nt*
eggplant ['egpla:nt] *n* aubergine *c*
egg-yolk ['egjouk] *n* eierdooier *c*
egoistic [,egou'istik] *adj* zelfzuchtig
Egypt ['i:dʒipt] Egypte
Egyptian [i'dʒipʃən] *adj* Egyptisch; *n*
Egyptenaar *c*

eiderdown ['aidədaun] *n* donzen dekbed
eight [eit] *num* acht
eighteen [,ei'ti:n] *num* achttien
eighteenth [,ei'ti:nθ] *num* achttiende
eighth [eitθ] *num* achtste
eighty ['eiti] *num* tachtig
either ['aiðə] *pron* een van beide; **either ... or** hetzij ... hetzij, of ... of
elaborate [i'læbəreit] *v* uitwerken
elastic [i'læstik] *adj* elastisch; rekbaar; elastiek *nt*
elasticity [,elæ'stisəti] *n* rek *c*
elbow ['elbou] *n* elleboog *c*
elder ['eldə] *adj* ouder
elderly ['eldəli] *adj* bejaard
eldest ['eldist] *adj* oudst
elect [i'lekt] *v* *kiezen, *verkiezen
election [i'lekʃən] *n* verkiezing *c*
electric [i'lektrik] *adj* elektrisch; ~
razor scheerapparaat *nt*; ~ **cord**
snoer *nt*
electrician [,ilek'triʃən] *n* elektricien *c*
electricity [,ilek'trisəti] *n* elektriciteit *c*
electronic [ilek'trɔnik] *adj* elektronisch; ~ **game** elektronisch spel
elegance ['eligəns] *n* elegantie *c*
elegant ['eligənt] *adj* elegant
element ['elimənt] *n* bestanddeel *nt*,
element *nt*
elephant ['elifənt] *n* olifant *c*
elevator ['eliveitə] *nAm* lift *c*
eleven [i'levən] *num* elf
eleventh [i'levənθ] *num* elfde
elf [elf] *n* (pl elves) elf *c*
eliminate [i'limineit] *v* elimineren
elm [elm] *n* iep *c*
else [els] *adv* anders
elsewhere [,el'sweə] *adv* elders
emancipation [i,mænsi'peiʃən] *n* emancipatie *c*
embankment [im'bæŋkmənt] *n* kade *c*
embargo [em'ba:gou] *n* (pl ~es) embargo *nt*

embark [im'bɑːk] v inschepen; instappen

embarkation [,embɑː'keiʃən] n inscheping c

embarrass [im'bærəs] v in verwarring brengen; in verlegenheid *brengen; hinderen; **embarrassed** verlegen, gegeneerd; **embarrassing** pijnlijk

embassy ['embəsi] n ambassade c

emblem ['embləm] n embleem nt

embrace [im'breis] v omhelzen; n omhelzing c

embroider [im'brɔidə] v borduren

embroidery [im'brɔidəri] n borduurwerk nt

emerald ['emərəld] n smaragd nt

emergency [i'məːdʒənsi] n spoedgeval nt, noodgeval nt; noodtoestand c; ~ **exit** nooduitgang c

emigrant ['emigrənt] n emigrant c

emigrate ['emigreit] v emigreren

emigration [,emi'greiʃən] n emigratie c

emotion [i'mouʃən] n ontroering c, emotie c

emperor ['empərə] n keizer c

emphasize ['emfəsaiz] v benadrukken

empire ['empaiə] n keizerrijk nt, rijk nt

employ [im'plɔi] v tewerkstellen; gebruiken

employee [,emplɔi'iː] n werknemer c, employé c

employer [im'plɔiə] n werkgever c

employment [im'plɔimənt] n tewerkstelling c, werk nt; ~ **exchange** arbeidsbureau nt

empress ['empris] n keizerin c

empty ['empti] adj leeg; v ledigen

enable [i'neibəl] v in staat stellen

enamel [i'næməl] n email nt

enamelled [i'næməld] adj geëmailleerd

enchanting [in'tʃɑːntiŋ] adj prachtig, betoverend

encircle [in'səːkəl] v omcirkelen, omringen; *insluiten

enclose [iŋ'klouz] v *bijsluiten, *insluiten

enclosure [iŋ'klouʒə] n bijlage c

encounter [iŋ'kauntə] v ontmoeten; n ontmoeting c

encourage [iŋ'kʌridʒ] v aanmoedigen

encyclopaedia [en,saiklə'piːdiə] n encyclopedie c

end [end] n einde nt; slot nt; v beëindigen; *aflopen

ending ['endiŋ] n einde nt

endless ['endləs] adj oneindig

endorse [in'dɔːs] v aftekenen, endosseren

endure [in'djuə] v *verdragen

enemy ['enəmi] n vijand c

energetic [,enə'dʒetik] adj energiek

energy ['enədʒi] n energie c; kracht c

engage [iŋ'geidʒ] v in dienst *nemen; *bespreken; zich *verbinden; **engaged** verloofd; bezig, bezet

engagement [iŋ'geidʒmənt] n verloving c; verplichting c; afspraak c; ~ **ring** verlovingsring c

engine ['endʒin] n machine c, motor c; locomotief c

engineer [,endʒi'niə] n ingenieur c

England ['iŋglənd] Engeland

English ['iŋgliʃ] adj Engels

Englishman ['iŋgliʃmən] n (pl -men) Engelsman c

engrave [iŋ'greiv] v graveren

engraver [iŋ'greivə] n graveur c

engraving [iŋ'greiviŋ] n prent c; gravure c

enigma [i'nigmə] n raadsel nt

enjoy [in'dʒɔi] v *genieten van

enjoyable [in'dʒɔiəbəl] adj fijn, prettig, leuk; lekker

enjoyment [in'dʒɔimənt] n genot nt

enlarge [in'lɑːdʒ] v vergroten; uitbreiden

enlargement [in'lɑːdʒmənt] n vergroting c

enormous [i'nɔ:məs] *adj* reusachtig, enorm

enough [i'nʌf] *adv* genoeg; *adj* voldoende

enquire [in'kwaiə] *v* informeren; *onderzoeken

enquiry [in'kwaiəri] *n* informatie c; onderzoek nt; enquête c

enter ['entə] *v* *betreden, *binnengaan; *inschrijven

enterprise ['entəpraiz] *n* onderneming c

entertain [,entə'tein] *v* vermaken, *onderhouden; *ontvangen

entertainer [,entə'teinə] *n* conferencier c

entertaining [,entə'teiniŋ] *adj* vermakelijk, amusant

entertainment [,entə'teinmənt] *n* vermaak nt, amusement nt

enthusiasm [in'θju:ziæzəm] *n* enthousiasme nt

enthusiastic [in,θju:zi'æstik] *adj* enthousiast

entire [in'taiə] *adj* heel, geheel

entirely [in'taiəli] *adv* helemaal

entrance ['entrəns] *n* ingang c; toegang c; binnenkomst c

entrance-fee ['entrənsfi:] *n* entree c

entry ['entri] *n* ingang c, entree c; toegang c; post c; **no ~** verboden toegang

envelope ['envəloup] *n* envelop c

envious ['enviəs] *adj* afgunstig, jaloers

environment [in'vaiərənmənt] *n* milieu nt; omgeving c

envoy ['envɔi] *n* gezant c

envy ['envi] *n* afgunst c; *v* benijden

epic ['epik] *n* epos nt; *adj* episch

epidemic [,epi'demik] *n* epidemie c

epilepsy ['epilepsi] *n* epilepsie c

epilogue ['epilɔg] *n* epiloog c

episode ['episoud] *n* episode c

equal ['i:kwəl] *adj* gelijk; *v* evenaren

equality [i'kwɔləti] *n* gelijkheid c

equalize ['i:kwəlaiz] *v* gelijk maken

equally ['i:kwəli] *adv* even

equator [i'kweitə] *n* evenaar c

equip [i'kwip] *v* uitrusten

equipment [i'kwipmənt] *n* uitrusting c

equivalent [i'kwivələnt] *adj* equivalent, gelijkwaardig

eraser [i'reizə] *n* gom c/nt

erect [i'rekt] *v* opbouwen, oprichten; *adj* overeind, rechtopstaand

err [ə:] *v* zich vergissen; dwalen

errand ['erənd] *n* boodschap c

error ['erə] *n* fout c, vergissing c

escalator ['eskəleitə] *n* roltrap c

escape [i'skeip] *v* ontsnappen; vluchten, ontvluchten; *ontgaan; *n* ontsnapping c

escort¹ ['eskɔ:t] *n* escorte nt

escort² [i'skɔ:t] *v* escorteren

especially [i'speʃəli] *adv* voornamelijk, vooral

esplanade [,esplə'neid] *n* promenade c

essay ['esei] *n* essay nt; verhandeling c, opstel nt

essence ['esəns] *n* essentie c; kern c, wezen nt

essential [i'senʃəl] *adj* onontbeerlijk; wezenlijk, essentieel

essentially [i'senʃəli] *adv* vooral

establish [i'stæbliʃ] *v* vestigen; vaststellen

estate [i'steit] *n* landgoed nt

esteem [i'sti:m] *n* respect nt, achting c; *v* achten

estimate¹ ['estimeit] *v* taxeren, schatten

estimate² ['estimət] *n* schatting c

estuary ['estʃuəri] *n* riviermonding c

etcetera [et'setərə] enzovoort

etching ['etʃiŋ] *n* ets c

eternal [i'tə:nəl] *adj* eeuwig

eternity [i'tə:nəti] *n* eeuwigheid c

ether ['i:θə] *n* ether *c*
Ethiopia [iθi'oupiə] Ethiopië
Ethiopian [iθi'oupiən] *adj* Ethiopisch; *n* Ethiopiër *c*
Europe ['juərəp] Europa
European [juərə'pi:ən] *adj* Europees; *n* Europeaan *c*
European Union [juərə'pi:ən 'ju:njən] Europese Unie
evacuate [i'vækjueit] *v* evacueren
evaluate [i'væljueit] *v* schatten
evaporate [i'væpəreit] *v* verdampen
even ['i:vən] *adj* effen, plat, gelijk; constant; even; *adv* zelfs
evening ['i:vniŋ] *n* avond *c*; ~ **dress** avondkleding *c*
event [i'vent] *n* gebeurtenis *c*; geval *nt*
eventual [i'ventʃuəl] *adj* eventueel; uiteindelijk
ever ['evə] *adv* ooit; altijd
every ['evri] *adj* ieder, elk
everybody ['evri,bɔdi] *pron* iedereen
everyday ['evridei] *adj* alledaags
everyone ['evriwʌn] *pron* ieder, iedereen
everything ['evriθiŋ] *pron* alles
everywhere ['evriwɛə] *adv* overal
evidence ['evidəns] *n* bewijs *nt*
evident ['evidənt] *adj* duidelijk
evil ['i:vəl] *n* kwaad *nt*; *adj* slecht
evolution [,i:və'lu:ʃən] *n* evolutie *c*
exact [ig'zækt] *adj* nauwkeurig, precies
exactly [ig'zæktli] *adv* precies
exaggerate [ig'zædʒəreit] *v* *overdrijven
examination [ig,zæmi'neiʃən] *n* examen *nt*; onderzoek *nt*; verhoor *nt*
examine [ig'zæmin] *v* *onderzoeken
example [ig'zɑ:mpəl] *n* voorbeeld *nt*; **for** ~ bijvoorbeeld
exceed [ik'si:d] *v* *overschrijden; *overtreffen
excel [ik'sel] *v* *uitblinken

excellent ['eksələnt] *adj* voortreffelijk, uitstekend
except [ik'sept] *prep* uitgezonderd, behalve
exception [ik'sepʃən] *n* uitzondering *c*
exceptional [ik'sepʃənəl] *adj* buitengewoon, uitzonderlijk
excerpt ['eksə:pt] *n* passage *c*
excess [ik'ses] *n* exces *nt*
excessive [ik'sesiv] *adj* buitensporig
exchange [iks'tʃeindʒ] *v* uitwisselen, wisselen, ruilen; *n* ruil *c*; beurs *c*; ~ **office** wisselkantoor *nt*; ~ **rate** koers *c*
excite [ik'sait] *v* *opwinden
excitement [ik'saitmənt] *n* drukte *c*, opwinding *c*
exciting [ik'saitiŋ] *adj* spannend
exclaim [ik'skleim] *v* *uitroepen
exclamation [,eksklə'meiʃən] *n* uitroep *c*
exclude [ik'sklu:d] *v* *uitsluiten
exclusive [ik'sklu:siv] *adj* exclusief
exclusively [ik'sklu:sivli] *adv* uitsluitend
excursion [ik'skə:ʃən] *n* uitstapje *nt*, excursie *c*
excuse¹ [ik'skju:s] *n* excuus *nt*
excuse² [ik'skju:z] *v* verontschuldigen, excuseren
execute ['eksikju:t] *v* uitvoeren
execution [,eksi'kju:ʃən] *n* terechtstelling *c*
executioner [,eksi'kju:ʃənə] *n* beul *c*
executive [ig'zekjutiv] *adj* uitvoerend; *n* uitvoerende macht; directeur *c*
exempt [ig'zempt] *v* *ontheffen, vrijstellen; *adj* vrijgesteld
exemption [ig'zempʃən] *n* vrijstelling *c*
exercise ['eksəsaiz] *n* oefening *c*; thema *nt*; *v* oefenen; uitoefenen
exhale [eks'heil] *v* uitademen
exhaust [ig'zɔ:st] *n* uitlaatpijp *c*, uitlaat *c*; *v* uitputten; ~ **gases** uit-

exhibit 53 extraordinary

laatgassen *pl*

exhibit [ig'zibit] *v* tentoonstellen; vertonen

exhibition [,eksi'biʃən] *n* expositie *c*, tentoonstelling *c*

exile ['eksail] *n* ballingschap *c*; balling *c*

exist [ig'zist] *v* *bestaan

existence [ig'zistəns] *n* bestaan *nt*

exit ['eksit] *n* uitgang *c*; uitrit *c*

exotic [ig'zɔtik] *adj* exotisch

expand [ik'spænd] *v* uitbreiden; uitspreiden; ontplooien

expect [ik'spekt] *v* verwachten

expectation [,ekspek'teiʃən] *n* verwachting *c*

expedition [,ekspə'diʃən] *n* verzending *c*; expeditie *c*

expel [ik'spel] *v* *uitwijzen

expenditure [ik'spenditʃə] *n* kosten *pl*, uitgave *c*

expense [ik'spens] *n* uitgave *c*; **expenses** *pl* onkosten *pl*

expensive [ik'spensiv] *adj* prijzig, duur; kostbaar

experience [ik'spiəriəns] *n* ervaring *c*; *v* ervaren, *ondervinden, beleven; **experienced** ervaren

experiment [ik'sperimənt] *n* proef *c*, experiment *nt*; *v* experimenteren

expert ['ekspə:t] *n* deskundige *c*, vakman *c*, expert *c*; *adj* deskundig

expire [ik'spaiə] *v* *vervallen, *aflopen, *verstrijken; uitademen; **expired** vervallen

expiry [ik'spaiəri] *n* vervaldag *c*, afloop *c*

explain [ik'splein] *v* verklaren, uitleggen

explanation [,eksplə'neiʃən] *n* toelichting *c*, uitleg *c*, verklaring *c*

explicit [ik'splisit] *adj* uitdrukkelijk, expliciet

explode [ik'sploud] *v* ontploffen

exploit [ik'splɔit] *v* uitbuiten, exploiteren

explore [ik'splɔ:] *v* verkennen, *onderzoeken

explosion [ik'splouʒən] *n* explosie *c*

explosive [ik'splousiv] *adj* explosief; *n* springstof *c*

export[1] [ik'spɔ:t] *v* uitvoeren, exporteren

export[2] ['ekspɔ:t] *n* export *c*

exportation [,ekspɔ:'teiʃən] *n* uitvoer *c*

exports ['ekspɔ:ts] *pl* export *c*

exposition [,ekspə'ziʃən] *n* tentoonstelling *c*

exposure [ik'spouʒə] *n* blootstelling *c*; belichting *c*; ~ **meter** belichtingsmeter *c*

express [ik'spres] *v* uitdrukken; betuigen, uiten; *adj* expresse-; uitdrukkelijk; ~ **train** sneltrein *c*

expression [ik'spreʃən] *n* uitdrukking *c*; uiting *c*

exquisite [ik'skwizit] *adj* voortreffelijk

extend [ik'stend] *v* verlengen; uitbreiden; verlenen

extension [ik'stenʃən] *n* verlenging *c*; uitbreiding *c*; toestel *nt*; ~ **cord** verlengsnoer *nt*

extensive [ik'stensiv] *adj* omvangrijk; veelomvattend, uitgebreid

extent [ik'stent] *n* omvang *c*

exterior [ek'stiəriə] *adj* uiterlijk; *n* buitenkant *c*

external [ek'stə:nəl] *adj* uiterlijk

extinguish [ik'stiŋgwiʃ] *v* blussen, doven

extort [ik'stɔ:t] *v* *afdwingen

extortion [ik'stɔ:ʃən] *n* afpersing *c*

extra ['ekstrə] *adj* extra

extract[1] [ik'strækt] *v* *uittrekken, *trekken

extract[2] ['ekstrækt] *n* fragment *nt*

extradite ['ekstrədait] *v* uitleveren

extraordinary [ik'strɔ:dənri] *adj* buitengewoon

extravagant [ik'strævəgənt] *adj* overdreven, extravagant

extreme [ik'stri:m] *adj* extreem; hoogst, uiterst; *n* uiterste *nt*

exuberant [ig'zju:bərənt] *adj* uitbundig

eye [ai] *n* oog *nt*

eyebrow ['aibrau] *n* wenkbrauw *c*

eyelash ['ailæʃ] *n* wimper *c*

eyelid ['ailid] *n* ooglid *nt*

eye-pencil ['ai,pensəl] *n* wenkbrauwstift *c*

eye-shadow ['ai,ʃædou] *n* ogenschaduw *c*

eye-witness ['ai,witnəs] *n* ooggetuige *c*

F

fable ['feibəl] *n* fabel *c*

fabric ['fæbrik] *n* stof *c*; structuur *c*

façade [fə'sa:d] *n* gevel *c*

face [feis] *n* gezicht *nt*; *v* het hoofd *bieden aan; ~ **massage** gezichtsmassage *c*; **facing** tegenover

face-cream ['feiskri:m] *n* gezichtscrème *c*

face-pack ['feispæk] *n* schoonheidsmasker *nt*

face-powder ['feis,paudə] *n* gezichtspoeder *nt/c*

facility [fə'siləti] *n* faciliteit *c*

fact [fækt] *n* feit *nt*; **in** ~ in feite

factor ['fæktə] *n* factor *c*

factory ['fæktəri] *n* fabriek *c*

factual ['fæktʃuəl] *adj* feitelijk

faculty ['fækəlti] *n* vermogen *nt*; gave *c*, talent *nt*, bekwaamheid *c*; faculteit *c*

fad [fæd] *n* gril *c*

fade [feid] *v* verkleuren, *verschieten

faience [fai'ɑ̃:s] *n* aardewerk *nt*, faience *c*

fail [feil] *v* falen; tekort *schieten; *ontbreken; *nalaten; zakken; **without** ~ beslist

failure ['feiljə] *n* mislukking *c*; fiasco *nt*

faint [feint] *v* *flauwvallen; *adj* zwak, vaag, flauw

fair [feə] *n* kermis *c*; beurs *c*; *adj* billijk, eerlijk; blond; mooi

fairly ['feəli] *adv* vrij, nogal, tamelijk

fairy ['feəri] *n* fee *c*

fairytale ['feəriteil] *n* sprookje *nt*

faith [feiθ] *n* geloof *nt*; vertrouwen *nt*

faithful ['feiθful] *adj* trouw

fake [feik] *n* vervalsing *c*

fall [fɔ:l] *n* val *c*; *nAm* herfst *c*

***fall** [fɔ:l] *v* *vallen

false [fɔ:ls] *adj* vals; verkeerd, onwaar, onecht; ~ **teeth** kunstgebit *nt*

falter ['fɔ:ltə] *v* wankelen; stamelen

fame [feim] *n* faam *c*, roem *c*; reputatie *c**

familiar [fə'miljə] *adj* vertrouwd; familiaar

family ['fæməli] *n* gezin *nt*; familie *c*; ~ **name** achternaam *c*

famous ['feiməs] *adj* beroemd

fan [fæn] *n* ventilator *c*; waaier *c*; fan *c*; ~ **belt** ventilatorriem *c*

fanatical [fə'nætikəl] *adj* fanatiek

fancy ['fænsi] *v* lusten, zin *hebben in; zich verbeelden, zich voorstellen; *n* gril *c*; fantasie *c*

fantastic [fæn'tæstik] *adj* fantastisch

fantasy ['fæntəzi] *n* fantasie *c*

far [fɑ:] *adj* ver; *adv* veel; **by** ~ verreweg; **so** ~ tot nu toe

far-away ['fɑ:rəwei] *adj* ver

farce [fɑ:s] *n* klucht *c*, farce *c*

fare [feə] *n* reiskosten *pl*; tarief *nt*; kost *c*, voedsel *nt*

farm [fɑ:m] *n* boerderij *c*

farmer ['fɑ:mə] *n* boer *c*; **farmer's**

wife boerin c

farmhouse ['fɑ:mhaus] n boerderij c

far-off ['fɑ:rɔf] adj afgelegen

fascinate ['fæsineit] v boeien

fascism ['fæsizəm] n fascisme nt

fascist ['fæsist] adj fascistisch; n fascist c

fashion ['fæʃən] n mode c; manier c

fashionable ['fæʃənəbəl] adj modieus

fast [fɑ:st] adj vlug, snel; vast

fasten ['fɑ:sən] v vastmaken, bevestigen; *sluiten

fastener ['fɑ:sənə] n sluiting c

fat [fæt] adj vet, dik; n vet nt

fatal ['feitəl] adj fataal, dodelijk, noodlottig

fate [feit] n lot nt, noodlot nt

father ['fɑ:ðə] n vader c; pater c

father-in-law ['fɑ:ðərinlɔ:] n (pl fathers-) schoonvader c

fatherland ['fɑ:ðələnd] n vaderland nt

fatness ['fætnəs] n dikte c

fatty ['fæti] adj vettig

faucet ['fɔ:sit] nAm kraan c

fault [fɔ:lt] n schuld c; fout c, defect nt, gebrek nt

faultless ['fɔ:ltləs] adj foutloos; feilloos

faulty ['fɔ:lti] adj gebrekkig, defect

favour ['feivə] n gunst c; v begunstigen, bevoorrechten

favourable ['feivərəbəl] adj gunstig

favourite ['feivərit] n lieveling c, favoriet c; adj lievelings-

fawn [fɔ:n] adj lichtbruin; n reekalf nt

fax [fæks] n fax c; send a ~ een fax versturen

fear [fiə] n vrees c, angst c; v vrezen

feasible ['fi:zəbəl] adj uitvoerbaar

feast [fi:st] n feest nt

feat [fi:t] n prestatie c

feather ['feðə] n veer c

feature ['fi:tʃə] n kenmerk nt; gelaats-

trek c

February ['februəri] februari

federal ['fedərəl] adj federaal

federation [,fedə'reiʃən] n federatie c; bond c

fee [fi:] n honorarium nt

feeble ['fi:bəl] adj zwak

*feed [fi:d] v voeden; fed up with beu

*feel [fi:l] v voelen; betasten; ~ like zin *hebben in

feeling ['fi:liŋ] n gevoel nt

fell [fel] v (p fall)

fellow ['felou] n kerel c

felt¹ [felt] n vilt nt

felt² [felt] v (p, pp feel)

female ['fi:meil] adj vrouwelijk

feminine ['feminin] adj vrouwelijk

fence [fens] n omheining c; hek nt; v schermen

fender ['fendə] n bumper c

ferment [fə'ment] v gisten

ferry-boat ['feribout] n veerboot c

fertile ['fə:tail] adj vruchtbaar

festival ['festivəl] n festival nt

festive ['festiv] adj feestelijk

fetch [fetʃ] v halen; afhalen

feudal ['fju:dəl] adj feodaal

fever ['fi:və] n koorts c

feverish ['fi:vəriʃ] adj koortsig

few [fju:] adj weinig

fiancé [fi'ɑ:sei] n verloofde c

fiancée [fi'ɑ:sei] n verloofde c

fibre ['faibə] n vezel c

fiction ['fikʃən] n fictie c, verzinsel nt

field [fi:ld] n akker c, veld nt; gebied nt; ~ glasses veldkijker c

fierce [fiəs] adj wild; woest, fel

fifteen [,fif'ti:n] num vijftien

fifteenth [,fif'ti:nθ] num vijftiende

fifth [fifθ] num vijfde

fifty ['fifti] num vijftig

fig [fig] n vijg c

fight [fait] n strijd c, gevecht nt

*fight [fait] v *strijden, *vechten

figure ['figǝ] n gestalte c, figuur c; cijfer nt

file [fail] n vijl c; dossier nt; rij c

Filipino [,fili'pi:nou] n Filippijn c

fill [fil] v vullen; ~ **in** invullen; **filling station** benzinestation nt; ~ **out** Am invullen; ~ **up** opvullen

filling ['filiŋ] n vulling c

film [film] n film c; v filmen

filter ['filtǝ] n filter nt

filthy ['filθi] adj smerig, vuil

f·nal ['fainǝl] adj laatst

finance [fai'næns] v financieren

finances [fai'nænsiz] pl financiën pl

financial [fai'nænʃǝl] adj financieel

finch [fintʃ] n vink c

*find [faind] v *vinden

fine [fain] n boete c; adj fijn; mooi; uitstekend, prachtig; ~ **arts** schone kunsten

finger ['fiŋgǝ] n vinger c; **little** ~ pink c

fingerprint ['fiŋgǝprint] n vingerafdruk c

finish ['finiʃ] v afmaken, beëindigen; eindigen; n einde nt; eindstreep c; **finished** af; op

Finland ['finlǝnd] Finland

Finn [fin] n Fin c

Finnish ['finiʃ] adj Fins

fire [faiǝ] n vuur nt; brand c; v *schieten; *ontslaan

fire-alarm ['faiǝrǝ,la:m] n brandalarm nt

fire-brigade ['faiǝbri,geid] n brandweer c

fire-escape ['faiǝri,skeip] n brandtrap c

fire-extinguisher ['faiǝrik,stiŋgwiʃǝ] n brandblusapparaat nt

fireplace ['faiǝpleis] n haard c

fireproof ['faiǝpru:f] adj brandvrij; vuurvast

firm [fǝ:m] adj vast; stevig; n firma c

first [fǝ:st] num eerst; **at** ~ eerst; aanvankelijk; ~ **name** voornaam c

first-aid [,fǝ:st'eid] n eerste hulp; ~ **kit** verbandkist c; ~ **post** eerste hulppost

first-class [,fǝ:st'kla:s] adj eersteklas

first-rate [,fǝ:st'reit] adj eersterangs, prima

fir-tree ['fǝ:tri:] n denneboom c, den c

fish¹ [fiʃ] n (pl ~, ~es) vis c; ~ **shop** viswinkel c

fish² [fiʃ] v vissen; hengelen; **fishing gear** vistuig nt; **fishing hook** vishaak c; **fishing industry** visserij c; **fishing licence** visakte c; **fishing line** vislijn c; **fishing net** visnet nt; **fishing rod** hengel c; **fishing tackle** vistuig nt

fishbone ['fiʃboun] n graat c, visgraat c

fisherman ['fiʃǝmǝn] n (pl -men) visser c

fist [fist] n vuist c

fit [fit] adj geschikt; n aanval c; v passen; **fitting room** paskamer c

five [faiv] num vijf

fix [fiks] v repareren

fixed [fikst] adj vast

fizz [fiz] n prik c

fjord [fjɔ:d] n fjord c

flag [flæg] n vlag c

flame [fleim] n vlam c

flamingo [flǝ'miŋgou] n (pl ~s, ~es) flamingo c

flannel ['flænǝl] n flanel nt

flash [flæʃ] n flits c

flash-bulb ['flæʃbʌlb] n flitslampje nt

flash-light ['flæʃlait] n zaklantaarn c

flask [fla:sk] n flacon c; **thermos** ~ thermosfles c

flat [flæt] adj vlak, plat; n flat c; ~ **tyre** lekke band

flavour ['fleivǝ] n smaak c; v kruiden

fleet [fli:t] n vloot c

flesh [fleʃ] n vlees nt

flew [flu:] v (p fly)

flex [fleks] n snoer nt

flexible ['fleksibəl] adj buigbaar; soepel

flight [flait] n vlucht c; **charter ~** chartervlucht c

flint [flint] n vuursteen c

float [flout] v *drijven; n vlotter c

flock [flɔk] n kudde c

flood [flʌd] n overstroming c; vloed c

floor [flɔ:] n vloer c; etage c, verdieping c; **~ show** floor-show c

florist ['flɔrist] n bloemist c

flour [flauə] n bloem c, meel nt

flow [flou] v vloeien, stromen

flower [flauə] n bloem c

flowerbed ['flauəbed] n bloemperk nt

flower-shop ['flauəʃɔp] n bloemenwinkel c

flown [floun] v (pp fly)

flu [flu:] n griep c

fluent ['flu:ənt] adj vloeiend

fluid ['flu:id] adj vloeibaar; n vloeistof c

flute [flu:t] n fluit c

fly [flai] n vlieg c; gulp c

***fly** [flai] v *vliegen

foam [foum] n schuim nt; v schuimen

foam-rubber ['foum,rʌbə] n schuimrubber nt

focus ['foukəs] n brandpunt nt

fog [fɔg] n mist c

foggy ['fɔgi] adj mistig

foglamp ['fɔglæmp] n mistlamp c

fold [fould] v *vouwen; *opvouwen; n vouw c

folk [fouk] n volk nt; **~ song** volkslied nt

folk-dance ['foukda:ns] n volksdans c

folklore ['fouklɔ:] n folklore c

follow ['fɔlou] v volgen; **following** adj eerstvolgend, volgend

***be fond of** [bi: fɔnd ɔv] *houden van

food [fu:d] n voedsel nt; eten nt, kost c; **~ poisoning** voedselvergiftiging c

foodstuffs ['fu:dstʌfs] pl levensmiddelen pl

fool [fu:l] n gek c, dwaas c; v foppen

foolish ['fu:liʃ] adj mal, dwaas

foot [fut] n (pl feet) voet c; **~ powder** voetpoeder nt/c; **on ~** te voet

football ['futbɔ:l] n voetbal c; **~ match** voetbalwedstrijd c

foot-brake ['futbreik] n voetrem c

footpath ['futpɑ:θ] n voetpad nt

footwear ['futweə] n schoeisel nt

for [fɔ:, fə] prep voor; gedurende; naar; vanwege, wegens, uit; conj want

***forbid** [fə'bid] v *verbieden

force [fɔ:s] v noodzaken, *dwingen; forceren; n macht c, kracht c; geweld nt; **by ~** noodgedwongen; **driving ~** drijfkracht c

ford [fɔ:d] n doorwaadbare plaats

forecast ['fɔ:kɑ:st] n voorspelling c; v voorspellen

foreground ['fɔ:graund] n voorgrond c

forehead ['fɔred] n voorhoofd nt

foreign ['fɔrin] adj buitenlands; vreemd

foreigner ['fɔrinə] n buitenlander c; vreemdeling c

foreman ['fɔ:mən] n (pl -men) voorman c

foremost ['fɔ:moust] adj hoogst

foresail ['fɔ:seil] n fok c

forest ['fɔrist] n woud nt, bos nt

forester ['fɔristə] n boswachter c

forge [fɔ:dʒ] v vervalsen

***forget** [fə'get] v *vergeten

forgetful [fə'getful] adj vergeetachtig

***forgive** [fə'giv] v *vergeven

fork [fɔ:k] n vork c; tweesprong c; v zich splitsen

form [fɔ:m] n vorm c; formulier nt;

klas *c*; *v* vormen
formal ['fɔ:məl] *adj* formeel
formality [fɔ:'mæləti] *n* formaliteit *c*
former ['fɔ:mə] *adj* voormalig; vroeger; **formerly** voorheen, vroeger
formula ['fɔ:mjulə] *n* (pl ~e, ~s) formule *c*
fort [fɔ:t] *n* fort *nt*
fortnight ['fɔ:tnait] *n* veertien dagen
fortress ['fɔ:tris] *n* vesting *c*
fortunate ['fɔ:tʃənət] *adj* gelukkig
fortune ['fɔ:tʃu:n] *n* fortuin *nt*; lot *nt*, geluk *nt*
forty ['fɔ:ti] *num* veertig
forward ['fɔ:wəd] *adv* vooruit, voorwaarts; *v* *nazenden
foster-parents ['fɔstə,peərənts] *pl* pleegouders *pl*
fought [fɔ:t] *v* (p, pp fight)
foul [faul] *adj* smerig; gemeen
found[1] [faund] *v* (p, pp find)
found[2] [faund] *v* oprichten, stichten
foundation [faun'deiʃən] *n* stichting *c*; ~ **cream** basiscrème *c*
fountain ['fauntin] *n* fontein *c*; bron *c*
fountain-pen ['fauntinpen] *n* vulpen *c*
four [fɔ:] *num* vier
fourteen [,fɔ:'ti:n] *num* veertien
fourteenth [,fɔ:'ti:nθ] *num* veertiende
fourth [fɔ:θ] *num* vierde
fowl [faul] *n* (pl ~s, ~) gevogelte *nt*
fox [fɔks] *n* vos *c*
foyer ['fɔiei] *n* foyer *c*
fraction ['frækʃən] *n* fractie *c*
fracture ['fræktʃə] *v* *breken; *n* breuk *c*
fragile ['frædʒail] *adj* breekbaar; broos
fragment ['frægmənt] *n* fragment *nt*; stuk *nt*
frame [freim] *n* lijst *c*; montuur *nt*
France [fra:ns] Frankrijk
franchise ['fræntʃaiz] *n* kiesrecht *nt*
fraternity [frə'tə:nəti] *n* broederschap *c*

fraud [frɔ:d] *n* fraude *c*, bedrog *nt*
fray [frei] *v* rafelen
free [fri:] *adj* vrij; gratis; ~ **of charge** gratis; ~ **ticket** vrijkaart *c*
freedom ['fri:dəm] *n* vrijheid *c*
* **freeze** [fri:z] *v* *vriezen; *bevriezen
freezing ['fri:ziŋ] *adj* ijskoud
freezing-point ['fri:ziŋpɔint] *n* vriespunt *nt*
freight [freit] *n* lading *c*, vracht *c*
freight-train ['freittrein] *nAm* goederentrein *c*
French [frentʃ] *adj* Frans
Frenchman ['frentʃmən] *n* (pl -men) Fransman *c*
frequency ['fri:kwənsi] *n* frequentie *c*
frequent ['fri:kwənt] *adj* veelvuldig, frequent; **frequently** dikwijls
fresh [freʃ] *adj* vers; fris; ~ **water** zoet water
friction ['frikʃən] *n* wrijving *c*
Friday ['fraidi] vrijdag *c*
fridge [fridʒ] *n* koelkast *c*, ijskast *c*
friend [frend] *n* vriend *c*; vriendin *c*
friendly ['frendli] *adj* vriendelijk; amicaal, vriendschappelijk
friendship ['frendʃip] *n* vriendschap *c*
fright [frait] *n* angst *c*, schrik *c*
frighten ['fraitən] *v* *doen schrikken
frightened ['fraitənd] *adj* bang; *be ~ *schrikken
frightful ['fraitfəl] *adj* verschrikkelijk, vreselijk
fringe [frindʒ] *n* franje *c*
frock [frɔk] *n* jurk *c*
frog [frɔg] *n* kikker *c*
from [frɔm] *prep* van; uit; vanaf
front [frʌnt] *n* voorkant *c*; **in ~ of** voor
frontier ['frʌntiə] *n* grens *c*
frost [frɔst] *n* vorst *c*
froth [frɔθ] *n* schuim *nt*
frozen ['frouzən] *adj* bevroren; ~ **food** diepvries produkten

fruit [fru:t] *n* fruit *nt*; vrucht *c*
fry [frai] *v* *bakken; *braden
frying-pan ['fraiiŋpæn] *n* koekepan *c*
fuel ['fju:əl] *n* brandstof *c*; benzine *c*; ~ **pump** *Am* benzinepomp *c*
full [ful] *adj* vol; ~ **board** vol pension; ~ **stop** punt *c*; ~ **up** vol
fun [fʌn] *n* plezier *nt*, pret *c*; lol *c*
function ['fʌŋkʃən] *n* functie *c*
fund [fʌnd] *n* fonds *nt*
fundamental [,fʌndə'mentəl] *adj* fundamenteel
funeral ['fju:nərəl] *n* begrafenis *c*
funnel ['fʌnəl] *n* trechter *c*
funny ['fʌni] *adj* leuk, grappig; zonderling
fur [fə:] *n* pels *c*; ~ **coat** bontjas *c*; **furs** bont *nt*
furious ['fjuəriəs] *adj* razend, woedend
furnace ['fə:nis] *n* oven *c*
furnish ['fə:niʃ] *v* leveren, verschaffen; inrichten, meubileren; ~ **with** *voorzien van
furniture ['fə:nitʃə] *n* meubilair *nt*
furrier ['fʌriə] *n* bontwerker *c*
further ['fə:ðə] *adj* verder; nader
furthermore ['fə:ðəmɔ:] *adv* bovendien
furthest ['fə:ðist] *adj* verst
fuse [fju:z] *n* zekering *c*; lont *c*
fuss [fʌs] *n* drukte *c*; ophef *c*, herrie *c*
future ['fju:tʃə] *n* toekomst *c*; *adj* toekomstig

G

gable ['geibəl] *n* geveltop *c*
gadget ['gædʒit] *n* technisch snufje
gaiety ['geiəti] *n* vrolijkheid *c*, pret *c*
gain [gein] *v* *winnen; *n* winst *c*
gait [geit] *n* gang *c*, loop *c*
gale [geil] *n* storm *c*

gall [gɔ:l] *n* gal *c*; ~ **bladder** galblaas *c*
gallery ['gæləri] *n* galerij *c*
gallop ['gæləp] *n* galop *c*
gallows ['gælouz] *pl* galg *c*
gallstone ['gɔ:lstoun] *n* galsteen *c*
game [geim] *n* spel *nt*; wild *nt*; ~ **reserve** wildpark *nt*
gang [gæŋ] *n* bende *c*; ploeg *c*
gangway ['gæŋwei] *n* loopplank *c*
gaol [dʒeil] *n* gevangenis *c*
gap [gæp] *n* bres *c*
garage ['gæra:ʒ] *n* garage *c*; *v* stallen
garbage ['ga:bidʒ] *n* vuilnis *nt*, afval *nt*
garden ['ga:dən] *n* tuin *c*; **public** ~ plantsoen *nt*; **zoological gardens** dierentuin *c*
gardener ['ga:dənə] *n* tuinman *c*
gargle ['ga:gəl] *v* gorgelen
garlic ['ga:lik] *n* knoflook *nt/c*
gas [gæs] *n* gas *nt*; *nAm* benzine *c*; ~ **cooker** gasstel *nt*; ~ **pump** *Am* benzinepomp *c*; ~ **station** *Am* benzinestation *nt*; ~ **stove** gaskachel *c*
gasoline ['gæsəli:n] *nAm* benzine *c*
gastric ['gæstrik] *adj* maag-; ~ **ulcer** maagzweer *c*
gasworks ['gæswə:ks] *n* gasfabriek *c*
gate [geit] *n* poort *c*; hek *nt*
gather ['gæðə] *v* verzamelen; *bijeenkomen; oogsten
gauge [geidʒ] *n* meter *c*
gauze [gɔ:z] *n* gaas *nt*
gave [geiv] *v* (p give)
gay [gei] *adj* vrolijk; bont
gaze [geiz] *v* staren
gear [giə] *n* versnelling *c*; uitrusting *c*; **change** ~ schakelen; ~ **lever** versnellingspook *c*
gear-box ['giəbɔks] *n* versnellingsbak *c*
gem [dʒem] *n* juweel *nt*, edelsteen *c*; kleinood *nt*

gender ['dʒendə] n geslacht nt

general ['dʒenərəl] adj algemeen; n generaal c; ~ **practitioner** huisarts c; **in** ~ in het algemeen

generate ['dʒenəreit] v verwekken

generation [,dʒenə'reiʃən] n generatie c

generator ['dʒenəreitər] n generator c

generosity [,dʒenə'rɔsəti] n edelmoedigheid c

generous ['dʒenərəs] adj gul, royaal

genital ['dʒenitəl] adj geslachtelijk

genius ['dʒi:niəs] n genie nt

gentle ['dʒentəl] adj zacht; teer, licht; voorzichtig

gentleman ['dʒentəlmən] n (pl -men) heer c

genuine ['dʒenjuin] adj echt

geography [dʒi'ɔɡrəfi] n aardrijkskunde c

geology [dʒi'ɔlədʒi] n geologie c

geometry [dʒi'ɔmətri] n meetkunde c

germ [dʒə:m] n bacil c; kiem c

German ['dʒə:mən] adj Duits; n Duitser c

Germany ['dʒə:məni] Duitsland

gesticulate [dʒi'stikjuleit] v gebaren

* **get** [get] v *krijgen; halen; *worden; ~ **back** *teruggaan; ~ **off** uitstappen; ~ **on** instappen; vorderen; ~ **up** *opstaan

ghost [ɡoust] n spook nt; geest c

giant ['dʒaiənt] n reus c

giddiness ['ɡidinəs] n duizeligheid c

giddy ['ɡidi] adj duizelig

gift [ɡift] n geschenk nt, cadeau nt; gave c

gifted ['ɡiftid] adj begaafd

gigantic [dʒai'ɡæntik] adj reusachtig

giggle ['ɡiɡəl] v giechelen

gill [ɡil] n kieuw c

gilt [ɡilt] adj verguld

ginger ['dʒindʒə] n gember c

gipsy ['dʒipsi] n zigeuner c

girdle ['ɡə:dəl] n step-in c

girl [ɡə:l] n meisje nt; ~ **guide** padvindster c

* **give** [ɡiv] v *geven; *aangeven; ~ **away** verklappen; ~ **in** *toegeven; ~ **up** *opgeven

glacier ['ɡlæsiə] n gletsjer c

glad [ɡlæd] adj verheugd, blij; **gladly** graag, gaarne

gladness ['ɡlædnəs] n vreugde c

glamorous ['ɡlæmərəs] adj betoverend, fascinerend

glamour ['ɡlæmə] n charme c

glance [ɡlɑ:ns] n blik c; v een blik *werpen

gland [ɡlænd] n klier c

glare [ɡleə] n scherp licht; schittering c

glaring ['ɡleəriŋ] adj verblindend

glass [ɡlɑ:s] n glas nt; glazen; **glasses** bril c; **magnifying** ~ vergrootglas nt

glaze [ɡleiz] v emailleren

glen [ɡlen] n bergkloof c

glide [ɡlaid] v *glijden

glider ['ɡlaidə] n zweefvliegtuig nt

glimpse [ɡlimps] n blik c; glimp c; v even *zien

global ['ɡloubəl] adj wereldomvattend

globe [ɡloub] n wereldbol c, aardbol c

gloom [ɡlu:m] n duister nt

gloomy ['ɡlu:mi] adj somber

glorious ['ɡlɔ:riəs] adj prachtig

glory ['ɡlɔ:ri] n glorie c, roem c; eer c, lof c

gloss [ɡlɔs] n glans c

glossy ['ɡlɔsi] adj glanzend

glove [ɡlʌv] n handschoen c

glow [ɡlou] v gloeien; n gloed c

glue [ɡlu:] n lijm c

* **go** [ɡou] v *gaan; *lopen; *worden; ~ **ahead** *doorgaan; ~ **away** *weggaan; ~ **back** *teruggaan; ~ **home** naar huis *gaan; ~ **in** *binnengaan;

~ **on** *doorgaan; ~ **out** *uitgaan;
~ **through** meemaken, doormaken
goal [goul] *n* doel *nt*; doelpunt *nt*
goalkeeper ['goul,ki:pə] *n* doelman *c*
goat [gout] *n* bok *c*, geit *c*
god [gɔd] *n* god *c*
goddess ['gɔdis] *n* godin *c*
godfather ['gɔd,fɑ:ðə] *n* peetvader *c*
goggles ['gɔgəlz] *pl* duikbril *c*
gold [gould] *n* goud *nt*; ~ **leaf** bladgoud *nt*
golden ['gouldən] *adj* gouden
goldmine ['gouldmain] *n* goudmijn *c*
goldsmith ['gouldsmiθ] *n* goudsmid *c*
golf [gɔlf] *n* golf *nt*
golf-club ['gɔlfklʌb] *n* golfclub *c*
golf-course ['gɔlfkɔ:s] *n* golfbaan *c*
golf-links ['gɔlfliŋks] *n* golfbaan *c*
gondola ['gɔndələ] *n* gondel *c*
gone [gɔn] *adv* (pp go) weg
good [gud] *adj* goed; lekker; zoet,
braaf
good-bye! [,gud'bai] dag!
good-humoured [,gud'hju:məd] *adj* opgeruimd
good-looking [,gud'lukiŋ] *adj* knap
good-natured [,gud'neitʃəd] *adj* goedhartig
goods [gudz] *pl* waren *pl*, goederen
pl; ~ **train** goederentrein *c*
good-tempered [,gud'tempəd] *adj*
goedgestemd
goodwill [,gud'wil] *n* welwillendheid *c*
goose [gu:s] *n* (pl geese) gans *c*
gooseberry ['guzbəri] *n* kruisbes *c*
goose-flesh ['gu:sfleʃ] *n* kippevel *nt*
gorge [gɔ:dʒ] *n* ravijn *nt*
gorgeous ['gɔ:dʒəs] *adj* prachtig
gospel ['gɔspəl] *n* evangelie *nt*
gossip ['gɔsip] *n* geroddel *nt*; *v* roddelen
got [gɔt] *v* (p, pp get)
gourmet ['guəmei] *n* fijnproever *c*
gout [gaut] *n* jicht *c*

govern ['gʌvən] *v* regeren
governess ['gʌvənis] *n* gouvernante
c
government ['gʌvənmənt] *n* bewind
nt, regering *c*
governor ['gʌvənə] *n* gouverneur *c*
gown [gaun] *n* japon *c*
grab [græb] *n* greep *c*; roof *c*
grace [greis] *n* gratie *c*; genade *c*
graceful ['greisfəl] *adj* bevallig
grade [greid] *n* graad *c*; *v* rangschikken
gradient ['greidiənt] *n* helling *c*
gradual ['grædʒuəl] *adj* geleidelijk;
gradually *adv* langzamerhand
graduate ['grædʒueit] *v* een diploma
behalen
grain [grein] *n* korrel *c*, graan *nt*, koren *nt*
gram [græm] *n* gram *nt*
grammar ['græmə] *n* grammatica *c*
grammatical [grə'mætikəl] *adj* grammaticaal
grand [grænd] *adj* groots
granddad ['grændæd] *n* opa *c*
granddaughter ['græn,dɔ:tə] *n* kleindochter *c*
grandfather ['græn,fɑ:ðə] *n* grootvader
c; opa *c*
grandmother ['græn,mʌðə] *n* grootmoeder *c*; oma *c*
grandparents ['græn,peərənts] *pl* grootouders *pl*
grandson ['grænsʌn] *n* kleinzoon *c*
granite ['grænit] *n* graniet *nt*
grant [grɑ:nt] *v* gunnen, verlenen; inwilligen; *n* toelage *c*, beurs *c*
grapefruit ['greipfru:t] *n* pompelmoes
c
grapes [greips] *pl* druiven *pl*
graph [græf] *n* grafiek *c*
graphic ['græfik] *adj* grafisch
grasp [grɑ:sp] *v* *grijpen; *n* greep *c*
grass [grɑ:s] *n* gras *nt*

grasshopper ['grɑ:s,hɔpə] n sprinkhaan c

grate [greit] n rooster nt; v raspen

grateful ['greitfəl] adj erkentelijk,
dankbaar

grater ['greitə] n rasp c

gratis ['grætis] adj gratis

gratitude ['grætitju:d] n dankbaarheid
c

gratuity [grə'tju:əti] n fooi c

grave [greiv] n graf nt; adj ernstig

gravel ['grævəl] n kiezel c, grind nt

gravestone ['greivstoun] n grafsteen c

graveyard ['greivjɑ:d] n kerkhof nt

gravity ['grævəti] n zwaartekracht c;
ernst c

gravy ['greivi] n jus c

graze [greiz] v grazen; n schaafwond
c

grease [gri:s] n vet nt; v smeren

greasy ['gri:si] adj vet, vettig

great [greit] adj groot; **Great Britain**
Groot-Brittannië

Greece [gri:s] Griekenland

greed [gri:d] n hebzucht c

greedy ['gri:di] adj hebzuchtig; gulzig

Greek [gri:k] adj Grieks; n Griek c

green [gri:n] adj groen; ~ **card** groene kaart

greengrocer ['gri:n,grousə] n groenteboer c

greenhouse ['gri:nhaus] n broeikas c,
kas c

greens [gri:nz] pl groente c

greet [gri:t] v groeten

greeting ['gri:tiŋ] n groet c

grey [grei] adj grijs; grauw

greyhound ['greihaund] n hazewind c

grief [gri:f] n verdriet nt; bedroefdheid c, smart c

grieve [gri:v] v treuren

grill [gril] n grill c; v roosteren

grill-room ['grilru:m] n grillroom c

grin [grin] v grijnzen; n grijns c

*grind [graind] v *malen; fijnmalen

grip [grip] v *grijpen; n houvast nt,
greep c; nAm handkoffertje nt

grit [grit] n gruis nt

groan [groun] v kreunen

grocer ['grousə] n kruidenier c; **grocer's** kruidenierswinkel c

groceries ['grousəriz] pl kruidenierswaren pl

groin [grɔin] n lies c

groove [gru:v] n groef c

gross¹ [grous] n (pl ~) gros nt

gross² [grous] adj grof; bruto

grotto ['grɔtou] n (pl ~es, ~s) grot c

ground¹ [graund] n bodem c, grond c;
~ **floor** begane grond; **grounds** terrein nt

ground² [graund] v (p, pp grind)

group [gru:p] n groep c

grouse [graus] n (pl ~) korhoen nt

grove [grouv] n bosje nt

*grow [grou] v groeien; kweken;
*worden

growl [graul] v grommen

grown-up ['grounʌp] adj volwassen; n
volwassene c

growth [grouθ] n groei c; gezwel nt

grudge [grʌdʒ] v misgunnen

grumble ['grʌmbəl] v mopperen

guarantee [,gærən'ti:] n garantie c;
waarborg c; v garanderen

guarantor [,gærən'tɔ:] n borg c

guard [gɑ:d] n bewaker c; v bewaken

guardian ['gɑ:diən] n voogd c

guess [ges] v *raden; *denken, gissen; n gissing c

guest [gest] n logé c, gast c

guest-house ['gesthaus] n pension nt

guest-room ['gestru:m] n logeerkamer
c

guide [gaid] n gids c; v leiden

guidebook ['gaidbuk] n gids c

guide-dog ['gaiddɔg] n geleidehond c

guilt [gilt] n schuld c

guilty ['gilti] *adj* schuldig
guinea-pig ['ginipig] *n* cavia *c*
guitar [gi'tɑ:] *n* gitaar *c*
gulf [gʌlf] *n* golf *c*
gull [gʌl] *n* meeuw *c*
gum [gʌm] *n* tandvlees *nt*; gom *c*; lijm *c*
gun [gʌn] *n* geweer *nt*, revolver *c*; kanon *nt*
gunpowder ['gʌn,paudə] *n* kruit *nt*
gust [gʌst] *n* windstoot *c*
gusty ['gʌsti] *adj* winderig
gut [gʌt] *n* darm *c*; **guts** lef *nt*
gutter ['gʌtə] *n* goot *c*
guy [gai] *n* vent *c*
gymnasium [dʒim'neiziəm] *n* (pl ~s, -sia) gymnastiekzaal *c*
gymnast ['dʒimnæst] *n* gymnast *c*
gymnastics [dʒim'næstiks] *pl* gymnastiek *c*
gynaecologist [,gainə'kɔlədʒist] *n* gynaecoloog *c*, vrouwenarts *c*

H

haberdashery ['hæbədæʃəri] *n* garen- en bandwinkel
habit ['hæbit] *n* gewoonte *c*
habitable ['hæbitəbəl] *adj* bewoonbaar
habitual [hə'bitʃuəl] *adj* gewoon
had [hæd] *v* (p, pp have)
haddock ['hædək] *n* (pl ~) schelvis *c*
haemorrhage ['heməridʒ] *n* bloeding *c*
haemorrhoids ['heməroidz] *pl* aambeien *pl*
hail [heil] *n* hagel *c*
hair [hɛə] *n* haar *nt*; ~ **cream** haarcrème *c*; ~ **gel** haargel; ~ **piece** haarstukje *nt*; ~ **tonic** haartonic *c*
hairbrush ['hɛəbrʌʃ] *n* haarborstel *c*
hair-do ['hɛədu:] *n* kapsel *nt*, coiffure *c*

hairdresser ['hɛə,dresə] *n* kapper *c*
hair-dryer ['hɛədraiə] *n* haardroger *c*
hair-grip ['hɛəgrip] *n* haarspeld *c*
hair-net ['hɛənet] *n* haarnetje *nt*
hair-oil ['hɛərɔil] *n* haarolie *c*
hairpin ['hɛəpin] *n* haarspeld *c*
hair-spray ['hɛəsprei] *n* haarlak *c*
hairy ['hɛəri] *adj* harig
half[1] [hɑ:f] *adj* half
half[2] [hɑ:f] *n* (pl halves) helft *c*
half-time [,hɑ:f'taim] *n* rust *c*
halfway [,hɑ:f'wei] *adv* halverwege
halibut ['hælibət] *n* (pl ~) heilbot *c*
hall [hɔ:l] *n* hal *c*; zaal *c*
halt [hɔ:lt] *v* stoppen
halve [hɑ:v] *v* halveren
ham [hæm] *n* ham *c*
hamlet ['hæmlət] *n* gehucht *nt*
hammer ['hæmə] *n* hamer *c*
hammock ['hæmək] *n* hangmat *c*
hamper ['hæmpə] *n* mand *c*
hand [hænd] *n* hand *c*; *v* *aangeven; ~ **cream** handcrème *c*
handbag ['hændbæg] *n* handtas *c*
handbook ['hændbuk] *n* handboek *nt*
hand-brake ['hændbreik] *n* handrem *c*
handcuffs ['hændkʌfs] *pl* handboeien *pl*
handful ['hændful] *n* handvol *c*
handicraft ['hændikrɑ:ft] *n* handenarbeid *c*; handwerk *nt*
handkerchief ['hæŋkətʃif] *n* zakdoek *c*
handle ['hændəl] *n* steel *c*, handvat *nt*; *v* hanteren; behandelen
hand-made [,hænd'meid] *adj* met de hand gemaakt
handshake ['hændʃeik] *n* handdruk *c*
handsome ['hænsəm] *adj* knap
handwork ['hændwɔ:k] *n* handwerk *nt*
handwriting ['hænd,raitiŋ] *n* handschrift *nt*
handy ['hændi] *adj* handig
*hang [hæŋ] *v* *ophangen; *hangen
hanger ['hæŋə] *n* kleerhanger *c*

hangover ['hæŋ,ouvə] n kater c

happen ['hæpən] v *voorkomen, gebeuren

happening ['hæpəniŋ] n gebeurtenis c

happiness ['hæpinəs] n geluk nt

happy ['hæpi] adj blij, gelukkig

harbour ['haːbə] n haven c

hard [haːd] adj hard; moeilijk; **hardly** nauwelijks

hardware ['haːdwɛə] n ijzerwaren pl; ~ **store** handel in ijzerwaren

hare [hɛə] n haas c

harm [haːm] n schade c; kwaad nt; v schaden

harmful ['haːmfəl] adj nadelig, schadelijk

harmless ['haːmləs] adj onschadelijk

harmony ['haːməni] n harmonie c

harp [haːp] n harp c

harpsichord ['haːpsikɔːd] n clavecimbel c

harsh [haːʃ] adj ruw; streng; wreed

harvest ['haːvist] n oogst c

has [hæz] v (pr have)

haste [heist] n spoed c, haast c

hasten ['heisən] v zich haasten

hasty ['heisti] adj haastig

hat [hæt] n hoed c; ~ **rack** kapstok c

hatch [hætʃ] n luik nt

hate [heit] v een hekel *hebben aan; haten; n haat c

hatred ['heitrid] n haat c

haughty ['hɔːti] adj hooghartig

haul [hɔːl] v slepen

***have** [hæv] v *hebben; *laten; ~ **to** *moeten

haversack ['hævəsæk] n broodzak c

hawk [hɔːk] n havik c; valk c

hay [hei] n hooi nt; ~ **fever** hooikoorts c

hazard ['hæzəd] n risico nt

haze [heiz] n nevel c; waas nt

hazelnut ['heizəlnʌt] n hazelnoot c

hazy ['heizi] adj heiig; wazig

he [hiː] pron hij

head [hed] n hoofd nt; kop c; v leiden; ~ **of state** staatshoofd nt; ~ **teacher** schoolhoofd nt, hoofdonderwijzer c

headache ['hedeik] n hoofdpijn c

heading ['hediŋ] n titel c

headlamp ['hedlæmp] n koplamp c

headland ['hedlənd] n landtong c

headlight ['hedlait] n koplamp c

headline ['hedlain] n kop c

headmaster [,hed'maːstə] n schoolhoofd nt; rector c, directeur c

headquarters [,hed'kwɔːtəz] pl hoofdkwartier nt

head-strong ['hedstrɔŋ] adj koppig

head-waiter [,hed'weitə] n maître d'hôtel

heal [hiːl] v *genezen

health [helθ] n gezondheid c; ~ **centre** consultatiebureau nt; ~ **certificate** gezondheidsattest nt

healthy ['helθi] adj gezond

heap [hiːp] n stapel c, hoop c

***hear** [hiə] v horen

hearing ['hiəriŋ] n gehoor nt

heart [haːt] n hart nt; kern c; **by** ~ uit het hoofd; ~ **attack** hartaanval c

heartburn ['haːtbəːn] n maagzuur nt

hearth [haːθ] n haard c

heartless ['haːtləs] adj harteloos

hearty ['haːti] adj hartelijk

heat [hiːt] n warmte c, hitte c; v verwarmen; **heating pad** elektrisch kussen

heater ['hiːtə] n kachel c; **immersion** ~ dompelaar c

heath [hiːθ] n heide c

heathen ['hiːðən] n heiden c; heidens

heather ['heðə] n heide c

heating ['hiːtiŋ] n verwarming c

heaven ['hevən] n hemel c

heavy ['hevi] adj zwaar

Hebrew ['hi:bru:] *n* Hebreeuws *nt*

hedge [hedʒ] *n* heg *c*

hedgehog ['hedʒhɔg] *n* egel *c*

heel [hi:l] *n* hiel *c*; hak *c*

height [hait] *n* hoogte *c*; toppunt *nt*, hoogtepunt *nt*

hell [hel] *n* hel *c*

hello! [he'lou] hallo!; dag!

helm [helm] *n* roer *nt*

helmet ['helmit] *n* helm *c*

helmsman ['helmzmən] *n* stuurman *c*

help [help] *v* *helpen; *n* hulp *c*

helper ['helpə] *n* helper *c*

helpful ['helpfəl] *adj* hulpvaardig

helping ['helpiŋ] *n* portie *c*

hem [hem] *n* zoom *c*

hemp [hemp] *n* hennep *c*

hen [hen] *n* hen *c*; kip *c*

henceforth [,hens'fɔ:θ] *adv* voortaan

her [hə:] *pron* haar

herb [hə:b] *n* kruid *nt*

herd [hə:d] *n* kudde *c*

here [hiə] *adv* hier; ~ you are alstublieft

hereditary [hi'reditəri] *adj* erfelijk

hernia ['hə:niə] *n* breuk *c*

hero ['hiərou] *n* (pl ~es) held *c*

heron ['herən] *n* reiger *c*

herring ['heriŋ] *n* (pl ~, ~s) haring *c*

herself [hə:'self] *pron* zich; zelf

hesitate ['heziteit] *v* aarzelen

heterosexual [,hetərə'sekʃuəl] *adj* heteroseksueel

hiccup ['hikʌp] *n* hik *c*

hide [haid] *n* huid *c*

***hide** [haid] *v* *verbergen; verstoppen

hideous ['hidiəs] *adj* afschuwelijk

hierarchy ['haiəra:ki] *n* hiërarchie *c*

high [hai] *adj* hoog

highway ['haiwei] *n* hoofdweg *c*; *nAm* autoweg *c*

hijack ['haidʒæk] *v* kapen

hijacker ['haidʒækə] *n* kaper *c*

hike [haik] *v* *trekken

hill [hil] *n* heuvel *c*

hillock ['hilək] *n* lage heuvel *nt*

hillside ['hilsaid] *n* helling *c*

hilltop ['hiltɔp] *n* heuveltop *c*

hilly ['hili] *adj* heuvelachtig

him [him] *pron* hem

himself [him'self] *pron* zich; zelf

hinder ['hində] *v* hinderen

hinge [hindʒ] *n* scharnier *nt*

hip [hip] *n* heup *c*

hire [haiə] *v* huren; for ~ te huur

hire-purchase [,haiə'pə:tʃəs] *n* huurkoop *c*

his [hiz] *adj* zijn

historian [hi'stɔ:riən] *n* geschiedkundige *c*

historic [hi'stɔrik] *adj* historisch

historical [hi'stɔrikəl] *adj* geschiedkundig

history ['histəri] *n* geschiedenis *c*

hit [hit] *n* hit *c*

***hit** [hit] *v* *slaan; raken; *treffen

hitchhike ['hitʃhaik] *v* liften

hitchhiker ['hitʃ,haikə] *n* lifter *c*

hoarse [hɔ:s] *adj* schor, hees

hobby ['hɔbi] *n* liefhebberij *c*, hobby *c*

hobby-horse ['hɔbihɔ:s] *n* stokpaardje *nt*

hockey ['hɔki] *n* hockey *nt*

hoist [hɔist] *v* *hijsen

hold [hould] *n* ruim *nt*

***hold** [hould] *v* *vasthouden, *houden; bewaren; ~ on zich *vasthouden; ~ up ondersteunen

hold-up ['houldʌp] *n* overval *c*

hole [houl] *n* kuil *c*, gat *nt*

holiday ['hɔlədi] *n* vakantie *c*; feestdag *c*; ~ camp vakantiekamp *nt*; ~ resort vakantieoord *nt*; on ~ met vakantie

Holland ['hɔlənd] Holland

hollow ['hɔlou] *adj* hol

holy ['houli] *adj* heilig

homage ['hɔmidʒ] *n* hulde *c*

home [houm] *n* thuis *nt*; tehuis *nt*, huis *nt*; *adv* thuis, naar huis; **at ~** thuis

home-made [‚houm'meid] *adj* eigengemaakt

homesickness ['houm‚siknəs] *n* heimwee *nt*

homosexual [‚houmə'sekʃuəl] *adj* homoseksueel

honest ['ɔnist] *adj* eerlijk; oprecht

honesty ['ɔnisti] *n* eerlijkheid *c*

honey ['hʌni] *n* honing *c*

honeymoon ['hʌnimu:n] *n* huwelijksreis *c*, wittebroodsweken *pl*

honk [hʌŋk] *vAm* claxonneren

honour ['ɔnə] *n* eer *c*; *v* eren, huldigen

honourable ['ɔnərəbəl] *adj* eervol, eerzaam; rechtschapen

hood [hud] *n* kap *c*; *nAm* motorkap *c*

hoof [hu:f] *n* hoef *c*

hook [huk] *n* haak *c*

hoot [hu:t] *v* claxonneren

hooter ['hu:tə] *n* claxon *c*

hoover ['hu:və] *v* stofzuigen

hop[1] [hɔp] *v* huppelen; *n* sprong *c*

hop[2] [hɔp] *n* hop *c*

hope [houp] *n* hoop *c*; *v* hopen

hopeful ['houpfəl] *adj* hoopvol

hopeless ['houpləs] *adj* hopeloos

horizon [hə'raizən] *n* kim *c*, horizon *c*

horizontal [‚hɔri'zɔntəl] *adj* horizontaal

horn [hɔ:n] *n* hoorn *c*; claxon *c*

horrible ['hɔribəl] *adj* vreselijk; verschrikkelijk, gruwelijk, afschuwelijk

horror ['hɔrə] *n* afgrijzen *nt*, afschuw *c*

hors-d'œuvre [ɔ:'də:vr] *n* hors d'œuvre *c*, voorgerecht *nt*

horse [hɔ:s] *n* paard *nt*

horseman ['hɔ:smən] *n* (pl -men) ruiter *c*

horsepower ['hɔ:‚pauə] *n* paardekracht *c*

horserace ['hɔ:sreis] *n* harddraverij *c*

horseradish ['hɔ:s‚rædiʃ] *n* mierikswortel *c*

horseshoe ['hɔ:sʃu:] *n* hoefijzer *nt*

horticulture ['hɔ:tikʌltʃə] *n* tuinbouw *c*

hosiery ['houʒəri] *n* tricotgoederen *pl*

hospitable ['hɔspitəbəl] *adj* gastvrij

hospital ['hɔspitəl] *n* hospitaal *nt*, ziekenhuis *nt*

hospitality [‚hɔspi'tæləti] *n* gastvrijheid *c*

host [houst] *n* gastheer *c*

hostage ['hɔstidʒ] *n* gijzelaar *c*

hostel ['hɔstəl] *n* herberg *c*

hostess ['houstis] *n* gastvrouw *c*

hostile ['hɔstail] *adj* vijandig

hot [hɔt] *adj* warm, heet

hotel [hou'tel] *n* hotel *nt*

hot-tempered [‚hɔt'tempəd] *adj* driftig

hour [auə] *n* uur *nt*

hourly ['auəli] *adj* uur-

house [haus] *n* huis *nt*; woning *c*; pand *nt*; **~ agent** makelaar *c*; **~ block** *Am* huizenblok *nt*; **public ~** kroeg *c*

houseboat ['hausbout] *n* woonboot *c*

household ['haushould] *n* huishouden *nt*

housekeeper ['haus‚ki:pə] *n* huishoudster *c*

housekeeping ['haus‚ki:piŋ] *n* huishouden *nt*

housemaid ['hausmeid] *n* meid *c*

housewife ['hauswaif] *n* huisvrouw *c*

housework ['hauswə:k] *n* huishouden *nt*

how [hau] *adv* hoe; wat; **~ many** hoeveel; **~ much** hoeveel

however [hau'evə] *conj* evenwel, echter

hug [hʌg] *v* omhelzen; *n* omhelzing *c*

huge [hju:dʒ] *adj* geweldig, enorm, reusachtig

hum [hʌm] v neuriën
human ['hju:mən] adj menselijk; ~ **being** menselijk wezen
humanity [hju'mænəti] n mensheid c
humble ['hʌmbəl] adj nederig
humid ['hju:mid] adj vochtig
humidity [hju'midəti] n vochtigheid c
humorous ['hju:mərəs] adj grappig, geestig, humoristisch
humour ['hju:mə] n humor c
hundred ['hʌndrəd] n honderd
Hungarian [hʌŋ'gɛəriən] adj Hongaars; n Hongaar c
Hungary ['hʌŋgəri] Hongarije
hunger ['hʌŋgə] n honger c
hungry ['hʌŋgri] adj hongerig
hunt [hʌnt] v jagen; n jacht c; ~ **for** *zoeken
hunter ['hʌntə] n jager c
hurricane ['hʌrikən] n orkaan c; ~ **lamp** stormlamp c
hurry ['hʌri] v *opschieten, zich haasten; n haast c; **in a ~** haastig
***hurt** [hə:t] v pijn *doen, bezeren; kwetsen
hurtful ['hə:tfəl] adj schadelijk
husband ['hʌzbənd] n echtgenoot c, man c
hut [hʌt] n hut c
hydrogen ['haidrədʒən] n waterstof c
hygiene ['haidʒi:n] n hygiëne c
hygienic [hai'dʒi:nik] adj hygiënisch
hymn [him] n gezang nt
hyphen ['haifən] n koppelteken nt
hypocrisy [hi'pɔkrəsi] n huichelarij c
hypocrite ['hipəkrit] n huichelaar c
hypocritical [,hipə'kritikəl] adj huichelachtig, hypocriet, schijnheilig
hysterical [hi'sterikəl] adj hysterisch

I

I [ai] pron ik
ice [ais] n ijs nt
ice-bag ['aisbæg] n koeltas c
ice-cream ['aiskri:m] n ijs nt, ijsje nt
Iceland ['aislənd] IJsland
Icelander ['aisləndə] n IJslander c
Icelandic [ais'lændik] adj IJslands
icon ['aikɔn] n ikoon c
idea [ai'diə] n idee nt/c; inval c, gedachte c; denkbeeld nt, begrip nt
ideal [ai'diəl] adj ideaal; n ideaal nt
identical [ai'dentikəl] adj identiek
identification [ai,dentifi'keiʃən] n identificatie c
identify [ai'dentifai] v identificeren
identity [ai'dentəti] n identiteit c; ~ **card** identiteitskaart c
idiom ['idiəm] n idioom nt
idiomatic [,idiə'mætik] adj idiomatisch
idiot ['idiət] n idioot c
idiotic [,idi'ɔtik] adj idioot
idle ['aidəl] adj werkeloos; lui; ijdel
idol ['aidəl] n afgod c; idool nt
if [if] conj als; indien
ignition [ig'niʃən] n ontsteking c; ~ **coil** ontsteking c
ignorant ['ignərənt] adj onwetend
ignore [ig'nɔ:] v negeren
ill [il] adj ziek; slecht; kwaad
illegal [i'li:gəl] adj illegaal, onwettig
illegible [i'ledʒəbəl] adj onleesbaar
illiterate [i'litərət] n analfabeet c
illness ['ilnəs] n ziekte c
illuminate [i'lu:mineit] v verlichten
illumination [i,lu:mi'neiʃən] n verlichting c
illusion [i'lu:ʒən] n illusie c; droombeeld nt
illustrate ['iləstreit] v illustreren
illustration [,ilə'streiʃən] n illustratie c
image ['imidʒ] n beeld nt

imaginary [i'mædʒinəri] *adj* denkbeeldig

imagination [i,mædʒi'neiʃən] *n* verbeelding *c*

imagine [i'mædʒin] *v* zich voorstellen; zich verbeelden; zich *indenken

imitate ['imiteit] *v* nabootsen, imiteren

imitation [,imi'teiʃən] *n* namaak *c*, imitatie *c*

immediate [i'mi:djət] *adj* onmiddellijk

immediately [i'mi:djətli] *adv* meteen, dadelijk, onmiddellijk

immense [i'mens] *adj* oneindig, reusachtig, onmetelijk

immigrant ['imigrənt] *n* immigrant *c*

immigrate ['imigreit] *v* immigreren

immigration [,imi'greiʃən] *n* immigratie *c*

immodest [i'mɔdist] *adj* onbescheiden

immunity [i'mju:nəti] *n* immuniteit *c*

immunize ['imjunaiz] *v* immuun maken

impartial [im'pɑ:ʃəl] *adj* onpartijdig

impassable [im'pɑ:səbəl] *adj* onbegaanbaar

impatient [im'peiʃənt] *adj* ongeduldig

impede [im'pi:d] *v* belemmeren

impediment [im'pedimənt] *n* beletsel *nt*

imperfect [im'pə:fikt] *adj* onvolmaakt

imperial [im'piəriəl] *adj* keizerlijk; rijks-

impersonal [im'pə:sənəl] *adj* onpersoonlijk

impertinence [im'pə:tinəns] *n* onbeschaamdheid *c*

impertinent [im'pə:tinənt] *adj* brutaal, onbeschoft, onbeschaamd

implement[1] ['implimənt] *n* werktuig *nt*, gereedschap *nt*

implement[2] ['impliment] *v* uitvoeren

imply [im'plai] *v* impliceren; *inhouden

impolite [,impə'lait] *adj* onbeleefd

import[1] [im'pɔ:t] *v* invoeren, importeren

import[2] ['impɔ:t] *n* import *c*, invoer *c*; ~ **duty** invoerrecht *nt*

importance [im'pɔ:təns] *n* belang *nt*

important [im'pɔ:tənt] *adj* gewichtig, belangrijk

importer [im'pɔ:tə] *n* importeur *c*

imposing [im'pouziŋ] *adj* indrukwekkend

impossible [im'pɔsəbəl] *adj* onmogelijk

impotence ['impətəns] *n* impotentie *c*

impotent ['impətənt] *adj* impotent

impound [im'paund] *v* beslag leggen op

impress [im'pres] *v* imponeren, indruk maken op

impression [im'preʃən] *n* indruk *c*

impressive [im'presiv] *adj* indrukwekkend

imprison [im'prizən] *v* gevangen zetten

imprisonment [im'prizənmənt] *n* gevangenschap *c*

improbable [im'prɔbəbəl] *adj* onwaarschijnlijk

improper [im'prɔpə] *adj* ongepast

improve [im'pru:v] *v* verbeteren

improvement [im'pru:vmənt] *n* verbetering *c*

improvise ['imprəvaiz] *v* improviseren

impudent ['impjudənt] *adj* onbeschaamd

impulse ['impʌls] *n* impuls *c*; prikkel *c*

impulsive [im'pʌlsiv] *adj* impulsief

in [in] *prep* in; over, op; *adv* binnen

inaccessible [i,næk'sesəbəl] *adj* ontoegankelijk

inaccurate [i'nækjurət] *adj* onnauwkeurig

inadequate [i'nædikwət] *adj* onvoldoende

incapable [in'keipəbəl] *adj* onbekwaam

incense ['insens] *n* wierook *c*

incident ['insidənt] *n* incident *nt*

incidental [,insi'dentəl] *adj* toevallig

incite [in'sait] *v* aansporen

inclination [,iŋkli'neiʃən] *n* neiging *c*

incline [iŋ'klain] *n* helling *c*

inclined [iŋ'klaind] *adj* genegen, geneigd; ***be ~ to** *v* neigen

include [iŋ'klu:d] *v* bevatten, *insluiten; **included** inbegrepen

inclusive [iŋ'klu:siv] *adj* inclusief

income ['iŋkəm] *n* inkomen *nt*

income-tax ['iŋkəmtæks] *n* inkomstenbelasting *c*

incompetent [iŋ'kɔmpətənt] *adj* onbekwaam

incomplete [,iŋkəm'pli:t] *adj* onvolledig, incompleet

inconceivable [,iŋkən'si:vəbəl] *adj* ondenkbaar

inconspicuous [,iŋkən'spikjuəs] *adj* onopvallend

inconvenience [,iŋkən'vi:njəns] *n* ongemak *nt*, ongerief *nt*

inconvenient [,iŋkən'vi:njənt] *adj* ongelegen; lastig

incorrect [,iŋkə'rekt] *adj* onnauwkeurig, onjuist

increase¹ [iŋ'kri:s] *v* vermeerderen; *oplopen, *toenemen

increase² ['iŋkri:s] *n* toename *c*; verhoging *c*

incredible [iŋ'kredəbəl] *adj* ongelofelijk

incurable [iŋ'kjuərəbəl] *adj* ongeneeslijk

indecent [in'di:sənt] *adj* onfatsoenlijk

indeed [in'di:d] *adv* inderdaad

indefinite [in'definit] *adj* onbepaald

indemnity [in'demnəti] *n* schadeloosstelling *c*, schadevergoeding *c*

independence [,indi'pendəns] *n* onafhankelijkheid *c*

independent [,indi'pendənt] *adj* onafhankelijk; zelfstandig

index ['indeks] *n* register *nt*, index *c*; ~ **finger** wijsvinger *c*

India ['indiə] India

Indian ['indiən] *adj* Indisch; Indiaans; *n* Indiër *c*; Indiaan *c*

indicate ['indikeit] *v* *aangeven, aanduiden

indication [,indi'keiʃən] *n* teken *nt*, aanwijzing *c*

indicator ['indikeitə] *n* richtingaanwijzer *c*

indifferent [in'difərənt] *adj* onverschillig

indigestion [,indi'dʒestʃən] *n* indigestie *c*

indignation [,indig'neiʃən] *n* verontwaardiging *c*

indirect [,indi'rekt] *adj* indirect

individual [,indi'vidʒuəl] *adj* afzonderlijk, individueel; *n* enkeling *c*, individu *nt*

Indonesia [,ində'ni:ziə] Indonesië

Indonesian [,ində'ni:ziən] *adj* Indonesisch; *n* Indonesiër *c*

indoor ['indɔ:] *adj* binnen

indoors [,in'dɔ:z] *adv* binnen

indulge [in'dʌldʒ] *v* *toegeven

industrial [in'dʌstriəl] *adj* industrieel; ~ **area** industriegebied *nt*

industrious [in'dʌstriəs] *adj* vlijtig

industry ['indəstri] *n* industrie *c*

inedible [i'nedibəl] *adj* oneetbaar

inefficient [,ini'fiʃənt] *adj* ondoeltreffend

inevitable [i'nevitəbəl] *adj* onvermijdelijk

inexpensive [,inik'spensiv] *adj* goedkoop

inexperienced [,inik'spiəriənst] *adj* onervaren

infant ['infənt] *n* zuigeling *c*

infantry ['infəntri] *n* infanterie *c*

infect [in'fekt] *v* besmetten, *aansteken

infection [in'fekʃən] n infectie c

infectious [in'fekʃəs] adj besmettelijk

infer [in'fə:] v afleiden

inferior [in'fiəriə] adj inferieur, minderwaardig; lager

infinite ['infinət] adj oneindig

infinitive [in'finitiv] n onbepaalde wijs

infirmary [in'fə:məri] n ziekenzaal c

inflammable [in'flæməbəl] adj ontvlambaar

inflammation [,inflə'meiʃən] n ontsteking c

inflatable [in'fleitəbəl] adj opblaasbaar

inflate [in'fleit] v *opblazen

inflation [in'fleiʃən] n inflatie c

influence ['influəns] n invloed c; v beïnvloeden

influential [,influ'enʃəl] adj invloedrijk

influenza [,influ'enzə] n griep c

inform [in'fɔ:m] v informeren; inlichten, mededelen

informal [in'fɔ:məl] adj informeel

information [,infə'meiʃən] n informatie c; inlichting c, mededeling c; ~ bureau inlichtingenkantoor nt

infra-red [,infrə'red] adj infrarood

infrequent [in'fri:kwənt] adj zeldzaam

ingredient [iŋ'gri:diənt] n ingrediënt nt, bestanddeel nt

inhabit [in'hæbit] v bewonen

inhabitable [in'hæbitəbəl] adj bewoonbaar

inhabitant [in'hæbitənt] n inwoner c; bewoner c

inhale [in'heil] v inademen

inherit [in'herit] v erven

inheritance [in'heritəns] n erfenis c

initial [i'niʃəl] adj begin-, eerst; n voorletter c; v paraferen

initiative [i'niʃətiv] n initiatief nt

inject [in'dʒekt] v *inspuiten

injection [in'dʒekʃən] n injectie c

injure ['indʒə] v verwonden, kwetsen; krenken

injured ['indʒəd] adj gewond

injury ['indʒəri] n verwonding c; letsel nt, blessure c

injustice [in'dʒʌstis] n onrecht nt

ink [iŋk] n inkt c

inlet ['inlet] n inham c

inn [in] n herberg c

inner ['inə] adj inwendig; ~ tube binnenband c

inn-keeper ['in,ki:pə] n herbergier c

innocence ['inəsəns] n onschuld c

innocent ['inəsənt] adj onschuldig

inoculate [i'nɔkjuleit] v inenten

inoculation [i,nɔkju'leiʃən] n inenting c

inquire [iŋ'kwaiə] v *navragen, informatie *inwinnen

inquiry [iŋ'kwaiəri] n vraag c, navraag c; onderzoek nt; ~ office informatiebureau nt

inquisitive [iŋ'kwizətiv] adj nieuwsgierig

insane [in'sein] adj krankzinnig

inscription [in'skripʃən] n inscriptie c

insect ['insekt] n insekt nt; ~ repellent insektenwerend middel

insecticide [in'sektisaid] n insekticide c

insensitive [in'sensətiv] adj ongevoelig

insert [in'sə:t] v invoegen

inside [,in'said] n binnenkant c; adj binnenst; adv binnen; van binnen; prep in, binnen; ~ out binnenste buiten; insides ingewanden pl

insight ['insait] n inzicht nt

insignificant [,insig'nifikənt] adj onbelangrijk; onbeduidend, nietsbetekenend; nietig

insist [in'sist] v *aandringen; *aanhouden, *volhouden

insolence ['insələns] n onbeschaamdheid c

insolent ['insələnt] adj brutaal, onbeschaamd

insomnia [in'sɔmniə] n slapeloosheid c

inspect [in'spekt] *v* inspecteren

inspection [in'spekʃən] *n* inspectie *c*; controle *c*

inspector [in'spektə] *n* inspecteur *c*

inspire [in'spaiə] *v* bezielen

install [in'stɔ:l] *v* installeren

installation [,instə'leiʃən] *n* installatie *c*

instalment [in'stɔ:lmənt] *n* afbetaling *c*

instance ['instəns] *n* voorbeeld *nt*; geval *nt*; **for ~** bijvoorbeeld

instant ['instənt] *n* ogenblik *nt*

instantly ['instəntli] *adv* ogenblikkelijk, onmiddellijk, meteen

instead of [in'sted ɔv] in plaats van

instinct ['instiŋkt] *n* instinct *nt*

institute ['institju:t] *n* instituut *nt*; instelling *c*; *v* instellen

institution [,insti'tju:ʃən] *n* inrichting *c*, instelling *c*

instruct [in'strʌkt] *v* onderrichten

instruction [in'strʌkʃən] *n* onderwijs *nt*

instructive [in'strʌktiv] *adj* leerzaam

instructor [in'strʌktə] *n* leraar *c*

instrument ['instrumənt] *n* instrument *nt*; **musical ~** muziekinstrument *nt*

insufficient ['insə'fiʃənt] *adj* onvoldoende

insulate ['insjuleit] *v* isoleren

insulation [,insju'leiʃən] *n* isolatie *c*

insulator ['insjuleitə] *n* isolator *c*

insult[1] [in'sʌlt] *v* beledigen

insult[2] ['insʌlt] *n* belediging *c*

insurance [in'ʃuərəns] *n* assurantie *c*, verzekering *c*; **~ policy** verzekeringspolis *c*

insure [in'ʃuə] *v* verzekeren

intact [in'tækt] *adj* intact

intellect ['intəlekt] *n* intellect *nt*

intellectual [,intə'lektʃuəl] *adj* intellectueel

intelligence [in'telidʒəns] *n* intelligen-tie *c*

intelligent [in'telidʒənt] *adj* intelligent

intend [in'tend] *v* van plan *zijn, bedoelen

intense [in'tens] *adj* intens; hevig

intention [in'tenʃən] *n* bedoeling *c*

intentional [in'tenʃənəl] *adj* opzettelijk

intercourse ['intəkɔ:s] *n* omgang *c*

interest ['intrəst] *n* interesse *c*, belangstelling *c*; belang *nt*; rente *c*; *v* interesseren; **interested** geïnteresseerd, belangstellend

interesting ['intrəstiŋ] *adj* interessant

interfere [,intə'fiə] *v* tussenbeide *komen; **~ with** zich bemoeien met

interference [,intə'fiərəns] *n* inmenging *c*

interim ['intərim] *n* tussentijd *c*

interior [in'tiəriə] *n* binnenkant *c*

interlude ['intəlu:d] *n* intermezzo *nt*

intermediary [,intə'mi:djəri] *n* tussenpersoon *c*

intermission [,intə'miʃən] *n* pauze *c*

internal [in'tə:nəl] *adj* intern, inwendig

international [,intə'næʃənəl] *adj* internationaal

interpret [in'tə:prit] *v* tolken; vertolken

interpreter [in'tə:pritə] *n* tolk *c*

interrogate [in'terəgeit] *v* *ondervragen

interrogation [in,terə'geiʃən] *n* verhoor *nt*

interrogative [,intə'rɔgətiv] *adj* vragend

interrupt [,intə'rʌpt] *v* *onderbreken

interruption [,intə'rʌpʃən] *n* onderbreking *c*

intersection [,intə'sekʃən] *n* kruispunt *nt*

interval ['intəvəl] *n* pauze *c*; tussenpoos *c*

intervene [,intə'vi:n] *v* *ingrijpen

interview ['intəvju:] n interview nt, vraaggesprek nt

intestine [in'testin] n darm c; **intestines** ingewanden pl

intimate ['intimət] adj intiem

into ['intu] prep in

intolerable [in'tɔlərəbəl] adj onuitstaanbaar

intoxicated [in'tɔksikeitid] adj dronken

intrigue [in'tri:g] n komplot nt

introduce [,intrə'dju:s] v introduceren, voorstellen; inleiden; invoeren

introduction [,intrə'dakʃən] n inleiding c

invade [in'veid] v *binnenvallen

invalid¹ ['invəli:d] n invalide c; adj invalide

invalid² [in'vælid] adj ongeldig

invasion [in'veiʒən] n inval c, invasie c

invent [in'vent] v *uitvinden; *verzinnen

invention [in'venʃən] n uitvinding c

inventive [in'ventiv] adj vindingrijk

inventor [in'ventə] n uitvinder c

inventory ['invəntri] n inventaris c

invert [in'və:t] v omdraaien

invest [in'vest] v investeren; beleggen

investigate [in'vestigeit] v *onderzoeken

investigation [in,vesti'geiʃən] n onderzoek nt

investment [in'vestmənt] n investering c; belegging c, geldbelegging c

investor [in'vestə] n investeerder c

invisible [in'vizəbəl] adj onzichtbaar

invitation [,invi'teiʃən] n uitnodiging c

invite [in'vait] v inviteren, uitnodigen

invoice ['invɔis] n factuur c

involve [in'vɔlv] v impliceren; **involved** betrokken

inwards ['inwədz] adv naar binnen

iodine ['aiədi:n] n jodium nt

Iran [i'ra:n] Iran

Iranian [i'reiniən] adj Iraans; n Iraniër c

Iraq [i'ra:k] Irak

Iraqi [i'ra:ki] adj Iraaks; n Irakees c

irascible [i'ræsibəl] adj driftig

Ireland ['aiələnd] Ierland

Irish ['aiəriʃ] adj Iers

Irishman ['aiəriʃmən] n (pl -men) Ier c

iron ['aiən] n ijzer nt; strijkijzer nt; ijzeren; v *strijken

ironical [ai'rɔnikəl] adj ironisch

ironworks ['aiənwə:ks] n hoogovens pl

irony ['aiərəni] n ironie c

irregular [i'regjulə] adj onregelmatig

irreparable [i'repərəbəl] adj onherstelbaar

irrevocable [i'revəkəbəl] adj onherroepelijk

irritable ['iritəbəl] adj prikkelbaar

irritate ['iriteit] v prikkelen, irriteren

is [iz] v (pr be)

island ['ailənd] n eiland nt

isolate ['aisəleit] v isoleren

isolation [,aisə'leiʃən] n isolement nt; isolatie c

Israel ['izreil] Israël

Israeli [iz'reili] adj Israëlisch; n Israëliër c

issue ['iʃu:] v *uitgeven; n uitgifte c, oplage c, uitgave c; kwestie c, punt nt; uitkomst c, resultaat nt, gevolg nt, slot nt, einde nt; uitgang c

isthmus ['ismɔs] n landengte c

it [it] pron het

Italian [i'tæljən] adj Italiaans; n Italiaan c

italics [i'tæliks] pl cursiefschrift nt

Italy ['itəli] Italië

itch [itʃ] n jeuk c; kriebel c; v jeuken

item ['aitəm] n artikel nt; punt nt

itinerant [ai'tinərənt] adj rondreizend

itinerary [ai'tinərəri] n reisplan nt, reisroute c

ivory ['aivəri] n ivoor nt

ivy ['aivi] n klimop c

J

jack [dʒæk] *n* krik *c*

jacket ['dʒækit] *n* jasje *nt*, colbert *c*, vest *nt*; omslag *c/nt*

jade [dʒeid] *n* jade *nt/c*

jail [dʒeil] *n* gevangenis *c*

jailer ['dʒeilə] *n* cipier *c*

jam [dʒæm] *n* jam *c*; verkeersopstopping *c*

janitor ['dʒænitə] *n* concierge *c*

January ['dʒænjuəri] januari

Japan [dʒə'pæn] Japan

Japanese [ˌdʒæpə'niːz] *adj* Japans; *n* Japanner *c*

jar [dʒɑː] *n* pot *c*

jaundice ['dʒɔːndis] *n* geelzucht *c*

jaw [dʒɔː] *n* kaak *c*

jealous ['dʒeləs] *adj* jaloers

jealousy ['dʒeləsi] *n* jaloezie *c*

jeans [dʒiːnz] *pl* spijkerbroek *c*

jelly ['dʒeli] *n* gelei *c*

jelly-fish ['dʒelifiʃ] *n* kwal *c*

jersey ['dʒəːzi] *n* jersey *c*; trui *c*

jet [dʒet] *n* straal *c*; straalvliegtuig *nt*

jetty ['dʒeti] *n* pier *c*

Jew [dʒuː] *n* jood *c*

jewel ['dʒuːəl] *n* juweel *nt*

jeweller ['dʒuːələ] *n* juwelier *c*

jewellery ['dʒuːəlri] *n* juwelen; bijouterie *c*

Jewish ['dʒuːiʃ] *adj* joods

job [dʒɔb] *n* karwei *nt*; betrekking *c*, baan *c*

jockey ['dʒɔki] *n* jockey *c*

join [dʒɔin] *v* *verbinden; zich voegen bij, zich *aansluiten bij; samenvoegen, verenigen

joint [dʒɔint] *n* gewricht *nt*; las *c*; *adj* verenigd, gezamenlijk

jointly ['dʒɔintli] *adv* gezamenlijk

joke [dʒouk] *n* mop *c*, grap *c*

jolly ['dʒɔli] *adj* leuk

Jordan ['dʒɔːdən] Jordanië

Jordanian [dʒɔː'deiniən] *adj* Jordaans; *n* Jordaniër *c*

journal ['dʒəːnəl] *n* tijdschrift *nt*

journalism ['dʒəːnəlizəm] *n* journalistiek *c*

journalist ['dʒəːnəlist] *n* journalist *c*

journey ['dʒəːni] *n* reis *c*

joy [dʒɔi] *n* genot *nt*, vreugde *c*

joyful ['dʒɔifəl] *adj* blij, vrolijk

jubilee ['dʒuːbiliː] *n* jubileum *nt*

judge [dʒʌdʒ] *n* rechter *c*; *v* oordelen; beoordelen

judgment ['dʒʌdʒmənt] *n* oordeel *nt*; beoordeling *c*

jug [dʒʌg] *n* kan *c*

juggle ['dʒʌgəl] *v* jongleren, goochelen

juice [dʒuːs] *n* sap *nt*

juicy ['dʒuːsi] *adj* sappig

July [dʒuː'lai] juli

jump [dʒʌmp] *v* *springen; *n* sprong *c*

jumper ['dʒʌmpə] *n* jumper *c*

junction ['dʒʌŋkʃən] *n* kruising *c*; knooppunt *nt*

June [dʒuːn] juni

jungle ['dʒʌŋgəl] *n* oerwoud *nt*, jungle *c*

junior ['dʒuːnjə] *adj* jonger

junk [dʒʌŋk] *n* rommel *c*

jury ['dʒuəri] *n* jury *c*

just [dʒʌst] *adj* terecht, rechtvaardig; juist; *adv* pas; precies; alleen, slechts

justice ['dʒʌstis] *n* recht *nt*; gerechtigheid *c*, rechtvaardigheid *c*

juvenile ['dʒuːvənail] *adj* jeugdig

K

kangaroo [ˌkæŋgəˈruː] *n* kangoeroe *c*
keel [kiːl] *n* kiel *c*
keen [kiːn] *adj* enthousiast; scherp
*keep [kiːp] *v* *houden; bewaren;
*blijven; ~ **away from** niet *betreden; ~ **off** *afblijven; ~ **on** *doorgaan met; ~ **quiet** *zwijgen; ~ **up**
*volhouden; ~ **up with** *bijhouden
keg [keg] *n* vaatje *nt*
kennel [ˈkenəl] *n* hondehok *nt*; kennel
c
Kenya [ˈkenjə] Kenya
kerosene [ˈkerəsiːn] *n* petroleum *c*
kettle [ˈketəl] *n* ketel *c*
key [kiː] *n* sleutel *c*
keyhole [ˈkiːhoul] *n* sleutelgat *nt*
khaki [ˈkɑːki] *n* kaki *nt*
kick [kik] *v* trappen, schoppen; *n* trap
c, schop *c*
kick-off [ˌkiˈkɔf] *n* aftrap *c*
kid [kid] *n* kind *nt*; geiteleer *nt*; *v*
*beetnemen
kidney [ˈkidni] *n* nier *c*
kill [kil] *v* *ombrengen, doden
kilogram [ˈkiləgræm] *n* kilo *nt*
kilometre [ˈkiləˌmiːtə] *n* kilometer *c*
kind [kaind] *adj* aardig, vriendelijk;
goed; *n* soort *c*/*nt*
kindergarten [ˈkindəˌgɑːtən] *n* kleuterschool *c*
king [kiŋ] *n* koning *c*
kingdom [ˈkiŋdəm] *n* koninkrijk *nt*;
rijk *nt*
kiosk [ˈkiːɔsk] *n* kiosk *c*
kiss [kis] *n* zoen *c*, kus *c*; *v* kussen
kit [kit] *n* uitrusting *c*
kitchen [ˈkitʃin] *n* keuken *c*; ~ **garden** moestuin *c*
knapsack [ˈnæpsæk] *n* knapzak *c*
knave [neiv] *n* boer *c*

knee [niː] *n* knie *c*
kneecap [ˈniːkæp] *n* knieschijf *c*
*kneel [niːl] *v* knielen
knew [njuː] *v* (p know)
knickers [ˈnikəz] *pl* onderbroek *c*
knife [naif] *n* (pl knives) mes *nt*
knight [nait] *n* ridder *c*
*knit [nit] *v* breien
knob [nɔb] *n* knop *c*
knock [nɔk] *v* kloppen; *n* klop *c*; ~
against *stoten tegen; ~ **down**
*neerslaan
knot [nɔt] *n* knoop *c*; *v* knopen
*know [nou] *v* *weten, kennen
knowledge [ˈnɔlidʒ] *n* kennis *c*
knuckle [ˈnʌkəl] *n* knokkel *c*

L

label [ˈleibəl] *n* etiket *nt*; *v* etiketteren
laboratory [ləˈbɔrətəri] *n* laboratorium
nt
labour [ˈleibə] *n* werk *nt*, arbeid *c*;
weeën *pl*; *v* zwoegen; **labor permit**
Am werkvergunning *c*
labourer [ˈleibərə] *n* arbeider *c*
labour-saving [ˈleibəˌseiviŋ] *adj* arbeidbesparend
labyrinth [ˈlæbərinθ] *n* doolhof *nt*
lace [leis] *n* kant *nt*; veter *c*
lack [læk] *n* gemis *nt*, gebrek *nt*; *v*
missen
lacquer [ˈlækə] *n* lak *c*
lad [læd] *n* jongen *c*, joch *nt*
ladder [ˈlædə] *n* ladder *c*
lady [ˈleidi] *n* dame *c*; **ladies' room**
damestoilet *c*
lagoon [ləˈguːn] *n* lagune *c*
lake [leik] *n* meer *nt*
lamb [læm] *n* lam *nt*; lamsvlees *nt*
lame [leim] *adj* lam, mank, kreupel
lamentable [ˈlæməntəbəl] *adj* erbarme-

lijk
lamp [læmp] *n* lamp *c*
lamp-post ['læmppoust] *n* lantaarnpaal *c*
lampshade ['læmpʃeid] *n* lampekap *c*
land [lænd] *n* land *nt*; *v* landen; aan land *gaan
landlady ['lænd,leidi] *n* hospita *c*
landlord ['lændlɔ:d] *n* huisbaas *c*; hospes *c*
landmark ['lændmɑ:k] *n* baken *nt*; mijlpaal *c*
landscape ['lændskeip] *n* landschap *nt*
lane [lein] *n* steeg *c*, pad *nt*; rijstrook *c*
language ['læŋgwidʒ] *n* taal *c*; ~ **laboratory** talenpracticum *nt*
lantern ['læntən] *n* lantaarn *c*
lapel [lə'pel] *n* revers *c*
larder ['lɑ:də] *n* provisiekast *c*
large [lɑ:dʒ] *adj* groot; ruim
lark [lɑ:k] *n* leeuwerik *c*
laryngitis [,lærin'dʒaitis] *n* keelontsteking *c*
last [lɑ:st] *adj* laatst; vorig; *v* duren; **at ~** eindelijk; tenslotte, uiteindelijk
lasting ['lɑ:stiŋ] *adj* blijvend, duurzaam
latchkey ['lætʃki:] *n* huissleutel *c*
late [leit] *adj* laat; te laat
lately ['leitli] *adv* de laatste tijd, onlangs, laatst
lather ['lɑ:ðə] *n* schuim *nt*
Latin America ['lætin ə'merikə] Latijns-Amerika
Latin-American [,lætinə'merikən] *adj* Latijns-Amerikaans
latitude ['lætitju:d] *n* breedtegraad *c*
laugh [lɑ:f] *v* *lachen; *n* lach *c*
laughter ['lɑ:ftə] *n* gelach *nt*
launch [lɔ:ntʃ] *v* inzetten; lanceren; *n* motorschip *nt*
launching ['lɔ:ntʃiŋ] *n* tewaterlating *c*

launderette [,lɔ:ndə'ret] *n* wasserette *c*
laundry ['lɔ:ndri] *n* wasserij *c*; was *c*
lavatory ['lævətəri] *n* toilet *nt*
lavish ['læviʃ] *adj* kwistig
law [lɔ:] *n* wet *c*; recht *nt*; ~ **court** gerecht *nt*
lawful ['lɔ:fəl] *adj* wettig
lawn [lɔ:n] *n* grasveld *nt*, gazon *nt*
lawsuit ['lɔ:su:t] *n* proces *nt*, geding *nt*
lawyer ['lɔ:jə] *n* advocaat *c*; jurist *c*
laxative ['læksətiv] *n* laxeermiddel *nt*
***lay** [lei] *v* plaatsen, zetten, leggen; ~ **bricks** metselen
layer [leiə] *n* laag *c*
layman ['leimən] *n* leek *c*
lazy ['leizi] *adj* lui
lead[1] [li:d] *n* voorsprong *c*; leiding *c*; riem *c*
lead[2] [led] *n* lood *nt*
***lead** [li:d] *v* leiden
leader ['li:də] *n* aanvoerder *c*, leider *c*
leadership ['li:dəʃip] *n* leiderschap *nt*
leading ['li:diŋ] *adj* vooraanstaand, voornaamst
leaf [li:f] *n* (pl leaves) blad *nt*
league [li:g] *n* bond *c*
leak [li:k] *v* lekken; *n* lek *nt*
leaky ['li:ki] *adj* lek
lean [li:n] *adj* mager
***lean** [li:n] *v* leunen
leap [li:p] *n* sprong *c*
***leap** [li:p] *v* *springen
leap-year ['li:pjiə] *n* schrikkeljaar *nt*
***learn** [lə:n] *v* leren
learner ['lə:nə] *n* beginneling *c*, beginner *c*
lease [li:s] *n* huurcontract *nt*; pacht *c*; *v* verpachten, verhuren; huren
leash [li:ʃ] *n* lijn *c*
least [li:st] *adj* geringst, minst; kleinst; **at ~** minstens; tenminste
leather ['leðə] *n* leer *nt*; lederen, leren
leave [li:v] *n* verlof *nt*

*leave [li:v] *v* *vertrekken, *verlaten; *laten; ~ **behind** *achterlaten; ~ **out** *weglaten

Lebanese [,lebə'ni:z] *adj* Libanees; *n* Libanees *c*

Lebanon ['lebənən] Libanon

lecture ['lektʃə] *r* college *nt*, lezing *c*

left[1] [left] *adj* links

left[2] [left] *v* (p, pp leave)

left-hand ['lefthænd] *adj* links

left-handed [,left'hændid] *adj* linkshandig

leg [leg] *n* poot *c*, been *nt*

legacy ['legəsi] *n* erfenis *c*

legal ['li:gəl] *adj* wettig, wettelijk; juridisch

legalization [,li:gəlai'zeiʃən] *n* legalisatie *c*

legation [li'geiʃən] *n* legatie *c*

legible ['ledʒibəl] *adj* leesbaar

legitimate [li'dʒitimət] *adj* wettig

leisure ['leʒə] *n* vrije tijd; gemak *nt*

lemon ['lemən] *n* citroen *c*

lemonade [,lemə'neid] *n* limonade *c*

*lend [lend] *v* lenen, uitlenen

length [leŋθ] *n* lengte *c*

lengthen ['leŋθən] *v* verlengen

lengthways ['leŋθweiz] *adv* in de lengte

lens [lenz] *n* lens *c*; **telephoto** ~ telelens *c*; **zoom** ~ zoomlens *c*

leprosy ['leprəsi] *n* lepra *c*

less [les] *adv* minder

lessen ['lesən] *v* verminderen

lesson ['lesən] *n* les *c*

*let [let] *v* *laten; verhuren; ~ **down** teleurstellen

letter ['letə] *n* brief *c*; letter *c*; ~ **of credit** kredietbrief *c*; ~ **of recommendation** aanbevelingsbrief *c*

letter-box ['letəbɔks] *n* brievenbus *c*

lettuce ['letis] *n* sla *c*

level ['levəl] *adj* egaal; plat, vlak, effen, gelijk; *n* peil *nt*, niveau *nt*; waterpas *c*; *v* egaliseren, nivelleren; ~ **crossing** overweg *c*

lever ['li:və] *n* hefboom *c*, hendel *c*

Levis ['li:vaiz] *pl* jeans *pl*

liability [,laiə'biləti] *n* aansprakelijkheid *c*

liable ['laiəbəl] *adj* aansprakelijk; ~ **to** onderhevig aan

liberal ['libərəl] *adj* liberaal; mild, royaal, vrijgevig

liberation [,libə'reiʃən] *n* bevrijding *c*

Liberia [lai'biəriə] Liberia

Liberian [lai'biəriən] *adj* Liberiaans; *n* Liberiaan *c*

liberty ['libəti] *n* vrijheid *c*

library ['laibrəri] *n* bibliotheek *c*

licence ['laisəns] *n* licentie *c*; vergunning *c*; **driving** ~ rijbewijs *nt*; ~ **number** *Am* kenteken *nt*; ~ **plate** *Am* nummerbord *nt*

license ['laisəns] *v* een vergunning verlenen

lick [lik] *v* likken

lid [lid] *n* deksel *nt*

lie [lai] *v* *liegen; *n* leugen *c*

*lie [lai] *v* *liggen; ~ **down** *gaan liggen

life [laif] *n* (pl lives) leven *nt*; ~ **insurance** levensverzekering *c*

lifebelt ['laifbelt] *n* reddingsgordel *c*

lifetime ['laiftaim] *n* leven *nt*

lift [lift] *v* optillen; *n* lift *c*

light [lait] *n* licht *nt*; *adj* licht; ~ **bulb** peer *c*

*light [lait] *v* *aansteken

lighter ['laitə] *n* aansteker *c*

lighthouse ['laithaus] *n* vuurtoren *c*

lighting ['laitiŋ] *n* verlichting *c*

lightning ['laitniŋ] *n* bliksem *c*

like [laik] *v* *houden van; *mogen, lusten; *adj* gelijk; *conj* zoals; *prep* als

likely ['laikli] *adj* waarschijnlijk

like-minded [,laik'maindid] *adj* gelijkgezind

likewise ['laikwaiz] *adv* evenzo, eveneens

lily ['lili] *n* lelie *c*

limb [lim] *n* ledemaat *c*

lime [laim] *n* kalk *c*; linde *c*; limoen *c*

limetree ['laimtri:] *n* linde *c*

limit ['limit] *n* limiet *c*; *v* beperken

limp [limp] *v* hinken; *adj* slap

line [lain] *n* regel *c*; streep *c*; snoer *nt*; lijn *c*; rij *c*; **stand in ~** *Am* in de rij *staan

linen ['linin] *n* linnen *nt*; linnengoed *nt*

liner ['lainə] *n* lijnboot *c*

lingerie ['lõʒəri:] *n* lingerie *c*

lining ['lainiŋ] *n* voering *c*

link [liŋk] *v* *verbinden; *n* verbinding *c*; schakel *c*

lion ['laiən] *n* leeuw *c*

lip [lip] *n* lip *c*

lipsalve ['lipsa:v] *n* lippenboter *c*

lipstick ['lipstik] *n* lippenstift *c*

liqueur [li'kjuə] *n* likeur *c*

liquid ['likwid] *adj* vloeibaar; *n* vloeistof *c*

liquor ['likə] *n* sterke drank

liquorice ['likəris] *n* drop *c*

list [list] *n* lijst *c*; *v* noteren

listen ['lisən] *v* aanhoren, luisteren

listener ['lisnə] *n* luisteraar *c*

literary ['litrəri] *adj* letterkundig, literair

literature ['litrətʃə] *n* literatuur *c*

litre ['li:tə] *n* liter *c*

litter ['litə] *n* afval *nt*; rommel *c*; nest *nt*

little ['litəl] *adj* klein; weinig

live[1] [liv] *v* leven; wonen

live[2] [laiv] *adj* levend

livelihood ['laivlihud] *n* kost *c*

lively ['laivli] *adj* levendig

liver ['livə] *n* lever *c*

living-room ['liviŋru:m] *n* huiskamer *c*, woonkamer *c*

load [loud] *n* lading *c*; last *c*; *v* *laden

loaf [louf] *n* (pl loaves) brood *nt*

loan [loun] *n* lening *c*

lobby ['lɔbi] *n* hal *c*; foyer *c*

lobster ['lɔbstə] *n* kreeft *c*

local ['loukəl] *adj* lokaal, plaatselijk; **~ call** lokaal gesprek; **~ train** stoptrein *c*

locality [lou'kæləti] *n* plaats *c*

locate [lou'keit] *v* plaatsen

location [lou'keiʃən] *n* ligging *c*

lock [lɔk] *v* op slot *doen; *n* slot *nt*; sluis *c*; **~ up** *opsluiten

locomotive [,loukə'moutiv] *n* locomotief *c*

lodge [lɔdʒ] *v* herbergen; *n* jachthuis *nt*

lodger ['lɔdʒə] *n* kamerbewoner *c*

lodgings ['lɔdʒiŋz] *pl* logies *nt*

log [lɔg] *n* houtblok *nt*

logic ['lɔdʒik] *n* logica *c*

logical ['lɔdʒikəl] *adj* logisch

lonely ['lounli] *adj* eenzaam

long [lɔŋ] *adj* lang; langdurig; **~ for** verlangen naar; **no longer** niet meer

longing ['lɔŋiŋ] *n* verlangen *nt*

longitude ['lɔndʒitju:d] *n* lengtegraad *c*

look [luk] *v* *kijken; *lijken, er uit *zien; *n* kijkje *nt*, blik *c*; uiterlijk *nt*, voorkomen *nt*; **~ after** verzorgen, zorgen voor, passen op; **~ at** *aankijken, *kijken naar; **~ for** *zoeken; **~ out** *uitkijken, oppassen; **~ up** *opzoeken

looking-glass ['lukiŋgla:s] *n* spiegel *c*

loop [lu:p] *n* lus *c*

loose [lu:s] *adj* los

loosen ['lu:sən] *v* losmaken

lord [lɔ:d] *n* lord *c*

lorry ['lɔri] *n* vrachtwagen *c*

***lose** [lu:z] *v* kwijtraken, *verliezen

loss [lɔs] *n* verlies *nt*

lost [lɔst] *adj* verdwaald; weg; ~ **and found** gevonden voorwerpen; ~ **property office** bureau voor gevonden voorwerpen

lot [lɔt] *n* lot *nt*; hoop *c*, boel *c*

lotion ['louʃən] *n* lotion *c*; **aftershave** ~ after shave

lottery ['lɔtəri] *n* loterij *c*

loud [laud] *adj* hard, luid

loud-speaker [,laud'spi:kə] *n* luidspreker *c*

lounge [laundʒ] *n* salon *c*

louse [laus] *n* (pl lice) luis *c*

love [lʌv] *v* *houden van, *liefhebben; *n* liefde *c*; **in** ~ verliefd

lovely ['lʌvli] *adj* heerlijk, prachtig, mooi

lover ['lʌvə] *n* minnaar *c*

love-story ['lʌv,stɔ:ri] *n* liefdesgeschiedenis *c*

low [lou] *adj* laag; diep; neerslachtig; ~ **tide** eb *c*

lower ['louə] *v* *neerlaten; verlagen; *strijken; *adj* onderst, lager

lowlands ['louləndz] *pl* laagland *nt*

loyal ['lɔiəl] *adj* loyaal

lubricate ['lu:brikeit] *v* oliën, smeren

lubrication [,lu:bri'keiʃən] *n* smering *c*; ~ **oil** smeerolie *c*; ~ **system** smeersysteem *nt*

luck [lʌk] *n* geluk *nt*; toeval *nt*; **bad** ~ pech *c*

lucky charm amulet *c*

ludicrous ['lu:dikrəs] *adj* belachelijk, bespottelijk

luggage ['lʌgidʒ] *n* bagage *c*; **hand** ~ handbagage *c*; **left** ~ **office** bagagedepot *nt*; ~ **rack** bagagerek *nt*, bagagenet *nt*; ~ **van** bagagewagen *c*

lukewarm ['lu:kwɔ:m] *adj* lauw

lumbago [lʌm'beigou] *n* spit *nt*

luminous ['lu:minəs] *adj* lichtgevend

lump [lʌmp] *n* brok *nt*, klont *c*, stuk *nt*; bult *c*; ~ **of sugar** suikerklontje *nt*; ~ **sum** ronde som

lumpy ['lʌmpi] *adj* klonterig

lunacy ['lu:nəsi] *n* krankzinnigheid *c*

lunatic ['lu:nətik] *adj* krankzinnig; *n* krankzinnige *c*

lunch [lʌntʃ] *n* lunch *c*, middageten *nt*

luncheon ['lʌntʃən] *n* middageten *nt*

lung [lʌŋ] *n* long *c*

lust [lʌst] *n* wellust *c*

luxurious [lʌg'ʒuəriəs] *adj* luxueus

luxury ['lʌkʃəri] *n* luxe *c*

M

machine [mə'ʃi:n] *n* apparaat *nt*, machine *c*

machinery [mə'ʃi:nəri] *n* machinerie *c*; mechanisme *nt*

mackerel ['mækrəl] *n* (pl ~) makreel *c*

mackintosh ['mækintɔʃ] *n* regenjas *c*

mad [mæd] *adj* krankzinnig, waanzinnig, gek; kwaad

madam ['mædəm] *n* mevrouw

madness ['mædnəs] *n* waanzin *c*

magazine [,mægə'zi:n] *n* blad *nt*

magic ['mædʒik] *n* toverkunst *c*, magie *c*; *adj* tover-

magician [mə'dʒiʃən] *n* goochelaar *c*

magistrate ['mædʒistreit] *n* magistraat *c*

magnetic [mæg'netik] *adj* magnetisch

magneto [mæg'ni:tou] *n* (pl ~s) magneet *c*

magnificent [mæg'nifisənt] *adj* prachtig; groots, luisterrijk

magpie ['mægpai] *n* ekster *c*

maid [meid] *n* meid *c*

maiden name ['meidən neim] meisjesnaam *c*

mail [meil] *n* post *c*; *v* posten; ~ **order** *Am* postwissel *c*

mailbox ['meilbɔks] *nAm* brievenbus *c*

main [mein] *adj* hoofd-, voornaamst; grootst; ~ **deck** bovendek *nt*; ~ **line** hoofdlijn *c*; ~ **road** hoofdweg *c*; ~ **street** hoofdstraat *c*

mainland ['meinlənd] *n* vasteland *nt*

mainly ['meinli] *adv* hoofdzakelijk

mains [meinz] *pl* hoofdleiding *c*

maintain [mein'tein] *v* handhaven

maintenance ['meintənəns] *n* onderhoud *nt*

maize [meiz] *n* maïs *c*

major ['meidʒə] *adj* groter; grootst; *n* majoor *c*

majority [mə'dʒɔrəti] *n* meerderheid *c*

***make** [meik] *v* maken; verdienen; halen; ~ **do with** zich **behelpen met; ~ **good** vergoeden; ~ **up** opstellen

make-up ['meikʌp] *n* make-up *c*

malaria [mə'lɛəriə] *n* malaria *c*

Malay [mə'lei] *n* Maleis *c*

Malaysia [mə'leiziə] Maleisië

Malaysian [mə'leiziən] *adj* Maleisisch

male [meil] *adj* mannelijk

malicious [mə'liʃəs] *adj* boosaardig

malignant [mə'lignənt] *adj* kwaadaardig

mallet ['mælit] *n* houten hamer

malnutrition [,mælnju'triʃən] *n* ondervoeding *c*

mammal ['mæməl] *n* zoogdier *nt*

mammoth ['mæməθ] *n* mammoet *c*

man [mæn] *n* (pl men) man *c*; mens *c*; **men's room** herentoilet *nt*

manage ['mænidʒ] *v* beheren; slagen

manageable ['mænidʒəbəl] *adj* hanteerbaar

management ['mænidʒmənt] *n* directie *c*; beheer *nt*

manager ['mænidʒə] *n* chef *c*, directeur *c*

mandarin ['mændərin] *n* mandarijn *c*

mandate ['mændeit] *n* mandaat *nt*

manger ['meindʒə] *n* kribbe *c*

manicure ['mænikjuə] *n* manicure *c*; *v* manicuren

mankind [mæn'kaind] *n* mensheid *c*

mannequin ['mænəkin] *n* mannequin *c*

manner ['mænə] *n* wijze *c*, manier *c*; **manners** *pl* manieren

man-of-war [,mænəv'wɔ:] *n* oorlogsschip *nt*

manor-house ['mænəhaus] *n* herenhuis *nt*

mansion ['mænʃən] *n* herenhuis *nt*

manual ['mænjuəl] *adj* hand-

manufacture [,mænju'fæktʃə] *v* vervaardigen, fabriceren

manufacturer [,mænju'fæktʃərə] *n* fabrikant *c*

manure [mə'njuə] *n* mest *c*

manuscript ['mænjuskript] *n* manuscript *nt*

many ['meni] *adj* veel

map [mæp] *n* kaart *c*; landkaart *c*; plattegrond *c*

maple ['meipəl] *n* esdoorn *c*

marble ['ma:bəl] *n* marmer *nt*; knikker *c*

March [ma:tʃ] maart

march [ma:tʃ] *v* marcheren; *n* mars *c*

mare [mɛə] *n* merrie *c*

margarine [,ma:dʒə'ri:n] *n* margarine *c*

margin ['ma:dʒin] *n* kantlijn *c*, marge *c*

maritime ['mæritaim] *adj* maritiem

mark [ma:k] *v* aankruisen; merken; kenmerken; *n* merkteken *nt*; cijfer *nt*; schietschijf *c*

market ['ma:kit] *n* markt *c*

market-place ['ma:kitpleis] *n* marktplein *nt*

marmalade ['ma:məleid] *n* marmelade *c*

marriage ['mæridʒ] *n* huwelijk *nt*

marrow ['mærou] *n* merg *nt*

marry ['mæri] *v* huwen, trouwen;
married couple echtpaar *nt*

marsh [mɑ:ʃ] *n* moeras *c*

marshy ['mɑ:ʃi] *adj* moerassig

martyr ['mɑ:tə] *n* martelaar *c*

marvel ['mɑ:vəl] *n* wonder *nt*; *v* zich
verbazen

marvellous ['mɑ:vələs] *adj* prachtig

mascara [mæ'skɑ:rə] *n* mascara *c*

masculine ['mæskjulin] *adj* mannelijk

mash [mæʃ] *v* fijnstampen

mask [mɑ:sk] *n* masker *nt*

Mass [mæs] *n* mis *c*

mass [mæs] *n* massa *c*; ~ production
massaproduktie *c*

massage ['mæsɑ:ʒ] *n* massage *c*; *v*
masseren

masseur [mæ'sə:] *n* masseur *c*

massive ['mæsiv] *adj* massief

mast [mɑ:st] *n* mast *c*

master ['mɑ:stə] *n* meester *c*; baas *c*;
leraar *c*, onderwijzer *c*; *v* beheersen

masterpiece ['mɑ:stəpi:s] *n* meesterwerk *nt*

mat [mæt] *n* mat *c*; *adj* mat, dof

match [mætʃ] *n* lucifer *c*; wedstrijd *c*;
v passen bij

match-box ['mætʃbɔks] *n* lucifersdoosje *nt*

material [mə'tiəriəl] *n* materiaal *nt*;
stof *c*; *adj* stoffelijk, materieel

mathematical [,mæθə'mætikəl] *adj*
wiskundig

mathematics [,mæθə'mætiks] *n* wiskunde *c*

matrimonial [,mætri'mouniəl] *adj* echtelijk

matrimony ['mætriməni] *n* echt *c*

matter ['mætə] *n* stof *c*, materie *c*;
aangelegenheid *c*, kwestie *c*, zaak *c*;
v van belang *zijn; as a ~ of fact
feitelijk, eigenlijk

matter-of-fact [,mætərəv'fækt] *adj*

nuchter

mattress ['mætrəs] *n* matras *c*

mature [mə'tjuə] *adj* rijp

maturity [mə'tjuərəti] *n* rijpheid *c*

mausoleum [,mɔ:sə'li:əm] *n* mausoleum *nt*

mauve [mouv] *adj* lichtpaars

May [mei] mei

*may [mei] *v* *kunnen; *mogen

maybe ['meibi:] *adv* misschien

mayor [mɛə] *n* burgemeester *c*

maze [meiz] *n* doolhof *nt*

me [mi:] *pron* me

meadow ['medou] *n* wei *c*

meal [mi:l] *n* maaltijd *c*, maal *nt*

mean [mi:n] *adj* gemeen; *n* gemiddelde *nt*

*mean [mi:n] *v* betekenen; bedoelen;
menen

meaning ['mi:niŋ] *n* betekenis *c*

meaningless ['mi:niŋləs] *adj* nietszeggend

means [mi:nz] *n* middel *nt*; by no ~
zeker niet, geenszins

in the meantime [in ðə 'mi:ntaim] inmiddels, ondertussen

meanwhile ['mi:nwail] *adv* intussen,
ondertussen

measles ['mi:zəlz] *n* mazelen *pl*

measure ['meʒə] *v* *meten; *n* maat *c*;
maatregel *c*

meat [mi:t] *n* vlees *nt*

mechanic [mi'kænik] *n* monteur *c*

mechanical [mi'kænikəl] *adj* mechanisch

mechanism ['mekənizəm] *n* mechanisme *nt*

medal ['medəl] *n* medaille *c*

mediaeval [,medi'i:vəl] *adj* middeleeuws

mediate ['mi:dieit] *v* bemiddelen

mediator ['mi:dieitə] *n* bemiddelaar *c*

medical ['medikəl] *adj* geneeskundig,
medisch

medicine ['medsin] n geneesmiddel nt; geneeskunde c

meditate ['mediteit] v mediteren

Mediterranean [,meditə'reiniən] Middellandse Zee

medium ['mi:diəm] adj middelmatig, gemiddeld, midden-

*** meet** [mi:t] v ontmoeten; *tegenkomen

meeting ['mi:tiŋ] n vergadering c, bijeenkomst c; ontmoeting c

meeting-place ['mi:tiŋpleis] n trefpunt nt

melancholy ['melənkəli] n weemoed c

mellow ['melou] adj zacht

melodrama ['melə,drɑ:mə] n melodrama nt

melody ['melədi] n melodie c

melon ['melən] n meloen c

melt [melt] v *smelten

member ['membə] n lid nt; **Member of Parliament** kamerlid nt

membership ['membəʃip] n lidmaatschap nt

memo ['memou] n (pl ~s) memorandum nt

memorable ['memərəbəl] adj gedenkwaardig

memorial [mə'mɔ:riəl] n gedenkteken nt

memorize ['meməraiz] v uit het hoofd leren

memory ['meməri] n geheugen nt; herinnering c; nagedachtenis c

mend [mend] v herstellen, repareren

menstruation [,menstru'eiʃən] n menstruatie c

mental ['mentəl] adj geestelijk

mention ['menʃən] v noemen, vermelden; n melding c, vermelding c

menu ['menju:] n spijskaart c, menukaart c

merchandise ['mə:tʃəndaiz] n handelswaar c, koopwaar c

merchant ['mə:tʃənt] n handelaar c, koopman c

merciful ['mə:sifəl] adj barmhartig

mercury ['mə:kjuri] n kwik nt

mercy ['mə:si] n genade c, clementie c

mere [miə] adj louter

merely ['miəli] adv slechts

merger ['mə:dʒə] n fusie c

merit ['merit] v verdienen; n verdienste c

mermaid ['mə:meid] n zeemeermin c

merry ['meri] adj vrolijk

merry-go-round ['merigou,raund] n draaimolen c

mesh [meʃ] n maas c

mess [mes] n rommel c, warboel c; ~ **up** *bederven

message ['mesidʒ] n boodschap c, bericht nt

messenger ['mesindʒə] n bode c

metal ['metəl] n metaal nt; metalen

meter ['mi:tə] n meter c

method ['meθəd] n aanpak c, methode c; orde c

methodical [mə'θɔdikəl] adj methodisch

methylated spirits ['meθəleitid 'spirits] brandspiritus c

metre ['mi:tə] n meter c

metric ['metrik] adj metrisch

Mexican ['meksikən] adj Mexicaans; n Mexicaan c

Mexico ['meksikou] Mexico

mezzanine ['mezəni:n] n entresol c

microphone ['maikrəfoun] n microfoon c

midday ['middei] n middag c

middle ['midəl] n midden nt; adj middelst; **Middle Ages** middeleeuwen pl; **middle-class** adj burgerlijk

midnight ['midnait] n middernacht c

midst [midst] n midden nt

midsummer ['mid,sʌmə] n midzomer c

midwife ['midwaif] n (pl -wives) vroedvrouw c

might [mait] n macht c

*might [mait] v *kunnen

mighty ['maiti] adj machtig

migraine ['migrein] n migraine c

mild [maild] adj zacht

mildew ['mildju] n schimmel c

mile [mail] n mijl c

mileage ['mailidʒ] n afstand in mijlen

milepost ['mailpoust] n wegwijzer c

milestone ['mailstoun] n mijlpaal c

milieu ['mi:ljə:] n milieu nt

military ['militəri] adj militair; ~ **force** krijgsmacht c

milk [milk] n melk c

milkman ['milkmən] n (pl -men) melkboer c

milk-shake ['milkʃeik] n milk shake

mill [mil] n molen c; fabriek c

miller ['milə] n molenaar c

milliner ['milinə] n modiste c

million ['miljən] n miljoen nt

millionaire [,miljə'nɛə] n miljonair c

mince [mins] v fijnhakken

mind [maind] n geest c; v bezwaar *hebben tegen; letten op, *geven om

mine [main] n mijn c

miner ['mainə] n mijnwerker c

mineral ['minərəl] n delfstof c, mineraal nt; ~ **water** mineraalwater nt

miniature ['minjətʃə] n miniatuur c

minimum ['miniməm] n minimum nt

mining ['mainiŋ] n mijnbouw c

minister ['ministə] n minister c; predikant c; **Prime Minister** premier c

ministry ['ministri] n ministerie nt

mink [miŋk] n nerts nt

minor ['mainə] adj klein, gering, kleiner; ondergeschikt; n minderjarige c

minority [mai'nɔrəti] n minderheid c

mint [mint] n munt c

minus ['mainəs] prep min

minute[1] ['minit] n minuut c; **minutes** notulen pl

minute[2] [mai'nju:t] adj minuscuul

miracle ['mirəkəl] n wonder nt

miraculous [mi'rækjuləs] adj wonderbaarlijk

mirror ['mirə] n spiegel c

misbehave [,misbi'heiv] v zich *misdragen

miscarriage [mis'kæridʒ] n miskraam c

miscellaneous [,misə'leiniəs] adj gemengd

mischief ['mistʃif] n kattekwaad nt; onheil nt, schade c, kwaad nt

mischievous ['mistʃivəs] adj ondeugend

miserable ['mizərəbəl] adj beroerd, ellendig

misery ['mizəri] n narigheid c, ellende c; nood c

misfortune [mis'fɔ:tʃən] n tegenslag c, ongeluk nt

*mislay [mis'lei] v kwijtraken

misplaced [mis'pleist] adj misplaatst

mispronounce [,misprə'nauns] v verkeerd *uitspreken

miss[1] [mis] mejuffrouw, juffrouw c

miss[2] [mis] v missen

missing ['misiŋ] adj ontbrekend; ~ **person** vermiste c

mist [mist] n nevel c, mist c

mistake [mi'steik] n abuis nt, vergissing c, fout c

*mistake [mi'steik] v verwarren

mistaken [mi'steikən] adj fout; ***be ~** zich vergissen

mister ['mistə] n meneer, mijnheer c

mistress ['mistrəs] n vrouw des huizes; meesteres c; maîtresse c

mistrust [mis'trʌst] v wantrouwen

misty ['misti] adj mistig

*misunderstand [,misʌndə'stænd] v *misverstaan

misunderstanding [,misʌndə'stændiŋ] *n* misverstand *nt*

misuse [mis'ju:s] *n* misbruik *nt*

mittens ['mitənz] *pl* wanten *pl*

mix [miks] *v* mengen; ~ **with** *omgaan met

mixed [mikst] *adj* gemêleerd, gemengd

mixer ['miksə] *n* mixer *c*

mixture ['mikstʃə] *n* mengsel *nt*

moan [moun] *v* kreunen

moat [mout] *n* gracht *c*

mobile ['moubail] *adj* beweeglijk, mobiel

mock [mɔk] *v* bespotten

mockery ['mɔkəri] *n* spot *c*

model ['mɔdəl] *n* model *nt*; mannequin *c*; *v* modelleren, boetseren

moderate ['mɔdərət] *adj* gematigd, matig; middelmatig

modern ['mɔdən] *adj* modern

modest ['mɔdist] *adj* discreet, bescheiden

modesty ['mɔdisti] *n* bescheidenheid *c*

modify ['mɔdifai] *v* wijzigen

mohair ['mouhɛə] *n* mohair *nt*

moist [mɔist] *adj* nat, vochtig

moisten ['mɔisən] *v* bevochtigen

moisture ['mɔistʃə] *n* vochtigheid *c*; **moisturizing cream** vochtinbrengende crème

molar ['moulə] *n* kies *c*

moment ['moumənt] *n* moment *nt*, ogenblik *nt*

momentary ['mouməntəri] *adj* kortstondig

monarch ['mɔnək] *n* vorst *c*

monarchy ['mɔnəki] *n* monarchie *c*

monastery ['mɔnəstri] *n* klooster *nt*

Monday ['mʌndi] maandag *c*

monetary ['mʌnitəri] *adj* monetair; ~ **unit** munteenheid *c*

money ['mʌni] *n* geld *nt*; ~ **exchange** wisselkantoor *nt*; ~ **order** overschrijving *c*

monk [mʌŋk] *n* monnik *c*

monkey ['mʌŋki] *n* aap *c*

monologue ['mɔnəlɔg] *n* monoloog *c*

monopoly [mə'nɔpəli] *n* monopolie *nt*

monotonous [mə'nɔtənəs] *adj* eentonig

month [mʌnθ] *n* maand *c*

monthly ['mʌnθli] *adj* maandelijks; ~ **magazine** maandblad *nt*

monument ['mɔnjumənt] *n* gedenkteken *nt*, monument *nt*

mood [mu:d] *n* humeur *nt*, stemming *c*

moon [mu:n] *n* maan *c*

moonlight ['mu:nlait] *n* maanlicht *nt*

moor [muə] *n* heide *c*, veen *nt*

moose [mu:s] *n* (pl ~, ~s) eland *c*

moped ['mouped] *n* bromfiets *c*

moral ['mɔrəl] *n* moraal *c*; *adj* zedelijk, moreel; **morals** zeden *pl*

morality [mə'ræləti] *n* moraliteit *c*

more [mɔ:] *adj* meer; **once** ~ nogmaals

moreover [mɔ:'rouvə] *adv* voorts, bovendien

morning ['mɔ:niŋ] *n* ochtend *c*, morgen *c*; ~ **paper** ochtendblad *nt*; **this** ~ vanmorgen

Moroccan [mə'rɔkən] *adj* Marokkaans; *n* Marokkaan *c*

Morocco [mə'rɔkou] Marokko

morphia ['mɔ:fiə] *n* morfine *c*

morphine ['mɔ:fi:n] *n* morfine *c*

morsel ['mɔ:səl] *n* brok *nt*

mortal ['mɔ:təl] *adj* dodelijk, sterfelijk

mortgage ['mɔ:gidʒ] *n* hypotheek *c*

mosaic [mə'zeiik] *n* mozaïek *nt*

mosque [mɔsk] *n* moskee *c*

mosquito [mə'ski:tou] *n* (pl ~es) mug *c*; muskiet *c*

mosquito-net [mə'ski:tounet] *n* muskietennet *nt*

moss [mɔs] *n* mos *nt*

most [moust] *adj* meest; **at** ~ hoogstens, hooguit; ~ **of all** vooral

mostly ['moustli] adv meestal

motel [mou'tel] n motel nt

moth [mɔθ] n mot c

mother ['mʌðə] n moeder c; ~ tongue moedertaal c

mother-in-law ['mʌðərinlɔ:] n (pl mothers-) schoonmoeder c

mother-of-pearl [,mʌðərəv'pə:l] n paarlemoer nt

motion ['mouʃən] n beweging c; motie c

motive ['moutiv] n motief nt

motor ['moutə] n motor c; v *autorijden; ~ body Am carrosserie c; starter ~ startmotor c

motorbike ['moutəbaik] nAm brommer c

motor-boat ['moutəbout] n motorboot c

motor-car ['moutəkɑ:] n auto c

motor-cycle ['moutə,saikəl] n motorfiets c

motoring ['moutəriŋ] n automobilisme nt

motorist ['moutərist] n automobilist c

motorway ['moutəwei] n snelweg c

motto ['motou] n (pl ~es, ~s) devies nt

mouldy ['mouldi] adj beschimmeld

mound [maund] n heuvel c

mount [maunt] v *bestijgen; n berg c

mountain ['mauntin] n berg c; ~ pass bergpas c; ~ range bergketen c

mountaineering [,maunti'niəriŋ] n bergsport c

mountainous ['mauntinəs] adj bergachtig

mourning ['mɔ:niŋ] n rouw c

mouse [maus] n (pl mice) muis c

moustache [mə'stɑ:ʃ] n snor c

mouth [mauθ] n mond c; muil c, bek c; monding c

mouthwash ['mauθwɔʃ] n mondspoeling c

movable ['mu:vəbəl] adj roerend

move [mu:v] v *bewegen; verplaatsen; verhuizen; ontroeren; n zet c, stap c; verhuizing c

movement ['mu:vmənt] n beweging c

movie ['mu:vi] n film c; movies Am bioscoop c; ~ theater Am bioscoop c

much [mʌtʃ] adj veel; as ~ evenveel; evenzeer

muck [mʌk] n drek c

mud [mʌd] n modder c

muddle ['mʌdəl] n wirwar c, warboel c; v verknoeien

muddy ['mʌdi] adj modderig

mud-guard ['mʌdgɑ:d] n spatbord nt

muffler ['mʌflə] nAm knalpot c

mug [mʌg] n beker c, kroes c

mulberry ['mʌlbəri] n moerbei c

mule [mju:l] n muildier nt, muilezel c

mullet ['mʌlit] n mul c

multiplication [,mʌltipli'keiʃən] n vermenigvuldiging c

multiply ['mʌltiplai] v vermenigvuldigen

mumps [mʌmps] n bof c

municipal [mju:'nisipəl] adj gemeentelijk

municipality [mju:,nisi'pæləti] n gemeentebestuur nt

murder ['mə:də] n moord c; v vermoorden

murderer ['mə:dərə] n moordenaar c

muscle ['mʌsəl] n spier c

muscular ['mʌskjulə] adj gespierd

museum [mju:'zi:əm] n museum nt

mushroom ['mʌʃru:m] n champignon c; paddestoel c

music ['mju:zik] n muziek c; ~ academy conservatorium nt

musical ['mju:zikəl] adj muzikaal; n musical c

music-hall ['mju:zikhɔ:l] n variététheater nt

musician [mju:'ziʃən] *n* musicus *c*

muslin ['mʌzlin] *n* mousseline *c*

mussel ['mʌsəl] *n* mossel *c*

***must** [mʌst] *v* *moeten

mustard ['mʌstəd] *n* mosterd *c*

mute [mju:t] *adj* stom

mutiny ['mju:tini] *n* muiterij *c*

mutton ['mʌtən] *n* schapevlees *nt*

mutual ['mju:tʃuəl] *adj* onderling, wederzijds

my [mai] *adj* mijn

myself [mai'self] *pron* me; zelf

mysterious [mi'stiəriəs] *adj* mysterieus, geheimzinnig

mystery ['mistəri] *n* raadsel *nt*, mysterie *nt*

myth [miθ] *n* mythe *c*

N

nail [neil] *n* nagel *c*; spijker *c*

nailbrush ['neilbrʌʃ] *n* nagelborstel *c*

nail-file ['neilfail] *n* nagelvijl *c*

nail-polish ['neil,pɔliʃ] *n* nagellak *c*

nail-scissors ['neil,sizəz] *pl* nagelschaar *c*

naïve [na:'i:v] *adj* naïef

naked ['neikid] *adj* bloot, naakt; kaal

name [neim] *n* naam *c*; *v* noemen; **in the ~ of** namens

namely ['neimli] *adv* namelijk

nap [næp] *n* dutje *nt*

napkin ['næpkin] *n* servet *nt*

nappy ['næpi] *n* luier *c*

narcosis [na:'kousis] *n* (pl -ses) narcose *c*

narcotic [na:'kɔtik] *n* narcoticum *nt*

narrow ['nærou] *adj* eng, smal, nauw

narrow-minded [,nærou'maindid] *adj* bekrompen

nasty ['na:sti] *adj* naar, akelig

nation ['neiʃən] *n* natie *c*; volk *nt*

national ['næʃənəl] *adj* nationaal; volks-; staats-; ~ **anthem** volkslied *nt*; ~ **dress** nationale klederdracht; ~ **park** natuurreservaat *nt*

nationality [,næʃə'næləti] *n* nationaliteit *c*

nationalize ['næʃənəlaiz] *v* nationaliseren

native ['neitiv] *n* inboorling *c*; *adj* inheems; ~ **country** vaderland *nt*, geboorteland *nt*; ~ **language** moedertaal *c*

natural ['nætʃərəl] *adj* natuurlijk; aangeboren

naturally ['nætʃərəli] *adv* natuurlijk, uiteraard

nature ['neitʃə] *n* natuur *c*; aard *c*

naughty ['nɔ:ti] *adj* ondeugend, stout

nausea ['nɔ:siə] *n* misselijkheid *c*

naval ['neivəl] *adj* marine-

navel ['neivəl] *n* navel *c*

navigable ['nævigəbəl] *adj* bevaarbaar

navigate ['nævigeit] *v* *varen; sturen

navigation [,nævi'geiʃən] *n* navigatie *c*; scheepvaart *c*

navy ['neivi] *n* marine *c*

near [niə] *prep* bij; *adj* nabij, dichtbij

nearby ['niəbai] *adj* nabijzijnd

nearly ['niəli] *adv* haast, bijna

neat [ni:t] *adj* keurig, net; puur

necessary ['nesəsəri] *adj* nodig, noodzakelijk

necessity [nə'sesəti] *n* noodzaak *c*

neck [nek] *n* hals *c*; **nape of the ~** nek *c*

necklace ['nekləs] *n* halsketting *c*

necktie ['nektai] *n* das *c*

need [ni:d] *v* hoeven, behoeven, nodig *hebben; *n* nood *c*, behoefte *c*; noodzaak *c*; ~ **to** *moeten

needle ['ni:dəl] *n* naald *c*

needlework ['ni:dəlwə:k] *n* handwerk *nt*

negative ['negətiv] *adj* ontkennend,

negatief; *n* negatief *nt*

neglect [ni'glekt] *v* verwaarlozen; *n* verwaarlozing *c*

neglectful [ni'glektfəl] *adj* nalatig

negligee ['negliʒei] *n* negligé *c*

negotiate [ni'gouʃieit] *v* onderhandelen

negotiation [ni,gouʃi'eiʃən] *n* onderhandeling *c*

Negro ['ni:grou] *n* (pl -es) neger *c*

neighbour ['neibə] *n* buur *c*, buurman *c*

neighbourhood ['neibəhud] *n* buurt *c*

neighbouring ['neibəriŋ] *adj* aangrenzend, naburig

neither ['naiðə] *pron* geen van beide; **neither ... nor** noch ... noch

neon ['ni:ɔn] *n* neon *nt*

nephew ['nefju:] *n* neef *c*

nerve [nə:v] *n* zenuw *c*; durf *c*

nervous ['nə:vəs] *adj* nerveus, zenuwachtig

nest [nest] *n* nest *nt*

net [net] *n* net *nt*; *adj* netto

the Netherlands ['neðələndz] Nederland

network ['netwə:k] *n* netwerk *nt*

neuralgia [njuə'rældʒə] *n* zenuwpijn *c*

neurosis [njuə'rousis] *n* neurose *c*

neuter ['nju:tə] *adj* onzijdig

neutral ['nju:trəl] *adj* neutraal

never ['nevə] *adv* nimmer, nooit

nevertheless [,nevəðə'les] *adv* niettemin

new [nju:] *adj* nieuw; **New Year** nieuwjaar

news [nju:z] *n* nieuwsberichten *pl*, nieuws *nt*; journaal *nt*

newsagent ['nju:,zeidʒənt] *n* krantenverkoper *c*

newspaper ['nju:z,peipə] *n* krant *c*

newsreel ['nju:zri:l] *n* filmjournaal *nt*

newsstand ['nju:zstænd] *n* krantenkiosk *c*

New Zealand [nju: 'zi:lənd] Nieuw-Zeeland

next [nekst] *adj* volgend; ~ **to** naast

nice [nais] *adj* aardig, mooi, prettig; lekker; sympathiek

nickel ['nikəl] *n* nikkel *nt*

nickname ['nikneim] *n* bijnaam *c*

nicotine ['nikəti:n] *n* nicotine *c*

niece [ni:s] *n* nicht *c*

Nigeria [nai'dʒiəriə] Nigeria

Nigerian [nai'dʒiəriən] *adj* Nigeriaans; *n* Nigeriaan *c*

night [nait] *n* nacht *c*; avond *c*; **by** ~ 's nachts; ~ **flight** nachtvlucht *c*; ~ **rate** nachttarief *nt*; ~ **train** nachttrein *c*

nightclub ['naitklʌb] *n* nachtclub *c*

night-cream ['naitkri:m] *n* nachtcrème *c*

nightdress ['naitdres] *n* nachtjapon *c*

nightingale ['naitiŋgeil] *n* nachtegaal *c*

nightly ['naitli] *adj* nachtelijk

nil [nil] niets

nine [nain] *num* negen

nineteen [,nain'ti:n] *num* negentien

nineteenth [,nain'ti:nθ] *num* negentiende

ninety ['nainti] *num* negentig

ninth [nainθ] *num* negende

nitrogen ['naitrədʒən] *n* stikstof *c*

no [nou] neen, nee; *adj* geen; ~ **one** niemand

nobility [nou'biləti] *n* adel *c*

noble ['noubəl] *adj* adellijk; edel

nobody ['noubɔdi] *pron* niemand

nod [nɔd] *n* knik *c*; *v* knikken

noise [nɔiz] *n* geluid *nt*; herrie *c*, rumoer *nt*, lawaai *nt*

noisy ['nɔizi] *adj* lawaaierig; gehorig

nominal ['nɔminəl] *adj* nominaal

nominate ['nɔmineit] *v* benoemen

nomination [,nɔmi'neiʃən] *n* nominatie *c*; benoeming *c*

none [nʌn] *pron* geen

nonsense ['nɔnsəns] *n* onzin *c*

noon [nu:n] *n* middag *c*

normal ['nɔ:məl] *adj* gewoon, normaal

north [nɔ:θ] *n* noorden *nt*; noord *c*; *adj* noordelijk; **North Pole** noordpool *c*

north-east [,nɔ:θ'i:st] *n* noordoosten *nt*

northerly ['nɔ:ðəli] *adj* noordelijk

northern ['nɔ:ðən] *adj* noordelijk

north-west [,nɔ:θ'west] *n* noordwesten *nt*

Norway ['nɔ:wei] Noorwegen

Norwegian [nɔ:'wi:dʒən] *adj* Noors; *n* Noor *c*

nose [nouz] *n* neus *c*

nosebleed ['nouzbli:d] *n* neusbloeding *c*

nostril ['nɔstril] *n* neusgat *nt*

not [nɔt] *adv* niet

notary ['noutəri] *n* notaris *c*

note [nout] *n* aantekening *c*, notitie *c*; noot *c*; toon *c*; *v* noteren; opmerken, constateren

notebook ['noutbuk] *n* notitieboek *nt*

noted ['noutid] *adj* befaamd

notepaper ['nout,peipə] *n* schrijfpapier *nt*, briefpapier *nt*

nothing ['nʌθiŋ] *n* niks, niets

notice ['noutis] *v* bemerken, merken, opmerken; *zien; *n* aankondiging *c*, bericht *nt*; notitie *c*, aandacht *c*

noticeable ['noutisəbəl] *adj* merkbaar; opmerkelijk

notify ['noutifai] *v* mededelen; waarschuwen

notion ['noufən] *n* begrip *nt*, notie *c*

notorious [nou'tɔ:riəs] *adj* berucht

nougat ['nu:ga:] *n* noga *c*

nought [nɔ:t] *n* nul *c*

noun [naun] *n* zelfstandig naamwoord *nt*

nourishing ['nʌrifiŋ] *adj* voedzaam

novel ['nɔvəl] *n* roman *c*

novelist ['nɔvəlist] *n* romanschrijver *c*

November [nou'vembə] november

now [nau] *adv* nu; thans; ~ **and then** nu en dan

nowadays ['nauədeiz] *adv* tegenwoordig

nowhere ['nouwɛə] *adv* nergens

nozzle ['nɔzəl] *n* tuit *c*

nuance [nju:'ã:s] *n* nuance *c*

nuclear ['nju:kliə] *adj* kern-, nucleair; ~ **energy** kernenergie *c*

nucleus ['nju:kliəs] *n* kern *c*

nude [nju:d] *adj* naakt; *n* naakt *nt*

nuisance ['nju:səns] *n* last *c*

numb [nʌm] *adj* gevoelloos; verstijfd

number ['nʌmbə] *n* nummer *nt*; cijfer *nt*, getal *nt*; aantal *nt*

numeral ['nju:mərəl] *n* telwoord *nt*

numerous ['nju:mərəs] *adj* talrijk

nun [nʌn] *n* non *c*

nunnery ['nʌnəri] *n* nonnenklooster *nt*

nurse [nɔ:s] *n* zuster *c*, verpleegster *c*; kinderjuffrouw *c*; *v* verplegen; zogen

nursery ['nɔ:səri] *n* kinderkamer *c*; crèche *c*; boomkwekerij *c*

nut [nʌt] *n* noot *c*; moer *c*

nutcrackers ['nʌt,krækəz] *pl* notekraker *c*

nutmeg ['nʌtmeg] *n* nootmuskaat *c*

nutritious [nju:'trifəs] *adj* voedzaam

nutshell ['nʌtfel] *n* notedop *c*

nylon ['nailɔn] *n* nylon *nt*

O

oak [ouk] *n* eik *c*

oar [ɔ:] *n* roeiriem *c*

oasis [ou'eisis] *n* (pl oases) oase *c*

oath [ouθ] *n* eed *c*

oats [outs] *pl* haver *c*

obedience [ə'bi:diəns] *n* gehoorzaamheid *c*

obedient [ə'bi:diənt] *adj* gehoorzaam

obey [ə'bei] *v* gehoorzamen

object[1] ['obdʒikt] *n* object *nt*; voorwerp *nt*; doel *nt*

object[2] [əb'dʒekt] *v* *tegenwerpen; ~ **to** bezwaar *hebben tegen

objection [əb'dʒekʃən] *n* bezwaar *nt*, tegenwerping *c*

objective [əb'dʒektiv] *adj* objectief; *n* doel *nt*

obligatory [ə'bligətəri] *adj* verplicht

oblige [ə'blaidʒ] *v* verplichten; ***be obliged to** verplicht *zijn om; *moeten

obliging [ə'blaidʒiŋ] *adj* voorkomend

oblong ['obloŋ] *adj* langwerpig; *n* rechthoek *c*

obscene [əb'si:n] *adj* obsceen

obscure [əb'skjuə] *adj* obscuur, duister

observation [,obzə'veiʃən] *n* observatie *c*, waarneming *c*

observatory [əb'zə:vətri] *n* observatorium *nt*

observe [əb'zə:v] *v* observeren, *waarnemen

obsession [əb'seʃən] *n* obsessie *c*

obstacle ['obstəkəl] *n* hindernis *c*

obstinate ['obstinət] *adj* koppig; hardnekkig

obtain [əb'tein] *v* behalen, *verkrijgen

obtainable [əb'teinəbəl] *adj* verkrijgbaar

obvious ['obviəs] *adj* duidelijk

occasion [ə'keiʒən] *n* gelegenheid *c*; aanleiding *c*

occasionally [ə'keiʒənəli] *adv* af en toe, nu en dan

occupant ['okjupənt] *n* bewoner *c*

occupation [,okju'peiʃən] *n* werk *nt*; bezetting *c*

occupy ['okjupai] *v* *innemen, bezetten; **occupied** *adj* bezet

occur [ə'kə:] *v* gebeuren, *voorkomen, zich *voordoen

occurrence [ə'kʌrəns] *n* gebeurtenis *c*

ocean ['ouʃən] *n* oceaan *c*

October [ok'toubə] oktober

octopus ['oktəpəs] *n* octopus *c*

oculist ['okjulist] *n* oogarts *c*

odd [od] *adj* raar, vreemd; oneven

odour ['oudə] *n* geur *c*

of [ov, əv] *prep* van

off [of] *adv* af; weg; *prep* van

offence [ə'fens] *n* overtreding *c*; belediging *c*, aanstoot *c*

offend [ə'fend] *v* krenken, beledigen; *overtreden

offensive [ə'fensiv] *adj* offensief; beledigend, aanstootgevend; *n* offensief *nt*

offer ['ofə] *v* *aanbieden; *bieden; *n* aanbieding *c*, aanbod *nt*

office ['ofis] *n* bureau *nt*, kantoor *nt*; ambt *nt*; ~ **hours** kantooruren *pl*

officer ['ofisə] *n* officier *c*

official [ə'fiʃəl] *adj* officieel

off-licence ['of,laisəns] *n* slijterij *c*

often ['ofən] *adv* vaak, dikwijls

oil [oil] *n* olie *c*; **fuel** ~ stookolie *c*; ~ **filter** oliefilter *nt*; ~ **pressure** oliedruk *c*

oil-painting [,oil'peintiŋ] *n* olieverfschilderij *nt*

oil-refinery ['oilri,fainəri] *n* olieraffinaderij *c*

oil-well ['oilwel] *n* oliebron *c*

oily ['oili] *adj* olieachtig

ointment ['ointmənt] *n* zalf *c*

okay! [,ou'kei] in orde!

old [ould] *adj* oud; ~ **age** ouderdom *c*

old-fashioned [,ould'fæʃənd] *adj* ouderwets

olive ['oliv] *n* olijf *c*; ~ **oil** olijfolie *c*

omelette ['omlət] *n* omelet *nt*

ominous ['ominəs] *adj* onheilspellend

omit [ə'mit] *v* *weglaten

omnipotent [om'nipətənt] *adj* almachtig

on [ɔn] *prep* op; aan

once [wʌns] *adv* eenmaal, eens; **at ~** meteen, dadelijk; **~ more** nog eens

oncoming ['ɔn,kʌmiŋ] *adj* tegemoetkomend, naderend

one [wʌn] *num* een; *pron* men

oneself [wʌn'self] *pron* zelf

onion ['ʌnjən] *n* ui *c*

only ['ounli] *adj* enig; *adv* slechts, alleen, maar; *conj* maar

onwards ['ɔnwədz] *adv* voorwaarts

onyx ['ɔniks] *n* onyx *nt*

opal ['oupəl] *n* opaal *c*

open ['oupən] *v* openen; *adj* open; openhartig

opening ['oupəniŋ] *n* opening *c*

opera ['ɔpərə] *n* opera *c*; **~ house** opera *c*

operate ['ɔpəreit] *v* opereren, werken

operation [,ɔpə'reiʃən] *n* werking *c*; operatie *c*

operator ['ɔpəreitə] *n* telefoniste *c*

operetta [,ɔpə'retə] *n* operette *c*

opinion [ə'pinjən] *n* opinie *c*, mening *c*

opponent [ə'pounənt] *n* tegenstander *c*

opportunity [,ɔpə'tju:nəti] *n* gelegenheid *c*, kans *c*

oppose [ə'pouz] *v* zich verzetten

opposite ['ɔpəzit] *prep* tegenover; *adj* tegengesteld

opposition [,ɔpə'ziʃən] *n* oppositie *c*

oppress [ə'pres] *v* beklemmen, verdrukken

optician [ɔp'tiʃən] *n* opticien *c*

optimism ['ɔptimizəm] *n* optimisme *nt*

optimist ['ɔptimist] *n* optimist *c*

optimistic [,ɔpti'mistik] *adj* optimistisch

optional ['ɔpʃənəl] *adj* facultatief

or [ɔ:] *conj* of

oral ['ɔ:rəl] *adj* mondeling

orange ['ɔrindʒ] *n* sinaasappel *c*; *adj* oranje

orchard ['ɔ:tʃəd] *n* boomgaard *c*

orchestra ['ɔ:kistrə] *n* orkest *nt*; **~ seat** *Am* stalles *pl*

order ['ɔ:də] *v* *bevelen; bestellen; *n* volgorde *c*, orde *c*; opdracht *c*, bevel *nt*; bestelling *c*; **in ~** in orde; **in ~ to** om te; **made to ~** op maat gemaakt; **out of ~** buiten werking; **postal ~** postwissel *c*

order-form ['ɔ:dəfɔ:m] *n* bestelformulier *nt*

ordinary ['ɔ:dənri] *adj* alledaags, gewoon

ore [ɔ:] *n* erts *nt*

organ ['ɔ:gən] *n* orgaan *nt*; orgel *nt*

organic [ɔ:'gænik] *adj* organisch

organization [,ɔ:gənai'zeiʃən] *n* organisatie *c*

organize ['ɔ:gənaiz] *v* organiseren

Orient ['ɔ:riənt] *n* Oosten *nt*

oriental [,ɔ:ri'entəl] *adj* oosters

orientate ['ɔ:riənteit] *v* zich oriënteren

origin ['ɔridʒin] *n* origine *c*, oorsprong *c*; afstamming *c*, herkomst *c*

original [ə'ridʒinəl] *adj* oorspronkelijk, origineel

originally [ə'ridʒinəli] *adv* aanvankelijk

orlon ['ɔ:lɔn] *n* orlon *nt*

ornament ['ɔ:nəmənt] *n* versiersel *nt*

ornamental [,ɔ:nə'mentəl] *adj* ornamenteel

orphan ['ɔ:fən] *n* wees *c*

orthodox ['ɔ:θədɔks] *adj* orthodox

ostrich ['ɔstritʃ] *n* struisvogel *c*

other ['ʌðə] *adj* ander

otherwise ['ʌðəwaiz] *conj* anders

*ought to [ɔ:t] *moeten

our [auə] *adj* ons

ourselves [auə'selvz] *pron* ons; zelf

out [aut] *adv* buiten, uit; **~ of** buiten, uit

outbreak ['autbreik] *n* uitbarsting *c*

outcome ['autkʌm] *n* resultaat *nt*

*outdo [,aut'du:] *v* *overtreffen

outdoors [,aut'dɔ:z] *adv* buiten

outfit ['autfit] *n* uitrusting *c*

outline ['autlain] *n* omtrek *c* ; *v* schetsen

outlook ['autluk] *n* verwachting *c* ; zienswijze *c*

output ['autput] *n* produktie *c*

outrage ['autreidʒ] *n* gewelddaad *c*

outside [,aut'said] *adv* buiten ; *prep* buiten ; *n* uiterlijk *nt*, buitenkant *c*

outsize ['autsaiz] *n* extra grote maat

outskirts ['autskə:ts] *pl* buitenwijk *c*

outstanding [,aut'stændiŋ] *adj* eminent, vooraanstaand

outward ['autwəd] *adj* uiterlijk

outwards ['autwədz] *adv* naar buiten

oval ['ouvəl] *adj* ovaal

oven ['ʌvən] *n* oven *c* ; **microwave ~** mikrogolf oven

over ['ouvə] *prep* boven, over ; meer dan ; *adv* over ; omver ; *adj* voorbij ; **~ there** ginds

overall ['ouvərɔ:l] *adj* totaal

overalls ['ouvərɔ:lz] *pl* overall *c*

overcast ['ouvəka:st] *adj* betrokken

overcoat ['ouvəkout] *n* overjas *c*

*overcome** [,ouvə'kʌm] *v* *overwinnen

overdue [,ouvə'dju:] *adj* te laat ; achterstallig

overgrown [,ouvə'groun] *adj* begroeid

overhaul [,ouvə'hɔ:l] *v* reviseren

overlook [,ouvə'luk] *v* over het hoofd *zien

overnight [,ouvə'nait] *adv* 's nachts

overseas [,ouvə'si:z] *adj* overzees

oversight ['ouvəsait] *n* vergissing *c*

*oversleep** [,ouvə'sli:p] *v* zich *verslapen

overstrung [,ouvə'strʌŋ] *adj* overspannen

*overtake** [,ouvə'teik] *v* inhalen ; **no overtaking** inhalen verboden

over-tired [,ouvə'taiəd] *adj* oververmoeid

overture ['ouvətʃə] *n* ouverture *c*

overweight ['ouvəweit] *n* bagageoverschot *nt*

overwhelm [,ouvə'welm] *v* onthutsen, overweldigen

overwork [,ouvə'wə:k] *v* zich overwerken

owe [ou] *v* verschuldigd *zijn, schuldig *zijn ; te danken *hebben aan ; **owing to** vanwege, ten gevolge van

owl [aul] *n* uil *c*

own [oun] *v* *bezitten ; *adj* eigen

owner ['ounə] *n* bezitter *c*, eigenaar *c*

ox [ɔks] *n* (pl oxen) os *c*

oxygen ['ɔksidʒən] *n* zuurstof *c*

oyster ['ɔistə] *n* oester *c*

P

pace [peis] *n* gang *c* ; schrede *c*, stap *c* ; tempo *nt*

Pacific Ocean [pə'sifik 'ouʃən] Stille Oceaan

pacifism ['pæsifizəm] *n* pacifisme *nt*

pacifist ['pæsifist] *n* pacifist *c* ; pacifistisch

pack [pæk] *v* inpakken ; **~ up** inpakken

package ['pækidʒ] *n* pak *nt*

packet ['pækit] *n* pakje *nt*

packing ['pækiŋ] *n* verpakking *c*

pad [pæd] *n* kussentje *nt* ; blocnote *c*

paddle ['pædəl] *n* peddel *c*

padlock ['pædlɔk] *n* hangslot *nt*

pagan ['peigən] *adj* heidens ; *n* heiden *c*

page [peidʒ] *n* pagina *c*, bladzijde *c*

page-boy ['peidʒbɔi] *n* piccolo *c*

pail [peil] *n* emmer *c*

pain [pein] *n* pijn *c* ; **pains** moeite *c*

painful ['peinfəl] *adj* pijnlijk

painless ['peinləs] *adj* pijnloos

paint [peint] n verf c; v schilderen; verven

paint-box ['peintbɔks] n verfdoos c

paint-brush ['peintbrʌʃ] n penseel nt

painter ['peintə] n schilder c

painting ['peintiŋ] n schilderij nt

pair [peə] n paar nt

Pakistan [ˌpɑ:ki'stɑ:n] Pakistan

Pakistani [ˌpɑ:ki'stɑ:ni] adj Pakistaans; n Pakistaan c

palace ['pæləs] n paleis nt

pale [peil] adj bleek; licht

palm [pɑ:m] n palm c; handpalm c

palpable ['pælpəbəl] adj tastbaar

palpitation [ˌpælpi'teiʃən] n hartklopping c

pan [pæn] n pan c

pane [pein] n ruit c

panel ['pænəl] n paneel nt

panelling ['pænəliŋ] n lambrizering c

panic ['pænik] n paniek c

pant [pænt] v hijgen

panties ['pæntiz] pl onderbroek c, slip c

pants [pænts] pl onderbroek c; plAm broek c

pant-suit ['pæntsu:t] n broekpak nt

panty-hose ['pæntihouz] n panty c

paper ['peipə] n papier nt; krant c; papieren; **carbon ~** carbonpapier nt; **~ bag** papieren zak; **~ napkin** papieren servet; **typing ~** schrijfmachinepapier nt; **wrapping ~** pakpapier nt

paperback ['peipəbæk] n pocketboek nt

paper-knife ['peipənaif] n briefopener c

parade [pə'reid] n parade c, optocht c

paraffin ['pærəfin] n petroleum c

paragraph ['pærəgrɑ:f] n alinea c, paragraaf c

parakeet ['pærəki:t] n parkiet c

paralise ['pærəlaiz] v verlammen

parallel ['pærəlel] adj evenwijdig, parallel; n parallel c

parcel ['pɑ:səl] n pakket nt, pakje nt

pardon ['pɑ:dən] n vergiffenis c; gratie c

parents ['peərənts] pl ouders pl

parents-in-law ['peərəntsinlɔ:] pl schoonouders pl

parish ['pæriʃ] n parochie c

park [pɑ:k] n park nt; v parkeren; **no parking** verboden te parkeren; **parking fee** parkeertarief nt; **parking light** stadslicht nt; **parking lot** Am parkeerplaats c; **parking meter** parkeermeter c; **parking zone** parkeerzone c

parliament ['pɑ:ləmənt] n parlement nt

parliamentary [ˌpɑ:lə'mentəri] adj parlementair

parrot ['pærət] n papegaai c

parsley ['pɑ:sli] n peterselie c

parson ['pɑ:sən] n dominee c

parsonage ['pɑ:sənidʒ] n pastorie c

part [pɑ:t] n gedeelte nt, deel nt; stuk nt; v *scheiden; **spare ~** onderdeel nt

partial ['pɑ:ʃəl] adj gedeeltelijk; partijdig

participant [pɑ:'tisipənt] n deelnemer c

participate [pɑ:'tisipeit] v *deelnemen

particular [pə'tikjulə] adj bijzonder, speciaal; kieskeurig; **in ~** in het bijzonder

parting ['pɑ:tiŋ] n afscheid nt; scheiding c

partition [pɑ:'tiʃən] n tussenschot nt

partly ['pɑ:tli] adv deels, gedeeltelijk

partner ['pɑ:tnə] n partner c; compagnon c

partridge ['pɑ:tridʒ] n patrijs c

party ['pɑ:ti] n partij c; fuif c, feestje nt; groep c

pass [pɑːs] v *voorbijgaan, passeren; *aangeven; slagen; vAm inhalen; **no passing** Am inhalen verboden; ~ **by** passeren; ~ **through** *gaan door

passage ['pæsidʒ] n doorgang c; overtocht c; passage c; doorreis c

passenger ['pæsəndʒə] n passagier c; ~ **car** Am wagon c; ~ **train** personentrein c

passer-by [,pɑːsə'bai] n voorbijganger c

passion ['pæʃən] n hartstocht c, passie c; drift c

passionate ['pæʃənət] adj hartstochtelijk

passive ['pæsiv] adj passief

passport ['pɑːspɔːt] n paspoort nt; ~ **control** paspoortcontrole c; ~ **photograph** pasfoto c

password ['pɑːswəːd] n wachtwoord nt

past [pɑːst] n verleden nt; adj vorig, afgelopen, voorbij; prep langs, voorbij

paste [peist] n pasta c; v plakken

pastry ['peistri] n gebak nt; ~ **shop** banketbakkerij c

pasture ['pɑːstʃə] n weiland nt

patch [pætʃ] v verstellen

patent ['peitənt] n patent nt, octrooi nt

path [pɑːθ] n pad nt

patience ['peiʃəns] n geduld nt

patient ['peiʃənt] adj geduldig; n patiënt c

patriot ['peitriət] n patriot c

patrol [pə'troul] n patrouille c; v patrouilleren; surveilleren

pattern ['pætən] n motief nt, patroon nt

pause [pɔːz] n pauze c; v pauzeren

pave [peiv] v plaveien, bestraten

pavement ['peivmənt] n trottoir nt; plaveisel nt

pavilion [pə'viljən] n paviljoen nt

paw [pɔː] n poot c

pawn [pɔːn] v verpanden; n pion c

pawnbroker ['pɔːn,broukə] n pandjesbaas c

pay [pei] n salaris nt, loon nt

*pay [pei] v betalen; lonen; ~ **attention to** letten op; **paying** rendabel; ~ **off** aflossen; ~ **on account** afbetalen

pay-desk ['peidesk] n kassa c

payee [pei'iː] n begunstigde c

payment ['peimənt] n betaling c

pea [piː] n erwt c

peace [piːs] n vrede c

peaceful ['piːsfəl] adj vreedzaam

peach [piːtʃ] n perzik c

peacock ['piːkɔk] n pauw c

peak [piːk] n top c; spits c; ~ **hour** spitsuur nt; ~ **season** hoogseizoen nt

peanut ['piːnʌt] n pinda c

pear [peə] n peer c

pearl [pəːl] n parel c

peasant ['pezənt] n boer c

pebble ['pebəl] n kiezel c

peculiar [pi'kjuːljə] adj eigenaardig; speciaal, bijzonder

peculiarity [pi,kjuːli'ærəti] n eigenaardigheid c

pedal ['pedəl] n pedaal nt/c

pedestrian [pi'destriən] n voetganger c; **no pedestrians** verboden voor voetgangers; ~ **crossing** zebrapad nt

pedicure ['pedikjuə] n pedicure c

peel [piːl] v schillen c; n schil c

peep [piːp] v gluren

peg [peg] n klerenhaak c

pelican ['pelikən] n pelikaan c

pelvis ['pelvis] n bekken nt

pen [pen] n pen c

penalty ['penəlti] n boete c; straf c; ~

kick strafschop c
pencil ['pensəl] n potlood nt
pencil-sharpener ['pensəl,ʃɑ:pnə] n
punteslijper c
penetrate ['penitreit] v *doordringen
penguin ['peŋgwin] n pinguin c
penicillin [,peni'silin] n penicilline c
peninsula [pə'ninsjulə] n schiereiland
nt
penknife ['pennaif] n (pl -knives) zakmes nt
pension¹ ['pɑ̃:siɔ̃:] n pension nt
pension² ['penʃən] n pensioen nt
people ['pi:pəl] pl mensen; n volk nt
pepper ['pepə] n peper c
peppermint ['pepəmint] n pepermunt
c
perceive [pə'si:v] v bemerken
percent [pə'sent] n procent nt
percentage [pə'sentidʒ] n percentage
nt
perceptible [pə'septibəl] adj merkbaar
perception [pə'sepʃən] n gewaarwording c
perch [pə:tʃ] (pl ~) baars c
percolator ['pə:kəleitə] n percolator c
perfect ['pə:fikt] adj volkomen, volmaakt
perfection [pə'fekʃən] n perfectie c,
volmaaktheid c
perform [pə'fɔ:m] v uitvoeren, verrichten
performance [pə'fɔ:məns] n voorstelling c
perfume ['pə:fju:m] n parfum nt
perhaps [pə'hæps] adv misschien; wellicht
peril ['peril] n gevaar nt
perilous ['periləs] adj gevaarlijk
period ['piəriəd] n tijdperk nt, periode
c; punt c
periodical [,piəri'ɔdikəl] n tijdschrift
nt; adj periodiek
perish ['periʃ] v *omkomen

perishable ['periʃəbəl] adj aan bederf
onderhevig
perjury ['pə:dʒəri] n meineed c
permanent ['pə:mənənt] adj blijvend,
permanent, duurzaam; bestendig,
vast; ~ press plooihoudend; ~
wave permanent c
permission [pə'miʃən] n toestemming
c, permissie c; verlof nt, vergunning c
permit¹ [pə'mit] v *toestaan, veroorloven
permit² ['pə:mit] n vergunning c
peroxide [pə'rɔksaid] n waterstofperoxyde nt
perpendicular [,pə:pən'dikjulə] adj
loodrecht
Persia ['pə:ʃə] Perzië
Persian ['pə:ʃən] adj Perzisch; n Pers
c
person ['pə:sən] n persoon c; per ~
per persoon
personal ['pə:sənəl] adj persoonlijk
personality [,pə:sə'næləti] n persoonlijkheid c
personnel [,pə:sə'nel] n personeel nt
perspective [pə'spektiv] n perspectief
nt
perspiration [,pə:spə'reiʃən] n transpiratie c, zweet nt
perspire [pə'spaiə] v transpireren, zweten
persuade [pə'sweid] v overreden, overhalen; overtuigen
persuasion [pə'sweiʒən] n overtuiging
c
pessimism ['pesimizəm] n pessimisme
nt
pessimist ['pesimist] n pessimist c
pessimistic [,pesi'mistik] adj pessimistisch
pet [pet] n huisdier nt; lieveling c
petal ['petəl] n bloemblad nt
petition [pi'tiʃən] n petitie c

petrol ['petrəl] n benzine c; **unleaded** ~ loodvrije benzine c; ~ **pump** benzinepomp c; ~ **station** benzinestation nt; ~ **tank** benzinetank c

petroleum [pi'trouliəm] n petroleum c

petty ['peti] adj klein, nietig, onbeduidend; ~ **cash** kleingeld nt

pewter ['pju:tə] n tin nt

phantom ['fæntəm] n spook nt

pharmacology [ˌfɑ:mə'kɔlədʒi] n farmacologie c

pharmacy ['fɑ:məsi] n apotheek c; drogisterij c

phase [feiz] n fase c

pheasant ['fezənt] n fazant c

Philippine ['filipain] adj Filippijns

Philippines ['filipi:nz] pl Filippijnen pl

philosopher [fi'lɔsəfə] n wijsgeer c, filosoof c

philosophy [fi'lɔsəfi] n wijsbegeerte c, filosofie c

phone [foun] n telefoon c; v opbellen, telefoneren

phonetic [fə'netik] adj fonetisch

photo ['foutou] n (pl ~s) foto c

photocopy ['foutəkɔpi] n fotocopie c

photograph ['foutəgrɑ:f] n foto c; v fotograferen

photographer [fə'tɔgrəfə] n fotograaf c

photography [fə'tɔgrəfi] n fotografie c

phrase [freiz] n uitdrukking c

phrase-book ['freizbuk] n taalgids c

physical ['fizikəl] adj fysiek

physician [fi'ziʃən] n dokter c

physicist ['fizisist] n natuurkundige c

physics ['fiziks] n fysica c, natuurkunde c

physiology [ˌfizi'ɔlədʒi] n fysiologie c

pianist ['pi:ənist] n pianist c

piano [pi'ænou] n piano c; **grand** ~ vleugel c

pick [pik] v plukken; *kiezen; n keus c; ~ **up** oprapen; ophalen; **pick-up**

van bestelauto c

pick-axe ['pikæks] n houweel nt

pickles ['pikəlz] pl zoetzuur nt, pickles pl

picnic ['piknik] n picknick c; v picknicken

picture ['piktʃə] n schilderij nt; plaat c, prent c; beeld nt, afbeelding c; ~ **postcard** ansichtkaart c, prentbriefkaart c; **pictures** bioscoop c

picturesque [ˌpiktʃə'resk] adj pittoresk, schilderachtig

piece [pi:s] n stuk nt

pier [piə] n pier c

pierce [piəs] v doorboren

pig [pig] n varken nt; zwijn nt

pigeon ['pidʒən] n duif c

pig-headed [ˌpig'hedid] adj eigenwijs

piglet ['piglət] n big c

pigskin ['pigskin] n varkensleer nt

pike [paik] (pl ~) snoek c

pile [pail] n stapel c; v opstapelen; **piles** pl aambeien pl

pilgrim ['pilgrim] n pelgrim c

pilgrimage ['pilgrimidʒ] n bedevaart c

pill [pil] n pil c

pillar ['pilə] n zuil c, pilaar c

pillar-box ['piləbɔks] n brievenbus c

pillow ['pilou] n kussen nt, hoofdkussen nt

pillow-case ['piloukeis] n kussensloop c/nt

pilot ['pailət] n piloot c; loods c

pimple ['pimpəl] n puistje nt

pin [pin] n speld c; v vastspelden; **bobby** ~ Am haarspeld c

pincers ['pinsəz] pl nijptang c

pinch [pintʃ] v *knijpen

pineapple ['pai,næpəl] n ananas c

ping-pong ['piŋpɔŋ] n tafeltennis nt

pink [piŋk] adj roze

pioneer [ˌpaiə'niə] n pionier c

pious ['paiəs] adj vroom

pip [pip] n pit c

pipe [paip] *n* pijp *c*; leiding *c*; ~ **cleaner** pijpestoker *c*; ~ **tobacco** pijptabak *c*

pirate ['paiərət] *n* piraat *c*

pistol ['pistəl] *n* pistool *nt*

piston ['pistən] *n* zuiger *c*; ~ **ring** zuigerring *c*

piston-rod ['pistənrɔd] *n* zuigerstang *c*

pit [pit] *n* kuil *c*; groeve *c*

pitcher ['pitʃə] *n* kruik *c*

pity ['piti] *n* medelijden *nt*; *v* medelijden *hebben met, beklagen; **what a pity!** jammer!

placard ['plækɑ:d] *n* aanplakbiljet *nt*

place [pleis] *n* plaats *c*; *v* zetten, plaatsen; ~ **of birth** geboorteplaats *c*; ***take** ~ *plaatshebben

plague [pleig] *n* plaag *c*

plaice [pleis] (pl ~) schol *c*

plain [plein] *adj* duidelijk; gewoon, eenvoudig; *n* vlakte *c*

plan [plæn] *n* plan *nt*; plattegrond *c*; *v* plannen

plane [plein] *adj* vlak; *n* vliegtuig *nt*; ~ **crash** vliegramp *c*

planet ['plænit] *n* planeet *c*

planetarium [,plæni'teəriəm] *n* planetarium *nt*

plank [plæŋk] *n* plank *c*

plant [plɑ:nt] *n* plant *c*; bedrijf *nt*; *v* planten

plantation [plæn'teiʃən] *n* plantage *c*

plaster ['plɑ:stə] *n* pleister *nt*, gips *nt*; pleister *c*

plastic ['plæstik] *adj* plastic; *n* plastic *nt*

plate [pleit] *n* bord *nt*; plaat *c*

plateau ['plætou] *n* (pl ~x, ~s) hoogvlakte *c*

platform ['plætfɔ:m] *n* perron *nt*; ~ **ticket** perronkaartje *nt*

platinum ['plætinəm] *n* platina *nt*

play [plei] *v* spelen; bespelen; *n* spel *nt*; toneelstuk *nt*; **one-act** ~ eenakter *c*; ~ **truant** spijbelen

player [pleiə] *n* speler *c*

playground ['pleigraund] *n* speelplaats *c*

playing-card ['pleiiŋkɑ:d] *n* speelkaart *c*

playwright ['pleirait] *n* toneelschrijver *c*

plea [pli:] *n* pleidooi *nt*

plead [pli:d] *v* pleiten

pleasant ['plezənt] *adj* prettig, aardig, aangenaam

please [pli:z] alstublieft; *v* *bevallen; **pleased** ingenomen; **pleasing** aangenaam

pleasure ['pleʒə] *n* genoegen *nt*, pret *c*, plezier *nt*

plentiful ['plentifəl] *adj* overvloedig

plenty ['plenti] *n* overvloed *c*; heleboel *c*

pliers [plaiəz] *pl* tang *c*

plimsolls ['plimsəlz] *pl* gymschoenen *pl*

plot [plɔt] *n* samenzwering *c*, komplot *nt*; handeling *c*; perceel *nt*

plough [plau] *n* ploeg *c*; *v* ploegen

plucky ['plʌki] *adj* flink

plug [plʌg] *n* stekker *c*; ~ **in** inschakelen

plum [plʌm] *n* pruim *c*

plumber ['plʌmə] *n* loodgieter *c*

plump [plʌmp] *adj* mollig

plural ['pluərəl] *n* meervoud *nt*

plus [plʌs] *prep* plus

pneumatic [nju:'mætik] *adj* pneumatisch

pneumonia [nju:'mouniə] *n* longontsteking *c*

poach [poutʃ] *v* stropen

pocket ['pɔkit] *n* zak *c*

pocket-book ['pɔkitbuk] *n* portefeuille *c*

pocket-comb ['pɔkitkoum] *n* zakkam *c*

pocket-knife ['pɔkitnaif] *n* (pl -knives)

zakmes *nt*

pocket-watch ['pɔkitwɔtʃ] *n* zakhorloge *nt*

poem ['pouim] *n* gedicht *nt*

poet ['pouit] *n* dichter *c*

poetry ['pouitri] *n* dichtkunst *c*

point [point] *n* punt *nt*; punt *c*; *v* *wijzen; ~ **of view** standpunt *nt*; ~ **out** *aanwijzen

pointed ['pointid] *adj* spits

poison ['pɔizən] *n* vergif *nt*; *v* vergiftigen

poisonous ['pɔizənəs] *adj* giftig

Poland ['poulənd] Polen

Pole [poul] *n* Pool *c*

pole [poul] *n* paal *c*

police [pə'li:s] *pl* politie *c*

policeman [pə'li:smən] *n* (pl -men) agent *c*, politieagent *c*

police-station [pə'li:s,steiʃən] *n* politiebureau *nt*

policy ['pɔlisi] *n* beleid *nt*, politiek *c*; polis *c*

polio ['pouliou] *n* polio *c*, kinderverlamming *c*

Polish ['pouliʃ] *adj* Pools

polish ['pɔliʃ] *v* poetsen

polite [pə'lait] *adj* beleefd

political [pə'litikəl] *adj* politiek

politician [,pɔli'tiʃən] *n* politicus *c*

politics ['pɔlitiks] *n* politiek *c*

pollution [pə'lu:ʃən] *n* vervuiling *c*, verontreiniging *c*

pond [pɔnd] *n* vijver *c*

pony ['pouni] *n* pony *c*

poor [puə] *adj* arm; armoedig; slecht

pope [poup] *n* paus *c*

poplin ['pɔplin] *n* popeline *nt/c*

pop music [pɔp 'mju:zik] popmuziek *c*

poppy ['pɔpi] *n* klaproos *c*; papaver *c*

popular ['pɔpjulə] *adj* populair; volks-

population [,pɔpju'leiʃən] *n* bevolking *c*

populous ['pɔpjuləs] *adj* dichtbevolkt

porcelain ['pɔ:səlin] *n* porselein *nt*

porcupine ['pɔ:kjupain] *n* stekelvarken *nt*

pork [pɔ:k] *n* varkensvlees *nt*

port [pɔ:t] *n* haven *c*; bakboord *nt*

portable ['pɔ:təbəl] *adj* draagbaar

porter ['pɔ:tə] *n* kruier *c*; portier *c*

porthole ['pɔ:thoul] *n* patrijspoort *c*

portion ['pɔ:ʃən] *n* portie *c*

portrait ['pɔ:trit] *n* portret *nt*

Portugal ['pɔ:tjugəl] Portugal

Portuguese [,pɔ:tju'gi:z] *adj* Portugees; *n* Portugees *c*

position [pə'ziʃən] *n* positie *c*; houding *c*; betrekking *c*

positive ['pɔzətiv] *adj* positief; *n* positief *nt*

possess [pə'zes] *v* *bezitten; **possessed** *adj* bezeten

possession [pə'zeʃən] *n* bezit *nt*; **possessions** eigendom *nt*

possibility [,pɔsə'biləti] *n* mogelijkheid *c*

possible ['pɔsəbəl] *adj* mogelijk; eventueel

post [poust] *n* paal *c*; betrekking *c*; post *c*; *v* posten; **post-office** postkantoor *nt*

postage ['poustidʒ] *n* frankering *c*; ~ **paid** franko; ~ **stamp** postzegel *c*

postcard ['poustka:d] *n* briefkaart *c*; ansichtkaart *c*

poster ['poustə] *n* affiche *nt*, poster *c*

poste restante [poust re'stã:t] poste restante

postman ['poustmən] *n* (pl -men) postbode *c*

post-paid [,poust'peid] *adj* franko

postpone [pə'spoun] *v* uitstellen

pot [pɔt] *n* pot *c*

potato [pə'teitou] *n* (pl ~es) aardappel *c*

pottery ['pɔtəri] *n* aardewerk *nt*

pouch [pautʃ] *n* buidel *c*

poulterer ['poultərə] n poelier c

poultry ['poultri] n gevogelte nt

pound [paund] n pond nt

pour [pɔ:] v *inschenken, *schenken, *gieten

poverty ['povəti] n armoede c

powder ['paudə] n poeder nt/c; ~ compact poederdoos c; talc ~ talkpoeder nt/c

powder-puff ['paudəpʌf] n poederdons c

powder-room ['paudəru:m] n damestoilet nt

power [pauə] n kracht c; energie c; macht c; mogendheid c

powerful ['pauəfəl] adj machtig; sterk

powerless ['pauələs] adj machteloos

power-station ['pauə,steiʃən] n electriciteitscentrale c

practical ['præktikəl] adj praktisch

practically ['præktikli] adv vrijwel

practice ['præktis] n praktijk c

practise ['præktis] v beoefenen; oefenen

praise [preiz] v *prijzen; n lof c

pram [præm] n kinderwagen c

prawn [prɔ:n] n garnaal c, steurgarnaal c

pray [prei] v *bidden

prayer [prɛə] n gebed nt

preach [pri:tʃ] v preken

precarious [pri'kɛəriəs] adj hachelijk

precaution [pri'kɔ:ʃən] n voorzorg c; voorzorgsmaatregel c

precede [pri'si:d] v *voorafgaan

preceding [pri'si:diŋ] adj voorgaand

precious ['preʃəs] adj kostbaar; dierbaar

precipice ['presipis] n afgrond c

precipitation [pri,sipi'teiʃən] n neerslag c

precise [pri'sais] adj precies, exact, nauwkeurig; secuur

predecessor ['pri:disesə] n voorganger c

predict [pri'dikt] v voorspellen

prefer [pri'fə:] v de voorkeur *geven aan, liever *hebben

preferable ['prefərəbəl] adj te verkiezen, verkieselijker, de voorkeur verdienend

preference ['prefərəns] n voorkeur c

prefix ['pri:fiks] n voorvoegsel nt

pregnant ['pregnənt] adj in verwachting, zwanger

prejudice ['predʒədis] n vooroordeel nt

preliminary [pri'liminəri] adj inleidend; voorlopig

premature ['premətʃuə] adj voorbarig

premier ['premiə] n premier c

premises ['premisiz] pl pand nt

premium ['pri:miəm] n premie c

prepaid [,pri:'peid] adj vooruitbetaald

preparation [,prepə'reiʃən] n voorbereiding c

prepare [pri'pɛə] v voorbereiden; klaarmaken

prepared [pri'pɛəd] adj bereid

preposition [,prepə'ziʃən] n voorzetsel nt

prescribe [pri'skraib] v *voorschrijven

prescription [pri'skripʃən] n recept nt

presence ['prezəns] n aanwezigheid c; tegenwoordigheid c

present[1] ['prezənt] n geschenk nt, cadeau nt; heden nt; adj tegenwoordig; aanwezig

present[2] [pri'zent] v voorstellen; *aanbieden

presently ['prezəntli] adv meteen, dadelijk

preservation [,prezə'veiʃən] n bewaring c

preserve [pri'zə:v] v bewaren; inmaken

president ['prezidənt] n president c; voorzitter c

press [pres] n pers c; v indrukken,

drukken; persen; ~ **conference** persconferentie c

pressing ['presiŋ] adj urgent, dringend

pressure ['preʃə] n druk c; spanning c; **atmospheric** ~ luchtdruk c

pressure-cooker ['preʃə,kukə] n snelkookpan c

prestige [pre'sti:ʒ] n prestige nt

presumable [pri'zju:məbəl] adj vermoedelijk

presumptuous [pri'zʌmpʃəs] adj overmoedig; arrogant

pretence [pri'tens] n voorwendsel nt

pretend [pri'tend] v *doen alsof, voorwenden

pretext ['pri:tekst] n voorwendsel nt

pretty ['priti] adj mooi, knap; adv vrij, tamelijk, nogal

prevent [pri'vent] v beletten, verhinderen; *voorkomen

preventive [pri'ventiv] adj preventief

previous ['pri:viəs] adj verleden, vroeger, voorgaand

pre-war [,pri:'wɔ:] adj vooroorlogs

price [prais] v prijzen; ~ **list** prijslijst c

priceless ['praisləs] adj onschatbaar

price-list ['prais,list] n prijs c

prick [prik] v prikken

pride [praid] n trots c

priest [pri:st] n priester c

primary ['praiməri] adj primair; eerst, hoofd-; elementair

prince [prins] n prins c

princess [prin'ses] n prinses c

principal ['prinsəpəl] adj voornaamst; n rector c, directeur c

principle ['prinsəpəl] n beginsel nt, principe n

print [print] v drukken; n afdruk c; prent c; **printed matter** drukwerk nt

prior [praiə] adj vroeger

priority [prai'ɔrəti] n prioriteit c, voor-

rang c

prison ['prizən] n gevangenis c

prisoner ['prizənə] n gedetineerde c, gevangene c; ~ **of war** krijgsgevangene c

privacy ['praivəsi] n privacy c, privéleven nt

private ['praivit] adj particulier, privé; persoonlijk

privilege ['privilidʒ] n voorrecht nt

prize [praiz] n prijs c; beloning c

probable ['prɔbəbəl] adj vermoedelijk, waarschijnlijk

probably ['prɔbəbli] adv waarschijnlijk

problem ['prɔbləm] n probleem nt; vraagstuk nt

procedure [prə'si:dʒə] n procedure c

proceed [prə'si:d] v *voortgaan; te werk *gaan

process ['prouses] n proces nt, procédé nt

procession [prə'seʃən] n processie c, stoet c

proclaim [prə'kleim] v afkondigen

produce[1] [prə'dju:s] v produceren

produce[2] ['prɔdju:s] n opbrengst c, produkt nt

producer [prə'dju:sə] n producent c

product ['prɔdʌkt] n produkt nt

production [prə'dʌkʃən] n produktie c

profession [prə'feʃən] n vak nt, beroep nt

professional [prə'feʃənəl] adj beroeps-

professor [prə'fesə] n hoogleraar c, professor c

profit ['prɔfit] n voordeel nt, winst c; baat c; v profiteren

profitable ['prɔfitəbəl] adj winstgevend

profound [prə'faund] adj diepzinnig

programme ['prougræm] n programma nt

progress[1] ['prougres] n vooruitgang c

progress[2] [prə'gres] v vorderen

progressive [prə'gresiv] adj vooruit-

strevend, progressief; toenemend
prohibit [prə'hibit] v *verbieden
prohibition [ˌproui'biʃən] n verbod nt
prohibitive [prə'hibitiv] adj onoverkomelijk
project ['prɔdʒekt] n plan nt, project nt
promenade [ˌprɔmə'na:d] n promenade c
promise ['prɔmis] n belofte c; v beloven
promote [prə'mout] v bevorderen
promotion [prə'mouʃən] n promotie c
prompt [prɔmpt] adj onmiddellijk, prompt
pronoun ['prounaun] n voornaamwoord nt
pronounce [prə'nauns] v *uitspreken
pronunciation [ˌprənʌnsi'eiʃən] n uitspraak c
proof [pru:f] n bewijs nt
propaganda [ˌprɔpə'gændə] n propaganda c
propel [prə'pel] v *aandrijven
propeller [prə'pelə] n schroef c, propeller c
proper ['prɔpə] adj juist; behoorlijk, passend, geschikt, gepast
property ['prɔpəti] n bezit nt, eigendom nt; eigenschap c
prophet ['prɔfit] n profeet c
proportion [prə'pɔ:ʃən] n proportie c
proportional [prə'pɔ:ʃənəl] adj evenredig
proposal [prə'pouzəl] n voorstel nt
propose [prə'pouz] v voorstellen
proposition [ˌprɔpə'ziʃən] n voorstel nt
proprietor [prə'praiətə] n eigenaar c
prospect ['prɔspekt] n vooruitzicht nt
prospectus [prə'spektəs] n prospectus c
prosperity [prɔ'sperəti] n voorspoed c, welvaart c
prosperous ['prɔspərəs] adj welvarend

prostitute ['prɔstitju:t] n prostituée c
protect [prə'tekt] v beschermen
protection [prə'tekʃən] n bescherming c
protein ['prouti:n] n eiwit nt
protest[1] ['proutest] n protest nt
protest[2] [prə'test] v protesteren
Protestant ['prɔtistənt] adj protestants
proud [praud] adj trots; hoogmoedig
prove [pru:v] v aantonen, *bewijzen; *blijken
proverb ['prɔvə:b] n spreekwoord nt
provide [prə'vaid] v leveren, verschaffen; **provided that** mits
province ['prɔvins] n provincie c; gewest nt
provincial [prə'vinʃəl] adj provinciaal
provisional [prə'viʒənəl] adj voorlopig
provisions [prə'viʒənz] pl voorraad c
prune [pru:n] n pruim c
psychiatrist [sai'kaiətrist] n psychiater c
psychic ['saikik] adj psychisch
psychoanalyst [ˌsaikou'ænəlist] n analyticus c
psychological [ˌsaikə'lɔdʒikəl] adj psychologisch
psychologist [sai'kɔlədʒist] n psycholoog c
psychology [sai'kɔlədʒi] n psychologie c
pub [pʌb] n café nt; kroeg c
public ['pʌblik] adj publiek, openbaar; algemeen; n publiek nt; ~ **garden** plantsoen nt; ~ **house** café nt
publication [ˌpʌbli'keiʃən] n publikatie c
publicity [pʌ'blisəti] n reclame c
publish ['pʌbliʃ] v publiceren, *uitgeven
publisher ['pʌbliʃə] n uitgever c
puddle ['pʌdəl] n plas c
pull [pul] v *trekken; ~ **out** *vertrekken; ~ **up** stoppen

pulley ['puli] n (pl ~s) katrol c
Pullman ['pulmən] n slaaprijtuig nt
pullover ['pu,louvə] n pullover c
pulpit ['pulpit] n kansel c, preekstoel c
pulse [pʌls] n polsslag c, pols c
pump [pʌmp] n pomp c; v pompen
punch [pʌntʃ] v stompen; n vuistslag c
punctual ['pʌŋktʃuəl] adj stipt, punctueel
puncture ['pʌŋktʃə] n lekke band, bandepech c
punctured ['pʌŋktʃəd] adj lek
punish ['pʌniʃ] v straffen
punishment ['pʌniʃmənt] n straf c
pupil ['pju:pəl] n leerling c
puppet-show ['pʌpitʃou] n poppenkast c
purchase ['pə:tʃəs] v *kopen; n aankoop c, koop c; ~ **price** koopprijs c; ~ **tax** omzetbelasting c
purchaser ['pə:tʃəsə] n koper c
pure [pjuə] adj rein, zuiver
purple ['pə:pəl] adj paars
purpose ['pə:pəs] n bedoeling c, doel nt; **on** ~ opzettelijk
purse [pə:s] n beurs c, portemonnee c
pursue [pə'sju:] v vervolgen; nastreven
pus [pʌs] n etter c
push [puʃ] n zet c, duw c; v duwen; *schuiven; *dringen
push-button ['puʃ,bʌtən] n drukknop c
***put** [put] v plaatsen, leggen, zetten; stoppen; stellen; ~ **away** *opbergen; ~ **off** opschorten; ~ **on** *aantrekken; ~ **out** *uitdoen
puzzle ['pʌzəl] n puzzel c; raadsel nt; v in verwarring *brengen; **jigsaw** ~ legpuzzel c
puzzling ['pʌzliŋ] adj onbegrijpelijk
pyjamas [pə'dʒɑ:məz] pl pyjama c

Q

quack [kwæk] n kwakzalver c, charlatan c
quail [kweil] n (pl ~, ~s) kwartel c
quaint [kweint] adj raar; ouderwets
qualification [,kwɔlifi'keiʃən] n bevoegdheid c; voorbehoud nt, restrictie c
qualified ['kwɔlifaid] adj gediplomeerd; bevoegd
qualify ['kwɔlifai] v geschikt *zijn
quality ['kwɔləti] n kwaliteit c; eigenschap c
quantity ['kwɔntəti] n hoeveelheid c; aantal nt
quarantine ['kwɔrənti:n] n quarantaine c
quarrel ['kwɔrəl] v twisten, ruzie maken; n twist c, ruzie c
quarry ['kwɔri] n steengroeve c
quarter ['kwɔ:tə] n kwart nt; kwartaal nt; wijk c; ~ **of an hour** kwartier nt
quarterly ['kwɔ:təli] adj driemaandelijks
quay [ki:] n kade c
queen [kwi:n] n koningin c
queer [kwiə] adj zonderling, raar; vreemd
query ['kwiəri] n vraag c; v *navragen; betwijfelen
question ['kwestʃən] n vraag c; kwestie c, vraagstuk nt; v *ondervragen; in twijfel *trekken; ~ **mark** vraagteken nt
queue [kju:] n rij c; v in de rij *staan
quick [kwik] adj vlug
quick-tempered [,kwik'tempəd] adj driftig
quiet ['kwaiət] adj stil, kalm, bedaard, rustig; n stilte c, rust c

quilt [kwilt] n sprei c

quinine [kwi'ni:n] n kinine c

quit [kwit] v *ophouden met, *uitscheiden

quite [kwait] adv helemaal; tamelijk, vrij, nogal; zeer, heel

quiz [kwiz] n (pl ~zes) quiz c

quota ['kwoutə] n quota c

quotation [kwou'teiʃən] n citaat nt; ~ **marks** aanhalingstekens pl

quote [kwout] v citeren, aanhalen

R

rabbit ['ræbit] n konijn nt

rabies ['reibiz] n hondsdolheid c

race [reis] n wedloop c, race c; ras nt

race-course ['reiskɔ:s] n renbaan c

race-horse ['reishɔ:s] n renpaard nt

race-track ['reistræk] n renbaan c

racial ['reiʃəl] adj rassen-

racket ['rækit] n kabaal nt

racquet ['rækit] n racket nt

radiator ['reidieitə] n radiator c

radical ['rædikəl] adj radicaal

radio ['reidiou] n radio c

radish ['rædiʃ] n radijs c

radius ['reidiəs] n (pl radii) straal c

raft [rɑ:ft] n vlot nt

rag [ræg] n vod nt

rage [reidʒ] n razernij c, woede c; v razen, woeden

raid [reid] n inval c

rail [reil] n leuning c, reling c

railing ['reiliŋ] n hek nt

railroad ['reilroud] nAm spoorbaan c, spoorweg c

railway ['reilwei] n spoorweg c, spoorbaan c

rain [rein] n regen c; v regenen

rainbow ['reinbou] n regenboog c

raincoat ['reinkout] n regenjas c

rainproof ['reinpru:f] adj waterdicht

rainy ['reini] adj regenachtig

raise [reiz] v optillen; verhogen; *grootbrengen, verbouwen, fokken; *heffen; nAm loonsverhoging c, opslag c

raisin ['reizən] n rozijn c

rake [reik] n hark c

rally ['ræli] n bijeenkomst c

ramp [ræmp] n glooiing c

ramshackle ['ræmˌʃækəl] adj gammel

rancid ['rænsid] adj ranzig

rang [ræŋ] v (p ring)

range [reindʒ] n bereik nt

range-finder ['reindʒˌfaində] n afstandsmeter c

rank [ræŋk] n rang c; rij c

ransom ['rænsəm] n losgeld nt

rape [reip] v verkrachten

rapid ['ræpid] adj vlug, snel

rapids ['ræpidz] pl stroomversnelling c

rare [reə] adj zeldzaam

rarely ['reəli] adv zelden

rascal ['rɑ:skəl] n schelm c, deugniet c

rash [ræʃ] n uitslag c, huiduitslag c; adj overhaast, onbezonnen

raspberry ['rɑ:zbəri] n framboos c

rat [ræt] n rat c

rate [reit] n prijs c, tarief nt; snelheid c; **at any ~** hoe dan ook, in elk geval; ~ **of exchange** wisselkoers c

rather ['rɑ:ðə] adv vrij, tamelijk, nogal; liever, eerder

ration ['ræʃən] n rantsoen nt

rattan [ræ'tæn] n rotan c

raven ['reivən] n raaf c

raw [rɔ:] adj rauw; ~ **material** grondstof c

ray [rei] n straal c

rayon ['reiɔn] n kunstzijde c

razor ['reizə] n scheerapparaat nt

razor-blade ['reizəbleid] n scheermesje nt

reach [ri:tʃ] v bereiken; n bereik nt

reaction [riˈækʃən] *n* reactie *c*
* **read** [riːd] *v* *lezen
reading-lamp [ˈriːdiŋlæmp] *n* leeslamp *c*
reading-room [ˈriːdiŋruːm] *n* leeszaal *c*
ready [ˈredi] *adj* gereed, klaar
ready-made [ˌrediˈmeid] *adj* confectie-
real [riəl] *adj* echt
reality [riˈæləti] *n* werkelijkheid *c*
realizable [ˈriəlaizəbəl] *adj* haalbaar
realize [ˈriəlaiz] *v* beseffen; tot stand *brengen, verwezenlijken
really [ˈriəli] *adv* echt, werkelijk; eigenlijk
rear [riə] *n* achterkant *c*; *v* *groot-brengen
rear-light [riəˈlait] *n* achterlicht *nt*
reason [ˈriːzən] *n* oorzaak *c*, reden *c*; verstand *nt*, rede *c*; *v* redeneren
reasonable [ˈriːzənəbəl] *adj* redelijk; billijk
reassure [ˌriːəˈʃuə] *v* geruststellen
rebate [ˈriːbeit] *n* korting *c*, reductie *c*
rebellion [riˈbeljən] *n* opstand *c*, op-roer *nt*
recall [riˈkɔːl] *v* zich herinneren; *te-rugroepen; *herroepen
receipt [riˈsiːt] *n* kwitantie *c*, reçu *nt*; ontvangst *c*
receive [riˈsiːv] *v* *krijgen, *ontvangen
receiver [riˈsiːvə] *n* telefoonhoorn *c*
recent [ˈriːsənt] *adj* recent
recently [ˈriːsəntli] *adv* kort geleden, onlangs
reception [riˈsepʃən] *n* ontvangst *c*; onthaal *nt*; ~ **office** receptie *c*
receptionist [riˈsepʃənist] *n* receptioni-ste *c*
recession [riˈseʃən] *n* teruggang *c*
recipe [ˈresipi] *n* recept *nt*
recital [riˈsaitəl] *n* recital *nt*
reckon [ˈrekən] *v* rekenen; beschou-wen; *denken
recognition [ˌrekəgˈniʃən] *n* erkenning *c*

recognize [ˈrekəgnaiz] *v* herkennen; erkennen
recollect [ˌrekəˈlekt] *v* zich herinneren
recommence [ˌriːkəˈmens] *v* hervatten
recommend [ˌrekəˈmend] *v* *aanprij-zen, *aanbevelen; *aanraden
recommendation [ˌrekəmenˈdeiʃən] *n* aanbeveling *c*
reconciliation [ˌrekənsiliˈeiʃən] *n* ver-zoening *c*
record[1] [ˈrekɔːd] *n* grammofoonplaat *c*; record *nt*; register *nt*
record[2] [riˈkɔːd] *v* aantekenen
recorder [riˈkɔːdə] *n* bandrecorder *c*
recording [riˈkɔːdiŋ] *n* opname *c*
record-player [ˈrekɔːdˌpleiə] *n* platen-speler *c*, pick-up *c*
recover [riˈkʌvə] *v* *terugvinden; zich herstellen, *genezen
recovery [riˈkʌvəri] *n* genezing *c*, her-stel *nt*
recreation [ˌrekriˈeiʃən] *n* recreatie *c*, ontspanning *c*; ~ **centre** recreatie-centrum *nt*; ~ **ground** speelterrein *nt*
recruit [riˈkruːt] *n* rekruut *c*
rectangle [ˈrektæŋgəl] *n* rechthoek *c*
rectangular [rekˈtæŋgjulə] *adj* recht-hoekig
rectory [ˈrektəri] *n* pastorie *c*
rectum [ˈrektəm] *n* endeldarm *c*
recyclable [ˌriːˈsaikləbəl] *adj* recycleer-bar
recycle [ˌriːˈsaikəl] *v* recycleren
red [red] *adj* rood
redeem [riˈdiːm] *v* verlossen
reduce [riˈdjuːs] *v* reduceren, vermin-deren, verlagen
reduction [riˈdʌkʃən] *n* korting *c*, re-ductie *c*
redundant [riˈdʌndənt] *adj* overbodig
reed [riːd] *n* riet *nt*
reef [riːf] *n* rif *nt*

reference ['refrəns] n referentie c, verwijzing c; betrekking c; **with ~ to** met betrekking tot

refer to [ri'fə:] *verwijzen naar

refill ['ri:fil] n vulling c

refinery [ri'fainəri] n raffinaderij c

reflect [ri'flekt] v weerkaatsen

reflection [ri'flekʃən] n weerkaatsing c; spiegelbeeld n

reflector [ri'flektə] n reflector c

reformation [,refə'meiʃən] n reformatie c

refresh [ri'freʃ] v verfrissen

refreshment [ri'freʃmənt] n verfrissing c

refrigerator [ri'fridʒəreitə] n koelkast c, ijskast c

refund¹ [ri'fʌnd] v terugbetalen

refund² ['ri:fʌnd] n terugbetaling c

refusal [ri'fju:zəl] n weigering c

refuse¹ [ri'fju:z] v weigeren

refuse² ['refju:s] n afval nt

regard [ri'gɑ:d] v beschouwen; *bekijken; n respect nt; **as regards** betreffende, aangaande, wat betreft

regarding [ri'gɑ:diŋ] prep met betrekking tot, betreffende; ten aanzien van

regatta [ri'gætə] n regatta c

régime [rei'ʒi:m] n regime nt

region ['ri:dʒən] n streek c; gebied nt

regional ['ri:dʒənəl] adj plaatselijk

register ['redʒistə] v zich *inschrijven; aantekenen; **registered letter** aangetekende brief

registration [,redʒi'streiʃən] n registratie c; ~ **form** inschrijvingsformulier nt; ~ **number** kenteken nt; ~ **plate** nummerbord nt

regret [ri'gret] v betreuren; n spijt c

regular ['regjulə] adj geregeld, regelmatig; gewoon, normaal

regulate ['regjuleit] v regelen

regulation [,regju'leiʃən] n reglement nt, voorschrift nt; regeling c

rehabilitation [,ri:hə,bili'teiʃən] n revalidatie c

rehearsal [ri'hə:səl] n repetitie c

rehearse [ri'hə:s] v repeteren

reign [rein] n regering c; v regeren

reimburse [,ri:im'bə:s] v terugbetalen, vergoeden

reindeer ['reindiə] n (pl ~) rendier nt

reject [ri'dʒekt] v *afwijzen, *verwerpen; afkeuren

relate [ri'leit] v vertellen

related [ri'leitid] adj verwant

relation [ri'leiʃən] n relatie c, verband nt; verwante c

relative ['relətiv] n familielid nt; adj betrekkelijk, relatief

relax [ri'læks] v zich ontspannen

relaxation [,rilæk'seiʃən] n ontspanning c

reliable [ri'laiəbəl] adj betrouwbaar

relic ['relik] n relikwie c

relief [ri'li:f] n verademing c, verlichting c; steun c; reliëf nt

relieve [ri'li:v] v verlichten; aflossen

religion [ri'lidʒən] n godsdienst c

religious [ri'lidʒəs] adj godsdienstig

rely on [ri'lai] vertrouwen op

remain [ri'mein] v *blijven; *overblijven

remainder [ri'meində] n restant nt, rest c

remaining [ri'meiniŋ] adj overig, overblijvend

remark [ri'mɑ:k] n opmerking c; v opmerken

remarkable [ri'mɑ:kəbəl] adj opmerkelijk

remedy ['remədi] n geneesmiddel nt; middel nt

remember [ri'membə] v zich herinneren; *onthouden

remembrance [ri'membrəns] n aandenken nt, herinnering c

remind [ri'maind] v herinneren

remit [ri'mit] v overmaken

remittance [ri'mitəns] n storting c

remnant ['remnənt] n overblijfsel nt, restant nt, rest c

remote [ri'mout] adj afgelegen, ver

removal [ri'mu:vəl] n verwijdering c

remove [ri'mu:v] v verwijderen

remunerate [ri'mju:nəreit] v vergoeden

remuneration [ri,mju:nə'reifən] n vergoeding c

renew [ri'nju:] v vernieuwen; verlengen

rent [rent] v huren; n huur c

repair [ri'pɛə] v herstellen, repareren; n herstel nt

reparation [,repə'reifən] n reparatie c

***repay** [ri'pei] v terugbetalen

repayment [ri'peimənt] n terugbetaling c

repeat [ri'pi:t] v herhalen

repellent [ri'pelənt] adj weerzinwekkend, afstotelijk

repentance [ri'pentəns] n berouw nt

repertory ['repətəri] n repertoire nt

repetition [,repə'tifən] n herhaling c

replace [ri'pleis] v *vervangen

reply [ri'plai] v antwoorden; n antwoord nt; **in ~** als antwoord

report [ri'pɔ:t] v rapporteren; melden; zich aanmelden; n verslag nt, rapport nt

reporter [ri'pɔ:tə] n verslaggever c

represent [,repri'zent] v vertegenwoordigen; voorstellen

representation [,reprizen'teifən] n vertegenwoordiging c

representative [,repri'zentətiv] adj representatief

reprimand ['reprimɑ:nd] v berispen

reproach [ri'proutf] n verwijt nt; v *verwijten

reproduce [,ri:prə'dju:s] v reproduceren

reproduction [,ri:prə'dʌkfən] n reproductie c

reptile ['reptail] n reptiel nt

republic [ri'pʌblik] n republiek c

republican [ri'pʌblikən] adj republikeins

repulsive [ri'pʌlsiv] adj weerzinwekkend

reputation [,repju'teifən] n reputatie c; naam c

request [ri'kwest] n verzoek nt; v *verzoeken

require [ri'kwaiə] v vereisen

requirement [ri'kwaiəmənt] n vereiste c

requisite ['rekwizit] adj vereist

rescue ['reskju:] v redden; n redding c

research [ri'sə:tf] n onderzoek nt

resemblance [ri'zembləns] n gelijkenis c

resemble [ri'zembəl] v *lijken op

resent [ri'zent] v kwalijk *nemen

reservation [,rezə'veifən] n reservering c

reserve [ri'zə:v] v reserveren; *bespreken; n reserve c

reserved [ri'zə:vd] adj gereserveerd

reservoir ['rezəvwɑ:] n reservoir nt

reside [ri'zaid] v wonen

residence ['rezidəns] n woonplaats c; **~ permit** verblijfsvergunning c

resident ['rezidənt] n inwoner c; adj woonachtig; intern

resign [ri'zain] v ontslag *nemen

resignation [,rezig'neifən] n ontslagneming c

resin ['rezin] n hars nt/c

resist [ri'zist] v zich verzetten

resistance [ri'zistəns] n verzet nt

resolute ['rezəlu:t] adj resoluut, vastberaden

respect [ri'spekt] n respect nt; ontzag nt, achting c, eerbied c; v respecteren

respectable [ri'spektəbəl] *adj* eerzaam, respectabel

respectful [ri'spektfəl] *adj* eerbiedig

respective [ri'spektiv] *adj* respectievelijk

respiration [,respə'reiʃən] *n* ademhaling *c*

respite ['respait] *n* uitstel *nt*

responsibility [ri,sponsə'biləti] *n* verantwoordelijkheid *c*; aansprakelijkheid *c*

responsible [ri'sponsəbəl] *adj* verantwoordelijk; aansprakelijk

rest [rest] *n* rust *c*; rest *c*; *v* uitrusten, rusten

restaurant ['restərɔ̃:] *n* restaurant *nt*

restful ['restfəl] *adj* rustig

rest-home ['resthoum] *n* rusthuis *nt*

restless ['restləs] *adj* onrustig; ongedurig

restrain [ri'strein] *v* *inhouden, *weerhouden

restriction [ri'strikʃən] *n* beperking *c*

result [ri'zʌlt] *n* resultaat *nt*; gevolg *nt*; uitslag *c*; *v* resulteren

resume [ri'zju:m] *v* hervatten

résumé ['rezjumei] *n* samenvatting *c*

retail ['ri:teil] *v* in het klein *verkopen; ~ **trade** kleinhandel *c*, detailhandel *c*

retailer ['ri:teilə] *n* detaillist *c*, kleinhandelaar *c*; wederverkoper *c*

retina ['retinə] *n* netvlies *nt*

retired [ri'taiəd] *adj* gepensioneerd

return [ri'tə:n] *v* *terugkomen, terugkeren; *n* terugkeer *c*; ~ **flight** retourvlucht *c*; ~ **journey** terugreis *c*

reunite [,ri:ju:'nait] *v* herenigen

reveal [ri'vi:l] *v* openbaren, onthullen

revelation [,revə'leiʃən] *n* onthulling *c*

revenge [ri'vendʒ] *n* wraak *c*

revenue ['revənju:] *n* inkomen *nt*

reverse [ri'və:s] *n* tegendeel *nt*; keerzijde *c*; omkeer *c*, tegenslag *c*; *adj* omgekeerd; *v* *achteruitrijden

review [ri'vju:] *n* bespreking *c*; tijdschrift *nt*

revise [ri'vaiz] *v* *herzien

revision [ri'viʒən] *n* herziening *c*

revival [ri'vaivəl] *n* herstel *nt*

revolt [ri'voult] *v* in opstand *komen; *n* opstand *c*, oproer *nt*

revolting [ri'voultiŋ] *adj* walgelijk, stuitend, weerzinwekkend

revolution [,revə'lu:ʃən] *n* revolutie *c*; omwenteling *c*

revolutionary [,revə'lu:ʃənəri] *adj* revolutionair

revolver [ri'volvə] *n* revolver *c*

revue [ri'vju:] *n* revue *c*

reward [ri'wɔ:d] *n* beloning *c*; *v* belonen

rheumatism ['ru:mətizəm] *n* reumatiek *c*

rhinoceros [rai'nosərəs] *n* (pl ~, ~es) neushoorn *c*

rhubarb ['ru:bɑ:b] *n* rabarber *c*

rhyme [raim] *n* rijm *nt*

rhythm ['riðəm] *n* ritme *nt*

rib [rib] *n* rib *c*

ribbon ['ribən] *n* lint *nt*

rice [rais] *n* rijst *c*

rich [ritʃ] *adj* rijk

riches ['ritʃiz] *pl* rijkdom *c*

riddle ['ridəl] *n* raadsel *nt*

ride [raid] *n* rit *c*

* **ride** [raid] *v* *rijden; *paardrijden

rider ['raidə] *n* ruiter *c*

ridge [ridʒ] *n* bergrug *c*

ridicule ['ridikju:l] *v* bespotten

ridiculous [ri'dikjuləs] *adj* bespottelijk, belachelijk

riding ['raidiŋ] *n* paardesport *c*

riding-school ['raidiŋsku:l] *n* manege *c*

rifle ['raifəl] *v* geweer *nt*

right [rait] *n* recht *nt*; *adj* goed, juist; recht; rechts; billijk, rechtvaardig; **all right!** in orde!; * **be** ~ gelijk *hebben; ~ **of way** voorrang *c*

righteous ['raitʃəs] *adj* rechtvaardig

right-hand ['raithænd] *adj* rechter, rechts

rightly ['raitli] *adv* terecht

rim [rim] *n* velg *c*; rand *c*

ring [riŋ] *n* ring *c*; kring *c*; piste *c*

* **ring** [riŋ] *v* bellen; ~ **up** opbellen

rinse [rins] *v* spoelen; *n* spoeling *c*

riot ['raiət] *n* rel *c*

rip [rip] *v* scheuren

ripe [raip] *adj* rijp

rise [raiz] *n* opslag *c*, verhoging *c*; stijging *c*; opkomst *c*

* **rise** [raiz] *v* *opstaan; *opgaan; *stijgen

rising ['raiziŋ] *n* opstand *c*

risk [risk] *n* risico *nt*; gevaar *nt*; *v* wagen

risky ['riski] *adj* gewaagd, riskant

rival ['raivəl] *n* rivaal *c*; concurrent *c*; *v* rivaliseren

rivalry ['raivəlri] *n* rivaliteit *c*; concurrentie *c*

river ['rivə] *n* rivier *c*; ~ **bank** oever *c*

riverside ['rivəsaid] *n* rivieroever *c*

roach [routʃ] *n* (pl ~) blankvoren *c*

road [roud] *n* straat *c*, weg *c*; ~ **fork** *n* tweesprong *c*; ~ **map** wegenkaart *c*; ~ **system** wegennet *nt*; ~ **up** werk in uitvoering

roadhouse ['roudhaus] *n* wegrestaurant *nt*

roadside ['roudsaid] *n* wegkant *c*; ~ **restaurant** wegrestaurant *nt*

roadway ['roudwei] *nAm* rijbaan *c*

roam [roum] *v* *zwerven

roar [rɔː] *v* loeien, brullen; *n* gebrul *nt*, geraas *nt*

roast [roust] *v* *braden, roosteren

rob [rɔb] *v* beroven

robber ['rɔbə] *n* dief *c*

robbery ['rɔbəri] *n* roof *c*, diefstal *c*, beroving *c*

robe [roub] *n* jurk *c*; gewaad *nt*

robin ['rɔbin] *n* roodborstje *nt*

robust [rou'bʌst] *adj* fors

rock [rɔk] *n* rots *c*; *v* schommelen

rocket ['rɔkit] *n* raket *c*

rock-'n-roll [,rɔkən'roul] *n* rock en roll *c*

rocky ['rɔki] *adj* rotsachtig

rod [rɔd] *n* stang *c*, roede *c*

roe [rou] *n* kuit *c*, viskuit *c*

roll [roul] *v* rollen; *n* rol *c*; broodje *nt*

Roman Catholic ['roumən 'kæθəlik] rooms-katholiek

romance [rə'mæns] *n* romance *c*

romantic [rə'mæntik] *adj* romantisch

roof [ruːf] *n* dak *nt*; **thatched** ~ strodak *nt*

room [ruːm] *n* vertrek *nt*, kamer *c*; ruimte *c*, plaats *c*; ~ **and board** kost en inwoning; ~ **service** bediening op de kamer; ~ **temperature** kamertemperatuur *c*

roomy ['ruːmi] *adj* ruim

root [ruːt] *n* wortel *c*

rope [roup] *n* touw *c*

rosary ['rouzəri] *n* rozenkrans *c*

rose [rouz] *n* roos *c*; *adj* roze

rotten ['rɔtən] *adj* rot

rouge [ruːʒ] *n* rouge *c/nt*

rough [rʌf] *adj* ruw

roulette [ruː'let] *n* roulette *c*

round [raund] *adj* rond; *prep* rondom, om; *n* ronde *c*; ~ **trip** *Am* retour

roundabout ['raundəbaut] *n* rotonde *c*

rounded ['raundid] *adj* afgerond

route [ruːt] *n* route *c*

routine [ruː'tiːn] *n* routine *c*

row¹ [rou] *n* rij *c*; *v* roeien

row² [rau] *n* ruzie *c*

rowdy ['raudi] *adj* baldadig

rowing-boat ['rouiŋbout] *n* roeiboot *c*

royal ['rɔiəl] *adj* koninklijk

rub [rʌb] *v* *wrijven

rubber ['rʌbə] *n* rubber *nt*; vlakgom

c/nt ; ~ **band** elastiek *nt*

rubbish ['rʌbiʃ] *n* afval *nt* ; geklets *nt*, onzin *c* ; **talk** ~ kletsen

rubbish-bin ['rʌbiʃbin] *n* vuilnisbak *c*

ruby ['ru:bi] *n* robijn *c*

rucksack ['rʌksæk] *n* rugzak *c*

rudder ['rʌdə] *n* roer *nt*

rude [ru:d] *adj* grof

rug [rʌg] *n* kleedje *nt*

ruin ['ru:in] *v* ruïneren ; *n* ondergang *c* ; **ruins** ruïne *c*

ruination [,ru:i'neiʃən] *n* ondergang *c*

rule [ru:l] *n* regel *c* ; bewind *nt*, bestuur *nt*, heerschappij *c* ; *v* heersen, regeren ; **as a** ~ gewoonlijk, in de regel

ruler ['ru:lə] *n* vorst *c*, heerser *c* ; liniaal *c*

Rumania [ru:'meiniə] Roemenië

Rumanian [ru:'meiniən] *adj* Roemeens ; *n* Roemeen *c*

rumour ['ru:mə] *n* gerucht *nt*

*****run** [rʌn] *v* rennen ; ~ **into** *tegenkomen

runaway ['rʌnəwei] *n* ontsnapte gevangene

rung [rʌŋ] *v* (pp ring)

runway ['rʌnwei] *n* startbaan *c*

rural ['ruərəl] *adj* plattelands-

ruse [ru:z] *n* list *c*

rush [rʌʃ] *v* zich haasten ; *n* bies *c*

rush-hour ['rʌʃauə] *n* spitsuur *nt*

Russia ['rʌʃə] Rusland

Russian ['rʌʃən] *adj* Russisch ; *n* Rus *c*

rust [rʌst] *n* roest *nt*

rustic ['rʌstik] *adj* rustiek

rusty ['rʌsti] *adj* roestig

S

saccharin ['sækərin] *n* sacharine *c*

sack [sæk] *n* zak *c*

sacred ['seikrid] *adj* heilig

sacrifice ['sækrifais] *n* offer *nt* ; *v* opofferen

sacrilege ['sækrilidʒ] *n* heiligschennis *c*

sad [sæd] *adj* bedroefd ; verdrietig, droevig, treurig

saddle ['sædəl] *n* zadel *nt*

sadness ['sædnəs] *n* bedroefdheid *c*

safe [seif] *adj* veilig ; *n* brandkast *c*, kluis *c*

safety ['seifti] *n* veiligheid *c*

safety-belt ['seiftibelt] *n* veiligheidsgordel *c*

safety-pin ['seiftipin] *n* veiligheidsspeld *c*

safety-razor ['seifti,reizə] *n* scheerapparaat *nt*

sail [seil] *v* *bevaren, *varen ; *n* zeil *nt*

sailing-boat ['seiliŋbout] *n* zeilboot *c*

sailor ['seilə] *n* matroos *c*

saint [seint] *n* heilige *c*

salad ['sæləd] *n* sla *c*

salad-oil ['sælədɔil] *n* slaolie *c*

salary ['sæləri] *n* loon *c*, salaris *nt*

sale [seil] *n* verkoop *c* ; **clearance** ~ opruiming *c* ; **for** ~ te koop ; **sales** uitverkoop *c* ; **sales tax** omzetbelasting *c*

saleable ['seiləbəl] *adj* verkoopbaar

salesgirl ['seilzgə:l] *n* verkoopster *c*

salesman ['seilzmən] *n* (pl -men) verkoper *c*

salmon ['sæmən] *n* (pl ~) zalm *c*

salon ['sælɔ̃:] *n* salon *c*

saloon [sə'lu:n] *n* bar *c*

salt [sɔ:lt] *n* zout *nt*

salt-cellar ['sɔ:lt,selə] *n* zoutvaatje *nt*

salty ['sɔ:lti] *adj* zout

salute [sə'lu:t] v groeten

salve [sɑ:v] n zalf c

same [seim] adj zelfde

sample ['sɑ:mpəl] n monster nt

sanatorium [,sænə'tɔ:riəm] n (pl ~s, -ria) sanatorium nt

sand [sænd] n zand nt

sandal ['sændəl] n sandaal c

sandpaper ['sænd,peipə] n schuurpapier nt

sandwich ['sænwidʒ] n boterham c

sandy ['sændi] adj zanderig

sanitary ['sænitəri] adj sanitair; ~ **towel** maandverband nt

sapphire ['sæfaiə] n saffier nt

sardine [sɑ:'di:n] n sardine c

satchel ['sætʃəl] n schooltas c

satellite ['sætəlait] n satelliet c

satin ['sætin] n satijn nt

satisfaction [,sætis'fækʃən] n bevrediging c, voldoening c

satisfy ['sætisfai] v bevredigen; **satisfied** voldaan, tevreden

Saturday ['sætədi] zaterdag c

sauce [sɔ:s] n saus c

saucepan ['sɔ:spən] n steelpan c

saucer ['sɔ:sə] n schoteltje nt

Saudi Arabia [,saudiə'reibiə] Saoedi-Arabië

Saudi Arabian [,saudiə'reibiən] adj Saoedi-Arabisch

sauna ['sɔ:nə] n sauna c

sausage ['sɔsidʒ] n worst c

savage ['sævidʒ] adj wild

save [seiv] v redden; sparen

savings ['seiviŋz] pl spaargeld nt; ~ **bank** spaarbank c

saviour ['seivjə] n redder c

savoury ['seivəri] adj smakelijk; pikant

saw[1] [sɔ:] v (p see)

saw[2] [sɔ:] n zaag c

sawdust ['sɔ:dʌst] n zaagsel nt

saw-mill ['sɔ:mil] n houtzagerij c

* **say** [sei] v *zeggen

scaffolding ['skæfəldiŋ] n steigers pl

scale [skeil] n schaal c; toonladder c; schub c; **scales** pl weegschaal c

scandal ['skændəl] n schandaal nt

Scandinavia [,skændi'neiviə] Scandinavië

Scandinavian [,skændi'neiviən] adj Scandinavisch; n Scandinaviër c

scapegoat ['skeipgout] n zondebok c

scar [skɑ:] n litteken nt

scarce [skɛəs] adj schaars

scarcely ['skɛəsli] adv nauwelijks

scarcity ['skɛəsəti] n schaarste c

scare [skɛə] v *doen schrikken; n schrik c

scarf [skɑ:f] n (pl ~s, scarves) das c, sjaal c

scarlet ['skɑ:lət] adj vuurrood

scary ['skɛəri] adj griezelig

scatter ['skætə] v verspreiden

scene [si:n] n scène c

scenery ['si:nəri] n landschap nt

scenic ['si:nik] adj schilderachtig

scent [sent] n geur c

schedule ['ʃedju:l] n dienstregeling c, rooster nt

scheme [ski:m] n schema nt; plan nt

scholar ['skɔlə] n geleerde c; leerling c

scholarship ['skɔləʃip] n studiebeurs c

school [sku:l] n school c

schoolboy ['sku:lbɔi] n schooljongen c

schoolgirl ['sku:lgə:l] n schoolmeisje nt

schoolmaster ['sku:l,mɑ:stə] n onderwijzer c, meester c

schoolteacher ['sku:l,ti:tʃə] n onderwijzer c

science ['saiəns] n wetenschap c

scientific [,saiən'tifik] adj wetenschappelijk

scientist ['saiəntist] n geleerde c

scissors ['sizəz] pl schaar c

scold [skould] v berispen; *schelden

scooter ['sku:tə] *n* scooter *c*; autoped *c*

score [skɔ:] *n* stand *c*; *v* scoren

scorn [skɔ:n] *n* hoon *c*, verachting *c*; *v* verachten

Scot [skɔt] *n* Schot *c*

Scotch [skɔtʃ] *adj* Schots; **scotch tape** plakband *nt*

Scotland ['skɔtlənd] Schotland

Scottish ['skɔtiʃ] *adj* Schots

scout [skaut] *n* padvinder *c*

scrap [skræp] *n* snipper *c*

scrap-book ['skræpbuk] *n* plakboek *nt*

scrape [skreip] *v* schrappen

scrap-iron ['skræpaiən] *n* schroot *nt*

scratch [skrætʃ] *v* krassen, krabben; *n* kras *c*, schram *c*

scream [skri:m] *v* gillen, schreeuwen; *n* gil *c*, schreeuw *c*

screen [skri:n] *n* scherm *nt*; beeldscherm *nt*

screw [skru:] *n* schroef *c*; *v* schroeven

screw-driver ['skru:,draivə] *n* schroevedraaier *c*

scrub [skrʌb] *v* schrobben; *n* struik *c*

sculptor ['skʌlptə] *n* beeldhouwer *c*

sculpture ['skʌlptʃə] *n* beeldhouwwerk *nt*

sea [si:] *n* zee *c*

sea-bird ['si:bə:d] *n* zeevogel *c*

sea-coast ['si:koust] *n* zeekust *c*

seagull ['si:gʌl] *n* meeuw *c*, zeemeeuw *c*

seal [si:l] *n* zegel *nt*; rob *c*, zeehond *c*

seam [si:m] *n* naad *c*

seaman ['si:mən] *n* (pl -men) zeeman *c*

seamless ['si:mləs] *adj* naadloos

seaport ['si:pɔ:t] *n* zeehaven *c*

search [sə:tʃ] *v* *zoeken; fouilleren, *doorzoeken

searchlight ['sə:tʃlait] *n* schijnwerper *c*

seascape ['si:skeip] *n* zeegezicht *nt*

sea-shell ['si:ʃel] *n* zeeschelp *c*

seashore ['si:ʃɔ:] *n* kust *c*

seasick ['si:sik] *adj* zeeziek

seasickness ['si:,siknəs] *n* zeeziekte *c*

seaside ['si:said] *n* kust *c*; ~ **resort** badplaats *c*

season ['si:zən] *n* jaargetijde *nt*, seizoen *nt*; **high** ~ hoogseizoen *nt*; **low** ~ naseizoen *nt*; **off** ~ buiten het seizoen

season-ticket ['si:zən,tikit] *n* abonnementskaart *c*

seat [si:t] *n* stoel *c*; plaats *c*, zitplaats *c*; zetel *c*

seat-belt ['si:tbelt] *n* veiligheidsgordel *c*

sea-urchin ['si:,ə:tʃin] *n* zeeëgel *c*

sea-water ['si:,wɔ:tə] *n* zeewater *nt*

second ['sekənd] *num* tweede; *n* seconde *c*; tel *c*

secondary ['sekəndəri] *adj* secundair, ondergeschikt; ~ **school** middelbare school

second-hand [,sekənd'hænd] *adj* tweedehands

secret ['si:krət] *n* geheim *nt*; *adj* geheim

secretary ['sekrətri] *n* secretaresse *c*; secretaris *c*

section ['sekʃən] *n* sectie *c*; afdeling *c*, vak *nt*

secure [si'kjuə] *adj* veilig; *v* bemachtigen

security [si'kjuərəti] *n* veiligheid *c*; pand *nt*

sedate [si'deit] *adj* kalm

sedative ['sedətiv] *n* kalmerend middel

seduce [si'dju:s] *v* verleiden

***see** [si:] *v* *zien, *begrijpen, *inzien; ~ **to** zorgen voor

seed [si:d] *n* zaad *nt*

***seek** [si:k] *v* *zoeken

seem [si:m] *v* *lijken, *schijnen

seen [si:n] *v* (pp see)

seesaw ['si:sɔ:] *n* wip *c*

seize [si:z] *v* *grijpen

seldom ['seldəm] *adv* zelden

select [si'lekt] *v* selecteren, *uitkiezen; *adj* select, uitgelezen

selection [si'lekʃən] *n* keuze *c*, selectie *c*

self-centred [,self'sentəd] *adj* egocentrisch

self-employed [,selfim'plɔid] *adj* zelfstandig

self-evident [,sel'fevidənt] *adj* vanzelfsprekend

self-government [,self'gʌvəmənt] *n* zelfbestuur *nt*

selfish ['selfiʃ] *adj* egoïstisch

selfishness ['selfiʃnəs] *n* egoïsme *nt*

self-service [,self'sə:vis] *n* zelfbediening *c*; ~ **restaurant** zelfbedieningsrestaurant *nt*

*sell [sel] *v* *verkopen

semblance ['sembləns] *n* schijn *c*

semi- ['semi] half

semicircle ['semi,sə:kəl] *n* halve cirkel

semi-colon [,semi'koulən] *n* puntkomma *c*

senate ['senət] *n* senaat *c*

senator ['senətə] *n* senator *c*

*send [send] *v* sturen, *zenden; ~ **back** terugsturen, *terugzenden; ~ **for** *laten halen; ~ **off** versturen

senile ['si:nail] *adj* seniel

sensation [sen'seiʃən] *n* sensatie *c*; gewaarwording *c*, gevoel *nt*

sensational [sen'seiʃənəl] *adj* sensationeel, opzienbarend

sense [sens] *n* zintuig *nt*; gezond verstand, rede *c*; zin *c*, betekenis *c*; *v* voelen; ~ **of honour** eergevoel *nt*

senseless ['sensləs] *adj* zinloos

sensible ['sensəbəl] *adj* verstandig

sensitive ['sensitiv] *adj* gevoelig

sentence ['sentəns] *n* zin *c*; vonnis *nt*; *v* veroordelen

sentimental [,senti'mentəl] *adj* sentimenteel

separate¹ ['sepəreit] *v* *scheiden

separate² ['sepərət] *adj* afzonderlijk, gescheiden

separately ['sepərətli] *adv* apart

September [sep'tembə] september

septic ['septik] *adj* septisch; **become ~ *ontsteken

sequel ['si:kwəl] *n* vervolg *nt*

sequence ['si:kwəns] *n* volgorde *c*; reeks *c*

serene [sə'ri:n] *adj* kalm; helder

serial ['siəriəl] *n* feuilleton *nt*

series ['siəri:z] *n* (pl ~) reeks *c*, serie *c*

serious ['siəriəs] *adj* serieus, ernstig

seriousness ['siəriəsnəs] *n* ernst *c*

sermon ['sə:mən] *n* preek *c*

serum ['siərəm] *n* serum *c*

servant ['sə:vənt] *n* bediende *c*

serve [sə:v] *v* bedienen

service ['sə:vis] *n* dienst *c*; bediening *c*; ~ **charge** bedieningsgeld *nt*; ~ **station** benzinestation *nt*

serviette [,sə:vi'et] *n* servet *nt*

session ['seʃən] *n* zitting *c*

set [set] *n* stel *nt*, groep *c*

*set [set] *v* zetten; ~ **menu** vast menu; ~ **out** *vertrekken

setting ['setiŋ] *n* omgeving *c*; ~ **lotion** haarversteviger *c*

settle ['setəl] *v* afhandelen, regelen; ~ **down** zich vestigen

settlement ['setəlmənt] *n* regeling *c*, schikking *c*, overeenkomst *c*

seven ['sevən] *num* zeven

seventeen [,sevən'ti:n] *num* zeventien

seventeenth [,sevən'ti:nθ] *num* zeventiende

seventh ['sevənθ] *num* zevende

seventy ['sevənti] *num* zeventig

several ['sevərəl] *adj* ettelijk, verscheidene

severe [si'viə] *adj* hevig, streng, ernstig

sew [sou] v naaien; ~ up hechten

sewer ['su:ə] n riool nt

sewing-machine ['souiŋmə‚ʃi:n] n naaimachine c

sex [seks] n geslacht nt; sex c

sexton ['sekstən] n koster c

sexual ['sekʃuəl] adj seksueel

sexuality [‚sekʃu'æləti] n seksualiteit c

shade [ʃeid] n schaduw c; tint c

shadow ['ʃædou] n schaduw c

shady ['ʃeidi] adj schaduwrijk

*shake [ʃeik] v schudden

shaky ['ʃeiki] adj gammel

*shall [ʃæl] v *zullen; *moeten

shallow ['ʃælou] adj ondiep

shame [ʃeim] n schaamte c; schande c; shame! foei!

shampoo [ʃæm'pu:] n shampoo c

shamrock ['ʃæmrɔk] n klaver c

shape [ʃeip] n vorm c; v vormen

share [ʃɛə] v delen; n deel nt; aandeel nt

shark [ʃɑ:k] n haai c

sharp [ʃɑ:p] adj scherp

sharpen ['ʃɑ:pən] v *slijpen

shave [ʃeiv] v zich *scheren

shaver ['ʃeivə] n scheerapparaat nt

shaving-brush ['ʃeiviŋbrʌʃ] n scheerkwast c

shaving-cream ['ʃeiviŋkri:m] n scheercrème c

shaving-soap ['ʃeiviŋsoup] n scheerzeep c

shawl [ʃɔ:l] n omslagdoek c, sjaal c

she [ʃi:] pron ze

shed [ʃed] n schuur c

*shed [ʃed] v storten; verspreiden

sheep [ʃi:p] n (pl ~) schaap nt

sheer [ʃiə] adj absoluut, puur; dun, doorzichtig

sheet [ʃi:t] n laken nt; blad nt; plaat c

shelf [ʃelf] n (pl shelves) plank c

shell [ʃel] n schelp c; dop c

shellfish ['ʃelfiʃ] n schaaldier nt

shelter ['ʃeltə] n beschutting c, schuilplaats c; v beschutten

shepherd ['ʃepəd] n herder c

shift [ʃift] n ploeg c

*shine [ʃain] v *schijnen; glanzen, *blinken

ship [ʃip] n schip nt; v verschepen; shipping line scheepvaartlijn c

shipowner ['ʃi‚pounə] n reder c

shipyard ['ʃipjɑ:d] n scheepswerf c

shirt [ʃə:t] n hemd nt, overhemd nt

shiver ['ʃivə] v bibberen, rillen; n rilling c

shivery ['ʃivəri] adj rillerig

shock [ʃɔk] n schok c; v schokken; ~ absorber schokbreker c

shocking ['ʃɔkiŋ] adj schokkend

shoe [ʃu:] n schoen c; gym shoes gymschoenen pl; ~ polish schoensmeer c

shoe-lace ['ʃu:leis] n schoenveter c

shoemaker ['ʃu:‚meikə] n schoenmaker c

shoe-shop ['ʃu:ʃɔp] n schoenwinkel c

shook [ʃuk] v (p shake)

*shoot [ʃu:t] v *schieten

shop [ʃɔp] n winkel c; v winkelen; ~ assistant verkoper c; shopping bag boodschappentas c; shopping centre winkelcentrum nt

shopkeeper ['ʃɔp‚ki:pə] n winkelier c

shop-window [‚ʃɔp'windou] n etalage c

shore [ʃɔ:] n oever c, kust c

short [ʃɔ:t] adj kort; klein; ~ circuit kortsluiting c

shortage ['ʃɔ:tidʒ] n tekort nt, gebrek nt

shortcoming ['ʃɔ:t‚kʌmiŋ] n tekortkoming c

shorten ['ʃɔ:tən] v verkorten

shorthand ['ʃɔ:thænd] n stenografie c

shortly ['ʃɔ:tli] adv weldra, binnenkort, spoedig

shorts [ʃɔːts] *pl* korte broek; *plAm* onderbroek *c*

short-sighted [‚ʃɔːˈtsaitid] *adj* bijziend

shot [ʃɔt] *n* schot *nt*; injectie *c*; opname *c*

*****should** [ʃud] *v* *moeten

shoulder [ˈʃouldə] *n* schouder *c*

shout [ʃaut] *v* schreeuwen, *roepen; *n* schreeuw *c*

shovel [ˈʃʌvəl] *n* schop *c*

show [ʃou] *n* voorstelling *c*; tentoonstelling *c*

*****show** [ʃou] *v* tonen; *laten zien, tentoonstellen; aantonen

show-case [ˈʃoukeis] *n* vitrine *c*

shower [ʃauə] *n* douche *c*; bui *c*, regenbui *c*

showroom [ˈʃouruːm] *n* toonzaal *c*

shriek [ʃriːk] *v* gillen; *n* gil *c*

shrimp [ʃrimp] *n* garnaal *c*

shrine [ʃrain] *n* heiligdom *nt*, schrijn *c*

*****shrink** [ʃriŋk] *v* *krimpen

shrinkproof [ˈʃriŋkpruːf] *adj* krimpvrij

shrub [ʃrʌb] *n* struik *c*

shudder [ˈʃʌdə] *n* rilling *c*

shuffle [ˈʃʌfəl] *v* schudden

*****shut** [ʃʌt] *v* *sluiten; **shut** dicht, gesloten; ~ **in** *insluiten

shutter [ˈʃʌtə] *n* luik *nt*, blind *nt*

shy [ʃai] *adj* schuw, verlegen

shyness [ˈʃainəs] *n* verlegenheid *c*

Siam [saiˈæm] Siam

Siamese [‚saiəˈmiːz] *adj* Siamees; *n* Siamees *c*

sick [sik] *adj* ziek; misselijk

sickness [ˈsiknəs] *n* ziekte *c*; misselijkheid *c*

side [said] *n* kant *c*, zijde *c*; partij *c*; **one-sided** *adj* eenzijdig

sideburns [ˈsaidbəːnz] *pl* bakkebaarden *pl*

sidelight [ˈsaidlait] *n* zijlicht *nt*

side-street [ˈsaidstriːt] *n* zijstraat *c*

sidewalk [ˈsaidwɔːk] *nAm* stoep *c*, trottoir *nt*

sideways [ˈsaidweiz] *adv* opzij

siege [siːdʒ] *n* belegering *c*

sieve [siv] *n* zeef *c*; *v* zeven

sift [sift] *v* zeven

sight [sait] *n* zicht *nt*; gezicht *nt*, aanblik *c*; bezienswaardigheid *c*

sign [sain] *n* teken *nt*; gebaar *nt*, wenk *c*; *v* ondertekenen, tekenen

signal [ˈsignəl] *n* signaal *nt*; sein *nt*, teken *nt*; *v* seinen

signature [ˈsignətʃə] *n* handtekening *c*

significant [sigˈnifikənt] *adj* veelbetekenend

signpost [ˈsainpoust] *n* wegwijzer *c*

silence [ˈsailəns] *n* stilte *c*; *v* tot zwijgen *brengen

silencer [ˈsailənsə] *n* knalpot *c*

silent [ˈsailənt] *adj* zwijgend, stil; *be ~ *zwijgen

silk [silk] *n* zijde *c*

silken [ˈsilkən] *adj* zijden

silly [ˈsili] *adj* mal, dwaas

silver [ˈsilvə] *n* zilver *nt*; zilveren

silversmith [ˈsilvəsmiθ] *n* zilversmid *c*

silverware [ˈsilvəwɛə] *n* zilverwerk *nt*

similar [ˈsimilə] *adj* dergelijk, overeenkomstig

similarity [‚simiˈlærəti] *n* gelijkenis *c*

simple [ˈsimpəl] *adj* simpel, eenvoudig; gewoon

simply [ˈsimpli] *adv* eenvoudig, gewoonweg

simulate [ˈsimjuleit] *v* huichelen

simultaneous [‚siməlˈteiniəs] *adj* gelijktijdig; **simultaneously** *adv* tegelijkertijd

sin [sin] *n* zonde *c*

since [sins] *prep* sedert; *adv* sindsdien; *conj* sinds; aangezien

sincere [sinˈsiə] *adj* oprecht

sinew [ˈsinjuː] *n* pees *c*

*****sing** [siŋ] *v* *zingen

singer [ˈsiŋə] *n* zanger *c*; zangeres *c*

single ['siŋgəl] *adj* enkel; ongetrouwd

singular ['siŋgjulə] *n* enkelvoud *nt*; *adj* eigenaardig

sinister ['sinistə] *adj* onheilspellend

sink [siŋk] *n* gootsteen *c*

*sink [siŋk] *v* *zinken

sip [sip] *n* slokje *nt*

siphon ['saifən] *n* sifon *c*

sir [sə:] *meneer*

siren ['saiərən] *n* sirene *c*

sister ['sistə] *n* zuster *c*, zus *c*

sister-in-law ['sistərinlɔ:] *n* (pl sisters-) schoonzuster *c*

*sit [sit] *v* *zitten; ~ **down** *gaan zitten

site [sait] *n* plaats *c*; ligging *c*

sitting-room ['sitiŋru:m] *n* zitkamer *c*

situated ['sitʃueitid] *adj* gelegen

situation [,sitʃu'eiʃən] *n* situatie *c*; ligging *c*

six [siks] *num* zes

sixteen [,siks'ti:n] *num* zestien

sixteenth [,siks'ti:nθ] *num* zestiende

sixth [siksθ] *num* zesde

sixty ['siksti] *num* zestig

size [saiz] *n* grootte *c*, maat *c*; afmeting *c*, omvang *c*; formaat *nt*

skate [skeit] *v* schaatsen; *n* schaats *c*

skating-rink ['skeitiŋriŋk] *n* kunstijsbaan *c*, ijsbaan *c*

skeleton ['skelitən] *n* skelet *nt*, geraamte *nt*

sketch [sketʃ] *n* tekening *c*, schets *c*; *v* tekenen, schetsen

sketch-book ['sketʃbuk] *n* schetsboek *nt*

ski¹ [ski:] *v* skiën

ski² [ski:] *n* (pl ~, ~s) ski *c*; ~ **boots** skischoenen *pl*; ~ **pants** skibroek *c*; ~ **poles** *Am* skistokken *pl*; ~ **sticks** skistokken *pl*

skid [skid] *v* slippen

skier ['ski:ə] *n* skiër *c*

skilful ['skilfəl] *adj* bekwaam, behen-

dig, vaardig

ski-lift ['ski:lift] *n* skilift *c*

skill [skil] *n* vaardigheid *c*

skilled [skild] *adj* vaardig, vakkundig

skin [skin] *n* vel *nt*, huid *c*; schil *c*; ~ **cream** huidcrème *c*

skip [skip] *v* huppelen; *overslaan

skirt [skə:t] *n* rok *c*

skull [skʌl] *n* schedel *c*

sky [skai] *n* hemel *c*; lucht *c*

skyscraper ['skai,skreipə] *n* wolkenkrabber *c*

slack [slæk] *adj* traag

slacks [slæks] *pl* broek *c*

slam [slæm] *v* *dichtslaan

slander ['slɑ:ndə] *n* laster *c*

slant [slɑ:nt] *v* hellen

slanting ['slɑ:ntiŋ] *adj* schuin, hellend, scheef

slap [slæp] *v* *slaan; *n* klap *c*

slate [sleit] *n* lei *c*

slave [sleiv] *n* slaaf *c*

sledge [sledʒ] *n* slee *c*, slede *c*

sleep [sli:p] *n* slaap *c*

*sleep [sli:p] *v* *slapen

sleeping-bag ['sli:piŋbæg] *n* slaapzak *c*

sleeping-car ['sli:piŋkɑ:] *n* slaapwagen *c*

sleeping-pill ['sli:piŋpil] *n* slaappil *c*

sleepless ['sli:pləs] *adj* slapeloos

sleepy ['sli:pi] *adj* slaperig

sleeve [sli:v] *n* mouw *c*; hoes *c*

sleigh [slei] *n* slee *c*, ar *c*

slender ['slendə] *adj* slank

slice [slais] *n* snee *c*

slide [slaid] *n* glijbaan *c*; dia *c*

*slide [slaid] *v* *glijden

slight [slait] *adj* licht; gering

slim [slim] *adj* slank; *v* vermageren

slip [slip] *v* slippen, *uitglijden; ontglippen; *n* misstap *c*; onderrok *c*

slipper ['slipə] *n* slof *c*, pantoffel *c*

slippery ['slipəri] *adj* glibberig, glad

slogan ['slougən] *n* leus *c*, slagzin *c*

slope [sloup] n helling c; v glooien
sloping ['sloupiŋ] adj afhellend
sloppy ['slɔpi] adj slordig
slot [slɔt] n gleuf c
slot-machine ['slɔt,məʃi:n] n automaat c
slovenly ['slʌvənli] adj slordig
slow [slou] adj traag, langzaam; ~ **down** vertragen; afremmen
sluice [slu:s] n sluis c
slum [slʌm] n achterbuurt c
slump [slʌmp] n prijsdaling c
slush [slʌʃ] n sneeuwslik nt
sly [slai] adj listig
smack [smæk] v *slaan; n klap c
small [smɔ:l] adj klein; gering
smallpox ['smɔ:lpɔks] n pokken pl
smart [smɑ:t] adj chic; knap, pienter
smell [smel] n geur c
***smell** [smel] v *ruiken; *stinken
smelly ['smeli] adj stinkend
smile [smail] v glimlachen; n glimlach c
smith [smiθ] n smid c
smoke [smouk] v roken; n rook c; **no smoking** verboden te roken
smoker ['smoukə] n roker c; rookcoupé c
smoking-compartment ['smoukiŋkəm,pɑ:tmənt] n coupé voor rokers
smoking-room ['smoukiŋru:m] n rookkamer c
smooth [smu:ð] adj effen, vlak, glad; zacht
smuggle ['smʌgəl] v smokkelen
snack [snæk] n snack c
snack-bar ['snækbɑ:] n snackbar c
snail [sneil] n slak c
snake [sneik] n slang c
snapshot ['snæpʃɔt] n kiekje nt, momentopname c
sneakers ['sni:kəz] plAm gymschoenen pl
sneeze [sni:z] v niezen

sniper ['snaipə] n sluipschutter c
snooty ['snu:ti] adj verwaand
snore [snɔ:] v snurken
snorkel ['snɔ:kəl] n snorkel c
snout [snaut] n snuit c
snow [snou] n sneeuw c; v sneeuwen
snowstorm ['snoustɔ:m] n sneeuwstorm c
snowy ['snoui] adj besneeuwd
so [sou] conj dus; adv zo; dermate; **and ~ on** enzovoort; ~ **far** tot zover; ~ **that** zodat, opdat
soak [souk] v weken, doorweken
soap [soup] n zeep c; ~ **powder** zeeppoeder nt
sober ['soubə] adj nuchter; bezonnen
so-called [,sou'kɔ:ld] adj zogenaamd
soccer ['sɔkə] n voetbal nt; ~ **team** elftal nt
social ['souʃəl] adj maatschappelijk, sociaal
socialism ['souʃəlizəm] n socialisme nt
socialist ['souʃəlist] adj socialistisch; n socialist c
society [sə'saiəti] n maatschappij c; genootschap nt, vereniging c; gezelschap nt
sock [sɔk] n sok c
socket ['sɔkit] n fitting c
soda-water ['soudə,wɔ:tə] n spuitwater nt, sodawater nt
sofa ['soufə] n sofa c
soft [sɔft] adj zacht; ~ **drink** frisdrank c
soften ['sɔfən] v verzachten
soil [sɔil] n grond c; bodem c, aarde c
soiled [sɔild] adj bevuild
sold [sould] v (p, pp sell); ~ **out** uitverkocht
solder ['sɔldə] v solderen
soldering-iron ['sɔldəriŋaiən] n soldeerbout c
soldier ['souldʒə] n militair c, soldaat c

sole[1] [soul] *adj* enig

sole[2] [soul] *n* zool *c*; tong *c*

solely ['soulli] *adv* uitsluitend

solemn ['soləm] *adj* plechtig

solicitor [sə'lisitə] *n* raadsman *c*, advocaat *c*

solid ['solid] *adj* stevig, solide; massief; *n* vaste stof

soluble ['soljubəl] *adj* oplosbaar

solution [sə'lu:ʃən] *n* oplossing *c*

solve [solv] *v* oplossen

sombre ['sombə] *adj* somber

some [sʌm] *adj* enige, enkele; *pron* sommige; iets; ~ **day** eens; ~ **more** nog wat; ~ **time** eens

somebody ['sʌmbədi] *pron* iemand

somehow ['sʌmhau] *adv* op de een of andere manier

someone ['sʌmwʌn] *pron* iemand

something ['sʌmθiŋ] *pron* iets

sometimes ['sʌmtaimz] *adv* soms

somewhat ['sʌmwot] *adv* enigszins

somewhere ['sʌmweə] *adv* ergens

son [sʌn] *n* zoon *c*

song [soŋ] *n* lied *nt*

son-in-law ['sʌninlɔ:] *n* (pl sons-) schoonzoon *c*

soon [su:n] *adv* vlug, gauw, weldra, spoedig; **as** ~ **as** zodra

sooner ['su:nə] *adv* liever

sore [sɔ:] *adj* pijnlijk, zeer; *n* zere plek; zweer *c*; ~ **throat** keelpijn *c*

sorrow ['sorou] *n* droefheid *c*, leed *nt*, verdriet *nt*

sorry ['sori] *adj* bedroefd; **sorry!** neem me niet kwalijk!, sorry!, pardon!

sort [sɔ:t] *v* sorteren, rangschikken; *n* slag *nt*, soort *c/nt*; **all sorts of** allerlei

soul [soul] *n* ziel *c*; geest *c*

sound [saund] *n* klank *c*, geluid *nt*; *v* *klinken; *adj* degelijk

soundproof ['saundpru:f] *adj* geluiddicht

soup [su:p] *n* soep *c*

soup-plate ['su:ppleit] *n* soepbord *nt*

soup-spoon ['su:pspu:n] *n* soeplepel *c*

sour [sauə] *adj* zuur

source [sɔ:s] *n* bron *c*

south [sauθ] *n* zuid *c*, zuiden *nt*; **South Pole** zuidpool *c*

South Africa [sauθ 'æfrikə] Zuid-Afrika

south-east [,sauθ'i:st] *n* zuidoosten *nt*

southerly ['sʌðəli] *adj* zuidelijk

southern ['sʌðən] *adj* zuidelijk

south-west [,sauθ'west] *n* zuidwesten *nt*

souvenir ['su:vəniə] *n* souvenir *nt*; ~ **shop** souvenirwinkel *c*

sovereign ['sovrin] *n* vorst *c*

Soviet ['souviət] *adj* Sovjet-

*sow [sou] *v* zaaien

spa [spa:] *n* geneeskrachtige bron

space [speis] *n* ruimte *c*; afstand *c*, tussenruimte *c*; *v* spatiëren

spacious ['speiʃəs] *adj* ruim

spade [speid] *n* schop *c*, spade *c*

Spain [spein] Spanje

Spaniard ['spænjəd] *n* Spanjaard *c*

Spanish ['spæniʃ] *adj* Spaans

spanking ['spæŋkiŋ] *n* pak slaag

spanner ['spænə] *n* schroefsleutel *c*; moersleutel *c*

spare [speə] *adj* reserve-, extra; *v* missen; ~ **part** onderdeel *nt*; ~ **room** logeerkamer *c*; ~ **time** vrije tijd; ~ **tyre** reserveband *c*; ~ **wheel** reservewiel *nt*

spark [spa:k] *n* vonk *c*

sparking-plug ['spa:kiŋplʌg] *n* bougie *c*

sparkling ['spa:kliŋ] *adj* fonkelend; mousserend

sparrow ['spærou] *n* mus *c*

*speak [spi:k] *v* *spreken

spear [spiə] *n* speer *c*

special ['speʃəl] *adj* bijzonder, speciaal; ~ **delivery** expresse-

specialist ['speʃəlist] n specialist c

speciality [,speʃi'æləti] n specialiteit c

specialize ['speʃəlaiz] v zich specialiseren

specially ['speʃəli] adv in het bijzonder

species ['spi:ʃi:z] n (pl ~) soort c/nt

specific [spə'sifik] adj specifiek

specimen ['spesimən] n exemplaar nt,
specimen nt

speck [spek] n spat c

spectacle ['spektəkəl] n schouwspel
nt; **spectacles** bril c

spectator [spek'teitə] n kijker c, toeschouwer c

speculate ['spekjuleit] v speculeren

speech [spi:tʃ] n spraak c; rede c, toespraak c; taal c

speechless ['spi:tʃləs] adj sprakeloos

speed [spi:d] n snelheid c; vaart c,
spoed c; **cruising** ~ kruissnelheid
c; ~ **limit** maximum snelheid, snelheidsbeperking c

* **speed** [spi:d] v hard *rijden; te hard
*rijden

speeding ['spi:diŋ] n snelheidsovertreding c

speedometer [spi:'dɔmitə] n snelheidsmeter c

spell [spel] n betovering c

* **spell** [spel] v spellen

spelling ['speliŋ] n spelling c

* **spend** [spend] v *uitgeven, besteden;
*doorbrengen

sphere [sfiə] n bol c; sfeer c

spice [spais] n specerij c; **spices** kruiden

spiced [spaist] adj gekruid

spicy ['spaisi] adj pikant

spider ['spaidə] n spin c; **spider's
web** spinneweb nt

* **spill** [spil] v morsen

* **spin** [spin] v *spinnen; draaien

spinach ['spinidʒ] n spinazie c

spine [spain] n ruggegraat c

spinster ['spinstə] n oude vrijster

spire [spaiə] n spits c

spirit ['spirit] n geest c; bui c; **spirits**
sterke drank; stemming c; ~ **stove**
spiritusbrander c

spiritual ['spiritʃuəl] adj geestelijk

spit [spit] n spuug nt, speeksel nt;
spit nt

* **spit** [spit] v spuwen

in spite of [in spait ɔv] ongeacht, ondanks

spiteful ['spaitfəl] adj hatelijk

splash [splæʃ] v spatten

splendid ['splendid] adj schitterend,
prachtig

splendour ['splendə] n pracht c

splint [splint] n spalk c

splinter ['splintə] n splinter c

* **split** [split] v *splijten

* **spoil** [spɔil] v *bederven; verwennen

spoke[1] [spouk] v (p speak)

spoke[2] [spouk] n spaak c

sponge [spʌndʒ] n spons c

spook [spu:k] n spook nt

spool [spu:l] n spoel c

spoon [spu:n] n lepel c

sport [spɔ:t] n sport c

sports-car ['spɔ:tska:] n sportwagen c

sports-jacket ['spɔ:ts,dʒækit] n sportjasje nt

sportsman ['spɔ:tsmən] n (pl -men)
sportman c

sportswear ['spɔ:tswɛə] n sportkleding
c

spot [spɔt] n spat c, vlek c; plek c,
plaats c

spotless ['spɔtləs] adj vlekkeloos

spotlight ['spɔtlait] n schijnwerper c

spotted ['spɔtid] adj gespikkeld

spout [spaut] n straal c

sprain [sprein] v verstuiken, verzwikken; n verstuiking c

* **spread** [spred] v spreiden

spring [spriŋ] n voorjaar nt, lente c; veer c; bron c

springtime ['spriŋtaim] n voorjaar nt

sprouts [sprauts] pl spruitjes pl

spy [spai] n spion c

squadron ['skwɔdrən] n eskader nt

square [skwɛə] adj vierkant; n kwadraat nt, vierkant nt; plein c

squash [skwɔʃ] n vruchtensap nt

squirrel ['skwirəl] n eekhoorn c

squirt [skwə:t] n straal c

stable ['steibəl] adj stabiel; n stal c

stack [stæk] n stapel c

stadium ['steidiəm] n stadion nt

staff [sta:f] n staf c

stage [steidʒ] n toneel nt; fase c, stadium nt; etappe c

stain [stein] v vlekken; n spat c, vlek c; **stained glass** gebrandschilderd glas; ~ **remover** vlekkenwater nt

stainless ['steinləs] adj vlekkeloos; ~ **steel** roestvrij staal

staircase ['stɛəkeis] n trap c

stairs [stɛəz] pl trap c

stale [steil] adj oudbakken

stall [stɔ:l] n kraam c; stalles pl

stamina ['stæminə] n uithoudingsvermogen nt

stamp [stæmp] n postzegel c; stempel c; v frankeren; stampen; ~ **machine** postzegelautomaat c

stand [stænd] n kraam c; tribune c

***stand** [stænd] v *staan

standard ['stændəd] n norm c, maatstaf c; standaard-; ~ **of living** levensstandaard c

stanza ['stænzə] n couplet nt

staple ['steipəl] n nietje nt

star [sta:] n ster c

starboard ['sta:bəd] n stuurboord nt

starch [sta:tʃ] n stijfsel nt; v *stijven

stare [stɛə] v staren

starling ['sta:liŋ] n spreeuw c

start [sta:t] v *beginnen; n begin nt;

starter motor startmotor c

starting-point ['sta:tiŋpoint] n uitgangspunt nt

state [steit] n staat c; toestand c; v verklaren

the States Verenigde Staten

statement ['steitmənt] n verklaring c

statesman ['steitsmən] n (pl -men) staatsman c

station ['steiʃən] n station nt; plaats c

stationary ['steiʃənəri] adj stilstaand

stationer's ['steiʃənəz] n kantoorboekhandel c

stationery ['steiʃənəri] n schrijfbehoeften pl

station-master ['steiʃən,ma:stə] n stationschef c

statistics [stə'tistiks] pl statistiek c

statue ['stætʃu:] n standbeeld nt

stay [stei] v *blijven; logeren, *verblijven; n verblijf nt

steadfast ['stedfa:st] adj standvastig

steady ['stedi] adj vast

steak [steik] n biefstuk c

***steal** [sti:l] v *stelen

steam [sti:m] n stoom c

steamer ['sti:mə] n stoomboot c

steel [sti:l] n staal c

steep [sti:p] adj steil

steeple ['sti:pəl] n kerktoren c

steering-column ['stiəriŋ,kɔləm] n stuurkolom c

steering-wheel ['stiəriŋwi:l] n stuurwiel nt

steersman ['stiəzmən] n (pl -men) stuurman c

stem [stem] n steel c

stenographer [ste'nɔgrəfə] n stenograaf c

step [step] n pas c, stap c; trede c; v stappen

stepchild ['steptʃaild] n (pl -children) stiefkind nt

stepfather ['step,fa:ðə] n stiefvader c

stepmother ['step,mʌðə] n stiefmoeder c

sterile ['sterail] adj steriel

sterilize ['sterilaiz] v steriliseren

steward ['stju:əd] n steward c

stewardess ['stju:ədes] n stewardess c

stick [stik] n stok c

*stick [stik] v kleven, plakken

sticky ['stiki] adj kleverig

stiff [stif] adj stijf

still [stil] adv nog; toch; adj stil

stillness ['stilnəs] n stilte c

stimulant ['stimjulənt] n stimulerend middel

stimulate ['stimjuleit] v stimuleren

sting [stiŋ] n prik c, steek c

*sting [stiŋ] v *steken

stingy ['stindʒi] adj gierig

*stink [stiŋk] v *stinken

stipulate ['stipjuleit] v bepalen

stipulation [,stipju'leiʃən] n bepaling c

stir [stə:] v *bewegen; roeren

stirrup ['stirəp] n stijgbeugel c

stitch [stitʃ] n steek c; hechting c

stock [stɔk] n voorraad c; v in voorraad *hebben; ~ **exchange** effectenbeurs c, beurs c; ~ **market** effectenbeurs c; **stocks and shares** effecten

stocking ['stɔkiŋ] n kous c

stole¹ [stoul] v (p steal)

stole² [stoul] n stola c

stomach ['stʌmək] n maag c

stomach-ache ['stʌməkeik] n buikpijn c, maagpijn c

stone [stoun] n steen c; edelsteen c; pit c; stenen; **pumice ~** puimsteen nt

stood [stud] v (p, pp stand)

stop [stɔp] v stoppen; *ophouden met, staken; n halte c; **stop!** halt!

stopper ['stɔpə] n stop c

storage ['stɔ:ridʒ] n opslag c

store [stɔ:] n voorraad c; winkel c; v *opslaan

store-house ['stɔ:haus] n magazijn nt

storey ['stɔ:ri] n etage c, verdieping c

stork [stɔ:k] n ooievaar c

storm [stɔ:m] n storm c

stormy ['stɔ:mi] adj stormachtig

story ['stɔ:ri] n verhaal nt

stout [staut] adj dik, gezet, corpulent

stove [stouv] n kachel c; fornuis nt

straight [streit] adj recht; eerlijk; adv recht; ~ **ahead** rechtdoor; ~ **away** direct, meteen; ~ **on** rechtdoor

strain [strein] n inspanning c; spanning c; v forceren; zeven

strainer ['streinə] n vergiet nt

strange [streindʒ] adj vreemd; raar

stranger ['streindʒə] n vreemdeling c; vreemde c

strangle ['stræŋgəl] v wurgen

strap [stræp] n riem c

straw [strɔ:] n stro nt

strawberry ['strɔ:bəri] n aardbei c

stream [stri:m] n beek c; stroom c; v stromen

street [stri:t] n straat c

streetcar ['stri:tkɑ:] nAm tram c

street-organ ['stri:,tɔ:gən] n draaiorgel nt

strength [streŋθ] n sterkte c, kracht c

stress [stres] n spanning c; nadruk c; v benadrukken

stretch [stretʃ] v rekken; n stuk nt

strict [strikt] adj strikt; streng

strife [straif] n strijd c

strike [straik] n staking c

*strike [straik] v *slaan; *toeslaan; *treffen; staken; *strijken

striking ['straikiŋ] adj frappant, opmerkelijk, opvallend

string [striŋ] n touw nt; snaar c

strip [strip] n strook c

stripe [straip] n streep c

striped [straipt] adj gestreept

stroke [strouk] n beroerte c

stroll [stroul] v wandelen; n wandeling c

strong [strɔŋ] adj sterk; krachtig

stronghold ['strɔŋhould] n burcht c

structure ['strʌktʃə] n structuur c

struggle ['strʌgəl] n strijd c, worsteling c; v worstelen, *strijden

stub [stʌb] n controlestrook c

stubborn ['stʌbən] adj hardnekkig

student ['stju:dənt] n student c; studente c

study ['stʌdi] v studeren; n studie c; studeerkamer c

stuff [stʌf] n stof c; spul nt

stuffed [stʌft] adj gevuld

stuffing ['stʌfiŋ] n vulling c

stuffy ['stʌfi] adj benauwd

stumble ['stʌmbəl] v struikelen

stung [stʌŋ] v (p, pp sting)

stupid ['stju:pid] adj dom

style [stail] n stijl c

subject¹ ['sʌbdʒikt] n onderwerp nt; onderdaan c; ~ to onderhevig aan

subject² [səb'dʒekt] v *onderwerpen

submit [səb'mit] v zich *onderwerpen

subordinate [sə'bɔ:dinət] adj ondergeschikt; bijkomstig

subscriber [səb'skraibə] n abonnee c

subscription [səb'skripʃən] n abonnement nt

subsequent ['sʌbsikwənt] adj volgend

subsidy ['sʌbsidi] n subsidie c

substance ['sʌbstəns] n substantie c

substantial [səb'stænʃəl] adj stoffelijk; werkelijk; aanzienlijk

substitute ['sʌbstitju:t] v *vervangen; n vervanging c; plaatsvervanger c

subtitle ['sʌb,taitəl] n ondertitel c

subtle ['sʌtəl] adj subtiel

subtract [səb'trækt] v *aftrekken

suburb ['sʌbə:b] n buitenwijk c, voorstad c

suburban [sə'bə:bən] adj van de voorstad

subway ['sʌbwei] nAm ondergrondse c

succeed [sək'si:d] v slagen; opvolgen

success [sək'ses] n succes nt

successful [sək'sesfəl] adj succesvol

succumb [sə'kʌm] v *bezwijken

such [sʌtʃ] adj dergelijk, zulk; adv zo; ~ as zoals

suck [sʌk] v *zuigen

sudden ['sʌdən] adj plotseling

suddenly ['sʌdənli] adv opeens

suede [sweid] n suède nt/c

suffer ['sʌfə] v *lijden; *ondergaan

suffering ['sʌfəriŋ] n lijden nt

suffice [sə'fais] v voldoende *zijn

sufficient [sə'fiʃənt] adj voldoende, genoeg

suffrage ['sʌfridʒ] n stemrecht nt, kiesrecht nt

sugar ['ʃugə] n suiker c

suggest [sə'dʒest] v voorstellen

suggestion [sə'dʒestʃən] n voorstel nt

suicide ['su:isaid] n zelfmoord c

suit [su:t] v schikken; aanpassen; goed *staan; n kostuum nt

suitable ['su:təbəl] adj gepast, geschikt

suitcase ['su:tkeis] n koffer c

suite [swi:t] n suite c

sum [sʌm] n som c

summary ['sʌməri] n resumé nt, samenvatting c

summer ['sʌmə] n zomer c; ~ **time** zomertijd c

summit ['sʌmit] n top c

summons ['sʌmənz] n (pl ~es) dagvaarding c

sun [sʌn] n zon c

sunbathe ['sʌnbeiθ] v zonnebaden

sunburn ['sʌnbə:n] n zonnebrand c

Sunday ['sʌndi] n zondag c

sun-glasses ['sʌn,glɑ:siz] pl zonnebril c

sunlight ['sʌnlait] n zonlicht nt

sunny ['sʌni] adj zonnig

sunrise ['sʌnraiz] n zonsopgang c

sunset ['sʌnset] n zonsondergang c

sunshade ['sʌnʃeid] n parasol c

sunshine ['sʌnʃain] n zonneschijn c

sunstroke ['sʌnstrouk] n zonnesteek c

suntan oil ['sʌntænɔil] zonnebrandolie c

superb [su'pə:b] adj groots, prachtig

superficial [,su:pə'fiʃəl] adj oppervlakkig

superfluous [su'pə:fluəs] adj overbodig

superior [su'piəriə] adj beter, groter, hoger, superieur

superlative [su'pə:lətiv] adj overtreffend; n superlatief c

supermarket ['su:pə,ma:kit] n supermarkt c

superstition [,su:pə'stiʃən] n bijgeloof nt

supervise ['su:pəvaiz] v toezicht *houden op

supervision [,su:pə'viʒən] n controle c, toezicht nt

supervisor ['su:pəvaizə] n opzichter c

supper ['sʌpə] n avondeten nt

supple ['sʌpəl] adj soepel, lenig, buigzaam

supplement ['sʌplimənt] n supplement nt

supply [sə'plai] n aanvoer c, levering c; voorraad c; aanbod nt; v leveren, bezorgen

support [sə'pɔ:t] v ondersteunen, steunen; n steun c; ~ **hose** steunkousen pl

supporter [sə'pɔ:tə] n supporter c

suppose [sə'pouz] v *aannemen, veronderstellen; **supposing that** aangenomen dat

suppository [sə'pɔzitəri] n zetpil c

suppress [sə'pres] v onderdrukken

surcharge ['sə:tʃa:dʒ] n toeslag c

sure [ʃuə] adj zeker

surely ['ʃuəli] adv zeker

surface ['sə:fis] n oppervlakte c

surf-board ['sə:fbɔ:d] n surfplank c

surgeon ['sə:dʒən] n chirurg c; **veterinary ~** veearts c

surgery ['sə:dʒəri] n operatie c; spreekkamer c

surname ['sə:neim] n achternaam c

surplus ['sə:pləs] n overschot nt

surprise [sə'praiz] n verrassing c; verbazing c; v verrassen; verbazen

surrender [sə'rendə] v zich *overgeven; n overgave c

surround [sə'raund] v omringen, *omgeven

surrounding [sə'raundiŋ] adj omliggend

surroundings [sə'raundiŋz] pl omgeving c

survey ['sə:vei] n overzicht nt

survival [sə'vaivəl] n overleving c

survive [sə'vaiv] v overleven

suspect[1] [sə'spekt] v *verdenken; vermoeden

suspect[2] ['sʌspekt] n verdachte c

suspend [sə'spend] v schorsen

suspenders [sə'spendəz] plAm bretels pl; **suspender belt** jarretelgordel c

suspension [sə'spenʃən] n vering c, ophanging c; ~ **bridge** hangbrug c

suspicion [sə'spiʃən] n verdenking c; wantrouwen nt, argwaan c

suspicious [sə'spiʃəs] adj verdacht; argwanend, achterdochtig

sustain [sə'stein] v *verdragen

Swahili [swɑ'hi:li] n Swahili nt

swallow ['swɔlou] v inslikken, slikken; n zwaluw c

swam [swæm] v (p swim)

swamp [swɔmp] n moeras nt

swan [swɔn] n zwaan c

swap [swɔp] v ruilen

***swear** [sweə] v *zweren; vloeken

sweat [swet] n zweet nt; v zweten

sweater ['swetə] n sweater c

Swede [swi:d] *n* Zweed *c*

Sweden ['swi:dən] Zweden

Swedish ['swi:diʃ] *adj* Zweeds

*****sweep** [swi:p] *v* vegen

sweet [swi:t] *adj* zoet; lief; *n* snoepje *nt*; toetje *nt*; **sweets** snoep *nt*, snoepgoed *nt*

sweeten ['swi:tən] *v* zoet maken

sweetheart ['swi:tha:t] *n* liefje *nt*, lieveling *c*

sweetshop ['swi:tʃɔp] *n* snoepwinkel *c*

swell [swel] *adj* prachtig

*****swell** [swel] *v* *zwellen

swelling ['sweliŋ] *n* zwelling *c*

swift [swift] *adj* snel

*****swim** [swim] *v* *zwemmen

swimmer ['swimə] *n* zwemmer *c*

swimming ['swimiŋ] *n* zwemsport *c*; ~ **pool** zwembad *nt*

swimming-trunks ['swimiŋtrʌŋks] *n* zwembroek *c*

swim-suit ['swimsu:t] *n* zwempak *nt*

swindle ['swindəl] *v* oplichten; *n* zwendelarij *c*

swindler ['swindlə] *n* oplichter *c*

swing [swiŋ] *n* schommel *c*

*****swing** [swiŋ] *v* zwaaien; schommelen

Swiss [swis] *adj* Zwitsers; *n* Zwitser *c*

switch [switʃ] *n* schakelaar *c*; *v* omwisselen; ~ **off** uitschakelen; ~ **on** inschakelen

switchboard ['switʃbɔ:d] *n* schakelbord *nt*

Switzerland ['switsələnd] Zwitserland

sword [sɔ:d] *n* zwaard *nt*

swum [swʌm] *v* (pp swim)

syllable ['siləbəl] *n* lettergreep *c*

symbol ['simbəl] *n* symbool *nt*

sympathetic [,simpə'θetik] *adj* hartelijk, begrijpend

sympathy ['simpəθi] *n* sympathie *c*; medegevoel *nt*

symphony ['simfəni] *n* symfonie *c*

symptom ['simtəm] *n* symptoom *nt*

synagogue ['sinəgɔg] *n* synagoge *c*

synonym ['sinənim] *n* synoniem *nt*

synthetic [sin'θetik] *adj* synthetisch

syphon ['saifən] *n* sifon *c*

Syria ['siriə] Syrië

Syrian ['siriən] *adj* Syrisch; *n* Syriër *c*

syringe [si'rindʒ] *n* spuit *c*

syrup ['sirəp] *n* stroop *c*, siroop *c*

system ['sistəm] *n* systeem *nt*; stelsel *nt*; **decimal** ~ tientallig stelsel

systematic [,sistə'mætik] *adj* systematisch

T

table ['teibəl] *n* tafel *c*; tabel *c*; ~ **of contents** inhoudsopgave *c*; ~ **tennis** tafeltennis *nt*

table-cloth ['teibəlklɔθ] *n* tafellaken *nt*

tablespoon ['teibəlspu:n] *n* eetlepel *c*

tablet ['tæblit] *n* tablet *c*

taboo [tə'bu:] *n* taboe *nt*

tactics ['tæktiks] *pl* tactiek *c*

tag [tæg] *n* etiket *nt*

tail [teil] *n* staart *c*

tail-light ['teillait] *n* achterlicht *nt*

tailor ['teilə] *n* kleermaker *c*

tailor-made ['teiləmeid] *adj* op maat gemaakt

*****take** [teik] *v* *nemen; pakken; *brengen; *begrijpen, snappen; ~ **away** *meenemen; *afnemen, *wegnemen; ~ **off** starten; ~ **out** *wegnemen; ~ **over** *overnemen; ~ **place** *plaatshebben; ~ **up** *innemen

take-off ['teikɔf] *n* start *c*

tale [teil] *n* verhaal *nt*, vertelling *c*

talent ['tælənt] *n* aanleg *c*, talent *nt*

talented ['tæləntid] *adj* begaafd

talk [tɔ:k] *v* *spreken, praten; *n* gesprek *nt*

talkative ['tɔːkətiv] *adj* spraakzaam

tall [tɔːl] *adj* hoog; lang, groot

tame [teim] *adj* mak, tam; *v* temmen

tampon ['tæmpən] *n* tampon *c*

tangerine [,tændʒə'riːn] *n* mandarijn *c*

tangible ['tændʒibəl] *adj* tastbaar

tank [tæŋk] *n* tank *c*

tanker ['tæŋkə] *n* tankschip *nt*

tanned [tænd] *adj* gebruind

tap [tæp] *n* kraan *c*; klop *c*; *v* kloppen

tape [teip] *n* band *c*; lint *nt*; **adhesive ~** plakband *nt*; hechtpleister *c*

tape-measure ['teip,meʒə] *n* centimeter *c*

tape-recorder ['teipri,kɔːdə] *n* bandrecorder *c*

tapestry ['tæpistri] *n* wandkleed *nt*, gobelin *c*

tar [taː] *n* teer *c/nt*

target ['taːgit] *n* doel *nt*, mikpunt *nt*

tariff ['tærif] *n* tarief *nt*

tarpaulin [taː'pɔːlin] *n* dekzeil *nt*

task [taːsk] *n* taak *c*

taste [teist] *n* smaak *c*; *v* smaken; proeven

tasteless ['teistləs] *adj* smakeloos

tasty ['teisti] *adj* lekker, smakelijk

taught [tɔːt] *v* (p, pp teach)

tavern ['tævən] *n* herberg *c*

tax [tæks] *n* belasting *c*; *v* belasten

taxation [tæk'seiʃən] *n* belasting *c*

tax-free ['tæksfriː] *adj* belastingvrij

taxi ['tæksi] *n* taxi *c*; **~ rank** taxistandplaats *c*; **~ stand** *Am* taxistandplaats *c*

taxi-driver ['tæksi,draivə] *n* taxichauffeur *c*

taxi-meter ['tæksi,miːtə] *n* taximeter *c*

tea [tiː] *n* thee *c*

***teach** [tiːtʃ] *v* leren, *onderwijzen

teacher ['tiːtʃə] *n* docent *c*, leraar *c*; lerares *c*; onderwijzer *c*, meester *c*, schoolmeester *c*

teachings ['tiːtʃiŋz] *pl* leer *c*

tea-cloth ['tiːklɔθ] *n* theedoek *c*

teacup ['tiːkʌp] *n* theekopje *nt*

team [tiːm] *n* equipe *c*, ploeg *c*

teapot ['tiːpɔt] *n* theepot *c*

tear¹ [tiə] *n* traan *c*

tear² [tɛə] *n* scheur *c*; ***tear** *v* scheuren

tear-jerker ['tiə,dʒəːkə] *n* smartlap *c*

tease [tiːz] *v* plagen

tea-set ['tiːset] *n* theeservies *nt*

tea-shop ['tiːʃɔp] *n* tearoom *c*

teaspoon ['tiːspuːn] *n* theelepel *c*

teaspoonful ['tiːspuːn,ful] *n* theelepel *c*

technical ['teknikəl] *adj* technisch

technician [tek'niʃən] *n* technicus *c*

technique [tek'niːk] *n* techniek *c*

technology [tek'nɔlədʒi] *n* technologie *c*

teenager ['tiː,neidʒə] *n* tiener *c*

teetotaller [tiː'toutələ] *n* geheelonthouder *c*

telegram ['teligræm] *n* telegram *nt*

telegraph ['teligraːf] *v* telegraferen

telepathy [ti'lepəθi] *n* telepathie *c*

telephone ['telifoun] *n* telefoon *c*; **~ book** *Am* telefoongids *c*, telefoonboek *nt*; **~ booth** telefooncel *c*; **~ call** telefoongesprek *nt*; **~ directory** telefoonboek *nt*, telefoongids *c*; **~ operator** telefoniste *c*

television ['teliviʒən] *n* televisie *c*; **~ set** televisietoestel *nt*; **cable ~** kabel-tv; **satellite ~** satelliet-tv

telex ['teleks] *n* telex *c*

***tell** [tel] *v* *zeggen; vertellen

temper ['tempə] *n* boosheid *c*

temperature ['temprətʃə] *n* temperatuur *c*

tempest ['tempist] *n* storm *c*

temple ['tempəl] *n* tempel *c*; slaap *c*

temporary ['tempərəri] *adj* voorlopig, tijdelijk

tempt [tempt] v *aantrekken

temptation [temp'teiʃən] n verleiding c

ten [ten] num tien

tenant ['tenənt] n huurder c

tend [tend] v de neiging *hebben; verzorgen; ~ **to** neigen tot

tendency ['tendənsi] n neiging c, tendens c

tender ['tendə] adj teder, teer; mals

tendon ['tendən] n pees c

tennis ['tenis] n tennis nt; ~ **shoes** tennisschoenen pl

tennis-court ['teniskɔːt] n tennisbaan c

tense [tens] adj gespannen

tension ['tenʃən] n spanning c

tent [tent] n tent c

tenth [tenθ] num tiende

tepid ['tepid] adj lauw

term [təːm] n term c; periode c, termijn c; voorwaarde c

terminal ['təːminəl] n eindpunt nt

terrace ['terəs] n terras nt

terrain [te'rein] n terrein nt

terrible ['teribəl] adj verschrikkelijk, ontzettend, vreselijk

terrific [tə'rifik] adj geweldig

terrify ['terifai] v schrik *aanjagen; **terrifying** angstwekkend

territory ['teritəri] n gebied nt

terror ['terə] n angst c

terrorism ['terərizəm] n terrorisme nt, terreur c

terrorist ['terərist] n terrorist c

terylene ['teriliːn] n terylene nt

test [test] n proef c, test c; v proberen, testen

testify ['testifai] v getuigen

text [tekst] n tekst c

textbook ['teksbuk] n leerboek nt

textile ['tekstail] n textiel c/nt

texture ['tekstʃə] n structuur c

Thai [tai] adj Thailands; n Thailander c

Thailand ['tailænd] Thailand

than [ðæn] conj dan

thank [θæŋk] v bedanken, danken; ~ **you** dank u

thankful ['θæŋkfəl] adj dankbaar

that [ðæt] adj die, dat; conj dat

thaw [θɔː] v dooien, ontdooien; n dooi c

the [ðə,ði] art de art; **the ... the** hoe ... hoe

theatre ['θiətə] n schouwburg c, theater nt

theft [θeft] n diefstal c

their [ðeə] adj hun

them [ðem] pron hen

theme [θiːm] n thema nt, onderwerp nt

themselves [ðəm'selvz] pron zich; zelf

then [ðen] adv toen; vervolgens, dan

theology [θi'ɔlədʒi] n theologie c

theoretical [θiə'retikəl] adj theoretisch

theory ['θiəri] n theorie c

therapy ['θerəpi] n therapie c

there [ðeə] adv daar; daarheen

therefore ['ðeəfɔː] conj daarom

thermometer [θə'mɔmitə] n thermometer c

thermostat ['θəːməstæt] n thermostaat c

these [ðiːz] adj deze

thesis ['θiːsis] n (pl theses) stelling c

they [ðei] pron ze

thick [θik] adj dik; dicht

thicken ['θikən] v verdikken

thickness ['θiknəs] n dikte c

thief [θiːf] n (pl thieves) dief c

thigh [θai] n dij c

thimble ['θimbəl] n vingerhoed c

thin [θin] adj dun; mager

thing [θiŋ] n ding nt

* **think** [θiŋk] v *denken; *nadenken; ~ **of** *denken aan; *bedenken; ~ **over** *overdenken

thinker ['θiŋkə] n denker c

third [θəːd] *num* derde

thirst [θəːst] *n* dorst *c*

thirsty ['θəːsti] *adj* dorstig

thirteen [,θəː'tiːn] *num* dertien

thirteenth [,θəː'tiːnθ] *num* dertiende

thirtieth ['θəːtiəθ] *num* dertigste

thirty ['θəːti] *num* dertig

this [ðis] *adj* dit, deze

thistle ['θisəl] *n* distel *c*

thorn [θɔːn] *n* doorn *c*

thorough ['θʌrə] *adj* grondig, degelijk

thoroughbred ['θʌrəbred] *adj* volbloed

thoroughfare ['θʌrəfeə] *n* hoofdweg *c*, hoofdstraat *c*

those [ðouz] *adj* die

though [ðou] *conj* hoewel, ofschoon, alhoewel; *adv* overigens

thought¹ [θɔːt] *v* (p, pp think)

thought² [θɔːt] *n* gedachte *c*

thoughtful ['θɔːtfəl] *adj* nadenkend; zorgzaam

thousand ['θauzənd] *num* duizend

thread [θred] *n* draad *c*; garen *nt*; *v* *rijgen

threadbare ['θredbeə] *adj* versleten

threat [θret] *n* dreigement *nt*, bedreiging *c*

threaten ['θretən] *v* dreigen, bedreigen; **threatening** dreigend

three [θriː] *num* drie

three-quarter [,θriː'kwɔːtə] *adj* driekwart

threshold ['θreʃould] *n* drempel *c*

threw [θruː] *v* (p throw)

thrifty ['θrifti] *adj* zuinig

throat [θrout] *n* keel *c*; hals *c*

throne [θroun] *n* troon *c*

through [θruː] *prep* door

throughout [θruː'aut] *adv* overal

throw [θrou] *n* gooi *c*

*throw [θrou] *v* *werpen, gooien

thrush [θrʌʃ] *n* lijster *c*

thumb [θʌm] *n* duim *c*

thumbtack ['θʌmtæk] *nAm* punaise *c*

thump [θʌmp] *v* stampen

thunder ['θʌndə] *n* donder *c*; *v* donderen

thunderstorm ['θʌndəstɔːm] *n* onweer *nt*

thundery ['θʌndəri] *adj* onweerachtig

Thursday ['θəːzdi] donderdag *c*

thus [ðʌs] *adv* zo

thyme [taim] *n* tijm *c*

tick [tik] *n* streepje *nt*; ~ **off** aanstrepen

ticket ['tikit] *n* kaartje *nt*; bon *c*; ~ **collector** conducteur *c*; ~ **machine** kaartenautomaat *c*

tickle ['tikəl] *v* kietelen

tide [taid] *n* getij *nt*; **high** ~ hoog water; **low** ~ laag water

tidings ['taidiŋz] *pl* nieuws *nt*

tidy ['taidi] *adj* net; ~ **up** opruimen

tie [tai] *v* knopen, *binden; *n* das *c*

tiger ['taigə] *n* tijger *c*

tight [tait] *adj* strak; nauw, krap; *adv* vast

tighten ['taitən] *v* aanhalen, *aantrekken; strakker maken; strakker *worden

tights [taits] *pl* maillot *c*

tile [tail] *n* tegel *c*; dakpan *c*

till [til] *prep* tot aan, tot; *conj* tot, totdat

timber ['timbə] *n* timmerhout *nt*

time [taim] *n* tijd *c*; maal *c*, keer *c*; **all the** ~ aldoor; **in** ~ op tijd; ~ **of arrival** aankomsttijd *c*; ~ **of departure** vertrektijd *c*

time-saving ['taim,seiviŋ] *adj* tijdbesparend

timetable ['taim,teibəl] *n* dienstregeling *c*

timid ['timid] *adj* bedeesd

timidity [ti'midəti] *n* verlegenheid *c*

tin [tin] *n* tin *nt*; bus *c*, blik *nt*; **tinned food** conserven *pl*

tinfoil ['tinfɔil] *n* zilverpapier *nt*

tin-opener ['ti,noupənə] n blikopener c
tiny ['taini] adj minuscuul
tip [tip] n punt c; fooi c
tire¹ [taiə] n band c
tire² [taiə] v vermoeien
tired [taiəd] adj vermoeid, moe; ~ of beu
tiring ['taiəriŋ] adj vermoeiend
tissue ['tiʃu:] n weefsel nt; papieren zakdoek
title ['taitəl] n titel c
to [tu:] prep tot; aan, voor, bij, naar; om te
toad [toud] n pad c
toadstool ['toudstu:l] n paddestoel c
toast [toust] n toast c
tobacco [tə'bækou] n (pl ~s) tabak c; ~ pouch tabakszak c
tobacconist [tə'bækənist] n sigarenwinkelier c; **tobacconist's** tabakswinkel c
today [tə'dei] adv vandaag
toddler ['tɔdlə] n peuter c
toe [tou] n teen c
toffee ['tɔfi] n toffee c
together [tə'geðə] adv bijeen, samen
toilet ['tɔilət] n toilet nt; ~ case toilettas c
toilet-paper ['tɔilət,peipə] n closetpapier nt, toiletpapier nt
toiletry ['tɔilətri] n toiletbenodigdheden pl
token ['toukən] n teken nt; bewijs nt; munt c
told [tould] v (p, pp tell)
tolerable ['tɔlərəbəl] adj draaglijk
toll [toul] n tol c
tomato [tə'mɑ:tou] n (pl ~es) tomaat c
tomb [tu:m] n graf nt
tombstone ['tu:mstoun] n grafsteen c
tomorrow [tə'mɔrou] adv morgen
ton [tʌn] n ton c
tone [toun] n toon c; klank c

tongs [tɔŋz] pl tang c
tongue [tʌŋ] n tong c
tonic ['tɔnik] n tonicum nt
tonight [tə'nait] adv vannacht, vanavond
tonsilitis [,tɔnsə'laitis] n amandelontsteking c
tonsils ['tɔnsəlz] pl amandelen
too [tu:] adv te; ook
took [tuk] v (p take)
tool [tu:l] n werktuig nt, gereedschap nt; ~ kit gereedschapskist c
toot [tu:t] vAm claxonneren
tooth [tu:θ] n (pl teeth) tand c
toothache ['tu:θeik] n tandpijn c
toothbrush ['tu:θbrʌʃ] n tandenborstel c
toothpaste ['tu:θpeist] n tandpasta c/nt
toothpick ['tu:θpik] n tandestoker c
toothpowder ['tu:θ,paudə] n tandpoeder nt/c
top [tɔp] n top c; bovenkant c; deksel nt; bovenst; **on ~ of** bovenop; ~ **side** bovenkant c
topcoat ['tɔpkout] n overjas c
topic ['tɔpik] n onderwerp nt
topical ['tɔpikəl] adj actueel
torch [tɔ:tʃ] n fakkel c; zaklantaarn c
torment¹ [tɔ:'ment] v kwellen
torment² ['tɔ:ment] n kwelling c
torture ['tɔ:tʃə] n marteling c; v martelen
toss [tɔs] v gooien
tot [tɔt] n kleuter c
total ['toutəl] adj totaal; geheel, volslagen; n totaal nt
totalitarian [,toutæli'tɛəriən] adj totalitair
totalizator ['toutəlaizeitə] n totalisator c
touch [tʌtʃ] v aanraken; *betreffen; n contact nt, aanraking c; tastzin c
touching ['tʌtʃiŋ] adj aandoenlijk

tough [tʌf] *adj* taai
tour [tuə] *n* rondreis *c*
tourism ['tuərizəm] *n* toerisme *nt*
tourist ['tuərist] *n* toerist *c*; ~ **class** toeristenklasse *c*; ~ **office** verkeersbureau *nt*
tournament ['tuənəmənt] *n* toernooi *nt*
tow [tou] *v* slepen
towards [tə'wɔ:dz] *prep* naar; jegens
towel [tauəl] *n* handdoek *c*
towelling ['tauəliŋ] *n* badstof *c*
tower [tauə] *n* toren *c*
town [taun] *n* stad *c*; ~ **centre** stadscentrum *nt*; ~ **hall** stadhuis *nt*
townspeople ['taunz,pi:pəl] *pl* stadsmensen *pl*
toxic ['tɔksik] *adj* vergiftig
toy [tɔi] *n* speelgoed *nt*
toyshop ['tɔiʃɔp] *n* speelgoedwinkel *c*
trace [treis] *n* spoor *nt*; *v* opsporen
track [træk] *n* spoor *nt*; renbaan *c*
tractor ['træktə] *n* tractor *c*
trade [treid] *n* koophandel *c*, handel *c*; ambacht *nt*, vak *nt*; *v* handel *drijven
trademark ['treidma:k] *n* handelsmerk *nt*
trader ['treidə] *n* handelaar *c*
tradesman ['treidzmən] *n* (pl -men) handelaar *c*
trade-union [,treid'ju:njən] *n* vakbond *c*
tradition [trə'diʃən] *n* traditie *c*
traditional [trə'diʃənəl] *adj* traditioneel
traffic ['træfik] *n* verkeer *nt*; ~ **jam** verkeersopstopping *c*; ~ **light** stoplicht *nt*
trafficator ['træfikeitə] *n* richtingaanwijzer *c*
tragedy ['trædʒədi] *n* tragedie *c*
tragic ['trædʒik] *adj* tragisch
trail [treil] *n* spoor *nt*, pad *nt*
trailer ['treilə] *n* aanhangwagen *c*;

nAm kampeerwagen *c*
train [trein] *n* trein *c*; *v* dresseren, trainen; **stopping** ~ stoptrein *c*; **through** ~ doorgaande trein
training ['treiniŋ] *n* training *c*
trait [treit] *n* trek *c*
traitor ['treitə] *n* verrader *c*
tram [træm] *n* tram *c*
tramp [træmp] *n* landloper *c*, vagebond *c*; *v* *rondtrekken
tranquil ['træŋkwil] *adj* rustig
tranquillizer ['træŋkwilaizə] *n* kalmerend middel
transaction [træn'zækʃən] *n* transactie *c*
transatlantic [,trænzət'læntik] *adj* transatlantisch
transfer [træns'fə:] *v* *overbrengen
transform [træns'fɔ:m] *v* veranderen
transformer [træns'fɔ:mə] *n* transformator *c*
transition [træn'siʃən] *n* overgang *c*
translate [træns'leit] *v* vertalen
translation [træns'leiʃən] *n* vertaling *c*
translator [træns'leitə] *n* vertaler *c*
transmission [trænz'miʃən] *n* uitzending *c*
transmit [trænz'mit] *v* *uitzenden
transmitter [trænz'mitə] *n* zender *c*
transparent [træn'spɛərənt] *adj* doorzichtig
transport[1] ['trænspɔ:t] *n* vervoer *nt*
transport[2] [træn'spɔ:t] *v* transporteren
transportation [,trænspɔ:'teiʃən] *n* transport *nt*
trap [træp] *n* val *c*
trash [træʃ] *n* rommel *c*; ~ **can** *Am* vuilnisbak *c*
travel ['trævəl] *v* reizen; ~ **agency** reisbureau *nt*; ~ **agent** reisagent *c*; ~ **insurance** reisverzekering *c*; **travelling expenses** reiskosten *pl*
traveller ['trævələ] *n* reiziger *c*; **traveller's cheque** reischeque *c*

tray [trei] *n* dienblad *nt*
treason ['tri:zən] *n* verraad *nt*
treasure ['treʒə] *n* schat *c*
treasurer ['treʒərə] *n* penningmeester *c*
treasury ['treʒəri] *n* schatkist *c*
treat [tri:t] *v* behandelen
treatment ['tri:tmənt] *n* behandeling *c*
treaty ['tri:ti] *n* verdrag *nt*
tree [tri:] *n* boom *c*
tremble ['trembəl] *v* rillen, beven; trillen
tremendous [tri'mendəs] *adj* enorm
trespasser ['trespəsə] *n* indringer *c*
trial [traiəl] *n* rechtszaak *c*; proef *c*
triangle ['traiæŋgəl] *n* driehoek *c*
triangular [trai'æŋgjulə] *adj* driehoekig
tribe [traib] *n* stam *c*
tributary ['tribjutəri] *n* zijrivier *c*
tribute ['tribju:t] *n* hulde *c*
trick [trik] *n* streek *c*; foefje *nt*, kunstje *nt*
trigger ['trigə] *n* trekker *c*
trim [trim] *v* bijknippen
trip [trip] *n* uitstapje *nt*, reis *c*
triumph ['traiəmf] *n* triomf *c*; *v* zegevieren
triumphant [trai'ʌmfənt] *adj* triomfantelijk
trolley-bus ['trɔlibʌs] *n* trolleybus *c*
troops [tru:ps] *pl* troepen *pl*
tropical ['trɔpikəl] *adj* tropisch
tropics ['trɔpiks] *pl* tropen *pl*
trouble ['trʌbəl] *n* zorg *c*, moeite *c*, last *c*; *v* storen
troublesome ['trʌbəlsəm] *adj* lastig
trousers ['trauzəz] *pl* broek *c*
trout [traut] *n* (pl ~) forel *c*
truck [trʌk] *nAm* vrachtwagen *c*
true [tru:] *adj* waar; werkelijk, echt; getrouw, trouw
trumpet ['trʌmpit] *n* trompet *c*
trunk [trʌŋk] *n* koffer *c*; stam *c*; *nAm* kofferruimte *c*; **trunks** *pl*

gymnastiekbroek *c*
trunk-call ['trʌŋkkɔ:l] *n* interlokaal gesprek
trust [trʌst] *v* vertrouwen; *n* vertrouwen *nt*
trustworthy ['trʌst,wə:ði] *adj* betrouwbaar
truth [tru:θ] *n* waarheid *c*
truthful ['tru:θfəl] *adj* waarheidsgetrouw
try [trai] *v* proberen; trachten, pogen; *n* poging *c*; ~ **on** passen
tube [tju:b] *n* pijp *c*, buis *c*; tube *c*
tuberculosis [tju:,bə:kju'lousis] *n* tuberculose *c*
Tuesday ['tju:zdi] dinsdag *c*
tug [tʌg] *v* slepen; *n* sleepboot *c*; ruk *c*
tuition [tju:'iʃən] *n* onderwijs *nt*
tulip ['tju:lip] *n* tulp *c*
tumbler ['tʌmblə] *n* beker *c*
tumour ['tju:mə] *n* gezwel *nt*, tumor *c*
tuna ['tju:nə] *n* (pl ~, ~s) tonijn *c*
tune [tju:n] *n* wijs *c*, melodie *c*; ~ **in** afstemmen
tuneful ['tju:nfəl] *adj* melodieus
tunic ['tju:nik] *n* tuniek *c*
Tunisia [tju:'niziə] Tunesië
Tunisian [tju:'niziən] *adj* Tunesisch; *n* Tunesiër *c*
tunnel ['tʌnəl] *n* tunnel *c*
turbine ['tə:bain] *n* turbine *c*
turbojet [,tə:bou'dʒet] *n* straalvliegtuig *nt*
Turk [tə:k] *n* Turk *c*
Turkey ['tə:ki] Turkije
turkey ['tə:ki] *n* kalkoen *c*
Turkish ['tə:kiʃ] *adj* Turks; ~ **bath** Turks bad
turn [tə:n] *v* draaien, keren; omkeren, omdraaien; *n* wending *c*, draai *c*; bocht *c*; beurt *c*; ~ **back** terugkeren; ~ **down** *verwerpen; ~ **into** veranderen in; ~ **off** dichtdraaien;

~ **on** aanzetten; opendraaien; ~
over omkeren; ~ **round** omkeren;
zich omdraaien

turning ['tə:niŋ] *n* bocht *c*

turning-point ['tə:niŋpɔint] *n* keerpunt
nt

turnover ['tə:ˌnouvə] *n* omzet *c*; ~ **tax**
omzetbelasting *c*

turnpike ['tə:npaik] *nAm* tolweg *c*

turpentine ['tə:pəntain] *n* terpentijn *c*

turtle ['tə:təl] *n* schildpad *c*

tutor ['tju:tə] *n* huisonderwijzer *c*;
voogd *c*

tuxedo [tʌk'si:dou] *nAm* (pl ~s, ~es)
smoking *c*

tweed [twi:d] *n* tweed *nt*

tweezers ['twi:zəz] *pl* pincet *c*

twelfth [twelfθ] *num* twaalfde

twelve [twelv] *num* twaalf

twentieth ['twentiəθ] *num* twintigste

twenty ['twenti] *num* twintig

twice [twais] *adv* tweemaal

twig [twig] *n* twijg *c*

twilight ['twailait] *n* schemering *c*

twine [twain] *n* touw *nt*

twins [twinz] *pl* tweeling *c*; **twin beds**
lits-jumeaux *nt*

twist [twist] *v* *winden; draaien; *n*
draai *c*

two [tu:] *num* twee

two-piece [ˌtu:'pi:s] *adj* tweedelig

type [taip] *v* tikken, typen; *n* type *nt*

typewriter ['taipˌraitə] *n* schrijfmachine *c*

typewritten ['taipˌritən] getypt

typhoid ['taifɔid] *n* tyfus *c*

typical ['tipikəl] *adj* kenmerkend, typisch

typist ['taipist] *n* typiste *c*

tyrant ['taiərənt] *n* tiran *c*

tyre [taiə] *n* band *c*; ~ **pressure** bandenspanning *c*

U

ugly ['ʌgli] *adj* lelijk

ulcer ['ʌlsə] *n* zweer *c*

ultimate ['ʌltimət] *adj* laatst

ultraviolet [ˌʌltrə'vaiələt] *adj* ultraviolet

umbrella [ʌm'brelə] *n* paraplu *c*

umpire ['ʌmpaiə] *n* scheidsrechter *c*

unable [ʌ'neibəl] *adj* onbekwaam

unacceptable [ˌʌnək'septəbəl] *adj* onaanvaardbaar

unaccountable [ˌʌnə'kauntəbəl] *adj* onverklaarbaar

unaccustomed [ˌʌnə'kʌstəmd] *adj* niet
gewend

unanimous [ju:'næniməs] *adj* unaniem

unanswered [ˌʌ'nɑ:nsəd] *adj* onbeantwoord

unauthorized [ˌʌ'nɔ:θəraizd] *adj* onbevoegd

unavoidable [ˌʌnə'vɔidəbəl] *adj* onvermijdelijk

unaware [ˌʌnə'wɛə] *adj* onbewust

unbearable [ʌn'bɛərəbəl] *adj* ondraaglijk

unbreakable [ˌʌn'breikəbəl] *adj* onbreekbaar

unbroken [ˌʌn'broukən] *adj* heel

unbutton [ˌʌn'bʌtən] *v* losknopen

uncertain [ʌn'sə:tən] *adj* onzeker

uncle ['ʌŋkəl] *n* oom *c*

unclean [ˌʌn'kli:n] *adj* onrein

uncomfortable [ʌn'kʌmfətəbəl] *adj* ongemakkelijk

uncommon [ʌn'kɔmən] *adj* ongewoon,
zeldzaam

unconditional [ˌʌnkən'diʃənəl] *adj* onvoorwaardelijk

unconscious [ʌn'kɔnʃəs] *adj* bewusteloos

uncork [ˌʌn'kɔ:k] *v* ontkurken

uncover [ʌn'kʌvə] *v* blootleggen

uncultivated [ˌʌnˈkʌltiveitid] *adj* onbebouwd

under [ˈʌndə] *prep* beneden, onder

undercurrent [ˈʌndəˌkʌrənt] *n* onderstroom *c*

underestimate [ˌʌndəˈrestimeit] *v* onderschatten

underground [ˈʌndəgraund] *adj* ondergronds; *n* metro *c*

underline [ˌʌndəˈlain] *v* onderstrepen

underneath [ˌʌndəˈniːθ] *adv* beneden

underpants [ˈʌndəpænts] *plAm* onderbroek *c*

undershirt [ˈʌndəʃəːt] *n* hemd *nt*

undersigned [ˈʌndəsaind] *n* ondergetekende *c*

* **understand** [ˌʌndəˈstænd] *v* *begrijpen

understanding [ˌʌndəˈstændiŋ] *n* begrip *nt*

* **undertake** [ˌʌndəˈteik] *v* *ondernemen

undertaking [ˌʌndəˈteikiŋ] *n* onderneming *c*

underwater [ˈʌndəˌwɔːtə] *adj* onderwater-

underwear [ˈʌndəweə] *n* ondergoed *nt*

undesirable [ˌʌndiˈzaiərəbəl] *adj* ongewenst

* **undo** [ˌʌnˈduː] *v* losmaken

undoubtedly [ʌnˈdautidli] *adv* ongetwijfeld

undress [ˌʌnˈdres] *v* zich uitkleden

undulating [ˈʌndjuleitiŋ] *adj* golvend

unearned [ˌʌˈnəːnd] *adj* onverdiend

uneasy [ʌˈniːzi] *adj* onbehaaglijk

uneducated [ˌʌˈnedjukeitid] *adj* ongeschoold

unemployed [ˌʌnimˈplɔid] *adj* werkeloos

unemployment [ˌʌnimˈplɔimənt] *n* werkeloosheid *c*

unequal [ˌʌˈniːkwəl] *adj* ongelijk

uneven [ˌʌˈniːvən] *adj* ongelijk, oneffen

unexpected [ˌʌnikˈspektid] *adj* onvoorzien, onverwacht

unfair [ˌʌnˈfeə] *adj* oneerlijk, onbillijk

unfaithful [ˌʌnˈfeiθfəl] *adj* ontrouw

unfamiliar [ˌʌnfəˈmiljə] *adj* onbekend

unfasten [ˌʌnˈfɑːsən] *v* losmaken

unfavourable [ˌʌnˈfeivərəbəl] *adj* ongunstig

unfit [ˌʌnˈfit] *adj* ongeschikt

unfold [ʌnˈfould] *v* ontvouwen

unfortunate [ʌnˈfɔːtʃənət] *adj* ongelukkig

unfortunately [ʌnˈfɔːtʃənətli] *adv* helaas, ongelukkigerwijs

unfriendly [ˌʌnˈfrendli] *adj* onvriendelijk

unfurnished [ˌʌnˈfəːniʃt] *adj* ongemeubileerd

ungrateful [ʌnˈgreitfəl] *adj* ondankbaar

unhappy [ʌnˈhæpi] *adj* ongelukkig

unhealthy [ʌnˈhelθi] *adj* ongezond

unhurt [ˌʌnˈhəːt] *adj* heelhuids

uniform [ˈjuːnifɔːm] *n* uniform *nt/c*; *adj* uniform

unimportant [ˌʌnimˈpɔːtənt] *adj* onbelangrijk

uninhabitable [ˌʌninˈhæbitəbəl] *adj* onbewoonbaar

uninhabited [ˌʌninˈhæbitid] *adj* onbewoond

unintentional [ˌʌninˈtenʃənəl] *adj* onopzettelijk

union [ˈjuːnjən] *n* vereniging *c*; verbond *nt*, unie *c*

unique [juːˈniːk] *adj* uniek

unit [ˈjuːnit] *n* eenheid *c*

unite [juːˈnait] *v* verenigen

United States [juːˈnaitid steits] Verenigde Staten

unity [ˈjuːnəti] *n* eenheid *c*

universal [ˌjuːniˈvəːsəl] *adj* algemeen, universeel

universe ['ju:nivə:s] *n* heelal *nt*

university [ˌju:ni'və:səti] *n* universiteit *c*

unjust [ˌʌn'dʒʌst] *adj* onrechtvaardig

unkind [ʌn'kaind] *adj* onaardig, onvriendelijk

unknown [ˌʌn'noun] *adj* onbekend

unlawful [ˌʌn'lɔ:fəl] *adj* onwettig

unlearn [ˌʌn'lə:n] *v* afleren

unless [ən'les] *conj* tenzij

unlike [ˌʌn'laik] *adj* verschillend

unlikely [ʌn'laikli] *adj* onwaarschijnlijk

unlimited [ʌn'limitid] *adj* grenzeloos, onbeperkt

unload [ˌʌn'loud] *v* lossen, *uitladen

unlock [ˌʌn'lɔk] *v* openen

unlucky [ʌn'lʌki] *adj* ongelukkig

unnecessary [ʌn'nesəsəri] *adj* onnodig

unoccupied [ˌʌ'nɔkjupaid] *adj* onbezet

unofficial [ˌʌnə'fiʃəl] *adj* officieus

unpack [ˌʌn'pæk] *v* uitpakken

unpleasant [ʌn'plezənt] *adj* onaangenaam, onplezierig; naar, vervelend

unpopular [ˌʌn'pɔpjulə] *adj* impopulair, onbemind

unprotected [ˌʌnprə'tektid] *adj* onbeschermd

unqualified [ˌʌn'kwɔlifaid] *adj* onbevoegd

unreal [ˌʌn'riəl] *adj* onwerkelijk

unreasonable [ʌn'ri:zənəbəl] *adj* onredelijk

unreliable [ˌʌnri'laiəbəl] *adj* onbetrouwbaar

unrest [ˌʌn'rest] *n* onrust *c*; rusteloosheid *c*

unsafe [ˌʌn'seif] *adj* onveilig

unsatisfactory [ˌʌnsætis'fæktəri] *adj* onbevredigend

unscrew [ˌʌn'skru:] *v* losschroeven

unselfish [ˌʌn'selfiʃ] *adj* onzelfzuchtig

unskilled [ˌʌn'skild] *adj* ongeschoold

unsound [ˌʌn'saund] *adj* ongezond

unstable [ˌʌn'steibəl] *adj* labiel

unsteady [ˌʌn'stedi] *adj* wankel, onvast; onevenwichtig

unsuccessful [ˌʌnsək'sesfəl] *adj* mislukt

unsuitable [ˌʌn'su:təbəl] *adj* ongepast

unsurpassed [ˌʌnsə'pa:st] *adj* onovertroffen

untidy [ʌn'taidi] *adj* slordig

untie [ˌʌn'tai] *v* losknopen

until [ən'til] *prep* tot

untrue [ˌʌn'tru:] *adj* onwaar

untrustworthy [ˌʌn'trʌst,wə:ði] *adj* onbetrouwbaar

unusual [ʌn'ju:ʒuəl] *adj* ongebruikelijk, ongewoon

unwell [ˌʌn'wel] *adj* onwel

unwilling [ˌʌn'wiliŋ] *adj* onwillig

unwise [ˌʌn'waiz] *adj* onverstandig

unwrap [ˌʌn'ræp] *v* uitpakken

up [ʌp] *adv* naar boven, omhoog, op

upholster [ʌp'houlstə] *v* bekleden

upkeep ['ʌpki:p] *n* onderhoud *nt*

uplands ['ʌpləndz] *pl* hoogvlakte *c*

upon [ə'pɔn] *prep* op

upper ['ʌpə] *adj* hoger, bovenst

upright ['ʌprait] *adj* rechtopstaand; *adv* overeind

upset [ʌp'set] *v* verstoren; *adj* overstuur

upside-down [ˌʌpsaid'daun] *adv* ondersteboven

upstairs [ˌʌp'stɛəz] *adv* boven; naar boven

upstream [ˌʌp'stri:m] *adv* stroomopwaarts

upwards ['ʌpwədz] *adv* naar boven

urban ['ə:bən] *adj* stedelijk

urge [ə:dʒ] *v* aansporen; *n* drang *c*

urgency ['ə:dʒənsi] *n* urgentie *c*

urgent ['ə:dʒənt] *adj* dringend

urine ['juərin] *n* urine *c*

Uruguay ['juərəgwai] Uruguay

Uruguayan [juərə'gwaiən] *adj* Uruguayaans; *n* Uruguayaan *c*

us [ʌs] *pron* ons

usable ['juːzəbəl] *adj* bruikbaar

usage ['juːzidʒ] *n* gebruik *nt*

use¹ [juːz] *v* gebruiken; *be used to gewoon *zijn; ~ up verbruiken

use² [juːs] *n* gebruik *nt*; nut *nt*; *be of ~ baten

useful ['juːsfəl] *adj* bruikbaar, nuttig

useless ['juːsləs] *adj* nutteloos

user ['juːzə] *n* gebruiker *c*

usher ['ʌʃə] *n* suppoost *c*

usherette [ˌʌʃə'ret] *n* ouvreuse *c*

usual ['juːʒuəl] *adj* gebruikelijk

usually ['juːʒuəli] *adv* gewoonlijk

utensil [juː'tensəl] *n* gereedschap *nt*, werktuig *nt*; gebruiksvoorwerp *nt*

utility [juː'tiləti] *n* nut *nt*

utilize ['juːtilaiz] *v* benutten

utmost ['ʌtmoust] *adj* uiterst

utter ['ʌtə] *adj* volslagen, totaal; *v* uiten

V

vacancy ['veikənsi] *n* vacature *c*

vacant ['veikənt] *adj* vacant

vacate [və'keit] *v* ontruimen

vacation [və'keiʃən] *n* vakantie *c*

vaccinate ['væksineit] *v* inenten

vaccination [ˌvæksi'neiʃən] *n* inenting *c*

vacuum ['vækjuəm] *n* vacuüm *nt*; *vAm* stofzuigen; ~ **cleaner** stofzuiger *c*; ~ **flask** thermosfles *c*

vagrancy ['veigrənsi] *n* landloperij *c*

vague [veig] *adj* vaag

vain [vein] *adj* ijdel; vergeefs; **in ~** vergeefs, tevergeefs

valet ['vælit] *n* bediende *c*

valid ['vælid] *adj* geldig

valley ['væli] *n* dal *nt*, vallei *c*

valuable ['væljubəl] *adj* waardevol, kostbaar; **valuables** *pl* kostbaarheden *pl*

value ['vælju:] *n* waarde *c*; *v* schatten

valve [vælv] *n* ventiel *nt*

van [væn] *n* bestelauto *c*

vanilla [və'nilə] *n* vanille *c*

vanish ['væniʃ] *v* *verdwijnen

vapour ['veipə] *n* damp *c*

variable ['vɛəriəbəl] *adj* veranderlijk

variation [ˌvɛəri'eiʃən] *n* afwisseling *c*; verandering *c*

varied ['vɛərid] *adj* gevarieerd

variety [və'raiəti] *n* verscheidenheid *c*; ~ **show** variétévoorstelling *c*; ~ **theatre** variététheater *nt*

various ['vɛəriəs] *adj* allerlei, verscheidene

varnish ['vɑːniʃ] *n* lak *c*, vernis *nt/c*; *v* lakken

vary ['vɛəri] *v* variëren, afwisselen; veranderen; verschillen

vase [vɑːz] *n* vaas *c*

vaseline ['væsəliːn] *n* vaseline *c*

vast [vɑːst] *adj* onmetelijk, uitgestrekt

vault [vɔːlt] *n* gewelf *nt*; kluis *c*

veal [viːl] *n* kalfsvlees *nt*

vegetable ['vedʒətəbəl] *n* groente *c*; ~ **merchant** groenteboer *c*

vegetarian [ˌvedʒi'tɛəriən] *n* vegetariër *c*

vegetation [ˌvedʒi'teiʃən] *n* plantengroei *c*

vehicle ['viːəkəl] *n* voertuig *nt*

veil [veil] *n* sluier *c*

vein [vein] *n* ader *c*; **varicose ~** spatader *c*

velvet ['velvit] *n* fluweel *nt*

velveteen [ˌvelvi'tiːn] *n* katoenfluweel *nt*

venerable ['venərəbəl] *adj* eerbiedwaardig

venereal disease [vi'niəriəl di'ziːz] geslachtsziekte *c*

Venezuela [ˌveniˈzweilə] Venezuela

Venezuelan [ˌveniˈzweilən] adj Venezo-laans; n Venezolaan c

ventilate [ˈventileit] v ventileren; luchten

ventilation [ˌventiˈleiʃən] n ventilatie c; luchtverversing c

ventilator [ˈventileitə] n ventilator c

venture [ˈventʃə] v wagen

veranda [vəˈrændə] n veranda c

verb [vəːb] n werkwoord nt

verbal [ˈvəːbəl] adj mondeling

verdict [ˈvəːdikt] n vonnis nt, uitspraak c

verge [vəːdʒ] n rand c

verify [ˈverifai] v verifiëren

verse [vəːs] n vers nt

version [ˈvəːʃən] n versie c; vertaling c

versus [ˈvəːsəs] prep contra

vertical [ˈvəːtikəl] adj verticaal

vertigo [ˈvəːtigou] n duizeling c

very [ˈveri] adv erg, zeer; adj precies, waar, werkelijk; uiterst

vessel [ˈvesəl] n vaartuig nt, schip nt; vat nt

vest [vest] n hemd nt; nAm vest nt

veterinary surgeon [ˈvetrinəri ˈsəːdʒən] dierenarts c

via [vaiə] prep via

viaduct [ˈvaiədʌkt] n viaduct c/nt

vibrate [vaiˈbreit] v trillen

vibration [vaiˈbreiʃən] n vibratie c

vicinity [viˈsinəti] n nabijheid c, buurt c

vicious [ˈviʃəs] adj boosaardig

victim [ˈviktim] n slachtoffer nt; dupe c

victory [ˈviktəri] n overwinning c

video [ˈvidiou] n video c; ~ camera video camera; ~ cassette video cassette; ~ recorder video recorder

view [vjuː] n uitzicht nt; opvatting c, mening c; v *bekijken

view-finder [ˈvjuːˌfaində] n zoeker c

vigilant [ˈvidʒilənt] adj waakzaam

villa [ˈvilə] n villa c

village [ˈvilidʒ] n dorp nt

villain [ˈvilən] n boef c

vine [vain] n wijnstok c

vinegar [ˈvinigə] n azijn c

vineyard [ˈvinjəd] n wijngaard c

vintage [ˈvintidʒ] n wijnoogst c

violation [vaiəˈleiʃən] n schending c

violence [ˈvaiələns] n geweld nt

violent [ˈvaiələnt] adj gewelddadig; hevig, heftig

violet [ˈvaiələt] n viooltje nt; adj violet

violin [vaiəˈlin] n viool c

virgin [ˈvəːdʒin] n maagd c

virtue [ˈvəːtʃuː] n deugd c

visa [ˈviːzə] n visum nt

visibility [ˌvizəˈbiləti] n zicht nt

visible [ˈvizəbəl] adj zichtbaar

vision [ˈviʒən] n visie c

visit [ˈvizit] v *bezoeken; n visite c, bezoek nt; **visiting hours** bezoekuren pl

visiting-card [ˈvizitiŋkaːd] n visitekaartje nt

visitor [ˈvizitə] n bezoeker c

vital [ˈvaitəl] adj essentieel

vitamin [ˈvitəmin] n vitamine c

vivid [ˈvivid] adj levendig

vocabulary [vəˈkæbjuləri] n vocabulaire nt, woordenschat c; woordenlijst c

vocal [ˈvoukəl] adj vocaal

vocalist [ˈvoukəlist] n zanger c

voice [vois] n stem c

void [void] adj nietig

volcano [vɔlˈkeinou] n (pl ~es, ~s) vulkaan c

volt [voult] n volt c

voltage [ˈvoultidʒ] n voltage c/nt

volume [ˈvɔljum] n volume nt; deel nt

voluntary ['volǝntǝri] *adj* vrijwillig
volunteer [,volǝn'tiǝ] *n* vrijwilliger *c*
vomit ['vomit] *v* braken, *overgeven
vote [vout] *v* stemmen; *n* stem *c*;
stemming *c*
voucher ['vautʃǝ] *n* bon *c*, bewijs *nt*
vow [vau] *n* gelofte *c*, eed *c*; *v* *zwe-ren
vowel ['vauǝl] *n* klinker *c*
voyage ['voiidʒ] *n* reis *c*
vulgar ['vʌlgǝ] *adj* vulgair; volks-, or-dinair
vulnerable ['vʌlnǝrǝbǝl] *adj* kwetsbaar
vulture ['vʌltʃǝ] *n* gier *c*

W

wade [weid] *v* waden
wafer ['weifǝ] *n* wafel *c*
waffle ['wɔfǝl] *n* wafel *c*
wages ['weidʒiz] *pl* loon *nt*
waggon ['wægǝn] *n* wagon *c*
waist [weist] *n* taille *c*, middel *nt*
waistcoat ['weiskout] *n* vest *nt*
wait [weit] *v* wachten; ~ **on** bedienen
waiter ['weitǝ] *n* ober *c*, kelner *c*
waiting *n* het wachten
waiting-list ['weitiŋlist] *n* wachtlijst *c*
waiting-room ['weitiŋru:m] *n* wachtka-mer *c*
waitress ['weitris] *n* serveerster *c*
***wake** [weik] *v* wekken; ~ **up** ontwa-ken, wakker *worden
walk [wɔ:k] *v* *lopen; wandelen; *n* wandeling *c*; loop *c*; **walking** te voet
walker ['wɔ:kǝ] *n* wandelaar *c*
walking-stick ['wɔ:kiŋstik] *n* wandel-stok *c*
wall [wɔ:l] *n* muur *c*; wand *c*
wallet ['wɔlit] *n* portefeuille *c*
wallpaper ['wɔ:l,peipǝ] *n* behang *nt*

walnut ['wɔ:lnʌt] *n* walnoot *c*
waltz [wɔ:ls] *n* wals *c*
wander ['wɔndǝ] *v* *rondzwerven, *zwerven
want [wɔnt] *v* *willen; wensen; *n* be-hoefte *c*; gebrek *nt*, gemis *nt*
war [wɔ:] *n* oorlog *c*
warden ['wɔ:dǝn] *n* bewaker *c*, opzich-ter *c*
wardrobe ['wɔ:droub] *n* klerenkast *c*, garderobe *c*
warehouse ['wεǝhaus] *n* magazijn *nt*, pakhuis *nt*
wares [wεǝz] *pl* waren *pl*
warm [wɔ:m] *adj* heet, warm; *v* ver-warmen
warmth [wɔ:mθ] *n* warmte *c*
warn [wɔ:n] *v* waarschuwen
warning ['wɔ:niŋ] *n* waarschuwing *c*
wary ['wεǝri] *adj* behoedzaam
was [wɔz] *v* (p be)
wash [wɔʃ] *v* *wassen; ~ **and wear** zelfstrijkend; ~ **up** afwassen
washable ['wɔʃǝbǝl] *adj* wasbaar
wash-basin ['wɔʃ,beisǝn] *n* wasbekken *nt*
washing ['wɔʃiŋ] *n* was *c*; wasgoed *nt*
washing-machine ['wɔʃiŋmǝ,ʃi:n] *n* wasmachine *c*
washing-powder ['wɔʃiŋ,paudǝ] *n* was-poeder *nt*
washroom ['wɔʃru:m] *nAm* toilet *nt*
wash-stand ['wɔʃstænd] *n* wastafel *c*
wasp [wɔsp] *n* wesp *c*
waste [weist] *v* verspillen; *n* verspil-ling *c*; *adj* braak
wasteful ['weistfǝl] *adj* verkwistend
wastepaper-basket [weist'peipǝ,ba:-skit] *n* prullenmand *c*
watch [wɔtʃ] *v* *kijken naar, *gade-slaan; letten op; *n* horloge *nt*; ~ **for** *uitkijken naar; ~ **out** *uitkij-ken
watch-maker ['wɔtʃ,meikǝ] *n* horloge-

maker c

watch-strap ['wɔtʃstræp] n horlogebandje nt

water ['wɔːtə] n water nt; **iced** ~ ijswater nt; **running** ~ stromend water; ~ **pump** waterpomp c; ~ **ski**
waterski c

water-colour ['wɔːtə,kʌlə] n waterverf
c; aquarel c

watercress ['wɔːtəkres] n waterkers c

waterfall ['wɔːtəfɔːl] n waterval c

watermelon ['wɔːtə,melən] n watermeloen c

waterproof ['wɔːtəpruːf] adj waterdicht

water-softener [,wɔːtə,sɔfnə] n wasverzachter c

waterway ['wɔːtəwei] n vaarwater nt

watt [wɔt] n watt c

wave [weiv] n golf c; v zwaaien

wave-length ['weivleŋθ] n golflengte c

wavy ['weivi] adj golvend

wax [wæks] n was c

waxworks ['wækswəːks] pl wassenbeeldenmuseum nt

way [wei] n manier c, wijze c; weg c;
kant c, richting c; afstand c; **any** ~
hoe dan ook; **by the** ~ tussen twee
haakjes; **one-way traffic** eenricht-
tingsverkeer nt; **out of the** ~ afgelegen; **the other** ~ **round** andersom; ~ **back** terugweg c; ~ **in** ingang c; ~ **out** uitgang c

wayside ['weisaid] n wegkant c

we [wiː] pron we

weak [wiːk] adj zwak; slap

weakness ['wiːknəs] n zwakheid c

wealth [welθ] n rijkdom c

wealthy ['welθi] adj rijk

weapon ['wepən] n wapen nt

***wear** [weə] v *aanhebben, *dragen;
~ **out** *verslijten

weary ['wiəri] adj moe, vermoeid

weather ['weðə] n weer nt; ~ **fore-**

cast weerbericht nt

***weave** [wiːv] v *weven

weaver ['wiːvə] n wever c

wedding ['wediŋ] n huwelijk nt, bruiloft c

wedding-ring ['wediŋriŋ] n trouwring
c

wedge [wedʒ] n wig c

Wednesday ['wenzdi] woensdag c

weed [wiːd] n onkruid nt

week [wiːk] n week c

weekday ['wiːkdei] n weekdag c

weekly ['wiːkli] adj wekelijks

***weep** [wiːp] v huilen

weigh [wei] v *wegen

weighing-machine ['weiiŋməʃiːn] n
weegschaal c

weight [weit] n gewicht c

welcome ['welkəm] adj welkom; n
welkom nt; v verwelkomen

weld [weld] v lassen

welfare ['welfeə] n welzijn nt

well¹ [wel] adv goed; adj gezond; **as**
~ ook, eveneens; **as** ~ **as** evenals;
well! welnu!

well² [wel] n bron c, put c

well-founded [,wel'faundid] adj gegrond

well-known ['welnoun] adj bekend

well-to-do [,weltə'duː] adj bemiddeld

went [went] v (p go)

were [wəː] v (p be)

west [west] n west c, westen nt

westerly ['westəli] adj westelijk

western ['westən] adj westers

wet [wet] adj nat; vochtig

whale [weil] n walvis c

wharf [wɔːf] n (pl ~s, wharves) kade c

what [wɔt] pron wat; ~ **for** waarom

whatever [wɔ'tevə] pron wat dan ook

wheat [wiːt] n tarwe c

wheel [wiːl] n wiel nt

wheelbarrow ['wiːl,bærou] n kruiwagen c

wheelchair ['wi:ltʃɛə] n rolstoel c

when [wen] adv wanneer; conj als, toen, wanneer

whenever [we'nevə] conj wanneer ook

where [wɛə] adv waar; conj waar

wherever [wɛə'revə] conj waar ook

whether ['weðə] conj of; whether ... or of ... of

which [witʃ] pron welk; dat

whichever [wi'tʃevə] adj welk ook

while [wail] conj terwijl; n poosje nt

whilst [wailst] conj terwijl

whim [wim] n gril c, bevlieging c

whip [wip] n zweep c; v kloppen

whiskers ['wiskəz] pl bakkebaarden pl

whisper ['wispə] v fluisteren; n gefluister nt

whistle ['wisəl] v *fluiten; n fluitje nt

white [wait] adj wit; blank

whitebait ['waitbeit] n witvis c

whiting ['waitiŋ] n (pl ~) wijting c

Whitsun ['witsən] Pinksteren

who [hu:] pron wie; die

whoever [hu:'evə] pron wie ook

whole [houl] adj geheel, heel; n geheel nt

wholesale ['houlseil] n groothandel c; ~ **dealer** grossier c

wholesome ['houlsəm] adj gezond

wholly ['houlli] adv helemaal

whom [hu:m] pron wie

whore [hɔ:] n hoer c

whose [hu:z] pron wiens; van wie

why [wai] adv waarom

wicked ['wikid] adj slecht

wide [waid] adj wijd, breed

widen ['waidən] v verwijden

widow ['widou] n weduwe c

widower ['widouə] n weduwnaar c

width [widθ] n breedte c

wife [waif] n (pl wives) echtgenote c, vrouw c

wig [wig] n pruik c

wild [waild] adj wild; woest

will [wil] n wil c; testament nt

*** will** [wil] v *willen; *zullen

willing ['wiliŋ] adj bereid

willingly ['wiliŋli] adv graag

will-power ['wilpauə] n wilskracht c

*** win** [win] v *winnen

wind [wind] n wind c

*** wind** [waind] v kronkelen; *opwinden, *winden

winding ['waindiŋ] adj kronkelig

windmill ['windmil] n molen c, windmolen c

window ['windou] n raam nt

window-sill ['windousil] n vensterbank c

windscreen ['windskri:n] n voorruit c; ~ **wiper** ruitenwisser c

windshield ['windʃi:ld] nAm voorruit c; ~ **wiper** Am ruitenwisser c

windy ['windi] adj winderig

wine [wain] n wijn c

wine-cellar ['wain,selə] n wijnkelder c

wine-list ['wainlist] n wijnkaart c

wine-merchant ['wain,mə:tʃənt] n wijnkoper c

wine-waiter ['wain,weitə] n wijnkelner c

wing [wiŋ] n vleugel c

winkle ['wiŋkəl] n alikruik c

winner ['winə] n winnaar c

winning ['winiŋ] adj winnend; **winnings** pl winst c

winter ['wintə] n winter c; ~ **sports** wintersport c

wipe [waip] v vegen, afvegen

wire [waiə] n draad c; ijzerdraad nt

wireless ['waiələs] n radio c

wisdom ['wizdəm] n wijsheid c

wise [waiz] adj wijs

wish [wiʃ] v verlangen, wensen; n verlangen nt, wens c

witch [witʃ] n heks c

with [wið] prep met; bij; van

*** withdraw** [wið'drɔ:] v *terugtrekken

within [wi'ðin] *prep* binnen; *adv* van binnen

without [wi'ðaut] *prep* zonder

witness ['witnəs] *n* getuige *c*

wits [wits] *pl* verstand *nt*

witty ['witi] *adj* geestig

wolf [wulf] *n* (pl wolves) wolf *c*

woman ['wumən] *n* (pl women) vrouw *c*

womb [wu:m] *n* baarmoeder *c*

won [wʌn] *v* (p, pp win)

wonder ['wʌndə] *n* wonder *nt*; verwondering *c*; *v* zich *afvragen

wonderful ['wʌndəfəl] *adj* prachtig, verrukkelijk; heerlijk

wood [wud] *n* hout *nt*; bos *nt*

wood-carving ['wud,ka:viŋ] *n* houtsnijwerk *nt*

wooded ['wudid] *adj* bebost

wooden ['wudən] *adj* houten; ~ **shoe** klomp *c*

woodland ['wudlənd] *n* bebost gebied *nt*

wool [wul] *n* wol *c*; **darning** ~ stopgaren *nt*

woollen ['wulən] *adj* wollen

word [wə:d] *n* woord *nt*

wore [wɔ:] *v* (p wear)

work [wə:k] *n* werk *nt*; arbeid *c*; *v* werken; functioneren; **working day** werkdag *c*; ~ **of art** kunstwerk *nt*; ~ **permit** werkvergunning *c*

worker ['wə:kə] *n* arbeider *c*

working ['wə:kiŋ] *n* werking *c*

workman ['wə:kmən] *n* (pl -men) arbeider *c*

works [wə:ks] *pl* fabriek *c*

workshop ['wə:kʃɔp] *n* werkplaats *c*

world [wə:ld] *n* wereld *c*; ~ **war** wereldoorlog *c*

world-famous [,wə:ld'feiməs] *adj* wereldberoemd

world-wide ['wə:ldwaid] *adj* wereldomvattend

worm [wə:m] *n* worm *c*

worn [wɔ:n] *adj* (pp wear) versleten

worn-out [,wɔ:n'aut] *adj* versleten

worried ['wʌrid] *adj* ongerust

worry ['wʌri] *v* zich ongerust maken; *n* zorg *c*, bezorgdheid *c*

worse [wə:s] *adj* slechter; *adv* erger

worship ['wə:ʃip] *v* *aanbidden; *n* eredienst *c*

worst [wə:st] *adj* slechtst; *adv* ergst

worsted ['wustid] *n* kamgaren *nt*

worth [wə:θ] *n* waarde *c*; *be ~ waard *zijn; *be worth-while de moeite waard *zijn

worthless ['wə:θləs] *adj* waardeloos

worthy of ['wə:ði ɔv] waard

would [wud] *v* (p will) gewoon *zijn

wound¹ [wu:nd] *n* wond *c*; *v* kwetsen, verwonden

wound² [waund] *v* (p, pp wind)

wrap [ræp] *v* inpakken

wreck [rek] *n* wrak *nt*; *v* vernielen

wrench [rentʃ] *n* sleutel *c*; ruk *c*; *v* verdraaien

wrinkle ['riŋkəl] *n* rimpel *c*

wrist [rist] *n* pols *c*

wrist-watch ['ristwɔtʃ] *n* polshorloge *nt*

***write** [rait] *v* *schrijven; **in writing** schriftelijk; ~ **down** *opschrijven

writer ['raitə] *n* schrijver *c*

writing-pad ['raitiŋpæd] *n* blocnote *c*, schrijfblok *nt*

writing-paper ['raitiŋ,peipə] *n* schrijfpapier *nt*

written ['ritən] *adj* (pp write) schriftelijk

wrong [rɔŋ] *adj* verkeerd, fout; *n* onrecht *nt*; *v* onrecht *aandoen; *be ~ ongelijk *hebben

wrote [rout] *v* (p write)

X

Xmas ['krisməs] Kerstmis
X-ray ['eksrei] n röntgenfoto c; v
 doorlichten

Y

yacht [jɔt] n jacht nt
yacht-club ['jɔtklʌb] n zeilclub c
yachting ['jɔtiŋ] n zeilsport c
yard [jɑ:d] n erf nt
yarn [jɑ:n] n garen nt
yawn [jɔ:n] v gapen, geeuwen
year [jiə] n jaar nt
yearly ['jiəli] adj jaarlijks
yeast [ji:st] n gist c
yell [jel] v gillen; n gil c
yellow ['jelou] adj geel
yes [jes] ja
yesterday ['jestədi] adv gisteren
yet [jet] adv nog; conj toch, echter,
 maar
yield [ji:ld] v *opbrengen; *toegeven
yoke [jouk] n juk nt

yolk [jouk] n dooier c
you [ju:] pron je; jou; u; jullie
young [jʌŋ] adj jong
your [jɔ:] adj uw; jouw; jullie
yourself [jɔ:'self] pron je; zelf
yourselves [jɔ:'selvz] pron je; zelf
youth [ju:θ] n jeugd c; ~ hostel
 jeugdherberg c

Z

Zaire [zɑ:'iə] Zaïre
zeal [zi:l] n ijver c
zealous ['zeləs] adj ijverig
zebra ['zi:brə] n zebra c
zenith ['zeniθ] n zenit nt; toppunt nt
zero ['ziərou] n (pl ~s) nul c
zest [zest] n animo c
zinc [ziŋk] n zink nt
zip [zip] n ritssluiting c; ~ code Am
 postcode c
zipper ['zipə] n ritssluiting c
zodiac ['zoudiæk] n dierenriem c
zombie ['zɔmbi] n levend lijk nt
zone [zoun] n zone c; gebied nt
zoo [zu:] n (pl ~s) dierentuin c
zoology [zou'ɔlədʒi] n zoölogie c

Dutch-English Dictionary

Engels-Nederlands Woordenboek

Culinaire woordenlijst

Spijzen

almond amandel

anchovy ansjovis

angel food cake witte, ronde cake, gemaakt van suiker, eiwit en bloem

angels on horseback geroosterde, met spek omwikkelde oesters

appetizer borrelhapje

apple appel
~ **charlotte** lagen van appels en sneetjes boord met vanille en slagroom
~ **dumpling** appelbol
~ **sauce** appelmoes

apricot abrikoos

Arbroath smoky gerookte schelvis

artichoke artisjok

asparagus asperge
~ **tip** aspergepunt

aspic koude schotel in gelei

assorted gevarieerd, gemengd

bacon spek
~ **and eggs** spiegeleieren met spek

bagel klein kransvormig broodje

baked in de oven gebakken, gebraden
~ **Alaska** omelette sibérienne
~ **beans** witte bonen in tomatensaus

~ **potato** hele, ongeschilde aardappel, in de oven gebakken

Bakewell tart amandeltaart met jam

baloney worstsoort

banana banaan
~ **split** in de lengte gehalveerde banaan met ijs, noten en overgoten met vruchtensiroop of vloeibare chocolade

barbecue 1) gehakt rundvlees in tomatensaus in een broodje geserveerd 2) maaltijd van geroosterd vlees in de open lucht
~ **sauce** zeer scherpe tomatensaus

barbecued geroosterd op houtskool

basil basilicum

bass baars

bean boon

beef rundvlees
~ **olive** blinde vink

beefburger gehakte, geroosterde biefstuk geserveerd in een broodje

beet, beetroot rode biet

bilberry blauwe bosbes

bill rekening
~ **of fare** menu

biscuit 1) koekje (GB) 2) broodje (US)

black pudding bloedworst

blackberry braam

blackcurrant zwarte bes

bloater verse bokking

blood sausage bloedworst

blueberry blauwe bosbes

boiled gekookt

Bologna (sausage) worstsoort

bone bot

boned ontbeend

Boston baked beans witte bonen met stukjes spek en stroop

Boston cream pie taart met vla-vulling en chocoladeglazuur

brains hersenen

braised gestoofd

bramble pudding bramenpudding, vaak met schijfjes appel erin

braunschweiger gerookte lever-worst

bread brood

breaded gepaneerd

breakfast ontbijt

bream brasem

breast borst (stuk)

brisket borststuk

broad bean tuinboon

broth bouillon

brown Betty afwisselende lagen appel, perzik of kers en paneer-meel, met suiker en kruiderijen, in de oven gebakken

brunch ontbijt en lunch gecombi-neerd

brussels sprout spruitje

bubble and squeak soort panne-koek van gebakken aardappe-len en kool, soms met vlees

bun 1) krentebroodje (GB) 2) klein, luchtig broodje (US)

butter boter

buttered beboterd

cabbage kool

Caesar salad sla met gerooster-de, naar knoflook smakende brooddobbelsteentjes, anjovis en geraspte kaas

cake gebak, koek, cake, taart

cakes koekjes, taartjes

calf kalfsvlees

Canadian bacon gerookt spek in dikke plakken gesneden

canapé belegd sneetje brood

cantaloupe wratmeloen, kante-loep

caper kappertje

capercaillie, capercailzie auer-hoen

carp karper

carrot wortel

cashew vrucht van de cajouboom

casserole gestoofd

catfish meerval (vis)

catsup ketchup

cauliflower bloemkool

celery selderie

cereal graansoorten voor bij het ontbijt, zoals maïsvlokken, ha-vermout, met melk en suiker

hot ~ havermoutpap

chateaubriand dubbele biefstuk van de haas

check rekening

Cheddar (cheese) stevige kaas met een milde, zurige smaak

cheese kaas

~ board kaasassortiment

~ cake kaaskoekje

cheeseburger gehakte, gerooster-de biefstuk met schijfje kaas, opgediend in een broodje

chef's salad salade van ham, kip, eieren, tomaten, sla en kaas

cherry kers

chestnut tamme kastanje

chicken kip

chicory 1) Brussels lof (GB) 2) andijvie (US)

chili con carne gehakt rundvlees gestoofd met bruine bonen, Spaanse pepers en komijn

chili pepper rode Spaanse pepers

chips 1) patates frites (GB) 2) aardappel chips (US)

chitt(er)lings varkenspens

chive bieslook

chocolate chocolade

$\sim$ **pudding** 1) chocoladepudding bereid met verkruimelde koekjes, suiker, eieren en bloem (GB) 2) chocolademousse (US)

choice keus

chop kotelet

$\sim$ **suey** gerecht, bereid uit fijngesneden varkensvlees en kip, groenten en rijst (tjap tjoy)

chopped fijngehakt

chowder dikke soep van vis, schaal- en schelpdieren of kip, met groenten

Christmas pudding speciaal Kerstgebak, soms geflambeerd

chutney sterke Indische kruiderij

cinnamon kaneel

clam steenmossel

club sandwich dubbele sandwich met kip, spek, sla, tomaat en mayonaise

cobbler vruchtenmoes met deeg, soms met ijs

cock-a-leekie soup preisoep met kip

coconut kokosnoot

cod kabeljauw

Colchester oyster beste soort Engelse oester

cold cuts/meat koud vlees

coleslaw koolsla

compote vruchten op sap

condiment kruiderij

consommé heldere soep

cooked gekookt

cookie koekje

corn 1) koren (GB) 2) maïs (US)

$\sim$ **on the cob** maïskolf

cornflakes maïsvlokken

cottage cheese witte, verse kaas

cottage pie gehakt vlees met uien, bedekt met aardappelpuree in de oven gebakken

course gerecht

cover charge couvert

crab krab

cracker droog beschuit van bladerdeeg

cranberry veenbes

$\sim$ **sauce** veenbessengelei

crawfish, crayfish 1) rivierkreeft 2) langoest (GB) 3) steurgarnaal (US)

cream 1) room 2) vlaai (dessert) 3) gebonden soep

$\sim$ **cheese** roomkaas

$\sim$ **puff** roomsoes

creamed potatoes aardappelen in witte roomsaus

creole op Creoolse wijze bereid; over het algemeen zeer pikant, met tomaten, paprika's en uien, geserveerd met rijst

cress waterkers

crisps chips

croquette kroket

crumpet rond, licht broodje, geroosterd en beboterd

cucumber komkommer

Cumberland ham zeer fijne, gerookte Engelse ham

Cumberland sauce rode bessengelei, op smaak gemaakt met wijn, sinaasappelsap en kruiderijen

cupcake klein rond gebakje

cured gezouten, gerookt, gepekeld (vis en vlees)

currant krent
curried met kerrie
curry kerrie
custard custardvla
cutlet vleeslapje, kotelet
dab schar
Danish pastry soort luchtig koffie-brood
date dadel
Derby cheese gele kaas met pikante smaak
devilled sterk gekruid
devil's food cake machtige chocoladetaart
devils on horseback gekookte pruimen, gevuld met amandelen en ansjovis, omwikkeld met spek, geroosterd en geserveerd op toost
Devonshire cream dikke, klonterige room
diced in dobbelsteentjes gesneden
diet food volgens voedselleer bereid
dill dille
dinner diner, avondeten
dish schotel, gerecht
donut, doughnut soort oliebol
double cream volle room
Dover sole tong uit Dover, in Engeland zeer gewaardeerd
dressing 1) slasaus 2) vulsel voor kalkoen (US)
Dublin Bay prawn steurgarnaal
duck eend
duckling jonge eend
dumpling knoedel
Dutch apple pie appeltaart bedekt met een mengsel van boter en bruine suiker
éclair langwerpig, met chocolade of caramel geglaceerd roomtaartje
eel paling

egg ei
  boiled ~ gekookt
  fried ~ spiegelei
  hard-boiled ~ hardgekookt
  poached ~ gepocheerd
  scrambled ~ roerei
  soft-boiled ~ zachtgekookt
eggplant aubergine, eierplant
endive 1) andijvie (GB) 2) Brussels lof (US)
entrecôte tussenrib
entrée 1) voorgerecht (GB) 2) hoofdgerecht (US)
escalope schnitzel
fennel venkel
fig vijg
filet mignon kalfs- of varkenshaasje
fillet filet van vlees of vis
finnan haddock gerookte schelvis
fish vis
  ~ **and chips** gebakken vis met frites
  ~ **cake** viskoekje
flan vla, ronde taart met vruchten
flapjack (appel)flap
flounder bot
forcemeat farce, gehakt
fowl gevogelte
frankfurter knakworst
French bean slaboon
French bread stokbrood
French dressing 1) slasaus in olie, azijn en tuinkruiden (GB) 2) romige slasaus met ketchup (US)
french fries patates frites
French toast wentelteefje
fresh vers
fricassée ragoût, vleeshachee
fried gebakken in een koekepan of in de olie
fritter beignet, poffertje
frogs' legs kikkerbilletjes

frosting suikerglazuur
fruit vrucht
fry bakken
game wild
gammon gerookte ham
garfish geep (snoekachtige zeevis)
garlic knoflook
garnish garnituur
gherkin augurkje
giblets afval van gevogelte
ginger gember
goose gans
~ **berry** kruisbes
grape druif
~ **fruit** pompelmoes
grated geraspt
gravy vleesjus
grayling vlagzalm
green bean slaboon
green pepper groene paprika
green salad sla
greens groenten
grilled geroosterd
grilse jonge zalm
grouse korhoen
gumbo 1) groente van Afrikaanse afkomst 2) Creools gerecht van vlees, kip of vis, met *okra*zaden, uien, tomaten en kruiden
haddock gerookte schelvis
haggis hart, longen en lever van een schaap fijn gehakt en in de maag gekookt met reuzel, havermeel en uien
hake stokvis
halibut heilbot
ham and eggs spiegeleieren met ham
hamburger gehakt, geroosterd rundvlees opgediend in een broodje
hare haas
haricot bean prinsessenboon, witte boon

hash 1) gehakt of fijngesneden vlees 2) hachee met aardappelen en groenten
hazelnut hazelnoot
heart hart
herb tuinkruid
herring haring
home-made eigengemaakt, van het huis
hominy grits brij van maïsgrutten
honey honing
~ **dew melon** zoete meloen met geelgroen vruchtvlees
hors-d'œuvre voorgerecht (Engeland)
horse-radish mierikswortel
hot 1) heet, warm 2) sterk gekruid
~ **cross bun** fijn broodje gevuld met rozijnen en kruisvormig bedekt met glazuur, wordt in de vastentijd gegeten (brioche)
~ **dog** hot dog, warme worst in een broodje
huckleberry blauwe bosbes
hush puppy beignet van maïsmeel en uien
ice-cream ijs
iced gekoeld
icing suikerglazuur
Idaho baked potato soort bintje, ongeschild in de oven gepoft
Irish stew hutspot van schapevlees, aardappelen en uien
Italian dressing slasaus van olie, azijn en tuinkruiden
jellied in gelei
Jell-O gelatinedessert
jelly jam; gelei
Jerusalem artichoke aardpeer
John Dory zonnevis (zeevis)
jugged hare hazepeper
juice sap
juniper berry jeneverbes
junket gestremde melk (wrongel),

gesuikerd

kale boerenkool

kedgeree stukjes vis met rijst, eiren, boter, wordt vaak als warm gerecht aan het ontbijt geserveerd

kidney nier

kipper bokking

lamb lamsvlees

Lancashire hot pot schotel in de oven van ragoût van lamsvlees en nieren met uien, kruiderijen en aardappelen

larded gelardeerd

lean mager

leek prei

leg bout

lemon citroen

~ **sole** scharretong

lentil linze

lettuce kropsla, veldsla

lima bean tuinboon

lime limoen, kleine groene citroen

liver lever

loaf brood

lobster kreeft

loin lendestuk

Long Island duck eend van Long Island, in de VS zeer goed bekend staande soort

low-calorie laag caloriegehalte

lox gerookte zalm

macaroon bitterkoekje

mackerel makreel

maize maïs

mandarin mandarijntje

maple syrup ahornstroop

marinated gemarineerd

marjoram marjolein

marmalade marmelade van sinaasappelen of andere citrusvruchten

marrow beenmerg

~ **bone** mergpijp

marshmallow Amerikaans snoepgoed; *marshmallows* worden vaak aan warme chocola en allerlei soorten desserts toegevoegd

marzipan marsepein

mashed potatoes aardappelpuree

meal maaltijd

meat vlees

~ **ball** gehaktbal

~ **loaf** gehaktbrood

~ **pâté** vleespastei

medium (done) net gaar

melon meloen

melted gesmolten

Melton Mowbray pie pastei bestaande uit gehakt vlees en kruiden

meringue schuimgebak, schuimpje

milk melk

mince fijnhakken

~ **pie** pasteitje met krenten, rozijnen, fijngehakte geconfijte vruchten en appelen (met of zonder vlees)

minced fijngehakt

~ **meat** fijngehakt vlees

mint munt (kruid)

minute steak kort gebakken biefstuk

mixed gemengd

~ **grill** aan een stokje geregen, geroosterde stukjes vlees

molasses melasse, stroop

morel morille, zeer gewaardeerde paddestoelsoort

mousse 1) dessert van geklopte eieren en slagroom 2) luchtig pasteitje

mulberry moerbei

mullet harder (vis gelijkend op een karper)

mulligatawny soup zeer sterk ge-

kruide soep van Indische afkomst met wortels, uien, *chutney* en kip met kerrie
mushroom paddestoel
muskmelon meloen
mussel mossel
mustard mosterd
mutton schapevlees
noodle noedel
nut noot
oatmeal (porridge) havermoutpap
oil olie
okra zaad van de *gumbo*, wordt
gebruikt om soepen en ragoût-
sausen aan te dikken
olive olijf
onion ui
orange sinaasappel
ox tongue ossetong
oxtail ossestaart
oyster oester
pancake pannekoek
Parmesan (cheese) Parmezaanse
kaas
parsley peterselie
parsnip pastinaak, witte peen
partridge patrijs
pastry banket, gebakje, taartje
pasty pastei
pea doperwt
peach perzik
peanut olienoot, pinda
~ **butter** pindakaas
pear peer
pearl barley parelgerst
pepper peper
~ **mint** pepermunt
perch baars
persimmon dadelpruim
pheasant fazant
pickerel jonge snoek
pickle 1) groente of geconfijte
vrucht in pekelzuur 2) in het
bijzonder augurkje (US)

pickled in pekel bewaard
pie pastei, vaak met een deksel
van bladerdeeg, gevuld met
vlees, groenten of vruchten
pig varken
pigeon duif
pike snoek
pineapple ananas
plaice schol
plain natuur, zonder iets erin
plate bord, schaal
plum pruim
~ **pudding** speciaal Kerstgebak, soms geflambeerd
poached gepocheerd
popcorn gepofte maïskorrels
popover klein, luchtig broodje
pork varkensvlees
porridge havermoutpap
porterhouse steak biefstuk van de
haas
pot roast met groenten gesmoord
rundvlees
potato aardappel
~ **chips** 1) patates frites (GB)
2) aardappel chips (US)
~ **in its jacket** aardappel in de
schil gekookt en opgediend
potted shrimps garnalen in gesmolten boter, koud opgediend
in een vorm
poultry gevogelte, pluimvee
prawn grote garnaal
prune gedroogde pruim
ptarmigan sneeuwhoen
pudding soepel of stevig beslag
van meel en eieren, gegarneerd
met vlees, vis, groenten of
vruchten, in de oven gebakken
of gaargestoomd; nagerecht
pumpernickel zwart roggebrood
pumpkin pompoen
quail kwartel
quince kweepeer

rabbit konijn
radish radijs
rainbow trout regenboogforel
raisin rozijn
rare ongaar
raspberry framboos
raw rauw
red mullet soort harder (zeevis)
red (sweet) pepper rode paprika
redcurrant rode bes
relish kruiderij gemaakt van fijngesneden groente in azijn
rhubarb rabarber
rib (of beef) ribstuk (van het rund)
ribe-eye steak entrecôte
rice rijst
rissole vlees- of viskroket
river trout rivierforel
roast braadstuk
roasted gebraden
Rock Cornish hen piepkuiken
roe viskuit
roll broodje
rollmop herring rolmops, gemari-
   neerde haringfilet
round steak runderschijf
Rubens sandwich cornedbeef op
   een toostje, met zuurkool, kaas
   en slasaus; warm opgediend
rump steak biefstuk
rusk beschuit
rye bread roggebrood
saddle lendestuk
saffron saffraan
sage salie
salad sla
   ~ **bar** verschillende soorten
      slaatjes, tomaten, prinsessen-
      bonen
   ~ **cream** slasaus, licht gezoet
   ~ **dressing** slasaus
salmon zalm
   ~ **trout** zalmforel
salt zout

salted gezouten
sardine sardien
sauce saus
sauerkraut zuurkool
sausage worst
sauté(ed) snel in boter, olie of vet
   gebakken
scallop 1) kamschelp 2) kalfslapje
scampi steurgarnaal
scone zacht broodje, warm geserveerd, met boter en jam
Scotch broth runder- of schape-
   bouillon met groenten
Scotch woodcock toost met roerei
   en ansjovis
sea bass zeebaars
sea kale zeekool
seafood zeebanket
(in) season (in het) seizoen
seasoning kruiderij
service bediening
   ~ **charge** bedieningstarief
   ~ **included** inclusief bediening
   ~ **not included** exclusief bedie-
      ning
set menu menu van de dag
shad elft (zeevis)
shallot sjalot
shellfish schelp- en schaaldieren
sherbet sorbet
shoulder schouderstuk
shredded wheat gesponnen tarwe,
   wordt bij het ontbijt gegeten
shrimp garnaal
silverside (of beef) onderste deel
   van runderschenkel
sirloin steak lendestuk (van het
   rund)
skewer vleespen
slice sneet(je), plak
sliced in plakken gesneden
sloppy Joe gehakt vlees in scherpe
   tomatensaus, geserveerd in een
   broodje

smelt spiering
smoked gerookt
snack hapje, snack
sole tong (vis)
soup soep
sour zuur
soused herring gepekelde haring
spare rib krabbetje
spice kruiderij
spinach spinazie
spiny lobster langoest
(on a) spit (aan het) spit
sponge cake Moscovisch gebak
sprat sprot
squash mergpompoen
starter voorgerecht
steak and kidney pie pastei in bladerdeeg van niertjes en rundvlees
steamed gekookt
stew stoofschotel
Stilton (cheese) een van de beste Engelse kazen, wit of blauw geaderd
strawberry aardbei
string bean slaboon
stuffed gevuld
stuffing vulling
suck(l)ing pig speenvarken
sugar suiker
sugarless zonder suiker
sundae roomijs met vruchten, noten, slagroom en siroop
supper avondmaaltijd
swede knolraap
sweet 1) zoet 2) dessert
$\sim$ **corn** zoete maïs
$\sim$ **potato** bataat, knol van een oorspronkelijk tropisch gewas, rijk aan zetmeel en suiker
sweetbread zwezerik
Swiss cheese Emmentaler kaas
Swiss roll opgerold gebak met jam ertussen (koninginnebrood)

Swiss steak met groenten en kruiderijen gestoofde runderlappen
T-bone steak lendestuk van het rund met een T-vormig bot erin
table d'hôte open tafel in een hotel
tangerine mandarijntje
tarragon dragon
tart (vruchten)taart
tenderloin filet van vlees
Thousand Island dressing slasaus, bestaande uit mayonaise met piment, noten, olijven, selderie, uien, peterselie en eieren
thyme tijm
toad-in-the-hole rundvlees (of worstjes) in beslag gedoopt en in de oven gebakken
toast geroosterd brood
toasted getoost
$\sim$ **cheese** toost met gesmolten kaas
tomato tomaat
tongue tong (vlees)
tournedos ossehaas in dikke plakken
treacle melasse, stroop
trifle cake met amandelen en gelei, in sherry (of brandewijn) gedrenkt, opgediend met vla of slagroom
tripe pens
trout forel
truffle truffel (paddestoel)
tuna, tunny tonijn
turbot tarbot
turkey kalkoen
turnip raap, knol
turnover flap
turtle schildpad
underdone ongaar
vanilla vanille
veal kalfsvlees
$\sim$ **bird** blinde vink
$\sim$ **escalope** kalfsoester

vegetable groente
~ **marrow** mergpompoen, courgette
venison wildbraad
vichyssoise preisoep, koud geserveerd
vinegar azijn
Virginia baked ham ham in de oven geroosterd, in inkepingen in het vel worden stukjes ananas, kersen en kruidnagels gestoken waarna de ham met het vruchtesap geglaceerd wordt
wafer wafeltje
waffle warme wafel met boter, stroop of honing
walnut walnoot
water ice sorbet
watercress waterkers

watermelon watermeloen
well-done gaar
Welsh rabbit/rarebit gesmolten kaas op geroosterd brood
whelk kinkhoorn (wulk)
whipped cream slagroom
whitebait witvis
wine list wijnkaart
woodcock (hout)snip
Worcestershire sauce zoetzure saus bestaande uit soja en vele andere ingrediënten
York ham zeer goed bekend staande ham, opgediend in dunne plakken
Yorkshire pudding knappend gebakken deeg, geserveerd met rosbief
zucchini mergpompoen, courgette
zwieback beschuit

Dranken

ale donker, zoetachtig bier, onder hoge temperatuur gegist
bitter ~ bitter bier, nogal zwaar
brown ~ gebotteld, zoetachtig donker bier
light ~ gebotteld licht bier
mild ~ donker bier van het vat met een zeer uitgesproken smaak
pale ~ gebotteld licht bier
applejack Amerikaanse appelbrandewijn
Athol Brose haver vermengd met kokend water, honing en whisky

Bacardi cocktail cocktail van rum en gin met grenadinesiroop en limoensap
barley water frisdrank gemaakt van parelgerst met citroensmaak
barley wine donker bier met hoog alcoholgehalte
beer bier
bottled ~ gebotteld bier
draft, draught ~ getapt bier, bier van het vat
bitters kruidenaperitieven, de spijsvertering bevorderende alcoholische dranken

black velvet champagne met toevoeging van *stout* (vaak ter begeleiding van oesters)

bloody Mary cocktail van wodka, tomatesap en kruiderijen

bourbon Amerikaanse whisky, hoofdzakelijk van mais gestookt

brandy 1) verzamelnaam voor brandewijnsoorten gemaakt van druiven en andere vruchten 2) cognac

~ **Alexander** cocktail van brandewijn, crème de cacao en room

British wines wijnen in Engeland gegist; gemaakt van geïmporteerde druiven (of van geïmporteerd druivesap)

cherry brandy kersenlikeur

chocolate chocolademelk

cider cider

~ **cup** mengsel van cider, kruiderijen, suiker en ijs

claret rode Bordeauxwijn

cobbler *long drink* gemaakt van vruchten, waaraan men wijn of alcohol toevoegt

coffee koffie

~ **with cream** met room

black ~ zonder melk

caffeine-free ~ cafeïnevrij

white ~ half koffie, half melk; koffie verkeerd

cordial hartversterking

cream room

cup verfrissende drank gemaakt van gekoelde wijn, sodawater en een likeur of andere sterkedrank met een schijfje citroen of sinaasappel

daiquiri cocktail van rum, suiker, limoensap

double dubbele portie

Drambuie likeur gemaakt van

whisky en honing

dry martini 1) droge vermouth (GB) 2) cocktail van droge vermouth en gin (US)

egg-nog alcoholische drank op basis van rum of andere sterkedrank, vermengd met geklopt eigeel en suiker

gin and it gin met Italiaanse vermouth

gin-fizz gin met citroensap, sodawater en suiker

ginger ale frisdrank met gembersmaak

ginger beer gemberbier

grasshopper cocktail van crème de menthe, crème de cacao en room

Guinness (stout) donker zoetsmakend bier met een hoog mouten hopgehalte

half pint ongeveer 3 dl

highball alcoholische drank, zoals whisky, vermengd met water, sodawater of *ginger ale*

iced gekoeld, ijskoud

Irish coffee koffie met suiker en slagroom, waaraan men een scheut Ierse whisky toevoegt

Irish Mist Ierse likeur van whisky en honing

Irish whiskey Ierse whisky minder scherp dan Schotse whisky, bevat naast gerst ook rogge, haver en tarwe

juice sap

lager licht bier, koud geserveerd

lemon squash kwast

lemonade limonade

lime juice limoensap

liqueur likeur

liquor sterkedrank

long drink sterkedrank met tonic, sodawater of gewoon water en ijsblokjes

madeira madera

Manhattan cocktail van Amerikaanse whisky en vermouth met angostura

milk melk

mineral water mineraalwater

mulled wine bisschopswijn; warme, gekruide wijn

neat onvermengd, puur, zonder water of ijs

old-fashioned cocktail van whisky, angostura, sinaasappel schijfje, suiker en maraskijnkersen

on the rocks met ijsblokjes

Ovaltine ovomaltine

Pimm's cup(s) sterkedrank met vruchtesap, eventueel aangelengd met sodawater
~ **No. 1** met gin
~ **No. 2** met whisky
~ **No. 3** met rum
~ **No. 4** met brandewijn

pink champagne roze champagne

pink lady cocktail van eiwit, calvados, citroensap, grenadine en gin

pint ongeveer 6 dl

porter donker, bitter bier

quart 1,14 l (US 0.95 l)

root beer gezoete frisdrank met aromat uit plantenwortels en kruiden

rye (whiskey) whisky uit rogge gestookt; zwaarder en scherper van smaak dan *bourbon*

scotch (whisky) Schotse whisky, een uit gerst en maïs (grain whisky) gestookte sterkedrank,

vaak vermengd met malt whisky, uitsluitend uit gemoute gerst gestookt

screwdriver wodka met sinaasappelsap

shandy *bitter ale* vermengd met limonade of met *ginger beer*

short drink sterkedrank, onverdund gedronken

shot scheut sterkedrank

sloe gin-fizz sleepruimlikeur (vrucht van de sleedoorn) met citroensap en sodawater

soda water sodawater, spuitwater

soft drink frisdrank

spirits spiritualiën, gedistilleerde dranken

stinger cognac en crème de menthe

stout donker bier met veel hop gebrouwen

straight sterkedrank onverdund gedronken, puur

tea thee

toddy grog

Tom Collins *long drink* van gin, citroensap, spuitwater en suiker

tonic (water) tonic, spuitwater met kininesmaak

vodka wodka

whisky sour whisky, citroensap, suiker en sodawater

wine wijn
dessert ~ zoete
dry ~ droge
red ~ rode
sparkling ~ mousserende
sweet ~ zoete (dessertwijn)
white ~ witte

Mini-grammatica

Het lidwoord

Het bepaald lidwoord heeft slechts één vorm: *the*.

the room, the rooms   de kamer, de kamers

Het onbepaald lidwoord heeft twee vormen: *a* voor woorden die met een medeklinker beginnen en *an* voor woorden die met een klinker of stomme h beginnen.

a coat	een jas
an umbrella	een paraplu
an hour	een uur

Het zelfstandig naamwoord

Het meervoud van de meeste zelfstandige naamwoorden wordt gevormd door aan het enkelvoud *-(e)s* toe te voegen.

cup — cups (kopje — kopjes)   **dress — dresses** (jurk — jurken)

N.B. Wanneer een zelfstandig naamwoord op *-y* eindigt en de voorlaatste letter een medeklinker is, wordt de meervoudsuitgang *-ies*; als de voorlaatste letter echter een klinker is dan wordt het meervoud op de normale wijze gevormd.

lady — ladies (dame — dames)   **key — keys** (sleutel — sleutels)

Enkele zelfstandige naamwoorden met een onregelmatig meervoud zijn:

man — men (man — mannen)   **child — children** (kind — kinderen)
woman — women (vrouw — vrouwen)
foot — feet (voet — voeten)

Genitief

1. Als de bezitter een mens is en het zelfstandig naamwoord niet met *-s* eindigt, dan wordt *'s* toegevoegd.

the boy's room	de kamer van de jongen
the children's clothes	de kleren van de kinderen

Eindigt het zelfstandig naamwoord met *-s,* dan wordt alleen een apostrophe (') toegevoegd.

the boys' room   de kamer van de jongens

2. Als de bezitter een ding is, gebruikt men het voorzetsel *of*.

the key of the door   de sleutel van de deur

Het bijvoeglijk naamwoord

De bijvoeglijke naamwoorden staan gewoonlijk voor het zelfstandig naamwoord.

a large brown suitcase   een grote bruine koffer

De vergrotende en overtreffende trap van een bijvoeglijk naamwoord kunnen op twee manieren gevormd worden.

1. Alle bijvoeglijke naamwoorden van één lettergreep en vele van twee lettergrepen krijgen -(e)r en -(e)st.

small (klein) — **smaller** — **smallest**
pretty (aardig) — **prettier** — **prettiest***

2. Bijvoeglijke naamwoorden van drie of meer lettergrepen en enkele van twee die eindigen op -ful en -less maken de vergrotende en overtreffende trap met *more* en *most*.

expensive (duur) — **more expensive** — **most expensive**
careful (voorzichtig) — **more careful** — **most careful**

De volgende bijvoeglijke naamwoorden zijn onregelmatig:

good (goed)	better	best
bad (slecht)	worse	worst
little (weinig)	less	least
much/many (veel)	more	most

Het bijwoord

De meeste bijwoorden worden gemaakt door aan het bijvoeglijk naamwoord -ly toe te voegen.

quick/quickly (vlug)   **slow/slowly** (langzaam)
Uitzonderingen:
good/well (goed)   **fast/fast** (snel)

Voornaamwoorden

	persoonlijk voornaamwoord		bezittelijk voornaamwoord	
	onderwerp	lijdend en meew. vw.	1	2
ik	I	me	my	mine
jij	you	you	your	yours
hij	he	him	his	his
zij	she	her	her	hers
het	it	it	its	—
wij	we	us	our	ours
u	you	you	your	yours
zij	they	them	their	theirs

De vormen onder 1 worden gebruikt vóór een zelfstandig naamwoord, die onder 2 staan op zichzelf.

Where's my key?   Waar is mijn sleutel?
That's not mine.   Dat is niet de mijne.

N.B. Het Engels kent geen onderscheid tussen „jij" en „u", in beide gevallen zegt men *you*.

He came with you.   Hij kwam met jou/u.

---

* *y* wordt *i* als er een medeklinker aan voorafgaat.

Onregelmatige werkwoorden

De onderstaande lijst geeft de Engelse onregelmatige werkwoorden aan. De samengestelde werkwoorden of werkwoorden met een voorvoegsel worden als de grondwerkwoorden vervoegd, bijvoorbeeld: *withdraw* wordt vervoegd als *draw* en *rebuild* als *build*.

Onbepaalde wijs	Onvoltooid verleden tijd	Verleden deelwoord	
arise	arose	arisen	*opstaan*
awake	awoke	awoken	*ontwaken*
be	was	been	*zijn*
bear	bore	borne	*dragen*
beat	beat	beaten	*slaan*
become	became	become	*worden*
begin	began	begun	*aanvangen*
bend	bent	bent	*buigen*
bet	bet	bet	*wedden*
bid	bade/bid	bidden/bid	*verzoeken*
bind	bound	bound	*binden*
bite	bit	bitten	*bijten*
bleed	bled	bled	*bloeden*
blow	blew	blown	*blazen*
break	broke	broken	*breken*
breed	bred	bred	*fokken*
bring	brought	brought	*brengen*
build	built	built	*bouwen*
burn	burnt/burned	burnt/burned	*branden*
burst	burst	burst	*barsten*
buy	bought	bought	*kopen*
can*	could	—	*kunnen*
cast	cast	cast	*werpen*
catch	caught	caught	*vangen*
choose	chose	chosen	*kiezen*
cling	clung	clung	*vastklemmen*
clothe	clothed/clad	clothed/clad	*kleden*
come	came	come	*komen*
cost	cost	cost	*kosten*
creep	crept	crept	*kruipen*
cut	cut	cut	*snijden*
deal	dealt	dealt	*uitdelen*
dig	dug	dug	*graven*
do (he does)	did	done	*doen*
draw	drew	drawn	*trekken*
dream	dreamt/dreamed	dreamt/dreamed	*dromen*
drink	drank	drunk	*drinken*
drive	drove	driven	*rijden*
dwell	dwelt	dwelt	*vertoeven*

* tegenwoordige tijd

eat	ate	eaten	*eten*
fall	fell	fallen	*vallen*
feed	fed	fed	*voeden*
feel	felt	felt	*voelen*
fight	fought	fought	*vechten*
find	found	found	*vinden*
flee	fled	fled	*vluchten*
fling	flung	flung	*werpen*
fly	flew	flown	*vliegen*
forsake	forsook	forsaken	*verzaken*
freeze	froze	frozen	*vriezen*
get	got	got	*krijgen*
give	gave	given	*geven*
go	went	gone	*gaan*
grind	ground	ground	*malen*
grow	grew	grown	*groeien*
hang	hung	hung	*(op)hangen*
have	had	had	*hebben*
hear	heard	heard	*horen*
hew	hewed	hewed/hewn	*hakken*
hide	hid	hidden	*verstoppen*
hit	hit	hit	*slaan*
hold	held	held	*houden*
hurt	hurt	hurt	*pijn doen*
keep	kept	kept	*houden*
kneel	knelt	knelt	*knielen*
knit	knitted/knit	knitted/knit	*breien*
know	knew	known	*weten*
lay	laid	laid	*leggen*
lead	led	led	*leiden*
lean	leant/leaned	leant/leaned	*leunen*
leap	leapt/leaped	leapt/leaped	*springen*
learn	learnt/learned	learnt/learned	*leren*
leave	left	left	*verlaten*
lend	lent	lent	*lenen(aan)*
let	let	let	*laten*
lie	lay	lain	*liggen*
light	lit/lighted	lit/lighted	*aansteken*
lose	lost	lost	*verliezen*
make	made	made	*maken*
may*	might	—	*mogen, kunnen*
mean	meant	meant	*bedoelen*
meet	met	met	*ontmoeten*
mow	mowed	mowed/mown	*maaien*
must*	—	—	*moeten*
ought (to)*	—	—	*moeten*
pay	paid	paid	*betalen*
put	put	put	*zetten*
read	read	read	*lezen*

* tegenwoordige tijd

rid	rid	rid	*zich ontdoen (van)*
ride	rode	ridden	*rijden*
ring	rang	rung	*bellen*
rise	rose	risen	*opstaan*
run	ran	run	*rennen*
saw	sawed	sawn	*zagen*
say	said	said	*zeggen*
see	saw	seen	*zien*
seek	sought	sought	*zoeken*
sell	sold	sold	*verkopen*
send	sent	sent	*verzenden*
set	set	set	*zetten*
sew	sewed	sewed/sewn	*naaien*
shake	shook	shaken	*schudden*
shall*	should	—	*zullen*
shed	shed	shed	*vergieten*
shine	shone	shone	*schijnen*
shoot	shot	shot	*schieten*
show	showed	shown	*tonen*
shrink	shrank	shrunk	*krimpen*
shut	shut	shut	*sluiten*
sing	sang	sung	*zingen*
sink	sank	sunk	*zinken*
sit	sat	sat	*zitten*
sleep	slept	slept	*slapen*
slide	slid	slid	*glijden*
sling	slung	slung	*slingeren*
slink	slunk	slunk	*sluipen*
slit	slit	slit	*opensnijden*
smell	smelled/smelt	smelled/smelt	*ruiken*
sow	sowed	sown/sowed	*zaaien*
speak	spoke	spoken	*spreken*
speed	sped/speeded	sped/speeded	*zich haasten*
spell	spelt/spelled	spelt/spelled	*spellen*
spend	spent	spent	*uitgeven*
spill	spilt/spilled	spilt/spilled	*morsen*
spin	spun	spun	*spinnen*
spit	spat	spat	*spuwen*
split	split	split	*splijten*
spoil	spoilt/spoiled	spoilt/spoiled	*bederven*
spread	spread	spread	*spreiden*
spring	sprang	sprung	*ontspringen*
stand	stood	stood	*staan*
steal	stole	stolen	*stelen*
stick	stuck	stuck	*kleven*
sting	stung	stung	*steken*
stink	stank/stunk	stunk	*stinken*
strew	strewed	strewed/strewn	*strooien*
stride	strode	stridden	*schrijden*

* tegenwoordige tijd

strike	struck	struck/stricken	*slaan*
string	strung	strung	*rijgen*
strive	strove	striven	*streven*
swear	swore	sworn	*zweren*
sweep	swept	swept	*vegen*
swell	swelled	swollen	*zwellen*
swim	swam	swum	*zwemmen*
swing	swung	swung	*slingeren*
take	took	taken	*nemen*
teach	taught	taught	*onderwijzen*
tear	tore	torn	*scheuren*
tell	told	told	*vertellen*
think	thought	thought	*denken*
throw	threw	thrown	*werpen*
thrust	thrust	thrust	*duwen*
tread	trod	trodden	*treden*
wake	woke/waked	woken/waked	*wekken*
wear	wore	worn	*dragen*
weave	wove	woven	*weven*
weep	wept	wept	*huilen*
will*	would	—	*zullen*
win	won	won	*winnen*
wind	wound	wound	*opwinden*
wring	wrung	wrung	*wringen*
write	wrote	written	*schrijven*

* tegenwoordige tijd

Engelse afkortingen

AA	*Automobile Association*	Britse Automobielclub
AAA	*American Automobile Association*	Amerikaanse Automobielclub
ABC	*American Broadcasting Company*	Amerikaanse radio- en televisiemaatschappij
A.D.	*anno Domini*	na Christus
Am.	*America; American*	Amerika; Amerikaans
a.m.	*ante meridiem (before noon)*	de tijd tussen 0 en 12 uur
Amtrak	*American railroad corporation*	Amerikaanse spoorwegmaatschappij
AT & T	*American Telephone and Telegraph Company*	Amerikaanse telefoon- en telegraafmaatschappij
Ave.	*avenue*	avenue
BBC	*British Broadcasting Corporation*	Britse radio- en televisie-maatschappij
B.C.	*before Christ*	voor Christus
bldg.	*building*	gebouw
Blvd.	*boulevard*	boulevard
B.R.	*British Rail*	Britse Spoorwegen
Brit.	*Britain; British*	Groot-Brittannië, Brits
Bros.	*brothers*	gebroeders
¢	*cent*	1/100 van een dollar
Can.	*Canada; Canadian*	Canada; Canadees
CBS	*Columbia Broadcasting System*	Amerikaanse radio- en televisiemaatschappij
CID	*Criminal Investigation Department*	afdeling criminele recherche van Scotland Yard
CNR	*Canadian National Railway*	Canadese Nationale Spoorwegen
c/o	*(in) care of*	per adres
Co.	*company*	maatschappij
Corp.	*corporation*	vennootschap
CPR	*Canadian Pacific Railways*	Canadese spoorweg-maatschappij
D.C.	*District of Columbia*	district in de V.S. waarin de hoofdstad Washington ligt
DDS	*Doctor of Dental Science*	doctor in de tandheelkunde
dept.	*department*	departement, afdeling
EEC	*European Economic Community*	EEG, Europese Economische Gemeenschap
e.g.	*for instance*	bijvoorbeeld

Eng.	*England; English*	Engeland; Engels
excl.	*excluding; exclusive*	exclusief
ft.	*foot/feet*	voet
GB	*Great Britain*	Groot-Brittannië
H.E.	*His/Her Excellency;*	Zijne/Hare Excellentie;
	His Eminence	Zijne Eminentie
H.H.	*His Holiness*	Zijne Heiligheid
H.M.	*His/Her Majesty*	Zijne/Hare Majesteit
H.M.S.	*Her Majesty's ship*	Harer Majesteits schip
		(Brits oorlogsschip)
hp	*horsepower*	paardekracht
Hwy	*highway*	autoweg
i.e.	*that is to say*	d.w.z., dat wil zeggen
in.	*inch*	duim (2,54 cm)
Inc.	*incorporated*	naamloze vennootschap
incl.	*including, inclusive*	inclusief
£	*pound sterling*	pond sterling
L.A.	*Los Angeles*	Los Angeles
Ltd.	*limited*	naamloze vennootschap
M.D.	*Doctor of Medicine*	arts
M.P.	*Member of Parliament*	lid van het Lagerhuis
		(Engeland)
mph	*miles per hour*	Engelse mijl per uur
Mr.	*Mister*	meneer
Mrs.	*Missis*	mevrouw
Ms.	*Missis/Miss*	mevrouw/mejuffrouw
nat.	*national*	nationaal
NBC	*National Broadcasting*	Amerikaanse radio- en
	Company	televisiemaatschappij
No.	*number*	nummer
N.Y.C.	*New York City*	New York City
O.B.E.	*Officer (of the Order)*	Officier in de Orde
	of the British Empire	van het Britse Imperium
p.	*page; penny/pence*	bladzijde; 1/100 van een pond
p.a.	*per annum*	per jaar
Ph.D.	*Doctor of Philosophy*	doctor in de wijsbegeerte
p.m.	*post meridiem*	de tijd tussen 12 en 24 uur
	(after noon)	
PO	*Post Office*	postkantoor
POO	*post office order*	postorder
pop.	*population*	bevolking
P.T.O.	*please turn over*	zie ommezijde, a.u.b.
RAC	*Royal Automobile Club*	Koninklijke Britse
		Automobielclub

RCMP	*Royal Canadian Mounted Police*	Koninklijke Canadese Bereden Politie
Rd.	*road*	weg
ref.	*reference*	verwijzing
Rev.	*reverend*	dominee
RFD	*rural free delivery*	landelijke postbus
RR	*railroad*	spoorweg
RSVP	*please reply*	verzoeke gaarne antwoord
$	*dollar*	dollar
Soc.	*society*	maatschappij, genootschap
St.	*saint; street*	sint; straat
STD	*Subscriber Trunk Dialling*	automatisch telefoonverkeer
UN	*United Nations*	V.N., Verenigde Naties
UPS	*United Parcel Service*	Amerikaanse pakketdienst
US	*United States*	Verenigde Staten
USS	*United States Ship*	Amerikaans oorlogsschip
VAT	*value added tax*	B.T.W.
VIP	*very important person*	zeer belangrijke persoon
Xmas	*Christmas*	Kerstmis
yd.	*yard*	yard (91,44 cm)
YMCA	*Young Men's Christian Association*	Christelijke Jongeren Vereniging
YWCA	*Young Women's Christian Association*	Christelijke Meisjes Vereniging
ZIP	*ZIP code*	postnummer

Telwoorden

Hoofdtelwoorden		Rangtelwoorden	
0	zero	1st	first
1	one	2nd	second
2	two	3rd	third
3	three	4th	fourth
4	four	5th	fifth
5	five	6th	sixth
6	six	7th	seventh
7	seven	8th	eighth
8	eight	9th	ninth
9	nine	10th	tenth
10	ten	11th	eleventh
11	eleven	12th	twelfth
12	twelve	13th	thirteenth
13	thirteen	14th	fourteenth
14	fourteen	15th	fifteenth
15	fifteen	16th	sixteenth
16	sixteen	17th	seventeenth
17	seventeen	18th	eighteenth
18	eighteen	19th	nineteenth
19	nineteen	20th	twentieth
20	twenty	21st	twenty-first
21	twenty-one	22nd	twenty-second
22	twenty-two	23rd	twenty-third
23	twenty-three	24th	twenty-fourth
24	twenty-four	25th	twenty-fifth
25	twenty-five	26th	twenty-sixth
30	thirty	27th	twenty-seventh
40	forty	28th	twenty-eighth
50	fifty	29th	twenty-ninth
60	sixty	30th	thirtieth
70	seventy	40th	fortieth
80	eighty	50th	fiftieth
90	ninety	60th	sixtieth
100	a/one hundred	70th	seventieth
230	two hundred and thirty	80th	eightieth
		90th	ninetieth
1,000	a/one thousand	100th	hundredth
10,000	ten thousand	230th	two hundred and thirtieth
100,000	a/one hundred thousand		
1,000,000	a/one million	1,000th	thousandth

Tijd

De Engelsen en Amerikanen gebruiken het twaalf-uren systeem. De uit-drukking *a.m. (ante meridiem)* duidt op de uren tussen middernacht en 12 uur 's middags; *p.m. (post meridiem)* op de uren tussen 12 uur 's middags en middernacht. Engeland gaat momenteel geleidelijk over op het continentale systeem.

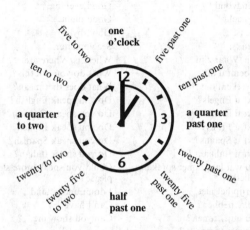

I'll come at seven a.m.   Ik kom om 7 uur 's morgens.
I'll come at two p.m.   Ik kom om 2 uur 's middags.
I'll come at eight p.m.   Ik kom om 8 uur 's avonds.

Dagen van de week

Sunday	zondag	*Thursday*	donderdag
Monday	maandag	*Friday*	vrijdag
Tuesday	dinsdag	*Saturday*	zaterdag
Wednesday	woensdag		

Enkele nuttige zinnen

Alstublieft.	Please.
Hartelijk dank.	Thank you very much.
Niets te danken.	Don't mention it.
Goedemorgen.	Good morning.
Goedemiddag.	Good afternoon.
Goedenavond.	Good evening.
Goedenacht.	Good night.
Tot ziens.	Good-bye.
Tot straks.	See you later.
Waar is/Waar zijn...?	Where is/Where are...?
Hoe noemt u dit?	What do you call this?
Wat betekent dat?	What does that mean?
Spreekt u Engels?	Do you speak English?
Spreekt u Duits?	Do you speak German?
Spreekt u Frans?	Do you speak French?
Spreekt u Spaans?	Do you speak Spanish?
Spreekt u Italiaans?	Do you speak Italian?
Kunt u wat langzamer spreken, alstublieft?	Could you speak more slowly, please?
Ik begrijp het niet.	I don't understand.
Mag ik...hebben?	Can I have...?
Kunt u mij...tonen?	Can you show me...?
Kunt u mij zeggen...?	Can you tell me...?
Kunt u me helpen?	Can you help me, please?
Ik wil graag...	I'd like...
Wij willen graag...	We'd like...
Geeft u me..., alstublieft.	Please give me...
Brengt u me..., alstublieft.	Please bring me...
Ik heb honger.	I'm hungry.
Ik heb dorst.	I'm thirsty.
Ik ben verdwaald.	I'm lost.
Vlug!	Hurry up!
Er is/Er zijn...	There is/There are...
Er is geen/Er zijn geen...	There isn't/There aren't...

Some Basic Phrases

Aankomst

Uw paspoort, alstublieft.

Hebt u iets aan te geven?

Nee, helemaal niets.

Kunt u me met mijn bagage helpen, alstublieft?

Waar is de bus naar het centrum?

Hierlangs, alstublieft.

Waar kan ik een taxi krijgen?

Wat kost het naar…?

Breng me naar dit adres, alstublieft.

Ik heb haast.

Arrival

Your passport, please.

Have you anything to declare?

No, nothing at all.

Can you help me with my luggage, please?

Where's the bus to the centre of town, please?

This way, please.

Where can I get a taxi?

What's the fare to…?

Take me to this address, please.

I'm in a hurry.

Hotel

Mijn naam is…

Hebt u gereserveerd?

Ik wil graag een kamer met bad.

Hoeveel kost het per nacht?

Mag ik de kamer zien?

Wat is mijn kamernummer?

Er is geen warm water.

Mag ik de directeur spreken, alstublieft?

Heeft er iemand voor mij opgebeld?

Is er post voor mij?

Mag ik de rekening, alstublieft?

Hotel

My name is…

Have you a reservation?

I'd like a room with a bath.

What's the price per night?

May I see the room?

What's my room number, please?

There's no hot water.

May I see the manager, please?

Did anyone telephone me?

Is there any mail for me?

May I have my bill (check), please?

Uit eten

Hebt u een menu à prix fixe?

Mag ik de spijskaart zien?

Kunt u ons een asbak brengen, alstublieft?

Eating out

Do you have a fixed-price menu?

May I see the menu?

May we have an ashtray, please?

Waar is het toilet?	Where's the toilet, please?
Ik wil graag een voorgerecht.	I'd like an hors d'œuvre (starter).
Hebt u soep?	Have you any soup?
Ik wil graag vis.	I'd like some fish.
Wat voor vis hebt u?	What kind of fish do you have?
Ik wil graag een biefstuk.	I'd like a steak.
Wat voor groenten hebt u?	What vegetables have you got?
Niets meer, dank u.	Nothing more, thanks.
Wat wilt u drinken?	What would you like to drink?
Een pils, alstublieft.	I'll have a beer, please.
Ik wil graag een fles wijn.	I'd like a bottle of wine.
Mag ik de rekening, alstublieft?	May I have the bill (check), please?
Is de bediening inbegrepen?	Is service included?
Dank u, het was een uitstekende maaltijd.	Thank you, that was a very good meal.

Reizen

Travelling

Waar is het station?	Where's the railway station, please?
Waar is het loket?	Where's the ticket office, please?
Ik wil graag een kaartje naar...	I'd like a ticket to...
Eerste of tweede klas?	First or second class?
Eerste klas, alstublieft.	First class, please.
Enkele reis of retour?	Single or return (one way or roundtrip)?
Moet ik overstappen?	Do I have to change trains?
Van welk perron vertrekt de trein naar...?	What platform does the train for... leave from?
Waar is het dichtstbijzijnde metrostation?	Where's the nearest underground (subway) station?
Waar is het busstation?	Where's the bus station, please?
Hoe laat vertrekt de eerste bus naar...?	When's the first bus to...?
Wilt u me bij de volgende halte laten uitstappen?	Please let me off at the next stop.

Ontspanning

Wat wordt er in de bioscoop gegeven?

Hoe laat begint de film?

Zijn er nog plaatsen vrij voor vanavond?

Waar kunnen we gaan dansen?

Relaxing

What's on at the cinema (movies)?

What time does the film begin?

Are there any tickets for tonight?

Where can we go dancing?

Ontmoetingen

Dag mevrouw/juffrouw/mijnheer.

Hoe maakt u het?

Uitstekend, dank u. En u?

Mag ik u... voorstellen?

Mijn naam is...

Prettig kennis met u te maken.

Hoelang bent u al hier?

Het was mij een genoegen.

Hindert het u als ik rook?

Hebt u een vuurtje, alstublieft?

Mag ik u iets te drinken aanbieden?

Mag ik u vanavond ten eten uitnodigen?

Waar spreken we af?

Meeting people

How do you do.

How are you?

Very well, thank you. And you?

May I introduce...?

My name is...

I'm very pleased to meet you.

How long have you been here?

It was nice meeting you.

Do you mind if I smoke?

Do you have a light, please?

May I get you a drink?

May I invite you for dinner tonight?

Where shall we meet?

Winkels en diensten

Waar is de dichtstbijzijnde bank?

Waar kan ik reischeques inwisselen?

Kunt u me wat kleingeld geven, alstublieft?

Waar is de dichtstbijzijnde apotheek?

Hoe kom ik daar?

Is het te lopen?

Shops, stores and services

Where's the nearest bank, please?

Where can I cash some travellers' cheques?

Can you give me some small change, please?

Where's the nearest chemist's (pharmacy)?

How do I get there?

Is it within walking distance?

Kunt u mij helpen, alstublieft?	Can you help me, please?
Hoeveel kost dit? En dat?	How much is this? And that?
Het is niet precies wat ik zoek.	It's not quite what I want.
Het bevalt me.	I like it.
Kunt u mij iets tegen zonnebrand aanbevelen?	Can you recommend something for sunburn?
Knippen, alstublieft.	I'd like a haircut, please.
Ik wil een manicure, alstublieft.	I'd like a manicure, please.

De weg vragen ## Street directions

Kunt u mij op de kaart aanwijzen waar ik ben?	Can you show me on the map where I am?
U bent op de verkeerde weg.	You are on the wrong road.
Rij/Ga rechtuit.	Go/Walk straight ahead.
Het is aan de linkerkant/aan de rechterkant.	It's on the left/on the right.

Spoedgevallen ## Emergencies

Roep vlug een dokter.	Call a doctor quickly.
Roep een ambulance.	Call an ambulance.
Roep de politie, alstublieft.	Please call the police.

dutch-english

nederlands-engels

Dutch-English Dictionary

Engels-Nederlands Woordenboek

Introduction

The dictionary has been designed to take account of your practical needs. Unnecessary linguistic information has been avoided. The entries are listed in alphabetical order regardless of whether the entry word is printed in a single word, is hyphened or is in two or more separate words. The only exception to this rule, reflexive verbs, are listed as main entries alphabetically according to the verb, e.g. *zich afvragen* is found under **a**.

When an entry is followed by sub-entries such as expressions and locutions, these, too, have been listed in alphabetical order.

Each main-entry word is followed by a phonetic transcription (see Guide to pronunciation). Following the transcription is the part of speech of the entry word whenever applicable. When an entry word may be used as more then one part of speech, the translations are grouped together after the respective part of speech.

Considering the complexity of the rules for constructing the plural of Dutch nouns, we have supplied the plural form whenever in current use.

Each time an entry word is repeated in plurals or in sub-entries, a tilde (~) is used to represent the full entry word.

In plurals of long words, only the part that changes is written out fully, whereas the unchanged part is represented by a hyphen.

Entry: beker (pl ~s)	Plural: bekers
kind (pl ~eren)	kinderen
leslokaal (pl -kalen)	leslokalen

An asterisk (*) in front of a verb indicates that the verb is irregular. For details, refer to the lists of irregular verbs.

Abbreviations

adj	adjective	*p*	past tense
adv	adverb	*pl*	plural
Am	American	*plAm*	plural (American)
art	article	*pp*	past participle
c	common gender	*pr*	present tense
conj	conjunction	*pref*	prefix
n	noun	*prep*	preposition
nAm	noun (American)	*pron*	pronoun
nt	neuter	*v*	verb
num	numeral	*vAm*	verb (American)

Guide to Pronunciation

Each main entry in this part of the dictionary is followed by a phonetic transcription which shows you how to pronounce the words. This transcription should be read as if it were English. It is based on Standard British pronunciation, though we have tried to take account of General American pronunciation also. Below, only those letters and symbols are explained which we consider likely to be ambiguous or not immediately understood.

The syllables are separated by hyphens, and stressed syllables are printed in *italics*.

Of course, the sounds of any two languages are never exactly the same, but if you follow carefully our indications, you should be able to pronounce the foreign words in such a way that you'll be understood. To make your task easier, our transcriptions occasionally simplify slightly the sound system of the language while still reflecting the essential sound differences.

Consonants

g	a **g**-sound where the tongue doesn't quite close the air passage between itself and the roof of the mouth, so that the escaping air produces audible friction; often fairly hard, so that it resembles **kh**
kh	like **g**, but based on a **k**-sound; therefore hard and voiceless, like **ch** in Scottish lo**ch**
ñ	as in Spanish se**ñ**or, or like **ni** in o**ni**on
s	always hard, as in **s**o
zh	a soft, voiced **sh**, like **s** in pleasure

1) In everyday speech, the **n** in the ending of verbs and plurals of nouns is usually dropped.

2) We use the transcription **v** for two different sounds (written **v** and **w** in Dutch) because the difference between them is often inaudible to foreigners.

Vowels and Diphthongs

aa	long **a**, as in c**ar**, without any **r**-sound
ah	a short version of **aa**; between **a** in c**a**t and **u** in c**u**t
ai	like **air**, without any **r**-sound

Dutch for English:

eh   like **e** in g**e**t

er   as in oth**er**, without any **r**-sound

ew   a "rounded **ee**-sound"; say the vowel sound **ee** (as in s**ee**), and while saying it, round your lips as for **oo** (as in s**oo**n), without moving your tongue; when your lips are in the **oo** position, but your tongue is in the **ee** position, you should be pronouncing the correct sound

ı   like **i** in b**i**t

igh   as in s**igh**

o   always as in h**o**t (British pronunciation)

ou   as in l**ou**d

ur   as in f**ur**, but with rounded lips and no **r**-sound

1) A bar over a vowel symbol (e.g. $\overline{oo}$) shows that this sound is long.

2) Raised letters (e.g. **aa**[ee], **t**[y], [y]**eh**) should be pronounced only fleetingly.

3) Dutch vowels (i.e. not diphthongs) are pure. Therefore, you should try to read a transcription like $\overline{oa}$ without moving tongue or lips while pronouncing the sound.

4) Some Dutch words borrowed from French contain nasal vowels, which we transcribe with a vowel symbol plus **ng** (e.g. **ahng**). This **ng** should *not* be pronounced, and serves solely to indicate nasal quality of the preceding vowel. A nasal vowel is pronounced simultaneously through the mouth and the nose.

Dutch-English
Dictionary

Engels-Nederlands
Woordenboek

A

aal (aal) *c* (pl alen) eel

aambeien (*aam*-bay-ern) *pl* haemorrhoids *pl*, piles *pl*

aan (aan) *prep* to; on

aanbetaling (*aam*-ber-taa-ling) *c* (pl ~en) down payment

*__aanbevelen__ (*aam*-ber-vāy-lern) *v* recommend

aanbeveling (*aam*-ber-vāy-ling) *c* (pl ~en) recommendation

aanbevelingsbrief (*aam*-ber-vāy-lings-breef) *c* (pl -brieven) letter of recommendation

*__aanbidden__ (*aam*-bi-dern) *v* worship

*__aanbieden__ (*aam*-bee-dern) *v* offer; present

aanbieding (*aam*-bee-ding) *c* (pl ~en) offer

aanblik (*aam*-blik) *c* sight; appearance

aanbod (*aam*-bot) *nt* offer; supply

aanbranden (*aam*-brahn-dern) *v* *burn

aandacht (*aan*-dahkht) *c* attention; notice, consideration; ~ **besteden aan** attend to

aandeel (*aan*-dāyl) *nt* (pl -delen) share

aandenken (*aan*-dehng-kern) *nt* (pl ~s) remembrance

aandoening (*aan*-dōō-ning) *c* (pl ~en) affection

aandoenlijk (aan-*dōōn*-lerk) *adj* touching

*__aandrijven__ (*aan*-dray-vern) *v* propel

*__aandringen__ (*aan*-dri-ngern) *v* insist

aanduiden (*aan*-dur^(ew)-dern) *v* indicate

*__aangaan__ (*aang*-gaan) *v* concern

aangaande (aang-*gaan*-der) *prep* as regards

aangeboren (*aang*-ger-bōa-rern) *adj* natural

aangelegenheid (aang-ger-*lāy*-gern-hayt) *c* (pl -heden) matter, concern; affair, business

aangenaam (*aang*-ger-naam) *adj* agreeable, pleasing, pleasant

aangesloten (*aang*-ger-slōa-tern) *adj* affiliated

*__aangeven__ (*aang*-gāy-vern) *v* indicate; declare; *give, hand, pass

aangezien (aang-ger-*zeen*) *conj* as, since; because

aangifte (*aang*-gif-ter) *c* (pl ~n) declaration

aangrenzend (aang-*grehn*-zernt) *adj* neighbouring

aanhalen (*aan*-haa-lern) *v* tighten; quote

aanhalingstekens (*aan*-haa-lings-tāy-kerns) *pl* quotation marks

aanhangwagen (*aan*-hahng-vaa-gern) *c* (pl ~s) trailer

aanhankelijk (aan-*hahng*-ker-lerk) *adj*

affectionate

*aanhebben (*aan*-heh-bern) *v* *wear

aanhechten (*aan*-hehkh-tern) *v* attach

aanhoren (*aan*-hōa-rern) *v* listen

*aanhouden (*aan*-hou-dern) *v* insist; **aanhoudend** constant

aanhouding (*aan*-hou-dıng) *c* (pl ~en) arrest

aankijken (*aang*-kay-kern) *v* look at

aanklacht (*aang*-klahkht) *c* (pl ~en) charge

aanklagen (*aang*-klaa-gern) *v* accuse, charge

aankleden (*aang*-klāy-dern) *v* dress; *get dressed

*aankomen (*aang*-kōa-mern) *v* arrive

aankomst (*aang*-komst) *c* arrival

aankomsttijd (*aang*-koms-tayt) *c* (pl ~en) time of arrival

aankondigen (*aang*-kon-der-gern) *v* announce

aankondiging (*aang*-kon-der-gıng) *c* (pl ~en) notice, announcement

aankoop (*aang*-kōap) *c* (pl -kopen) purchase

aankruisen (*aang*-krur^ew^-sern) *v* mark

aanleg (*aan*-lehkh) *c* talent

aanleggen (*aan*-leh-gern) *v* dock

aanleiding (*aan*-lay-dıng) *c* (pl ~en) cause, occasion

aanlengen (*aan*-leh-ngern) *v* dilute

zich aanmelden (*aan*-mehl-dern) report

aanmerkelijk (aa-*mehr*-ker-lerk) *adj* considerable

aanmerken (*aa*-mehr-kern) *v* comment

aanmoedigen (*aa*-mōo-der-gern) *v* encourage

*aannemen (*aa*-nāy-mern) *v* accept; assume, suppose; adopt; **aangenomen dat** supposing that

aannemer (*aa*-nāy-merr) *c* (pl ~s) contractor

aanpak (*aam*-pahk) *c* method, approach

aanpassen (*aam*-pah-sern) *v* adapt; suit; adjust

aanplakbiljet (*aam*-plahk-bıl-^y^eht) *nt* (pl ~ten) placard

*aanprijzen (*aan*-pray-zern) *v* recommend

*aanraden (*aan*-raa-dern) *v* advise, recommend

aanraken (*aan*-raa-kern) *v* touch

aanraking (*aan*-raa-kıng) *c* (pl ~en) touch; contact

aanranden (*aan*-rahn-dern) *v* assault

aanrichten (*aan*-rıkh-tern) *v* cause

aanrijding (*aan*-ray-dıng) *c* (pl ~en) collision

aanschaffen (*aan*-skhah-fern) *v* *buy

*aansluiten (*aan*-slur^ew^-tern) *v* connect

aansluiting (*aan*-slur^ew^-tıng) *c* (pl ~en) connection

aansporen (*aan*-spōa-rern) *v* incite; urge

aanspraak (*aan*-spraak) *c* (pl -spraken) claim

aansprakelijk (aan-*spraa*-ker-lerk) *adj* liable; responsible

aansprakelijkheid (aan-*spraa*-ker-lerk-hayt) *c* liability; responsibility

*aanspreken (*aan*-sprāy-kern) *v* address

aanstekelijk (aan-*stāy*-ker-lerk) *adj* contagious

*aansteken (*aan*-stāy-kern) *v* *light; infect

aansteker (*aan*-stāy-kerr) *c* (pl ~s) lighter, cigarette-lighter

aanstellen (*aan*-steh-lern) *v* appoint

aanstoot (*aan*-stōat) *c* offence

aanstootgevend (aan-stōat-*khāy*-vernt) *adj* offensive

aanstrepen (*aan*-strāy-pern) *v* tick off

aantal (*aan*-tahl) *nt* (pl ~len) number; quantity

aantekenen (aan-tāy-ker-nern) v record; register

aantekening (aan-tāy-ker-nɪng) c (pl ~en) note

aantonen (aan-tōa-nern) v prove; demonstrate, *show

aantrekkelijk (aan-treh-ker-lerk) adj attractive

*****aantrekken** (aan-treh-kern) v attract; tempt; *put on; tighten

aantrekking (aan-treh-kɪng) c attraction

aanvaarden (aan-vaar-dern) v accept

aanval (aan-vahl) c (pl ~len) attack; fit

*****aanvallen** (aan-vah-lern) v attack; assault

aanvang (aan-vahng) c beginning

*****aanvangen** (aan-vah-ngern) v *begin

aanvankelijk (aan-vahng-ker-lerk) adv originally, at first

aanvaring (aan-vaa-rɪng) c (pl ~en) collision

aanvoer (aan-vōōr) c supply

aanvoerder (aan-vōōr-derr) c (pl ~s) leader

aanvraag (aan-vraakh) c (pl -vragen) application

aanwezig (aan-vāy-zerkh) adj present

aanwezigheid (aan-vāy-zerkh-hayt) c presence

*****aanwijzen** (aan-vay-zern) v point out; designate

aanwijzing (aan-vay-zɪng) c (pl ~en) indication

aanzetten (aan-zeh-tern) v turn on

aanzien (aan-zeen) nt aspect; esteem; **ten ~ van** regarding

aanzienlijk (aan-zeen-lerk) adj considerable, substantial

aap (aap) c (pl apen) monkey

aard (aart) c nature

aardappel (aar-dah-perl) c (pl ~s, ~en) potato

aardbei (aart-bay) c (pl ~en) strawberry

aardbeving (aart-bāy-vɪng) c (pl ~en) earthquake

aardbol (aart-bol) c globe

aarde (aar-der) c earth; soil

aardewerk (aar-der-vehrk) nt crockery, pottery, faience, earthenware, ceramics pl

aardig (aar-derkh) adj pleasant; nice, kind

aardrijkskunde (aar-drayks-kern-der) c geography

aartsbisschop (aarts-bɪ-skhop) c (pl ~pen) archbishop

aarzelen (aar-zer-lern) v hesitate

aas (aass) nt bait

abces (ahp-sehss) nt (pl ~sen) abscess

abdij (ahb-day) c (pl ~en) abbey

abnormaal (ahp-nor-maal) adj abnormal

abonnee (ah-bo-nāy) c (pl ~s) subscriber

abonnement (ah-bo-ner-mehnt) nt (pl ~en) subscription

abonnementskaart (ah-bo-ner-mehnts-kaart) c (pl ~en) season-ticket

abortus (ah-bor-terss) c (pl ~sen) abortion

abrikoos (ah-bree-kōāss) c (pl -kozen) apricot

absoluut (ahp-sōa-lēwt) adj sheer; adv absolutely

abstract (ahp-strahkt) adj abstract

absurd (ahp-serrt) adj absurd

abuis (aa-burᵉʷss) nt (pl abuizen) mistake

academie (aa-kaa-dāy-mee) c (pl ~s) academy

accent (ahk-sehnt) nt (pl ~en) accent

accepteren (ahk-sehp-tāy-rern) v accept

accessoires (ahk-seh-svaa-rerss) pl accessories pl

accijns (ahk-*sayns*) c (pl -cijnzen) Customs duty

accommodatie (ah-ko-mōa-*daa*-tsee) c accommodation

accu (*ah*-kew) c (pl ~'s) battery

acht (ahkht) num eight

achteloos (*ahkh*-ter-lōass) adj careless

achten (*ahkh*-tern) v esteem; count

achter (*ahkh*-terr) prep behind; after

achteraan (ahkh-ter-*raan*) adv behind

achterbuurt (*ahkh*-terr-bewrt) c (pl ~en) slum

achterdochtig (ahkh-terr-*dokh*-terkh) adj suspicious

achtergrond (*ahkh*-terr-gront) c (pl ~en) background

achterkant (*ahkh*-terr-kahnt) c (pl ~en) rear

*****achterlaten** (*ahkh*-terr-laa-tern) v *leave behind

achterlicht (*ahkh*-terr-lıkht) nt (pl ~en) tail-light, rear-light

achternaam (*ahkh*-terr-naam) c (pl -namen) family name, surname

achterstallig (ahkh-terr-*stah*-lerkh) adj overdue

achteruit (ahkh-ter-*rur*^{ew}t) adv backwards

*****achteruitrijden** (ahkh-ter-*rur*^{ew}t-ray-dern) v reverse

achterwerk (*ahkh*-terr-vehrk) nt (pl ~en) bottom

achting (*ahkh*-tıng) c respect, esteem

achtste (*ahkht*-ster) num eighth

achttien (*ahkh*-teen) num eighteen

achttiende (*ahkh*-teen-der) num eighteenth

acne (*ahk*-nāy) c acne

acquisitie (ah-kvee-*zee*-tsee) c (pl ~s) acquisition

acteur (ahk-*tūrr*) c (pl ~s) actor

actie (*ahk*-see) c (pl ~s) action

actief (ahk-*teef*) adj active

activiteit (ahk-tee-vee-*tayt*) c (pl ~en) activity

actrice (ahk-*tree*-ser) c (pl ~s) actress

actueel (ahk-tew-*vāyl*) adj topical

acuut (ah-*kewt*) adj acute

adel (*aa*-derl) c nobility

adellijk (*aa*-der-lerk) adj noble

adem (*aa*-derm) c breath

ademen (*aa*-der-mern) v breathe

ademhaling (*aa*-derm-haa-lıng) c breathing, respiration

adequaat (ah-dāy-*kvaat*) adj adequate

ader (*aa*-derr) c (pl ~s, ~en) vein

administratie (aht-mee-nee-*straa*-tsee) c (pl ~s) administration

administratief (aht-mee-nee-straa-*teef*) adj administrative

admiraal (aht-mee-*raal*) c (pl ~s) admiral

adopteren (ah-dop-*tāy*-rern) v adopt

adres (aa-*drehss*) nt (pl ~sen) address

adresseren (aa-dreh-*sāy*-rern) v address

advertentie (aht-ferr-*tehn*-see) c (pl ~s) advertisement

advies (aht-*feess*) nt (pl adviezen) advice

adviseren (aht-fee-*zāy*-rern) v advise

advocaat (aht-fōa-*kaat*) c (pl -caten) lawyer; barrister; solicitor; attorney

af (ahf) adv off; finished; ~ **en toe** occasionally

afbeelding (*ahf*-bāyl-dıng) c (pl ~en) picture

afbetalen (*ahf*-ber-taa-lern) v *pay on account

afbetaling (*ahf*-ber-taa-lıng) c (pl ~en) instalment

*****afblijven** (*ahf*-blay-vern) v *keep off

afbraak (*ahf*-braak) c demolition

*****afbreken** (*ahf*-brāy-kern) v chip

afdaling (*ahf*-daa-lıng) c (pl ~en) descent

afdanken (*ahf*-dahng-kern) v discard

afdeling (ahf-day-ling) c (pl ~en) division, department; section

*afdingen** (ahf-di-ngern) v bargain

afdrogen (ahf-droa-gern) v dry

afdruk (ahf-drerk) c (pl ~ken) print

*afdwingen** (ahf-dvi-ngern) v extort

affaire (ah-fai-rer) c (pl ~s) deal; affair

affiche (ah-fee-sher) nt (pl ~s) poster

afgeladen (ahf-kher-laa-dern) adj packed, replete

afgelegen (ahf-kher-lay-gern) adj remote, far-off, out of the way

afgelopen (ahf-kher-loa-pern) adj past

afgerond (ahf-kher-ront) adj rounded

afgevaardigde (ahf-kher-vaar-derg-der) c (pl ~n) deputy

afgezien van (ahf-kher-zeen vahn) apart from

afgod (ahf-khot) c (pl ~en) idol

afgrijzen (ahf-khray-zern) nt horror

afgrond (ahf-khront) c (pl ~en) precipice, abyss

afgunst (ahf-khernst) c envy

afgunstig (ahf-khern-sterkh) adj envious

afhalen (ahf-haa-lern) v collect, fetch

afhandelen (ahf-hahn-der-lern) v settle

*afhangen van** (ahf-hah-ngern) depend on

afhankelijk (ahf-hahng-ker-lerk) adj dependant

afhellend (ahf-heh-lernt) adj sloping

afkeer (ahf-kayr) c dislike; antipathy

afkerig (ahf-kay-rerkh) adj averse

afkeuren (ahf-kur-rern) v disapprove; reject

afknippen (ahf-kni-pern) v *cut off

afkondigen (ahf-kon-der-gern) v proclaim

afkorting (ahf-kor-ting) c (pl ~en) abbreviation

afleiden (ahf-lay-dern) v deduce, infer

afleiding (ahf-lay-ding) c diversion

afleren (ahf-lay-rern) v unlearn

afleveren (ahf-lay-ver-rern) v deliver

afloop (ahf-loap) c expiry

*aflopen** (ahf-loa-pern) v end; expire

aflossen (ahf-lo-sern) v relieve; *pay off

afluisteren (ahf-lur^ew-ster-rern) v eavesdrop

afmaken (ahf-maa-kern) v finish

afmeting (ahf-may-ting) c (pl ~en) size

*afnemen** (ahf-nay-mern) v decrease; *take away

afpersing (ahf-pehr-sing) c (pl ~en) extortion

*afraden** (ahf-raa-dern) v dissuade from

afremmen (ahf-reh-mern) v slow down

Afrika (aa-free-kaa) Africa

Afrikaan (aa-free-kaan) c (pl -kanen) African

Afrikaans (aa-free-kaans) adj African

afschaffen (ahf-skhah-fern) v abolish

afscheid (ahf-skhayt) nt parting

afschrift (ahf-skhrift) nt (pl ~en) copy

afschuw (ahf-skhew^∞) c horror

afschuwelijk (ahf-skhew-ver-lerk) adj horrible, awful; hideous

*afsluiten** (ahf-slur^ew-tern) v *cut off

*afsnijden** (ahf-snay-dern) v *cut off; chip

afspraak (ahf-spraak) c (pl -spraken) date, appointment; engagement

afstammeling (ahf-stah-mer-ling) c (pl ~en) descendant

afstamming (ahf-stah-ming) c origin

afstand (ahf-stahnt) c (pl ~en) distance; space, way

afstandsmeter (ahf-stahnts-may-terr) c (pl ~s) range-finder

afstellen (ahf-steh-lern) v adjust

afstemmen (ahf-steh-mern) v tune in

afstotelijk (ahf-stoa-ter-lerk) adj repellent

aftekenen (*ahf*-tāy-ker-nern) *v* endorse
*****aftrekken** (*ahf*-treh-kern) *v* deduct; subtract
afvaardiging (ah-faar-der-gıng) *c* (pl ~en) delegation
afval (ah-fahl) *nt* garbage, litter, rubbish, refuse
afvegen (ah-fāy-gern) *v* wipe
afvoer (ah-fōōr) *c* drain
zich *****afvragen (ah-fraa-gern) *v* wonder
afwachten (*ahf*-vahkh-tern) *v* await
afwassen (*ahf*-vah-sern) *v* wash up
afwateren (*ahf*-vaa-ter-rern) *v* drain
afwenden (*ahf*-vehn-dern) *v* avert
afwezig (ahf-*vāy*-zerkh) *adj* absent
afwezigheid (ahf-*vāy*-zerkh-hayt) *c* absence
*****afwijken** (*ahf*-vay-kern) *v* deviate
afwijking (*ahf*-vay-kıng) *c* (pl ~en) aberration
*****afwijzen** (*ahf*-vay-zern) *v* reject
afwisselen (*ahf*-vı-ser-lern) *v* vary; **afwisselend** alternate
afwisseling (*ahf*-vı-ser-lıng) *c* variation
*****afzeggen** (*ahf*-seh-gern) *v* cancel
afzetting (*ahf*-seh-tıng) *c* (pl ~en) deposit
afzonderlijk (ahf-*son*-derr-lerk) *adj* individual; separate; *adv* apart
agenda (aa-*gehn*-daa) *c* (pl ~'s) diary; agenda
agent (aa-*gehnt*) *c* (pl ~en) policeman; distributor, agent
agentschap (aa-*gehnt*-skhahp) *nt* (pl ~pen) agency
agrarisch (aa-*graa*-reess) *adj* agrarian
agressief (ah-greh-*seef*) *adj* aggressive
AIDS (eets) *nt* AIDS
akelig (*aa*-ker-lerkh) *adj* nasty
akker (*ah*-kerr) *c* (pl ~s) field
akkoord (ah-*kōārt*) *nt* (pl ~en) agreement
akte (*ahk*-ter) *c* (pl ~n, ~s) act, certificate

aktentas (*ahk*-tern-tahss) *c* (pl ~sen) briefcase, attaché case
al (ahl) *adj* all; *adv* already
alarm (aa-*lahrm*) *nt* alarm
alarmeren (aa-lahr-*māy*-rern) *v* alarm
album (*ahl*-berm) *nt* (pl ~s) album
alcohol (*ahl*-kōa-hol) *c* alcohol
alcoholisch (ahl-kōa-*hōa*-leess) *adj* alcoholic
aldoor (*ahl*-dōar) *adv* all the time
alfabet (*ahl*-faa-beht) *nt* alphabet
algebra (*ahl*-ger-braa) *c* algebra
algemeen (ahl-ger-*māyn*) *adj* general; universal, public; **in het ~** in general
Algerije (ahl-ger-*ray*-er) Algeria
Algerijn (ahl-ger-*rayn*) *c* (pl ~en) Algerian
Algerijns (ahl-ger-*rayns*) *adj* Algerian
alhoewel (ahl-hōō-*vehl*) *conj* though
alikruik (*aa*-lee-krur^{ew}k) *c* (pl ~en) winkle
alimentatie (ah-lee-mehn-*taa*-tsee) *c* alimony
alinea (aa-*lee*-nāy-aa) *c* (pl ~'s) paragraph
alledaags (ah-ler-*daakhs*) *adj* ordinary; everyday
alleen (ah-*lāyn*) *adv* only; alone
allemaal (ah-ler-*maal*) *num* ALL
allergie (ah-lehr-*gee*) *c* (pl ~ën) allergy
allerlei (*ah*-lerr-lay) *adj* various; all sorts of
alles (*ah*-lerss) *pron* everything
almachtig (ahl-*mahkh*-terkh) *adj* omnipotent
almanak (*ahl*-maa-nahk) *c* (pl ~ken) almanac
als (ahls) *conj* if; when; as, like
alsof (ahl-*zof*) *conj* as if; *****doen ~** pretend
alstublieft (ahl-stēw-*bleeft*) here you

are; please

alt (ahlt) c (pl ~en) alto

altaar (ahl-taar) nt (pl altaren) altar

alternatief (ahl-terr-naa-teef) nt (pl -tieven) alternative

altijd (ahl-tayt) adv always, ever

amandel (aa-mahn-derl) c (pl ~en, ~s) almond; **amandelen** tonsils pl

amandelontsteking (aa-mahn-derl-ont-stāy-king) c (pl ~en) tonsilitis

ambacht (ahm-bahkht) nt (pl ~en) trade

ambassade (ahm-bah-saa-der) c (pl ~s) embassy

ambassadeur (ahm-bah-saa-dūrr) c (pl ~s) ambassador

ambitieus (ahm-bee-tsⁱūrss) adj ambitious

ambt (ahmt) nt (pl ~en) office

ambtenaar (ahm-ter-naar) c (pl -naren) civil servant

ambulance (aa-mbew-lahn-ser) c (pl ~s) ambulance

Amerika (aa-māy-ree-kaa) America

Amerikaan (aa-māy-ree-kaan) c (pl -kanen) American

Amerikaans (aa-māy-ree-kaans) adj American

amethist (ah-mer-tist) c (pl ~en) amethyst

amicaal (aa-mee-kaal) adj friendly

ammonia (ah-mōa-nee-ⁱaa) c ammonia

amnestie (ahm-nehss-tee) c amnesty

amulet (aa-mew-leht) c (pl ~ten) lucky charm, charm

amusant (aa-mew-zahnt) adj amusing; entertaining

amusement (aa-mew-zer-mehnt) nt amusement; entertainment

amuseren (aa-mew-zāy-rern) v amuse

analfabeet (ahn-ahl-faa-bāyt) c (pl -beten) illiterate

analist (ah-naa-list) c (pl ~en) analyst

analyse (ah-naa-lee-zer) c (pl ~n, ~s) analysis

analyseren (ah-naa-lee-zāy-rern) v analyse

analyticus (ah-naa-lee-tee-kerss) c (pl -ci) analyst, psychoanalyst

ananas (ah-nah-nahss) c (pl ~sen) pineapple

anarchie (ah-nahr-khee) c anarchy

anatomie (ah-naa-tōa-mee) c anatomy

ander (ahn-derr) adj other; different; **een ~** another; **onder andere** among other things

anders (ahn-derrs) adv else; otherwise

andersom (ahn-derr-som) adv the other way round

angst (ahngst) c (pl ~en) fright, fear; terror

angstig (ahng-sterkh) adj afraid

angstwekkend (ahngst-veh-kernt) adj terrifying

animo (aa-nee-mōa) c zest

anker (ahng-kerr) nt (pl ~s) anchor

annexeren (ah-nehk-sāy-rern) v annex

annonce (ah-nawng-ser) c (pl ~s) advertisement

annuleren (ah-new-lāy-rern) v cancel

annulering (ah-new-lāy-ring) c (pl ~en) cancellation

anoniem (ah-nōa-neem) adj anonymous

ansichtkaart (ahn-zikht-kaart) c (pl ~en) postcard, picture postcard

ansjovis (ahn-shōa-viss) c (pl ~sen) anchovy

antenne (ahn-teh-ner) c (pl ~s) aerial

antibioticum (ahn-tee-bee-ⁱōa-tee-kerm) nt (pl -ca) antibiotic

antiek (ahn-teek) adj antique

antipathie (ahn-tee-paa-tee) c dislike

antiquair (ahn-tee-kair) c (pl ~s) antique dealer

antiquiteit (ahn-tee-kvee-tayt) c (pl ~en) antique

antivries (ahn-tee-*vreess*) *c* antifreeze

antwoord (*ahnt*-vōart) *nt* (pl ~en) reply, answer; **als** ~ in reply

antwoorden (*ahnt*-vōar-dern) *v* reply, answer

apart (aa-*pahrt*) *adv* apart, separately

aperitief (aa-*pāy*-ree-teef) *nt/c* (pl -tieven) aperitif

apotheek (aa-pōa-*tāyk*) *c* (pl -theken) pharmacy, chemist's; drugstore *nAm*

apotheker (aa-pōa-*tāy*-kerr) *c* (pl ~s) chemist

apparaat (ah-paa-*raat*) *nt* (pl -raten) appliance; machine; apparatus

appartement (ah-pahr-ter-*mehnt*) *nt* (pl ~en) apartment *nAm*

appel (*ah*-perl) *c* (pl ~s) apple

applaudisseren (ah-plou-dee-*sāy*-rern) *v* clap

applaus (ah-*plouss*) *nt* applause

april (ah-*pril*) April

aquarel (aa-kvaa-*rehl*) *c* (pl ~len) water-colour

ar (ahr) *c* (pl ~ren) sleigh

Arabier (aa-raa-*beer*) *c* (pl ~en) Arab

Arabisch (aa-*raa*-beess) *adj* Arab

arbeid (*ahr*-bayt) *c* labour, work

arbeidbesparend (*ahr*-bayt-ber-spaa-rernt) *adj* labour-saving

arbeider (*ahr*-bay-derr) *c* (pl ~s) labourer, workman, worker

arbeidsbureau (*ahr*-bayts-bēw-rōa) *nt* (pl ~s) employment exchange

archeologie (ahr-khāy-ōa-lōa-*gee*) *c* archaeology

archeoloog (ahr-khāy-ōa-*lōakh*) *c* (pl -logen) archaeologist

archief (ahr-*kheef*) *nt* (pl -chieven) archives *pl*

architect (ahr-shee-*tehkt*) *c* (pl ~en) architect

architectuur (ahr-shee-tehk-*tēwr*) *c* architecture

arena (aa-*rāy*-naa) *c* (pl ~'s) bullring

arend (*aa*-rernt) *c* (pl ~en) eagle

Argentijn (ahr-gern-*tayn*) *c* (pl ~en) Argentinian

Argentijns (ahr-gern-*tayns*) *adj* Argentinian

Argentinië (ahr-gern-*tee*-nee-Yer) Argentina

argument (ahr-gēw-*mehnt*) *nt* (pl ~en) argument

argumenteren (ahr-gēw-mehn-*tāy*-rern) *v* argue

argwaan (*ahrkh*-vaan) *c* suspicion

argwanend (*ahrkh*-vaa-nernt) *adj* suspicious

arm¹ (ahrm) *adj* poor

arm² (ahrm) *c* (pl ~en) arm

armband (*ahrm*-bahnt) *c* (pl ~en) bracelet; bangle

armoede (*ahr*-mōo-der) *c* poverty

armoedig (*ahr*-mōo-derkh) *adj* poor

aroma (aa-*rōa*-maa) *nt* aroma

arrestatie (ah-rehss-*taa*-tsee) *c* (pl ~s) arrest

arresteren (ah-rehss-*tāy*-rern) *v* arrest

arrogant (ah-rōa-*gahnt*) *adj* presumptuous

artikel (ahr-*tee*-kerl) *nt* (pl ~en, ~s) article; item

artisjok (ahr-tee-*shok*) *c* (pl ~ken) artichoke

artistiek (ahr-tiss-*teek*) *adj* artistic

arts (ahrts) *c* (pl ~en) doctor

as¹ (ahss) *c* (pl ~sen) axle

as² (ahss) *c* ash

asbak (*ahss*-bahk) *c* (pl ~ken) ashtray

asbest (*ahss*-behst) *nt* asbestos

asfalt (*ahss*-fahlt) *nt* asphalt

asiel (aa-*zeel*) *nt* asylum

aspect (ahss-*pehkt*) *nt* (pl ~en) aspect

asperge (ahss-*pehr*-zher) *c* (pl ~s) asparagus

aspirine (ahss-pee-*ree*-ner) *c* aspirin

assistent (ah-see-*stehnt*) *c* (pl ~en)

assistant

associëren (ah-sōa-*shāy*-rern) *v* associate

assortiment (ah-sor-tee-*mehnt*) *nt* (pl ~en) assortment

assurantie (ah-sew-*rahn*-see) *c* (pl -ties, -tiën) insurance

astma (*ahss*-maa) *nt* asthma

atheïst (aa-tāy-*ist*) *c* (pl ~en) atheist

Atlantische Oceaan (aht-*lahn*-tee-ser ōa-say-*aan*) Atlantic

atleet (aht-*lāyt*) *c* (pl -leten) athlete

atletiek (aht-lāy-*teek*) *c* athletics *pl*

atmosfeer (aht-moss-*fāyr*) *c* atmosphere

atomisch (aa-*tōa*-meess) *adj* atomic

atoom (aa-*tōam*) *nt* (pl atomen) atom; **atoom-** atomic

attent (ah-*tehnt*) *adj* considerate

attest (ah-*tehst*) *nt* (pl ~en) certificate

attractie (ah-*trahk*-see) *c* (pl ~s) attraction

aubergine (ōa-behr-*zhee*-ner) *c* (pl ~s) eggplant

augustus (ou-*gerss*-terss) August

aula (*ou*-laa) *c* (pl ~'s) auditorium

Australië (ou-*straa*-lee-ᵞer) Australia

Australiër (ou-*straa*-lee-ᵞerr) *c* (pl ~s) Australian

Australisch (ou-*straa*-leess) *adj* Australian

auteur (ōa-*tūrr*) *c* (pl ~s) author

authentiek (ōa-tehn-*teek*) *adj* authentic

auto (*ōa*-tōa) *c* (pl ~'s) car; motorcar, automobile

automaat (ōa-tōa-*maat*) *c* (pl -maten) slot-machine

automatisch (ōa-tōa-*maa*-tees) *adj* automatic

automatisering (ōa-tōa-maa-tee-*zāy*-ring) *c* automation

automobielclub (ōa-tōa-mōa-*beel*-klerp) *c* (pl ~s) automobile club

automobilisme (ōa-tōa-mōa-bee-*liss*-mer) *nt* motoring

automobilist (ōa-tōa-mōa-bee-*list*) *c* (pl ~en) motorist

autonoom (ōa-tōa-*nōam*) *adj* autonomous

autoped (*ōa*-tōa-peht) *c* (pl ~s) scooter

autopsie (ōa-top-*see*) *c* autopsy

*autorijden (*ōa*-tōa-ray-dern) *v* motor

autorit (*ōa*-tōa-rɪt) *c* (pl ~ten) drive

autoritair (ōa-tōa-ree-*tair*) *adj* authoritarian

autoriteiten (ōa-tōa-ree-*tay*-tern) *pl* authorities *pl*

autoverhuur (*ōa*-tōa-verr-hewr) *c* car hire; car rental *Am*

autoweg (*ōa*-tōa-vehkh) *c* (pl ~en) highway *nAm*

avond *c* (pl ~en) night, evening

avondeten (*aa*-vernt-āy-tern) *nt* dinner; supper

avondkleding (*aa*-vernt-klāy-dɪng) *c* evening dress

avondschemering (*aa*-vernt-skhāy-mer-rɪng) *c* dusk

avontuur (aa-von-*tewr*) *nt* (pl -turen) adventure

Aziaat (aa-zee-ᵞ*aat*) *c* (pl Aziaten) Asian

Aziatisch (aa-zee-ᵞ*aa*-teess) *adj* Asian

Azië (*aa*-zee-ᵞer) Asia

azijn (aa-*zayn*) *c* vinegar

B

baai (baaᵉᵉ) *c* (pl ~en) bay

baan (baan) *c* (pl banen) job

baard (baart) *c* (pl ~en) beard

baarmoeder (*baar*-mōō-derr) *c* womb

baars (baars) *c* (pl baarzen) bass,

perch

baas (baass) c (pl bazen) boss; master

baat (baat) c benefit; profit

babbelen (bah-ber-lern) v chat

babbelkous (bah-berl-kouss) c (pl ~en) chatterbox

babbeltje (bah-berl-tᵞer) nt (pl ~s) chat

baby (baȳ-bee) c (pl ~'s) baby

bacil (bah-sil) c (pl ~len) germ

bacterie (bahk-tāȳ-ree) c (pl -riën) bacterium

bad (baht) nt (pl ~en) bath; een ~ *nemen bathe

baden (baa-dern) v bathe

badhanddoek (baht-hahn-dōōk) c (pl ~en) bath towel

badjas (baht-ᵞahss) c (pl ~sen) bathrobe

badkamer (baht-kaa-merr) c (pl ~s) bathroom

badmuts (baht-merts) c (pl ~en) bathing-cap

badpak (baht-pahk) nt (pl ~ken) bathing-suit

badplaats (baht-plaats) c (pl ~en) seaside resort

badstof (baht-stof) c towelling

badzout (baht-sout) nt bath salts

bagage (bah-gaa-zher) c baggage; luggage

bagagedepot (bah-gaa-zher-dāȳ-pōa) nt (pl ~s) left luggage office; baggage deposit office Am

bagagenet (bah-gaa-zher-neht) nt (pl ~ten) luggage rack

bagageoverschot (bah-gaa-zher-ōa-verr-skhot) nt overweight

bagagerek (bah-gaa-zher-rehk) nt (pl ~ken) luggage rack

bagageruimte (bah-gaa-zher-rur*ew*m-ter) c (pl ~n, ~s) boot

bagagewagen (bah-gaa-zher-vaa-gern) c (pl ~s) luggage van

bakboord (bahk-bōart) nt port

baken (baa-kern) nt (pl ~s) landmark

bakermat (baa-kerr-maht) c cradle

bakkebaarden (bah-ker-baar-dern) pl whiskers pl, sideburns pl

*****bakken** (bah-kern) v bake; fry

bakker (bah-kerr) c (pl ~s) baker

bakkerij (bah-ker-ray) c (pl ~en) bakery

baksteen (bahk-stāȳn) c (pl -stenen) brick

bal[1] (bahl) c (pl ~len) ball

bal[2] (bahl) nt (pl ~s) ball

balans (bah-lahns) c (pl ~en) balance

baldadig (bahl-daa-derkh) adj rowdy

balie (baa-lee) c (pl ~s) counter

balk (bahlk) c (pl ~en) beam

balkon (bahl-kon) nt (pl ~s) balcony; circle

ballet (bah-leht) nt (pl ~ten) ballet

balling (bah-ling) c (pl ~en) exile

ballingschap (bah-ling-skhahp) c exile

ballon (bah-lon) c (pl ~s) balloon

ballpoint (bol-poᵞnt) c (pl ~s) ball-point-pen; Biro

bamboe (bahm-bōō) nt bamboo

banaan (baa-naan) c (pl bananen) banana

band (bahnt) c (pl ~en) tape; band; tyre, tire; lekke ~ flat tyre, puncture

bandenspanning (bahn-der-spah-ning) c tyre pressure

bandepech (bahn-der-pehkh) c blow-out, puncture

bandiet (bahn-deet) c (pl ~en) bandit

bandrecorder (bahnt-rer-kor-derr) c (pl ~s) tape-recorder, recorder

bang (bahng) adj frightened, afraid

bank (bahngk) c (pl ~en) bank; bench

bankbiljet (bahngk-bil-ᵞeht) nt (pl ~ten) banknote

banket (bahng-keht) nt (pl ~ten) banquet

banketbakker (bahng-*keht*-bah-kerr) *c* (pl ~s) confectioner

banketbakkerij (bahng-keht-bah-ker-*ray*) *c* (pl ~en) pastry shop

banketzaal (bahng-*keht*-saal) *c* (pl -za-len) banqueting-hall

bankrekening (*bahngk*-rāy-ker-ning) *c* (pl ~en) bank account

bankroet (bahngk-*rōōt*) *adj* bankrupt

bar (bahr) *c* (pl ~s) bar; saloon

baret (baa-*reht*) *c* (pl ~ten) beret

bariton (*baa*-ree-ton) *c* (pl ~s) baritone

barjuffrouw (*bahr*-Yer-frou) *c* (pl ~en) barmaid

barman (*bahr*-mahn) *c* (pl ~nen) bartender, barman

barmhartig (bahr-*mahr*-terkh) *adj* merciful

barnsteen (*bahrn*-stāyn) *nt* amber

barok (baa-*rok*) *adj* baroque

barometer (bah-rōa-māy-terr) *c* (pl ~s) barometer

barrière (bah-ree-*Yai*-rer) *c* (pl ~s) barrier

barst (bahrst) *c* (pl ~en) crack

* **barsten** (*bahrs*-tern) *v* crack, *burst, *split; *get cracked

bas (bahss) *c* (pl ~sen) bass

baseren (baa-*zāy*-rern) *v* base

basiliek (baa-zee-*leek*) *c* (pl ~en) basilica

basis (*baa*-zerss) *c* (pl bases) basis; base

basiscrème (*baa*-zerss-kraim) *c* (pl ~s) foundation cream

bast (bahst) *c* (pl ~en) bark

bastaard (*bahss*-taart) *c* (pl ~en, ~s) bastard

baten (*baa*-tern) *v* *be of use

batterij (bah-ter-*ray*) *c* (pl ~en) battery

beambte (ber-*ahm*-ter) *c* (pl ~n) clerk

beantwoorden (ber-*ahnt*-vōar-dern) *v* answer

bebost (ber-*bost*) *adj* wooded

bebouwen (ber-*bou*-ern) *v* cultivate

bed (beht) *nt* (pl ~den) bed

bedaard (ber-*daart*) *adj* quiet

bedachtzaam (ber-*dahkht*-saam) *adj* cautious

bedanken (ber-*dahng*-kern) *v* thank

bedaren (ber-*daa*-rern) *v* calm down

beddegoed (*beh*-der-gōōt) *nt* bedding

bedeesd (ber-*dāyst*) *adj* timid

bedekken (ber-*deh*-kern) *v* cover

bedelaar (*bāy*-der-laar) *c* (pl ~s) beggar

bedelen (*bāy*-der-lern) *v* beg

* **bedelven** (ber-*dehl*-vern) *v* bury

* **bedenken** (ber-*dehng*-kern) *v* *think of

* **bederven** (ber-*dehr*-vern) *v* *spoil; mess up

bedevaart (*bāy*-der-vaart) *c* (pl ~en) pilgrimage

bediende (ber-*deen*-der) *c* (pl ~n, ~s) domestic, servant; valet; boy

bedienen (ber-*dee*-nern) *v* serve; wait on; attend on

bediening (ber-*dee*-ning) *c* service

bedieningsgeld (ber-*dee*-nings-khehlt) *nt* service charge

bedoelen (ber-*dōō*-lern) *v* *mean; intend

bedoeling (ber-*dōō*-ling) *c* (pl ~en) purpose, intention

bedrag (ber-*drahkh*) *nt* (pl ~en) amount

* **bedragen** (ber-*draa*-gern) *v* amount to

bedreigen (ber-*dray*-gern) *v* threaten

bedreiging (ber-*dray*-ging) *c* (pl ~en) threat

* **bedriegen** (ber-*dree*-gern) *v* deceive; cheat

bedrijf (ber-*drayf*) *nt* (pl bedrijven)

business, concern; plant; act

bedrijvig (ber-*dray*-verkh) *adj* active

bedroefd (ber-*drōōft*) *adj* sad, sorry

bedroefdheid (ber-*drōōft*-hayt) *c* sadness; grief

bedrog (ber-*drokh*) *nt* deceit; fraud

beëindigen (ber-*ayn*-der-gern) *v* end, finish

beek (bāyk) *c* (pl beken) brook, stream

beeld (bāylt) *nt* (pl ~en) picture, image

beeldhouwer (*bāylt*-hou-err) *c* (pl ~s) sculptor

beeldhouwwerk (*bāylt*-hou-vehrk) *nt* (pl ~en) sculpture

beeldscherm (*bāylt*-skhehrm) *nt* (pl ~en) screen

been¹ (bāyn) *nt* (pl benen) leg

been² (bāyn) *nt* (pl beenderen, benen) bone

beer (bāyr) *c* (pl beren) bear

beest (bāyst) *nt* (pl ~en) beast

beestachtig (*bāyst*-ahkh-terkh) *adj* brutal

beet (bāyt) *c* (pl beten) bite

beetje (*bāy*-tᵉer) *nt* bit

*****beetnemen** (*bāyt*-nāy-mern) *v* kid

beetwortel (*bāyt*-vor-terl) *c* (pl ~s, ~en) beetroot

befaamd (ber-*faamt*) *adj* noted

begaafd (ber-*gaaft*) *adj* gifted, talented

*****begaan** (ber-*gaan*) *v* commit

begeerlijk (ber-*gāyr*-lerk) *adj* desirable

begeerte (ber-*gāyr*-ter) *c* (pl ~n) desire

begeleiden (ber-ger-*lay*-dern) *v* accompany; conduct

begeren (ber-*gāy*-rern) *v* desire

begin (ber-*gin*) *nt* start, beginning; **begin-** initial

beginneling (ber-*gi*-ner-ling) *c* (pl ~en) learner, beginner

*****beginnen** (ber-*gi*-nern) *v* start, commence, *begin

beginner (ber-*gi*-nerr) *c* (pl ~s) learner

beginsel (ber-*gin*-serl) *nt* (pl ~en, ~s) principle

begraafplaats (ber-*graaf*-plaats) *c* (pl ~en) cemetery

begrafenis (ber-*graa*-fer-niss) *c* (pl ~sen) burial; funeral

*****begraven** (ber-*graa*-vern) *v* bury

*****begrijpen** (ber-*gray*-pern) *v* *understand; *see, *take; **begrijpend** sympathetic

begrip (ber-*grip*) *nt* (pl ~pen) notion; idea, conception; understanding

begroeid (ber-*grōō*ᵉᵉt) *adj* overgrown

begroting (ber-*grōā*-ting) *c* (pl ~en) budget

begunstigde (ber-*gern*-sterkh-der) *c* (pl ~n) payee

begunstigen (ber-*gern*-ster-gern) *v* favour

beha (bāy-*haa*) *c* (pl ~'s) brassiere, bra

behalen (ber-*haa*-lern) *v* obtain

behalve (ber-*hahl*-ver) *prep* but, except; beyond, besides

behandelen (ber-*hahn*-der-lern) *v* treat, handle

behandeling (ber-*hahn*-der-ling) *c* (pl ~en) treatment

behang (ber-*hahng*) *nt* wallpaper

beheer (ber-*hāyr*) *nt* management; administration

beheersen (ber-*hāyr*-sern) *v* master

beheksen (ber-*hehk*-sern) *v* bewitch

zich *behelpen met (ber-*hehl*-pern) *make do with

behendig (ber-*hehn*-derkh) *adj* skilful

beheren (ber-*hāy*-rern) *v* manage

behoedzaam (ber-*hōōt*-saam) *adj* wary

behoefte (ber-*hōōf*-ter) *c* (pl ~n) need, want

behoeven (ber-*hoō*-vern) v need; **ten behoeve van** on behalf of

behoorlijk (ber-*hōar*-lerk) adj proper

behoren (ber-*hōa*-rern) v belong to; *ought

behoudend (ber-*hou*-dernt) adj conservative

beide (*bay*-der) adj both; either; **een van ~** either; **geen van ~** neither

beige (*bai*-zher) adj beige

beïnvloeden (ber-*ın*-vlōō-dern) v influence; affect

beitel (*bay*-terl) c (pl ~s) chisel

bejaard (ber-*Yaart*) adj aged; elderly

bek (behk) c (pl ~ken) mouth; beak

bekend (ber-*kehnt*) adj well-known

bekende (ber-*kehn*-der) c (pl ~n) acquaintance

bekendmaken (ber-*kehnt*-maa-kern) v announce

bekendmaking (ber-*kehnt*-maa-kıng) c (pl ~en) announcement

bekennen (ber-*keh*-nern) v admit, confess

bekentenis (ber-*kehn*-ter-niss) c (pl ~sen) confession

beker (*bāy*-kerr) c (pl ~s) mug; tumbler; cup

bekeren (ber-*kāy*-rern) v convert

*bekijken** (ber-*kay*-kern) v regard, view

bekken (*beh*-kern) nt (pl ~s) basin; pelvis

beklagen (ber-*klaa*-gern) v pity

bekleden (ber-*klāy*-dern) v upholster

beklemmen (ber-*kleh*-mern) v oppress

*beklimmen** (ber-*klı*-mern) v ascend

beklimming (ber-*klı*-mıng) c (pl ~en) ascent

beknopt (ber-*knopt*) adj concise; brief

zich bekommeren om (ber-*ko*-mer-rern) care about

bekoring (ber-*kōa*-rıng) c (pl ~en) attraction, charm

bekritiseren (ber-kree-tee-*zāy*-rern) v criticize

bekrompen (ber-*krom*-pern) adj narrow-minded

bekronen (ber-*krōa*-nern) v crown

bekwaam (ber-*kvaam*) adj able, capable; skilful

bekwaamheid (ber-*kvaam*-hayt) c (pl -heden) ability, faculty, capacity

bel (behl) c (pl ~len) bell; bubble

belachelijk (ber-*lah*-kher-lerk) adj ridiculous, ludicrous

belang (ber-*lahng*) nt (pl ~en) interest; importance; **van ~ *zijn** matter

belangrijk (ber-*lahng*-rayk) adj important; capital

belangstellend (ber-lahng-*steh*-lernt) adj interested

belangstelling (ber-*lahng*-steh-lıng) c interest

belastbaar (ber-*lahst*-baar) adj dutiable

belasten (ber-*lahss*-tern) v charge; tax; **belast met** in charge of

belasting (ber-*lahss*-tıng) c (pl ~en) charge; tax; taxation

belastingvrij (ber-lahss-tıng-*vray*) adj duty-free; tax-free

beledigen (ber-*lāy*-der-gern) v insult; offend; **beledigend** offensive

belediging (ber-*lāy*-der-gıng) c (pl ~en) insult; offence

beleefd (ber-*lāyft*) adj polite; civil

belegering (ber-*lāy*-ger-rıng) c (pl ~en) siege

beleggen (ber-*leh*-gern) v invest

belegging (ber-*leh*-gıng) c (pl ~en) investment

beleid (ber-*layt*) nt policy

belemmeren (ber-*leh*-mer-rern) v impede

beletsel (ber-*leht*-serl) nt (pl ~s, ~en) impediment

beletten (ber-*leh*-tern) *v* prevent

beleven (ber-*lay*-vern) *v* experience

Belg (behlkh) *c* (pl ~en) Belgian

België (*behl*-gee-Yer) Belgium

Belgisch (*behl*-geess) *adj* Belgian

belichting (ber-*likh*-ting) *c* exposure

belichtingsmeter (ber-*likh*-tings-may-terr) *c* (pl ~s) exposure meter

*****belijden** (ber-*lay*-dern) *v* confess

bellen (*beh*-lern) *v* *****ring

belofte (ber-*lof*-ter) *c* (pl ~n) promise

belonen (ber-*loa*-nern) *v* reward

beloning (ber-*loa*-ning) *c* (pl ~en) reward; prize

beloven (ber-*loa*-vern) *v* promise

bemachtigen (ber-*mahkh*-ter-gern) *v* secure

bemanning (ber-*mah*-ning) *c* (pl ~en) crew

bemerken (ber-*mehr*-kern) *v* notice; perceive

bemiddelaar (ber-*mi*-der-laar) *c* (pl ~s) mediator

bemiddeld (ber-*mi*-derlt) *adj* well-to-do

bemiddelen (ber-*mi*-der-lern) *v* mediate

bemind (ber-*mint*) *adj* beloved

zich bemoeien met (ber-*mooee*-ern) interfere with

benadrukken (ber-*naa*-drer-kern) *v* emphasize, stress

benaming (ber-*naa*-ming) *c* (pl ~en) denomination

benauwd (ber-*nout*) *adj* stuffy

bende (*behn*-der) *c* (pl ~n, ~s) gang

beneden (ber-*nay*-dern) *prep* under, below; *adv* underneath, beneath; below; downstairs; **naar ~** downwards, down; downstairs

benieuwd (ber-*nee∞t*) *adj* curious

benijden (ber-*nay*-dern) *v* envy

benoemen (ber-*noo*-mern) *v* nominate, appoint

benoeming (ber-*noo*-ming) *c* (pl ~en) nomination, appointment

benutten (ber-*ner*-tern) *v* utilize

benzine (behn-*zee*-ner) *c* petrol; fuel; gasoline *nAm*; gas *nAm*; **loodvrije ~** unleaded petrol

benzinepomp (behn-*zee*-ner-pomp) *c* (pl ~en) petrol pump; fuel pump *Am*; gas pump *Am*

benzinestation (behn-*zee*-ner-staa-shon) *nt* (pl ~s) service station, petrol station; gas station *Am*

benzinetank (behn-*zee*-ner-tehngk) *c* (pl ~s) petrol tank

beoefenen (ber-*oo*-fer-nern) *v* practise

beogen (ber-*oa*-gern) *v* aim at

beoordelen (ber-*oar*-day-lern) *v* judge

beoordeling (ber-*oar*-day-ling) *c* (pl ~en) judgment

bepaald (ber-*paalt*) *adj* definite; certain

bepalen (ber-*paa*-lern) *v* define, determine; stipulate

bepaling (ber-*paa*-ling) *c* (pl ~en) stipulation; definition

beperken (ber-*pehr*-kern) *v* limit

beperking (ber-*pehr*-king) *c* (pl ~en) restriction

beproeven (ber-*proo*-vern) *v* attempt

beraad (ber-*raat*) *nt* deliberation

beraadslagen (ber-*raat*-slaa-gern) *v* deliberate

beramen (ber-*raa*-mern) *v* devise

bereid (ber-*rayt*) *adj* prepared, willing

bereiden (ber-*ray*-dern) *v* cook

bereidwillig (ber-rayt-*vi*-lerkh) *adj* cooperative

bereik (ber-*rayk*) *nt* reach; range

bereikbaar (ber-*rayk*-baar) *adj* attainable

bereiken (ber-*ray*-kern) *v* reach; achieve, accomplish, attain

berekenen (ber-*ray*-ker-nern) *v* calculate; charge

berekening (ber-*rāy*-ker-nıng) *c* (pl ~en) calculation

berg (behrkh) *c* (pl ~en) mountain; mount

bergachtig (*behrkh*-ahkh-terkh) *adj* mountainous

bergketen (*behrkh*-kāy-tern) *c* (pl ~s) mountain range

bergkloof (*behrkh*-klōaf) *c* (pl -kloven) glen

bergpas (*behrkh*-pahss) *c* (pl ~sen) mountain pass

bergplaats (*behrkh*-plaats) *c* (pl ~en) depository

bergrug (*behrkh*-rerg) *c* (pl ~gen) ridge

bergsport (*behrkh*-sport) *c* mountaineering

bericht (ber-*rıkht*) *nt* (pl ~en) message; notice

berispen (ber-*rıss*-pern) *v* reprimand, scold

berk (behrk) *c* (pl ~en) birch

beroemd (ber-*rōōmt*) *adj* famous

beroep (ber-*rōōp*) *nt* (pl ~en) profession; appeal; **beroeps-** professional

beroerd (ber-*rōōrt*) *adj* miserable

beroerte (ber-*rōōr*-ter) *c* (pl ~n, ~s) stroke

berouw (ber-*rou*) *nt* repentance

beroven (ber-*rōā*-vern) *v* rob

beroving (ber-*rōā*-vıng) *c* (pl ~en) robbery

berucht (ber-*rerkht*) *adj* notorious

bes (behss) *c* (pl ~sen) berry; currant; **zwarte ~** black-currant

beschaafd (ber-*skhaaft*) *adj* civilized; cultured

beschaamd (ber-*skhaamt*) *adj* ashamed

beschadigen (ber-*skhaa*-der-gern) *v* damage

beschaving (ber-*skhaa*-vıng) *c* (pl ~en) civilization; culture

bescheiden (ber-*skhay*-dern) *adj* modest

bescheidenheid (ber-*skhay*-dern-hayt) *c* modesty

beschermen (ber-*skhehr*-mern) *v* protect

bescherming (ber-*skhehr*-mıng) *c* protection

beschikbaar (ber-*skhık*-baar) *adj* available

beschikken over (ber-*skhı*-kern) dispose of

beschikking (ber-*skhı*-king) *c* disposal

beschimmeld (ber-*skhı*-merlt) *adj* mouldy

beschouwen (ber-*skhou*-ern) *v* consider; regard; reckon

*beschrijven** (ber-*skhray*-vern) *v* describe

beschrijving (ber-*skhray*-vıng) *c* (pl ~en) description

beschuldigen (ber-*skherl*-der-gern) *v* accuse; blame

beschutten (ber-*skher*-tern) *v* shelter

beschutting (ber-*skher*-tıng) *c* cover, shelter

beseffen (ber-*seh*-fern) *v* realize

beslag (ber-*slahkh*) *nt* batter; **beslag leggen op** impound, confiscate

beslissen (ber-*slı*-sern) *v* decide

beslissing (ber-*slı*-sıng) *c* (pl ~en) decision

beslist (ber-*slıst*) *adv* without fail

besluit (ber-*slur^{ew}t*) *nt* (pl ~en) decision

*besluiten** (ber-*slur^{ew}*-tern) *v* decide

besmettelijk (ber-*smeh*-ter-lerk) *adj* contagious, infectious

besmetten (ber-*smeh*-tern) *v* infect

besneeuwd (ber-*snāy^{oo}t*) *adj* snowy

bespelen (ber-*spāy*-lern) *v* play

bespottelijk (ber-*spo*-ter-lerk) *adj* ridiculous, ludicrous

bespotten (ber-*spo*-tern) v ridicule; mock

*bespreken (ber-*spray*-kern) v engage, reserve; discuss

bespreking (ber-*spray*-king) c (pl ~en) booking; review; discussion

best (behst) adj best

bestaan (ber-*staan*) nt existence

*bestaan (ber-*staan*) v exist; ~ **uit** consist of

bestanddeel (ber-*stahn-dayl*) nt (pl -delen) ingredient; element

besteden (ber-*stay*-dern) v *spend

bestek (ber-*stehk*) nt (pl ~ken) cutlery

bestelauto (ber-*stehl*-oa-toa) c (pl ~'s) van; delivery van, pick-up van

bestelformulier (ber-*stehl*-for-mew-leer) nt (pl ~en) order-form

bestellen (ber-*steh*-lern) v order

bestelling (ber-*steh*-ling) c (pl ~en) order

bestemmen (ber-*steh*-mern) v destine

bestemming (ber-*steh*-ming) c (pl ~en) destination

bestendig (ber-*stehn*-derkh) adj permanent

*bestijgen (ber-*stay*-gern) v mount

bestraten (ber-*straa*-tern) v pave

*bestrijden (ber-*stray*-dern) v combat

besturen (ber-*stew*-rern) v *drive

bestuur (ber-*stewr*) nt (pl besturen) direction; board; rule

bestuurlijk (ber-*stewr*-lerk) adj administrative

bestuursrecht (ber-*stewrs*-rehkht) nt administrative law

betalen (ber-*taa*-lern) v *pay

betaling (ber-*taa*-ling) c (pl ~en) payment

betasten (ber-*tahss*-tern) v *feel

betekenen (ber-*tay*-ker-nern) v *mean

betekenis (ber-*tay*-ker-niss) c (pl ~sen) meaning; sense

beter (*bay*-terr) adj better; superior

beteugelen (ber-*tur*-ger-lern) v curb

betogen (ber-*toa*-gern) v demonstrate

betoging (ber-*toa*-ging) c (pl ~en) demonstration

beton (ber-*ton*) nt concrete

betoveren (ber-*toa*-ver-rern) v bewitch; **betoverend** enchanting, glamorous

betovering (ber-*toa*-ver-ring) c (pl ~en) spell

betrappen (ber-*trah*-pern) v *catch

*betreden (ber-*tray*-dern) v enter

*betreffen (ber-*treh*-fern) v concern; affect, touch; **wat betreft** as regards

betreffende (ber-*treh*-fern-der) prep as regards, regarding, about, concerning

betrekkelijk (ber-*treh*-ker-lerk) adj relative

*betrekken (ber-*treh*-kern) v implicate, *get involved; obtain

betrekking (ber-*treh*-king) c (pl ~en) post, position, job; reference; **met ~ tot** regarding, with reference to

betreuren (ber-*trur*-rern) v regret

betrokken (ber-*tro*-kern) adj cloudy, overcast; concerned, involved

betrouwbaar (ber-*trou*-baar) adj trustworthy, reliable

betuigen (ber-*tur*ᵉʷ-gern) v express

betwijfelen (ber-*tvay*-fer-lern) v doubt, query

betwisten (ber-*tviss*-tern) v dispute

beu (bur) adj tired of, fed up with

beuk (burk) c (pl ~en) beech

beul (burl) c (pl ~en) executioner

beurs (burrs) c (pl beurzen) purse; stock exchange; fair; grant

beurt (burrt) c (pl ~en) turn

bevaarbaar (ber-*vaar*-baar) adj navigable

*bevallen (ber-*vah*-lern) v please

bevallig (ber-*vah*-lerkh) *adj* graceful

bevalling (ber-*vah*-ling) *c* (pl ~en) delivery, childbirth

bevaren (ber-*vaa*-rern) *v* sail

bevatten (ber-*vah*-tern) *v* contain; include

bevel (ber-*vehl*) *nt* (pl ~en) command, order

bevelen (ber-*vāy*-lern) *v* command, order

bevelhebber (ber-*vehl*-heh-berr) *c* (pl ~s) commander

beven (*bāy*-vern) *v* tremble

bever (*bāy*-verr) *c* (pl ~s) beaver

bevestigen (ber-*vehss*-ter-gern) *v* acknowledge, confirm; fasten; **bevestigend** affirmative

bevestiging (ber-*vehss*-ter-ging) *c* (pl ~en) confirmation

zich *bevinden (ber-*vin*-dern) *be

bevlieging (ber-*vlee*-ging) *c* (pl ~en) whim

bevochtigen (ber-*vokh*-ter-gern) *v* damp, moisten

bevoegd (ber-*vōōkht*) *adj* qualified

bevoegdheid (ber-*vōōkht*-hayt) *c* (pl -heden) qualification

bevolking (ber-*vol*-king) *c* population

bevoorrechten (ber-*vōa*-raykh-tern) *v* favour

bevorderen (ber-*vor*-der-rern) *v* promote

bevredigen (ber-*vrāy*-der-gern) *v* satisfy

bevrediging (ber-*vrāy*-der-ging) *c* (pl ~en) satisfaction

bevriezen (ber-*vree*-zern) *v* *freeze

bevrijding (ber-*vray*-ding) *c* liberation

bevuild (ber-*vur^ew^lt*) *adj* soiled

bewaken (ber-*vaa*-kern) *v* guard

bewaker (ber-*vaa*-kerr) *c* (pl ~s) guard; warden

bewapenen (ber-*vaa*-per-nern) *v* arm

bewaren (ber-*vaa*-rern) *v* *hold; preserve; *keep

bewaring (ber-*vaa*-ring) *c* preservation

beweeglijk (ber-*vāykh*-lerk) *adj* mobile

beweegreden (ber-*vāykh*-rāy-dern) *c* (pl ~en) cause

bewegen (ber-*vāy*-gern) *v* move; stir

beweging (ber-*vāy*-ging) *c* (pl ~en) movement; motion

beweren (ber-*vāy*-rern) *v* claim

bewijs (ber-*vayss*) *nt* (pl bewijzen) proof, evidence; token; voucher

bewijzen (ber-*vay*-zern) *v* prove

bewind (ber-*vint*) *nt* rule, government

bewolking (ber-*vol*-king) *c* clouds

bewolkt (ber-*volkt*) *adj* cloudy

bewonderen (ber-*von*-der-rern) *v* admire

bewondering (ber-*von*-der-ring) *c* admiration

bewonen (ber-*vōā*-nern) *v* inhabit

bewoner (ber-*vōā*-nerr) *c* (pl ~s) inhabitant; occupant

bewoonbaar (ber-*vōān*-baar) *adj* habitable, inhabitable

bewust (ber-*verst*) *adj* conscious, aware

bewusteloos (ber-*verss*-ter-lōass) *adj* unconscious

bewustzijn (ber-*verst*-sayn) *nt* consciousness

bezem (*bāy*-zerm) *c* (pl ~s) broom

bezeren (ber-*zāy*-rern) *v* *hurt

bezet (ber-*zeht*) *adj* engaged, occupied

bezetten (ber-*zeh*-tern) *v* occupy

bezetting (ber-*zeh*-ting) *c* (pl ~en) occupation

bezielen (ber-*zee*-lern) *v* inspire

bezienswaardigheid (ber-zeen-*svaar*-derkh-hayt) *c* (pl -heden) sight

bezig (*bāy*-zerkh) *adj* engaged, busy

zich *bezighouden met (*bāy*-zerkh-hou-dern) attend to

bezinksel (ber-*zingk*-serl) *nt* (pl ~s) deposit

bezit (ber-*zıt*) *nt* property; possession

*__bezitten__ (ber-*zı*-tern) *v* possess, own

bezitter (ber-*zı*-terr) *c* (pl ~s) owner

bezittingen (ber-*zı*-tıng-ern) *pl* belongings *pl*

bezoek (ber-*zōōk*) *nt* (pl ~en) call, visit

*__bezoeken__ (ber-*zōō*-kern) *v* visit; call on

bezoeker (ber-*zōō*-kerr) *c* (pl ~s) visitor

bezoekuren (ber-*zōōk*-ēw-rern) *pl* visiting hours

bezonnen (ber-*zo*-nern) *adj* sober

bezorgd (ber-*zorkht*) *adj* anxious, concerned

bezorgdheid (ber-*zorkht*-hayt) *c* worry, anxiety

bezorgen (ber-*zor*-gern) *v* deliver; supply

bezorging (ber-*zor*-gıng) *c* delivery

bezwaar (ber-*zvaar*) *nt* (pl bezwaren) objection; ~ *hebben tegen* object to; mind

*__bezwijken__ (ber-*zvay*-kern) *v* collapse; succumb

bibberen (bı-*ber*-rern) *v* shiver

bibliotheek (bee-blee-Yōa-*tāyk*) *c* (pl -theken) library

*__bidden__ (bı-dern) *v* pray

biecht (beekht) *c* (pl ~en) confession

biechten (beekh-tern) *v* confess

*__bieden__ (bee-dern) *v* offer

biefstuk (beef-sterk) *c* (pl ~ken) steak

bier (beer) *nt* (pl ~en) beer; ale

bies (beess) *c* (pl biezen) rush

bieslook (beess-lōak) *nt* chives *pl*

biet (beet) *c* (pl ~en) beet

big (bıkh) *c* (pl ~gen) piglet

bij[1] (bay) *prep* near, at, with, by; to

bij[2] (bay) *c* (pl ~en) bee

bijbel (*bay*-berl) *c* (pl ~s) bible

bijbetekenis (*bay*-ber-tāy-ker-nıss) *c* (pl ~sen) connotation

bijdrage (*bay*-draa-ger) *c* (pl ~n) contribution

bijeen (bay-*āyn*) *adv* together

*__bijeenbrengen__ (bay-*āyn*-breh-ngern) *v* assemble

*__bijeenkomen__ (bay-*āyng*-kōa-mern) *v* gather

bijeenkomst (bay-*āyng*-komst) *c* (pl ~en) meeting; rally; assembly, congress

bijenkorf (*bay*-er-korf) *c* (pl -korven) beehive

bijgebouw (*bay*-ger-bou) *nt* (pl ~en) annex

bijgeloof (*bay*-ger-lōaf) *nt* superstition

bijgevolg (bay-ger-*volkh*) *adv* consequently

*__bijhouden__ (*bay*-hou-dern) *v* *keep up with

bijknippen (*bay*-knı-pern) *v* trim

bijkomend (*bay*-kōa-mernt) *adj* additional

bijkomstig (bay-*kom*-sterkh) *adj* additional; subordinate

bijl (bayl) *c* (pl ~en) axe

bijlage (*bay*-laa-ger) *c* (pl ~n) annex; enclosure

bijna (*bay*-naa) *adv* nearly, almost

bijnaam (*bay*-naam) *c* (pl -namen) nickname

bijouterie (bee-zhōō-ter-*ree*) *c* jewellery

*__bijsluiten__ (*bay*-slur^{ew}-tern) *v* enclose

*__bijstaan__ (*bay*-staan) *v* assist, aid

bijstand (*bay*-stahnt) *c* assistance

*__bijten__ (*bay*-tern) *v* *bite

bijvoegen (*bay*-vōō-gern) *v* attach

bijvoeglijk naamwoord (bay-*vōōkh*-lerk naam-vōart) *nt* adjective

bijvoorbeeld (ber-*vōar*-bāylt) *adv* for instance, for example

bijwonen (*bay*-vōa-nern) *v* assist at, attend

bijwoord (*bay*-vōart) *nt* (pl ~en) adverb

bijziend (bay-*zeent*) *adj* short-sighted

bijzonder (bee-*zon*-derr) *adj* special, particular; peculiar; **in het ~** in particular, specially

bijzonderheid (bee-*zon*-derr-hayt) *c* (pl -heden) detail

bil (bɪl) *c* (pl ~len) buttock

biljart (bɪl-*Yahrt*) *nt* billiards *pl*

billijk (bɪ-lerk) *adj* right, fair, reasonable

***binden** (*bɪn*-dern) *v* *bind; tie

binnen (*bɪ*-nern) *prep* within, inside; *adv* inside, indoors; in; indoor; **naar ~** inwards; **van ~** within, inside

binnenband (*bɪ*-ner-bahnt) *c* (pl ~en) inner tube

***binnengaan** (*bɪ*-ner-gaan) *v* enter, *go in

binnenkant (*bɪ*-ner-kahnt) *c* interior, inside

***binnenkomen** (*bɪ*-nern-kōa-mern) *v* enter

binnenkomst (*bɪ*-ner-komst) *c* entrance

binnenkort (bɪ-ner-*kort*) *adv* shortly

binnenlands (*bɪ*-ner-lahnts) *adj* domestic

binnenst (*bɪ*-nerst) *adj* inside; **binnenste buiten** *adv* inside out

***binnenvallen** (*bɪ*-ner-vah-lern) *v* invade

biologie (bee-Yōa-lōa-*gee*) *c* biology

bioscoop (bee-Yoss-*kōap*) *c* (pl -scopen) cinema; pictures; movie theater *Am*, movies *Am*

biscuit (bɪss-*kvee*) *nt* (pl ~s) cookie *nAm*

bisschop (*bɪss*-khop) *c* (pl ~pen) bishop

bitter (*bɪ*-terr) *adj* bitter

blaar (blaar) *c* (pl blaren) blister

blaas (blaass) *c* (pl blazen) bladder;

blister

blaasontsteking (*blaass*-ont-stā̄y-kɪng) *c* (pl ~en) cystitis

blad¹ (blaht) *nt* (pl ~eren, blaren) leaf

blad² (blaht) *nt* (pl ~en) sheet; magazine

bladgoud (*blaht*-khout) *nt* gold leaf

bladzijde (*blaht*-say-der) *c* (pl ~n) page

blaffen (*blah*-fern) *v* bark; bay

blanco (*blahng*-kōa) *adj* blank

blank (blahngk) *adj* white

blankvoren (*blahngk*-fōa-rern) *c* (pl ~s) roach

blauw (blou) *adj* blue

***blazen** (*blaa*-zern) *v* *blow

blazer (*blā̄y*-zerr) *c* (pl ~s) blazer

bleek (blā̄yk) *adj* pale

bleken (*blā̄y*-kern) *v* bleach

blessure (bleh-*sēw*-rer) *c* (pl ~s) injury

blij (blay) *adj* glad; happy, joyful

blijkbaar (*blayk*-baar) *adv* apparently

***blijken** (*blay*-kern) *v* prove; appear

blijspel (*blay*-spehl) *nt* (pl ~en) comedy

***blijven** (*blay*-vern) *v* stay, remain; *keep; **blijvend** lasting; permanent

blik (blɪk) *nt* (pl ~ken) tin, can; *c* look; glimpse, glance; **een ~ *werpen** glance

blikopener (*blɪk*-ōa-per-nerr) *c* (pl ~s) tin-opener, can opener

bliksem (*blɪk*-serm) *c* lightning

blind¹ (blɪnt) *nt* (pl ~en) shutter

blind² (blɪnt) *adj* blind

blindedarm (blɪn-der-*dahrm*) *c* (pl ~en) appendix

blindedarmontsteking (blɪn-der-*dahrm*-ont-stā̄y-kɪng) *c* (pl ~en) appendicitis

***blinken** (*blɪng*-kern) *v* *shine; **blinkend** bright

blocnote (*blok*-nōat) *c* (pl ~s) writing-pad

bloed (blōōt) *nt* blood

bloedarmoede (blōōt-ahr-mōō-der) *c* anaemia

bloeddruk (blōō-drerk) *c* blood pressure

bloeden (blōō-dern) *v* *bleed

bloeding (blōō-dɪng) *c* (pl ~en) haemorrhage

bloedsomloop (blōōt-som-lōap) *c* circulation

bloedvat (blōōt-faht) *nt* (pl ~en) blood-vessel

bloedvergiftiging (blōōt-ferr-gɪf-ter-gɪng) *c* blood-poisoning

bloem¹ (blōōm) *c* flour

bloem² (blōōm) *c* (pl ~en) flower

bloemblad (blōōm-blaht) *nt* (pl ~en) petal

bloembol (blōōm-bol) *c* (pl ~len) bulb

bloemenwinkel (blōō-mer-vɪng-kerl) *c* (pl ~s) flower-shop

bloemist (blōōm-mɪst) *c* (pl ~en) florist

bloemkool (blōōm-kōal) *c* (pl -kolen) cauliflower

bloemlezing (blōōm-lāy-zɪng) *c* (pl ~en) anthology

bloemperk (blōōm-pehrk) *nt* (pl ~en) flowerbed

blok (blok) *nt* (pl ~ken) block; **blokje** *nt* cube

blokkeren (blo-kāy-rern) *v* block

blond (blont) *adj* fair

blondine (blon-dee-ner) *c* (pl ~s) blonde

bloot (blōat) *adj* bare; naked

blootleggen (blōat-leh-gern) *v* uncover

blootstelling (blōat-steh-lɪng) *c* (pl ~en) exposure

blouse (blōō-zer) *c* (pl ~s) blouse

blozen (blōa-zern) *v* blush

blussen (bler-sern) *v* extinguish

bocht (bokht) *c* (pl ~en) turning, bend; curve, turn

bode (bōa-der) *c* (pl ~n, ~s) messenger

bodem (bōa-derm) *c* (pl ~s) bottom; ground; soil

boef (bōōf) *c* (pl boeven) villain

boei (bōōee) *c* (pl ~en) buoy

boeien (bōōee-ern) *v* fascinate

boek (bōōk) *nt* (pl ~en) book

boeken (bōō-kern) *v* book

boekenstalletje (bōō-ker-stah-ler-tʸer) *nt* (pl ~s) bookstand

boeket (bōō-keht) *nt* (pl ~ten) bouquet

boekhandel (bōōk-hahn-derl) *c* (pl ~s) bookstore

boekhandelaar (bōōk-hahn-der-laar) *c* (pl -laren) bookseller

boekwinkel (bōōk-vɪng-kerl) *c* (pl ~s) bookstore

boel (bōōl) *c* lot

boer (bōōr) *c* (pl ~en) farmer; peasant; knave

boerderij (bōōr-der-ray) *c* (pl ~en) farm; farmhouse

boerin (bōō-rɪn) *c* (pl ~nen) farmer's wife

boete (bōō-ter) *c* (pl ~n, ~s) penalty, fine

boetseren (bōōt-sāy-rern) *v* model

bof (bof) *c* mumps

bok (bok) *c* (pl ~ken) goat

boksen (bok-sern) *v* box

bokswedstrijd (boks-veht-strayt) *c* (pl ~en) boxing match

bol (bol) *c* (pl ~len) bulb; sphere

Boliviaan (bōa-lee-vee-ʸaan) *c* (pl -vianen) Bolivian

Boliviaans (bōa-lee-vee-ʸaans) *adj* Bolivian

Bolivië (bōa-lee-vee-ʸer) Bolivia

bom (bom) *c* (pl ~men) bomb

bombarderen (bom-bahr-dāy-rern) *v* bomb

bon (bon) *c* (pl ~nen) coupon; ticket; voucher

bonbon (bom-*bon*) c (pl ~s) chocolate

bond (bont) c (pl ~en) league, federation

bondgenoot (*bont*-kher-nōāt) c (pl -noten) associate

bondgenootschap (*bont*-kher-nōāt-skhahp) nt (pl ~pen) alliance

bons (boᶇs) c (pl bonzen) bump

bont (bont) adj gay, colourful; nt furs

bontjas (*bon*-tᵞahss) c (pl ~sen) fur coat

bontwerker (*bon*-tvehr-kerr) c (pl ~s) furrier

bonzen (*bon*-zern) v bump

boodschap (*bōāt*-skhahp) c (pl ~pen) errand; message

boodschappentas (*bōāt*-skhah-per-tahss) c (pl ~sen) shopping bag

boog (bōākh) c (pl bogen) arch; bow

boogvormig (*bōākh*-for-merkh) adj arched

boom (bōām) c (pl bomen) tree

boomgaard (*bōām*-gaart) c (pl ~en) orchard

boomkwekerij (bōām-kvāy-ker-*ray*) c (pl ~en) nursery

boon (bōān) c (pl bonen) bean

boor (bōār) c (pl boren) drill

boord (bōārt) nt/c (pl ~en) collar; **aan boord** aboard; **van boord *gaan** disembark

boordeknoopje (*bōār*-der-knōā-pᵞer) nt (pl ~s) collar stud

boos (bōāss) adj cross

boosaardig (bōā-*zaar*-derkh) adj malicious, vicious

boosheid (*bōāss*-hayt) c anger, temper

boot (bōāt) c (pl boten) boat

bootje (*bōā*-tᵞer) nt (pl ~s) dinghy

boottocht (*bōā*-tokht) c (pl ~en) cruise

bord (bort) nt (pl ~en) dish, plate; board

bordeel (bor-*dāyl*) nt (pl -delen) brothel

borduren (bor-*dēw*-rern) v embroider

borduurwerk (bor-*dēw̄*-vehrk) nt (pl ~en) embroidery

boren (*bōā*-rern) v drill, bore

borg (borkh) c (pl ~en) guarantor

borgsom (*borkh*-som) c (pl ~men) bail

borrel (*boa*-rerl) c (pl ~s) drink

borrelhapje (*bo*-rerl-hahp-ᵞer) nt (pl ~s) appetizer

borst (borst) c (pl ~en) chest; breast, bosom

borstel (*bor*-sterl) c (pl ~s) brush

borstelen (*bor*-ster-lern) v brush

borstkas (*borst*-kahss) c (pl ~sen) chest

bos (boss) nt (pl ~sen) forest, wood; c bunch

bosje (*bo*-sher) nt (pl ~s) grove

boswachter (*boss*-vahkh-terr) c (pl ~s) forester

bot¹ (bot) adj dull, blunt

bot² (bot) nt (pl ~ten) bone

boter (*bōā*-terr) c butter

boterham (*bōā*-terr-hahm) c (pl ~men) sandwich

botsen (*bot*-sern) v bump; collide, crash

botsing (*bot*-sɪng) c (pl ~en) collision, crash

bougie (bōō-*zhee*) c (pl ~s) sparking-plug

bout (bout) c (pl ~en) bolt

boutique (bōō-*teek*) c (pl ~s) boutique

bouw (bou) c construction

bouwen (*bou*-ern) v *build; construct

bouwkunde (*bou*-kern-der) c architecture

bouwvallig (bou-*vah*-lerkh) adj dilapidated

boven (*bōā*-vern) prep above, over;

adv above; upstairs; **naar ~** upwards, up; upstairs

bovendek (*bōā-vern-*dehk) *nt* main deck

bovendien (boa-vern-*deen*) *adv* furthermore, moreover, besides

bovenkant (*bōā-*verng-kahnt) *c* (pl ~en) top side, top

bovenop (boa-vern-*op*) *prep* on top of

bovenst (*bōā-*verst) *adj* upper, top

braaf (braaf) *adj* good

braak (braak) *adj* waste

braam (braam) *c* (pl bramen) blackberry

***braden** (*braa-*dern) *v* fry; roast

braken (*braa-*kern) *v* vomit

brand (brahnt) *c* (pl ~en) fire

brandalarm (*brahnt-*aa-lahrm) *nt* fire-alarm

brandblusapparaat (*brahnt-*blerss-ah-paa-raat) *nt* (pl -raten) fire-extinguisher

branden (*brahn-*dern) *v* *burn

brandkast (*brahnt-*kahst) *c* (pl ~en) safe

brandmerk (*brahnt-*mehrk) *nt* (pl ~en) brand

brandpunt (*brahnt-*pernt) *nt* (pl ~en) focus

brandspiritus (*brahnt-*spee-ree-terss) *c* methylated spirits

brandstof (*brahnt-*stof) *c* (pl ~fen) fuel

brandtrap (*brahn-*trahp) *c* (pl ~pen) fire-escape

brandvrij (*brahnt-*fray) *adj* fireproof

brandweer (*brahn-*tvāȳr) *c* fire-brigade

brandwond (*brahn-*tvont) *c* (pl ~en) burn

brasem (*braa-*serm) *c* (pl ~s) bream

Braziliaan (braa-zee-lee-*ᵞaan*) *c* (pl -lianen) Brazilian

Braziliaans (braa-zee-lee-*ᵞaans*) *adj* Brazilian

Brazilië (braa-*zee-*lee-ᵞer) Brazil

breed (brāyt) *adj* broad, wide

breedte (*brāy-*ter) *c* (pl ~n, ~s) breadth, width

breedtegraad (*brāy-*ter-graat) *c* (pl -graden) latitude

breekbaar (*brāyk-*baar) *adj* fragile

breekijzer (*brāy-*kay-zerr) *nt* (pl ~s) crowbar

breien (*bray-*ern) *v* *knit

***breken** (*brāy-*kern) *v* *break; *burst, crack; fracture

***brengen** (*breh-*ngern) *v* *bring; *take

bres (brehss) *c* (pl ~sen) gap, breach

bretels (brer-*tehls*) *pl* braces *pl*; suspenders *plAm*

breuk (brurk) *c* (pl ~en) break; fracture; hernia

brief (breef) *c* (pl brieven) letter; **aangetekende ~** registered letter

briefkaart (*breef-*kaart) *c* (pl ~en) card, postcard

briefopener (*breef-*ōā-per-nerr) *c* (pl ~s) paper-knife

briefpapier (*breef-*paa-peer) *nt* notepaper

briefwisseling (*breef-*vɪ-ser-lɪng) *c* correspondence

bries (breess) *c* breeze

brievenbus (*bree-*ver-berss) *c* (pl ~sen) letter-box, pillar-box; mailbox *nAm*

bril (brɪl) *c* (pl ~len) spectacles, glasses

briljant (brɪl-*ᵞahnt*) *adj* brilliant

Brit (brɪt) *c* (pl ~ten) Briton

Brits (brɪts) *adj* British

broche (bro-*sher*) *c* (pl ~s) brooch

brochure (bro-*shēw̄-*rer) *c* (pl ~s) brochure

broeder (*brōō-*derr) *c* (pl ~s) brother

broederschap (*brōō-*derr-skhahp) *c*

fraternity

broeikas (*brōo͞ee*-kahss) *c* (pl ~sen) greenhouse

broek (brōōk) *c* (pl ~en) trousers *pl*, slacks *pl*; pants *plAm*; **korte ~** shorts *pl*

broekpak (*brōōk*-pahk) *nt* (pl ~ken) pant-suit

broer (brōōr) *c* (pl ~s) brother

brok (brok) *nt* (pl ~ken) morsel; lump

bromfiets (*brom*-feets) *c* (pl ~en) moped

brommer (*bro*-merr) *c* (pl ~s) motor-bike *nAm*

bron (bron) *c* (pl ~nen) well; fountain, source, spring; **geneeskrachtige ~** spa

bronchitis (brong-*khee*-terss) *c* bronchitis

brons (brons) *nt* bronze

bronzen (*bron*-zern) *adj* bronze

brood (brōat) *nt* (pl broden) bread; loaf

broodje (*brōa*-t^yer) *nt* (pl ~s) roll, bun

broos (brōass) *adj* fragile

brouwen (*brou*-ern) *v* brew

brouwerij (brou-er-*ray*) *c* (pl ~en) brewery

brug (brerkh) *c* (pl ~gen) bridge

bruid (brur^{ew}t) *c* (pl ~en) bride

bruidegom (*brur^{ew}*-der-gom) *c* (pl ~s) bridegroom

bruikbaar (*brur^{ew}k*-baar) *adj* usable; useful

bruiloft (*brur^{ew}*-loft) *c* (pl ~en) wedding

bruin (brur^{ew}n) *adj* brown

brullen (*brer*-lern) *v* roar

brunette (brew-*neh*-ter) *c* (pl ~s) brunette

brutaal (brew-*taal*) *adj* bold, impertinent, insolent

bruto (*brōō*-tōa) *adj* gross

budget (ber-*jeht*) *nt* (pl ~ten, ~s) budget

buffet (bew-*feht*) *nt* (pl ~ten) buffet

bui (bur^{ew}) *c* (pl ~en) shower; spirit

buidel (*bur^{ew}*-derl) *c* (pl ~s) pouch

buigbaar (*bur^{ew}kh*-baar) *adj* flexible

*buigen (*bur^{ew}*-gern) *v* *bend; bow

buigzaam (*bur^{ew}kh*-saam) *adj* supple

buik (bur^{ew}k) *c* (pl ~en) belly

buikpijn (*bur^{ew}k*-payn) *c* stomach-ache

buis (bur^{ew}ss) *c* (pl buizen) tube

buiten (*bur^{ew}*-tern) *prep* outside, out of; *adv* out; outside, outdoors; **naar ~** outwards

buitengewoon (*bur^{ew}*-ter-ger-vōan) *adj* extraordinary, exceptional

buitenhuis (*bur^{ew}*-ter-hur^{ew}ss) *nt* (pl -huizen) cottage

buitenkant (*bur^{ew}*-ter-kahnt) *c* (pl ~en) outside, exterior

in het buitenland (ın ert *bur^{ew}*-tern-lahnt) abroad

buitenlander (*bur^{ew}*-ter-lahn-derr) *c* (pl ~s) alien, foreigner

buitenlands (*bur^{ew}*-ter-lahnts) *adj* alien, foreign

buitensporig (bur^{ew}-ter-*spōa*-rerkh) *adj* excessive

buitenwijk (*bur^{ew}*-ter-vayk) *c* (pl ~en) suburb; outskirts *pl*

zich bukken (ber-kern) *bend down

Bulgaar (berl-*gaar*) *c* (pl -garen) Bulgarian

Bulgaars (berl-*gaars*) *adj* Bulgarian

Bulgarije (berl-gaa-*ray*-er) Bulgaria

bult (berlt) *c* (pl ~en) lump

bumper (*berm*-perr) *c* (pl ~s) bumper, fender

bundel (*bern*-derl) *c* (pl ~s) bundle

bundelen (*bern*-der-lern) *v* bundle

burcht (berrkht) *c* (pl ~en) stronghold

bureau (bew-*rōa*) *nt* (pl ~s) agency, office; bureau, desk; **~ voor ge-**

vonden voorwerpen lost property office

bureaucratie (bew-rōā-kraa-*tsee*) *c* bureaucracy

burgemeester (berr-ger-*mǟyss*-terr) *c* (pl ~s) mayor

burger (*berr*-gerr) *c* (pl ~s) citizen; civilian; **burger-** civilian, civic

burgerlijk (*berr*-gerr-lerk) *adj* bourgeois, middle-class; ~ **recht** civil law

bus (berss) *c* (pl ~sen) coach, bus; tin, canister

buste (*bew*-ster) *c* (pl ~s, ~n) bust

bustehouder (*bew*-ster-hou-derr) *c* (pl ~s) brassiere, bra

buur (bewr) *c* (pl buren) neighbour

buurman (*bewr*-mahn) *c* neighbour

buurt (bewrt) *c* (pl ~en) neighbourhood, vicinity

C

cabaret (kaa-bee-*reht*) *nt* (pl ~s) cabaret

cabine (kaa-*bee*-ner) *c* (pl ~s) cabin

cadeau (kaa-*dōā*) *nt* (pl ~s) gift, present

café (kah-*fǟy*) *nt* (pl ~s) café; public house, pub

cafetaria (kah-fer-*taa*-ree-Yaa) *c* (pl ~s) cafeteria

caissière (kah-*shai*-rer) *c* (pl ~s) cashier

cake (kǟyk) *c* (pl ~s) cake

calcium (*kahl*-see-Yerm) *nt* calcium

calorie (kah-lōā-*ree*) *c* (pl ~ën) calorie

calvinisme (kahl-vee-*niss*-mer) *nt* Calvinism

camee (kaa-*mǟy*) *c* (pl ~ën) cameo

campagne (kahm-*pah*-ñer) *c* (pl ~s) campaign

camping (*kehm*-ping) *c* (pl ~s) camping site, camping

Canada (*kaa*-naa-daa) Canada

Canadees (kaa-naa-*dǟyss*) *adj* Canadian

capabel (kaa-*paa*-berl) *adj* able

capaciteit (kaa-paa-see-*tayt*) *c* (pl ~en) capacity

cape (kǟyp) *c* (pl ~s) cape

capitulatie (kah-pee-tew-*laa*-tsee) *c* (pl ~s) capitulation

capsule (kahp-*sew*-ler) *c* (pl ~s) capsule

caravan (*keh*-rer-vern) *c* (pl ~s) caravan

carbonpapier (kahr-*bon*-paa-peer) *nt* carbon paper

carburateur (kahr-bew-raa-*tūr*) *c* (pl ~s) carburettor

carillon (kaa-ril-*Yon*) *nt* (pl ~s) chimes *pl*

carnaval (*kahr*-naa-vahl) *nt* carnival

carrière (kah-ree-*Yai*-rer) *c* (pl ~s) career

carrosserie (kah-ro-ser-*ree*) *c* (pl ~ën) coachwork; motor body *Am*

carter (*kahr*-terr) *nt* crankcase

casino (kaa-*zee*-nōā) *nt* (pl ~'s) casino

catacombe (kah-tah-*kom*-ber) *c* (pl ~n) catacomb

catalogus (kah-*taa*-lōā-gerss) *c* (pl -gussen, -gi) catalogue

catarre (kaa-*tahr*) *c* catarrh

catastrofe (kaa-taa-*straw*-fer) *c* (pl ~s) catastrophe, disaster

categorie (kaa-ter-gōā-*ree*) *c* (pl ~ën) category

cavia (*kaa*-vee-Yaa) *c* (pl ~'s) guinea-pig

cel (sehl) *c* (pl ~len) cell

celibaat (sǟy-lee-*baat*) *nt* celibacy

cellofaan (seh-loa-*faan*) *nt* cellophane

celsius (*sehl*-see-Yerss) centigrade

cement (ser-*mehnt*) *nt* cement

censuur (sehn-*zewr*) c censorship

centimeter (*sehn-tee-may-terr*) c (pl ~s) centimetre; tape-measure

centraal (sehn-*traal*) adj central; ~ **station** central station; **centrale verwarming** central heating

centraliseren (sehn-traa-lee-*zay*-rern) v centralize

centrifuge (sehn-tree-*few*-zher) c (pl ~s) dryer

centrum (*sehn*-trerm) nt (pl centra) centre

ceramiek (*say*-raa-*meek*) c ceramics pl

ceremonie (*say*-rer-*moa*-nee) c (pl -niën, -nies) ceremony

certificaat (sehr-tee-fee-*kaat*) nt (pl -caten) certificate

chalet (shaa-*leht*) nt (pl ~s) chalet

champagne (shahm-*pah*-ñer) c (pl ~s) champagne

champignon (shahm-pee-*ñon*) c (pl ~s) mushroom

chantage (shahn-*taa*-zher) c blackmail

chanteren (shahn-*tay*-rern) v blackmail

chaos (*khaa*-oss) c chaos

chaotisch (khaa-*oa*-teess) adj chaotic

charlatan (*shahr*-laa-tahn) c (pl ~s) quack

charmant (shahr-*mahnt*) adj charming

charme (*shahr*-mer) c (pl ~s) charm; glamour

chartervlucht (*chahr*-terr-vlerkht) c (pl ~en) charter flight

chassis (shah-*see*) nt (pl ~) chassis

chauffeur (shoa-*fūr*) c (pl ~s) driver, chauffeur

chef (shehf) c (pl ~s) boss, manager, chief

chef-kok (shehf-*kok*) c (pl ~s) chef

chemie (khay-*mee*) c chemistry

chemisch (*khay*-meess) adj chemical

cheque (shehk) c (pl ~s) cheque; check nAm

chequeboekje (shehk-*boo*-kᵞer) nt (pl ~s) cheque-book; check-book nAm

chic (sheek) adj smart

Chileen (shee-*layn*) c (pl -lenen) Chilean

Chileens (shee-*layns*) adj Chilean

Chili (*shee*-lee) Chile

China (*shee*-naa) China

Chinees (shee-*nayss*) adj Chinese

chirurg (shee-*rerrkh*) c (pl ~en) surgeon

chloor (khlōar) nt chlorine

chocola (shōa-kōa-*laa*) c chocolate

chocolademelk (shōa-kōa-*laa*-der-mehlk) c chocolate

christelijk (*kriss*-ter-lerk) adj Christian

christen (*kriss*-tern) c (pl ~en) Christian

Christus (*kriss*-terss) Christ

chronisch (*khrōa*-neess) adj chronic

chronologisch (khrōa-nōa-*lōa*-geess) adj chronological

chroom (khrōam) nt chromium

cijfer (*say*-ferr) nt (pl ~s) number, figure; digit; mark

cilinder (see-*lin*-derr) c (pl ~s) cylinder

cilinderkop (see-*lin*-derr-kop) c (pl ~pen) cylinder head

cipier (see-*peer*) c (pl ~s) jailer

circa (*sir*-kaa) adv approximately

circulatie (sir-kew-*laa*-tsee) c circulation

circus (*sir*-kerss) nt (pl ~sen) circus

cirkel (*sir*-kerl) c (pl ~s) circle

citaat (see-*taat*) nt (pl citaten) quotation

citeren (see-*tay*-rern) v quote

citroen (see-*trōon*) c (pl ~en) lemon

civiel (see-*veel*) adj civil

clausule (klou-*sew*-ler) c (pl ~s) clause

clavecimbel (klaa-ver-*sim*-berl) c (pl ~s) harpsichord

claxon (*klahk*-son) *c* (pl ~s) horn, hooter

claxonneren (klahk-so-*nāy*-rern) *v* hoot; toot *vAm*, honk *vAm*

clementie (klāy-*mehn*-tsee) *c* mercy

cliënt (klee-ᵞehnt) *c* (pl ~en) customer, client

closetpapier (klōa-*zeht*-pah-peer) *nt* toilet-paper

cocaïne (kōa-kaa-*ee*-ner) *c* cocaine

code (*kōa*-der) *c* (pl ~s) code

coffeïne (ko-fāy-*ee*-ner) *c* caffeine

coffeïnevrij (ko-fāy-*ee*-ner-vray) *adj* decaffeinated

cognac (ko-*ñahk*) *c* cognac

coiffure (kvah-*fēw*-rer) *c* (pl ~s) hairdo

colbert (kol-*bair*) *c* (pl ~s) jacket

collectant (ko-lehk-*tahnt*) *c* (pl ~en) collector

collecteren (ko-lehk-*tāy*-rern) *v* collect

collectie (ko-*lehk*-see) *c* (pl ~s) collection

collectief (ko-lehk-*teef*) *adj* collective

collega (ko-*lāy*-gaa) *c* (pl ~'s) colleague

college (ko-*lāy*-zher) *nt* (pl ~s) lecture

Colombia (kōa-*lom*-bee-ᵞaa) Colombia

Colombiaan (kōa-lom-bee-ᵞaan) *c* (pl -bianen) Colombian

Colombiaans (kōa-lom-bee-ᵞaans) *adj* Colombian

coma (*kōa*-maa) *nt* coma

combinatie (kom-bee-*naa*-tsee) *c* (pl ~s) combination

combineren (kom-bee-*nāy*-rern) *v* combine

comfortabel (kom-for-*taa*-berl) *adj* comfortable

comité (ko-mee-*tāy*) *nt* (pl ~s) committee

commentaar (ko-mehn-*taar*) *nt* (pl -taren) comment

commercieel (ko-mehr-*shāyl*) *adj* commercial

commissie (ko-*mi*-see) *c* (pl ~s) committee; commission

commode (ko-*mōa*-der) *c* (pl ~s) bureau *nAm*

commune (ko-*mēw*-ner) *c* (pl ~s) commune

communicatie (ko-mēw-nee-*kaa*-tsee) *c* communication

communiqué (ko-mēw-nee-*kāy*) *nt* (pl ~s) communiqué

communisme (ko-mēw-*niss*-mer) *nt* communism

compact (kom-*pahkt*) *adj* compact

compact disk (*kom*-pahkt disk) *c* compact disc; ~ **speler** CD-player

compagnon (kom-pah-*ñon*) *c* (pl ~s) partner

compensatie (kom-pehn-*zaa*-tsee) *c* (pl ~s) compensation

compenseren (kom-pehn-*zāy*-rern) *v* compensate

compleet (kom-*plāyt*) *adj* complete

compliment (kom-plee-*mehnt*) *nt* (pl ~en) compliment

componist (kom-pōa-*nist*) *c* (pl ~en) composer

compositie (kom-pōa-*zee*-tsee) *c* (pl ~s) composition

compromis (kom-prōa-*mee*) *nt* (pl ~sen) compromise

computer (kom-*pjoe*-terr) *nt* computer

concentratie (kon-sehn-*traa*-tsee) *c* (pl ~s) concentration

concentreren (kon-sehn-*trāy*-rern) *v* concentrate

conceptie (kon-*sehp*-see) *c* conception

concert (kon-*sehrt*) *nt* (pl ~en) concert

concertzaal (kon-*sehrt*-saal) *c* (pl -zalen) concert hall

concessie (kon-*seh*-see) *c* (pl ~s) concession

concierge (kon-*shehr*-zheh) *c* (pl ~s)
janitor; caretaker, concierge

conclusie (kong-*klew*-zee) *c* (pl ~s)
conclusion

concreet (kong-*krayt*) *adj* concrete

concurrent (kong-kew-*rehnt*) *c* (pl
~en) competitor; rival

concurrentie (kong-kew-*rehn*-tsee) *c*
competition; rivalry

conditie (kon-*dee*-tsee) *c* (pl ~s) condition

conditioner (kon-*disj*-er-nerr) *nt* conditioner

condoom (kon-*doom*) *nt* condom

conducteur (kon-derk-*tūrr*) *c* (pl ~s)
conductor; ticket collector

conferencier (kon-fer-rahng-*shay*) *c* (pl
~s) entertainer

conferentie (kon-fer-*rehn*-see) *c* (pl
~s) conference

conflict (kon-*flıkt*) *nt* (pl ~en) conflict

congregatie (kong-gray-*gaa*-tsee) *c* (pl
~s) congregation

congres (kong-*grehss*) *nt* (pl ~sen)
congress

consequentie (kon-ser-*kvehn*-see) *c*
(pl ~s) consequence

conservatief (kon-zerr-vaa-*teef*) *adj*
conservative

conserven (kon-*sehr*-vern) *pl* tinned
food

consideratie (kon-see-der-*raa*-tsee) *c*
consideration

constant (kon-*stahnt*) *adj* even

constateren (koan-staa-*tay*-rern) *v*
note, ascertain; diagnose

constipatie (kon-stee-*paa*-tsee) *c* constipation

constructie (kon-*strerk*-see) *c* (pl ~s)
construction

construeren (kon-strew°°-*ay*-rern) *v*
construct

consulaat (kon-zew-*laat*) *nt* (pl -laten)
consulate

consult (kon-*zerlt*) *nt* (pl ~en) consultation

consultatiebureau (kon-zerl-*taa*-tsee-
bew-roā) *nt* (pl ~s) health centre

consument (kon-zew-*mehnt*) *c* (pl
~en) consumer

contact (kon-*tahkt*) *nt* (pl ~en) contact; touch

contactlenzen (kon-*tahkt*-lehn-zern) *pl*
contact lenses

contanten (kon-*tahn*-tern) *pl* cash

continent (kon-tee-*nehnt*) *nt* (pl ~en)
continent

continentaal (kon-tee-nehn-*taal*) *adj*
continental

contra (*kon*-traa) *prep* versus

contract (kon-*trahkt*) *nt* (pl ~en)
agreement, contract

contrast (kon-*trahst*) *nt* (pl ~en) contrast

controle (kon-*traw*-ler) *c* (pl ~s) control; supervision, inspection

controleren (kon-troā-*lay*-rern) *v* control, check

controlestrook (kon-*traw*-ler-stroāk) *c*
(-stroken) counterfoil, stub

controversieel (kon-troā-vehr-*zhayl*)
adj controversial

conversatie (kon-verr-*zaa*-tsee) *c* (pl
~s) conversation

coöperatie (koā-oā-per-*raa*-tsee) *c* (pl
~s) co-operative

coöperatief (koā-oā-per-raa-*teef*) *adj*
co-operative

coördinatie (koā-or-dee-*naa*-tsee) *c* co-
ordination

coördineren (koā-or-dee-*nay*-rern) *v*
co-ordinate

corpulent (kor-pew-*lehnt*) *adj* corpulent, stout

correct (ko-*rehkt*) *adj* correct

correctie (ko-*rehk*-see) *c* (pl ~s) correction

correspondent (ko-rehss-pon-*dehnt*) *c*

(pl ~en) correspondent

correspondentie (ko-rehss-pon-*dehn*-see) *c* correspondence

corresponderen (ko-rehss-pon-*day*-rern) *v* correspond

corrigeren (ko-ree-*zhay*-rern) *v* correct

corrupt (ko-*rerpt*) *adj* corrupt

couchette (kōō-*sheh*-ter) *c* (pl ~s) berth

coupé (kōō-*pay*) *c* (pl ~s) compartment; ~ **voor rokers** smoking-compartment

couplet (kōō-*pleht*) *nt* (pl ~ten) stanza

coupon (kōō-*pon*) *c* (pl ~s) coupon

crèche (krehsh) *c* (pl ~s) nursery

crediteren (kray-dee-*tay*-rern) *v* credit

creëren (kray-*ay*-rern) *v* create

crematie (kray-*maa*-tsee) *c* (pl ~s) cremation

crème (kraim) *c* (pl ~s) cream; **vochtinbrengende** ~ moisturizing cream

cremeren (kray-*may*-rern) *v* cremate

criminaliteit (kree-mee-naa-lee-*tayt*) *c* criminality

crimineel (kree-mee-*nayl*) *adj* criminal

crisis (*kree*-serss) *c* (pl -ses) crisis

criticus (*kree*-tee-kerss) *c* (pl -ci) critic

croquant (krōa-*kahnt*) *adj* crisp

Cuba (*kēw*-baa) Cuba

Cubaan (kēw-*baan*) *c* (pl -banen) Cuban

Cubaans (kēw-*baans*) *adj* Cuban

cultuur (kerl-*tēwr*) *c* (pl -turen) culture

cursiefschrift (kerr-*zeef*-skhrift) *nt* italics *pl*

cursus (*kerr*-zerss) *c* (pl ~sen) course

cyclus (*see*-klerss) *c* (pl ~sen) cycle

D

daad (daat) *c* (pl daden) deed, act

daar (daar) *adv* there

daarheen (*daar*-hāyn) *adv* there

daarom (*daa*-rom) *conj* therefore

dadel (*daa*-derl) *c* (pl ~s) date

dadelijk (*daa*-der-lerk) *adv* at once, immediately; presently

dag (dahkh) *c* (pl ~en) day; **dag!** hello!; good-bye!; **per** ~ per day

dagblad (*dahkh*-blaht) *nt* (pl ~en) daily

dagboek (*dahkh*-bōōk) *nt* (pl ~en) diary

dagelijks (*daa*-ger-lerks) *adj* daily

dageraad (*daa*-ger-raat) *c* daybreak, dawn

daglicht (*dahkh*-likht) *nt* daylight

dagvaarding (*dahkh*-vaar-ding) *c* (pl ~en) summons

dak (dahk) *nt* (pl ~en) roof

dakpan (*dahk*-pahn) *c* (pl ~nen) tile

dal (dahl) *nt* (pl ~en) valley

dalen (*daa*-lern) *v* descend

dam (dahm) *c* (pl ~men) dam; dike

dambord (*dahm*-bort) *nt* (pl ~en) draught-board

dame (*daa*-mer) *c* (pl ~s) lady

damestoilet (*daa*-merss-tvah-leht) *nt* (pl ~ten) powder-room, ladies' room

damp (dahmp) *c* (pl ~en) vapour

damspel (*dahm*-spehl) *nt* draughts; checkers *plAm*

dan (dahn) *adv* then; *conj* than; **nu en** ~ occasionally

dankbaar (*dahngk*-baar) *adj* grateful, thankful

dankbaarheid (*dahngk*-baar-hayt) *c* gratitude

danken (*dahng*-kern) *v* thank; **dank u**

thank you; **te ~** *__hebben aan__ owe

dans (dahns) c (pl ~en) dance

dansen (dahn-sern) v dance

danszaal (dahn-saal) c (pl -zalen) ballroom

dapper (dah-perr) adj brave, courageous

dapperheid (dah-perr-hayt) c courage

darm (dahrm) c (pl ~en) gut, intestine; **darmen** bowels pl

das (dahss) c (pl ~sen) necktie, tie; scarf

dat (daht) pron which; conj that

datum (daa-term) c (pl data) date

dauw (dou) c dew

de (der) art the art

debat (der-baht) nt (pl ~ten) discussion, debate

debatteren (dāy-bah-tāy-rern) v argue

debet (dāy-beht) nt debit

december (dāy-sehm-berr) December

deeg (dāykh) nt dough

deel (dāyl) nt (pl delen) part; share; volume

__*deelnemen__ (dāyl-nāy-mern) v participate

deelnemer (dāyl-nāy-merr) c (pl ~s) participant

deels (dāyls) adv partly

Deen (dāyn) c (pl Denen) Dane

Deens (dāyns) adj Danish

defect[1] (der-fehkt) adj defective, faulty

defect[2] (der-fehkt) nt (pl ~en) fault

defensie (dāy-fehn-zee) c defence

definiëren (dāy-fi-ni-āy-rern) v define

definitie (dāy-fee-nee-tsee) c (pl ~s) definition

degelijk (dāy-ger-lerk) adj thorough; sound

dek (dehk) nt deck

deken (dāy-kern) c (pl ~s) blanket

dekhut (dehk-hert) c (pl ~ten) deck cabin

deksel (dehk-serl) nt (pl ~s) lid; cover, top

dekzeil (dehk-sayl) nt (pl ~en) tarpaulin

delegatie (dāy-ler-gaa-tsee) c (pl ~s) delegation

delen (dāy-lern) v divide; share

delfstof (dehlf-stof) c (pl ~fen) mineral

delicatessen (dāy-lee-kaa-teh-sern) pl delicatessen

delicatessenwinkel (dāy-lee-kaa-teh-ser-vɪng-kerl) c (pl ~s) delicatessen

delikaat (dāy-lee-kaat) adj delicate

deling (dāy-lɪng) c (pl ~en) division

delinquent (dāy-lɪng-kvehnt) c (pl ~en) criminal

__*delven__ (dehl-vern) v *dig

democratie (dāy-mōa-kraa-tsee) c (pl ~ën) democracy

democratisch (dāy-mōa-kraa-teess) adj democratic

demonstratie (dāy-mon-straa-tsee) c (pl ~s) demonstration

demonstreren (dāy-mon-strāy-rern) v demonstrate

den (dehn) c (pl ~nen) fir-tree

Denemarken (dāy-ner-mahr-kern) Denmark

denkbeeld (dehngk-bāyld) nt (pl ~en) idea

denkbeeldig (dehngk-bāyl-derkh) adj imaginary

__*denken__ (dehng-kern) v *think; guess, reckon; **~ aan** *think of

denker (dehng-kerr) c (pl ~s) thinker

denneboom (deh-ner-bōam) c (pl -bomen) fir-tree

deodorant (dāy-Yōa-dōa-rahnt) c deodorant

departement (dāy-pahr-ter-mehnt) nt (pl ~en) department

deponeren (dāy-pōa-nāy-rern) v bank

depressie (dāy-preh-see) c (pl ~s) depression

deprimeren (dāy-pree-*māy*-rern) *v* depress

derde (*dehr*-der) *num* third

dergelijk (*dehr*-ger-lerk) *adj* such; similar

dermate (*dehr*-maa-ter) *adv* so

dertien (*dehr*-teen) *num* thirteen

dertiende (*dehr*-teen-der) *num* thirteenth

dertig (*dehr*-terkh) *num* thirty

dertigste (*dehr*-terkh-ster) *num* thirtieth

deserteren (dāy-zehr-*tāy*-rern) *v* desert

deskundig (dehss-*kern*-derkh) *adj* expert

deskundige (dehss-*kern*-der-ger) *c* (pl ~n) expert

dessert (deh-*sair*) *nt* (pl ~s) dessert

detail (dāy-*tigh*) *nt* (pl ~s) detail

detailhandel (dāy-*tigh*-hahn-derl) *c* retail trade

detaillist (dāy-tah-*Yist*) *c* (pl ~en) retailer

detectiveroman (dāy-*tehk*-tif-rōa-mahn) *c* (pl ~s) detective story

deugd (dūrkht) *c* (pl ~en) virtue

deugniet (*dūrkh*-neet) *c* (pl ~en) rascal

deuk (dūrk) *c* (pl ~en) dent

deur (dūrr) *c* (pl ~en) door

deurbel (*dūrr*-behl) *c* (pl ~len) doorbell

deurwaarder (*dūrr*-vaar-derr) *c* (pl ~s) bailiff

devaluatie (dāy-vaa-lēw̄-*vaa*-tsee) *c* (pl ~s) devaluation

devalueren (dāy-vaa-lēw̄-*vāy*-rern) *v* devalue

devies (der-*veess*) *nt* (pl deviezen) motto

deze (*dāy*-zer) *pron* this; these

dia (*dee*-Yaa) *c* (pl ~'s) slide

diabetes (dee-Yaa-*bāy*-terss) *c* diabetes

diabeticus (dee-Yaa-*bāy*-tee-kerss) *c* (pl -ci) diabetic

diagnose (dee-Yahkh-*nō̄*-zer) *c* (pl ~n, ~s) diagnosis; **een ~ stellen** diagnose

diagonaal[1] (dee-Yaa-gō̄a-*naal*) *adj* diagonal

diagonaal[2] (dee-Yaa-gō̄a-*naal*) *c* (pl -nalen) diagonal

dialect (dee-Yaa-*lehkt*) *nt* (pl ~en) dialect

diamant (dee-Yaa-*mahnt*) *c* (pl ~en) diamond

diarree (dee-Yah-*rāy*) *c* diarrhoea

dicht (dikht) *adj* dense; thick; closed, shut

dichtbevolkt (dikht-ber-*volkt*) *adj* populous

dichtbij (dikht-*bay*) *adj* near

dichtdraaien (*dikh*-draa^ee-ern) *v* turn off

dichter (*dikh*-terr) *c* (pl ~s) poet

dichtkunst (*dikht*-kernst) *c* poetry

***dichtslaan** (*dikht*-slaan) *v* slam

dictaat (dik-*taat*) *nt* (pl -taten) dictation

dictafoon (dik-taa-*fōan*) *c* (pl ~s) dictaphone

dictator (dik-*taa*-tor) *c* (pl ~s) dictator

dictee (dik-*tāy*) *nt* (pl ~s) dictation

dicteren (dik-*tāy*-rern) *v* dictate

die (dee) *pron* that; those; who

dieet (dee-*Yāyt*) *nt* diet

dief (deef) *c* (pl dieven) robber, thief

diefstal (*deef*-stahl) *c* (pl ~len) robbery, theft

dienblad (*deen*-blaht) *nt* (pl ~en) tray

dienen (*dee*-nern) *v* serve

dienst (deenst) *c* (pl ~en) service; **in ~ *nemen** engage

dienstplichtige (deenst-*plikh*-ter-ger) *c* (pl ~n) conscript

dienstregeling (*deenst*-rāy-ger-ling) *c* (pl ~en) schedule, timetable

diep (deep) *adj* deep; low

diepte (*deep*-ter) *c* (pl ~n, ~s) depth

diepvrieskast (*deep*-freess-kahst) *c* (pl ~en) deep-freeze

diepzinnig (deep-*si*-nerkh) *adj* profound

dier (deer) *nt* (pl ~en) animal

dierbaar (*deer*-baar) *adj* dear; precious

dierenarts (*dee*-rern-ahrts) *c* (pl ~en) veterinary surgeon

dierenriem (*dee*-rer-reem) *c* zodiac

dierentuin (*dee*-rer-tur^{ew}n) *c* (pl ~en) zoological gardens; zoo

diesel (*dee*-serl) *c* diesel

difterie (dif-ter-*ree*) *c* diphtheria

digitaal (die-gie-*taal*) *adj* digital

dij (day) *c* (pl ~en) thigh

dijk (dayk) *c* (pl ~en) dike; dam

dik (dik) *adj* corpulent; thick; fat, stout, big

dikte (*dik*-ter) *c* (pl ~n, ~s) thickness; fatness

dikwijls (*dik*-verls) *adv* frequently, often

ding (ding) *nt* (pl ~en) thing

dinsdag (*dins*-dahkh) *c* Tuesday

diploma (dee-*plōa*-maa) *nt* (pl ~'s) certificate, diploma; **een ~ behalen** graduate

diplomaat (dee-plōa-*maat*) *c* (pl -maten) diplomat

direct (dee-*rehkt*) *adj* direct; *adv* straight away

directeur (dee-rerk-*tūrr*) *c* (pl ~en, ~s) executive, manager, director; headmaster, principal

directie (dee-*rehk*-see) *c* (pl ~s) management

dirigent (dee-ree-*gehnt*) *c* (pl ~en) conductor

dirigeren (dee-ree-*gāy*-rern) *v* conduct

disconto (diss-*kon*-tōa) *nt* (pl ~'s) bank-rate

discreet (diss-*krāyt*) *adj* modest

discussie (diss-*ker*-see) *c* (pl ~s) discussion, argument

discussiëren (diss-ker-shāy-rern) *v* discuss; argue

distel (*diss*-terl) *c* (pl ~s) thistle

district (diss-*trikt*) *nt* (pl ~en) district

dit (dit) *pron* this

divan (dee-vahn) *c* (pl ~s) couch

docent (dōa-*sehnt*) *c* (pl ~en) teacher

doch (dokh) *conj* but

dochter (*dokh*-terr) *c* (pl ~s) daughter

doctor (*dok*-tor) *c* (pl ~en, ~s) doctor

document (dōa-kew-*mehnt*) *nt* (pl ~en) document

dodelijk (*dōa*-der-lerk) *adj* mortal, fatal

doden (*dōa*-dern) *v* kill

doek (dōok) *c* (pl ~en) cloth; *nt* curtain

doel (dōol) *nt* (pl ~en) objective, aim, purpose; object, goal, design, target

doelman (*dōol*-mahn) *c* (pl ~nen) goalkeeper

doelmatig (dōol-*maa*-terkh) *adj* efficient

doelpunt (*dōol*-pernt) *nt* (pl ~en) goal

doeltreffend (dōol-*treh*-fernt) *adj* effective

*****doen** (dōon) *v* *do; cause to

dof (dof) *adj* mat, dim

dok (dok) *nt* (pl ~ken) dock

dokter (*dok*-terr) *c* (pl ~s) doctor, physician

dom¹ (dom) *adj* dumb, stupid

dom² (dom) *c* cathedral

dominee (*dōa*-mee-nāy) *c* (pl ~s) clergyman, parson, rector

dompelaar (*dom*-per-laar) *c* (pl ~s) immersion heater

donateur (dōa-naa-*tūrr*) *c* (pl ~s) donor

donder (*don*-derr) *c* thunder

donderdag (*don*-derr-dahkh) *c* Thursday

donderen (*don*-der-rern) *v* thunder

donker (*dong*-kerr) *adj* dark, dim

dons (dons) *nt* down; **donzen dekbed** eiderdown

dood (dōāt) *adj* dead; *c* death

doodstraf (*dōāt*-strahf) *c* death penalty

doof (dōāf) *adj* deaf

dooi (dōā^ee) *c* thaw

dooien (*dōā^ee*-ern) *v* thaw

dooier (*dōā^ee*-err) *c* (pl ~s) yolk

doolhof (*dōāl*-hof) *nt* (pl -hoven) maze; labyrinth

doop (dōāp) *c* baptism, christening

doopsel (*dōāp*-serl) *nt* baptism

door (dōār) *prep* through; by

doorboren (dōār-*bōā*-rern) *v* pierce

***doorbrengen** (*dōār*-breh-ngern) *v* *spend

doordat (dōār-*daht*) *conj* because

***doordringen** (*dōār*-drı-ngern) *v* penetrate

***doorgaan** (*dōār*-gaan) *v* continue, *go on; carry on; *go ahead; ~ **met** *keep on

doorgang (*dōār*-gahng) *c* (pl ~en) passage

doorlichten (*dōār*-lıkh-tern) *v* X-ray

doorlopend (dōār-*lōā*-pernt) *adj* continuous

doormaken (*dōār*-maa-kern) *v* *go through

doorn (dōārn) *c* (pl ~en, ~s) thorn

doorreis (*dōā*-rayss) *c* passage

doorslag (*dōār*-slahkh) *c* (pl ~en) carbon copy

doorweken (dōār-*vāy*-kern) *v* soak

doorzichtig (dōār-*zıkh*-terkh) *adj* transparent, sheer

***doorzoeken** (dōār-*zōō*-kern) *v* search

doos (dōāss) *c* (pl dozen) box

dop (dop) *c* (pl ~pen) shell

dopen (*dōā*-pern) *v* baptize, christen

dor (dor) *adj* arid

dorp (dorp) *nt* (pl ~en) village

dorst (dorst) *c* thirst

dorstig (dors-terkh) *adj* thirsty

dosis (*dōā*-zerss) *c* (pl doses) dose

dossier (do-*shāy*) *nt* (pl ~s) file

douane (dōō-*vaa*-ner) *c* Customs *pl*

douanebeambte (dōō-*vaa*-ner-ber-ahm-ter) *c* (pl ~n) Customs officer

douche (dōōsh) *c* (pl ~s) shower

doven (*dōā*-vern) *v* extinguish

dozijn (dōā-*zayn*) *nt* (pl ~en) dozen

draad (draat) *c* (pl draden) thread; wire

draagbaar (*draakh*-baar) *adj* portable

draaglijk (*draakh*-lerk) *adj* tolerable

draai (draa^ee) *c* (pl ~en) turn; twist

draaideur (draa^ee-dūrr) *c* (pl ~en) revolving door

draaien (*draa^ee*-ern) *v* turn; twist; *spin

draaimolen (*draa^ee*-mōā-lern) *c* (pl ~s) merry-go-round

draaiorgel (*draa^ee*-or-gerl) *nt* (pl ~s) street-organ

draak (draak) *c* (pl draken) dragon

***dragen** (*draa*-gern) *v* carry, *bear; *wear

drager (*draa*-gerr) *c* (pl ~s) bearer

drama (*draa*-maa) *nt* (pl ~'s) drama

dramatisch (draa-*maa*-teess) *adj* dramatic

drang (drahng) *c* urge

drank (drahngk) *c* (pl ~en) drink, beverage; **sterke** ~ spirits, liquor

dreigement (dray-ger-*mernt*) *nt* (pl ~en) threat

dreigen (*dray*-gern) *v* threaten

drek (drehk) *c* muck

drempel (*drehm*-perl) *c* (pl ~s) threshold

dresseren (dreh-*sāy*-rern) *v* train

drie (dree) *num* three

driehoek (*dree*-hōōk) *c* (pl ~en) triangle

driehoekig (dree-*hōō*-kerkh) adj triangular

driekwart (dree-kvahrt) adj three-quarter

driemaandelijks (dree-maan-der-lerks) adj quarterly

drift (drift) c passion

driftig (drif-terkh) adj quick-tempered; hot-tempered, irascible

drijfkracht (drayf-krahkht) c driving force

***drijven** (dray-vern) v float

***dringen** (dri-ngern) v push; **dringend** pressing, urgent

drinkbaar (dringk-baar) adj for drinking

***drinken** (dring-kern) v *drink

drinkwater (dringk-vaa-terr) nt drinking-water

droefheid (drōōf-hayt) c sorrow

droevig (drōō-verkh) adj sad

drogen (drōā-gern) v dry

drogisterij (drōā-giss-ter-ray) c (pl ~en) pharmacy, chemist's; drugstore nAm

dromen (drōā-mern) v *dream

dronken (drong-kern) adj drunk; intoxicated

droog (drōākh) adj dry

droogleggen (drōākh-leh-gern) v drain

droogte (drōākh-ter) c drought

droom (drōām) c (pl dromen) dream

droombeeld (drōām-baylt) nt (pl ~en) illusion

drop (drop) c liquorice

druiven (drur*ew*-vern) pl grapes pl

druk (drerk) adj busy; crowded; c pressure

drukken (drer-kern) v press; print

drukknop (drer-knop) c (pl ~pen) push-button

drukte (drerk-ter) c bustle; fuss, excitement

drukwerk (drerk-vehrk) nt printed matter

druppel (drer-perl) c (pl ~s) drop

dubbel (der-berl) adj double

dubbelzinnig (der-berl-zi-nerkh) adj ambiguous

duidelijk (dur*ew*-der-lerk) adj distinct, plain, clear; apparent, evident; obvious

duif (dur*ew*f) c (pl duiven) pigeon

duikbril (dur*ew*k-bril) c (pl ~len) goggles pl

***duiken** (dur*ew*-kern) v dive

duim (dur*ew*m) c (pl ~en) thumb

duin (dur*ew*n) nt (pl ~en) dune

duister (dur*ew*-sterr) adj obscure, dark; nt gloom

duisternis (dur*ew*-sterr-niss) c dark

Duits (dur*ew*ts) adj German

Duitser (dur*ew*t-serr) c (pl ~s) German

Duitsland (dur*ew*ts-lahnt) Germany

duivel (dur*ew*-verl) c (pl ~s) devil

duizelig (dur*ew*-zer-lerkh) adj giddy, dizzy

duizeligheid (dur*ew*-zer-lerkh-hayt) c giddiness, dizziness

duizeling (dur*ew*-zer-ling) c (pl ~en) vertigo

duizend (dur*ew*-zernt) num thousand

dulden (derl-dern) v *bear

dun (dern) adj thin; sheer

dupe (de*ẁ*-per) c (pl ~s) victim

duren (de*ẁ*-rern) v last

durf (derrf) c nerve

durven (derr-vern) v dare

dus (derss) conj so

dutje (der-t*y*er) nt (pl ~s) nap

duur (de*ẁ*r) adj dear, expensive; c duration

duurzaam (de*ẁ*r-zaam) adj lasting, permanent

duw (de*ẁ*ōō) c (pl ~en) push

duwen (de*ẁ*ōō-ern) v push

dwaas¹ (dvaass) *adj* foolish, crazy, silly

dwaas² (dvaass) *c* (pl dwazen) fool

dwalen (*dvaa*-lern) *v* err

dwerg (dvehrkh) *c* (pl ~en) dwarf

*dwingen (*dvı*-ngern) *v* force; compel

dynamo (dee-*naa*-mōa) *c* (pl ~'s) dynamo

dysenterie (dee-sehn-ter-*ree*) *c* dysentery

E

eb (ehp) *c* low tide

ebbehout (*eh*-ber-hout) *nt* ebony

echo (*eh*-khōa) *c* (pl ~'s) echo

echt (ehkht) *adj* genuine, true, authentic, real; *adv* really; *c* matrimony

echtelijk (*ehkh*-ter-lerk) *adj* matrimonial

echter (*ehkh*-terr) *conj* however, yet

echtgenoot (*ehkht*-kher-nōat) *c* (pl -noten) husband

echtgenote (*ehkht*-kher-nōa-ter) *c* (pl ~n) wife

echtpaar (*ehkht*-paar) *nt* (pl -paren) married couple

echtscheiding (*ehkht*-skhay-dıng) *c* (pl ~en) divorce

economie (āy-kōa-nōa-*mee*) *c* economy

economisch (āy-kōa-*nōa*-meess) *adj* economic

econoom (āy-kōa-*nōam*) *c* (pl -nomen) economist

Ecuador (āy-kvaa-*dor*) Ecuador

Ecuadoriaan (āy-kvaa-dōa-ree-ᵞaan) *c* (pl -rianen) Ecuadorian

eczeem (ehk-*sāym*) *nt* eczema

edel (*āy*-derl) *adj* noble

edelmoedigheid (āy-derl-*mōō*-derkh-hayt) *c* generosity

edelsteen (*āy*-derl-stāyn) *c* (pl -stenen) gem, stone

editie (āy-*dee*-tsee) *c* (pl ~s) edition

eed (āyt) *c* (pl eden) oath, vow

eekhoorn (*āyk*-hōarn) *c* (pl ~s) squirrel

eelt (āylt) *nt* callus

een¹ (ern) *art* a art

een² (āyn) *num* one

eenakter (*āyn*-ahk-terr) *c* (pl ~s) one-act play

eend (āynt) *c* (pl ~en) duck

eender (*āyn*-derr) *adj* alike

eenheid (*āyn*-hayt) *c* (pl -heden) unit; unity

eenmaal (*āyn*-maal) *adv* once

eenrichtingsverkeer (*āyn*-rıkh-tıngs-ferr-kāyr) *nt* one-way traffic

eens (āyns) *adv* once; some time, some day; **het ~ *zijn** agree

eentonig (āyn-*tōa*-nerkh) *adj* monotonous

eenvoudig (āyn-*vou*-derkh) *adj* plain, simple; *adv* simply

eenzaam (*āyn*-zaam) *adj* lonely

eenzijdig (āyn-*zay*-derkh) *adj* one-sided

eer (āyr) *c* honour; glory

eerbied (*āyr*-beet) *c* respect

eerbiedig (āyr-*bee*-derkh) *adj* respectful

eerbiedwaardig (āyr-beet-*vaar*-derkh) *adj* venerable

eerder (*āyr*-derr) *adv* before; rather

eergevoel (*āyr*-ger-vōōl) *nt* sense of honour

eergisteren (*āyr*-gıss-ter-rern) *adv* the day before yesterday

eerlijk (*āyr*-lerk) *adj* honest; fair, straight

eerlijkheid (*āyr*-lerk-hayt) *c* honesty

eerst (āyrst) *adj* first; primary, initial; *adv* at first

eersteklas (*āyr*-ster-klahss) *adj* first-class

eersterangs (*ā̄yr*-ster-rahngs) *adj* first-rate

eerstvolgend (*ā̄yrst*-*fol*-gernt) *adj* following

eervol (*ā̄yr*-vol) *adj* honourable

eerzaam (*ā̄yr*-zaam) *adj* respectable; honourable

eerzuchtig (*ā̄yr*-*zerkh*-terkh) *adj* ambitious

eetbaar (*ā̄yt*-baar) *adj* edible

eetkamer (*ā̄yt*-kaa-merr) *c* (pl ~s) dining-room

eetlepel (*ā̄yt*-lā̄y-perl) *c* (pl ~s) tablespoon

eetlust (*ā̄yt*-lerst) *c* appetite

eetservies (*ā̄yt*-sehr-veess) *nt* (pl -viezen) dinner-service

eetzaal (*ā̄yt*-saal) *c* (pl -zalen) dining-room

eeuw (ā̄y∞) *c* (pl ~en) century

eeuwig (*ā̄y∞*-erkh) *adj* eternal

eeuwigheid (*ā̄y∞*-erkh-hayt) *c* eternity

effect (eh-*fehkt*) *nt* (pl ~en) effect; **effecten** stocks and shares

effectenbeurs (eh-*fehk*-term-būrrs) *c* (pl -beurzen) stock market, stock exchange

effectief (eh-fehk-*teef*) *adj* effective

effen (*eh*-fern) *adj* level; smooth, even

efficiënt (eh-fee-*shehnt*) *adj* efficient

egaal (ā̄y-*gaal*) *adj* level

egaliseren (ā̄y-gaa-lee-*zā̄y*-rern) *v* level

egel (*ā̄y*-gerl) *c* (pl ~s) hedgehog

egocentrisch (ā̄y-gōa-*sehn*-treess) *adj* self-centred

egoïsme (ā̄y-gōa-*viss*-mer) *nt* selfishness

egoïstisch (ā̄y-gōa-*viss*-teess) *adj* selfish

Egypte (ā̄y-*gip*-ter) Egypt

Egyptenaar (ā̄y-*gip*-ter-naar) *c* (pl -naren) Egyptian

Egyptisch (ā̄y-*gip*-teess) *adj* Egyptian

ei (ay) *nt* (pl ~eren) egg

eierdooier (ay-err-dōa^(ee)-err) *c* (pl ~s) egg-yolk

eierdopje (ay-err-dop-ⱽer) *nt* (pl ~s) egg-cup

eigen (*ay*-gern) *adj* own

eigenaar (*ay*-ger-naar) *c* (pl ~s, -naren) owner, proprietor

eigenaardig (ay-ger-*naar*-derkh) *adj* singular, peculiar

eigenaardigheid (ay-ger-*naar*-derkh-hayt) *c* (pl -heden) peculiarity

eigendom (*ay*-gern-dom) *nt* (pl ~men) property; possessions

eigengemaakt (*ay*-gern-ger-maakt) *adj* home-made

eigenlijk (*ay*-gern-lerk) *adj* actual; *adv* as a matter of fact, really

eigenschap (*ay*-gern-skhahp) *c* (pl ~pen) property, quality

eigentijds (*ay*-gern-tayts) *adj* contemporary

eigenwijs (ay-gern-*vayss*) *adj* pigheaded

eik (ayk) *c* (pl ~en) oak

eikel (*ay*-kerl) *c* (pl ~s) acorn

eiland (*ay*-lahnt) *nt* (pl ~en) island

einde (*ayn*-der) *nt* end, finish; ending, issue

eindelijk (*ayn*-der-lerk) *adv* at last

eindigen (*ayn*-der-gern) *v* finish

eindpunt (*aynt*-pernt) *nt* (pl ~en) terminal

eindstreep (*aynt*-strā̄yp) *c* (pl -strepen) finish

eis (ayss) *c* (pl ~en) demand, claim

eisen (*ay*-sern) *v* demand

eiwit (*ay*-vit) *nt* (pl ~ten) protein

ekster (*ehk*-sterr) *c* (pl ~s) magpie

eksteroog (*ehk*-sterr-ōakh) *nt* (pl -ogen) corn

eland (*ā̄y*-lahnt) *c* (pl ~en) moose

elastiek (ā̄y-lahss-*tēek*) *nt* (pl ~en) rubber band, elastic

elastisch (āy-*lahss*-teess) *adj* elastic

elders (*ehl*-derrs) *adv* elsewhere

elegant (āy-ler-*gahnt*) *adj* elegant

elegantie (āy-ler-*gahnt*-see) *c* elegance

elektricien (āy-lehk-tree-*shang*) *c* (pl ~s) electrician

elektriciteit (āy-lehk-tree-see-*tayt*) *c* electricity

elektriciteitscentrale (āy-lehk-tree-see-*tayt*-sehn-traa-ler) *c* power-station

elektrisch (āy-*lehk*-treess) *adj* electric

elektronisch (āy-lehk-*trōā*-neess) *adj* electronic; ~ **spel** electronic game

element (āy-ler-*mehnt*) *nt* (pl ~en) element

elementair (āy-ler-mehn-*tair*) *adj* primary

elf[1] (ehlf) *num* eleven

elf[2] (ehlf) *c* (pl ~en) elf

elfde (*ehlf*-der) *num* eleventh

elftal (*ehlf*-tahl) *nt* (pl ~len) soccer team

elimineren (āy-lee-mee-*nāy*-rern) *v* eliminate

elk (ehlk) *adj* each, every

elkaar (ehl-*kaar*) *pron* each other

elleboog (*eh*-ler-bōākh) *c* (pl -bogen) elbow

ellende (eh-*lehn*-der) *c* misery

ellendig (eh-*lehn*-derkh) *adj* miserable

email (āy-*migh*) *nt* enamel

emailleren (āy-migh-*āy*-rern) *v* glaze

emancipatie (āy-mahn-see-*paa*-tsee) *c* emancipation

embargo (ehm-*bahr*-gōa) *nt* embargo

embleem (ehm-*blāym*) *nt* (pl -blemen) emblem

emigrant (āy-mee-*grahnt*) *c* (pl ~en) emigrant

emigratie (āy-mee-*graa*-tsee) *c* emigration

emigreren (āy-mee-*grāy*-rern) *v* emigrate

eminent (āy-mee-*nehnt*) *adj* outstanding

emmer (*eh*-merr) *c* (pl ~s) bucket, pail

emotie (āy-*mōā*-tsee) *c* (pl ~s) emotion

employé (ahm-plvah-*ᵞāy*) *c* (pl ~s) employee

en (ehn) *conj* and

encyclopedie (ehn-see-klōā-pāy-*dee*) *c* (pl ~ën) encyclopaedia

endeldarm (*ehn*-derl-dahrm) *c* (pl ~en) rectum

endosseren (ahn-do-*sāy*-rern) *v* endorse

energie (āy-nehr-*zhee*) *c* energy; power

energiek (āy-nehr-*zheek*) *adj* energetic

eng (ehng) *adj* narrow; creepy

engel (*eh*-ngerl) *c* (pl ~en) angel

Engeland (*eh*-nger-lahnt) England; Britain

Engels (*eh*-ngerls) *adj* English; British

Engelsman (*eh*-ngerls-mahn) *c* (pl Engelsen) Englishman; Briton

enig (*āy*-nerkh) *adj* sole, only; *pron* any; **enige** *pron* some

enigszins (*āy*-nerkh-sıns) *adv* somewhat

enkel[1] (*ehng*-kerl) *adj* single; **enkele** *pron* some

enkel[2] (*ehng*-kerl) *c* (pl ~s) ankle

enkeling (*ehng*-ker-ling) *c* (pl ~en) individual

enkelvoud (*ehng*-kerl-vout) *nt* singular

enorm (āy-*norm*) *adj* tremendous, enormous, huge

enquête (ahng-*kai*-ter) *c* (pl ~s) enquiry

enthousiasme (ahn-tōō-*zhahss*-mer) *nt* enthusiasm

enthousiast (ahn-tōō-*zhahst*) *adj* enthusiastic; keen

entree (ahn-*trāy*) *c* entry; entrance-fee

entresol (ahng-trer-*sol*) *c* (pl ~s) mezzanine

envelop (ahng-ver-*lop*) *c* (pl ~pen) envelope

enzovoort (ehn-zōa-vōārt) and so on, etcetera

epidemie (āy-pee-der-*mee*) *c* (pl ~ën) epidemic

epilepsie (āy-pee-lehp-*see*) *c* epilepsy

epiloog (āy-pee-*lōākh*) *c* (pl -logen) epilogue

episch (āy-peess) *adj* epic

episode (āy-pee-zōā-der) *c* (pl ~n, ~s) episode

epos (āy-poss) *nt* (pl epen, ~sen) epic

equipe (āy-*keep*) *c* (pl ~s) team

equivalent (āy-kvee-vaa-*lehnt*) *adj* equivalent

er (ehr) *adv* there; *pron* of them

erbarmelijk (ehr-*bahr*-mer-lerk) *adj* lamentable

eredienst (āy-rer-deenst) *c* (pl ~en) worship

eren (āy-rern) *v* honour

erf (ehrf) *nt* (pl erven) yard

erfelijk (*ehr*-fer-lerk) *adj* hereditary

erfenis (ehr-fer-niss) *c* (pl ~sen) inheritance; legacy

erg (ehrkh) *adj* bad; *adv* very; **erger** worse; **ergst** worst

ergens (ehrg-gerns) *adv* somewhere

ergeren (ehr-ger-rern) *v* annoy

ergernis (ehr-gerr-niss) *c* annoyance

erkennen (ehr-keh-nern) *v* recognize; acknowledge

erkenning (ehr-keh-ning) *c* (pl ~en) recognition

erkentelijk (ehr-*kehn*-ter-lerk) *adj* grateful

ernst (ehrnst) *c* seriousness; gravity

ernstig (*ehrn*-sterkh) *adj* serious; grave, bad, severe

erts (ehrts) *nt* (pl ~en) ore

*****ervaren** (ehr-*vaa*-rern) *v* experience

ervaring (ehr-*vaa*-ring) *c* (pl ~en) experience

erven (*ehr*-vern) *v* inherit

erwt (ehrt) *c* (pl ~en) pea

escorte (ehss-*kor*-ter) *nt* (pl ~s) escort

escorteren (ehss-kor-*tāy*-rern) *v* escort

esdoorn (ehss-dōārn) *c* (pl ~s) maple

essay (eh-*sāy*) *nt* (pl ~s) essay

essentie (eh-*sehn*-see) *c* essence

essentieel (eh-sehn-*shāyl*) *adj* vital, essential

etage (āy-*taa*-zher) *c* (pl ~s) floor, storey; apartment *nAm*

etalage (āy-taa-*laa*-zher) *c* (pl ~s) shop-window

etappe (āy-*tah*-per) *c* (pl ~n, ~s) stage

eten (āy-tern) *nt* food

*****eten** (āy-tern) *v* *eat

ether (āy-terr) *c* ether

Ethiopië (āy-tee-*yōā*-pee-*yer*) Ethiopia

Ethiopiër (āy-tee-*yōā*-pee-*yerr*) *c* (pl ~s) Ethiopian

Ethiopisch (āy-tee-*yōā*-peess) *adj* Ethiopian

etiket (āy-tee-*keht*) *nt* (pl ~ten) label, tag

etiketteren (āy-tee-keh-*tāy*-rern) *v* label

etmaal (*eht*-maal) *nt* (pl -malen) twenty-four hours

ets (ehts) *c* (pl ~en) etching

ettelijk (*eh*-ter-lerk) *adj* several

etter (*eh*-terr) *c* pus

etui (āy-*tvee*) *nt* (pl ~s) case

Europa (ūr-*rōā*-paa) Europe

Europeaan (ūr-rōā-pāy-*aan*) *c* (pl -anen) European

Europees (ūr-rōā-*pāyss*) *adj* European

Europese Unie (eur-oo-*peeser* y-nie) European Union

evacueren (āy-vaa-kēw-*vāy*-rern) *v* evacuate

evangelie (āy-vahng-*gāy*-lee) *nt* (pl -liën, ~s) gospel

even (*ay̅*-vern) *adj* even; *adv* equally, as

evenaar (*ay̅*-ver-naar) *c* equator

evenals (*ay̅*-ver-nahls) *conj* as well as

evenaren (*ay̅*-ver-naa-rern) *v* equal

eveneens (*ay̅*-ver-*nay̅ns*) *adv* as well, likewise, also

evenredig (*ay̅*-ver-*ray̅*-derkh) *adj* proportional

eventueel (*ay̅*-vern-tew̅-*vay̅l*) *adj* possible, eventual

evenveel (*ay̅*-ver-*vay̅l*) *adv* as much

evenwel (*ay̅*-ver-*vehl*) *adv* however

evenwicht (*ay̅*-ver-vikht) *nt* balance

evenwijdig (*ay̅*-ver-*vay*-derkh) *adj* parallel

evenzeer (*ay̅*-ver-*zay̅r*) *adv* as much

evenzo (*ay̅*-ver-*zo̅a*) *adv* likewise

evolutie (*ay̅*-vo̅a-*lew̅*-tsee) *c* (pl ~s) evolution

exact (ehk-*sahkt*) *adj* precise

examen (ehk-*saa*-mern) *nt* (pl ~s) examination

excentriek (ehk-sehn-*treek*) *adj* eccentric

exces (ehk-*sehss*) *nt* (pl ~sen) excess

exclusief (ehks-klew̅-*zeef*) *adj* exclusive

excursie (ehks-*kerr*-zee) *c* (pl ~s) day trip, excursion

excuseren (ehks-kew̅-*zay̅*-rern) *v* excuse

excuus (ehks-*kew̅ss*) *nt* (pl excuses) apology, excuse

exemplaar (ehk-serm-*plaar*) *nt* (pl -plaren) specimen; copy

exotisch (ehk-*so̅a*-teess) *adj* exotic

expeditie (ehks-per-*dee*-tsee) *c* (pl ~s) expedition

experiment (ehks-pay̅-ree-*mehnt*) *nt* (pl ~en) experiment

experimenteren (ehks-pay̅-ree-mehn-*tay̅*-rern) *v* experiment

expert (ehks-*pair*) *c* (pl ~s) expert

expliciet (ehks-plee-*seet*) *adj* explicit

exploiteren (ehks-plvah-*tay̅*-rern) *v* exploit

explosie (ehks-*plo̅a*-zee) *c* (pl ~s) blast, explosion

explosief (ehks-plo̅a-*zeef*) *adj* explosive

export (*ehk*-sport) *c* exports pl, export

exporteren (ehk-spor-*tay̅*-rern) *v* export

expositie (ehk-spo̅a-*zee*-tsee) *c* (pl ~s) exhibition; display

expresse- (ehk-*spreh*-ser) express; special delivery

extase (ehk-*staa*-zer) *c* ecstasy

extra (*ehk*-straa) *adj* additional, extra; spare

extravagant (ehk-straa-vaa-*gahnt*) *adj* extravagant

extreem (ehk-*stray̅m*) *adj* extreme

ezel (*ay̅*-zerl) *c* (pl ~s) ass; donkey

F

faam (faam) *c* fame

fabel (*faa*-berl) *c* (pl ~s, ~en) fable

fabriceren (faa-bree-*say̅*-rern) *v* manufacture

fabriek (faa-*breek*) *c* (pl ~en) factory; mill, works pl

fabrikant (faa-bree-*kahnt*) *c* (pl ~en) manufacturer

faciliteit (faa-see-lee-*tayt*) *c* (pl ~en) facility

factor (*fahk*-tor) *c* (pl ~en) factor

factureren (fahk-tew̅-*ray̅*-rern) *v* bill

factuur (fahk-*tew̅r*) *c* (pl -turen) invoice

facultatief (faa-kerl-taa-*teef*) *adj* optional

faculteit (faa-kerl-*tayt*) *c* (pl ~en) faculty

failliet (fah-*Yeet*) *adj* bankrupt

fakkel (fah-kerl) *c* (pl ~s) torch

falen (faa-lern) *v* fail

familiaar (fah-mee-lee-*Yaar*) *adj* familiar

familie (faa-*mee*-lee) *c* (pl ~s) family

familielid (faa-*mee*-lee-lıt) *nt* (pl -leden) relative

fanatiek (faa-naa-*teek*) *adj* fanatical

fanfarekorps (fahm-*faa*-rer-korps) *nt* (pl ~en) brass band

fantasie (fahn-taa-*zee*) *c* (pl ~ën) fantasy, fancy

fantastisch (fahn-*tahss*-teess) *adj* fantastic

farce (fahrs) *c* (pl ~n) farce

farmacologie (fahr-maa-kōa-lōa-*gee*) *c* pharmacology

fascinerend (fah-see-*nāy*-rernt) *adj* glamorous

fascisme (fah-*siss*-mer) *nt* fascism

fascist (fah-*sist*) *c* (pl ~en) fascist

fascistisch (fah-*siss*-teess) *adj* fascist

fase (*faa*-zer) *c* (pl ~s, ~n) stage, phase

fataal (faa-*taal*) *adj* fatal

fatsoen (faht-*sōōn*) *nt* decency

fatsoenlijk (faht-*sōōn*-lerk) *adj* decent

fauteuil (fōā-*turew*) *c* (pl ~s) armchair

favoriet (faa-vōā-*reet*) *c* (pl ~en) favourite

fax (faks) *c* fax; **een ~ versturen** send a fax

februari (fāy-brēw-*vaa*-ree) February

federaal (fāy-der-*raal*) *adj* federal

federatie (fāy-der-*raa*-tsee) *c* (pl ~s) federation

fee (fāy) *c* (pl ~ën) fairy

feest (fāyst) *nt* (pl ~en) feast

feestdag (*fāyss*-dahkh) *c* (pl ~en) holiday

feestelijk (*fāy*-ster-lerk) *adj* festive

feestje (*fāy*-sher) *nt* (pl ~s) party

feilloos (*fay*-lōass) *adj* faultless

feit (fayt) *nt* (pl ~en) fact; **in feite** in fact

feitelijk (*fay*-ter-lerk) *adj* factual; *adv* as a matter of fact, actually, in effect

felicitatie (fāy-lee-see-*taa*-tsee) *c* (pl ~s) congratulation

feliciteren (fāy-lee-see-*tāy*-rern) *v* congratulate; compliment

feodaal (fāy-*Yōa*-daal) *adj* feudal

festival (fehss-tee-vahl) *nt* (pl ~s) festival

feuilleton (fur*ew*-er-ton) *nt* (pl ~s) serial

fiasco (fee-*Yahss*-kōa) *nt* (pl ~'s) failure

fiche (*fee*-sher) *c* (pl ~s) chip

fictie (*fık*-see) *c* (pl ~s) fiction

fiets (feets) *c* (pl ~en) cycle, bicycle

fietser (*fee*-tserr) *c* (pl ~s) cyclist

figuur (fee-*gēwr*) *c* (pl -guren) figure; diagram

fijn (fayn) *adj* enjoyable; fine; delicate

fijnhakken (*fayn*-hah-kern) *v* mince

*fijnmalen (*fayn*-maa-lern) *v* *grind

fijnproever (*faym*-prōō-verr) *c* (pl ~s) gourmet

fijnstampen (*fayn*-stahm-pern) *v* mash

filiaal (fee-lee-*Yaal*) *nt* (-ialen) branch

Filippijn (fee-lı-*payn*) *c* (pl ~en) Filipino

Filippijnen (fee-lı-*pay*-nern) *pl* Philippines *pl*

Filippijns (fee-lı-*payns*) *adj* Philippine

film (fılm) *c* (pl ~s) film; movie

filmcamera (*fılm*-kaa-mer-raa) *c* (pl ~'s) camera

filmen (*fıl*-mern) *v* film

filmjournaal (*fılm*-zhōōr-naal) *nt* newsreel

filosofie (fee-lōā-zōā-*fee*) *c* (pl ~ën) philosophy

filosoof (fee-lōā-*zōāf*) c (pl -sofen) philosopher

filter (*fil*-terr) nt (pl ~s) filter

Fin (fin) c (pl ~nen) Finn

financieel (fee-nahn-*shāyl*) adj financial

financiën (fee-*nahn*-see-Yern) pl finances pl

financieren (fee-nahn-*see*-rern) v finance

Finland (*fin*-laht) Finland

Fins (fins) adj Finnish

firma (*fir*-maa) c (pl ~'s) company, firm

fitting (*fi*-ting) c (pl ~en) socket

fjord (fYort) c (pl ~en) fjord

flacon (flaa-*kon*) c (pl ~s) flask

flamingo (flaa-*ming*-gōā) c (pl ~'s) flamingo

flanel (flaa-*nehl*) nt flannel

flat (fleht) c (pl ~s) flat; apartment nAm

flatgebouw (*fleht*-kher-bou) nt (pl ~en) block of flats; apartment house Am

flauw (flou) adj faint

*flauwvallen (*flou*-vah-lern) v faint

fles (flehss) c (pl ~sen) bottle

flesopener (*fleh*-zōā-per-nerr) c (pl ~s) bottle opener

flessehals (*fleh*-ser-hahls) c bottleneck

flets (flehts) adj dull

flink (flingk) adj considerable; brave, plucky

flits (flits) c (pl ~en) flash

flitslampje (*flits*-lahm-pYer) nt (pl ~s) flash-bulb

fluisteren (*flurew*ss-ter-rern) v whisper

fluit (flurewt) c (pl ~en) flute

*fluiten (*flurew*-tern) v whistle

fluitje (*flurew*-tYer) nt (pl ~s) whistle

fluweel (flew-*vāyl*) nt velvet

foefje (*fōō*-fYer) nt (pl ~s) trick

foei! (fōōee) shame!

fok (fok) c (pl ~ken) foresail

fokken (*fo*-kern) v *breed; raise

folklore (fol-*klōā*-rer) c folklore

fonds (fons) nt (pl ~en) fund

fonetisch (fōā-*nāy*-teess) adj phonetic

fonkelend (*fong*-ker-lernt) adj sparkling

fontein (fon-*tayn*) c (pl ~en) fountain

fooi (fōāee) c (pl ~en) tip; gratuity

foppen (*fo*-pern) v fool

forceren (for-*sāy*-rern) v strain; force

forel (fōā-*rehl*) c (pl ~len) trout

forens (fōā-*rehns*) c (pl ~en, forenzen) commuter

formaat (for-*maat*) nt (pl -maten) size

formaliteit (for-maa-lee-*tayt*) c (pl ~en) formality

formeel (for-*māyl*) adj formal

formule (for-*mēw*-ler) c (pl ~s) formula

formulier (for-mēw-*leer*) nt (pl ~en) form

fornuis (for-*nurew*ss) nt (pl -nuizen) cooker, stove

fors (fors) adj robust

fort (fort) nt (pl ~en) fort

fortuin (for-*turew*n) nt (pl ~en) fortune

foto (*fōā*-tōā) c (pl ~'s) photograph, photo

fotocopie (fōā-tōā-kōā-*pee*) c (pl ~ën) photocopy

fotograaf (fōā-tōā-*graaf*) c (pl -grafen) photographer

fotograferen (fōā-tōā-graa-*fāy*-rern) v photograph

fotografie (fōā-tōā-graa-*fee*) c photography

fototoestel (*fōā*-tōā-tōō-stehl) nt (pl ~len) camera

fotowinkel (*fōā*-tōā-ving-kerl) c (pl ~s) camera shop

fouilleren (fōō-Yāy-rern) v search

fout¹ (fout) adj mistaken, wrong

fout² (fout) *c* (pl ~en) error, mistake, fault

foutloos (*fout*-lōass) *adj* faultless

foyer (fvah-*ʸaӯ*) *c* (pl ~s) foyer; lobby

fractie (*frahk*-see) *c* (pl ~s) fraction

fragment (frahkh-*mehnt*) *nt* (pl ~en) fragment; extract

framboos (frahm-*bōass*) *c* (pl -bozen) raspberry

franje (*frah*-ñer) *c* (pl ~s) fringe

frankeren (frahng-*kaӯ*-rern) *v* stamp

frankering (frahng-*kaӯ*-rɪng) *c* (pl ~en) postage

franko (*frahng*-kōa) *adj* postage paid, post-paid

Frankrijk (*frahng*-krayk) France

Frans (frahns) *adj* French

Fransman (*frahns*-mahn) *c* (pl Fransen) Frenchman

frappant (frah-*pahnt*) *adj* striking

fraude (*frou*-der) *c* (pl ~s) fraud

frequent (frer-*kvehnt*) *adj* frequent

frequentie (frer-*kvehn*-tsee) *c* (pl ~s) frequency

fris (frɪss) *adj* fresh

frisdrank (*frɪss*-drahngk) *c* soft drink

frites (freet) *pl* chips

fruit (frur*ew*t) *nt* fruit

fuif (fur*ew*f) *c* (pl fuiven) party

functie (*ferngk*-see) *c* (pl ~s) function

functioneren (ferngk-shōa-*naӯ*-rern) *v* work

fundamenteel (fern-daa-mehn-*taӯl*) *adj* fundamental, basic

fusie (*fe̅w*-zee) *c* (pl ~s) merger

fysica (*fee*-zee-kaa) *c* physics

fysiek (fee-*zeek*) *adj* physical

fysiologie (fee-zee-*ʸōa*-lōa-*gee*) *c* physiology

G

*gaan (gaan) *v* *go; *** ~ door** pass through

gaarne (*gaar*-ner) *adv* gladly

gaas (gaass) *nt* gauze

*gadeslaan (*gaa*-der-slaan) *v* watch

gal (gahl) *c* gall, bile

galblaas (*gahl*-blaass) *c* (pl -blazen) gall bladder

galerij (gah-ler-*ray*) *c* (pl ~en) arcade; gallery

galg (gahlkh) *c* (pl ~en) gallows *pl*

galop (gaa-*lop*) *c* gallop

galsteen (*gahl*-staӯn) *c* (pl -stenen) gallstone

gammel (*gah*-merl) *adj* ramshackle, shaky

gang (gahng) *c* (pl ~en) corridor; gait, pace; course

gangbaar (*gahng*-baar) *adj* current

gangpad (*gahng*-paht) *nt* (pl ~en) aisle

gans (gahns) *c* (pl ganzen) goose

gapen (*gaa*-pern) *v* yawn

garage (gaa-*raa*-zher) *c* (pl ~s) garage

garanderen (gaa-rahn-*daӯ*-rern) *v* guarantee

garantie (gaa-*rahn*-tsee) *c* (pl ~s) guarantee

garderobe (gahr-der-*raw*-ber) *c* (pl ~s) wardrobe, cloakroom; checkroom *nAm*

garen (*gaa*-rern) *nt* (pl ~s) thread, yarn; **garen- en bandwinkel** haberdashery

garnaal (gahr-*naal*) *c* (pl -nalen) prawn, shrimp

gas (gahss) *nt* (pl ~sen) gas

gasfabriek (*gahss*-faa-breek) *c* (pl ~en) gasworks

gasfornuis (*gahss*-for-nur*ew*ss) *nt* (pl

-nuizen) gas cooker

gaskachel (*gahss*-kah-kherl) *c* (pl ~s) gas stove

gaspedaal (*gahss*-per-daal) *nt* (pl -dalen) accelerator

gasstel (*gah*-stehl) *nt* (pl ~len) gas cooker

gast (gahst) *c* (pl ~en) guest

gastheer (*gahst*-hāȳr) *c* (pl -heren) host

gastvrij (gahst-*fray*) *adj* hospitable

gastvrijheid (gahst-*fray*-hayt) *c* hospitality

gastvrouw (*gahst*-frou) *c* (pl ~en) hostess

gat (gaht) *nt* (pl ~en) hole

gauw (gou) *adv* soon

gave (*gaa*-ver) *c* (pl ~n) gift, faculty

gazon (gaa-*zon*) *nt* (pl ~s) lawn

geacht (ger-*ahkht*) *adj* esteemed;
   geachte Heer Dear Sir

geadresseerde (ger-ah-dreh-*sāȳr*-der) *c* (pl ~n) addressee

geaffecteerd (ger-ah-fehk-*tāȳrt*) *adj* affected

gearmd (ger-*ahrmt*) *adv* arm-in-arm

gebaar (ger-*baar*) *nt* (pl gebaren) sign

gebak (ger-*bahk*) *nt* cake, pastry

gebaren (ger-*baa*-rern) *v* gesticulate

gebed (ger-*beht*) *nt* (pl ~en) prayer

gebergte *nt* mountain range

gebeuren (ger-*būr*-rern) *v* occur; happen

gebeurtenis (ger-*būrr*-ter-niss) *c* (pl ~sen) event; happening, occurrence

gebied (ger-*beet*) *nt* (pl ~en) region; zone, area, field, territory

geblokt (ger-*blokt*) *adj* chequered

gebogen (ger-*bōā*-gern) *adj* curved

geboorte (ger-*bōār*-ter) *c* (pl ~n) birth

geboorteland (ger-*bōār*-ter-lahnt) *nt* native country

geboorteplaats (ger-*bōār*-ter-plaats) *c* place of birth

geboren (ger-*bōā*-rern) *adj* born

gebouw (ger-*bou*) *nt* (pl ~en) construction, building

gebrek (ger-*brehk*) *nt* (pl ~en) deficiency, fault; want, lack, shortage

gebrekkig (ger-*breh*-kerkh) *adj* defective, faulty

gebruik (ger-*brur^{ew}k*) *nt* (pl ~en) use, usage; custom

gebruikelijk (ger-*brur^{ew}*-ker-lerk) *adj* customary; common, usual

gebruiken (ger-*brur^{ew}*-kern) *v* use; employ; apply

gebruiker (ger-*brur^{ew}*-kerr) *c* (pl ~s) user

gebruiksaanwijzing (ger-*brur^{ew}k*-saan-vay-zing) *c* (pl ~en) directions for use

gebruiksvoorwerp (ger-*brur^{ew}ks*-fōār-vehrp) *nt* (pl ~en) utensil

gebruind (ger-*brur^{ew}nt*) *adj* tanned

gebrul (ger-*brerl*) *nt* roar

gecompliceerd (ger-kom-plee-*sāȳrt*) *adj* complicated

gedachte (ger-*dahkh*-ter) *c* (pl ~n) thought; idea

gedachtenstreepje (ger-*dahkh*-ter-strāyp-Yer) *nt* (pl ~s) dash

gedeelte (ger-*dāȳl*-ter) *nt* (pl ~n, ~s) part

gedeeltelijk (ger-*dāȳl*-ter-lerk) *adj* partial; *adv* partly

gedelegeerde (ger-dāy-ler-*gāȳr*-der) *c* (pl ~n) delegate

gedenkteken (ger-*dehngk*-tāȳ-kern) *nt* (pl ~s) memorial; monument

gedenkwaardig (ger-dehngk-*vaar*-derkh) *adj* memorable

gedetailleerd (ger-dāy-tah-*Yāȳrt*) *adj* detailed

gedetineerde (ger-dāy-tee-*nāȳr*-der) *c* (pl ~n) prisoner

gedicht (ger-*dikht*) *nt* (pl ~en) poem

geding (ger-*ding*) *nt* (pl ~en) lawsuit

gediplomeerd (ger-dee-plōa-*mayrt*) *adj* qualified

gedrag (ger-*drahkh*) *nt* conduct, behaviour

zich *gedragen (ger-*draa*-gern) act, behave

geduld (ger-*derlt*) *nt* patience

geduldig (ger-*derl*-derkh) *adj* patient

gedurende (ger-*dēw*-rern-der) *prep* during; for

gedurfd (ger-*derrft*) *adj* daring

geel (gāyl) *adj* yellow

geelkoper (*gāyl*-kōa-perr) *nt* brass

geelzucht (*gāyl*-zerkht) *c* jaundice

geëmailleerd (ger-āȳ-mah-*Yayrt*) *adj* enamelled

geen (gāyn) *adj* no

geenszins (*gāyn*-sins) *adv* by no means

geest (gāyst) *c* (pl ~en) spirit, mind; soul; ghost

geestelijk (*gāy*-ster-lerk) *adj* spiritual, mental

geestelijke (*gāy*-ster-ler-ker) *c* (pl ~n) clergyman

geestig (*gāy*-sterkh) *adj* witty, humorous

geeuwen (*gāy*oo-ern) *v* yawn

gefluister (ger-*flur*ew-sterr) *nt* whisper

gegadigde (ger-*gaa*-derkh-der) *c* (pl ~n) candidate

gegeneerd (ger-zher-*nayrt*) *adj* embarrassed

gegeven (ger-*gāy*-vern) *nt* (pl ~s) data *pl*

gegrond (ger-*gront*) *adj* well-founded

gehandicapt (ger-*hehn*-dee-kehpt) *adj* disabled

geheel (ger-*hāyl*) *adj* entire, whole, total; *adv* completely; *nt* whole

geheelonthouder (ger-*hāyl*-ont-hou-derr) *c* (pl ~s) teetotaller

geheim[1] (ger-*haym*) *adj* secret

geheim[2] (ger-*haym*) *nt* (pl ~en) secret

geheimzinnig (ger-haym-*zi*-nerkh) *adj* mysterious

geheugen (ger-*hūr*-gern) *nt* memory

gehoor (ger-*hōar*) *nt* hearing

gehoorzaam (ger-*hōar*-zaam) *adj* obedient

gehoorzaamheid (ger-*hōar*-zaam-hayt) *c* obedience

gehoorzamen (ger-*hōar*-zaa-mern) *v* obey

gehorig (ger-*hōa*-rerkh) *adj* noisy

geïnteresseerd (ger-in-trer-*sayrt*) *adj* interested

geïsoleerd (ger-ee-zōa-*layrt*) *adj* isolated

geit (gayt) *c* (pl ~en) goat

geiteleer (*gay*-ter-lāyr) *nt* kid

gek[1] (gehk) *adj* crazy, mad

gek[2] (gehk) *c* (pl ~ken) fool

geklets (ger-*klehts*) *nt* chat; rubbish

gekleurd (ger-*klūrrt*) *adj* coloured

gekraak (ger-*kraak*) *nt* crack

gekruid (ger-*krur*ewt) *adj* spiced

gelaatstrek (ger-*laats*-trehk) *c* (pl ~ken) feature

gelach (ger-*lahkh*) *nt* laughter

geld (gehlt) *nt* money; **buitenlands ~** foreign currency; **contant ~** cash

geldautomaat (*gehlt*-oo-too-maat) *c* cash dispenser, ATM

geldbelegging (*gehlt*-ber-leh-ging) *c* (pl ~en) investment

*gelden (*gehl*-dern) *v* apply

geldig (*gehl*-derkh) *adj* valid

geldstuk (*gehlt*-sterk) *nt* (pl ~ken) coin

geleden (ger-*lāy*-dern) ago; **kort ~** recently

geleerde (ger-*lāyr*-der) *c* (pl ~n) scholar, scientist

gelegen (ger-*lay*-gern) *adj* situated

gelegenheid (ger-*lāy*-gern-hayt) *c* (pl -heden) occasion, chance, opportunity

gelei (zher-*lay*) c (pl ~en) jelly

geleidehond (ger-*lay*-der-hont) c (pl ~en) guide-dog

geleidelijk (ger-*lay*-der-lerk) adj gradual

gelijk (ger-*layk*) adj equal, like, alike; level, even; ~ *hebben * be right; ~ maken equalize

gelijkenis (ger-*lay*-ker-niss) c (pl ~sen) resemblance, similarity

gelijkgezind (ger-*layk*-kher-*zint*) adj like-minded

gelijkheid (ger-*layk*-hayt) c equality

gelijkstroom (ger-*layk*-strōam) c direct current

gelijktijdig (ger-*layk*-tay-derkh) adj simultaneous

gelijkwaardig (ger-*layk*-*vaar*-derkh) adj equivalent

gelofte (ger-*lof*-ter) c (pl ~n) vow

geloof (ger-*lōāf*) nt belief; faith

geloofwaardig (ger-lōāf-*vaar*-derkh) adj credible

geloven (ger-*lōā*-vern) v believe

geluid (ger-*lur*ᵉʷt) nt (pl ~en) sound; noise

geluiddicht (ger-lurᵉʷ-*dikht*) adj soundproof

geluk (ger-*lerk*) nt happiness; luck, fortune

gelukkig (ger-*ler*-kerkh) adj happy; fortunate

gelukwens (ger-*lerk*-vehns) c (pl ~en) congratulation

gelukwensen (ger-*lerk*-vehn-sern) v congratulate, compliment

gemak (ger-*mahk*) nt leisure; ease; comfort

gemakkelijk (ger-*mah*-ker-lerk) adj easy; convenient

gematigd (ger-*maa*-terkht) adj moderate

gember (*gehm*-berr) c ginger

gemeen (ger-*māyn*) adj foul, mean

gemeenschap (ger-*māyn*-skhahp) c (pl ~pen) community

gemeenschappelijk (ger-māyn-*skhah*-per-lerk) adj common

gemeente (ger-*māyn*-ter) c (pl ~n, ~s) congregation

gemeentebestuur (ger-*māyn*-ter-ber-stēwr) nt municipality

gemeentelijk (ger-*māyn*-ter-lerk) adj municipal

gemêleerd (ger-meh-*lāyrt*) adj mixed

gemengd (ger-*mehngt*) adj mixed; miscellaneous

gemiddeld (ger-mi-derlt) adj average, medium; adv on the average

gemiddelde (ger-mi-derl-der) nt (pl ~n) average, mean

gemis (ger-*miss*) nt want, lack

genade (ger-*naa*-der) c mercy; grace

geneeskunde (ger-*nāyss*-kern-der) c medicine

geneeskundig (ger-nāyss-*kern*-derkh) adj medical

geneesmiddel (ger-*nāyss*-mi-derl) nt (pl ~en) medicine; remedy, drug

genegen (ger-*nāy*-gern) adj inclined

genegenheid (ger-*nāy*-gern-hayt) c affection

geneigd (ger-*naykht*) adj inclined

generaal (gāy-ner-*raal*) c (pl ~s) general

generatie (gāy-ner-*raa*-tsee) c (pl ~s) generation

generator (gāy-ner-*raa*-tor) c (pl ~en, ~s) generator

*genezen (ger-*nāy*-zern) v heal; cure; recover

genezing (ger-*nāy*-zing) c (pl ~en) cure; recovery

genie (zher-*nee*) nt (pl ~ën) genius

*genieten van (ger-*nee*-tern) enjoy

genoeg (ger-*nōōkh*) adv enough; sufficient

genoegen (ger-*nōō*-gern) nt (pl ~s)

pleasure

genootschap (ger-*nōāt*-skhahp) *nt* (pl ~pen) society; association

genot (ger-*not*) *nt* joy; delight; enjoyment

geologie (gāy-Yōā-lōā-*gee*) *c* geology

gepast (ger-*pahst*) *adj* suitable, proper

gepensioneerd (ger-pehn-shōā-*nāȳrt*) *adj* retired

geraamte (ger-*raam*-ter) *nt* (pl ~n, ~s) skeleton

geraas (ger-*raass*) *nt* roar

gerecht (ger-*rehkht*) *nt* (pl ~en) dish; law court

gerechtigheid (ger-*rehkh*-terkh-hayt) *c* justice

gereed (ger-*rāȳt*) *adj* ready

gereedschap (ger-*rāȳt*-skhahp) *nt* (pl ~pen) tool; utensil, implement

gereedschapskist (ger-*rāȳt*-skhahps-kıst) *c* (pl ~en) tool kit

geregeld (ger-*rāȳ*-gerlt) *adj* regular

gereserveerd (ger-rāȳ-zehr-*vāȳrt*) *adj* reserved

gerief (ger-*reef*) *nt* comfort

gerieflijk (ger-*ree*-fer-lerk) *adj* comfortable, easy; convenient

gering (ger-*rıng*) *adj* minor; slight, small; **geringst** least

geroddel (ger-*ro*-derl) *nt* gossip

gerst (gehrst) *c* barley

gerucht (ger-*rerkht*) *nt* (pl ~en) rumour

geruit (ger-*rurew*t) *adj* chequered

gerust (ger-*rerst*) *adj* confident

geruststellen (ger-*rerst*-steh-lern) *v* reassure

gescheiden (ger-*skhay*-dern) *adj* separate

geschenk (ger-*skhehngk*) *nt* (pl ~en) gift, present

geschiedenis (ger-*skhee*-der-nıss) *c* history

geschiedkundig (ger-skheet-*kern*-derkh) *adj* historical

geschiedkundige (ger-skheet-*kern*-der-ger) *c* (pl ~n) historian

geschikt (ger-*skhıkt*) *adj* convenient, suitable, proper, appropriate, fit; ~ ***zijn** qualify

geschil (ger-*skhıl*) *nt* (pl ~len) dispute

geslacht (ger-*slahkht*) *nt* (pl ~en) sex; gender

geslachtsziekte (ger-*slahkht*-seek-ter) *c* (pl ~n, ~s) venereal disease

gesloten (ger-*slōā*-tern) *adj* closed, shut

gesp (gehsp) *c* (pl ~en) buckle

gespannen (ger-*spah*-nern) *adj* tense

gespierd (ger-*speert*) *adj* muscular

gespikkeld (ger-*spı*-kerlt) *adj* spotted

gesprek (ger-*sprehk*) *nt* (pl ~ken) discussion, conversation, talk; **interlokaal** ~ trunk-call; **lokaal** ~ local call

gestalte (ger-*stahl*-ter) *c* (pl ~n, ~s) figure

gesticht (ger-*stıkht*) *nt* (pl ~en) asylum

gestorven (ger-*stor*-vern) *adj* dead

gestreept (ger-*strāȳpt*) *adj* striped

getal (ger-*tahl*) *nt* (pl ~len) number

getij (ger-*tay*) *nt* (pl ~en) tide

getrouw (ger-*trou*) *adj* true

getuige (ger-*turew*-ger) *c* (pl ~n) witness

getuigen (ger-*turew*-gern) *v* testify

getuigschrift (ger-*turew*kh-skhrıft) *nt* (pl ~en) certificate

getypt (ger-*teept*) *adj* typewritten

geur (gūrr) *c* (pl ~en) smell, odour; scent

gevaar (ger-*vaar*) *nt* (pl -varen) danger; risk, peril

gevaarlijk (ger-*vaar*-lerk) *adj* dangerous; perilous

geval (ger-*vahl*) *nt* (pl ~len) case; instance; event; **in elk** ~ at any rate, anyway; **in ~ van** in case of

gevangene (ger-*vah*-nger-ner) *c* (pl ~n) prisoner

gevangenis (ger-*vah*-nger-niss) *c* (pl ~sen) prison; gaol, jail

gevangenschap (ger-*vah*-ngern-skhahp) *c* imprisonment

gevarieerd (ger-vaa-ree-*Yaȳ*rt) *adj* varied

gevecht (ger-*vehkht*) *nt* (pl ~en) combat, battle, fight

gevel (*gaȳ*-verl) *c* (pl ~s) façade

geveltop (*gaȳ*-verl-top) *c* (pl ~pen) gable

*****geven** (*gaȳ*-vern) *v* *give; **~ om** mind

gevoel (ger-*vōōl*) *nt* feeling; sensation

gevoelig (ger-*vōō*-lerkh) *adj* sensitive

gevoelloos (ger-*vōō*-lōass) *adj* numb

gevogelte (ger-*vōā*-gerl-ter) *nt* fowl; poultry

gevolg (ger-*volkh*) *nt* (pl ~en) result, consequence; issue, effect; **ten gevolge van** owing to

gevolgtrekking (ger-*volkh*-treh-king) *c* (pl ~en) conclusion

gevorderd (ger-*vor*-derrt) *adj* advanced

gevuld (ger-*verlt*) *adj* stuffed

gewaad (ger-*vaat*) *nt* (pl gewaden) robe

gewaagd (ger-*vaakht*) *adj* risky

gewaarwording (ger-*vaar*-vor-ding) *c* (pl ~en) perception; sensation

gewapend (ger-*vaa*-pernt) *adj* armed

geweer (ger-*vaȳr*) *nt* (pl geweren) rifle, gun

gewei (ger-*vay*) *nt* (pl ~en) antlers *pl*

geweld (ger-*vehlt*) *nt* violence; force

gewelddaad (ger-*vehl*-daat) *c* (pl -daden) outrage

gewelddadig (ger-vehl-*daa*-derkh) *adj* violent

geweldig (ger-*vehl*-derkh) *adj* terrific;

huge

gewelf (ger-*vehlf*) *nt* (pl gewelven) arch, vault

gewend (ger-*vehnt*) *adj* accustomed

gewest (ger-*vehst*) *nt* (pl ~en) province

geweten (ger-*vaȳ*-tern) *nt* conscience

gewicht (ger-*vikht*) *nt* (pl ~en) weight

gewichtig (ger-*vikh*-terkh) *adj* important; big

gewillig (ger-*vi*-lerkh) *adj* co-operative

gewond (ger-*vont*) *adj* injured

gewoon (ger-*vōān*) *adj* normal, ordinary; common, regular, plain, simple; customary, habitual; accustomed; **~ *zijn** *be used to; would

gewoonlijk (ger-*vōān*-lerk) *adj* customary; *adv* as a rule, usually

gewoonte (ger-*vōān*-ter) *c* (pl ~n, ~s) habit; custom

gewoonweg (ger-*vōān*-vehkh) *adv* simply

gewricht (ger-*vrikht*) *nt* (pl ~en) joint

gezag (ger-*zahkh*) *nt* authority

gezagvoerder (ger-*zahkh*-fōōr-derr) *c* (pl ~s) captain

gezamenlijk (ger-*zaa*-mer-lerk) *adj* joint

gezang (ger-*zahng*) *nt* (pl ~en) hymn

gezant (ger-*zahnt*) *c* (pl ~en) envoy

gezellig (ger-*zeh*-lerkh) *adj* cosy

gezelschap (ger-*zehl*-skhahp) *nt* (pl ~pen) company; society

gezet (ger-*zeht*) *adj* corpulent; stout

gezicht (ger-*zikht*) *nt* (pl ~en) face; sight

gezichtscrème (ger-*zikhts*-kraim) *c* (pl ~s) face-cream

gezichtsmassage (ger-*zikhts*-mah-saa-zher) *c* (pl ~s) face massage

gezichtspoeder (ger-*zikhts*-pōō-derr) *nt/c* (pl ~s) face-powder

gezien (ger-*zeen*) *prep* considering

gezin (ger-*zin*) *nt* (pl ~nen) family

gezond (ger-*zont*) *adj* healthy; well; wholesome

gezondheid (ger-*zont*-hayt) *c* health

gezondheidsattest (ger-*zont*-hayts-ah-tehst) *nt* (pl ~en) health certificate

gezwel (ger-*zvehl*) *nt* (pl ~len) tumour, growth

gids (gits) *c* (pl ~en) guide; guidebook

giechelen (*gee*-kher-lern) *v* giggle

gier (geer) *c* (pl ~en) vulture

gierig (*gee*-rerkh) *adj* avaricious; stingy

*__gieten__ (*gee*-tern) *v* pour

gietijzer (*gee*-tay-zerr) *nt* cast iron

gift (gift) *c* (pl ~en) donation

giftig (*gif*-terkh) *adj* poisonous

gijzelaar (*gay*-zer-laar) *c* (pl ~s) hostage

gil (gil) *c* (pl ~len) scream, yell, shriek

gillen (*gi*-lern) *v* scream, yell, shriek

ginds (gins) *adv* over there

gips (gips) *nt* plaster

gissen (*gi*-sern) *v* guess

gissing (*gi*-sing) *c* (pl ~en) guess

gist (gist) *c* yeast

gisten (*giss*-tern) *v* ferment

gisteren (*giss*-ter-rern) *adv* yesterday

gitaar (gee-*taar*) *c* (pl -taren) guitar

glad (glaht) *adj* slippery; smooth

glans (glahns) *c* gloss

glanzen (*glahn*-zern) *v* *shine; **glanzend** glossy

glas (glahss) *nt* (pl glazen) glass; **gebrandschilderd** ~ stained glass

glazen (*glaa*-zern) *adj* glass

gletsjer (*gleht*-sherr) *c* (pl ~s) glacier

gleuf (glūrf) *c* (pl gleuven) slot

glibberig (*gli*-ber-rerkh) *adj* slippery

glijbaan (*glay*-baan) *c* (pl -banen) slide

*__glijden__ (*glay*-dern) *v* glide, *slide

glimlach (*glim*-lahkh) *c* smile

glimlachen (*glim*-lah-khern) *v* smile

glimp (glimp) *c* glimpse

globaal (glōā-*baal*) *adj* broad

gloed (glōōt) *c* glow

gloeien (*glōō*ee-ern) *v* glow

gloeilamp (*glōō*ee-lahmp) *c* (pl ~en) light bulb

glooien (*glōā*ee-ern) *v* slope

glooiing (*glōā*ee-ing) *c* (pl ~en) ramp

glorie (*glōā*-ree) *c* glory

gluren (*glew*-rern) *v* peep

gobelin (gōā-ber-*lang*) *c* (pl ~s) tapestry

god (got) *c* (pl ~en) god

goddelijk (*go*-der-lerk) *adj* divine

godin (gōā-*din*) *c* (pl ~nen) goddess

godsdienst (gots-deenst) *c* (pl ~en) religion

godsdienstig (gots-*deen*-sterkh) *adj* religious

goed (gōōt) *adj* good; right, correct; kind; *adv* well; **goed!** all right!

goederen (*gōō*-der-rern) *pl* goods *pl*

goederentrein (*gōō*-der-rern-trayn) *c* (pl ~en) goods train; freight-train *nAm*

goedgelovig (gōōt-kher-*lōā*-verkh) *adj* credulous

goedgestemd (gōōt-kher-*stehmt*) *adj* good-tempered

goedhartig (gōōt-*hahr*-terkh) *adj* good-natured

goedkeuren (*gōōt*-kūr-rern) *v* approve

goedkeuring (*gōōt*-kur-ring) *c* (pl ~en) approval

goedkoop (gōōt-*kōāp*) *adj* cheap; inexpensive

gok (gok) *c* chance

golf[1] (golf) *c* (pl golven) wave; gulf

golf[2] (golf) *nt* golf

golfbaan (*golf*-baan) *c* (pl -banen) golf-links, golf-course

golfclub (*golf*-klerp) *c* (pl ~s) golf-club

golflengte (*golf*-lehng-ter) *c* (pl ~n, ~s) wave-length

golvend (*gol*-vernt) *adj* wavy, undulating

gom (gom) *c/nt* (pl ~men) eraser

gondel (*gon*-derl) *c* (pl ~s) gondola

goochelaar (*gōā*-kher-laar) *c* (pl ~s) magician

gooi (gōā^{ee}) *c* (pl ~en) throw

gooien (*gōā^{ee}*-ern) *v* *throw; *cast; toss

goot (gōāt) *c* (pl goten) gutter

gootsteen (*gōāt*-stāyn) *c* (pl -stenen) sink

gordijn (gor-*dayn*) *nt* (pl ~en) curtain

gorgelen (*gor*-ger-lern) *v* gargle

goud (gout) *nt* gold

gouden (*gou*-dern) *adj* golden

goudmijn (*gout*-mayn) *c* (pl ~en) goldmine

goudsmid (*gout*-smit) *c* (pl -smeden) goldsmith

gouvernante (gōō-verr-*nahn*-ter) *c* (pl ~s) governess

gouverneur (gōō-verr-*nūrr*) *c* (pl ~s) governor

graad (graat) *c* (pl graden) degree; grade

graaf (graaf) *c* (pl graven) count; earl

graafschap (*graaf*-skhahp) *nt* (pl ~pen) county

graag (graakh) *adv* gladly, willingly

graan (graan) *nt* (pl granen) corn, grain

graat (graat) *c* (pl graten) bone, fishbone

gracht (grahkht) *c* (pl ~en) canal; moat

graf (grahf) *nt* (pl graven) grave; tomb

grafiek (graa-*feek*) *c* (pl ~en) graph, diagram; chart

grafisch (*graa*-feess) *adj* graphic

grafsteen (*grahf*-stāyn) *c* (pl -stenen) tombstone, gravestone

gram (grahm) *nt* (pl ~men) gram

grammatica (grah-*maa*-tee-kaa) *c* grammar

grammaticaal (grah-maa-tee-*kaal*) *adj* grammatical

grammofoonplaat (grah-mōā-*fōān*-plaat) *c* (pl -platen) disc, record

graniet (graa-*neet*) *nt* granite

grap (grahp) *c* (pl ~pen) joke

grappig (*grah*-perkh) *adj* funny, humorous

gras (grahss) *nt* grass

grasspriet (*grahss*-spreet) *c* (pl ~en) blade of grass

grasveld (*grahss*-fehlt) *nt* (pl ~en) lawn

gratie (*graa*-tsee) *c* grace; pardon

gratis (*graa*-terss) *adv* free of charge, free, gratis

grauw (grou) *adj* grey

***graven** (*graa*-vern) *v* *dig

graveren (graa-*vāy*-rern) *v* engrave

graveur (graa-*vūrr*) *c* (pl ~s) engraver

gravin (graa-*vin*) *c* (pl ~nen) countess

gravure (graa-*vēw*-rer) *c* (pl ~s, ~n) engraving

grazen (*graa*-zern) *v* graze

greep (grāyp) *c* (pl grepen) grip; grasp, clutch

grendel (*grehn*-derl) *c* (pl ~s) bolt

grens (grehns) *c* (pl grenzen) frontier, border; boundary, bound

grenzeloos (grehn-zer-*lōāss*) *adj* unlimited

grenzen (*grehn*-zern) *v* border (on), adjoin; verge

greppel (*greh*-perl) *c* (pl ~s) ditch

Griek (greek) *c* (pl ~en) Greek

Griekenland (*gree*-kern-lahnt) Greece

Grieks (greeks) *adj* Greek

griep (greep) *c* flu, influenza

griet (greet) *c* (pl ~en) brill

griezelig (*gree*-zer-lerkh) *adj* scary,

creepy

grijns (grayns) c grin

grijnzen (grayn-zern) v grin

*grijpen (gray-pern) v *catch, grip, grasp, seize

grijs (grayss) adj grey

gril (grɪl) c (pl ~len) whim, fancy, fad

grind (grɪnt) nt gravel

grinniken (grɪ-ner-kern) v chuckle

groef (grōōf) c (pl groeven) groove

groei (grōō ee) c growth

groeien (grōō ee-ern) v *grow

groen (grōōn) adj green

groente c (pl ~n, ~s) greens pl, vegetable

groenteboer (grōōn-ter-bōōr) c (pl ~en) greengrocer; vegetable merchant

groep (grōōp) c (pl ~en) group; bunch, set, party

groet (grōōt) c (pl ~en) greeting

groeten (grōō-tern) v greet; salute

groeve (grōō-ver) c (pl ~n) pit

grof (grof) adj gross, coarse; rude

grommen (gro-mern) v growl

grond (gront) c ground; earth, soil; **begane ~** ground floor

grondig (gron-derkh) adj thorough

grondslag (gront-slahkh) c (pl ~en) basis, base

grondstof (gront-stof) c (pl ~fen) raw material

grondwet (gront-veht) c (pl ~ten) constitution

groot (grōāt) adj big; great, large, tall; major; **grootst** major, main; **groter** major; superior

*grootbrengen (grōāt-breh-ngern) v *bring up, raise; rear

Groot-Brittannië (grōāt-brɪ-tah-nee-ᵧer) Great Britain

groothandel (grōāt-hahn-derl) c wholesale

grootmoeder (grōāt-mōō-derr) c (pl

~s) grandmother

grootouders (grōāt-ou-derrs) pl grandparents pl

groots (grōāts) adj grand, superb, magnificent

grootte (grōā-ter) c (pl ~n, ~s) size

grootvader (grōāt-faa-derr) c (pl ~s) grandfather

gros (gross) nt (pl ~sen) gross

grossier (gro-seer) c (pl ~s) wholesale dealer

grot (grot) c (pl ~ten) cave; grotto

gruis (grurᵉʷss) nt grit

gruwelijk (grēw-ver-lerk) adj horrible

gul (gerl) adj generous

gulp (gerlp) c (pl ~en) fly

gulzig (gerl-zerkh) adj greedy

gunnen (ger-nern) v grant

gunst (gernst) c (pl ~en) favour

gunstig (gern-sterkh) adj favourable

guur (gēwr) adj bleak

gymnast (gɪm-nahst) c (pl ~en) gymnast

gymnastiek (gɪm-nahss-teek) c gymnastics pl

gymnastiekbroek (gɪm-nahss-teek-brōōk) c (pl ~en) trunks pl

gymnastiekzaal (gɪm-nahss-teek-saal) c (pl -zalen) gymnasium

gymschoenen (gɪm-skhōō-nern) pl gym shoes, plimsolls pl; sneakers plAm

gynaecoloog (gee-nāy-kōa-lōākh) c (pl -logen) gynaecologist

H

haai (haa ee) c (pl ~en) shark

haak (haak) c (pl haken) hook; **tussen twee haakjes** by the way

haalbaar (haal-baar) adj attainable, realizable

haan (haan) *c* (pl hanen) cock
haar¹ (haar) *nt* (pl haren) hair
haar² (haar) *pron* her
haarborstel (*haar*-bor-sterl) *c* (pl ~s) hairbrush
haarcrème (*haar*-kraim) *c* (pl ~s) hair cream
haard (haart) *c* (pl ~en) hearth, fireplace
haardroger (*haar*-drōā-gerr) *c* (pl ~s) hair-dryer
haargel (*haar*-zhel) *c* hair gel
haarlak (*haar*-lahk) *c* (pl ~ken) hair-spray
haarnetje (*haar*-neh-t^yer) *nt* (pl ~s) hair-net
haarspeld (*haar*-spehlt) *c* (pl ~en) hairpin, hair-grip; bobby pin *Am*
haarstukje (*haar*-ster-k^yer) *nt* (pl ~s) hair piece
haarversteviger (*haar*-verr-stāy-ver-gerr) *c* setting lotion
haas (haass) *c* (pl hazen) hare
haast¹ (haast) *adv* nearly, almost
haast² (haast) *c* haste, hurry
zich haasten (*haass*-tern) hasten, rush, hurry
haastig (*haass*-terkh) *adj* hasty; *adv* in a hurry
haat (haat) *c* hatred, hate
hachelijk (*hah*-kher-lerk) *adj* precarious, critical
hagel (*haa*-gerl) *c* hail
hak (hahk) *c* (pl ~ken) heel
haken (*haa*-kern) *v* crochet
hakken (*hah*-kern) *v* chop
hal (hahl) *c* (pl ~len) lobby, hall
halen (*haa*-lern) *v* *get, fetch; *make; *catch; *laten ~ *send for
half (hahlf) *adj* half; semi-; *adv* half
hallo! (hah-*lōā*) hello!
hals (hahls) *c* (pl halzen) throat; neck
halsband (*hahls*-bahnt) *c* (pl ~en) collar

halsketting (*hahls*-keh-tıng) *c* (pl ~en) necklace
halt! (hahlt) stop!
halte (*hahl*-ter) *c* (pl ~n, ~s) stop
halveren (hahl-*vāy*-rern) *v* halve
halverwege (*hahl*-verr-vāy-ger) *adv* halfway
ham (hahm) *c* (pl ~men) ham
hamer (*haa*-merr) *c* (pl ~s) hammer; **houten ~** mallet
hand (hahnt) *c* (pl ~en) hand; **hand-** manual; **met de ~ gemaakt** handmade
handbagage (*hahnt*-bah-gaa-zher) *c* hand luggage; hand baggage *Am*
handboeien (*hahnt*-bōō^{ee}-ern) *pl* handcuffs *pl*
handboek (*hahnt*-bōōk) *nt* (pl ~en) handbook
handcrème (*hahnt*-kraim) *c* (pl ~s) hand cream
handdoek (*hahn*-dōōk) *c* (pl ~en) towel
handdruk (*hahn*-drerk) *c* handshake
handel (*hahn*-derl) *c* commerce, trade; business; ~ *drijven trade; **handels-** commercial
handelaar (*hahn*-der-laar) *c* (pl ~s, -laren) tradesman, merchant; dealer, trader
handelen (*hahn*-der-lern) *v* act
handeling (*hahn*-der-lıng) *c* (pl ~en) action; deed, plot
handelsmerk (*hahn*-derls-mehrk) *nt* (pl ~en) trademark
handelsrecht (*hahn*-derls-rehkht) *nt* commercial law
handelswaar (*hahn*-derls-vaar) *c* merchandise
handenarbeid (*hahn*-der-nahr-bayt) *c* handicraft
handhaven (*hahnt*-haa-vern) *v* maintain
handig (*hahn*-derkh) *adj* handy

handkoffertje (*hahnt-ko-ferr-t^yer*) *nt* (pl ~s) grip *nAm*

handpalm (*hahnt-pahlm*) *c* (pl ~en) palm

handrem (*hahnt-rehm*) *c* (pl ~men) hand-brake

handschoen (*hahnt-skhōōn*) *c* (pl ~en) glove

handschrift (*hahnt-skhrift*) *nt* (pl ~en) handwriting

handtas (*hahn-tahss*) *c* (pl ~sen) handbag, bag

handtekening (*hahn-tāy-ker-ning*) *v* (pl ~en) signature

handvat (*hahnt-faht*) *nt* (pl ~ten) handle

handvol (*hahnt-fol*) *c* handful

handwerk (*hahnt-vehrk*) *nt* handwork, handicraft; needlework

hangbrug (*hahng-brerkh*) *c* (pl ~gen) suspension bridge

*__hangen__ (*hah-ngern*) *v* *hang

hangmat (*hahng-maht*) *c* (pl ~ten) hammock

hangslot (*hahng-slot*) *nt* (pl ~en) padlock

hanteerbaar (*hahn-tāyr-baar*) *adj* manageable

hanteren (*hahn-tāy-rern*) *v* handle

hap (*hahp*) *c* (pl ~pen) bite

hard (*hahrt*) *adj* hard; loud

harddraverij (*hahr-draa-ver-ray*) *c* (pl ~en) horserace

hardnekkig (*hahrt-neh-kerkh*) *adj* obstinate, dogged, stubborn

hardop (*hahrt-op*) *adv* aloud

harig (*haa-rerkh*) *adj* hairy

haring (*haa-ring*) *c* (pl ~en) herring

hark (*hahrk*) *c* (pl ~en) rake

harmonie (*hahr-mōa-nee*) *c* harmony

harnas (*hahr-nahss*) *nt* (pl ~sen) armour

harp (*hahrp*) *c* (pl ~en) harp

hars (*hahrs*) *nt/c* resin

hart (*hahrt*) *nt* (pl ~en) heart

hartaanval (*hahr-taan-vahl*) *c* (pl ~len) heart attack

hartelijk (*hahr-ter-lerk*) *adj* hearty, cordial; sympathetic

harteloos (*hahr-ter-lōass*) *adj* heartless

hartklopping (*hahrt-klo-ping*) *c* (pl ~en) palpitation

hartstocht (*hahrts-tokht*) *c* passion

hartstochtelijk (*hahrts-tokh-ter-lerk*) *adj* passionate

hatelijk (*haa-ter-lerk*) *adj* spiteful

haten (*haa-tern*) *v* hate

haven (*haa-vern*) *c* (pl ~s) port, harbour

havenarbeider (*haa-vern-ahr-bay-derr*) *c* (pl ~s) docker

haver (*haa-verr*) *c* oats *pl*

havik (*haa-vik*) *c* (pl ~en) hawk

hazelnoot (*haa-zerl-nōat*) *c* (pl -noten) hazelnut

hazewind (*haa-zer-vint*) *c* (pl ~en) greyhound

*__hebben__ (*heh-bern*) *v* *have

Hebreeuws (*hāy-brāy^{oo}ss*) *nt* Hebrew

hebzucht (*hehp-serkht*) *c* greed

hebzuchtig (*hehp-serkh-terkh*) *adj* greedy

hechten (*hehkh-tern*) *v* attach; sew up

hechtenis (*hehkh-ter-niss*) *c* custody

hechting (*hehkh-ting*) *c* (pl ~en) stitch

hechtpleister (*hehkht-play-sterr*) *c* (pl ~s) adhesive tape

heden (*hāy-dern*) *nt* present

hedendaags (*hāy-dern-daakhs*) *adj* contemporary

heel (*hāyl*) *adj* entire, whole; unbroken; *adv* quite

heelal (*hāy-lahl*) *nt* universe

heelhuids (*hāyl-hur^{ew}ts*) *adj* unhurt

*__heengaan__ (*hāyng-gaan*) *v* depart

heer (*hāyr*) *c* (pl heren) gentleman

heerlijk (*hāyr-lerk*) *adj* lovely, wonderful; delightful, delicious

heerschappij (hayr-skhah-*pay*) c (pl ~en) rule; dominion

heersen (*hayr*-sern) v rule

heerser (*hayr*-serr) c (pl ~s) ruler

hees (hayss) adj hoarse

heet (hayt) adj hot; warm

hefboom (*hehf*-bōm) c (pl -bomen) lever

*****heffen** (*heh*-fern) v raise

heftig (*hehf*-terkh) adj violent

heg (hehkh) c (pl ~gen) hedge

heide (*hay*-der) c (pl ~n) heath; moor; heather

heiden (*hay*-dern) c (pl ~en) heathen, pagan

heidens (*hay*-derns) adj heathen, pagan

heiig (*hay*-erkh) adj hazy

heilbot (*hayl*-bot) c (pl ~ten) halibut

heilig (*hay*-lerkh) adj holy, sacred

heiligdom (*hay*-lerkh-dom) nt (pl ~men) shrine

heilige (*hay*-ler-ger) c (pl ~n) saint

heiligschennis (*hay*-lerkh-skheh-nerss) c sacrilege

heimwee (*haym*-vay) nt homesickness

hek (hehk) nt (pl ~ken) fence; gate; railing

hekel (*hay*-kerl) c dislike; **een ~ *hebben aan** hate, dislike

heks (hehks) c (pl ~en) witch

hel (hehl) c hell

helaas (hay-*laass*) adv unfortunately

held (hehlt) c (pl ~en) hero

helder (*hehl*-derr) adj clear; serene; bright

heleboel (*hay*-ler-*bōōl*) c plenty

helemaal (*hay*-ler-maal) adv entirely, altogether, completely, wholly; quite; at all

helft (hehlft) c (pl ~en) half

hellen (*heh*-lern) v slant; **hellend** slanting

helling (*heh*-ling) c (pl ~en) slope; hillside; gradient, incline

helm (hehlm) c (pl ~en) helmet

*****helpen** (*hehl*-pern) v help; assist, aid

helper (*hehl*-perr) c (pl ~s) helper

hem (hehm) pron him

hemd (hehmt) nt (pl ~en) shirt; vest; undershirt

hemel (*hay*-merl) c (pl ~s, ~en) sky; heaven

hen[1] (hehn) pron them

hen[2] (hehn) c (pl ~nen) hen

hendel (*hehn*-derl) c (pl ~s) lever

hengel (*heh*-ngerl) c (pl ~s) fishing rod

hengelen (*heh*-nger-lern) v angle, fish

hennep (*heh*-nerp) c hemp

herberg (*hehr*-behrkh) c (pl ~en) hostel, tavern, inn

herbergen (*hehr*-behr-gern) v lodge

herbergier (hehr-behr-*geer*) c (pl ~s) inn-keeper

herdenking (hehr-*dehng*-king) c (pl ~en) commemoration

herder (*hehr*-derr) c (pl ~s) shepherd

herenhuis (*hay*-rern-hur^(ew)ss) nt (pl -huizen) mansion, manor-house

herenigen (heh-*ray*-ner-gern) v reunite

herentoilet (*hay*-rern-tvah-leht) nt (pl ~ten) men's room

herfst (hehrfst) c autumn; fall nAm

herhalen (hehr-*haa*-lern) v repeat

herhaling (hehr-*haa*-ling) c (pl ~en) repetition

herinneren (heh-*ri*-ner-rern) v remind; **zich ~** remember, recollect, recall

herinnering (heh-*ri*-ner-ring) c (pl ~en) memory; remembrance

herkennen (hehr-*keh*-nern) v recognize

herkomst (*hehr*-komst) c origin

hernia (*hehr*-nee-^(y)aa) c slipped disc

herrie (*heh*-ree) c noise; fuss

*****herroepen** (heh-*rōō*-pern) v recall

hersenen (*hehr*-ser-nern) *pl* brain

hersenschudding (*hehr*-sern-skher-dɪng) *c* (pl ~en) concussion

herstel (hehr-*stehl*) *nt* repair; recovery; revival

herstellen (hehr-*steh*-lern) *v* repair, mend; **zich ~** recover

hert (hehrt) *nt* (pl ~en) deer

hertog (*hehr*-tokh) *c* (pl ~en) duke

hertogin (hehr-tōa-gɪn) *c* (pl ~nen) duchess

hervatten (hehr-*vah*-tern) *v* resume, recommence

***herzien** (hehr-*zeen*) *v* revise

herziening (hehr-*zee*-nɪng) *c* (pl ~en) revision

het (heht, ert) *art* the; *pron* it

***heten** (*hāy*-tern) *v* *be called

heteroseksueel (hāy-ter-rōa-sehk-sēw-*vāyl*) *adj* heterosexual

hetzij ... hetzij (heht-*say*) either ... or

heup (hūrp) *c* (pl ~en) hip

heuvel (*hūr*-verl) *c* (pl ~s) hill; mound

heuvelachtig (*hūr*-ver-lahkh-terkh) *adj* hilly

heuveltop (*hūr*-verl-top) *c* (pl ~pen) hilltop

hevig (*hāy*-verkh) *adj* severe, violent; intense

hiel (heel) *c* (pl ~en) heel

hier (heer) *adv* here

hiërarchie (hee-ʸer-rahr-*khee*) *c* (pl ~ën) hierarchy

hij (hay) *pron* he

hijgen (*hay*-gern) *v* pant

***hijsen** (*hay*-sern) *v* hoist

hijskraan (*hayss*-kraan) *c* (pl -kranen) crane

hik (hɪk) *c* hiccup

hinderen (*hɪn*-der-rern) *v* hinder; bother, embarrass

hinderlaag (*hɪn*-derr-laakh) *c* (pl -lagen) ambush

hinderlijk (hɪn-derr-lerk) *adj* annoying

hindernis (hɪn-derr-nɪss) *c* (pl ~sen) obstacle

hinken (*hɪng*-kern) *v* limp

historisch (hee-*stōa*-reess) *adj* historic

hitte (hɪ-ter) *c* heat

hobbelig (ho-ber-lerkh) *adj* bumpy

hobby (*ho*-bee) *c* (pl ~'s) hobby

hoe (hōō) *adv* how; **~ ... hoe** the ... the; **~ dan ook** anyhow, any way; at any rate

hoed (hōōt) *c* (pl ~en) hat

hoede (*hōō*-der) *c* custody

zich hoeden (*hōō*-dern) beware

hoef (hōōf) *c* (pl hoeven) hoof

hoefijzer (*hōōf*-ay-zerr) *nt* (pl ~s) horseshoe

hoek (hōōk) *c* (pl ~en) corner; angle

hoer (hōōr) *c* (pl ~en) whore

hoes (hōōss) *c* (pl hoezen) sleeve

hoest (hōōst) *c* cough

hoesten (*hōōss*-tern) *v* cough

hoeveel (hōō-*vāyl*) *pron* how much; how many

hoeveelheid (hōō-*vāyl*-hayt) *c* (pl -heden) quantity; amount

hoeven (*hōō*-vern) *v* need

hoewel (hōō-*vehl*) *conj* although, though

hof (hof) *nt* (pl hoven) court

hoffelijk (*ho*-fer-lerk) *adj* courteous

hokje (*ho*-kʸer) *nt* (pl ~s) booth

hol¹ (hol) *nt* (pl ~en) den; cavern

hol² (hol) *adj* hollow

Holland (*ho*-lahnt) Holland

Hollander (*ho*-lahn-derr) *c* (pl ~s) Dutchman

Hollands (*ho*-lahnts) *adj* Dutch

holte (*hol*-ter) *c* (pl ~s, ~n) cavity

homoseksueel (hōa-mōa-sehk-sēw-*vāyl*) *adj* homosexual

hond (hont) *c* (pl ~en) dog

hondehok (*hon*-der-hok) *nt* (pl ~ken) kennel

honderd (*hon*-derrt) *num* hundred

hondsdolheid (honts-*dol*-hayt) *c* rabies

Hongaar (hong-*gaar*) *c* (pl -garen) Hungarian

Hongaars (hong-*gaars*) *adj* Hungarian

Hongarije (hong-gaa-*ray*-er) Hungary

honger (*ho*-ngerr) *c* hunger

hongerig (*ho*-nger-rerkh) *adj* hungry

honing (*hō̄a*-ning) *c* honey

honkbal (*hongk*-bahl) *nt* baseball

honorarium (hō̄a-nō̄a-*raa*-ree-Yerm) *nt* (pl -ria) fee

hoofd (hō̄aft) *nt* (pl ~en) head; **het ~ *bieden aan** face; **hoofd-** primary, main, chief; cardinal, capital; **over het ~ *zien** overlook; **uit het ~** by heart; **uit het ~ leren** memorize

hoofdkussen (*hō̄a*-ker-sern) *nt* (pl ~s) pillow

hoofdkwartier (*hō̄aft*-kvahr-teer) *nt* (pl ~en) headquarters *pl*

hoofdleiding (*hō̄aft*-lay-ding) *c* (pl ~en) mains *pl*

hoofdletter (*hō̄aft*-leh-terr) *c* (pl ~s) capital letter

hoofdlijn (*hō̄aft*-layn) *c* (pl ~en) main line

hoofdonderwijzer (*hō̄aft*-on-derr-vay-zerr) *c* (pl ~s) head teacher

hoofdpijn (*hō̄aft*-payn) *c* headache

hoofdstad (*hō̄aft*-staht) *c* (pl -steden) capital

hoofdstraat (*hō̄aft*-straat) *c* (pl -straten) main street, thoroughfare

hoofdweg (*hō̄aft*-vehkh) *c* (pl ~en) main road, thoroughfare; highway

hoofdzakelijk (*hō̄aft*-saa-ker-lerk) *adv* mainly

hoog (hō̄akh) *adj* high; tall; **hoger** upper; superior; **hoogst** foremost, extreme

hooghartig (hō̄akh-*hahr*-terkh) *adj* haughty

hoogleraar (hō̄akh-*lāy*-raar) *c* (pl -leraren, ~s) professor

hoogmoedig (hō̄akh-*mō̄o*-derkh) *adj* proud

hoogovens (*hō̄akh*-ōā-verns) *pl* ironworks

hoogseizoen (*hō̄akh*-say-zō̄on) *nt* high season, peak season

hoogstens (*hō̄akh*-sterns) *adv* at most

hoogte (*hō̄akh*-ter) *c* (pl ~n, ~s) height; altitude

hoogtepunt (*hō̄akh*-ter-pernt) *nt* (pl ~en) height

hooguit (hō̄akh-*ur*ᵉʷt) *adv* at most

hoogvlakte (*hō̄akh*-flahk-ter) *c* (pl ~n, ~s) uplands *pl*; plateau

hooi (hō̄aᵉᵉ) *nt* hay

hooikoorts (*hō̄a*ᵉᵉ-kō̄arts) *c* hay fever

hoon (hō̄an) *c* scorn

hoop¹ (hō̄ap) *c* (pl hopen) heap, lot

hoop² (hō̄ap) *c* hope

hoopvol (*hō̄ap*-fol) *adj* hopeful

hoorbaar (*hō̄ar*-baar) *adj* audible

hoorn (*hō̄a*-rern) *c* (pl ~en, ~s) horn

hop (hop) *c* hop

hopeloos (*hō̄a*-per-lō̄ass) *adj* hopeless

hopen (*hō̄a*-pern) *v* hope

horen (*hō̄a*-rern) *v* *hear

horizon (*hō̄a*-ree-zon) *c* horizon

horizontaal (hō̄a-ree-zon-*taal*) *adj* horizontal

horloge (hor-*lō̄a*-zher) *nt* (pl ~s) watch

horlogebandje (hor-*lō̄a*-zher-bahn-tYer) *nt* (pl ~s) watch-strap

horlogemaker (hor-*lō̄a*-zher-maa-kerr) *c* (pl ~s) watch-maker

hors d'œuvre (awr-*dūr*-vrer) *c* (pl ~s) hors-d'œuvre

hospes (*hoss*-perss) *c* (pl ~sen) landlord

hospita (*hoss*-pee-taa) *c* (pl ~'s) landlady

hospitaal (*hoss*-pee-taal) *nt* (pl -talen) hospital

hotel (hōa-*tehl*) *nt* (pl ~s) hotel

***houden** (*hou*-dern) *v* *hold; *keep; ~ **van** love; like, care for, *be fond of; **niet ~ van** dislike

houding (*hou*-dıng) *c* (pl ~en) position; attitude

hout (hout) *nt* wood

houtblok (*hout*-blok) *nt* (pl ~ken) log

houten (*hou*-tern) *adj* wooden

houtskool (*houts*-kōa̅l) *c* charcoal

***houtsnijden** (*hout*-snay-dern) *v* carve

houtsnijwerk (*hout*-snay-vehrk) *nt* wood-carving

houtzagerij (hout-saa-ger-*ray*) *c* (pl ~en) saw-mill

houvast (hou-*vahst*) *nt* grip

houweel (hou-*vāy̅l*) *nt* (pl -welen) pick-axe

huichelaar (*hur*ew-kher-laar) *c* (pl ~s) hypocrite

huichelachtig (*hur*ew-kherl-ahkh-terkh) *adj* hypocritical

huichelarij (hur*ew*-kher-laa-*ray*) *c* hypocrisy

huichelen (*hur*ew-kher-lern) *v* simulate

huid (hur*ew*t) *c* (pl ~en) skin; hide

huidcrème (*hur*ew t-kraim) *c* (pl ~s) skin cream

huidig (*hur*ew-derkh) *adj* current

huiduitslag (*hur*ew t-ur ew t-slahkh) *c* rash

huilen (*hur*ew-lern) *v* cry, *weep

huis (hur*ew*ss) *nt* (pl huizen) house; home; **naar ~** home

huisarts (*hur*ew ss-ahrts) *c* (pl ~en) general practitioner

huisbaas (*hur*ew ss-baass) *c* (pl -bazen) landlord

huisdier (*hur*ew ss-deer) *nt* (pl ~en) pet

huiselijk (*hur*ew-ser-lerk) *adj* domestic

huishouden (*hur*ew ss-hou-dern) *nt* (pl ~s) household; housework, housekeeping

huishoudster (*hur*ew ss-hout-sterr) *c* (pl ~s) housekeeper

huiskamer (*hur*ew ss-kaa-merr) *c* (pl ~s) living-room

huisonderwijzer (*hur*ew ss-on-derr-vay-zerr) *c* (pl ~s) tutor

huissleutel (*hur*ew-slu̅r-terl) *c* (pl ~s) latchkey

huisvrouw (*hur*ew ss-frou) *c* (pl ~en) housewife

huizenblok (*hur*ew-zern-blok) *nt* (pl ~ken) house block *Am*

hulde (*herl*-der) *c* tribute, homage

huldigen (*herl*-der-gern) *v* honour

hulp (herlp) *c* help; assistance, aid; **eerste ~** first-aid; **eerste hulppost** first-aid post

hulpvaardig (herlp-*faar*-derkh) *adj* helpful

humeur (hew-*mu̅rr*) *nt* (pl ~en) mood

humor (*hew*-mor) *c* humour

humoristisch (hew-mōa-*riss*-teess) *adj* humorous

hun (hern) *pron* their

huppelen (*her*-per-lern) *v* hop, skip

huren (*hew*-rern) *v* hire, rent; lease

hut (hert) *c* (pl ~ten) hut; cabin

huur (hew̅r) *c* (pl huren) rent; **te ~** for hire

huurcontract (*hew̅r*-kon-trahkt) *nt* (pl ~en) lease

huurder (*hew̅r*-derr) *c* (pl ~s) tenant

huurkoop (*hew̅r*-kōap) *c* hire-purchase

huwelijk (*hew̅*-ver-lerk) *nt* (pl ~en) wedding, marriage

huwelijksreis (*hew̅*-ver-lerks-rayss) *c* (pl -reizen) honeymoon

huwen (*hew̅*ᵒᵒ-ern) *v* marry

hygiëne (hee-gee-ʸā̅y̅-ner) *c* hygiene

hygiënisch (hee-gee-ʸā̅y̅-neess) *adj* hygienic

hypocriet (hee-pōa-*kreet*) *adj* hypocritical

hypotheek (hee-pōa-*tāy̅k*) *c* (pl -theken) mortgage

hysterisch (hee-*stay*-reess) *adj* hysterical

I

ideaal[1] (ee-day-*Yaal*) *adj* ideal

ideaal[2] (ee-day-*Yaal*) *nt* (pl idealen) ideal

idee (ee-*day*) *nt/c* (pl ~ën, ~s) idea

identiek (ee-dehn-*teek*) *adj* identical

identificatie (ee-dehn-tee-fi-*kaa*-tsee) *c* identification

identificeren (ee-dehn-tee-fee-*say*-rern) *v* identify

identiteit (ee-dehn-ti-*tayt*) *c* identity

identiteitskaart (ee-dehn-tee-*tayts*-kaart) *c* (pl ~en) identity card

idiomatisch (ee-dee-Yoa-*maa*-teess) *adj* idiomatic

idioom (ee-dee-*Yoam*) *nt* (pl idiomen) idiom

idioot[1] (ee-dee-*Yoat*) *adj* idiotic

idioot[2] (ee-dee-*Yoat*) *c* (pl idioten) idiot

idool (ee-*doal*) *nt* (pl idolen) idol

ieder (*ee*-derr) *pron* each, every; everyone

iedereen (ee-der-*rayn*) *pron* everyone, everybody; anyone

iemand (*ee*-mahnt) *pron* someone, somebody

iep (eep) *c* (pl ~en) elm

ler (eer) *c* (pl ~en) Irishman

lerland (*eer*-lahnt) Ireland

lers (eers) *adj* Irish

iets (eets) *pron* something; some

ijdel (*ay*-derl) *adj* vain; idle

ijs (ayss) *nt* ice; ice-cream

ijsbaan (*ayss*-baan) *c* (pl -banen) skating-rink

ijsje (*ay*-sher) *nt* (pl ~s) ice-cream

ijskast (*ayss*-kahst) *c* (pl ~en) fridge, refrigerator

ijskoud (ayss-kout) *adj* freezing

IJsland (*ayss*-lahnt) Iceland

IJslander (*ayss*-lahn-derr) *c* (pl ~s) Icelander

IJslands (*ayss*-lahnts) *adj* Icelandic

ijswater (*ayss*-vaa-terr) *nt* iced water

ijver (*ay*-verr) *c* zeal; diligence

ijverig (*ay*-ver-rerkh) *adj* zealous; diligent

ijzer (*ay*-zerr) *nt* iron

ijzerdraad (*ay*-zerr-draat) *nt* wire

ijzeren (*ay*-zer-rern) *adj* iron

ijzerwaren (*ay*-zerr-vaa-rern) *pl* hardware

ik (ɪk) *pron* I

ikoon (ee-*koan*) *c* (pl ikonen) icon

illegaal (ee-ler-*gaal*) *adj* illegal

illusie (ɪ-*lew*-zee) *c* (pl ~s) illusion

illustratie (ɪ-lew-*straa*-tsee) *c* (pl ~s) illustration

illustreren (ɪ-lew-*stray*-rern) *v* illustrate

imitatie (ee-mee-*taa*-tsee) *c* (pl ~s) imitation

imiteren (ee-mee-*tay*-rern) *v* imitate

immigrant (ɪ-mee-*grahnt*) *c* (pl ~en) immigrant

immigratie (ɪ-mee-*graa*-tsee) *c* immigration

immigreren (ɪ-mee-*gray*-rern) *v* immigrate

immuniteit (ɪ-*mew*-nee-*tayt*) *c* immunity

impliceren (ɪm-plee-*say*-rern) *v* imply, involve

imponeren (ɪm-poa-*nay*-rern) *v* impress

impopulair (ɪm-poa-pew-*lair*) *adj* unpopular

import (*ɪm*-port) *c* import

importeren (ɪm-por-*tay*-rern) *v* import

importeur (ɪm-por-*türr*) *c* (pl ~s) importer

impotent (im-pōa-*tehnt*) *adj* impotent

impotentie (im-pōa-*tehn*-see) *c* impotence

improviseren (im-prōa-vee-*say*-rern) *v* improvise

impuls (im-*perls*) *c* (pl ~en) impulse

impulsief (im-perl-*zeef*) *adj* impulsive

in (in) *prep* in; into, inside; at

inademen (*in*-aa-der-mern) *v* inhale

inbegrepen (*in*-ber-grāy-pern) *adj* included; **alles** ~ all in

inboorling (*im*-bōar-ling) *c* (pl ~en) native

*****inbreken** (*im*-brāy-kern) *v* burgle

inbreker (*im*-brāy-kerr) *c* (pl ~s) burglar

incasseren (ing-kah-*say*-rern) *v* cash

incident (in-see-*dehnt*) *nt* (pl ~en) incident

inclusief (ing-klew-*zeef*) *adv* inclusive

incompleet (ing-kom-*plāyt*) *adj* incomplete

indelen (*in*-dāy-lern) *v* classify

zich ***indenken (*in*-dehng-kern) imagine

inderdaad (in-derr-*daat*) *adv* indeed

index (*in*-dehks) *c* (pl ~en) index

India (*in*-dee-Yah) India

Indiaan (in-dee-*Yaan*) *c* (pl Indianen) Indian

Indiaans (in-dee-*Yaans*) *adj* Indian

indien (in-*deen*) *conj* in case, if

Indiër (*in*-dee-Yerr) *c* (pl ~s) Indian

indigestie (in-dee-*gehss*-tee) *c* indigestion

indirect (*in*-dee-rehkt) *adj* indirect

Indisch (*in*-deess) *adj* Indian

individu (in-dee-vee-*dew*) *nt* (pl ~en, ~'s) individual

individueel (in-dee-vee-dew-*vāyl*) *adj* individual

Indonesië (in-dōa-*nāy*-zee-Yer) Indonesia

Indonesiër (in-dōa-*nāy*-zee-Yerr) *c* (pl ~s) Indonesian

Indonesisch (in-dōa-*nāy*-zeess) *adj* Indonesian

indringer (*in*-dri-ngerr) *c* (pl ~s) trespasser

indruk (*in*-drerk) *c* (pl ~ken) impression; ~ **maken op** impress

indrukken (*in*-drer-kern) *v* press

indrukwekkend (in-drerk-*veh*-kernt) *adj* impressive, imposing

industrie (in-derss-*tree*) *c* (pl ~ën) industry

industrieel (in-derss-tree-*Yāyl*) *adj* industrial

industriegebied (in-derss-*tree*-ger-beet) *nt* (pl ~en) industrial area

ineens (i-*nāyns*) *adv* suddenly; at once

inenten (*in*-ehn-tern) *v* vaccinate, inoculate

inenting (*in*-ehn-ting) *c* (pl ~en) vaccination, inoculation

infanterie (*in*-fahn-ter-ree) *c* infantry

infectie (in-*fehk*-see) *c* (pl ~s) infection

inferieur (in-fāy-ree-*Yūrr*) *adj* inferior

inflatie (in-*flaa*-tsee) *c* inflation

informatie (in-for-*maa*-tsee) *c* (pl ~s) information; enquiry; ~ *****inwinnen** *v* inquire

informatiebureau (in-for-*maa*-tsee-bēw-rōa) *nt* (pl ~s) inquiry office

informeel (in-for-*māyl*) *adj* informal

informeren (in-for-*māy*-rern) *v* enquire; inform

infrarood (*in*-fraa-rōat) *adj* infra-red

*****ingaan** (*ing*-gaan) *v* enter; *take effect

ingang (*ing*-gahng) *c* (pl ~en) entrance, way in; entry; **met** ~ **van** as from

ingenieur (in-zhern-*Yūrr*) *c* (pl ~s) engineer

ingenomen (*ing*-ger-nōa-mern) *adj*

pleased

ingevolge (ing-ger-*vol*-ger) *prep* in accordance with

ingewanden (*ing*-ger-vahn-dern) *pl* bowels *pl*, intestines, insides

ingewikkeld (ing-ger-*vi*-kerlt) *adj* complicated; complex

ingrediënt (ing-grāy-dee-*ʸehnt*) *nt* (pl ~en) ingredient

*ingrijpen** (*ing*-gray-pern) *v* intervene

inhalen (*in*-haa-lern) *v* *overtake; pass *vAm*; ~ **verboden** no overtaking; no passing *Am*

inham (*in*-hahm) *c* (pl ~men) creek, inlet

inheems (in-*hāyms*) *adj* native

inhoud (*in*-hout) *c* contents *pl*

*inhouden** (*in*-hou-dern) *v* contain; imply; restrain

inhoudsopgave (*in*-houts-op-khaa-ver) *c* (pl ~n) table of contents

initiatief (ee-nee-shaa-*teef*) *nt* (pl -tieven) initiative

injectie (in-*ʸehk*-see) *c* (pl ~s) shot, injection

inkomen (*ing*-kōa-mern) *nt* (pl ~s) revenue, income

inkomsten (*ing*-kom-stern) *pl* earnings *pl*

inkomstenbelasting (*ing*-kom-ster-ber-lahss-ting) *c* income-tax

inkt (ingkt) *c* ink

inleiden (*in*-lay-dern) *v* introduce; **inleidend** preliminary

inleiding (*in*-lay-ding) *c* (pl ~en) introduction

inlichten (*in*-likh-tern) *v* inform

inlichting (*in*-likh-ting) *c* (pl ~en) information

inlichtingenkantoor (*in*-likh-ti-nger-kahn-tōar) *nt* (pl -toren) information bureau

inmaken (*in*-maa-kern) *v* preserve

inmenging (*in*-mehng-ing) *c* (pl ~en) interference

inmiddels (*in*-*mi*-derls) *adv* in the meantime

*innemen** (*i*-nāy-mern) *v* *take up; occupy; capture

inneming (*i*-nāy-ming) *c* capture

innen (*i*-nern) *v* cash

inpakken (*im*-pah-kern) *v* wrap; pack up, pack

inrichten (*in*-rikh-tern) *v* furnish

inrichting (*in*-rikh-ting) *c* (pl ~en) institution

inschakelen (*in*-skhaa-ker-lern) *v* switch on; plug in

*inschenken** (*in*-skhehng-kern) *v* pour

inschepen (*in*-skhāy-pern) *v* embark

inscheping (*in*-skhāy-ping) *c* embarkation

*inschrijven** (*in*-skhray-vern) *v* enter, book; zich ~ register, check in

inschrijvingsformulier (*in*-skhray-vings-for-mēw-leer) *nt* (pl ~en) registration form

inscriptie (in-*skrip*-see) *c* (pl ~s) inscription

insekt (in-*sehkt*) *nt* (pl ~en) insect; bug *nAm*

insekticide (in-sehk-tee-*see*-der) *c* (pl ~n) insecticide

inslikken (*in*-sli-kern) *v* swallow

*insluiten** (*in*-slur^ew-tern) *v* *shut in; encircle; include; enclose

inspanning (*in*-spah-ning) *c* (pl ~en) strain, effort

inspecteren (in-spehk-*tāy*-rern) *v* inspect

inspecteur (in-spehk-*tūrr*) *c* (pl ~s) inspector

inspectie (in-*spehk*-see) *c* (pl ~s) inspection

*inspuiten** (*in*-spur^ew-tern) *v* inject

installatie (in-stah-*laa*-tsee) *c* (pl ~s) installation

installeren (in-stah-*lāy*-rern) *v* install

instappen (*in*-stah-pern) *v* *get on; embark

instellen (*in*-steh-lern) *v* institute

instelling (*in*-steh-ling) *c* (pl ~en) institution, institute

instemmen (*in*-steh-mern) *v* consent; ~ **met** approve of

instemming (*in*-steh-ming) *c* approval, consent

instinct (in-*stingkt*) *nt* (pl ~en) instinct

instituut (in-stee-*tewt*) *nt* (pl -tuten) institute

instorten (*in*-stor-tern) *v* collapse

instructie (in-*strerk*-see) *c* (pl ~s) direction

instrument (in-strew-*mehnt*) *nt* (pl ~en) instrument

intact (in-*tahkt*) *adj* intact

integendeel (in-*tay*-gern-dayl) on the contrary

intellect (in-ter-*lehkt*) *nt* intellect

intellectueel (in-ter-lehk-tew-*vayl*) *adj* intellectual

intelligent (in-ter-lee-*gehnt*) *adj* clever, intelligent

intelligentie (in-ter-lee-*gehn*-see) *c* intelligence

intens (in-*tehns*) *adj* intense

interessant (in-ter-rer-*sahnt*) *adj* interesting

interesse (in-ter-*reh*-ser) *c* interest

interesseren (in-ter-reh-*say*-rern) *v* interest

intermezzo (in-terr-*mehd*-zoa) *nt* (pl ~'s) interlude

intern (in-*tehrn*) *adj* internal; resident

internaat (in-terr-*naat*) *nt* (pl -naten) boarding-school

internationaal (in-terr-naht-shoa-*naal*) *adj* international

intiem (in-*teem*) *adj* intimate

introduceren (in-troa-dew-*say*-rern) *v* introduce

intussen (in-*ter*-sern) *adv* meanwhile

inval (*in*-vahl) *c* (pl ~len) brain-wave, idea; raid, invasion

invalide[1] (in-vaa-*lee*-der) *adj* disabled, invalid

invalide[2] (in-vaa-*lee*-der) *c* (pl ~n) invalid

invasie (in-*vaa*-zee) *c* (pl ~s) invasion

inventaris (in-vehn-*taa*-rerss) *c* (pl ~sen) inventory

investeerder (in-vehss-*tayr*-derr) *c* (pl ~s) investor

investeren (in-vehss-*tay*-rern) *v* invest

investering (in-vehss-*tay*-ring) *c* (pl ~en) investment

inviteren (in-vee-*tay*-rern) *v* invite

invloed (*in*-vloot) *c* (pl ~en) influence

invloedrijk (*in*-vloot-rayk) *adj* influential

invoegen (*in*-voo-gern) *v* insert

invoer (*in*-voor) *c* import

invoeren (*in*-voo-rern) *v* introduce; import

invoerrecht (*in*-voo-rehkht) *nt* (pl ~en) duty, import duty

invullen (*in*-ver-lern) *v* fill in; fill out *Am*

inwendig (in-*vehn*-derkh) *adj* inner; internal

inwilligen (*in*-vi-ler-gern) *v* grant

inwoner (*in*-voa-nerr) *c* (pl ~s) inhabitant; resident

inzet (*in*-zeht) *c* (pl ~ten) bet

inzetten (*in*-zeh-tern) *v* launch

inzicht (*in*-zikht) *nt* (pl ~en) insight

*inzien (*in*-zeen) *v* *see

Iraaks (ee-*raaks*) *adj* Iraqi

Iraans (ee-*raans*) *adj* Iranian

Irak (ee-*raak*) Iraq

Irakees (ee-raa-*kayss*) *c* (pl -kezen) Iraqi

Iran (ee-*raan*) Iran

Iraniër (ee-*raa*-nee-Yerr) *c* (pl ~s) Iranian

ironie (ee-rōa-*nee*) *c* irony

ironisch (ee-*rōa*-neess) *adj* ironical

irriteren (ı-ree-*tāy*-rern) *v* annoy, irritate

isolatie (ee-zōa-*laa*-tsee) *c* insulation; isolation

isolator (ee-zōa-*laa*-tor) *c* (pl ~en, ~s) insulator

isolement (ee-zōa-ler-*mehnt*) *nt* isolation

isoleren (ee-zōa-*lāy*-rern) *v* insulate; isolate

Israël (*ıss*-raa-ehl) Israel

Israëliër (ıss-raa-*āȳ*-lee-ᵞerr) *c* (pl ~s) Israeli

Israëlisch (ıss-raa-*āȳ*-leess) *adj* Israeli

Italiaan (ee-taa-lee-*ᵞaan*) *c* (pl -lianen) Italian

Italiaans (ee-taa-lee-*ᵞaans*) *adj* Italian

Italië (ee-*taa*-lee-ᵞer) Italy

ivoor (ee-*vōār*) *nt* ivory

J

ja (ᵞaa) yes

jaar (ᵞaar) *nt* (pl jaren) year

jaarboek (ᵞaar-bōōk) *nt* (pl ~en) annual

jaargetijde (ᵞaar-ger-tay-der) *nt* (pl ~n) season

jaarlijks (ᵞaar-lerks) *adj* annual, yearly; *adv* per annum

jacht¹ (ᵞahkht) *c* hunt; chase

jacht² (ᵞahkht) *nt* (pl ~en) yacht

jachthuis (ᵞahkht-hurᵉᵂss) *nt* (pl -huizen) lodge

jade (ᵞaa-der) *nt/c* jade

jagen (ᵞaa-gern) *v* hunt

jager (ᵞaa-gerr) *c* (pl ~s) hunter

jaloers (ᵞaa-*lōōrs*) *adj* envious, jealous

jaloezie (ᵞaa-lōō-*zee*) *c* (pl ~ën) jealousy; blind

jam (zhehm) *c* jam

jammer! (ᵞah-merr) what a pity!

janboel (ᵞahn-bōōl) *c* mess, shambles

janken (ᵞahn-kern) *v* yelp; whine, whimper

januari (ᵞah-nēᵂ-*vaa*-ree) January

Japan (ᵞaa-*pahn*) Japan

Japanner (ᵞaa-*pah*-nerr) *c* (pl ~s) Japanese

Japans (ᵞaa-*pahns*) *adj* Japanese

japon (ᵞaa-*pon*) *c* (pl ~nen) dress; gown

jarretelgordel (zhah-rer-*tehl*-gor-derl) *c* (pl ~s) suspender belt; garter belt *Am*

jas (ᵞahss) *c* (pl ~sen) coat

jasje (ᵞah-sher) *nt* (pl ~s) jacket

jassenhanger (ᵞass-en-hahng-err) *c* coathanger

je (ᵞer) *pron* you; yourself; yourselves

jegens (ᵞāȳ-gerns) *prep* towards

jeugd (ᵞūrkht) *c* youth

jeugdherberg (ᵞūrkht-hehr-behrkh) *c* (pl ~en) youth hostel

jeugdig (ᵞūrkh-derkh) *adj* juvenile

jeuk (ᵞūrk) *c* itch

jeuken (ᵞūr-kern) *v* itch

jicht (ᵞıkht) *c* gout

jij (ᵞay) *pron* you

joch (ᵞokh) *nt* boy, lad

jodium (ᵞ*ōa*-dee-ᵞerm) *nt* iodine

jong (ᵞong) *adj* young; **jonger** junior

jongen (ᵞo-ngern) *c* (pl ~s) boy; lad

jood (ᵞōat) *c* (pl joden) Jew

joods (ᵞōats) *adj* Jewish

Jordaans (ᵞor-*daans*) *adj* Jordanian

Jordanië (ᵞor-*daa*-nee-ᵞer) Jordan

Jordaniër (ᵞor-*daa*-nee-ᵞerr) *c* (pl ~s) Jordanian

jou (ᵞou) *pron* you

journaal (zhōōr-*naal*) *nt* news

journalist (zhōōr-naa-*lıst*) *c* (pl ~en) journalist

journalistiek (zhóor-naa-liss-*teek*) c
journalism

jouw (Vou) *pron* your

jubileum (Yew-bee-*láy*-Yerm) *nt* (pl ~s,
-lea) jubilee

juffrouw (Yer-frou) c (pl ~en) miss

juichen (Yurew-khern) v cheer

juist (Yurewst) *adj* right, correct, just;
proper, appropriate

juistheid (Yurewst-hayt) c correctness

juk (Yerk) *nt* (pl ~ken) yoke

jukbeen (Yerk-bàyn) *nt* (pl ~deren,
-benen) cheek-bone

juli (Yew-lee) July

jullie (Yer-lee) *pron* you; your

juni (Yew-nee) June

juridisch (Yew-ree-deess) *adj* legal

jurist (Yew-rist) c (pl ~en) lawyer

jurk (Yerrk) c (pl ~en) frock, robe,
dress

jury (zhew-ree) c (pl ~'s) jury

jus (zhew) c gravy

juweel (Yew-vàyl) *nt* (pl -welen) jewel; gem; **juwelen** jewellery

juwelier (Yew-ver-*leer*) c (pl ~s) jeweller

K

kaak (kaak) c (pl kaken) jaw

kaal (kaal) *adj* bald; naked, bare

kaap (kaap) c (pl kapen) cape

kaars (kaars) c (pl ~en) candle

kaart (kaart) c (pl ~en) map; card;
groene ~ green card

kaartenautomaat (*kaar*-tern-òa-tòa-
maat) c (pl -maten) ticket machine

kaartje (*kaar*-tYer) *nt* (pl ~s) ticket

kaas (kaass) c (pl kazen) cheese

kabaal (kaa-*baal*) *nt* racket

kabel (*kaa*-berl) c (pl ~s) cable

kabeljauw (kah-berl-Vou) c (pl ~en)
cod

kabinet (kaa-bee-*neht*) *nt* (pl ~ten)
cabinet

kachel (*kah*-kherl) c (pl ~s) heater;
stove

kade (*kaa*-der) c (pl ~n) quay; embankment; dock, wharf

kader (*kaa*-derr) *nt* (pl ~s) cadre

kajuit (kaa-Yurewt) c (pl ~en) cabin

kaki (*kaa*-kee) *nt* khaki

kalender (kaa-*lehn*-derr) c (pl ~s) calendar

kalf (kahlf) *nt* (pl kalveren) calf

kalfsleer (*kahlfs*-làyr) *nt* calf skin

kalfsvlees (*kahlfs*-flàyss) *nt* veal

kalk (kahlk) c lime

kalkoen (kahl-*koōn*) c (pl ~en) turkey

kalm (kahlm) *adj* calm; sedate, quiet,
serene

kalmeren (kahl-*máy*-rern) v calm
down

kam (kahm) c (pl ~men) comb

kameel (kaa-*máyl*) c (pl kamelen)
camel

kamer (*kaa*-merr) c (pl ~s) room;
chamber

kameraad (kah-mer-*raat*) c (pl -raden)
comrade

kamerbewoner (*kaa*-merr-ber-vòa-nerr)
c (pl ~s) lodger

kamerjas (*kaa*-merr-Yahss) c (pl ~sen)
dressing-gown

kamerlid (*kaa*-merr-lit) *nt* (pl -leden)
Member of Parliament

kamermeisje (*kaa*-merr-may-sher) *nt*
(pl ~s) chambermaid

kamertemperatuur (*kaa*-merr-tehm-
per-raa-tewr) c room temperature

kamgaren (*kahm*-gaa-rern) *nt* worsted

kammen (*kah*-mern) v comb

kamp (kahmp) *nt* (pl ~en) camp

kampeerder (kahm-*páyr*-derr) c (pl
~s) camper

kampeerterrein (kahm-*páyr*-teh-rayn)

nt (pl ~en) camping site

kampeerwagen (kahm-*pāyr*-vaa-gern)
c (pl ~s) trailer *nAm*

kamperen (kahm-*pāy*-rern) *v* camp

kampioen (kahm-pee-*yōōn*) *c* (pl ~en)
champion

kan (kahn) *c* (pl ~nen) jug

kanaal (kaa-*naal*) *nt* (pl kanalen) canal; channel; **het Kanaal** English
Channel

kanarie (kaa-*naa*-ree) *c* (pl ~s) canary

kandelaber (kahn-der-*laa*-berr) *c* (pl
~s) candelabrum

kandidaat (kahn-dee-*daat*) *c* (pl -da-
ten) candidate

kaneel (kaa-*nāyl*) *c* cinnamon

kangoeroe (*kahng*-ger-rōō) *c* (pl ~s)
kangaroo

kanker (*kahng*-kerr) *c* cancer

kano (*kaa*-nōa) *c* (pl ~'s) canoe

kanon (kaa-*non*) *nt* (pl ~nen) gun

kans (kahns) *c* (pl ~en) chance; opportunity

kansel (*kahn*-serl) *c* (pl ~s) pulpit

kant[1] (kahnt) *c* (pl ~en) side; way;
edge; **aan de andere ~ van** across

kant[2] (kahnt) *nt* lace

kantine (kahn-*tee*-ner) *c* (pl ~s) canteen

kantlijn (*kahnt*-layn) *c* (pl ~en) margin

kantoor (kahn-*tōar*) *nt* (pl -toren) office

kantoorbediende (kahn-*tōar*-ber-deen-
der) *c* (pl ~n, ~s) clerk

kantoorboekhandel (kahn-*tōar*-bōōk-
hahn-derl) *c* (pl ~s) stationer's

kantooruren (kahn-*tōar*-ēw-rern) *pl*
business hours, office hours

kap (kahp) *c* (pl ~pen) hood

kapel (kaa-*pehl*) *c* (pl ~len) chapel

kapelaan (kah-per-*laan*) *c* (pl ~s)
chaplain

kapen (*kaa*-pern) *v* hijack

kaper (*kaa*-perr) *c* (pl ~s) hijacker

kapitaal (kah-pee-*taal*) *nt* capital

kapitalisme (kah-pee-taa-*liss*-mer) *nt*
capitalism

kapitein (kah-pee-*tayn*) *c* (pl ~s) captain

kapot (kaa-*pot*) *adj* broken

kapper (*kah*-perr) *c* (pl ~s) barber;
hairdresser

kapsel (*kahp*-serl) *nt* (pl ~s) hair-do

kapstok (*kahp*-stok) *c* (pl ~ken) hat
rack

kar (kahr) *c* (pl ~ren) cart

karaat (kaa-*raat*) *nt* carat

karaf (kaa-*rahf*) *c* (pl ~fen) carafe

karakter (kaa-*rahk*-terr) *nt* (pl ~s)
character

karakteristiek (kaa-rahk-ter-riss-*teek*)
adj characteristic

karaktertrek (kaa-*rahk*-terr-trehk) *c* (pl
~ken) characteristic

karamel (kaa-raa-*mehl*) *c* (pl ~s, ~len)
caramel

kardinaal[1] (kahr-dee-*naal*) *c* (pl -na-
len) cardinal

kardinaal[2] (kahr-dee-*naal*) *adj* cardinal

karper (*kahr*-perr) *c* (pl ~s) carp

karton (kahr-*ton*) *nt* cardboard

kartonnen (kahr-*to*-nern) *adj* cardboard; ~ **doos** carton

karwei (kahr-*vay*) *nt* (pl ~en) job

kas (kahss) *c* (pl ~sen) greenhouse

kasjmier (*kahsh*-meer) *nt* cashmere

kassa (*kah*-saa) *c* (pl ~'s) pay-desk;
box-office

kassier (kah-*seer*) *c* (pl ~s) cashier

kast (kahst) *c* (pl ~en) cupboard,
closet

kastanje (kahss-*tah*-ñer) *c* (pl ~s)
chestnut

kastanjebruin (kahss-*tah*-ñer-brur^{ew}n)
adj auburn

kasteel (kahss-*tāyl*) *nt* (pl -telen) castle

kat (kaht) *c* (pl ~ten) cat

kathedraal (kaa-tāy-*draal*) *c* (pl -dralen) cathedral

katholiek (kaa-tōa-*leek*) *adj* catholic

katoen (kaa-*tōōn*) *nt/c* cotton

katoenen (kaa-*tōō*-nern) *adj* cotton

katoenfluweel (kaa-*tōōn*-flēw-vāyl) *nt* velveteen

katrol (kaa-*trol*) *c* (pl ~len) pulley

kattekwaad (*kah*-ter-kvaat) *nt* mischief

kauwen (*kou*-ern) *v* chew

kauwgom (*kou*-gom) *c/nt* chewing-gum

kaviaar (*kaa*-vee-Yaar) *c* caviar

kazerne (kaa-*zehr*-ner) *c* (pl ~s, ~n) barracks *pl*

keel (kāyl) *c* (pl kelen) throat

keelontsteking (*kāyl*-ont-stāy-king) *c* (pl ~en) laryngitis

keelpijn (*kāyl*-payn) *c* sore throat

keer (kāyr) *c* (pl keren) time

keerpunt (*kāyr*-pernt) *nt* (pl ~en) turning-point

keerzijde (*kāyr*-zay-der) *c* (pl ~n) reverse

kegelbaan (*kāy*-gerl-baan) *c* (pl -banen) bowling alley

kegelspel (*kāy*-gerl-spehl) *nt* bowling

keizer (*kay*-zerr) *c* (pl ~s) emperor

keizerin (kay-zer-*rin*) *c* (pl ~nen) empress

keizerlijk (*kay*-zer-lerk) *adj* imperial

keizerrijk (*kay*-zer-rayk) *nt* (pl ~en) empire

kelder (*kehl*-derr) *c* (pl ~s) cellar

kelner (*kehl*-nerr) *c* (pl ~s) waiter

kenmerk (*kehn*-mehrk) *nt* (pl ~en) characteristic, feature

kenmerken (*kehn*-mehr-kern) *v* characterize, mark; **kenmerkend** characteristic, typical

kennel (*keh*-nerl) *c* (pl ~s) kennel

kennen (*keh*-nern) *v* *know

kenner (*keh*-nerr) *c* (pl ~s) connoisseur

kennis[1] (*keh*-nerss) *c* knowledge

kennis[2] (*keh*-nerss) *c* (pl ~sen) acquaintance

kenteken (*kehn*-tāy-kern) *nt* (pl ~s) registration number; licence number *Am*

Kenya (*kāy*-nee-Yaa) Kenya

kerel (*kāy*-rerl) *c* (pl ~s) fellow

keren (*kāy*-rern) *v* turn

kerk (kehrk) *c* (pl ~en) church; chapel

kerkhof (*kehrk*-hof) *nt* (pl -hoven) cemetery, graveyard, churchyard

kerktoren (*kehrk*-tōa-rern) *c* (pl ~s) steeple

kermis (*kehr*-merss) *c* (pl ~sen) fair

kern (kehrn) *c* (pl ~en) nucleus; heart, core; essence; **kern-** nuclear

kernenergie (*kehrn*-āy-nehr-zhee) *c* nuclear energy

kerrie (*keh*-ree) *c* curry

kers (kehrs) *c* (pl ~en) cherry

Kerstmis (*kehrs*-merss) Xmas, Christmas

kerven (*kehr*-vern) *v* carve

ketel (*kāy*-terl) *c* (pl ~s) kettle

keten (*kāy*-tern) *c* (pl ~s, ~en) chain

ketting (*keh*-ting) *c* (pl ~en) chain

keuken (*kūr*-kern) *c* (pl ~s) kitchen

keurig (*kūr*-rerkh) *adj* neat

keus (kūrss) *c* (pl keuzen) pick, choice

keuze (*kūr*-zer) *c* (pl ~n) selection, choice

kever (*kāy*-verr) *c* (pl ~s) beetle; bug

kiekje (*keek*-Yer) *nt* (pl ~s) snapshot

kiel (keel) *c* (pl ~en) keel

kiem (keem) *c* (pl ~en) germ

kier (keer) *c* (pl ~en) chink

kies (keess) *c* (pl kiezen) molar

kiesdistrict (*keess*-diss-trikt) *nt* (pl

~en) constituency

kieskeurig (keess-*kūr*-rerkh) *adj* particular

kiesrecht (*keess*-rehkht) *nt* franchise, suffrage

kietelen (*kee*-ter-lern) *v* tickle

kieuw (kee°°) *c* (pl ~en) gill

kievit (*kee*-veet) *c* (pl ~en) pewit

kiezel (*kee*-zerl) *c* (pl ~s) pebble; gravel

*__kiezen__ (*kee*-zern) *v* *choose; pick; elect

*__kijken__ (*kay*-kern) *v* look at; ~ **naar** look at; watch

kijker (*kay*-kerr) *c* (pl ~s) spectator

kijkje (*kayk*-Yer) *nt* (pl ~s) look

kikker (*kɪ*-kerr) *c* (pl ~s) frog

kil (kɪl) *adj* chilly

kilo (*kee*-lōā) *nt* (pl ~'s) kilogram

kilometer (*kee*-lōā-māy-terr) *c* (pl ~s) kilometre

kilometertal (*kee*-lōā-māy-terr-tahl) *nt* distance in kilometres

kim (kɪm) *c* horizon

kin (kɪn) *c* (pl ~nen) chin

kind (kɪnt) *nt* (pl ~eren) child; kid

kinderjuffrouw (*kɪn*-derr-Yer-frou) *c* (pl ~en) nurse

kinderkamer (*kɪn*-derr-kaa-merr) *c* (pl ~s) nursery

kinderverlamming (*kɪn*-derr-verr-lah-mɪng) *c* polio

kinderwagen (*kɪn*-derr-vaa-gern) *c* (pl ~s) pram; baby carriage *Am*

kinine (kee-*nee*-ner) *c* quinine

kiosk (kee-Yosk) *c* (pl ~en) kiosk

kip (kɪp) *c* (pl ~pen) hen; chicken

kippevel (*kɪ*-per-vehl) *nt* goose-flesh

kist (kɪst) *c* (pl ~en) chest

klaar (klaar) *adj* ready

klaarblijkelijk (klaar-*blay*-ker-lerk) *adv* apparently

klaarmaken (*klaar*-maa-kern) *v* prepare; cook

klacht (klahkht) *c* (pl ~en) complaint

klachtenboek (*klahkh*-tern-bōōk) *nt* (pl ~en) complaints book

klagen (*klaa*-gern) *v* complain

klank (klahngk) *c* (pl ~en) sound; tone

klant (klahnt) *c* (pl ~en) customer; client

klap (klahp) *c* (pl ~pen) blow; smack, slap

klappen (*klah*-pern) *v* clap

klaproos (*klahp*-rōāss) *c* (pl -rozen) poppy

klas (klahss) *c* (pl ~sen) class; form

klasgenoot (*klahss*-kher-nōāt) *c* (pl -noten) class-mate

klasse (*klah*-ser) *c* (pl ~n) class

klassiek (klah-*seek*) *adj* classical

klauw (klou) *c* (pl ~en) claw

klaver (*klaa*-verr) *c* (pl ~s) clover; shamrock

zich kleden (*klāy*-dern) dress

kleding (*klāy*-dɪng) *c* clothes *pl*

kleedhokje (*klāyt*-hok-Yer) *nt* (pl ~s) cabin

kleedje (*klāy*-tYer) *nt* (pl ~s) rug

kleedkamer (*klāyt*-kaa-merr) *c* (pl ~s) dressing-room

kleerborstel (*klāyr*-bor-sterl) *c* (pl ~s) clothes-brush

kleerhanger (*klāyr*-hah-ngerr) *c* (pl ~s) hanger, coat-hanger

kleerkast (*klāyr*-kahst) *c* (pl ~en) closet *nAm*

kleermaker (*klāyr*-maa-kerr) *c* (pl ~s) tailor

klei (klay) *c* clay

klein (klayn) *adj* little, small; minor, petty, short; **kleiner** minor; **kleinst** least

kleindochter (*klayn*-dokh-terr) *c* (pl ~s) granddaughter

kleingeld (*klayn*-gehlt) *nt* change, petty cash

kleinhandel (*klayn*-hahn-derl) *c* retail trade

kleinhandelaar (*klayn*-hahn-der-laar) *c* (pl -laren, ~s) retailer

kleinood (*klay*-nōat) *nt* (pl -noden) gem

kleinzoon (*klayn*-zōan) *c* (pl -zonen) grandson

klem (klehm) *c* (pl ~men) clamp

klemschroef (*klehm*-skhrōōf) *c* (pl -schroeven) clamp

kleren (*klay*-rern) *pl* clothes *pl*

klerenhaak (*klay*-rern-haak) *c* (pl -haken) peg

klerenkast (*klay*-rer-kahst) *c* (pl ~en) wardrobe

klerk (klehrk) *c* (pl ~en) clerk

kletsen (*kleht*-sern) *v* chat; talk rubbish

kleur (klurr) *c* (pl ~en) colour

kleurecht (*klurr*-ehkht) *adj* fast-dyed

kleurenblind (*klur*-rerm-blint) *adj* colour-blind

kleurenfilm (*klur*-rer-film) *c* (pl ~s) colour film

kleurrijk (*klur*-rayk) *adj* colourful

kleurstof (*klurr*-stof) *c* (pl ~fen) colourant

kleuter (*klur*-terr) *c* (pl ~s) tot

kleuterschool (*klur*-terr-skhōal) *c* (pl -scholen) kindergarten

kleven (*klay*-vern) *v* *stick

kleverig (*klay*-ver-rerkh) *adj* sticky

klier (kleer) *c* (pl ~en) gland

klimaat (klee-*maat*) *nt* (pl -maten) climate

*klimmen** (*kli*-mern) *v* climb

klimop (kli-*mop*) *c* ivy

kliniek (klee-*neek*) *c* (pl ~en) clinic

*klinken** (*kling*-kern) *v* sound

klinker (*kling*-kerr) *c* (pl ~s) vowel

klip (klip) *c* (pl ~pen) cliff

klok (klok) *c* (pl ~ken) clock; bell

klokhuis (*klok*-hur^{ew}ss) *nt* (pl -huizen) core

klomp (klomp) *c* (pl ~en) wooden shoe

klont (klont) *c* (pl ~en) lump

klonterig (*klon*-ter-rerkh) *adj* lumpy

kloof (klōaf) *c* (pl kloven) cleft; chasm

klooster (*klōa*-sterr) *nt* (pl ~s) monastery; convent, cloister

klop (klop) *c* (pl ~pen) knock, tap

kloppen (*klo*-pern) *v* knock, tap; whip

klucht (klerkht) *c* (pl ~en) farce

kluis (klur^{ew}ss) *c* (pl kluizen) safe, vault

knaap (knaap) *c* (pl knapen) boy

knalpot (*knahl*-pot) *c* (pl ~ten) silencer; muffler *nAm*

knap (knahp) *adj* smart, clever; pretty, handsome, good-looking

knappend (*knah*-pernt) *adj* crisp

knapzak (*knahp*-sahk) *c* (pl ~ken) knapsack

kneuzen (*knūr*-zern) *v* bruise

kneuzing (*knūr*-zing) *c* (pl ~en) bruise

knie (knee) *c* (pl ~ën) knee

knielen (*knee*-lern) *v* *kneel

knieschijf (*knee*-skhayf) *c* (pl -schijven) kneecap

*knijpen** (*knay*-pern) *v* pinch

knik (knik) *c* nod

knikken (*kni*-kern) *v* nod

knikker (*kni*-kerr) *c* (pl ~s) marble

knippen (*kni*-pern) *v* *cut

knoflook (*knof*-lōak) *nt/c* garlic

knokkel (*kno*-kerl) *c* (pl ~s) knuckle

knoop (knōap) *c* (pl knopen) button; knot

knooppunt (*knōa*-pernt) *nt* (pl ~en) junction

knoopsgat (*knōaps*-khaht) *nt* (pl ~en) buttonhole

knop (knop) *c* (pl ~pen) bud; knob

knopen (*knōa*-pern) *v* button; tie, knot

knots (knots) c (pl ~en) club

knuffelen (kner-fer-lern) v cuddle

knuppel (kner-perl) c (pl ~s) club; cudgel

knus (knerss) adj cosy

koe (koo) c (pl koeien) cow

koeiehuid (koo͞ee-er-hurᵉʷt) c (pl ~en) cow-hide

koek (kook) c (pl ~en) cake

koekepan (koo͞-ker-pahn) c (pl ~nen) frying-pan

koekje (kook-ᵧer) nt (pl ~s) biscuit; cracker nAm

koekoek (koo͞-kook) c (pl ~en) cuckoo

koel (kool) adj cool

koelkast (kool-kahst) c (pl ~en) fridge, refrigerator

koelsysteem (kool-see-staym) nt (pl -temen) cooling system

koeltas (kool-tahss) c (pl ~sen) ice-bag

koepel (koo͞-perl) c (pl ~s) dome

koers (koorss) c (pl ~en) exchange rate; course

koets (koots) c (pl ~en) carriage, coach

koffer (ko-ferr) c (pl ~s) case, suit-case, bag; trunk

kofferruimte (ko-fer-rurᵉʷm-ter) c trunk nAm

koffie (ko-fee) c coffee

kogel (koa-gerl) c (pl ~s) bullet

kok (kok) c (pl ~s) cook

koken (koa-kern) v cook; boil

kokosnoot (koa-koss-noat) c (pl -noten) coconut

kolen (koa-lern) pl coal

kolom (koa-lom) c (pl ~men) column

kolonel (koa-loa-nehl) c (pl ~s) colonel

kolonie (koa-loa-nee) c (pl ~s, -niën) colony

kolonne (koa-lo-ner) c (pl ~s) column

kom (kom) c (pl ~men) basin

komedie (koa-may-dee) c (pl ~s) comedy

*komen (koa-mern) v *come

komfort (koam-foar) nt comfort

komiek (koa-meek) c (pl ~en) comedian

komisch (koa-meess) adj comic

komkommer (kom-ko-merr) c (pl ~s) cucumber

komma (ko-maa) c (pl ~'s) comma

kompas (kom-pahss) nt (pl ~sen) compass

komplot (kom-plot) nt (pl ~ten) plot, intrigue

komst (komst) c coming; arrival

konijn (koa-nayn) nt (pl ~en) rabbit

koning (koa-ning) c (pl ~en) king

koningin (koa-nɪ-ngin) c (pl ~nen) queen

koninklijk (koa-ning-klerk) adj royal

koninkrijk (koa-ning-krayk) nt (pl ~en) kingdom

kooi (koaee) c (pl ~en) cage; bunk, berth

kookboek (koak-book) nt (pl ~en) cookery-book; cookbook nAm

kool (koal) c (pl kolen) cabbage

koop (koap) c purchase; **te ~** for sale

koophandel (koap-hahn-derl) c trade

koopje (koap-ᵧer) nt (pl ~s) bargain

koopman (koap-mahn) c (pl kooplie-den) dealer, merchant

koopprijs (koap-prayss) c (pl -prijzen) purchase price

koopwaar (koap-vaar) c merchandise

koor (koar) nt (pl koren) choir

koord (koart) nt (pl ~en) cord

koorts (koarts) c fever

koortsig (koart-serkh) adj feverish

kop (kop) c (pl ~pen) head; headline

*kopen (koa-pern) v *buy; purchase

koper¹ (koa-perr) nt brass; copper

koper² (koa-perr) c (pl ~s) buyer, purchaser

koperwerk (kōā-perr-vehrk) nt brassware

kopie (kōā-pee) c (pl ~ën) copy

kopiëren (kōā-pee-Yāy-rern) v copy

kopje (kop-Yer) nt (pl ~s) cup

koplamp (kop-lahmp) c (pl ~en) headlight, headlamp

koppeling (ko-per-ling) c clutch

koppelteken (ko-perl-tāy-kern) nt (pl ~s) hyphen

koppig (ko-perkh) adj obstinate, headstrong

koraal (kōā-raal) c (pl -ralen) coral

koren (kōā-rern) nt corn, grain

korenveld (kōā-rer-vehlt) nt (pl ~en) cornfield

korhoen (kor-hōōn) nt (pl ~ders) grouse

korrel (ko-rerl) c (pl ~s) corn, grain

korset (kor-seht) nt (pl ~ten) corset

korst (korst) c (pl ~en) crust

kort (kort) adj brief, short

korting (kor-ting) c (pl ~en) discount, reduction, rebate

kortsluiting (kort-slur ew-ting) c short circuit

kortstondig (kort-ston-derkh) adj momentary

kosmetica (koss-māy-tee-kaa) pl cosmetics pl

kost (kost) c food, fare; livelihood; ~ **en inwoning** room and board, board and lodging, bed and board

kostbaar (kost-baar) adj precious, valuable, expensive

kostbaarheden (kost-baar-hāy-dern) pl valuables pl

kosteloos (koss-ter-lōass) adj free of charge

kosten (koss-tern) v *cost; pl cost, expenditure

koster (koss-terr) c (pl ~s) sexton

kostganger (kost-khah-ngerr) c (pl ~s) boarder

kostuum (koss-tewm) nt (pl ~s) suit

kotelet (kōā-ter-leht) c (pl ~ten) chop

kou (kou) c cold; ~ **vatten** catch a cold

koud (kout) adj cold

kous (kouss) c (pl ~en) stocking

kraag (kraakh) c (pl kragen) collar

kraai (kraa ee) c (pl ~en) crow

kraakbeen (kraak-bāyn) nt cartilage

kraal (kraal) c (pl kralen) bead

kraam (kraam) c (pl kramen) stand, stall; booth

kraan (kraan) c (pl kranen) tap; faucet nAm

krab (krahp) c (pl ~ben) crab

krabben (krah-bern) v scratch

kracht (krahkht) c (pl ~en) force, strength; energy, power

krachtig (krahkh-terkh) adj strong

kraken (kraa-kern) v creak, crack

kralensnoer (kraa-ler-snōōr) nt (pl ~en) beads pl

kramp (krahmp) c (pl ~en) cramp; convulsion

krankzinnig (krahngk-si-nerkh) adj insane; lunatic, crazy, mad

krankzinnige (krahngk-si-ner-ger) c (pl ~n) lunatic

krankzinnigheid (krahngk-si-nerkh-hayt) c lunacy

krant (krahnt) c (pl ~en) newspaper, paper

krantenkiosk (krahn-ter-kee-Yosk) c (pl ~en) newsstand

krantenverkoper (krahn-ter-verr-kōā-perr) c (pl ~s) newsagent

krap (krahp) adj tight

kras (krahss) c (pl ~sen) scratch

krassen (krah-sern) v scratch

krat (kraht) nt (pl ~ten) crate

krater (kraa-terr) c (pl ~s) crater

krediet (krer-deet) nt (pl ~en) credit

kredietbrief (krer-deet-breef) c (pl -brieven) letter of credit

kreeft (*krāyft*) *c* (pl ~en) lobster

kreek (*krāyk*) *c* (pl kreken) creek

kreet (*krāyt*) *c* (pl kreten) cry

krekel (*krāy*-kerl) *c* (pl ~s) cricket

krenken (*krehng*-kern) *v* offend, injure

krent (krehnt) *c* (pl ~en) currant

kreuken (*krūr*-kern) *v* crease

kreunen (*krūr*-nern) *v* moan, groan

kreupel (*krūr*-perl) *adj* lame, crippled

kribbe (*kri*-ber) *c* (pl ~n) manger

kriebel (*kree*-berl) *c* (pl ~s) itch

*krijgen (*kray*-gern) *v* *get; receive

krijgsgevangene (*kraykhs*-kher-vah-nger-ner) *c* (pl ~n) prisoner of war

krijgsmacht (*kraykhs*-mahkht) *c* (pl ~en) military force

krijt (krayt) *nt* chalk

krik (krik) *c* (pl ~ken) jack

*krimpen (*krim*-pern) *v* *shrink

krimpvrij (*krimp*-vray) *adj* shrinkproof

kring (kring) *c* (pl ~en) ring, circle

kringloop (*kring*-lōap) *c* (pl -lopen) cycle

kristal (kriss-*tahl*) *nt* (pl ~len) crystal

kristallen (kriss-*tah*-lern) *adj* crystal

kritiek (kree-*teek*) *adj* critical; *c* criticism

kritisch (*kree*-teess) *adj* critical

kroeg (krōōkh) *c* (pl ~en) public house; pub

kroes (krōōss) *c* (pl kroezen) mug

krokodil (krō-kō-*dil*) *c* (pl ~len) crocodile

krom (krom) *adj* crooked; curved, bent

kromming (*kro*-ming) *c* (pl ~en) curve, bend

kronen (*krōa*-nern) *v* crown

kronkelen (*krong*-ker-lern) *v* *wind

kronkelig (*krong*-ker-lerkh) *adj* winding

kroon (krōan) *c* (pl kronen) crown

kruid (krur^{ew}t) *nt* (pl ~en) herb; **kruiden** spices; *v* flavour

kruidenier (krur^{ew}-der-*neer*) *c* (pl ~s) grocer

kruidenierswaren (krur^{ew}-der-*neers*-vaa-rern) *pl* groceries *pl*

kruidenierswinkel (krur^{ew}-der-*neers*-ving-kerl) *c* (pl ~s) grocer's

kruier (*krur^{ew}*-err) *c* (pl ~s) porter

kruik (krur^{ew}k) *c* (pl ~en) pitcher

kruimel (*krur^{ew}*-merl) *c* (pl ~s) crumb

*kruipen (*krur^{ew}*-pern) *v* *creep, crawl

kruis (krur^{ew}ss) *nt* (pl ~en) cross

kruisbeeld (*krur^{ew}ss*-bāylt) *nt* (pl ~en) crucifix

kruisbes (*krur^{ew}ss*-behss) *c* (pl ~sen) gooseberry

kruisigen (*krur^{ew}*-ser-gern) *v* crucify

kruisiging (*krur^{ew}*-ser-ging) *c* (pl ~en) crucifixion

kruising (*krur^{ew}*-sing) *c* (pl ~en) crossing, junction

kruispunt (*krur^{ew}ss*-pernt) *nt* (pl ~en) crossroads, intersection

kruissnelheid (*krur^{ew}*-snehl-hayt) *c* cruising speed

kruistocht (*krur^{ew}ss*-tokht) *c* (pl ~en) crusade

kruit (krur^{ew}t) *nt* gunpowder

kruiwagen (*krur^{ew}*-vaa-gern) *c* (pl ~s) wheelbarrow

kruk (krerk) *c* (pl ~ken) crutch

krukas (*krerk*-ahss) *c* crankshaft

krul (krerl) *c* (pl ~len) curl

krullen (*krer*-lern) *v* curl; **krullend** curly

krulspeld (*krerl*-spehlt) *c* (pl ~en) curler

krultang (*krerl*-tahng) *c* (pl ~en) curling-tongs *pl*

kubus (*kew̄*-berss) *c* (pl ~sen) cube

kudde (*ker*-der) *c* (pl ~n, ~s) herd, flock

kuiken (*kur^{ew}*-kern) *nt* (pl ~s) chicken

kuil (kur^{ew}l) *c* (pl ~en) hole; pit

kuis (kur^{ew}ss) *adj* chaste

kuit¹ (kur^ew t) *c* roe

kuit² (kur^ew t) *c* (pl ~en) calf

kundig (*kern*-derkh) *adj* capable

*****kunnen** (*ker*-nern) *v* *can, *be able to; *might, *may

kunst (kernst) *c* (pl ~en) art; **schone kunsten** fine arts

kunstacademie (*kernst*-ah-kaa-dā́y-mee) *c* (pl ~s) art school

kunstenaar (*kern*-ster-naar) *c* (pl ~s) artist

kunstenares (kern-ster-naa-*rehss*) *c* (pl ~sen) artist

kunstgalerij (*kernst*-khah-ler-ray) *c* (pl ~en) art gallery

kunstgebit (*kernst*-kher-bɪt) *nt* (pl ~ten) denture, false teeth

kunstgeschiedenis (*kernst*-kher-skhee-der-nɪss) *c* art history

kunstijsbaan (*kernst*-ayss-baan) *c* (pl ~banen) skating-rink

kunstje (*kern*-sher) *nt* (pl ~s) trick

kunstmatig (kernst-*maa*-terkh) *adj* artificial

kunstnijverheid (kernst-*nay*-verr-hayt) *c* arts and crafts

kunsttentoonstelling (*kerns*-tern-tōan-steh-lɪng) *c* (pl ~en) art exhibition

kunstverzameling (*kernst*-ferr-zaa-mer-lɪng) *c* (pl ~en) art collection

kunstwerk (*kernst*-vehrk) *nt* (pl ~en) work of art

kunstzijde (*kernst*-say-der) *c* rayon

kunstzinnig (kernst-*sɪ*-nerkh) *adj* artistic

kurk (kerrk) *c* (pl ~en) cork

kurketrekker (*kerr*-ker-treh-kerr) *c* (pl ~s) corkscrew

kus (kerss) *c* (pl ~sen) kiss

kussen¹ (*ker*-sern) *v* kiss

kussen² (*ker*-sern) *nt* (pl ~s) cushion; pillow; **kussentje** *nt* pad

kussensloop (*ker*-ser-slōap) *c*/*nt* (pl ~slopen) pillow-case

kust (kerst) *c* (pl ~en) coast, shore; seaside, seashore

kuur (kewr) *c* (pl kuren) cure

kwaad¹ (kvaat) *adj* angry, cross; mad; ill

kwaad² (kvaat) *nt* (pl kwaden) evil; mischief, harm

kwaadaardig (kvaa-*daar*-derkh) *adj* malignant

kwaal (kvaal) *c* (pl kwalen) ailment

kwadraat (kvaa-*draat*) *nt* (pl -draten) square

kwakzalver (*kvahk*-sahl-verr) *c* (pl ~s) quack

kwal (kvahl) *c* (pl ~len) jelly-fish

kwalijk *nemen (*kvaa*-lerk *nāy*-mern) resent; **neem me niet kwalijk!** sorry!

kwaliteit (kvaa-lee-*tayt*) *c* (pl ~en) quality

kwart (kvahrt) *nt* (pl ~en) quarter

kwartaal (kvahr-*taal*) *nt* (pl -talen) quarter

kwartel (*kvahr*-terl) *c* (pl ~s) quail

kwartier (kvahr-*teer*) *nt* quarter of an hour

kwast (kvahst) *c* (pl ~en) brush

kweken (*kvāy*-kern) *v* cultivate, *grow

kwellen (*kveh*-lern) *v* torment

kwelling (*kveh*-lɪng) *c* (pl ~en) torment

kwestie (*kvehss*-tee) *c* (pl ~s) matter, question, issue

kwetsbaar (*kvehts*-baar) *adj* vulnerable

kwetsen (*kveht*-sern) *v* injure; *hurt, wound

kwijtraken (*kvayt*-raa-kern) *v* *lose; *mislay

kwik (kvɪk) *nt* mercury

kwistig (*kvɪss*-terkh) *adj* lavish

kwitantie (kvee-*tahn*-see) *c* (pl ~s) receipt

L

la (laa) *c* (pl ~den) drawer

laag¹ (laakh) *adj* low; **lager** *adj* inferior

laag² (laakh) *c* (pl lagen) layer

laagland (*laakh*-lahnt) *nt* lowlands *pl*

laan (laan) *c* (pl lanen) avenue

laars (laars) *c* (pl laarzen) boot

laat (laat) *adj* late; **laatst** *adj* last; ultimate, final; *adv* lately; **later** *adv* afterwards; **te ~** late; overdue

labiel (laa-*beel*) *adj* unstable

laboratorium (laa-bōa-raa-*tōa*-ree-ᵞᵉʳm) *nt* (pl -ria) laboratory

lach (lahkh) *c* laugh

*lachen (*lah*-khern) *v* laugh

ladder (*lah*-derr) *c* (pl ~s) ladder

lade (*laa*-der) *c* (pl ~n) drawer

*laden (*laa*-dern) *v* load; charge

ladenkast (*laa*-der-kahst) *c* (pl ~en) chest of drawers

lading (*laa*-ding) *c* (pl ~en) charge, load; freight, cargo

laf (lahf) *adj* cowardly

lafaard (*lah*-faart) *c* (pl ~s) coward

lagune (laa-*gēw*-ner) *c* (pl ~s) lagoon

lak (lahk) *c* (pl ~ken) lacquer, varnish

laken (*laa*-kern) *nt* (pl ~s) sheet

lakken (*lah*-kern) *v* varnish

lam¹ (lahm) *adj* lame

lam² (lahm) *nt* (pl ~meren) lamb

lambrizering (lahm-bree-*zāy*-rɪng) *c* panelling

lamp (lahmp) *c* (pl ~en) lamp

lampekap (*lahm*-per-kahp) *c* (pl ~pen) lampshade

lamsvlees (*lahms*-flāyss) *nt* lamb

lanceren (lahn-*sāy*-rern) *v* launch

land (lahnt) *nt* (pl ~en) country, land; **aan ~** ashore; **aan ~ *gaan** land

landbouw (*lahnt*-bou) *c* agriculture; **landbouw-** agrarian

landen (*lahn*-dern) *v* land

landengte (*lahnt*-ehng-ter) *c* (pl ~n, ~s) isthmus

landgenoot (*lahnt*-kher-nōat) *c* (pl -noten) countryman

landgoed (*lahnt*-khōot) *nt* (pl ~eren) estate

landhuis (*lahnt*-hurᵉʷss) *nt* (pl -huizen) country house

landkaart (*lahnt*-kaart) *c* (pl ~en) map

landloper (*lahnt*-lōa-perr) *c* (pl ~s) tramp

landloperij (lahnt-lōa-per-*ray*) *c* vagrancy

landschap (*lahnt*-skhahp) *nt* (pl ~pen) scenery, landscape

landsgrens (*lahnts*-khrehns) *c* (pl -grenzen) boundary

landtong (*lahn*-tong) *c* (pl ~en) headland

lang (lahng) *adj* long; tall

langdurig (lahng-*dēw*-rerkh) *adj* long

langs (lahngs) *prep* along; past

langspeelplaat (*lahng*-spāyl-plaat) *c* (pl -platen) long-playing record

langwerpig (lahng-*vehr*-perkh) *adj* oblong

langzaam (*lahng*-zaam) *adj* slow

langzamerhand (lahng-zaa-merr-*hahnt*) *adv* gradually

lantaarn (lahn-*taa*-rern) *c* (pl ~s) lantern

lantaarnpaal (lahn-*taa*-rerm-paal) *c* (pl -palen) lamp-post

las (lahss) *c* (pl ~sen) joint

lassen (*lah*-sern) *v* weld

last (lahst) *c* (pl ~en) charge; load, burden; trouble, nuisance, bother

laster (*lahss*-terr) *c* slander

lastig (*lahss*-terkh) *adj* troublesome, inconvenient; difficult

*laten (*laa*-tern) *v* *let; allow to;

*leave; *have

Latijns-Amerika (lah-tayn-zaa-*māy*-ree-kaa) Latin America

Latijns-Amerikaans (lah-tayn-zaa-*māy*-ree-*kaans*) adj Latin-American

lauw (lou) adj lukewarm, tepid

lawaai (laa-*vaa^ee*) nt noise

lawaaierig (laa-*vaa^ee*-er-rerkh) adj noisy

lawine (laa-*vee*-ner) c (pl ~s, ~n) avalanche

laxeermiddel (lahk-*sāyr*-mɪ-derl) nt (pl ~en) laxative

ledemaat (*lāy*-der-maat) c (pl maten) limb

lederen (*lāy*-der-rern) adj leather

ledigen (*lāy*-der-gern) v empty

leed (lāyt) nt affliction, sorrow

leeftijd (*lāyf*-tayt) c (pl ~en) age

leeg (lāykh) adj empty

leek (lāyk) c (pl leken) layman

leer[1] (lāyr) c teachings pl

leer[2] (lāyr) nt leather

leerboek (*lāyr*-bōōk) nt (pl ~en) textbook

leerling (*lāyr*-lɪng) c (pl ~en) pupil; scholar

leerzaam (*lāyr*-zaam) adj instructive

leesbaar (*lāyss*-baar) adj legible

leeslamp (*lāyss*-lahmp) c (pl ~en) reading-lamp

leeszaal (*lāy*-saal) c (pl -zalen) reading-room

leeuw (lāy^∞) c (pl ~en) lion

leeuwerik (*lāy^∞*-er-rɪk) c (pl ~en) lark

lef (lehf) nt guts

legalisatie (lāy-gaa-lee-*zaa*-tsee) c legalization

legatie (ler-*gaa*-tsee) c (pl ~s) legation

leger (*lāy*-gerr) nt (pl ~s) army

leggen (*leh*-gern) v *lay, *put

legpuzzel (*lehkh*-per-zerl) c (pl ~s) jigsaw puzzle

lei (lay) nt slate

leiden (*lay*-dern) v head, direct; guide, *lead, conduct

leider (*lay*-derr) c (pl ~s) leader

leiderschap (*lay*-derr-skhahp) nt leadership

leiding[1] (*lay*-dɪng) c lead

leiding[2] (*lay*-dɪng) c (pl ~en) pipe

lek[1] (lehk) adj leaky; punctured

lek[2] (lehk) nt (pl ~ken) leak

lekken (*leh*-kern) v leak

lekker (*leh*-kerr) adj good; nice, enjoyable, delicious, tasty

lekkernij (leh-kerr-*nay*) c (pl ~en) delicacy

lelie (*lāy*-lee) c (pl ~s) lily

lelijk (*lāy*-lerk) adj ugly

lemmet (*leh*-mert) nt (pl ~en) blade

lenen (*lāy*-nern) v *lend; borrow

lengte (*lehng*-ter) c (pl ~n, ~s) length; **in de** ~ lengthways

lengtegraad (*lehng*-ter-graat) c (pl -graden) longitude

lenig (*lāy*-nerkh) adj supple

lening (*lāy*-nɪng) c (pl ~en) loan

lens (lehns) c (pl lenzen) lens

lente (*lehn*-ter) c (pl ~s) spring

lepel (*lāy*-perl) c (pl ~s) spoon; spoonful

lepra (*lāy*-praa) c leprosy

leraar (*lāy*-raar) c (pl leraren, ~s) master, teacher; instructor

lerares (lāy-raa-*rehss*) c (pl ~sen) teacher

leren[1] (*lāy*-rern) v *teach; *learn

leren[2] (*lāy*-rern) adj leather

les (lehss) c (pl ~sen) lesson

leslokaal (lehss-lōā-kaal) nt (pl -kalen) classroom

lessenaar (*leh*-ser-naar) c (pl ~s) desk

letsel (*leht*-serl) nt (pl ~s) injury

letten op (*leh*-tern) attend to, *pay attention to; watch, mind

letter (*leh*-terr) c (pl ~s) letter

lettergreep (*leh*-terr-grāyp) *c* (pl -grepen) syllable

letterkundig (leh-terr-*kern*-derkh) *adj* literary

leugen (*lūr*-gern) *c* (pl ~s) lie

leuk (lūrk) *adj* enjoyable; funny, jolly

leunen (*lūr*-nern) *v* *lean

leuning (*lūr*-nɪng) *c* (pl ~en) arm; rail

leunstoel (*lūrn*-stōōl) *c* (pl ~en) easy chair, armchair

leus (lūrss) *c* (pl leuzen) slogan

leven[1] (*lāy*-vern) *v* live; **levend** alive; live

leven[2] (*lāy*-vern) *nt* (pl ~s) life; lifetime; **in** ~ alive

levendig (*lāy*-vern-derkh) *adj* lively; brisk, vivid

levensmiddelen (*lāy*-verns-mɪ-der-lern) *pl* foodstuffs *pl*

levensstandaard (*lāy*-vern-stahn-daart) *c* standard of living

levensverzekering (*lāy*-verns-ferr-zāy-ker-rɪng) *c* (pl ~en) life insurance

lever (*lāy*-verr) *c* (pl ~s) liver

leveren (*lāy*-ver-rern) *v* furnish, provide, supply

levering (*lāy*-ver-rɪng) *c* (pl ~en) delivery, supply

***lezen** (*lāy*-zern) *v* *read

lezing (*lāy*-zɪng) *c* (pl ~en) lecture

Libanees[1] (lee-baa-*nāyss*) *adj* Lebanese

Libanees[2] (lee-bah-*nāyss*) *c* (pl -nezen) Lebanese

Libanon (lee-baa-non) Lebanon

liberaal (lee-ber-*raal*) *adj* liberal

Liberia (lee-*bāy*-ree-Yaa) Liberia

Liberiaan (lee-bāy-ree-Yaan) *c* (pl -rianen) Liberian

Liberiaans (lee-bāy-ree-Yaans) *adj* Liberian

licentie (lee-*sehn*-see) *c* (pl ~s) licence

lichaam (*lɪ*-khaam) *nt* (pl lichamen) body

licht[1] (lɪkht) *adj* light; pale; gentle, slight

licht[2] (lɪkht) *nt* (pl ~en) light

lichtbruin (*lɪkht*-brur^{ew}n) *adj* fawn

lichtgevend (*lɪkht*-kher-vernt) *adj* luminous

lichting (*lɪkh*-tɪng) *c* (pl ~en) collection

lichtpaars (*lɪkht*-paars) *adj* mauve

lid (lɪt) *nt* (pl leden) member; associate

lidmaatschap (*lɪt*-maat-skhahp) *nt* membership

lidwoord (*lɪt*-vōart) *nt* (pl ~en) article

lied (leet) *nt* (pl ~eren) song

lief (leef) *adj* dear; sweet; affectionate, adorable

liefdadigheid (leef-*daa*-derkh-hayt) *c* charity

liefde (*leef*-der) *c* (pl ~s) love

liefdesgeschiedenis (*leef*-derss-kher-skhee-der-nɪss) *c* (pl ~sen) love-story

***liefhebben** (*leef*-heh-bern) *v* love

liefhebberij (leef-heh-ber-*ray*) *c* (pl ~en) hobby

liefje (*leef*-Yer) *nt* (pl ~s) sweetheart

***liegen** (*lee*-gern) *v* lie

lies (leess) *c* (pl liezen) groin

lieveling (*lee*-ver-lɪng) *c* (pl ~en) darling, sweetheart; favourite, pet; **lievelings-** favourite, pet

liever (*lee*-verr) *adv* sooner, rather; ~ ***hebben** prefer

lift (lɪft) *c* (pl ~en) lift; elevator *nAm*

liften (*lɪf*-tern) *v* hitchhike

lifter (*lɪf*-terr) *c* (pl ~s) hitchhiker

***liggen** (*lɪ*-gern) *v* *lie; ***gaan** ~ *lie down

ligging (*lɪ*-gɪng) *c* location; situation, site

ligstoel (*lɪkh*-stōōl) *c* (pl ~en) deck chair

lijden (*lay*-dern) *nt* suffering

*lijden (*lay*-dern) v suffer

lijf (layf) nt (pl lijven) body

lijfwacht (*layf*-vahkht) c (pl ~en) bodyguard

lijk (layk) nt (pl ~en) corpse

*lijken (lay-kern) v seem, appear; look; ~ **op** resemble

lijm (laym) c glue, gum

lijn (layn) c (pl ~en) line; leash

lijnboot (*layn*-bōat) c (pl -boten) liner

lijst (layst) c (pl ~en) list; frame

lijster (*lay*-sterr) c (pl ~s) thrush

lijvig (*lay*-verkh) adj bulky

likdoorn (*lik*-dōa-rern) c (pl ~s) corn

likeur (lee-*kūrr*) c (pl ~en) liqueur

likken (*li*-kern) v lick

limiet (lee-*meet*) c (pl ~en) limit

limoen (lee-*mōon*) c (pl ~en) lime

limonade (lee-mōa-*naa*-der) c (pl ~s) lemonade

linde (*lin*-der) c (pl ~n) limetree, lime

lingerie (lang-zher-*ree*) c lingerie

liniaal (lee-nee-*Yaal*) c (pl -alen) ruler

links (lingks) adj left; left-hand

linkshandig (lingks-*hahn*-derkh) adj left-handed

linnen (*li*-nern) nt linen

linnengoed (*li*-ner-gōot) nt linen

lint (lint) nt (pl ~en) ribbon; tape

lip (lip) c (pl ~pen) lip

lippenboter (*li*-per-bōa-terr) c lipsalve

lippenstift (*li*-per-stift) c lipstick

list (list) c (pl ~en) ruse, artifice

listig (*liss*-terkh) adj sly

liter (*lee*-terr) c (pl ~s) litre

literair (lee-ter-*rair*) adj literary

literatuur (lee-ter-raa-*tēwr*) c literature

lits-jumeaux (lee-zhēw-*mōa*) nt twin beds

litteken (*li*-tāy-kern) nt (pl ~s) scar

locomotief (lōa-kōa-mōa-*teef*) c (pl -tieven) engine, locomotive

loeien (*lōō*ᵉᵉ-ern) v roar

lof (lof) c glory, praise

logé (lōa-*zhāy*) c (pl ~'s) guest

logeerkamer (lōa-*zhāyr*-kaa-merr) c (pl ~s) spare room, guest-room

logeren (lōa-*zhāy*-rern) v stay

logica (*lōa*-gee-kaa) c logic

logies (lōa-*zheess*) nt lodgings pl, accommodation; ~ **en ontbijt** bed and breakfast

logisch (*lōa*-geess) adj logical

lokaal (lōa-*kaal*) adj local

lol (lol) c fun

lonen (*lōa*-nern) v *pay

long (long) c (pl ~en) lung

longontsteking (*long*-ont-stāy-king) c (pl ~en) pneumonia

lont (lont) c (pl ~en) fuse

lood (lōat) nt lead

loodgieter (*lōat*-khee-terr) c (pl ~s) plumber

loodrecht (*lōat*-rehkht) adj perpendicular

loods (lōats) c (pl ~en) pilot

loon (lōan) nt (pl lonen) wages pl; salary, pay

loonsverhoging (*lōans*-ferr-hōa-ging) c (pl ~en) raise nAm

loop (lōap) c course; gait, walk

loopbaan (*lōa*-baan) c (pl -banen) career

loopplank (*lōa*-plahngk) c (pl ~en) gangway

*lopen (*lōa*-pern) v walk; *go

los (loss) adj loose

losgeld (*loass*-khehlt) nt (pl ~en) ransom

losknopen (*loss*-knōa-pern) v unbutton; untie

losmaken (*loss*-maa-kern) v unfasten, *undo, detach; loosen

losschroeven (*lo*-skhrōo-vern) v unscrew

lossen (*lo*-sern) v unload, discharge

lot¹ (lot) nt lot, fortune, destiny, fate

lot² (lot) nt (pl ~en) lot

loterij (loa-ter-*ray*) *c* (pl ~en) lottery
lotion (loa-*shon*) *c* (pl ~s) lotion
loyaal (loa-*Yaal*) *adj* loyal
lucht (lerkht) *c* air; breath; sky
luchtdicht (*lerkh*-dıkht) *adj* airtight
luchtdruk (*lerkh*-drerk) *c* atmospheric pressure
luchten (*lerkh*-tern) *v* air, ventilate
luchtfilter (*lerkht*-fıl-terr) *nt* (pl ~s) air-filter
luchthaven (*lerkht*-haa-vern) *c* (pl ~s) airport
luchtig (*lerkh*-terkh) *adj* airy
luchtpost (*lerkht*-post) *c* airmail
luchtvaartmaatschappij (*lerkht*-faart-maat-skhah-pay) *c* (pl ~en) airline
luchtverversing (*lerkht*-ferr-vehr-sıng) *c* air-conditioning, ventilation
luchtziekte (*lerkht*-seek-ter) *c* air-sickness
lucifer (*lew*-see-fehr) *c* (pl ~s) match
lucifersdoosje (*lew*-see-fehrs-doa-sher) *nt* (pl ~s) match-box
lui (lur*ew*) *adj* lazy; idle
luid (lur*ew*t) *adj* loud
luidspreker (*lurew*t-spray-kerr) *c* (pl ~s) loud-speaker
luier (*lurew*-err) *c* (pl ~s) nappy; diaper *nAm*
luik (lur*ew*k) *nt* (pl ~en) hatch; shutter
luis (lur*ew*ss) *c* (pl luizen) louse
luisteraar (*lurew*ss-ter-raar) *c* (pl ~s) listener
luisteren (*lurew*ss-ter-rern) *v* listen
luisterrijk (*lurew*ss-ter-rayk) *adj* magnificent
lukken (*ler*-kern) *v* succeed
lunch (lernsh) *c* (pl ~es) lunch
lus (lerss) *c* (pl ~sen) loop
lusten (*lerss*-tern) *v* like; fancy
luxe (*lewk*-ser) *c* luxury
luxueus (lewk-sew-*ürss*) *adj* luxurious

M

maag (maakh) *c* (pl magen) stomach; **maag-** gastric
maagd (maakht) *c* (pl ~en) virgin
maagpijn (*maakh*-payn) *c* stomach-ache
maagzuur (*maakh*-sewr) *nt* heartburn
maagzweer (*maakh*-svayr) *c* (pl -zweren) gastric ulcer
maal[1] (maal) *nt* (pl malen) meal
maal[2] (maal) *c* (pl malen) time
maal[3] (maal) *prep* times
maaltijd (*maal*-tayt) *c* (pl ~en) meal; **warme ~** dinner
maan (maan) *c* (pl manen) moon
maand (maant) *c* (pl ~en) month
maandag (*maan*-dahkh) *c* Monday
maandblad (*maant*-blaht) *nt* (pl ~en) monthly magazine
maandelijks (*maan*-der-lerks) *adj* monthly
maandverband (*maant*-ferr-bahnt) *nt* sanitary towel
maanlicht (*maan*-lıkht) *nt* moonlight
maar (maar) *conj* but; yet; *adv* only
maart (maart) March
maas (maass) *c* (pl mazen) mesh
maat (maat) *c* (pl maten) size, measure; **extra grote ~** outsize; **op ~ gemaakt** tailor-made; made to order
maatregel (*maat*-ray-gerl) *c* (pl ~en, ~s) measure
maatschappelijk (maat-*skhah*-per-lerk) *adj* social
maatschappij (maat-skhah-*pay*) *c* (pl ~en) company; society
maatstaf (*maat*-stahf) *c* (pl -staven) standard
machine (mah-*shee*-ner) *c* (pl ~s) engine, machine

machinerie (mah-shee-ner-*ree*) c machinery

macht (mahkht) c (pl ~en) power; force, might; authority

machteloos (*mahkh*-ter-lōass) adj powerless

machtig (*mahkh*-terkh) adj powerful, mighty

machtiging (*mahkh*-ter-gɪng) c (pl ~en) authorization

magazijn (maa-gaa-*zayn*) nt (pl ~en) store-house, warehouse

mager (*maa*-gerr) adj lean, thin

magie (maa-*gee*) c magic

magistraat (maa-gɪss-*traat*) c (pl -straten) magistrate

magneet (mahkh-*nāyt*) c (pl -neten) magneto

magnetisch (mahkh-*nāy*-teess) adj magnetic

maillot (maa-*Yōā*) c (pl ~s) tights pl

maïs (mighss) c maize

maïskolf (*mighss*-kolf) c (pl -kolven) corn on the cob

maître d'hôtel (mai-trer-dōā-*tehl*) head-waiter

maîtresse (meh-*tray*-ser) c (pl ~s, ~n) mistress

majoor (maa-*Yōār*) c (pl ~s) major

mak (mahk) adj tame

makelaar (*maa*-ker-laar) c (pl ~s) broker, house agent

maken (*maa*-kern) v *make; **te** ~ *hebben met** *deal with

makreel (maa-*krāyl*) c (pl -relen) mackerel

mal (mahl) adj foolish, silly

malaria (maa-*laa*-ree-Yaa) c malaria

Maleis (maa-*layss*) nt Malay

Maleisië (maa-*lay*-zee-Yer) Malaysia

Maleisisch (maa-*lay*-zeess) adj Malaysian

***malen** (*maa*-lern) v *grind

mals (mahls) adj tender

mammoet (*mah*-mōot) c (pl ~en, ~s) mammoth

man (mahn) c (pl ~nen) man; husband

manchet (mahn-*sheht*) c (pl ~ten) cuff

manchetknopen (mahn-*sheht*-knōā-pern) pl cuff-links pl

mand (mahnt) c (pl ~en) hamper, basket

mandaat (mahn-*daat*) nt (pl -daten) mandate

mandarijn (mahn-daa-*rayn*) c (pl ~en) mandarin, tangerine

manege (maa-*nāy*-zher) c (pl ~s) riding-school

manicure (maa-nee-*kēw*-rer) c (pl ~s) manicure

manicuren (maa-nee-*kēw*-rern) v manicure

manier (maa-*neer*) c (pl ~en) manner; way, fashion

mank (mahngk) adj lame

mannelijk (*mah*-ner-lerk) adj male; masculine

mannequin (mah-ner-*kang*) c (pl ~s) model, mannequin

mantel (*mahn*-terl) c (pl ~s) coat, cloak

manufacturier (mah-nēw-fahk-tēw-*reer*) c (pl ~s) draper

manuscript (maa-nerss-*krɪpt*) nt (pl ~en) manuscript

marcheren (mahr-*shāy*-rern) v march

margarine (mahr-gaa-*ree*-ner) c margarine

marge (*mahr*-zher) c (pl ~s) margin

marine (maa-*ree*-ner) c navy; **marine**-naval

maritiem (mah-ree-*teem*) adj maritime

markt (mahrkt) c (pl ~en) market; **zwarte** ~ black market

marktplein (*mahrkt*-playn) nt (pl ~en) market-place

marmelade (mahr-mer-*laa*-der) *c* (pl ~s, ~n) marmalade

marmer (*mahr*-merr) *nt* marble

Marokkaan (mah-ro-*kaan*) *c* (pl -kanen) Moroccan

Marokkaans (mah-ro-*kaans*) *adj* Moroccan

Marokko (maa-*ro*-kōā) Morocco

mars (mahrs) *c* (pl ~en) march

martelaar (*mahr*-ter-laar) *c* (pl ~s, -laren) martyr

martelen (*mahr*-ter-lern) *v* torture

marteling (*mahr*-ter-lıng) *c* (pl ~en) torture

mascara (mahss-*kaa*-raa) *c* mascara

masker (*mahss*-kerr) *nt* (pl ~s) mask

massa (*mah*-saa) *c* (pl ~'s) bulk, mass; crowd

massage (mah-*saa*-zher) *c* (pl ~s) massage

massaproduktie (*mah*-saa-prōā-derk-see) *c* mass production

masseren (mah-*sāy*-rern) *v* massage

masseur (mah-*sūrr*) *c* (pl ~s) masseur

massief (mah-*seef*) *adj* solid, massive

mast (mahst) *c* (pl ~en) mast

mat[1] (maht) *adj* dull, mat, dim

mat[2] (maht) *c* (pl ~ten) mat

materiaal (maa-tree-*Yaal*) *nt* (pl -rialen) material

materie (mah-*tāy*-ree) *c* (pl -riën, ~s) matter

materieel (maa-tree-*Yāyl*) *adj* material

matig (*maa*-terkh) *adj* moderate

matras (maa-*trahss*) *c* (pl ~sen) mattress

matroos (maa-*trōāss*) *c* (pl matrozen) sailor

mausoleum (mou-sōā-*lāy*-Yerm) *nt* (pl ~s, -lea) mausoleum

mazelen (*maa*-zer-lern) *pl* measles

me (mer) *pron* me; myself

mechanisch (māy-*khaa*-neess) *adj* mechanical

mechanisme (māy-khaa-*nıss*-mer) *nt* (pl ~n) mechanism; machinery

medaille (māy-*dah*-Yer) *c* (pl ~s) medal

mededelen (*māy*-der-dāy-lern) *v* notify, communicate, inform

mededeling (*māy*-der-dāy-lıng) *c* (pl ~en) communication, information

medegevoel (*māy*-der-ger-vōōl) *nt* sympathy

medelijden (*māy*-der-lay-dern) *nt* pity; ~ ***hebben met** pity

medeplichtige (māy-der-*plıkh*-ter-ger) *c* (pl ~n) accessary

medewerking (*māy*-der-vehr-kıng) *c* co-operation

medisch (*māy*-deess) *adj* medical

mediteren (māy-dee-*tāy*-rern) *v* meditate

***meebrengen** (*māy*-breh-ngern) *v* ***bring**

meedelen (*māy*-dāy-lern) *v* communicate

meel (māyl) *nt* flour

meemaken (*māy*-maa-kern) *v* ***go through**

***meenemen** (*māy*-nāy-mern) *v* ***take away**

meer[1] (māyr) *adj* more; ~ **dan** over; **niet** ~ no longer

meer[2] (māyr) *nt* (pl meren) lake

meerderheid (*māyr*-derr-hayt) *c* majority; bulk

meerderjarig (māyr-derr-*Yaa*-rerkh) *adj* of age

meervoud (*māyr*-vout) *nt* (pl ~en) plural

meest (māyst) *adj* most

meestal (māy-*stahl*) *adv* mostly

meester (*māy*-sterr) *c* (pl ~s) master; schoolmaster, teacher

meesteres (māy-ster-*rehss*) *c* (pl ~sen) mistress

meesterwerk (*māy*-sterr-vehrk) *nt* (pl

~en) masterpiece

meetellen (*may*-teh-lern) v count

meetkunde (*mayt*-kern-der) c geometry

meeuw (may^{oo}) c (pl ~en) gull; seagull

mei (may) May

meid (mayt) c (pl ~en) housemaid, maid

meineed (*may*-nayt) c (pl -eden) perjury

meisje (*may*-sher) nt (pl ~s) girl

meisjesnaam (*may*-sherss-naam) c (pl -namen) maiden name

mejuffrouw (mer-*Yer*-frou) miss

melden (*mehl*-dern) v report

melding (*mehl*-ding) c (pl ~en) mention

melk (mehlk) c milk

melkboer (*mehlk*-boor) c (pl ~en) milkman

melodie (may-loa-*dee*) c (pl ~ën) melody; tune

melodieus (may-loa-dee-*Yurss*) adj tuneful

melodrama (may-loa-*draa*-maa) nt (pl ~'s) melodrama

meloen (mer-*loon*) c (pl ~en) melon

memorandum (may-moa-*rahn*-derm) nt (pl -randa) memo

men (mehn) pron one

meneer (mer-*nayr*) mister; sir

menen (*may*-nern) v consider; *mean

mengen (*meh*-ngern) v mix

mengsel (*mehng*-serl) nt (pl ~s) mixture

menigte (*may*-nerkh-ter) c (pl ~n, ~s) crowd

mening (*may*-ning) c (pl ~en) opinion; view; **van ~ verschillen** disagree

mens (mehns) c (pl ~en) man; **mensen** people pl

menselijk (*mehn*-ser-lerk) adj human;

~ **wezen** human being

mensheid (*mehns*-hayt) c humanity, mankind

menstruatie (mehn-strew-*vaa*-tsee) c menstruation

menukaart (mer-*new*-kaart) c (pl ~en) menu

merel (*may*-rerl) c (pl ~s) blackbird

merg (mehrkh) nt marrow

merk (mehrk) nt (pl ~en) brand

merkbaar (*mehrk*-baar) adj noticeable, perceptible

merken (*mehr*-kern) v notice; mark

merkteken (*mehrk*-tay-kern) nt (pl ~s) mark

merrie (*meh*-ree) c (pl ~s) mare

mes (mehss) nt (pl ~sen) knife

messing (*meh*-sing) nt brass

mest (mehst) c dung, manure

mesthoop (*mehst*-hoap) c (pl -hopen) dunghill

met (meht) prep with; by

metaal (may-*taal*) nt (pl metalen) metal

metalen (may-*taa*-lern) adj metal

meteen (mer-*tayn*) adv at once, straight away, immediately, instantly; presently

*meten** (*may*-tern) v measure

meter (*may*-terr) c (pl ~s) metre; meter; gauge

metgezel (*meht*-kher-zehl) c (pl ~len) companion

methode (may-*toa*-der) c (pl ~n, ~s) method

methodisch (may-*toa*-deess) adj methodical

metrisch (*may*-treess) adj metric

metro (*may*-troa) c (pl ~'s) underground

metselaar (*meht*-ser-laar) c (pl ~s) bricklayer

metselen (*meht*-ser-lern) v *lay bricks

meubilair (mūr-bee-*lair*) nt furniture

meubileren (mūr-bee-*lay*-rern) *v* furnish

mevrouw (mer-*vrou*) madam

Mexicaan (mehk-see-*kaan*) *c* (pl -canen) Mexican

Mexicaans (mehk-see-*kaans*) *adj* Mexican

Mexico (*mehk*-see-kōa) Mexico

microfoon (mee-krōa-*fōan*) *c* (pl ~s) microphone

middag (*mı*-dahkh) *c* (pl ~en) afternoon; midday; noon

middageten (*mı*-dahkh-*ay*-tern) *nt* luncheon, lunch; dinner

middel¹ (*mı*-derl) *nt* (pl ~en) means; remedy; **antiseptisch** ~ antiseptic; **insektenwerend** ~ insect repellent; **kalmerend** ~ tranquillizer, sedative; **pijnstillend** ~ anaesthetic; **stimulerend** ~ stimulant; **verdovend** ~ drug

middel² (*mı*-derl) *nt* (pl ~s) waist

middeleeuwen (*mı*-derl-*ay*ᵒᵒ-ern) *pl* Middle Ages

middeleeuws (*mı*-derl-*ay*ᵒᵒss) *adj* mediaeval

Middellandse Zee (*mı*-der-lahnt-ser-*zay*) Mediterranean

middelmatig (*mı*-derl-*maa*-terkh) *adj* moderate; medium

middelpunt (*mı*-derl-pernt) *nt* (pl ~en) centre

middelst (*mı*-derlst) *adj* middle

midden (*mı*-dern) *nt* midst, middle; **midden-** medium-; ~ **in** amid; **te** ~ **van** amid; among

middernacht (*mı*-derr-*nahkht*) *c* midnight

midzomer (*mı*t-*sōa*-merr) *c* midsummer

mier (meer) *c* (pl ~en) ant

mierikswortel (*mee*-rıks-vor-terl) *c* (pl ~s) horseradish

migraine (mee-*grai*-ner) *c* migraine

mijl (mayl) *c* (pl ~en) mile

mijlpaal (*mayl*-paal) *c* (pl -palen) milestone; landmark

mijn¹ (mayn) *pron* my

mijn² (mayn) *c* (pl ~en) mine

mijnbouw (*mayn*-bou) *c* mining

mijnheer (mer-*nayr*) mister

mijnwerker (*mayn*-vehr-kerr) *c* (pl ~s) miner

mikken op (*mı*-kern) aim at

mikpunt (*mı*k-pernt) *nt* (pl ~en) target

mild (mılt) *adj* liberal

milieu (meel-*ʸūr*) *nt* (pl ~s) milieu; environment

militair¹ (mee-lee-*tair*) *adj* military

militair² (mee-lee-*tair*) *c* (pl ~en) soldier

miljoen (mıl-*ʸōōn*) *nt* million

miljonair (mıl-ʸōa-*nair*) *c* (pl ~s) millionaire

min (mın) *prep* minus

minachting (*mın*-ahkh-tıng) *c* contempt

minder (*mın*-derr) *adv* less

minderheid (*mın*-derr-hayt) *c* (pl -heden) minority

minderjarig (mın-derr-*ʸaa*-rerkh) *adj* under age

minderjarige (mın-derr-*ʸaa*-rer-ger) *c* (pl ~n) minor

minderwaardig (mın-derr-*vaar*-derkh) *adj* inferior

mineraal (mee-ner-*raal*) *nt* (pl -ralen) mineral

mineraalwater (mee-ner-*raal*-vaa-terr) *nt* mineral water

miniatuur (mee-nee-ʸaa-*tewr*) *c* (pl -turen) miniature

minimum (*mee*-nee-merm) *nt* (pl -ma) minimum

minister (mee-*nıss*-terr) *c* (pl ~s) minister

ministerie (mee-nıss-*tay*-ree) *nt* (pl

~s) ministry

minnaar (*mı*-naar) *c* (pl ~s) lover

minst (mınst) *adj* least

minstens (*mın*-sterns) *adv* at least

minuscuul (mee-nerss-*kēwl*) *adj* tiny, minute

minuut (mee-*nēwt*) *c* (pl minuten) minute

mis (mıss) *c* (pl ~sen) Mass

misbruik (*mıss*-brur^{ew}k) *nt* misuse, abuse

misdaad (*mıss*-daat) *c* (pl -daden) crime

misdadig (mıss-*daa*-derkh) *adj* criminal

misdadiger (*mıss*-daa-der-gerr) *c* (pl ~s) criminal

zich *misdragen** (mıss-*draa*-gern) misbehave

misgunnen (mıss-*kher*-nern) *v* grudge

mishagen (mıss-*haa*-gern) *v* displease

miskraam (*mıss*-kraam) *c* (pl -kramen) miscarriage

mislukking (mıss-*ler*-kıng) *c* (pl ~en) failure

mislukt (mıss-*lerkt*) *adj* unsuccessful

mismaakt (mıss-*maakt*) *adj* deformed

misplaatst (mıss-*plaatst*) *adj* misplaced

misschien (mı-*skheen*) *adv* perhaps; maybe

misselijk (*mı*-ser-lerk) *adj* sick; disgusting

misselijkheid (*mı*-ser-lerk-hayt) *c* nausea, sickness

missen (*mı*-sern) *v* lack; miss; spare

misstap (*mı*-stahp) *c* (pl ~pen) slip

mist (mıst) *c* fog, mist

mistig (*mıss*-terkh) *adj* foggy, misty

mistlamp (*mıst*-lahmp) *c* (pl ~en) foglamp

*misverstaan** (mıss-ferr-*staan*) *v* *misunderstand

misverstand (*mıss*-ferr-stahnt) *nt* (pl

~en) misunderstanding

misvormd (mıss-*formt*) *adj* deformed

mits (mıts) *conj* provided that

mobiel (mōa-*beel*) *adj* mobile

modder (*mo*-derr) *c* mud

modderig (*mo*-der-rerkh) *adj* muddy

mode (*mōa*-der) *c* (pl ~s) fashion

model (mōa-*dehl*) *nt* (pl ~len) model

modelleren (mōa-deh-*lāy*-rern) *v* model

modern (mōa-*dehrn*) *adj* modern

modieus (mōa-dee-*Yūrss*) *adj* fashionable

modiste (mōa-*dıss*-ter) *c* (pl ~s) milliner

moe (mōo) *adj* tired; weary

moed (mōot) *c* courage

moeder (*mōo*-derr) *c* (pl ~s) mother

moedertaal (*mōo*-derr-taal) *c* native language, mother tongue

moedig (*mōo*-derkh) *adj* brave, courageous

moeilijk (*mōo^{ee}*-lerk) *adj* difficult; hard

moeilijkheid (*mōo^{ee}*-lerk-hayt) *c* (pl -heden) difficulty

moeite (*mōo^{ee}*-ter) *c* (pl ~n) trouble; pains, difficulty; **de ~ waard *zijn** *be worth-while; ~ *doen** bother

moer (mōor) *c* (pl ~en) nut

moeras (mōo-*rahss*) *nt* (pl ~sen) swamp; bog, marsh

moerassig (mōo-*rah*-serkh) *adj* marshy

moerbei (*mōor*-bay) *c* (pl ~en) mulberry

moestuin (*mōoss*-tur^{ew}n) *c* (pl ~en) kitchen garden

*moeten** (*mōo*-tern) *v* *must; *have to; need to, *ought to, *be obliged to, *should

mogelijk (*mōa*-ger-lerk) *adj* possible

mogelijkheid (*mōa*-ger-lerk-hayt) *c* (pl -heden) possibility

*mogen** (*mōa*-gern) *v* *be allowed;

*may; like

mogendheid (*mōā*-gernt-hayt) *c* (pl -heden) power

mohair (*mōā*-hair) *nt* mohair

molen (*mōā*-lern) *c* (pl ~s) mill; windmill

molenaar (*mōā*-ler-naar) *c* (pl ~s) miller

mollig (*mo*-lerkh) *adj* plump

moment (*mōā*-mehnt) *nt* (pl ~en) moment

momentopname (*mōā*-mehnt-op-naa-mer) *c* (pl ~n) snapshot

monarchie (*mōā*-nahr-khee) *c* (pl ~ën) monarchy

mond (mont) *c* (pl ~en) mouth

mondeling (*mon*-der-ling) *adj* oral, verbal

monding (*mon*-dɪng) *c* (pl ~en) mouth

mondspoeling (*mont*-spōō-ling) *c* mouthwash

monetair (mōā-nāy-*tair*) *adj* monetary

monnik (*mo*-nerk) *c* (pl ~en) monk

monoloog (mōā-nōā-*lōākh*) *c* (pl -logen) monologue

monopolie (mōā-nōā-*pōā*-lee) *nt* (pl ~s) monopoly

monster (*mon*-sterr) *nt* (pl ~s) sample

monteren (mon-*tāy*-rern) *v* assemble

monteur (mon-*tūrr*) *c* (pl ~s) mechanic

montuur (mon-*tewr*) *nt* (pl -turen) frame

monument (mōā-new-*mehnt*) *nt* (pl ~en) monument

mooi (mōā ee) *adj* beautiful; pretty, fine; nice, lovely, fair

moord (mōārt) *c* (pl ~en) assassination, murder

moordenaar (*mōār*-der-naar) *c* (pl ~s) murderer

mop (mop) *c* (pl ~pen) joke

mopperen (*mo*-per-rern) *v* grumble

moraal (mōā-*raal*) *c* moral

moraliteit (mōā-raa-lee-*tayt*) *c* morality

moreel (mōā-*rāyl*) *adj* moral

morfine (mor-*fee*-ner) *c* morphine, morphia

morgen¹ (*mor*-gern) *adv* tomorrow

morgen² (*mor*-gern) *c* (pl ~s) morning

morsen (*mor*-sern) *v* *spill

mos (moss) *nt* (pl ~sen) moss

moskee (moss-*kāy*) *c* (pl ~ën) mosque

mossel (*mo*-serl) *c* (pl ~s, ~en) mussel

mosterd (*moss*-terrt) *c* mustard

mot (mot) *c* (pl ~ten) moth

motel (mōā-*tehl*) *nt* (pl ~s) motel

motie (*mōā*-tsee) *c* (pl ~s) motion

motief (mōā-*teef*) *nt* (pl motieven) motive; pattern

motor (*mōā*-terr) *c* (pl ~en, ~s) engine, motor

motorboot (*mōā*-terr-bōāt) *c* (pl -boten) motor-boat

motorfiets (*mōā*-terr-feets) *c* (pl ~en) motor-cycle

motorkap (*mōā*-terr-kahp) *c* (pl ~pen) bonnet; hood *nAm*

motorpech (*mōā*-terr-pehkh) *c* breakdown

motorschip (*mōā*-terr-skhɪp) *nt* (pl -schepen) launch

motregen (*mot*-rāy-gern) *c* drizzle

mousseline (mōō-ser-*lee*-ner) *c* muslin

mousserend (mōō-*sāy*-rernt) *adj* sparkling

mouw (mou) *c* (pl ~en) sleeve

mozaïek (mōā-zaa-*eek*) *nt* (pl ~en) mosaic

mug (merkh) *c* (pl ~gen) mosquito

muil (mur^ew^l) *c* (pl ~en) mouth

muildier (mur^ew^l-deer) *nt* (pl ~en) mule

muilezel (*mur^ewl*-āy-zerl) *c* (pl ~s) mule

muis (mur^ewss) *c* (pl muizen) mouse

muiterij (mur^ew-ter-*ray*) *c* (pl ~en) mutiny

mul (merl) *c* mullet

munt (mernt) *c* (pl ~en) coin; token; mint

munteenheid (*mernt*-āyn-hayt) *c* (pl -heden) monetary unit

muntstuk (*mernt*-sterk) *nt* (pl ~ken) coin

mus (merss) *c* (pl ~sen) sparrow

museum (mēw-*zāy*-Υerm) *nt* (pl ~s, -sea) museum

musical (*m^Υōō*-zi-kerl) *c* (pl ~s) musical comedy, musical

musicus (mēw-zee-kerss) *c* (pl -ci) musician

muskiet (merss-*keet*) *c* (pl ~en) mosquito

muskietennet (merss-*kee*-ter-neht) *nt* (pl ~ten) mosquito-net

muts (merts) *c* (pl ~en) cap

muur (mēwr) *c* (pl muren) wall

muziek (mēw-*zeek*) *c* music

muziekinstrument (mēw-*zeek*-ın-strēw-mehnt) *nt* (pl ~en) musical instrument

muzikaal (mēw-zee-*kaal*) *adj* musical

mysterie (mee-*stāy*-ree) *nt* (pl ~s) mystery

mysterieus (mee-stāy-ree-*Υūrss*) *adj* mysterious

mythe (*mee*-ter) *c* (pl ~n) myth

N

na (naa) *prep* after

naad (naat) *c* (pl naden) seam

naadloos (*naat*-lōäss) *adj* seamless

naaien (*naa^ee*-ern) *v* sew

naaimachine (*naa^ee*-mah-shee-ner) *c* (pl ~s) sewing-machine

naaister (*naa^ee*-sterr) *c* (pl ~s) dressmaker

naakt (naakt) *adj* nude, naked, bare

naaktstrand (*naakt*-strahnt) *nt* (pl ~en) nudist beach

naald (naalt) *c* (pl ~en) needle

naam (naam) *c* (pl namen) name; reputation; denomination; in ~ van on behalf of

naar¹ (naar) *prep* to, towards; at, for

naar² (naar) *adj* nasty, unpleasant

naast (naast) *prep* next to, beside

nabij (naa-*bay*) *adj* near, close

nabijheid (naa-*bay*-hayt) *c* vicinity

nabijzijnd (naa-*bay*-zaynt) *adj* nearby

nabootsen (*naa*-bōät-sern) *v* imitate

naburig (naa-*bōō*-rerkh) *adj* neighbouring

nacht (nahkht) *c* (pl ~en) night; 's nachts by night; overnight

nachtclub (*nahkht*-klerp) *c* (pl ~s) nightclub, cabaret

nachtcrème (*nahkht*-kraim) *c* (pl ~s) night-cream

nachtegaal (*nahkh*-ter-gaal) *c* (pl -galen) nightingale

nachtelijk (*nahkh*-ter-lerk) *adj* nightly

nachtjapon (*nahkht*-Υaa-pon) *c* (pl ~nen) nightdress

nachttarief (*nahkh*-taa-reef) *nt* (pl -rieven) night rate

nachttrein (*nahkh*-trayn) *c* (pl ~en) night train

nachtvlucht (*nahkht*-flerkht) *c* (pl ~en) night flight

nadat (naa-*daht*) *conj* after

nadeel (naa-*dāyl*) *nt* (pl -delen) disadvantage

nadelig (naa-*dāy*-lerkh) *adj* harmful

*nadenken (*naa*-dehng-kern) *v* *think; nadenkend thoughtful

nader (*naa*-derr) *adj* further

naderen (*naa*-der-rern) v approach; **naderend** oncoming

naderhand (*naa*-derr-*hahnt*) adv afterwards

nadien (*naa*-*deen*) adv afterwards

nadruk (*naa*-drerk) c stress; accent

nagedachtenis (*naa*-ger-dahkh-ter-niss) c memory

nagel (*naa*-gerl) c (pl ~s) nail

nagelborstel (*naa*-gerl-bors-terl) c (pl ~s) nailbrush

nagellak (*naa*-ger-lahk) c nail-polish

nagelschaar (*naa*-gerl-skhaar) c (pl -scharen) nail-scissors pl

nagelvijl (*naa*-gerl-vayl) c (pl ~en) nail-file

naïef (naa-*eef*) adj naïve

najaar (*naa*-Yaar) nt autumn

*****najagen** (*naa*-Yaa-gern) v chase

*****nakijken** (*naa*-kay-kern) v check

*****nalaten** (*naa*-laa-tern) v fail

nalatig (*naa*-laa-terkh) adj neglectful

namaak (*naa*-maak) c imitation

namaken (*naa*-maa-kern) v copy

namelijk (*naa*-mer-lerk) adv namely

namens (*naa*-merns) adv on behalf of, in the name of

namiddag (naa-*mɪ*-dahkh) c (pl ~en) afternoon

narcis (nahr-*siss*) c (pl ~sen) daffodil

narcose (nahr-*kōā*-zer) c narcosis

narcoticum (nahr-*kōā*-tee-kerm) nt (pl -ca) narcotic

narigheid (*naa*-rerkh-hayt) c (pl -heden) misery

naseizoen (*naa*-say-zōōn) nt low season

nastreven (*naa*-strāy-vern) v aim at, pursue

nat (naht) adj wet; damp, moist

natie (*naa*-tsee) c (pl ~s) nation

nationaal (naa-tshōā-*naal*) adj national; **nationale klederdracht** national dress

nationaliseren (naa-tshōā-naa-lee-*zāy*-rern) v nationalize

nationaliteit (naa-tshōā-naa-lee-*tayt*) c (pl ~en) nationality

natuur (naa-*tewr*) c nature

natuurkunde (naa-*tewr*-kern-der) c physics

natuurkundige (naa-*tewr*-*kern*-der-ger) c (pl ~n) physicist

natuurlijk (naa-*tewr*-lerk) adj natural; adv of course, naturally

natuurreservaat (naa-*tew*-rāy-zerr-vaat) nt (pl -vaten) national park

nauw (nou) adj narrow; tight

nauwelijks (*nou*-er-lerks) adv hardly; scarcely, barely

nauwkeurig (*nou*-er-rerkh) adj accurate; precise, careful, exact

navel (*naa*-verl) c (pl ~s) navel

navigatie (naa-vee-*gaa*-tsee) c navigation

navraag (*naa*-vraakh) c inquiry; demand

*****navragen** (*naa*-vraa-gern) v query, inquire

*****nazenden** (*naa*-zehn-dern) v forward

nederig (*nāy*-der-rerkh) adj humble

nederlaag (*nāy*-derr-laakh) c (pl -lagen) defeat

Nederland (*nāy*-derr-lahnt) the Netherlands

Nederlander (*nāy*-derr-lahn-derr) c (pl ~s) Dutchman

Nederlands (*nāy*-derr-lahnts) adj Dutch

nee (nāy) no

neef (nāyf) c (pl neven) cousin; nephew

neen (nāyn) no

neer (nāyr) adv down; downwards

*****neerlaten** (*nāyr*-laa-tern) v lower

*****neerslaan** (*nāyr*-slaan) v knock down

neerslachtig (nāyr-*slahkh*-terkh) adj

down, low, blue, depressed

neerslachtigheid (*nāȳr-slahkh*-terkh-hayt) *c* depression

neerslag (*nāȳr*-slahkh) *c* precipitation

neerstorten (*nāȳr*-stor-tern) *v* crash

negatief (nay-gaa-*teef*) *adj* negative

negen (*nāȳ*-gern) *num* nine

negende (*nāȳ*-gern-der) *num* ninth

negentien (*nāȳ*-gern-teen) *num* nineteen

negentiende (*nāȳ*-gern-teen-der) *num* nineteenth

negentig (*nāȳ*-gern-terkh) *num* ninety

neger (*nāȳ*-gerr) *c* (pl ~s) Negro

negeren (ner-*gāȳ*-rern) *v* ignore

negligé (nāȳ-glee-*zhāȳ*) *nt* (pl ~s) negligee

neigen (nay-gern) *v* *be inclined to; ~ tot *v* tend to

neiging (nay-gıng) *c* (pl ~en) inclination, tendency; **de ~** *hebben tend

nek (nehk) *c* (pl ~ken) nape of the neck

***nemen** (*nāȳ*-mern) *v* *take; **op zich ~** *take charge of

neon (*nāȳ*-ᵞon) *nt* neon

nergens (*nehr*-gerns) *adv* nowhere

nerts (nehrts) *nt* (pl ~en) mink

nerveus (nehr-*vūrss*) *adj* nervous

nest (nehst) *nt* (pl ~en) nest; litter

net¹ (neht) *adj* tidy, neat

net² (neht) *nt* (pl ~ten) net

netnummer (*neht*-ner-merr) *nt* (pl ~s) area code

netto (*neh*-tōa) *adj* net

netvlies (*neht*-fleess) *nt* (pl -vliezen) retina

netwerk (*neht*-vehrk) *nt* (pl ~en) network

neuriën (*nūr*-ree-ᵞern) *v* hum

neurose (nūr-*rōa*-zer) *c* (pl ~n, ~s) neurosis

neus (nūrss) *c* (pl neuzen) nose

neusbloeding (*nūrss*-blōō-dıng) *c* (pl

~en) nosebleed

neusgat (*nūrss*-khaht) *nt* (pl ~en) nostril

neushoorn (*nūrss*-hōärn) *c* (pl ~s) rhinoceros

neutraal (nūr-*traal*) *adj* neutral

nevel (*nāȳ*-verl) *c* (pl ~s, ~en) haze, mist

nicht (nıkht) *c* (pl ~en) cousin; niece

nicotine (nee-kōa-*tee*-ner) *c* nicotine

niemand (*nee*-mahnt) *pron* nobody, no one

nier (neer) *c* (pl ~en) kidney

niet (neet) *adv* not

nietig (*nee*-terkh) *adj* petty, insignificant; void

nietje (*nee*-tᵞer) *nt* (pl ~s) staple

niets (neets) *pron* nothing; nil

nietsbetekenend (neets-ber-*tāȳ*-ker-nernt) *adj* insignificant

nietszeggend (neet-*seh*-gernt) *adj* meaningless

niettemin (nee-ter-*mın*) *adv* nevertheless

nieuw (nee∞) *adj* new

nieuwjaar (nee∞-*ᵞaar*) New Year

nieuws (nee∞ss) *nt* news; tidings *pl*

nieuwsberichten (nee∞ss-ber-rıkh-tern) *pl* news

nieuwsgierig (nee∞-*skhee*-rerkh) *adj* curious, inquisitive

nieuwsgierigheid (nee∞-*skhee*-rerkh-hayt) *c* curiosity

Nieuw-Zeeland (nee∞-*zāȳ*-lahnt) New Zealand

niezen (*nee*-zern) *v* sneeze

Nigeria (nee-*gāȳ*-ree-ᵞaa) Nigeria

Nigeriaan (nee-gāȳ-ree-ᵞaan) *c* (pl -rianen) Nigerian

Nigeriaans (nee-gāȳ-ree-ᵞaans) *adj* Nigerian

nijptang (*nayp*-tahng) *c* (pl ~en) pincers *pl*

nikkel (*nı*-kerl) *nt* nickel

niks (niks) *pron* nothing

nimmer (*ni*-merr) *adv* never

niveau (nee-*voā*) *nt* (pl ~s) level

nivelleren (nee-ver-*lāy*-rern) *v* level

noch ... noch (nokh) neither ... nor

nodig (*nōā*-derkh) *adj* necessary; ~ **hebben** need

noemen (*nōō*-mern) *v* call; name, mention

nog (nokh) *adv* still, yet; ~ **een** another; ~ **eens** once more; ~ **wat** some more

noga (*nōā*-gaa) *c* nougat

nogal (*no*-gahl) *adv* pretty, fairly, rather, quite

nogmaals (*nokh*-maals) *adv* once more

nokkenas (*no*-ker-nahss) *c* (pl ~sen) camshaft

nominaal (*nōā*-mee-*naal*) *adj* nominal

nominatie (*nōā*-mee-*naa*-tsee) *c* (pl ~s) nomination

non (non) *c* (pl ~nen) nun

nonnenklooster (*no*-ner-klōass-terr) *nt* (pl ~s) nunnery

nood (nōāt) *c* (pl noden) distress; misery; need

noodgedwongen (nōāt-kher-*dvo*-ngern) *adv* by force

noodgeval (*nōāt*-kher-vahl) *nt* (pl ~len) emergency

noodlot (*nōāt*-lot) *nt* destiny, fate

noodlottig (nōāt-*lo*-terkh) *adj* fatal

noodsein (*nōāt*-sayn) *nt* (pl ~en) distress signal

noodtoestand (*nōā*-tōō-stahnt) *c* emergency

nooduitgang (*nōāt*-ur^(ew)t-khahng) *c* (pl ~en) emergency exit

noodzaak (*nōāt*-saak) *c* need, necessity

noodzakelijk (nōāt-*saa*-ker-lerk) *adj* necessary

noodzaken (*nōāt*-saa-kern) *v* force

nooit (nōā^(eet)) *adv* never

Noor (nōar) *c* (pl Noren) Norwegian

noord (nōart) *c* north

noordelijk (*nōar*-der-lerk) *adj* northern, northerly, north

noorden (*nōar*-dern) *nt* north

noordoosten (nōart-*ōass*-tern) *nt* north-east

noordpool (*nōart*-pōal) *c* North Pole

noordwesten (nōart-*vehss*-tern) *nt* north-west

Noors (nōars) *adj* Norwegian

Noorwegen (*nōar*-vāy-gern) Norway

noot (nōat) *c* (pl noten) nut; note

nootmuskaat (nōat-merss-*kaat*) *c* nutmeg

norm (norm) *c* (pl ~en) standard

normaal (nor-*maal*) *adj* normal, regular

nota (*nōā*-taa) *c* (pl ~'s) bill

notaris (nōā-*taa*-rerss) *c* (pl ~sen) notary

notedop (*nōā*-ter-dop) *c* (pl ~pen) nutshell

notekraker (*nōā*-ter-kraa-kerr) *c* (pl ~s) nutcrackers *pl*

noteren (nōā-*tāy*-rern) *v* note; list

notie (*nōā*-tsee) *c* notion

notitie (nōā-*tee*-tsee) *c* (pl ~s) note

notitieboek (nōā-*tee*-tsee-bōōk) *nt* (pl ~en) notebook

notulen (*nōā*-tēw-lern) *pl* minutes

nou (nou) *adv* now

november (nōā-*vehm*-berr) November

nu (nēw) *adv* now; ~ **en dan** now and then; **tot** ~ **toe** so far

nuance (nēw-*ahng*-ser) *c* (pl ~s, ~n) nuance

nuchter (*nerkh*-terr) *adj* sober; down-to-earth, matter-of-fact

nucleair (nēw-klāy-*Υair*) *adj* nuclear

nul (nerl) *c* (pl ~len) nought, zero

nummer (*ner*-merr) *nt* (pl ~s) number; act

nummerbord (*ner*-merr-bort) *nt* (pl ~en) registration plate; licence plate *Am*

nut (nert) *nt* utility, use

nutteloos (*ner*-ter-lōass) *adj* useless

nuttig (*ner*-terkh) *adj* useful

nylon (*nay*-lon) *nt* nylon

O

oase (ōā-*vaa*-zer) *c* (pl ~n, ~s) oasis

ober (*ōā*-berr) *c* (pl ~s) waiter

object (op-*Yehkt*) *nt* (pl ~en) object

objectief (op-*Yehk-teef*) *adj* objective

obligatie (ōā-blee-*gaa*-tsee) *c* (pl ~s) bond

obsceen (op-*sāyn*) *adj* obscene

obscuur (op-*skewr*) *adj* obscure

observatie (op-sehr-*vaa*-tsee) *c* (pl ~s) observation

observatorium (op-sehr-vaa-*tōā*-ree-Yerm) *nt* (pl -ria) observatory

observeren (op-sehr-*vāy*-rern) *v* observe

obsessie (op-*seh*-see) *c* (pl ~s) obsession

obstipatie (op-stee-*paa*-tsee) *c* constipation

oceaan (ōā-sāy-*Yaan*) *c* (pl oceanen) ocean

ochtend (*okh*-ternt) *c* (pl ~en) morning

ochtendblad (*okh*-ternt-blaht) *nt* (pl ~en) morning paper

ochtendeditie (*okh*-ternt-āy-dee-tsee) *c* (pl ~s) morning edition

ochtendschemering (*okh*-ternt-skhāy-mer-rıng) *c* dawn

octopus (*ok*-tōā-perss) *c* (pl ~sen) octopus

octrooi (ok-*trōāee*) *nt* (pl ~en) patent

oefenen (*ōō*-fer-nern) *v* practise, exercise

oefening (*ōō*-fer-nıng) *c* (pl ~en) exercise

oeroud (*ōōr*-out) *adj* ancient

oerwoud (*ōōr*-vout) *nt* (pl ~en) jungle

oester (*ōōss*-terr) *c* (pl ~s) oyster

oever (*ōō*-verr) *c* (pl ~s) river bank; bank, shore

of (of) *conj* or; whether; ~ ... **of** either ... or; whether ... or

offensief[1] (o-fehn-*seef*) *adj* offensive

offensief[2] (o-fehn-*seef*) *nt* (pl -sieven) offensive

offer (*o*-ferr) *nt* (pl ~s) sacrifice

officieel (o-fee-*shāyl*) *adj* official

officier (o-fee-*seer*) *c* (pl ~en, ~s) officer

officieus (o-fee-*shurss*) *adj* unofficial

ofschoon (of-*skhōān*) *conj* although, though

ogenblik (*ōā*-germ-blık) *nt* (pl ~ken) moment, instant

ogenblikkelijk (*ōā*-germ-*blı*-ker-lerk) *adv* instantly

ogenschaduw (*ōā*-ger-skhaa-dēwōō) *c* eye-shadow

oktober (ok-*tōā*-berr) October

olie (*ōā*-lee) *c* oil

olieachtig (*ōā*-lee-ahkh-terkh) *adj* oily

oliebron (*ōā*-lee-bron) *c* (pl ~nen) oil-well

oliedruk (*ōā*-lee-drerk) *c* oil pressure

oliefilter (*ōā*-lee-fıl-terr) *nt* (pl ~s) oil filter

oliën (*ōā*-lee-Yern) *v* lubricate

olieraffinaderij (*ōā*-lee-rah-fee-naa-der-ray) *c* (pl ~en) oil-refinery

olieverfschilderij (*ōā*-lee-vehrf-skhıl-der-ray) *nt* (pl ~en) oil-painting

olifant (*ōā*-lee-fahnt) *c* (pl ~en) elephant

olijf (*ōā*-layf) *c* (pl olijven) olive

olijfolie (*ōā*-layf-ōā-lee) *c* olive oil

om (om) *prep* round, about, around;

~ **te** to, in order to

oma (*ōa*-maa) *c* (pl ~'s) grandmother

***ombrengen** (*om*-breh-ngern) *v* kill

omcirkelen (*om*-*sir*-ker-lern) *v* encircle

omdat (om-*daht*) *conj* because; as

omdraaien (*om*-draa^{ee}-ern) *v* turn; invert; **zich ~** turn round

omelet (ōa-mer-*leht*) *nt* (pl ~ten) omelette

***omgaan met** (*om*-gaan) associate with, mix with

omgang (*om*-gahng) *c* intercourse

omgekeerd (om-ger-*kāyrt*) *adj* reverse

***omgeven** (om-*gāy*-vern) *v* surround, circle

omgeving (om-*gāy*-ving) *c* environment, surroundings *pl*; setting

omheen (om-*hāyn*) *adv* about

omheining (om-*hay*-ning) *c* (pl ~en) fence

omhelzen (om-*hehl*-zern) *v* hug, embrace

omhelzing (om-*hehl*-zing) *c* (pl ~en) hug, embrace

omhoog (om-*hōakh*) *adv* up; ~ ***gaan** ascend

omkeer (*om*-kāyr) *c* reverse

omkeren (*om*-kāy-rern) *v* turn over, turn, turn round

***omkomen** (*om*-kōa-mern) *v* perish

***omkopen** (*om*-kōa-pern) *v* bribe, corrupt

omkoping (*om*-kōa-ping) *c* (pl ~en) bribery, corruption

omlaag (om-*laakh*) *adv* down

omleiding (*om*-lay-ding) *c* (pl ~en) detour

omliggend (*om*-li-gernt) *adj* surrounding

omloop (*om*-lōap) *c* circulation

omrekenen (*om*-rāy-ker-nern) *v* convert

omrekentabel (*om*-rāy-ker-taa-behl) *c* (pl ~len) conversion chart

omringen (om-*ring*-ern) *v* encircle, surround, circle

***omschrijven** (oam-*skhray*-vern) *v* define

omslag (*om*-slahkh) *c/nt* (pl ~en) cover, jacket

omslagdoek (*om*-slahkh-dōok) *c* (pl ~en) shawl

omstandigheid (om-*stahn*-derkh-hayt) *c* (pl -heden) circumstance; condition

omstreden (om-*strāy*-dern) *adj* controversial

omstreeks (om-*strāyks*) *adv* about

omtrek (*om*-trehk) *c* (pl ~ken) contour, outline

omtrent (om-*trehnt*) *prep* about, concerning

omvang (*om*-vahng) *c* bulk, size; extent

omvangrijk (om-*vahng*-rayk) *adj* bulky, big; extensive

omvatten (om-*vah*-tern) *v* comprise

omver (om-*vehr*) *adv* down, over

omweg (*om*-vehkh) *c* (pl ~en) detour

omwenteling (om-*vehn*-ter-ling) *c* (pl ~en) revolution

omwisselen (*om*-vi-ser-lern) *v* switch

omzet (*om*-zeht) *c* (pl ~ten) turnover

omzetbelasting (*om*-zeht-ber-lahss-ting) *c* turnover tax; sales tax

onaangenaam (on-*aan*-ger-naam) *adj* unpleasant, disagreeable

onaanvaardbaar (on-aan-*vaart*-baar) *adj* unacceptable

onaardig (on-*aar*-derkh) *adj* unkind

onafgebroken (on-*ahf*-kher-brōa-kern) *adj* continuous

onafhankelijk (on-ahf-*hahng*-ker-lerk) *adj* independent

onafhankelijkheid (on-ahf-*hahng*-ker-lerk-hayt) *c* independence

onbeantwoord (on-ber-*ahnt*-vōart) *adj* unanswered

onbebouwd (om-ber-*bout*) *adj* uncultivated

onbeduidend (om-ber-*dur*ew-dernt) *adj* petty, insignificant

onbegaanbaar (om-ber-*gaam*-baar) *adj* impassable

onbegrijpelijk (om-ber-*gray*-per-lerk) *adj* puzzling

onbehaaglijk (om-ber-*haakh*-lerk) *adj* uneasy

onbekend (om-ber-*kehnt*) *adj* unfamiliar, unknown

onbekwaam (om-ber-*kvaam*) *adj* unable, incompetent, incapable

onbelangrijk (om-ber-*lahng*-rayk) *adj* unimportant; insignificant

onbeleefd (om-ber-*layft*) *adj* impolite

onbemind (om-ber-*mint*) *adj* unpopular

onbepaald (om-ber-*paalt*) *adj* indefinite; **onbepaalde wijs** infinitive

onbeperkt (om-ber-*pehrkt*) *adj* unlimited

onbeschaamd (om-ber-*skhaamt*) *adj* impudent, impertinent, insolent

onbeschaamdheid (om-ber-*skhaamt*-hayt) *c* impertinence, insolence

onbescheiden (om-ber-*skhay*-dern) *adj* immodest

onbeschermd (om-ber-*skhehrmt*) *adj* unprotected

onbeschoft (oam-ber-*skhoft*) *adj* impertinent

onbetrouwbaar (om-ber-*trou*-baar) *adj* untrustworthy, unreliable

onbevoegd (om-ber-*vōōkht*) *adj* unqualified; unauthorized

onbevredigend (om-ber-*vray*-der-gernt) *adj* unsatisfactory

onbewoonbaar (om-ber-*vōam*-baar) *adj* uninhabitable

onbewoond (om-ber-*vōant*) *adj* uninhabited

onbewust (om-ber-*verst*) *adj* unaware

onbezet (om-ber-*zeht*) *adj* unoccupied

onbezonnen (om-ber-*zo*-nern) *adj* rash

onbezorgd (om-ber-*zorkht*) *adj* carefree

onbillijk (om-bι-lerk) *adj* unfair

onbreekbaar (om-*brāyk*-baar) *adj* unbreakable

ondankbaar (on-*dahngk*-baar) *adj* ungrateful

ondanks (*on*-dahngks) *prep* despite, in spite of

ondenkbaar (on-*dehngk*-baar) *adj* inconceivable

onder (*on*-derr) *prep* under; beneath, below; among, amid

onderaan (on-der-*raan*) *adv* below

*****onderbreken** (on-derr-*brāy*-kern) *v* interrupt

onderbreking (on-derr-*brāy*-kιng) *c* (pl ~en) interruption

*****onderbrengen** (*on*-derr-breh-ngern) *v* accommodate

onderbroek (*on*-derr-brōōk) *c* (pl ~en) briefs *pl*, pants *pl*, panties *pl*; shorts *plAm*; underpants *plAm*

onderdaan (*on*-derr-daan) *c* (pl -danen) subject

onderdak (*on*-derr-dahk) *nt* accommodation

onderdeel (*on*-derr-dāyl) *nt* (pl -delen) spare part

onderdrukken (on-derr-*drer*-kern) *v* suppress

*****ondergaan** (on-derr-*gaan*) *v* suffer

ondergang (*on*-derr-gahng) *c* destruction; ruination, ruin

ondergeschikt (on-derr-ger-*skhιkt*) *adj* subordinate; secondary, minor

ondergetekende (on-derr-ger-*tāy*-kern-der) *c* (pl ~n) undersigned

ondergoed (*on*-derr-gōōt) *nt* underwear

ondergronds (on-derr-*gronts*) *adj* underground

ondergrondse (on-derr-*gron*-tser) *c*
subway *nAm*

onderhandelen (on-derr-*hahn*-der-lern)
v negotiate

onderhandeling (on-derr-*hahn*-der-ling) *c* (pl ~en) negotiation

onderhevig aan (on-derr-*hay*-verkh
aan) subject to; liable to; **aan bederf onderhevig** perishable

onderhoud (*on*-derr-hout) *nt* upkeep;
maintenance

onderhouden (on-derr-*hou*-dern) *v*
entertain

onderling (*on*-derr-ling) *adj* mutual

ondernemen (on-derr-*nay*-mern) *v*
*undertake

onderneming (on-derr-*nay*-ming) *c* (pl ~en) enterprise, undertaking; concern, company

onderrichten (on-der-*rikh*-tern) *v* instruct

onderrok (*on*-derr-rok) *c* (pl ~ken)
slip

onderschatten (on-derr-*skhah*-tern) *v*
underestimate

onderscheid (*on*-derr-skhayt) *nt* distinction; difference; ~ **maken** distinguish

onderscheiden (on-derr-*skhay*-dern)
v distinguish

onderst (*on*-derrst) *adj* bottom

ondersteboven (on-derr-ster-*boa*-vern)
adv upside-down

ondersteunen (on-derr-*stur*-nern) *v*
*hold up, support

onderstrepen (on-derr-*stray*-pern) *v*
underline

onderstroom (*on*-derr-stroam) *c* (pl -stromen) undercurrent

ondertekenen (on-derr-*tay*-ker-nern) *v*
sign

ondertitel (*on*-derr-tee-terl) *c* (pl ~s)
subtitle

ondertussen (on-derr-*ter*-sern) *adv* in

the meantime, meanwhile

ondervinden (on-derr-*vin*-dern) *v* experience

ondervoeding (on-derr-*voo*-ding) *c*
malnutrition

ondervragen (on-derr-*vraa*-gern) *v*
interrogate

onderwerp (*on*-derr-vehrp) *nt* (pl ~en)
subject; topic, theme

onderwerpen (on-derr-*vehr*-pern) *v*
subject; **zich ~** submit

onderwijs (*on*-derr-vayss) *nt* tuition;
education, instruction

onderwijzen (on-derr-*vay*-zern) *v*
*teach

onderwijzer (on-derr-*vay*-zerr) *c* (pl ~s) schoolteacher, schoolmaster,
master, teacher

onderzoek (*on*-derr-zook) *nt* (pl ~en)
enquiry, investigation, inquiry;
check-up, examination; research

onderzoeken (on-derr-*zoo*-kern) *v* enquire, investigate, examine; explore

ondeugend (on-*dur*-gernt) *adj* naughty, mischievous

ondiep (on-*deep*) *adj* shallow

ondoeltreffend (on-*dool*-*treh*-fehnt)
adj inefficient

ondraaglijk (on-*draakh*-lerk) *adj* unbearable

onduidelijk (on-*dur^(ew)*-der-lerk) *adj*
ambiguous

onecht (on-*ehkht*) *adj* false

het oneens *zijn (ert on-*ayns* zayn) *v*
disagree

oneerlijk (on-*ayr*-lerk) *adj* crooked,
dishonest; unfair

oneetbaar (on-*ayt*-baar) *adj* inedible

oneffen (on-*eh*-fern) *adj* uneven

oneindig (on-*ayn*-derkh) *adj* infinite,
endless; immense

onenigheid (on-*ay*-nerkh-hayt) *c* (pl
-heden) dispute

onervaren (on-ehr-*vaa*-rern) *adj* inexperienced

oneven (on-*āy*-vern) *adj* odd

onevenwichtig (on-*āy*-ver-*vikh*-terkh)
adj unsteady

onfatsoenlijk (om-faht-*soōn*-lerk) *adj*
indecent

ongeacht (ong-*ger*-ahkht) *prep* in
spite of

ongebruikelijk (ong-ger-*brur^ew*-ker-
lerk) *adj* unusual

ongeduldig (ong-ger-*derl*-derkh) *adj*
impatient; eager

ongedurig (ong-ger-*dēw*-rerkh) *adj*
restless

ongedwongen (ong-ger-*dvo*-ngern)
adj casual

ongedwongenheid (ong-ger-*dvo*-nger-
hayt) *c* ease

ongeldig (ong-*gehl*-derkh) *adj* invalid

ongelegen (ong-ger-*lāy*-gern) *adj* inconvenient

ongelijk (ong-ger-*layk*) *adj* unequal;
uneven; ~ *hebben *be wrong

ongelofelijk (ong-ger-*lōā*-fer-lerk) *adj*
incredible

ongeluk (*ong*-ger-lerk) *nt* (pl ~ken)
accident; misfortune

ongelukkig (ong-ger-*ler*-kerkh) *adj* unhappy; unlucky, unfortunate

ongelukkigerwijs (ong-ger-ler-ker-gerr-
vayss) *adv* unfortunately

ongemak (*ong*-ger-mahk) *nt* (pl ~ken)
inconvenience

ongemakkelijk (ong-ger-*mah*-ker-lerk)
adj uncomfortable

ongemeubileerd (ong-ger-mūr-bee-
lāyrt) *adj* unfurnished

ongeneeslijk (ong-ger-*nāyss*-lerk) *adj*
incurable

ongepast (ong-ger-*pahst*) *adj* unsuitable; improper

ongerief (*ong*-ger-reef) *nt* inconvenience

ongerijmd (ong-ger-*raymt*) *adj* absurd

ongerust (ong-ger-*rerst*) *adj* worried;
zich ~ **maken** worry

ongeschikt (ong-ger-*skhikt*) *adj* unfit

ongeschoold (ong-ger-*skhoālt*) *adj* uneducated; unskilled

ongetrouwd (ong-ger-*trout*) *adj* single

ongetwijfeld (ong-ger-*tvay*-ferlt) *adv*
undoubtedly

ongeval (*ong*-ger-vahl) *nt* (pl ~len)
accident

ongeveer (ong-ger-*vāyr*) *adv* about,
approximately

ongevoelig (ong-ger-*vōō*-lerkh) *adj* insensitive

ongewenst (ong-ger-*vehnst*) *adj* undesirable

ongewoon (ong-ger-*vōān*) *adj* uncommon, unusual

ongezond (ong-ger-*zont*) *adj* unhealthy, unsound

ongunstig (ong-*gerns*-terkh) *adj* unfavourable

onhandig (on-*hahn*-derkh) *adj* clumsy,
awkward

onheil (*on*-hayl) *nt* calamity, disaster;
mischief

onheilspellend (on-hayl-*speh*-lernt)
adj sinister; ominous

onherroepelijk (on-heh-*rōō*-per-lerk)
adj irrevocable

onherstelbaar (on-hehr-*stehl*-baar) *adj*
irreparable

onjuist (oñ-*ur^ew*st) *adj* incorrect

onkosten (*ong*-koss-tern) *pl* expenses
pl

onkruid (*ong*-krur^ewt) *nt* weed

onlangs (*on*-lahngs) *adv* recently;
lately

onleesbaar (on-*lāyss*-baar) *adj* illegible

onmetelijk (o-*māy*-ter-lerk) *adj* vast,
immense

onmiddellijk (o-*mi*-der-lerk) *adj* immediate, prompt; *adv* immediately,

instantly

onmogelijk (o-*mōā*-ger-lerk) *adj* impossible

onnauwkeurig (o-nou-*kūr*-rerkh) *adj* inaccurate; incorrect

onnodig (o-*nōā*-derkh) *adj* unnecessary

onontbeerlijk (on-ont-*bāyr*-lerk) *adj* essential

onopvallend (on-op-*fah*-lernt) *adj* inconspicuous

onopzettelijk (on-op-*seh*-ter-lerk) *adj* unintentional

onoverkomelijk (on-ōā-verr-*kōā*-mer-lerk) *adj* prohibitive

onovertroffen (on-ōā-verr-*tro*-fern) *adj* unsurpassed

onpartijdig (om-pahr-*tay*-derkh) *adj* impartial

onpersoonlijk (om-pehr-*sōān*-lerk) *adj* impersonal

onplezierig (om-pler-*zee*-rerkh) *adj* unpleasant

onrecht (*on*-rehkht) *nt* injustice; wrong; ~ **aandoen wrong

onrechtvaardig (on-rehkht-*faar*-derkh) *adj* unjust

onredelijk (on-*rāy*-der-lerk) *adj* unreasonable

onregelmatig (on-rāy-gerl-*maa*-terkh) *adj* irregular

onrein (on-*rayn*) *adj* unclean

onrust (*on*-rerst) *c* unrest

onrustig (on-*rerss*-terkh) *adj* restless

ons (ons) *pron* our; us; ourselves

onschadelijk (on-*skhaa*-der-lerk) *adj* harmless

onschatbaar (on-*skhaht*-baar) *adj* priceless

onschuld (*on*-skherlt) *c* innocence

onschuldig (on-*skherl*-derkh) *adj* innocent

ontbijt (ont-*bayt*) *nt* breakfast

***ontbinden** (ont-*bin*-dern) *v* dissolve

***ontbreken** (ont-*brāy*-kern) *v* fail; **ontbrekend** missing

ontdekken (on-*deh*-kern) *v* detect, discover

ontdekking (on-*deh*-king) *c* (pl ~en) discovery

ontdooien (on-*dōā*ᵉᵉ-ern) *v* thaw

ontevreden (on-ter-*vrāy*-dern) *adj* dissatisfied; discontented

***ontgaan** (ont-*khaan*) *v* escape

ontglippen (ont-*khli*-pern) *v* slip

onthaal (ont-*haal*) *nt* reception

***ontheffen** (ont-*heh*-fern) *v* exempt; ~ **van** discharge of

***onthouden** (ont-*hou*-dern) *v* remember; deny; **zich ~ van** abstain from

onthullen (ont-*her*-lern) *v* reveal

onthulling (ont-*her*-ling) *c* (pl ~en) revelation

onthutsen (ont-*hert*-sern) *v* overwhelm

ontkennen (ont-*keh*-nern) *v* deny; **ontkennend** negative

ontkoppelen (ont-*ko*-per-lern) *v* disconnect

ontkurken (ont-*kerr*-kern) *v* uncork

ontleden (ont-*lāy*-dern) *v* analyse; ***break down

ontlenen (ont-*lāy*-nern) *v* borrow

ontmoeten (ont-*mōō*-tern) *v* encounter; ***meet

ontmoeting (ont-*mōō*-ting) *c* (pl ~en) encounter, meeting

***ontnemen** (ont-*nāy*-mern) *v* deprive of

ontoegankelijk (on-tōō-*gahng*-ker-lerk) *adj* inaccessible

ontploffen (ont-*plo*-fern) *v* explode

ontplooien (ont-*plōā*ᵉᵉ-ern) *v* expand

ontroeren (oant-*rōō*-rern) *v* move

ontroering (oant-*rōō*-ring) *c* emotion

ontrouw (*on*-trou) *adj* unfaithful

ontruimen (ont-*rur*ᵉʷ-mern) *v* vacate

ontschepen (ont-*skhāy*-pern) *v* disembark

* **ontslaan** (ont-*slaan*) *v* dismiss, fire
ontslag * **nemen** (ont-*slahkh nāy*-mern) resign
ontslagneming (ont-*slahkh*-nāy-ming) *c* resignation
ontsmetten (ont-*smeh*-tern) *v* disinfect
ontsmettingsmiddel (ont-*smeh*-tings-mi-derl) *nt* (pl ~en) disinfectant
ontsnappen (ont-*snah*-pern) *v* escape
ontsnapping (ont-*snah*-ping) *c* (pl ~en) escape
ontspannen (ont-*spah*-nern) *adj* easygoing
zich ontspannen (ont-*spah*-nern) relax
ontspanning (ont-*spah*-ning) *c* relaxation; recreation
* **ontstaan** (ont-*staan*) *v* *arise
* **ontsteken** (ont-*stāy*-kern) *v* *become septic
ontsteking (ont-*stāy*-king) *c* (pl ~en) ignition; ignition coil; inflammation
ontstemmen (ont-*steh*-mern) *v* displease
* **ontvangen** (ont-*fah*-ngern) *v* receive; entertain
ontvangst (ont-*fahngst*) *c* (pl ~en) receipt; reception
ontvlambaar (ont-*flahm*-baar) *adj* inflammable
ontvluchten (ont-*flerkh*-tern) *v* escape
ontvouwen (ont-*fou*-ern) *v* unfold
ontwaken (ont-*vaa*-kern) *v* wake up
ontwerp (ont-*vehrp*) *nt* (pl ~en) design
* **ontwerpen** (ont-*vehr*-pern) *v* design
* **ontwijken** (ont-*vay*-kern) *v* avoid
ontwikkelen (ont-*vi*-ker-lern) *v* develop
ontwikkeling (ont-*vi*-ker-ling) *c* (pl ~en) development
ontwricht (ont-*frikht*) *adj* dislocated

ontzag (ont-*sahkh*) *nt* respect
* **ontzeggen** (ont-*seh*-gern) *v* deny
ontzettend (ont-*seh*-ternt) *adj* dreadful, terrible
onuitstaanbaar (on-ur^{ewt}-*staam*-baar) *adj* intolerable
onvast (*on*-vahst) *adj* unsteady
onveilig (on-*vay*-lerkh) *adj* unsafe
onverdiend (*on*-verr-deent) *adj* unearned
onverklaarbaar (on-verr-*klaar*-baar) *adj* unaccountable
onvermijdelijk (on-verr-*may*-der-lerk) *adj* unavoidable, inevitable
onverschillig (on-verr-*skhi*-lerkh) *adj* indifferent
onverstandig (on-verr-*stahn*-derkh) *adj* unwise
onverwacht (*on*-verr-vahkht) *adj* unexpected
onvoldoende (on-vol-*dōōn*-der) *adj* insufficient; inadequate
onvolledig (on-vo-*lāy*-derkh) *adj* incomplete
onvolmaakt (on-vol-*maakt*) *adj* imperfect
onvoorwaardelijk (on-vōar-*vaar*-der-lerk) *adj* unconditional
onvoorzien (on-vōar-*zeen*) *adj* unexpected
onvriendelijk (on-*vreen*-der-lerk) *adj* unkind, unfriendly
onwaar (*on*-vaar) *adj* untrue, false
onwaarschijnlijk (on-vaar-*skhayn*-lerk) *adj* unlikely, improbable
onweer (*on*-vāyr) *nt* thunderstorm
onweerachtig (*on*-vāyr-ahkh-terkh) *adj* thundery
onwel (on-*vehl*) *adj* unwell
onwerkelijk (on-*vehr*-ker-lerk) *adj* unreal
onwetend (on-*vāy*-ternt) *adj* ignorant
onwettig (on-*veh*-terkh) *adj* unlawful, illegal

onwillig (on-*vi*-lerkh) *adj* unwilling

onyx (*ōā*-niks) *nt* onyx

onzeker (on-*zāy*-kerr) *adj* doubtful, uncertain

onzelfzuchtig (on-zehlf-*serkh*-terkh) *adj* unselfish

onzichtbaar (on-*zikht*-baar) *adj* invisible

onzijdig (on-*zay*-derkh) *adj* neuter

onzin (*on*-zin) *c* nonsense, rubbish

oog (ōakh) *nt* (pl ogen) eye

oogarts (*ōākh*-ahrts) *c* (pl ~en) oculist

ooggetuige (*ōā*-kher-tur^ew-ger) *c* (pl ~n) eye-witness

ooglid (*ōākh*-lit) *nt* (pl -leden) eyelid

oogst (*ōā*khst) *c* (pl ~en) harvest; crop

ooievaar (*ōā*^ee-vaar) *c* (pl ~s) stork

ooit (*ōā*^ee t) *adv* ever

ook (ōāk) *adv* also, too; as well

oom (ōām) *c* (pl ~s) uncle

oor (ōār) *nt* (pl oren) ear

oorbel (*ōār*-behl) *c* (pl ~len) earring

oordeel (*ōār*-dāyl) *nt* (pl -delen) judgment

oordelen (*ōār*-dāy-lern) *v* judge

oorlog (*ōār*-lokh) *c* (pl ~en) war

oorlogsschip (*ōār*-lokh-skhip) *nt* (pl -schepen) man-of-war

oorpijn (*ōār*-payn) *c* earache

oorsprong (*ōār*-sprong) *c* (pl ~en) origin

oorspronkelijk (*ōār*-*sprong*-ker-lerk) *adj* original

oorzaak (*ōār*-zaak) *c* (pl -zaken) cause; reason

oost (ōāst) *c* east; oost- eastern

oostelijk (*o*-ster-lerk) *adj* eastern, easterly

oosten (*ōā*-stern) *nt* east

Oostenrijk (*ōā*-stern-rayk) Austria

Oostenrijker (*ōā*-stern-ray-kerr) *c* (pl ~s) Austrian

Oostenrijks (*ōā*-stern-rayks) *adj* Aus-

trian

oosters (*ōā*-sterrs) *adj* oriental

op (op) *prep* on, upon; at, in; *adv* up; finished

opa (*ōā*-paa) *c* (pl ~'s) grandfather, granddad

opaal (ōā-*paal*) *c* (pl opalen) opal

opbellen (*o*-beh-lern) *v* call, ring up, phone; call up *Am*

*opbergen (*o*-behr-gern) *v* *put away

opblaasbaar (o-*blaass*-baar) *adj* inflatable

*opblazen (*o*-blaa-zern) *v* inflate

opbouw (*o*-bou) *c* construction

opbouwen (*o*-bou-ern) *v* erect; construct

opbrengst (*o*-brehngst) *c* (pl ~en) produce

opdat (ob-*daht*) *conj* so that

opdracht (*op*-drahkht) *c* (pl ~en) order; assignment

*opdragen aan (*oap*-draa-gern) assign to

opeens (op-*āyns*) *adv* suddenly

opeisen (*op*-ay-sern) *v* claim

open (*ōā*-pern) *adj* open

openbaar (*ōā*-perm-*baar*) *adj* public

openbaren (*ōā*-perm-*baa*-rern) *v* reveal

opendraaien (*ōā*-per-draa^ee ern) *v* turn on

openen (*ōā*-per-nern) *v* unlock; open

openhartig (ōā-per-*hahr*-terkh) *adj* open

opening (*ōā*-per-ning) *c* (pl ~en) opening

openingstijden (*ōā*-per-nings-tay-dern) *pl* business hours

opera (*ōā*-per-raa) *c* (pl ~'s) opera; opera house

operatie (*ōā*-per-*raa*-tsee) *c* (pl ~s) operation, surgery

opereren (*ōā*-per-*rāy*-rern) *v* operate

operette (*ōā*-per-*reh*-ter) *c* (pl ~s) operette

*opgaan (*op*-khaan) *v* *rise

opgeruimd (*op*-kher-rur^{ew}mt) *adj* good-humoured

opgetogen (*oap*-kher-tōā-gern) *adj* delighted

*opgeven (*oap*-khāy-vern) *v* declare; *give up

opgewekt (*op*-kher-vehkt) *adj* cheerful

opgraving (*op*-khraa-vɪng) *c* (pl ~en) excavation

ophaalbrug (*op*-haal-brerkh) *c* (pl ~gen) drawbridge

ophalen (*op*-haa-lern) *v* collect, pick up

*ophangen (*op*-hah-ngern) *v* *hang

ophanging (*op*-hah-ngɪng) *c* suspension

ophef (*op*-hehf) *c* fuss

*opheffen (*op*-heh-fern) *v* discontinue

*ophelderen (*op*-hehl-der-rern) *v* clarify

*ophouden (*op*-hou-dern) *v* cease; ~ **met** stop; quit

opinie (ōa-*pee*-nee) *c* (pl ~s) opinion

opkomst (*op*-komst) *c* rise; attendance

oplage (*op*-laa-ger) *c* (pl ~n) issue

opleiden (*op*-lay-dern) *v* educate

opletten (*op*-leh-tern) *v* *pay attention; **oplettend** attentive

oplichten (*op*-lɪkh-tern) *v* cheat, swindle

oplichter (*op*-lɪkh-terr) *c* (pl ~s) swindler

*oplopen (*op*-lōā-pern) *v* increase; contract

oplosbaar (op-*loss*-baar) *adj* soluble

oplossen (*op*-lo-sern) *v* dissolve; solve

oplossing (*op*-lo-sɪng) *c* (pl ~en) solution

opmerkelijk (op-*mehr*-ker-lerk) *adj* remarkable; noticeable, striking

opmerken (*op*-mehr-kern) *v* notice, note; remark

opmerking (*op*-mehr-kɪng) *c* (pl ~en) remark

opname (*op*-naa-mer) *c* (pl ~n) recording; shot

*opnemen (*op*-nāy-mern) *v* *draw

opnieuw (op-*nee*^{oo}) *adv* again

opoffern (*op*-o-fer-rern) *v* sacrifice

oponthoud (*op*-ont-hout) *nt* delay

oppassen (*o*-pah-sern) *v* look out, beware

oppasser (*o*-pah-serr) *c* (pl ~s) attendant

opperhoofd (*o*-perr-hōāft) *nt* (pl ~en) chieftain

oppervlakkig (o-perr-*vlah*-kerkh) *adj* superficial

oppervlakte (*o*-perr-vlahk-ter) *c* (pl ~n, ~s) surface; area

oppositie (o-pōā-*see*-tsee) *c* (pl ~s) opposition

oprapen (*op*-raa-pern) *v* pick up

oprecht (op-*rehkht*) *adj* honest, sincere

oprichten (*op*-rɪkh-tern) *v* found; erect

*oprijzen (*op*-ray-zern) *v* *arise

oproer (*op*-rōōr) *nt* revolt, rebellion

opruimen (*op*-rur^{ew}-mern) *v* tidy up

opruiming (*op*-rur^{ew}-mɪng) *c* clearance sale

opscheppen (*op*-skheh-pern) *v* boast

*opschieten (*op*-skhee-tern) *v* hurry

opschorten (*op*-skhor-tern) *v* *put off

*opschrijven (*op*-skhray-vern) *v* *write down

*opslaan (*op*-slaan) *v* store

opslag¹ (*op*-slahkh) *c* storage

opslag² (*op*-slahkh) *c* rise; raise *nAm*

opslagplaats (*op*-slahkh-plaats) *c* (pl ~en) depot

*opsluiten (*op*-slur^{ew}-tern) *v* lock up

opsporen (*op*-spōā-rern) *v* trace

*opstaan (*op*-staan) *v* *get up, *rise

opstand (*op*-stahnt) *c* (pl ~en) rising, revolt, rebellion; **in** ~ **komen** revolt

opstapelen (*op*-staa-per-lern) *v* pile

opstel (*op*-stehl) *nt* (pl ~len) essay

opstellen (*op*-steh-lern) *v* *draw up, *make up

•opstijgen (*op*-stay-gern) *v* ascend

optellen (*op*-teh-lern) *v* add; count

optelling (*op*-teh-ling) *c* (pl ~en) addition

opticien (op-tee-*shang*) *c* (pl ~s) optician

optillen (*op*-ti-lern) *v* lift; raise

optimisme (op-tee-*miss*-mer) *nt* optimism

optimist (op-tee-*mist*) *c* (pl ~en) optimist

optimistisch (op-tee-*miss*-teess) *adj* optimistic

optocht (*op*-tokht) *c* (pl ~en) parade

optreden (*op*-trāy-dern) *nt* (pl ~s) appearance

•optreden (*op*-trāy-dern) *v* act; appear

•opvallen (*op*-fah-lern) *v* attract attention; **opvallend** striking

opvatten (*op*-fah-tern) *v* conceive

opvatting (*op*-fah-ting) *c* (pl ~en) view

opvoeden (*op*-fōō-dern) *v* *bring up, educate

opvoeding (*op*-fōō-ding) *c* education

opvolgen (*op*-fol-gern) *v* succeed

•opvouwen (*op*-fou-ern) *v* fold

opvrolijken (*op*-frōa-ler-kern) *v* cheer up

opvullen (*op*-fer-lern) *v* fill up

•opwinden (*op*-vin-dern) *v* *wind; excite

opwinding (*op*-vin-ding) *c* excitement

opzettelijk (op-*seh*-ter-lerk) *adj* deliberate, intentional; on purpose

opzicht (*op*-sikht) *nt* (pl ~en) respect

opzichter (*op*-sikh-terr) *c* (pl ~s) supervisor; warden

opzienbarend (op-seen-*baa*-rernt) *adj* sensational

opzij (op-*say*) *adv* aside; sideways

•opzoeken (*op*-sōō-kern) *v* look up

oranje (ōa-*rah*-ñer) *adj* orange

orde¹ (*or*-der) *c* order; method; **in ~** in order; **in orde!** okay!, all right!

orde² (*or*-der) *c* (pl ~n, ~s) congregation

ordenen (*or*-der-nern) *v* arrange

ordinair (or-dee-*nair*) *adj* common, vulgar

orgaan (or-*gaan*) *nt* (pl organen) organ

organisatie (or-gaa-nee-*zaa*-tsee) *c* (pl ~s) organization

organisch (or-*gaa*-neess) *adj* organic

organiseren (or-gaa-nee-*zāy*-rern) *v* organize

orgel (*or*-gerl) *nt* (pl ~s) organ

zich oriënteren (ōa-ree-Yehn-*tāy*-rern) orientate

origine (ōa-ree-*zhee*-ner) *c* origin

origineel (ōa-ree-zhee-*nāyl*) *adj* original

orkaan (or-*kaan*) *c* (pl orkanen) hurricane

orkest (or-*kehst*) *nt* (pl ~en) orchestra; band

orlon (*or*-lon) *nt* orlon

ornamenteel (or-naa-mehn-*tāyl*) *adj* ornamental

orthodox (or-tōa-*doks*) *adj* orthodox

os (oss) *c* (pl ~sen) ox

oud (out) *adj* old; ancient; aged; **ouder** elder; **oudst** eldest, elder

oudbakken (out-*bah*-kern) *adj* stale

ouderdom (*ou*-derr-dom) *c* age; old age

ouders (*ou*-derrs) *pl* parents *pl*

ouderwets (ou-derr-*vehts*) *adj* old-fashioned, ancient; out of date; quaint

oudheden (*out*-hāy-dern) *pl* antiquities *pl*

Oudheid (*out*-hayt) c antiquity

oudheidkunde (*out*-hayt-kern-der) c archaeology

ouverture (ōō-verr-*tew*-rer) c (pl ~s, ~n) overture

ouvreuse (ōō-*vrūr*-zer) c (pl ~s) usherette

ovaal (ōā-*vaal*) adj oval

oven (ōā-vern) c (pl ~s) oven; furnace; **mikrogolf ~** microwave oven

over (ōā-verr) prep about; over; across; in; adv over

overal (ōā-verr-ahl) adv everywhere; anywhere; throughout

overall (ōā-ver-*rahl*) c (pl ~s) overalls pl

overblijfsel (ōā-verr-blayf-serl) nt (pl ~s, ~en) remnant

*** overblijven** (ōā-verr-blay-vern) v remain

overbodig (ōā-verr-*bōā*-derkh) adj superfluous; redundant

*** overbrengen** (ōā-verr-breh-ngern) v transfer

overdag (ōā-verr-*dahkh*) adv by day

*** overdenken** (ōā-verr-*dehng*-kern) v *think over

*** overdrijven** (ōā-verr-*dray*-vern) v exaggerate; **overdreven** extravagant

*** overeenkomen** (ōā-ver-*rāyng*-kōā-mern) v agree; correspond

overeenkomst (ōā-ver-*rāyng*-komst) c (pl ~en) agreement, settlement

overeenkomstig (ōā-ver-*rāyng*-kom-sterkh) adj similar; prep according to

overeenstemming (ōā-ver-*rāyn*-steh-ming) c agreement

overeind (ōā-ver-*raynt*) adv upright; erect

overgang (ōā-verr-gahng) c (pl ~en) transition

overgave (ōā-verr-gaa-ver) c surrender

*** overgeven** (ōā-verr-*gāy*-vern) v vomit; **zich *overgeven** surrender

overhaast (ōā-verr-*haast*) adj rash

overhalen (ōā-verr-haa-lern) v persuade

overheersing (ōā-verr-*hāyr*-sing) c domination

overheid (ōā-verr-hayt) c (pl -heden) authorities pl

overhemd (ōā-verr-hehmt) nt (pl ~en) shirt

overig (ōā-ver-rerkh) adj remaining

overigens (ōā-ver-rer-gerns) adv though

overjas (ōā-verr-Уahss) c (pl ~sen) topcoat, overcoat

aan de overkant (aan der ōā-verr-kahnt) across

overleg (ōā-verr-*lehkh*) nt deliberation

overleggen (ōā-verr-*leh*-gern) v deliberate

overleven (ōā-verr-*lāy*-vern) v survive

overleving (ōā-verr-*lāyving*) c survival

*** overlijden** (ōā-verr-lay-dern) v depart, die

overmaken (ōā-verr-maa-kern) v remit

overmoedig (ōā-verr-*mōō*-derkh) adj presumptuous

*** overnemen** (ōā-verr-nāy-mern) v *take over

overreden (ōā-ver-*rāy*-dern) v persuade

overschot (ōā-verr-skhot) nt (pl ~ten) surplus

*** overschrijden** (ōā-verr-*skhray*-dern) v exceed

overschrijving (ōā-verr-*skhray*-ving) c (pl ~en) money order

*** overslaan** (ōā-verr-slaan) v skip

overspannen (ōā-verr-*spah*-nern) adj overstrung

overstappen (ōā-verr-stah-pern) v change

oversteekplaats (ōā-verr-stāyk-plaats) c (pl ~en) crossing

oversteken (ōa-verr-stāy-kern) v
cross

overstroming (ōa-verr-strōa-ming) c
(pl ~en) flood

overstuur (ōa-verr-stewr) adj upset

overtocht (ōa-verr-tokht) c (pl ~en)
crossing, passage

*overtreden** (ōa-verr-trāy-dern) v offend

overtreding (ōa-verr-trāy-ding) c (pl
~en) offence

*overtreffen** (ōa-verr-treh-fern) v
*outdo, exceed

overtuigen (ōa-verr-tur^(ew)-gern) v convince; persuade

overtuiging (ōa-verr-tur^(ew)-ging) c (pl
~en) conviction; persuasion

overval (ōa-verr-vahl) c (pl ~len)
hold-up

oververmoeid (ōa-verr-verr-mōo^(ee)t)
adj over-tired

overvloed (ōa-verr-vlōot) c abundance; plenty

overvloedig (ōa-verr-vlōo-derkh) adj
abundant, plentiful

overvol (ōa-verr-vol) adj crowded

overweg (ōa-verr-vehkh) c (pl ~en)
level crossing, crossing

*overwegen** (ōa-verr-vāy-gern) v consider

overweging (ōa-verr-vāy-ging) c (pl
~en) consideration

overweldigen (ōa-verr-vehl-der-gern) v
overwhelm

zich overwerken (ōa-verr-vehr-kern) v
overwork

*overwinnen** (ōa-verr-vi-nern) v conquer; *overcome

overwinning (ōa-verr-vi-ning) c (pl
~en) victory

overzees (ōa-verr-zāyss) adj overseas

overzicht (ōa-verr-zikht) nt (pl ~en)
survey

P

paal (paal) c (pl palen) post, pole

paar (paar) nt (pl paren) pair; couple

paard (paart) nt (pl ~en) horse

paardebloem (paar-der-blōom) c (pl
~en) dandelion

paardekracht (paar-der-krahkht) c
horsepower

paardesport (paar-der-sport) c riding

*paardrijden** (paart-ray-dern) v *ride

paarlemoer (paar-ler-mōor) nt mother-of-pearl

paars (paars) adj purple

pacht (pahkht) c (pl ~en) lease

pacifisme (pah-see-fiss-mer) nt pacifism

pacifist (pah-see-fist) c (pl ~en) pacifist

pacifistisch (pah-see-fiss-teess) adj
pacifist

pad[1] (paht) nt (pl ~en) path; lane,
trail

pad[2] (paht) c (pl ~den) toad

paddestoel (pah-der-stōōl) c (pl ~en)
toadstool; mushroom

padvinder (paht-fin-derr) c (pl ~s)
scout, boy scout

padvindster (paht-fint-sterr) c (pl ~s)
girl guide

pagina (paa-gee-naa) c (pl ~'s) page

pak (pahk) nt (pl ~ken) package

pakhuis (pahk-hur^(ew)ss) nt (pl -huizen)
warehouse

Pakistaan (paa-kee-staan) c (pl -stanen) Pakistani

Pakistaans (paa-kee-staans) adj Pakistani

Pakistan (paa-kiss-tahn) Pakistan

pakje (pahk-Yer) nt (pl ~s) parcel,
packet

pakken (pah-kern) v *take

pakket (pah-*keht*) *nt* (pl ~ten) parcel

pakpapier (*pahk*-paa-peer) *nt* wrapping paper

paleis (paa-*layss*) *nt* (pl paleizen) palace

paling (*paa*-ling) *c* (pl ~en) eel

palm (pahlm) *c* (pl ~en) palm

pan (pahn) *c* (pl ~nen) pan

pand (pahnt) *nt* (pl ~en) security; house, premises *pl*

pandjesbaas (*pahn*-t^yerss-baass) *c* (pl -bazen) pawnbroker

paneel (paa-*nāyl*) *nt* (pl panelen) panel

paniek (paa-*neek*) *c* panic

panne (*pah*-ner) *c* breakdown

pantoffel (pahn-*to*-ferl) *c* (pl ~s) slipper

panty (*pehn*-tee) *c* (pl panties) panty-hose

papa (*pah*-paa) *c* (pl ~'s) daddy

papaver (paa-*paa*-verr) *c* (pl ~s) poppy

papegaai (pah-per-*gaa^{ee}*) *c* (pl ~en) parrot

papier (paa-*peer*) *nt* (pl ~en) paper

papieren (paa-*pee*-rern) *adj* paper; ~ **servet** paper napkin; ~ **zak** paper bag; ~ **zakdoek** tissue

parade (paa-*raa*-der) *c* (pl ~s) parade

paraferen (paa-raa-*fāy*-rern) *v* initial

paragraaf (paa-raa-*graaf*) *c* (pl -grafen) paragraph

parallel (paa-raa-*lehl*) *adj* parallel

paraplu (paa-raa-*plew*) *c* (pl ~'s) umbrella

parasol (paa-raa-*sol*) *c* (pl ~s) sunshade

pardon! (pahr-*don*) sorry!

parel (*paa*-rerl) *c* (pl ~s, ~en) pearl

parfum (pahr-*ferm*) *nt* (pl ~s) perfume

park (pahrk) *nt* (pl ~en) park

parkeermeter (pahr-*kāyr*-māy-terr) *c* (pl ~s) parking meter

parkeerplaats (pahr-*kāyr*-plaats) *c* (pl ~en) car park; parking lot *Am*

parkeertarief (pahr-*kāyr*-taa-reef) *nt* (pl -tarieven) parking fee

parkeerzone (pahr-*kāyr*-zaw-ner) *c* (pl ~s) parking zone

parkeren (pahr-*kāy*-rern) *v* park

parkiet (pahr-*keet*) *c* (pl ~en) parakeet

parlement (pahr-ler-*mehnt*) *nt* (pl ~en) parliament

parlementair (pahr-ler-mehn-*tair*) *adj* parliamentary

parochie (pah-*ro*-khee) *c* (pl ~s) parish

particulier (pahr-tee-kew-*leer*) *adj* private

partij (pahr-*tay*) *c* (pl ~en) party; side; batch

partijdig (pahr-*tay*-derkh) *adj* partial

partner (*pahrt*-nerr) *c* (pl ~s) partner; associate

pas[1] (pahss) *c* (pl ~sen) step

pas[2] (pahss) *adv* just

Pasen (*paa*-sern) Easter

pasfoto (*pahss*-fōa-tōa) *c* (pl ~'s) passport photograph

paskamer (*pahss*-kaa-merr) *c* (pl ~s) fitting room

paspoort (*pahss*-pōart) *nt* (pl ~en) passport

paspoortcontrole (*pahss*-pōart-kon-traw-ler) *c* passport control

passage (pah-*saa*-zher) *c* (pl ~s) excerpt; passage

passagier (pah-saa-*zheer*) *c* (pl ~s) passenger

passen (*pah*-sern) *v* try on; fit; ~ **bij** match; **passend** appropriate; convenient, adequate, proper; ~ **op** look after; attend to

passeren (pah-*sāy*-rern) *v* pass; by-pass, pass by

passie (*pah*-see) *c* passion

passief (pah-*seef*) *adj* passive

pasta (*pahss*-taa) *c* (pl ~'s) paste

pastorie (pahss-tōa-*ree*) *c* (pl ~ën)
parsonage, vicarage, rectory

patent (paa-*tehnt*) *nt* (pl ~en) patent

pater (*paa*-terr) *c* (pl ~s) father

patiënt (paa-*shehnt*) *c* (pl ~en) patient

patrijs (paa-*trayss*) *c* (pl patrijzen)
partridge

patrijspoort (paa-*trayss*-pōārt) *c* (pl
~en) porthole

patriot (paa-tree-*Yot*) *c* (pl ~ten) patriot

patroon (paa-*trōan*) *nt* (pl patronen)
pattern; *c* cartridge

patrouille (paa-*trōo-Yer*) *c* (pl ~s) patrol

patrouilleren (paa-trōo-*Yāy*-rern) *v* patrol

paus (pouss) *c* (pl ~en) pope

pauw (pou) *c* (pl ~en) peacock

pauze (*pou*-zer) *c* (pl ~s) pause;
break; interval, intermission

pauzeren (pou-*zāy*-rern) *v* pause

paviljoen (paa-vil-*Yōōn*) *nt* (pl ~en,
~s) pavilion

pech (pehkh) *c* bad luck

pedaal (per-*daal*) *nt/c* (pl pedalen)
pedal

peddel (*peh*-derl) *c* (pl ~s) paddle

pedicure (pāy-dee-*kew*-rer) *c* (pl ~s)
pedicure, chiropodist

peen (pāyn) *c* (pl penen) carrot

peer (pāyr) *c* (pl peren) pear; light
bulb

pees (pāyss) *c* (pl pezen) sinew, tendon

peetvader (*pāyt*-faa-derr) *c* (pl ~s)
godfather

peil (payl) *nt* (pl ~en) level

pelgrim (*pehl*-grim) *c* (pl ~s) pilgrim

pelikaan (pāy-lee-*kaan*) *c* (pl -kanen)
pelican

pels (pehls) *c* (pl pelzen) fur

pen (pehn) *c* (pl ~nen) pen

penicilline (pāy-nee-see-*lee*-ner) *c*
penicillin

penningmeester (*peh*-nɪng-māyss-terr)
c (pl ~s) treasurer

penseel (pehn-*sāyl*) *nt* (pl -selen)
paint-brush

pensioen (pehn-*shōōn*) *nt* (pl ~en)
pension

pension (pehn-*shon*) *nt* (pl ~s)
board; boarding-house, guest-
house, pension; **vol** ~ full board,
board and lodging, bed and board

peper (*pāy*-perr) *c* pepper

pepermunt (pāy-perr-*mernt*) *c* peppermint

per (pehr) *prep* by

perceel (pehr-*sāyl*) *nt* (pl -celen) plot

percentage (pehr-sehn-*taa*-zher) *nt* (pl
~s) percentage

percolator (pehr-kōa-*laa*-tor) *c* (pl ~s)
percolator

perfectie (pehr-*fehk*-see) *c* perfection

periode (pāy-ree-*Yōa*-der) *c* (pl ~s,
~n) period; term

periodiek (pāy-ree-*Yōa*-deek) *adj* periodical

permanent (pehr-maa-*nehnt*) *adj* permanent; *c* permanent wave

permissie (pehr-*mɪ*-see) *c* permission

perron (peh-*ron*) *nt* (pl ~s) platform

perronkaartje (peh-*ron*-kaar-t^Yer) *nt*
(pl ~s) platform ticket

Pers (pehrs) *c* (pl Perzen) Persian

pers (pehrs) *c* press

persconferentie (*pehrs*-kon-fer-rehn-
tsee) *c* (pl ~s) press conference

persen (*pehr*-sern) *v* press

personeel (pehr-sōa-*nāyl*) *nt* personnel

personentrein (pehr-*sōa*-ner-trayn) *c*
(pl ~en) passenger train

persoon (pehr-*sōan*) *c* (pl -sonen) person; **per ~** per person

persoonlijk (pehr-*sōān*-lerk) *adj* personal; private

persoonlijkheid (pehr-*sōān*-lerk-hayt) *c* (pl -heden) personality

perspectief (pehr-spehk-*teef*) *nt* (pl -tieven) perspective

Perzië (*pehr*-zee-Yer) Persia

perzik (*pehr*-zık) *c* (pl ~en) peach

Perzisch (*pehr*-zeess) *adj* Persian

pessimisme (peh-see-*miss*-mer) *nt* pessimism

pessimist (peh-see-*mist*) *c* (pl ~en) pessimist

pessimistisch (peh-see-*miss*-teess) *adj* pessimistic

pet (peht) *c* (pl ~ten) cap

peterselie (pāy-terr-*sāy*-lee) *c* parsley

petitie (per-*tee*-tsee) *c* (pl ~s) petition

petroleum (pāy-*trōā*-lāy-Yerm) *c* petroleum; kerosene, paraffin

peuter (*pūr*-terr) *c* (pl ~s) toddler

pianist (pee-Yaa-*nist*) *c* (pl ~en) pianist

piano (pee-*Yaa*-nōā) *c* (pl ~'s) piano

piccolo (*pee*-kōā-lōā) *c* (pl ~'s) pageboy, bellboy

picknick (*pık*-nık) *c* (pl ~s) picnic

picknicken (*pık*-nı-kern) *v* picnic

pick-up (pık-*erp*) *c* (pl ~s) recordplayer

pienter (*peen*-terr) *adj* bright, smart, clever

pier (peer) *c* (pl ~en) pier, jetty

pijl (payl) *c* (pl ~en) arrow

pijn (payn) *c* (pl ~en) ache, pain; **~ *doen** *hurt; ache

pijnlijk (*payn*-lerk) *adj* sore, painful; embarrassing, awkward

pijnloos (*payn*-lōāss) *adj* painless

pijp (payp) *c* (pl ~en) pipe; tube

pijpestoker (*pay*-per-stōā-kerr) *c* (pl ~s) pipe cleaner

pijptabak (*payp*-taa-bahk) *c* pipe tobacco

pikant (pee-*kahnt*) *adj* spicy; savoury

pil (pıl) *c* (pl ~len) pill

pilaar (pee-*laar*) *c* (pl pilaren) column, pillar

piloot (pee-*lōāt*) *c* (pl piloten) pilot

pils (pıls) *nt* beer

pincet (pın-*seht*) *c* (pl ~ten) tweezers *pl*

pinda (*pın*-daa) *c* (pl ~'s) peanut

pinguïn (*pın*-gvın) *c* (pl ~s) penguin

pink (pıngk) *c* (pl ~en) little finger

Pinksteren (*pıngk*-ster-rern) Whitsun

pion (pee-Yon) *c* (pl ~nen) pawn

pionier (pee-Yōā-*neer*) *c* (pl ~s) pioneer

piraat (pee-*raat*) *c* (pl piraten) pirate

piste (*peess*-ter) *c* (pl ~s) ring

pistool (peess-*tōāl*) *nt* (pl pistolen) pistol

pit (pıt) *c* (pl ~ten) stone, pip

pittoresk (pee-tōā-*rehsk*) *adj* picturesque

plaag (plaakh) *c* (pl plagen) plague

plaat (plaat) *c* (pl platen) plate, sheet; picture

plaats (plaats) *c* (pl ~en) place; spot, locality, site; seat; room; **in ~ van** instead of

plaatselijk (*plaat*-ser-lerk) *adj* local; regional

plaatsen (*plaat*-sern) *v* *lay, *put, place; locate

*plaatshebben (*plaats*-heh-bern) *v* *take place

plaatskaartenbureau (*plaats*-kaar-ter-bēw-rōā) *nt* (pl ~s) box-office

plaatsvervanger (*plaats*-ferr-vah-ngerr) *c* (pl ~s) deputy, substitute

plafond (plaa-*font*) *nt* (pl ~s) ceiling

plagen (*plaa*-gern) *v* tease

plakband (*plahk*-bahnt) *nt* scotch tape, adhesive tape

plakboek (*plahk*-bōōk) *nt* (pl ~en)

scrap-book

plakken (*plah*-kern) *v* *stick; paste

plan (plahn) *nt* (pl ~nen) plan; project, scheme; **van ~ *zijn** intend

planeet (plaa-*nayt*) *c* (pl -neten) planet

planetarium (plaa-ner-*taa*-ree-Yerm) *nt* (pl ~s, -ria) planetarium

plank (plahngk) *c* (pl ~en) board, plank; shelf

plannen (*pleh*-nern) *v* plan

plant (plahnt) *c* (pl ~en) plant

plantage (plahn-*taa*-zher) *c* (pl ~s) plantation

planten (*plahn*-tern) *v* plant

plantengroei (*plahn*-ter-grōō ee) *c* vegetation

plantkunde (*plahnt*-kern-der) *c* botany

plantsoen (plahnt-*sōōn*) *nt* (pl ~en) public garden

plas (plahss) *c* (pl ~sen) puddle

plastic (*pleh*-stik) *adj* plastic

plat (plaht) *adj* flat; even, level

platenspeler (*plaa*-ter-spāy-lerr) *c* (pl ~s) record-player

platina (*plaa*-tee-naa) *nt* platinum

plattegrond (plah-ter-*gront*) *c* (pl ~en) map, plan

platteland (plah-ter-*lahnt*) *nt* countryside, country; **plattelands-** rural

platzak (*plaht*-sahk) broke

plaveien (plaa-*vay*-ern) *v* pave

plaveisel (plaa-*vay*-serl) *nt* pavement

plechtig (*plehkh*-terkh) *adj* solemn

pleegouders (*plāykh*-ou-derrs) *pl* foster-parents *pl*

plegen (*plāy*-gern) *v* commit

pleidooi (play-*dōā*ee) *nt* (pl ~en) plea

plein (playn) *nt* (pl ~en) square

pleister¹ (*play*-sterr) *c* (pl ~s) plaster

pleister² (*play*-sterr) *nt* plaster

pleiten (*play*-tern) *v* plead

plek (plehk) *c* (pl ~ken) spot; **blauwe ~** bruise; **zere ~** sore

plezier (pler-*zeer*) *nt* pleasure; fun

plicht (plikht) *c* (pl ~en) duty

ploeg¹ (plōōkh) *c* (pl ~en) plough

ploeg² (plōōkh) *c* (pl ~en) team; shift; gang

ploegen (*plōō*-gern) *v* plough

plooi (plōā ee) *c* (pl ~en) crease

plooihoudend (plōā ee-*hou*-dernt) *adj* permanent press

plotseling (*plot*-ser-ling) *adj* sudden

plukken (*pler*-kern) *v* pick

plus (plerss) *prep* plus

pneumatisch (pnūr-*maa*-teess) *adj* pneumatic

pocketboek (*po*-kert-bōōk) *nt* (pl ~en) paperback

poeder (*pōō*-derr) *nt/c* (pl ~s) powder

poederdons (*pōō*-derr-dons) *c* (pl -donzen) powder-puff

poederdoos (*pōō*-derr-dōāss) *c* (pl -dozen) powder compact

poelier (pōō-*leer*) *c* (pl ~s) poulterer

poes (pōōss) *c* (pl poezen) pussy-cat

poetsen (*pōō*-tsern) *v* brush; polish

pogen (*pōā*-gern) *v* try

poging (*pōā*-ging) *c* (pl ~en) try, attempt; effort

pokken (*po*-kern) *pl* smallpox

Polen (*pōā*-lern) Poland

polio (*pōā*-lee-Yōā) *c* polio

polis (*pōā*-lerss) *c* (pl ~sen) policy

politicus (pōā-*lee*-tee-kerss) *c* (pl -ci) politician

politie (pōā-*lee*-tsee) *c* police *pl*

politieagent (pōā-*lee*-tsi-aa-gehnt) *c* (pl ~en) policeman

politiebureau (pōā-*lee*-tsee-bēw-rōā) *nt* (pl ~s) police-station

politiek (pōā-lee-*teek*) *adj* political; *c* policy; politics

pols (pols) *c* (pl ~en) wrist; pulse

polshorloge (pols-hor-lōā-zher) *nt* (pl ~s) wrist-watch

polsslag (*pol*-slahkh) *c* pulse

pomp (pomp) *c* (pl ~en) pump

pompelmoes (*pom-perl-mōoss*) *c* (pl -moezen) grapefruit

pompen (*pom-pern*) *v* pump

pond (pont) *nt* pound

Pool (pōal) *c* (pl Polen) Pole

Pools (pōals) *adj* Polish

poort (pōart) *c* (pl ~en) gate

poosje (*pōa-sher*) *nt* while

poot (pōat) *c* (pl poten) leg; paw

pop (pop) *c* (pl ~pen) doll

popeline (pōa-per-*lee*-ner) *nt/c* poplin

popmuziek (*pop-mēw-zeek*) *c* pop music

poppenkast (*po-per-kahst*) *c* puppet-show

populair (pōa-pew-*lair*) *adj* popular

porselein (por-seh-*layn*) *nt* porcelain, china

portefeuille (por-ter-*fur*ᵉʷ-Yer) *c* (pl ~s) pocket-book, wallet

portemonnee (por-ter-mo-*nāy*) *c* (pl ~s) purse

portie (*por*-see) *c* (pl ~s) portion; helping

portier (por-*teer*) *c* (pl ~s) doorman, door-keeper, porter

portret (por-*treht*) *nt* (pl ~ten) portrait

Portugal (*por*-tew-gahl) Portugal

Portugees (por-tew-*gāyss*) *adj* Portuguese

positie (pōa-*zee*-tsee) *c* (pl ~s) position

positief (pōa-zee-*teef*) *adj* positive

post[1] (post) *c* mail, post

post[2] (post) *c* (pl ~en) entry

postbode (*post*-bōa-der) *c* (pl ~s, ~n) postman

postcode (*post*-kōa-der) *c* (pl ~s) zip code *Am*

posten (*poss*-tern) *v* mail, post

poste restante (post-rehss-*tahnt*) poste restante

posterijen (poss-ter-*ray*-ern) *pl* postal service

postkantoor (*post*-kahn-tōar) *nt* (pl -toren) post-office

postwissel (*post*-vi-serl) *c* (pl ~s) postal order; mail order *Am*

postzegel (*post*-sāy-gerl) *c* (pl ~s) postage stamp, stamp

postzegelautomaat (*post*-sāy-gerl-ōa-tōa-maat) *c* (pl -maten) stamp machine

pot (pot) *c* (pl ~ten) pot; jar

potlood (*pot*-lōat) *nt* (pl -loden) pencil

praatje (*praa*-tYer) *nt* (pl ~s) chat

pracht (prahkht) *c* splendour

prachtig (*prahkh*-terkh) *adj* lovely, wonderful, marvellous; splendid, gorgeous, fine

praktijk (prahk-*tayk*) *c* (pl ~en) practice

praktisch (*prahk*-teess) *adj* practical

praten (*praa*-tern) *v* talk

precies (prer-*seess*) *adj* precise, very, exact; *adv* exactly; just

predikant (*prāy*-dee-kahnt) *c* (pl ~en) clergyman, minister, vicar, rector

preek (prāyk) *c* (pl preken) sermon

preekstoel (*prāyk*-stōol) *c* (pl ~en) pulpit

preken (*prāy*-kern) *v* preach

premie (*prāy*-mee) *c* (pl ~s) premium

premier (prer-m[ʸ]*āy*) *c* (pl ~s) premier, Prime Minister

prent (prehnt) *c* (pl ~en) picture; print, engraving

prentbriefkaart (*prehnt*-breef-kaart) *c* (pl ~en) picture postcard

president (prāy-zee-*dehnt*) *c* (pl ~en) president

prestatie (prehss-*taa*-tsee) *c* (pl ~s) achievement; feat

presteren (prehss-*tāy*-rern) *v* achieve

prestige (prehss-*tee*-zher) *nt* prestige

pret (preht) *c* fun; gaiety, pleasure

prettig (*preh*-terkh) *adj* enjoyable, pleasant ; nice

preventief (prāy-vehn-*teef*) *adj* preventive

priester (*pree*-sterr) *c* (pl ~s) priest

prijs (prayss) *c* (pl prijzen) price-list ; charge, cost, rate ; prize, award ; **op ~ stellen** appreciate

prijsdaling (*prayss*-daa-lıng) *c* (pl ~en) slump

prijslijst (*prayss*-layst) *c* (pl ~en) price list

prijzen (*pray*-zern) *v* price

***prijzen** (*pray*-zern) *v* praise

prijzig (*pray*-zerkh) *adj* expensive

prik[1] (prık) *c* (pl ~ken) sting

prik[2] (prık) *c* fizz

prikkel (*prı*-kerl) *c* (pl ~s) impulse

prikkelbaar (*prı*-kerl-baar) *adj* irritable

prikkelen (*prı*-ker-lern) *v* irritate

prikken (*prı*-kern) *v* prick

prima (*pree*-maa) *adj* first-rate

primair (*pree*-mair) *adj* primary

principe (prın-*see*-per) *nt* (pl ~s) principle

prins (prıns) *c* (pl ~en) prince

prinses (prın-*sehss*) *c* (pl ~sen) princess

prioriteit (pree-Ỵōa-ree-*tayt*) *c* (pl ~en) priority

privé (pree-*vāy*) *adj* private

privéleven (pree-*vāy*-lāy-vern) *nt* privacy

proberen (prōa-*bāy*-rern) *v* try ; attempt ; test

probleem (prōa-*blāym*) *nt* (pl -blemen) problem

procédé (prōa-ser-*dāy*) *nt* (pl ~s) process

procedure (prōa-ser-*dēw*-rer) *c* (pl ~s) procedure

procent (prōa-*sehnt*) *nt* (pl ~en) percent

proces (prōa-*sehss*) *nt* (pl ~sen) process ; lawsuit

processie (prōa-*seh*-see) *c* (pl ~s) procession

producent (prōa-dēw-*sehnt*) *c* (pl ~en) producer

produceren (prōa-dēw-*sāy*-rern) *v* produce

produkt (prōa-*derkt*) *nt* (pl ~en) product ; produce

produktie (prōa-*derk*-see) production ; output

proef (prōof) *c* (pl proeven) experiment ; trial, test

proeven (*prōo*-vern) *v* taste

profeet (prōa-*fāyt*) *c* (pl -feten) prophet

professor (prōa-*feh*-sor) *c* (pl ~en, ~s) professor

profiteren (prōa-fee-*tāy*-rern) *v* profit, benefit

programma (prōa-*grah*-maa) *nt* (pl ~'s) programme

progressief (prōa-greh-*seef*) *adj* progressive

project (prōa-Ỵ*ehkt*) *nt* (pl ~en) project

promenade (pro-mer-*naa*-der) *c* (pl ~s) esplanade, promenade

promotie (prōa-*mōa*-tsee) *c* (pl ~s) promotion

prompt (prompt) *adj* prompt

propaganda (prōa-paa-*gahn*-daa) *c* propaganda

propeller (prōa-*peh*-lerr) *c* (pl ~s) propeller

proportie (prōa-*por*-see) *c* (pl ~s) proportion

prospectus (pro-*spehk*-terss) *c* (pl ~sen) prospectus

prostituée (pro-stee-tēw-*vāy*) *c* (pl ~s) prostitute

protest (prōa-*tehst*) *nt* (pl ~en) protest

protestants (prōa-terss-*tahnts*) *adj*

Protestant

protesteren (prōa-tehss-*tay*-rern) *v* protest

provinciaal (prōa-vın-*shaal*) *adj* provincial

provincie (prōa-*vın*-see) *c* (pl ~s) province

provisiekast (prōa-*vee*-zee-kahst) *c* (pl ~en) larder

pruik (prur^ewk) *c* (pl ~en) wig

pruim (prur^ewm) *c* (pl ~en) plum; prune

prullenmand (*prer*-ler-mahnt) *c* (pl ~en) wastepaper-basket

psychiater (psee-khee-*Yaa*-terr) *c* (pl ~s) psychiatrist

psychisch (*psee*-kheess) *adj* psychic

psychologie (psee-khōa-lōa-*gee*) *c* psychology

psychologisch (psee-khōa-*lōa*-geess) *adj* psychological

psycholoog (psee-khōa-*lōakh*) *c* (pl -logen) psychologist

publiceren (pēw-blee-*say*-rern) *v* publish

publiek (pēw-*bleek*) *adj* public; *nt* audience, public

publikatie (pēw-blee-*kaa*-tsee) *c* (pl ~s) publication

puimsteen (*pur^ew*m-stāyn) *nt* pumice stone

puistje (*pur^ew*-sher) *nt* (pl ~s) pimple

punaise (pēw-*nai*-zer) *c* (pl ~s) drawing-pin; thumbtack *nAm*

punctueel (perngk-tēw-*vāyl*) *adj* punctual

punt (pernt) *nt* (pl ~en) point; item, issue; *c* full stop, period; tip

puntesliijper (*pern*-ter-slay-perr) *c* (pl ~s) pencil-sharpener

puntkomma (pernt-*ko*-maa) *c* semicolon

put (pert) *c* (pl ~ten) well

puur (pēwr) *adj* neat; sheer

puzzel (*per*-zerl) *c* (pl ~s) puzzle

pyjama (pee-*Yaa*-maa) *c* (pl ~'s) pyjamas *pl*

Q

quarantaine (kaa-rahn-*tai*-ner) *c* quarantine

quota (*kvōa*-taa) *c* (pl ~'s) quota

R

raad¹ (raat) *c* advice, counsel

raad² (raat) *c* (pl raden) council

raadplegen (*raat*-plāy-gern) *v* consult

raadpleging (*raat*-plāy-gıng) *c* (pl ~en) consultation

raadsel (*raat*-serl) *nt* (pl ~s, ~en) riddle, puzzle; mystery, enigma

raadslid (*raats*-lıt) *nt* (pl -leden) councillor

raadsman (*raats*-mahn) *c* (pl -lieden) counsellor; solicitor

raaf (raaf) *c* (pl raven) raven

raam (raam) *nt* (pl ramen) window

raar (raar) *adj* curious, odd, strange, queer, quaint

rabarber (raa-*bahr*-berr) *c* rhubarb

racket (*reh*-kert) *nt* (pl ~s) racquet

***raden** (*raa*-dern) *v* guess

radiator (raa-dee-*Yaa*-tor) *c* (pl ~s, ~en) radiator

radicaal (raa-dee-*kaal*) *adj* radical

radijs (raa-*dayss*) *c* (pl radijzen) radish

radio (*raa*-dee-*Yōa*) *c* (pl ~'s) wireless, radio

rafelen (*raa*-fer-lern) *v* fray

raffinaderij (rah-fee-naa-der-*ray*) *c* (pl ~en) refinery

rage (*raa*-zher) *c* (pl ~s) craze

raken (*raa*-kern) *v* *hit

raket (raa-*keht*) *c* (pl ~ten) rocket

ramp (rahmp) *c* (pl ~en) calamity, disaster

rampzalig (rahm-*psaa*-lerkh) *adj* disastrous

rand (rahnt) *c* (pl ~en) edge, border; brim, rim, verge

rang (rahng) *c* (pl ~en) rank; class

rangschikken (*rahng*-skhi-kern) *v* arrange; sort, grade

rantsoen (rahnt-*soōn*) *nt* (pl ~en) ration

ranzig (*rahn*-zerkh) *adj* rancid

rapport (rah-*port*) *nt* (pl ~en) report

rapporteren (rah-por-*tāy*-rern) *v* report

rariteit (raa-ree-*tayt*) *c* (pl ~en) curio

ras (rahss) *nt* (pl ~sen) race; breed; **rassen-** racial

rasp (rahsp) *c* (pl ~en) grater

raspen (*rahss*-pern) *v* grate

rat (raht) *c* (pl ~ten) rat

rauw (rou) *adj* raw

ravijn (raa-*vayn*) *nt* (pl ~en) gorge

razen (*raa*-zern) *v* rage

razend (*raa*-zernt) *adj* furious

razernij (raa-zerr-*nay*) *c* rage

reactie (rāy-*Yahk*-see) *c* (pl ~s) reaction

reageren (rāy-Yah-*gāy*-rern) *v* react

recent (rer-*sehnt*) *adj* recent

recept (rer-*sehpt*) *nt* (pl ~en) recipe; prescription

receptie (rer-*sehp*-see) *c* (pl ~s) reception office

receptioniste (rer-sehp-shoā-*niss*-ter) *c* (pl ~s) receptionist

recht¹ (rehkht) *nt* (pl ~en) right; law, justice

recht² (rehkht) *adj* straight

rechtbank (*rehkht*-bahngk) *c* (pl ~en) court

rechtdoor (rehkht-*doār*) *adv* straight on, straight ahead

rechter¹ (*rehkh*-terr) *adj* right-hand

rechter² (*rehkh*-terr) *c* (pl ~s) judge

rechthoek (*rehkht*-hoōk) *c* (pl ~en) oblong, rectangle

rechtopstaand (rehkh-*top*-staant) *adj* erect, upright

rechts (rehkhts) *adj* right-hand, right

rechtschapen (rehkht-*skhaa*-pern) *adj* honourable

rechtstreeks (*rehkh*-strāyks) *adj* direct

rechtszaak (*rehkht*-saak) *c* (pl -zaken) trial

rechtuit (rehkh-*tur^{ew}t*) *adv* straight ahead

rechtvaardig (raykht-*faar*-derkh) *adj* just, righteous, right

rechtvaardigheid (rehkht-*faar*-derkh-hayt) *c* justice

reclame (rer-*klaa*-mer) *c* advertising

reclamespot (rer-*klaa*-mer-spot) *c* (pl ~s) commercial

record (rer-*kawr*) *nt* (pl ~s) record

recreatie (rāy-krāy-*Yaa*-tsee) *c* recreation

recreatiecentrum (rāy-krāy-*Yaa*-tsee-sehn-trerm) *nt* (pl -tra) recreation centre

rector (*rehk*-tor) *c* (pl ~en, ~s) headmaster, principal

reçu (rer-*sēw*) *nt* (pl ~'s) receipt

recycleerbar (ree-sie-*kleer*-bar) *adj* recyclable

recycleren (ree-sie-*klee*-rern) *v* recycle

redakteur (rāy-dahk-*tūrr*) *c* (pl ~en, ~s) editor

redden (*reh*-dern) *v* save, rescue

redder (*reh*-derr) *c* (pl ~s) saviour

redding (*reh*-ding) *c* (pl ~en) rescue

reddingsgordel (*reh*-dings-khor-derl) *c* (pl ~s) lifebelt

rede¹ (*rāy*-der) *c* sense; reason

rede² (*rāy*-der) *c* (pl ~s) speech

redelijk (*rāy*-der-lerk) *adj* reasonable

reden (*rāy*-dern) *c* (pl ~en) reason

redeneren (rāy-der-nāy-rern) v reason

reder (rāy-derr) c (pl ~s) shipowner

redetwisten (rāy-der-tvɪss-tern) v argue

reduceren (rāy-dēw-sāy-rern) v reduce

reductie (rer-derk-see) c (pl ~s) discount, reduction, rebate

reeds (rāyts) adv already

reekalf (rāy-kahlf) nt (pl -kalveren) fawn

reeks (rāyks) c (pl ~en) series; sequence

referentie (rer-fer-rehn-tsee) c (pl ~s) reference

reflector (rer-flehk-tor) c (pl ~s, ~en) reflector

reformatie (rāy-for-maa-tsee) c reformation

regel (rāy-gerl) c (pl ~s) line; rule; **in de ~** as a rule

regelen (rāy-ger-lern) v arrange; settle; regulate

regeling (rāy-ger-lɪng) c (pl ~en) arrangement; settlement; regulation

regelmatig (rāy-gerl-maa-terkh) adj regular

regen (rāy-gern) c rain

regenachtig (rāy-gern-ahkh-terkh) adj rainy

regenboog (rāy-ger-bōakh) c (pl -bogen) rainbow

regenbui (rāy-ger-burᵉʷ) c (pl ~en) shower

regenen (rāy-ger-nern) v rain

regenjas (rāy-ger-ʸahss) c (pl ~sen) mackintosh, raincoat

regeren (rer-gāy-rern) v rule, govern, reign

regering (rer-gāy-rɪng) c (pl ~en) government; reign

regie (rer-gee) c (pl ~s) direction

regime (rer-zheem) nt (pl ~s) régime

regisseren (rāy-gee-sāy-rern) v direct

regisseur (rāy-gee-sūrr) c (pl ~s) director

rector

register (rer-gɪss-terr) nt (pl ~s) record; index

registratie (rāy-gɪss-traa-tsee) c registration

reglement (rāy-gler-mehnt) nt (pl ~en) regulation

rein (rayn) adj pure

reinigen (ray-ner-gern) v clean; **chemisch ~** dry-clean

reiniging (ray-ner-gɪng) c cleaning

reinigingsmiddel (ray-ner-gɪngs-mɪderl) nt (pl ~en) cleaning fluid

reis (rayss) c (pl reizen) journey; trip, voyage

reisagent (rayss-aa-gehnt) c (pl ~en) travel agent

reisbureau (rayss-bēw-rōa) nt (pl ~s) travel agency

reischeque (ray-shehk) c (pl ~s) traveller's cheque

reiskosten (rayss-koss-tern) pl fare

reisplan (rayss-plahn) nt (pl ~nen) itinerary

reisroute (rayss-rōō-ter) c (pl ~s, ~n) itinerary

reisverzekering (rayss-ferr-zāy-ker-rɪng) c travel insurance

reiswieg (rayss-veekh) c (pl ~en) carry-cot

reizen (ray-zern) v travel

reiziger (ray-zer-gerr) c (pl ~s) traveller

rek (rehk) c elasticity

rekbaar (rehk-baar) adj elastic

rekenen (rāy-ker-nern) v reckon

rekening (rāy-ker-nɪng) c (pl ~en) account; bill; check nAm

rekenkunde (rāy-kerng-kern-der) c arithmetic

rekenmachine (ree-kern-ma-sjiner) c calculator

rekken (reh-kern) v stretch

rekruut (rer-krēwt) c (pl rekruten) recruit

rel (rehl) *c* (pl ~len) riot

relatie (rer-*laa*-tsee) *c* (pl ~s) relation; connection

relatief (rer-laa-*teef*) *adj* relative; comparative

reliëf (rerl-*Yehf*) *nt* (pl ~s) relief

relikwie (rer-ler-*kvee*) *c* (pl ~ën) relic

reling (*rāy*-lıng) *c* (pl ~en) rail

rem (rehm) *c* (pl ~men) brake

remlichten (*rehm*-lıkh-tern) *pl* brake lights

remtrommel (*rehm*-tro-mehl) *c* (pl ~s) brake drum

renbaan (*rehn*-baan) *c* (pl -banen) race-course; track; race-track

rendabel (rehn-*daa*-berl) *adj* paying

rendier (*rehn*-deer) *nt* (pl ~en) reindeer

rennen (*reh*-nern) *v* *run

renpaard (*rehn*-paart) *nt* (pl ~en) race-horse

rente (*rehn*-ter) *c* (pl ~n, ~s) interest

reparatie (rāy-paa-*raa*-tsee) *c* (pl ~s) reparation

repareren (rāy-paa-*rāy*-rern) *v* repair, fix; mend

repertoire (rer-pehr-*tvaar*) *nt* (pl ~s) repertory

repeteren (rer-per-*tāy*-rern) *v* rehearse

repetitie (rer-per-*tee*-tsee) *c* (pl ~s) rehearsal

representatief (rer-prāy-zehn-taa-*teef*) *adj* representative

reproduceren (rāy-prōa-dēw-*sāy*-rern) *v* reproduce

reproduktie (rāy-prōa-*derk*-see) *c* (pl ~s) reproduction

reptiel (rehp-*teel*) *nt* (pl ~en) reptile

republiek (rāy-pēw-*bleek*) *c* (pl ~en) republic

republikeins (rāy-pēw-blee-*kayns*) *adj* republican

reputatie (rāy-pēw-*taa*-tsee) *c* reputa-

tion; fame

reserve (rer-*zehr*-ver) *c* (pl ~s) reserve; **reserve-** spare

reserveband (rer-*zehr*-ver-bahnt) *c* (pl ~en) spare tyre

reserveren (rer-zehr-*vāy*-rern) *v* reserve; book

reservering (rer-zehr-*vāy*-ring) *c* (pl ~en) reservation; booking

reservewiel (rer-*zehr*-ver-veel) *nt* (pl ~en) spare wheel

reservoir (rer-zerr-*vvaar*) *nt* (pl ~s) reservoir; container

resoluut (rāy-zōa-*lōōt*) *adj* resolute

respect (reh-*spehkt*) *nt* respect; esteem, regard

respectabel (reh-spehk-*taa*-berl) *adj* respectable

respecteren (reh-spehk-*tāy*-rern) *v* respect

respectievelijk (reh-spehk-*tee*-ver-lerk) *adj* respective

rest (rehst) *c* (pl ~en) rest; remainder; remnant

restant (rehss-*tahnt*) *nt* (pl ~en) remainder; remnant

restaurant (reh-stōa-*rahnt*) *nt* (pl ~s) restaurant

restauratiewagen (rehss-tōa-*raa*-tsee-vaa-gern) *c* (pl ~s) dining-car

restriktie (rer-*strık*-see) *c* (pl ~s) qualification

resultaat (rāy-zerl-*taat*) *nt* (pl -taten) result; outcome, issue

resulteren (rāy-zerl-*tāy*-rern) *v* result

resumé (rāy-zēw-*māy*) *nt* (pl ~s) summary

retour (rer-*tōōr*) round trip *Am*

retourvlucht (rer-*tōōr*-vlerkht) *c* (pl ~en) return flight

reumatiek (rūr-maa-*teek*) *c* rheumatism

reus (rūrss) *c* (pl reuzen) giant

reusachtig (rūr-*zahkh*-terkh) *adj* huge;

gigantic, enormous, immense

revalidatie (rāy-vaa-lee-*daa*-tsee) c re-habilitation

revers (rer-*vair*) c (pl ~) lapel

reviseren (rāy-vee-*zāy*-rern) v overhaul

revolutie (rāy-vōa-*lēw*-tsee) c (pl ~s) revolution

revolutionair (rāy-vōa-lēw-tshōa-*nair*) adj revolutionary

revolver (rer-*vol*-verr) c (pl ~s) gun, revolver

revue (rer-*vēw*) c (pl ~s) revue

rib (rip) c (pl ~ben) rib

ribfluweel (*rip*-flēw-vāyl) nt corduroy

richten (*rikh*-tern) v direct; ~ **op** aim at

richting (*rikh*-ting) c (pl ~en) direction; way

richtingaanwijzer (*rikh*-ting-aan-vay-zerr) c (pl ~s) trafficator, indicator; directional signal Am

richtlijn (*rikht*-layn) c (pl ~en) directive

ridder (*ri*-derr) c (pl ~s) knight

riem (reem) c (pl ~en) belt; strap; lead

riet (reet) nt reed; cane

rif (rif) nt (pl ~fen) reef

rij (ray) c (pl ~en) row, rank; line; file, queue; **in de ~** *staan queue; stand in line Am

rijbaan (*ray*-baan) c (pl -banen) carriageway; roadway nAm

rijbewijs (*ray*-ber-vayss) nt driving licence

*rijden** (*ray*-dern) v *drive; *ride

*rijgen** (*ray*-gern) v thread

rijk[1] (rayk) adj rich; wealthy

rijk[2] (rayk) nt (pl ~en) kingdom, empire; **rijks-** imperial

rijkdom (*rayk*-dom) c (pl ~men) wealth, riches pl

rijm (raym) nt (pl ~en) rhyme

rijp (rayp) adj ripe, mature

rijpheid (*rayp*-hayt) c maturity

rijst (rayst) c rice

rijstrook (*ray*-strōak) c (pl -stroken) lane

rijtuig (*ray*-tur^ew g) nt (pl ~en) carriage; coach

rijweg (*ray*-vehkh) c drive

rijwiel (*ray*-veel) nt (pl ~en) cycle; bicycle

rillen (*ri*-lern) v shiver; tremble

rillerig (*ri*-ler-rerkh) adj shivery

rilling (*ri*-ling) c (pl ~en) chill; shiver, shudder

rimpel (*rim*-perl) c (pl ~s) wrinkle

ring (ring) c (pl ~en) ring

ringweg (*ring*-vehkh) c (pl ~en) bypass

riool (ree-^Y*ōal*) nt (pl riolen) sewer

risico (*ree*-zee-kōa) nt (pl ~'s) risk; chance, hazard

riskant (riss-*kahnt*) adj risky

rit (rit) c (pl ~ten) ride

ritme (*rit*-mer) nt (pl ~n) rhythm

ritssluiting (*rit*-slur^ew -ting) c (pl ~en) zipper, zip

rivaal (ree-*vaal*) c (pl rivalen) rival

rivaliseren (ree-vaa-lee-*zāy*-rern) v rival

rivaliteit (ree-vaa-lee-*tayt*) c rivalry

rivier (ree-*veer*) c (pl ~en) river

riviermonding (ree-*veer*-mon-ding) c (pl ~en) estuary

rivieroever (ree-*veer*-ōō-verr) c (pl ~s) riverside

rob (rop) c (pl ~ben) seal

robijn (rōa-*bayn*) c (pl ~en) ruby

roddelen (*ro*-der-lern) v gossip

roede (*rōō*-der) c (pl ~n) rod

roeiboot (*rōō*^ee -bōat) c (pl -boten) rowing-boat

roeien (*rōō*^ee -ern) v row

roeiriem (*rōō*^ee -reem) c (pl ~en) oar

roem (rōōm) c glory; celebrity, fame

Roemeen (rōō-*māyn*) c (pl -menen)

Rumanian

Roemeens (rōō-*mᾱyns*) *adj* Rumanian

Roemenië (rōō-*mᾱy*-nee-ᵞer) Rumania

roep (rōōp) *c* call, cry

* roepen (*rōō*-pern) *v* call; cry, shout

roer (rōōr) *nt* rudder, helm

roeren (*rōō*-rern) *v* stir

roerend (*rōō*-rernt) *adj* movable

roest (rōōst) *nt* rust

roestig (*rōōss*-terkh) *adj* rusty

rok (rok) *c* (pl ~ken) skirt

roken (*rōᾱ*-kern) *v* smoke

roker (*rōᾱ*-kerr) *c* (pl ~s) smoker

rol (rol) *c* (pl ~len) roll

rolgordijn (*rol*-gor-dayn) *nt* (pl ~en) blind

rollen (*ro*-lern) *v* roll

rolstoel (*rol*-stōōl) *c* (pl ~en) wheelchair

roltrap (*rol*-trahp) *c* (pl ~pen) escalator

roman (rōᾱ-*mahn*) *c* (pl ~s) novel

romance (rōᾱ-*mahng*-ser) *c* (pl ~s, ~n) romance

romanschrijver (rōᾱ-*mahn*-skhray-verr) *c* (pl ~s) novelist

romantisch (rōᾱ-*mahn*-teess) *adj* romantic

romig (*rōᾱ*-merkh) *adj* creamy

rommel (*ro*-merl) *c* mess; litter; trash, junk

rond (ront) *adj* round; *prep* around

ronde (*ron*-der) *c* (pl ~n, ~s) round

rondom (ront-*om*) *adv* around; *prep* round

rondreis (*ront*-rayss) *c* (pl ~reizen) tour

rondreizend (*ront*-ray-zernt) *adj* itinerant

* rondtrekken (*ront*-treh-kern) *v* tramp

* rondzwerven (*ront*-svehr-vern) *v* wander

röntgenfoto (*rernt*-gern-fōᾱ-tōᾱ) *c* (pl ~'s) X-ray

rood (rōᾱt) *adj* red

roodborstje (*rōᾱt*-bor-sher) *nt* (pl ~s) robin

roodkoper (*rōᾱt*-kōᾱ-perr) *nt* copper

roof (rōᾱf) *c* robbery

roofdier (*rōᾱf*-deer) *nt* (pl ~en) beast of prey

rook (rōᾱk) *c* smoke

rookcoupé (*rōᾱ*-kōō-pᾱy) *c* (pl ~s) smoker

rookkamer (*rōᾱ*-kaa-merr) *c* smoking-room

room (rōᾱm) *c* cream

roomkleurig (rōᾱm-*klūr*-rerkh) *adj* cream

rooms-katholiek (rōᾱms-kah-tōᾱ-*leek*) *adj* Roman Catholic

roos[1] (rōᾱss) *c* (pl rozen) rose

roos[2] (rōᾱss) *c* dandruff

rooster (*rōᾱ*-sterr) *nt* (pl ~s) grate; schedule

roosteren (*rōᾱ*-ster-rern) *v* grill, roast

rot (rot) *adj* rotten

rotan (*rōᾱ*-tahn) *nt* rattan

rotonde (rōᾱ-*ton*-der) *c* (pl ~s) roundabout

rots (rots) *c* (pl ~en) rock; cliff

rotsachtig (*rot*-sahkh-terkh) *adj* rocky

rotsblok (*rots*-blok) *c* (pl ~ken) boulder

rouge (rōō-zher) *c/nt* rouge

roulette (rōō-*leh*-ter) *c* roulette

route (*rōō*-ter) *c* (pl ~s) route

routine (rōō-*tee*-ner) *c* routine

rouw (rou) *c* mourning

royaal (rōᾱ-ᵞaal) *adj* generous; liberal

roze (raw-zer) *adj* rose, pink

rozenkrans (*rōᾱ*-zer-krahns) *c* (pl ~en) rosary, beads *pl*

rozijn (rōᾱ-*zayn*) *c* (pl ~en) raisin

rubber (*rer*-berr) *nt* rubber

rubriek (rēw-*breek*) *c* (pl ~en) column

rug (rerkh) *c* (pl ~gen) back

ruggegraat (*rer*-ger-graat) *c* spine, backbone

rugpijn (rerkh-payn) c backache

rugzak (rerkh-sahk) c (pl ~ken) rucksack

*__ruiken__ (rur^{ew}-kern) v *smell

ruil (rur^{ew}l) c exchange

ruilen (rur^{ew}-lern) v exchange; swap

ruim¹ (rur^{ew}m) adj broad, large; roomy, spacious

ruim² (rur^{ew}m) nt (pl ~en) hold

ruimte (rur^{ew}m-ter) c room, space

ruïne (rēw-vee-ner) c (pl ~s) ruins

ruïneren (rēw-vee-na̅y̅-rern) v ruin

ruit (rur^{ew}t) c (pl ~en) check; pane

ruitenwisser (rur^{ew}-ter-vı-serr) c (pl ~s) windscreen wiper; windshield wiper Am

ruiter (rur^{ew}-terr) c (pl ~s) horseman; rider

ruk (rerk) c (pl ~ken) tug, wrench

rumoer (rēw-mo̅o̅r) nt noise

rundvlees (rernt-fla̅yss) nt beef

Rus (rerss) c (pl ~sen) Russian

Rusland (rerss-lahnt) Russia

Russisch (rer-seess) adj Russian

rust (rerst) c rest; quiet; half-time

rusteloosheid (rerss-ter-lo̅a̅ss-hayt) c unrest

rusten (rerss-tern) v rest

rusthuis (rerst-hur^{ew}ss) nt (pl -huizen) rest-home

rustiek (rerss-teek) adj rustic

rustig (rerss-terkh) adj calm, quiet; restful, tranquil

ruw (rēw^{oo}) adj rough, harsh

ruzie (rēw-zee) c (pl ~s) row, quarrel, dispute; ~ **maken** quarrel

S

saai (saa^{ee}) adj dull, boring

sacharine (sah-khaa-ree-ner) c saccharin

saffier (sah-feer) nt sapphire

salaris (saa-laa-rıss) nt (pl ~sen) salary; pay

saldo (sahl-do̅a̅) nt (pl ~'s, saldi) balance

salon (saa-lon) c (pl ~s) drawing-room, lounge; salon

samen (saa-mern) adv together

*__samenbinden__ (saa-mer-bın-dern) v bundle

*__samenbrengen__ (saa-mer-breh-ngern) v combine

samenhang (saa-mer-hahng) c coherence

samenleving (saa-mer-la̅y̅-vıng) c (pl ~en) community

samenloop (saa-mer-lo̅a̅p) c concurrence

samenstellen (saa-mer-steh-lern) v compose, compile

samenstelling (saa-mer-steh-lıng) c (pl ~en) composition

*__samenvallen__ (saa-mer-vah-lern) v coincide

samenvatting (saa-mer-vah-tıng) c (pl ~en) résumé, summary

samenvoegen (saa-mer-vo̅o̅-gern) v join

samenwerking (saa-mer-vehr-kıng) c co-operation

*__samenzweren__ (saa-mer-zva̅y̅-rern) v conspire

samenzwering (saa-mer-zva̅y̅-rıng) c (pl ~en) plot

sanatorium (saa-naa-to̅a̅-ree-^yerm) nt (pl ~s, -ria) sanatorium

sandaal (sahn-daal) c (pl -dalen) sandal

sanitair (saa-nee-tair) adj sanitary

Saoedi-Arabië (saa-o̅o̅-dee-aa-raa-bee-^yer) Saudi Arabia

Saoedi-Arabisch (saa-o̅o̅-dee-aa-raa-beess) adj Saudi Arabian

sap (sahp) nt (pl ~pen) juice

sappig (*sah*-perkh) *adj* juicy

sardine (sahr-*dee*-ner) *c* (pl ~s) sardine

satelliet (saa-ter-*leet*) *c* (pl ~en) satellite

satijn (saa-*tayn*) *nt* satin

sauna (*sou*-naa) *c* (pl ~'s) sauna

saus (souss) *c* (pl sauzen) sauce

Scandinavië (skahn-dee-*naa*-vee-ᵉr) Scandinavia

Scandinaviër (skahn-dee-*naa*-vee-ᵉrr) *c* (pl ~s) Scandinavian

Scandinavisch (skahn-dee-*naa*-veess) *adj* Scandinavian

scène (*sai*-ner) *c* (pl ~s) scene

schaafwond (*skhaaf*-vont) *c* (pl ~en) graze

schaak! (skhaak) check!

schaakbord (*skhaak*-bort) *nt* (pl ~en) checkerboard *nAm*

schaakspel (*skhaak*-spehl) *nt* chess

schaal (skhaal) *c* (pl schalen) dish; bowl; scale

schaaldier (*skhaal*-deer) *nt* (pl ~en) shellfish

schaamte (*skhaam*-ter) *c* shame

schaap (skhaap) *nt* (pl schapen) sheep

schaar (skhaar) *c* (pl scharen) scissors *pl*

schaars (skhaars) *adj* scarce

schaarste (*skhaar*-ster) *c* scarcity

schaats (skhaats) *c* (pl ~en) skate

schaatsen (*skhaat*-sern) *v* skate

schade (*skhaa*-der) *c* damage; harm, mischief

schadelijk (*skhaa*-der-lerk) *adj* harmful; hurtful

schadeloosstelling (*skhaa*-der-lōa-steh-lɪng) *c* (pl ~en) indemnity

schaden (*skhaa*-dern) *v* harm

schadevergoeding (*skhaa*-der-verr-gōo-dɪng) *c* (pl ~en) compensation, indemnity

schaduw (*skhaa*-dēw°°) *c* (pl ~en) shade; shadow

schaduwrijk (*skhaa*-dēw°°-rayk) *adj* shady

schakel (*skhaa*-kerl) *c* (pl ~s) link

schakelaar (*skhaa*-ker-laar) *c* (pl ~s) switch

schakelbord (*skhaa*-kerl-bort) *nt* switchboard

schakelen (*skhaa*-ker-lern) *v* change gear

zich schamen (*skhaa*-mern) *be ashamed

schandaal (skhahn-*daal*) *nt* (pl -dalen) scandal

schande (*skhahn*-deh) *c* disgrace, shame

schapevlees (*skhaa*-per-vlāyss) *nt* mutton

scharnier (skhahr-*neer*) *nt* (pl ~en) hinge

schat (skhaht) *c* (pl ~ten) treasure; darling

schatkist (*skhaht*-kɪst) *c* treasury

schatten (*skhah*-tern) *v* evaluate, estimate, value; appreciate

schatting (*skhah*-tɪng) *c* (pl ~en) estimate; appreciation

schedel (*skhāy*-derl) *c* (pl ~s) skull

scheef (skhāyf) *adj* slanting

scheel (skhāyl) *adj* cross-eyed

scheepswerf (*skhāyps*-vehrf) *c* (pl -werven) shipyard

scheepvaart (*skhāyp*-faart) *c* navigation

scheepvaartlijn (*skhāyp*-faart-layn) *c* (pl ~en) shipping line

scheerapparaat (*skhāyr*-ah-paa-raat) *nt* (pl -raten) safety-razor, electric razor, shaver

scheercrème (*skhāyr*-kraim) *c* (pl ~s) shaving-cream

scheerkwast (*skhāyr*-kvahst) *c* (pl ~en) shaving-brush

scheermesje (*skhāyr*-meh-sher) *nt* (pl

~s) razor-blade

scheerzeep (*skhayr-zayp*) c shaving-soap

* **scheiden** (*skhay-dern*) v separate; divide, part; divorce

scheiding (*skhay-ding*) c (pl ~en) division; parting

scheidsrechter (*skhayts-rehkh-terr*) c (pl ~s) umpire

scheikunde (*skhay-kern-der*) c chemistry

scheikundig (skhay-*kern*-derkh) adj chemical

* **schelden** (*skhehl*-dern) v scold

schelm (skhehlm) c (pl ~en) rascal

schelp (skhehlp) c (pl ~en) shell

schelvis (*skhehl*-viss) c haddock

schema (*skhay*-maa) nt (pl ~'s, ~ta) diagram; scheme

schemering (*skhay*-mer-ring) c twilight

schending (*skhehn*-ding) c (pl ~en) violation

* **schenken** (*skhehng*-kern) v pour; donate

schenking (*skhehng*-king) c (pl ~en) donation

* **scheppen** (*skheh*-pern) v create

schepsel (*skhehp*-serl) nt (pl ~s) creature

zich * scheren (*skhay*-rern) shave

scherm (skhehrm) nt (pl ~en) screen

schermen (*skhehr*-mern) v fence

scherp (skhehrp) adj sharp; keen

schets (skhehts) c (pl ~en) sketch

schetsboek (*skhehts*-book) nt (pl ~en) sketch-book

schetsen (*skheht*-sern) v sketch

scheur (skhurr) c (pl ~en) tear

scheuren (*skhur*-rern) v rip, *tear

schiereiland (*skheer*-ay-lahnt) nt peninsula

* **schieten** (*skhee*-tern) v *shoot, fire

schietschijf (*skheet*-skhayf) c (pl

-schijven) mark

schijf (skhayf) c (pl schijven) disc

schijn (skhayn) c semblance

schijnbaar (*skhaym*-baar) adj apparent

* **schijnen** (*skhay*-nern) v appear, seem; *shine

schijnheilig (skhayn-*hay*-lerkh) adj hypocritical

schijnwerper (*skhayn*-vehr-perr) c (pl ~s) spotlight, searchlight

schikken (*skhi*-kern) v suit

schikking (*skhi*-king) c (pl ~en) settlement

schil (skhil) c (pl ~len) skin; peel

schilder (*skhil*-derr) c (pl ~s) painter

schilderachtig (*skhil*-derr-ahkh-terkh) adj scenic, picturesque

schilderen (*skhil*-der-rern) v paint

schilderij (skhil-der-*ray*) nt (pl ~en) painting, picture

schildpad (*skhil*-paht) c (pl ~den) turtle

schilfer (*skhil*-ferr) c (pl ~s) chip

schillen (*skhi*-lern) c peel

schimmel (*skhi*-merl) c (pl ~s) mildew

schip (skhip) nt (pl schepen) ship; boat, vessel

schitterend (*skhi*-ter-rernt) adj brilliant, splendid

schittering (*skhi*-ter-ring) c (pl ~en) glare

schoeisel (*skhoo*ᵉᵉ-serl) nt footwear

schoen (skhoon) c (pl ~en) shoe

schoenmaker (*skhoon*-maa-kerr) c (pl ~s) shoemaker

schoensmeer (*skhoon*-smayr) c shoe polish

schoenveter (*skhoon*-fay-terr) c (pl ~s) shoe-lace

schoenwinkel (*skhoon*-ving-kerl) c (pl ~s) shoe-shop

schoft (skhoft) c (pl ~en) bastard

schok (skhok) c (pl ~ken) shock

schokbreker (*skhok*-brāy-kerr) *c* (pl
~s) shock absorber

schokken (*skho*-kern) *v* shock

schol (skhol) *c* (pl ~len) plaice

schommel (*skho*-merl) *c* (pl ~s) swing

schommelen (*skho*-mer-lern) *v* rock,
*swing

school (skhōal) *c* (pl scholen) school;
college; **middelbare** ~ secondary
school

schoolbank (*skhōal*-bahngk) *c* (pl
~en) desk

schoolbord (*skhōal*-bort) *nt* (pl ~en)
blackboard

schoolhoofd (*skhōal*-hōaft) *nt* (pl
~en) headmaster, head teacher

schooljongen (*skhōal*-ʸo-ngern) *c* (pl
~s) schoolboy

schoolmeester (*skhōal*-māyss-terr) *c*
(pl ~s) teacher

schoolmeisje (*skhōal*-may-sher) *nt* (pl
~s) schoolgirl

schoolslag (*skhōal*-slahkh) *c* breaststroke

schooltas (*skhōal*-tahss) *c* (pl ~sen)
satchel

schoon (skhōan) *adj* clean

schoonheid (*skhōan*-hayt) *c* (pl -he-
den) beauty

schoonheidsbehandeling (*skhōan*-
hayts-ber-hahn-der-ling) *c* (pl ~en)
beauty treatment

schoonheidsmasker (*skhōan*-hayts-
mahss-kerr) *nt* (pl ~s) face-pack

schoonheidsmiddelen (*skhōan*-hayts-
mi-der-lern) *pl* cosmetics *pl*

schoonheidssalon (*skhōan*-hayts-saa-
lon) *c* (pl ~s) beauty salon, beauty
parlour

schoonmaak (*skhōa*-maak) *c* cleaning

schoonmaken (*skhōa*-maa-kern) *v*
clean

schoonmoeder (*skhōa*-mōō-derr) *c* (pl
~s) mother-in-law

schoonouders (*skhōan*-ou-derrs) *pl*
parents-in-law *pl*

schoonvader (*skhōan*-vaa-derr) *c* (pl
~s) father-in-law

schoonzoon (*skhōan*-zōan) *c* (pl -zo-
nen) son-in-law

schoonzuster (*skhōan*-zerss-terr) *c* (pl
~s) sister-in-law

schoorsteen (*skhōar*-stāyn) *c* (pl -ste-
nen) chimney

schop (skhop) *c* (pl ~pen) kick;
spade, shovel

schoppen (*skho*-pern) *v* kick

schor (skhor) *adj* hoarse

schorsen (*skhor*-sern) *v* suspend

schort (skhort) *c* (pl ~en) apron

Schot (skhot) *c* (pl ~ten) Scot

schot (skhot) *nt* (pl ~en) shot

schotel (*skhōa*-terl) *c* (pl ~s) dish;
schoteltje *nt* saucer

Schotland (*skhot*-lahnt) Scotland

Schots (skhots) *adj* Scottish, Scotch

schouder (*skhou*-derr) *c* (pl ~s) shoulder

schouwburg (*skhou*-berrkh) *c* (pl ~en)
theatre

schouwspel (*skhou*-spehl) *nt* (pl ~en)
spectacle

schram (skhrahm) *c* (pl ~men)
scratch

schrappen (*skhrah*-pern) *v* scrape

schrede (*skhrāy*-der) *c* (pl ~n) pace

schreeuw (skhrāyᵒᵒ) *c* (pl ~en)
scream, cry, shout

schreeuwen (*skhrāyᵒᵒ*-ern) *v* scream,
cry, shout

schriftelijk (*skhrif*-ter-lerk) *adj* written; *adv* in writing

schrijfbehoeften (*skhrayf*-ber-hōōf-
tern) *pl* stationery

schrijfblok (*skhrayf*-blok) *nt* (pl ~ken)
writing-pad

schrijfmachine (*skhrayf*-mah-shee-ner)
c (pl ~s) typewriter

schrijfmachinepapier (*skhrayf*-mah-shee-ner-paa-peer) *nt* typing paper

schrijfpapier (*skhrayf*-paa-peer) *nt* notepaper; writing-paper

schrijftafel (*skhrayf*-taa-ferl) *c* (pl ~s) bureau

schrijn (skhrayn) *c* (pl ~en) shrine

*schrijven (*skhray*-vern) *v* *write

schrijver (*skhray*-vehr) *c* (pl ~s) author, writer

schrik (skhrɪk) *c* fright, scare; ~ *aanjagen terrify

schrikkeljaar (*skhrɪ*-kerl-Yaar) *nt* leap-year

*schrikken (*skhrɪ*-kern) *v* *be frightened; *doen ~ frighten, scare

schrobben (*skhro*-bern) *v* scrub

schroef (skhrōōf) *c* (pl schroeven) screw; propeller

schroefsleutel (*skhrōōf*-slʉr-terl) *c* (pl ~s) spanner

schroevedraaier (*skhrōō*-ver-draa-Yerr) *c* (pl ~s) screw-driver

schroeven (*skhrōō*-vern) *v* screw

schroot (skhrōāt) *nt* scrap-iron

schub (skherp) *c* (pl ~ben) scale

schudden (*skher*-dern) *v* *shake; shuffle

schuifdeur (*skhurew*f-dʉrr) *c* (pl ~en) sliding door

schuilplaats (*skhurew*l-plaats) *c* (pl ~en) cover; shelter

schuim (skhurewm) *nt* froth, lather, foam

schuimen (*skhurew*m-ern) *v* foam

schuimrubber (*skhurew*m-rer-berr) *nt* foam-rubber

schuin (skhurewn) *adj* slanting

*schuiven (*skhurew*-vern) *v* push

schuld¹ (skherlt) *c* guilt; fault, blame; de ~ *geven aan blame

schuld² (skherlt) *c* (pl ~en) debt

schuldeiser (*skherlt*·ay-serr) *c* (pl ~s) creditor

schuldig (*skherl*-derkh) *adj* guilty; ~ *bevinden convict; ~ *zijn owe

schuur (skhewr) *c* (pl schuren) barn; shed

schuurpapier (*skhewr*-paa-peer) *nt* sandpaper

schuw (skhew∞) *adj* shy

scoren (*skōā*-rern) *v* score

seconde (ser-*kon*-der) *c* (pl ~n) second

secretaresse (sɪ-krer-taa-*reh*-ser) *c* (pl ~n) secretary

secretaris (sɪ-krer-*taa*-rerss) *c* (pl ~sen) secretary; clerk

sectie (*sehk*-see) *c* (pl ~s) section

secundair (sāy-kern-*dair*) *adj* secondary

secuur (ser-*kewr*) *adj* precise

sedert (*sāy*-derrt) *prep* since

sein (sayn) *nt* (pl ~en) signal

seinen (*say*-nern) *v* signal

seizoen (say-*zōōn*) *nt* (pl ~en) season; buiten het ~ off season

seksualiteit (sehk-sew-vaa-lee-*tayt*) *c* sexuality

seksueel (sehk-sew-*vāyl*) *adj* sexual

selderij (*sehl*-der-ray) *c* celery

select (ser-*lehkt*) *adj* select

selecteren (sāy-lehk-*tāy*-rern) *v* select

selectie (sāy-*lehk*-see) *c* selection

senaat (ser-*naat*) *c* senate

senator (ser-*naa*-tor) *c* (pl ~en) senator

seniel (ser-*neel*) *adj* senile

sensatie (sehn-*zaa*-tsee) *c* (pl ~s) sensation

sensationeel (sehn-zaa-tshōā-*nāyl*) *adj* sensational

sentimenteel (sehn-tee-mehn-*tāyl*) *adj* sentimental

september (sehp-*tehm*-berr) September

septisch (*sehp*-teess) *adj* septic

serie (*sāy*-ree) *c* (pl ~s) series

serieus (sāy-ree-*y*ūrss) *adj* serious

serum (sāy-rerm) *nt* (pl ~s, sera) serum

serveerster (sehr-vāy-sterr) *c* (pl ~s) waitress

servet (sehr-*veht*) *nt* (pl ~ten) napkin, serviette

sfeer (sfāyr) *c* atmosphere; sphere

shag (shehk) *c* cigarette tobacco

shampoo (shahm-pōa) *c* shampoo

Siam (see-*y*ahm) Siam

Siamees (see-*y*aa-*māyss*) *adj* Siamese

sifon (see-*fon*) *c* (pl ~s) syphon, siphon

sigaar (see-*gaar*) *c* (pl sigaren) cigar

sigarenwinkel (see-*gaa*-rer-vɪng-kerl) *c* (pl ~s) cigar shop

sigarenwinkelier (see-*gaa*-rer-vɪng-ker-leer) *c* (pl ~s) tobacconist

sigaret (see-gaa-*reht*) *c* (pl ~ten) cigarette

sigarettenkoker (see-gaa-*reh*-ter-kōa-kehr) *c* (pl ~s) cigarette-case

sigarettepijpje (see-gaa-*reh*-ter-payp-*y*er) *nt* (pl ~s) cigarette-holder

signaal (see-*ñaal*) *nt* (pl -nalen) signal

signalement (see-ñaa-ler-*mehnt*) *nt* (pl ~en) description

simpel (sɪm-perl) *adj* simple

sinaasappel (*see*-naa-sah-perl) *c* (pl ~en, ~s) orange

sinds (sɪns) *conj* since

sindsdien (sɪns-*deen*) *adv* since

singel (sɪ-ngerl) *c* (pl ~s) canal

sirene (see-*rāy*-ner) *c* (pl ~s) siren

siroop (see-*rōap*) *c* syrup

situatie (see-tēw-*vaa*-tsee) *c* (pl ~s) situation

sjaal (shaal) *c* (pl ~s) shawl; scarf

skelet (sker-*leht*) *nt* (pl ~ten) skeleton

ski (skee) *c* (pl ~'s) ski

skibroek (*skee*-brōok) *c* (pl ~en) ski pants

skiën (*skee*-*y*ern) *v* ski

skiër (*skee*-*y*err) *c* (pl ~s) skier

skilift (*skee*-lɪft) *c* (pl ~en) ski-lift

skischoenen (*skee*-skhōō-nern) *pl* ski boots

skistokken (*skee*-sto-kern) *pl* ski sticks; ski poles *Am*

sla (slaa) *c* lettuce; salad

***slaan** (slaan) *v* *beat; *hit, *strike; smack, slap

slaap¹ (slaap) *c* sleep; **in ~** asleep

slaap² (slaap) *c* (pl slapen) temple

slaapkamer (*slaap*-kaa-merr) *c* (pl ~s) bedroom

slaappil (*slaa*-pɪl) *c* (pl ~len) sleeping-pill

slaapwagen (*slaap*-vaa-gern) *c* (pl ~s) sleeping-car

slaapzaal (*slaap*-saal) *c* (pl -zalen) dormitory

slaapzak (*slaap*-sahk) *c* (pl ~ken) sleeping-bag

slachtoffer (*slahkht*-o-ferr) *nt* (pl ~s) victim; casualty

slag¹ (slahkh) *c* (pl ~en) blow; battle

slag² (slahkh) *nt* sort

slagader (*slahkh*-aa-derr) *c* (pl ~s) artery

slagboom (*slahkh*-bōam) *c* (pl -bomen) barrier

slagen (*slaa*-gern) *v* manage, succeed; pass

slager (*slaa*-gerr) *c* (pl ~s) butcher

slagzin (*slahkh*-sɪn) *c* (pl ~nen) slogan

slak (slahk) *c* (pl ~ken) snail

slang (slahng) *c* (pl ~en) snake

slank (slahngk) *adj* slim, slender

slaolie (*slaa*-ōa-lee) *c* salad-oil

slap (slahp) *adj* limp; weak

slapeloos (*slaa*-per-lōass) *adj* sleepless

slapeloosheid (slaa-per-*lōass*-hayt) *c* insomnia

***slapen** (*slaa*-pern) *v* *sleep

slaperig (*slaa*-per-rerkh) *adj* sleepy

slecht (slehkht) *adj* bad; poor; ill;
 wicked, evil; **slechter** worse;
 slechtst worst
slechts (slehkhts) *adv* only, merely
slede (*slāy*-der) *c* (pl ~n) sledge
slee (slāy) *c* (pl ~ën) sleigh, sledge
sleepboot (*slāy*-bōat) *c* (pl -boten) tug
slepen (*slāy*-pern) *v* drag, haul; tug,
 tow
sleutel (*slūr*-terl) *c* (pl ~s) key;
 wrench
sleutelbeen (*slūr*-terl-bāyn) *nt* (pl
 -beenderen, -benen) collarbone
sleutelgat (*slūr*-terl-gaht) *nt* (pl ~en)
 keyhole
***slijpen** (*slay*-pern) *v* sharpen
slijterij (slay-ter-*ray*) *c* (pl ~en) off-licence
slikken (*sli*-kern) *v* swallow
slim (slim) *adj* clever
slip (slip) *c* (pl ~s) briefs *pl*; panties
 pl
slippen (*sli*-pern) *v* slip; skid
slof (slof) *c* (pl ~fen) slipper; carton
slokje (*slok*-ᵞer) *nt* (pl ~s) sip
sloot (slōat) *c* (pl sloten) ditch
slopen (*slōa*-pern) *v* demolish
slordig (*slor*-derkh) *adj* untidy;
 slovenly, sloppy, careless
slot¹ (slot) *nt* (pl ~en) lock; castle;
 op ~ *doen lock
slot² (slot) *nt* end, issue
sluier (*slur*ᵉʷ-err) *c* (pl ~s) veil
sluipschutter (*slur*ᵉʷp-skher-terr) *c* (pl
 ~s) sniper
sluis (*slur*ᵉʷss) *c* (pl sluizen) lock,
 sluice
***sluiten** (*slur*ᵉʷ-tern) *v* close, *shut;
 fasten
sluiting (*slur*ᵉʷ-ting) *c* (pl ~en)
 fastener
sluw (slewᵒᵒ) *adj* cunning
smaak (smaak) *c* (pl smaken) taste;
 flavour

smakelijk (*smaa*-ker-lerk) *adj* savoury,
 tasty; appetizing
smakeloos (*smaa*-ker-lōass) *adj* tasteless
smaken (*smaa*-kern) *v* taste
smal (smahl) *adj* narrow
smaragd (smaa-*rahkht*) *nt* emerald
smart (smahrt) *c* (pl ~en) grief
smartlap (*smahrt*-lahp) *c* (pl ~pen)
 tear-jerker
smeerolie (*smāyr*-ōa-lee) *c* lubrication
 oil
smeersysteem (*smāyr*-see-stāym) *nt*
 lubrication system
smeken (*smāy*-kern) *v* beg
***smelten** (*smehl*-tern) *v* melt
smeren (*smāy*-rern) *v* lubricate, grease
smerig (*smāy*-rerkh) *adj* dirty; foul,
 filthy
smering (*smāy*-ring) *c* lubrication
smet (smeht) *c* (pl ~ten) blot
smid (smit) *c* (pl smeden) smith,
 blacksmith
smoking (*smōa*-king) *c* (pl ~s) dinner-
 jacket; tuxedo *nAm*
smokkelen (*smo*-ker-lern) *v* smuggle
snaar (snaar) *c* (pl snaren) string
snavel (*snaa*-verl) *c* (pl ~s) beak
snee (snāy) *c* (pl ~ën) cut; slice
sneeuw (snāyᵒᵒ) *c* snow
sneeuwen (*snāy*ᵒᵒ-ern) *v* snow
sneeuwslik (*snāy*ᵒᵒ-slik) *nt* slush
sneeuwstorm (*snāy*ᵒᵒ-storm) *c* (pl
 ~en) snowstorm, blizzard
snel (snehl) *adj* fast, swift, rapid
snelheid (*snehl*-hayt) *c* (pl -heden)
 speed; **maximum ~** speed limit
snelheidsbeperking (*snehl*-hayts-ber-
 pehr-king) *c* speed limit
snelheidsmeter (*snehl*-hayts-māy-terr)
 c speedometer
snelheidsovertreding (*snehl*-hayts-ōa-
 verr-trāy-ding) *c* speeding
snelkookpan (*snehl*-kōak-pahn) *c* (pl

~nen) pressure-cooker

snellen (*sneh*-lern) *v* dash

sneltrein (*snehl*-trayn) *c* (pl ~en) express train

snelweg (*snehl*-vehkh) *c* (pl ~en) motorway

*snijden (*snay*-dern) *v* *cut; carve

snijwond (*snay*-vont) *c* (pl ~en) cut

snipper (*sni*-perr) *c* (pl ~s) scrap

snoek (snook) *c* (pl ~en) pike

snoep (snoop) *nt* sweets; candy *nAm*

snoepgoed (*snoop*-khoot) *nt* sweets; candy *nAm*

snoepje (*snoop*-Yer) *nt* (pl ~s) sweet; candy *nAm*

snoepwinkel (*snoop*-ving-kerl) *c* (pl ~s) sweetshop; candy store *Am*

snoer (snoor) *nt* (pl ~en) line, cord; flex; electric cord

snor (snor) *c* (pl ~ren) moustache

snorkel (*snor*-kerl) *c* (pl ~s) snorkel

snugger (*snur*-gerr) *adj* bright

snuit (snur^{ew}t) *c* (pl ~en) snout

snurken (*snerr*-kern) *v* snore

sociaal (soa-*shaal*) *adj* social

socialisme (soa-shaa-*liss*-mer) *nt* socialism

socialist (soa-shaa-*list*) *c* (pl ~en) socialist

socialistisch (soa-shaa-*liss*-teess) *adj* socialist

sociëteit (soa-see-Yer-*tayt*) *c* (pl ~en) club

sodawater (*soa*-daa-vaa-terr) *nt* sodawater

soep (soop) *c* (pl ~en) soup

soepbord (*soo*-bort) *nt* (pl ~en) soupplate

soepel (*soo*-perl) *adj* supple, flexible

soeplepel (*soop*-lāy-perl) *c* (pl ~s) soup-spoon

sofa (*soa*-faa) *c* (pl ~'s) sofa

sok (sok) *c* (pl ~ken) sock

soldaat (sol-*daat*) *c* (pl -daten) soldier

soldeerbout (sol-*dāy*r-bout) *c* (pl ~en) soldering-iron

solderen (sol-*dāy*-rern) *v* solder

solide (soa-*lee*-der) *adj* (pl ~en) solid

solitair (soa-lee-*tehr*) *adj* solitary

sollicitatie (so-lee-see-*taa*-tsee) *c* (pl ~s) application

solliciteren (so-lee-see-*tāy*-rern) *v* apply

som (som) *c* (pl ~men) sum; amount; **ronde ~** lump sum

somber (*som*-berr) *adj* gloomy, sombre

sommige (*so*-mer-ger) *pron* some

soms (soms) *adv* sometimes

soort (soart) *c/nt* (pl ~en) sort, kind; breed, species

sorteren (sor-*tāy*-rern) *v* assort, sort

sortering (sor-*tāy*-ring) *c* (pl ~en) assortment

souterrain (*soo*-ter-rang) *nt* (pl ~s) basement

souvenir (*soo*-ver-neer) *nt* (pl ~s) souvenir; **souvenirwinkel** souvenir shop

spaak (spaak) *c* (pl spaken) spoke

Spaans (spaans) *adj* Spanish

spaarbank (*spaar*-bahngk) *c* (pl ~en) savings bank

spaargeld (*spaar*-gehlt) *nt* savings *pl*

spaarzaam (*spaar*-zaam) *adj* economical

spade (*spaa*-der) *c* (pl ~n) spade

spalk (spahlk) *c* (pl ~en) splint

Spanjaard (*spah*-ñaart) *c* (pl ~en) Spaniard

Spanje (*spah*-ñer) Spain

spannend (*spah*-nernt) *adj* exciting

spanning (*spah*-ning) *c* (pl ~en) tension; pressure, strain, stress

sparen (*spaa*-rern) *v* save; economize

spat (spaht) *c* (pl ~ten) stain, spot, speck

spatader (*spaht*-aa-derr) *c* (pl ~s,

~en) varicose vein

spatbord (*spaht*-bort) *nt* (pl ~en) mud-guard

spatiëren (spaa-*tshāy*-rern) *v* space

spatten (*spah*-tern) *v* splash

specerij (spāy-ser-*ray*) *c* (pl ~en) spice

speciaal (spāy-*shaal*) *adj* special; particular, peculiar

zich specialiseren (spāy-shaa-lee-*zāy*-rern) specialize

specialist (spāy-shaa-*list*) *c* (pl ~en) specialist

specialiteit (spāy-shaa-lee-*tayt*) *c* (pl ~en) speciality

specifiek (spāy-see-*feek*) *adj* specific

specimen (*spāy*-see-mehn) *nt* (pl ~s) specimen

speculeren (spāy-kēw-*lāy*-rern) *v* speculate

speeksel (*spāyk*-serl) *nt* spit

speelgoed (*spāyl*-gōōt) *nt* toy

speelgoedwinkel (*spāyl*-gōōt-ving-kerl) *c* (pl ~s) toyshop

speelkaart (*spāyl*-kaart) *c* (pl ~en) playing-card

speelplaats (*spāyl*-plaats) *c* (pl ~en) playground

speelterrein (*spāyl*-teh-rayn) *nt* (pl ~en) recreation ground

speer (spāyr) *c* (pl speren) spear

spek (spehk) *nt* bacon

spel[1] (spehl) *nt* (pl ~en) game

spel[2] (spehl) *nt* (pl ~len) play

speld (spehlt) *c* (pl ~en) pin

spelen (*spāy*-lern) *v* play

speler (*spāy*-lerr) *c* (pl ~s) player

spellen (*speh*-lern) *v* *spell

spelling (*speh*-ling) *c* spelling

spelonk (spāy-*longk*) *c* (pl ~en) cave

spiegel (*spee*-gerl) *c* (pl ~s) looking-glass, mirror

spiegelbeeld (*spee*-gerl-bāylt) *nt* (pl ~en) reflection

spier (speer) *c* (pl ~en) muscle

spijbelen (*spay*-ber-lern) *v* play truant

spijker (*spay*-kerr) *c* (pl ~s) nail

spijkerbroek (*spay*-kerr-brōōk) *c* (pl ~en) jeans *pl*

spijskaart (*spayss*-kaart) *c* (pl ~en) menu

spijsvertering (*spayss*-ferr-tāy-ring) *c* digestion

spijt (spayt) *c* regret

spin (spin) *c* (pl ~nen) spider

spinazie (spee-*naa*-zee) *c* spinach

spinnen (*spi*-nern) *v* *spin

spinneweb (*spi*-ner-vehp) *nt* (pl ~ben) spider's web, cobweb

spion (spee-*Yon*) *c* (pl ~nen) spy

spiritusbrander (*spee*-ree-terss-brahn-derr) *c* (pl ~s) spirit stove

spit[1] (spit) *nt* (pl ~ten) spit

spit[2] (spit) *nt* lumbago

spits[1] (spits) *adj* pointed

spits[2] (spits) *c* (pl ~en) peak; spire

spitsuur (*spits*-ēwr) *nt* (pl -uren) rush-hour, peak hour

splijten (*splay*-tern) *v* *split

splinter (*splin*-terr) *c* (pl ~s) splinter

splinternieuw (*splin*-terr-nee∞) *adj* brand-new

zich splitsen (*split*-sern) fork

spoed (spōōt) *c* haste, speed

spoedcursus (*spōōt*-kerr-zerss) *c* (pl ~sen) intensive course

spoedgeval (*spōōt*-kher-vahl) *nt* (pl ~len) emergency

spoedig (*spōō*-derkh) *adv* soon, shortly

spoel (spōōl) *c* (pl ~en) spool

spoelen (*spōō*-lern) *v* rinse

spoeling (*spōō*-ling) *c* (pl ~en) rinse

spons (spons) *c* (pl sponzen) sponge

spook (spōāk) *nt* (pl spoken) ghost, phantom; spook

spoor (spōār) *nt* (pl sporen) trace; trail, track

spoorbaan (*spōār*-baan) *c* (pl -banen)

railway; railroad *nAm*

spoorweg (*spoār*-vehkh) *c* (pl ~en)
railway; railroad *nAm*

sport (sport) *c* sport

sportjasje (*sport*-Yah-sher) *nt* (pl ~s)
sports-jacket, blazer

sportkleding (*sport*-klāy-dıng) *c*
sportswear

sportman (*sport*-mahn) *c* (pl ~en)
sportsman

sportwagen (*sport*-vaa-gern) *c* (pl ~s)
sports-car

spot (spot) *c* mockery

spraak (spraak) *c* speech; **ter sprake
*brengen** *bring up

spraakzaam (*spraak*-saam) *adj* talkative

sprakeloos (*spraa*-ker-lōass) *adj*
speechless

spreekkamer (*sprāy*-kaa-merr) *c* (pl
~s) surgery

spreekuur (*sprāyk*-ēwr) *nt* (pl -uren)
consultation hours

spreekwoord (*sprāyk*-vōart) *nt* (pl
~en) proverb

spreeuw (sprāy∞) *c* (pl ~en) starling

sprei (spray) *c* (pl ~en) counterpane,
quilt

spreiden (*spray*-dern) *v* *spread

***spreken** (*sprāy*-kern) *v* *speak, talk

***springen** (*sprı*-ngern) *v* jump; *leap

springstof (*sprıng*-stof) *c* (pl ~fen) explosive

sprinkhaan (*sprıngk*-haan) *c* (pl -ha-
nen) grasshopper

sproeier (*sprōō^ee*-err) *c* (pl ~s) atomizer

sprong (sprong) *c* (pl ~en) jump;
hop, leap

sprookje (*sprōāk*-Yer) *nt* (pl ~s) fairytale

spruitjes (*sprur^ew*-t^Yerss) *pl* sprouts *pl*

spuit (spur^ewt) *c* (pl ~en) syringe

spuitbus (*spur^ewt*-berss) *c* (pl ~sen)
atomizer

spuitwater (*spur^ew*t-vaa-terr) *nt* sodawater

spuug (spe̅wkh) *nt* spit

spuwen (*spe̅w^∞*-ern) *v* *spit

staal (staal) *nt* steel; **roestvrij ~**
stainless steel

***staan** (staan) *v* *stand; **goed ~** *be-
come; suit

staart (staart) *c* (pl ~en) tail

staat (staat) *c* (pl staten) state; **in ~
stellen** enable; **in ~ *zijn om** *be
able to; **staats-** national

staatsburgerschap (*staats*-berr-gerr-
skhahp) *nt* citizenship

staatshoofd (*staats*-hōaft) *nt* (pl ~en)
head of state

staatsman (*staats*-mahn) *c* (pl -lieden)
statesman

stabiel (staa-*beel*) *adj* stable

stad (staht) *c* (pl steden) town; city

stadhuis (staht-*hur^ew*ss) *nt* (pl -hui-
zen) town hall

stadion (*staa*-dee-Yon) *nt* (pl ~s) stadium

stadium (*staa*-dee-Yerm) *nt* (pl stadia)
stage

stadscentrum (*staht*-sehn-trerm) *nt* (pl
-tra) town centre

stadslicht (*stahts*-lıkht) *nt* (pl ~en)
parking light

stadsmensen (*stahts*-mehn-sern) *pl*
townspeople *pl*

staf (stahf) *c* staff

staken (*staa*-kern) *v* *strike; stop, discontinue

staking (*staa*-kıng) *c* (pl ~en) strike

stal (stahl) *c* (pl ~len) stable

stallen (*stah*-lern) *v* garage

stalles (*stah*-lerss) *pl* stall; orchestra
seat *Am*

stam (stahm) *c* (pl ~men) trunk;
tribe

stamelen (*staa*-mer-lern) *v* falter

stampen (*stahm*-pern) *v* stamp, thump

stampvol (*stahmp*-fol) *adj* packed

stand (stahnt) *c* score; **tot ~ *brengen** realize

standbeeld (*stahnt*-baÿlt) *nt* (pl ~en) statue

standpunt (*stahnt*-pernt) *nt* (pl ~en) point of view

standvastig (stahnt-*fahss*-terkh) *adj* steadfast

stang (stahng) *c* (pl ~en) rod, bar

stap (stahp) *c* (pl ~pen) step; pace; move

stapel (*staa*-perl) *c* (pl ~s) stack, heap, pile

stappen (*stah*-pern) *v* step

staren (*staa*-rern) *v* gaze, stare

start (stahrt) *c* take-off

startbaan (*stahrt*-baan) *c* runway

starten (*stahr*-tern) *v* *take off

startmotor (*stahrt*-mōa-terr) *c* starter motor

statiegeld (*staa*-tsee-gehlt) *nt* deposit

station (staa-*shon*) *nt* (pl ~s) station; depot *nAm*

stationschef (staa-*shon*-shehf) *c* (pl ~s) station-master

statistiek (staa-tiss-*teek*) *c* (pl ~en) statistics *pl*

stedelijk (*staÿ*-der-lerk) *adj* urban

steeds (staÿts) *adv* continually

steeg (staÿkh) *c* (pl stegen) alley, lane

steek (staÿk) *c* (pl steken) stitch; sting, bite

steel (staÿl) *c* (pl stelen) stem; handle

steelpan (*staÿl*-pahn) *c* (pl ~nen) saucepan

steen (staÿn) *c* (pl stenen) stone; brick

steengroeve (*staÿn*-grōō-ver) *c* (pl ~n) quarry

steenpuist (*staÿn*-pur^ew st) *c* (pl ~en) boil

steigers (*stay*-gerrs) *pl* scaffolding

steil (stayl) *adj* steep

stekelvarken (*staÿ*-kerl-vahr-kern) *nt* (pl ~s) porcupine

*steken (*staÿ*-kern) *v* *sting

stekker (*staÿ*-kerr) *c* (pl ~s) plug

stel (stehl) *nt* (pl ~len) set

*stelen (*staÿ*-lern) *v* *steal

stellen (*steh*-lern) *v* *put

stelling (*steh*-ling) *c* (pl ~en) thesis

stelsel (*stehl*-serl) *nt* (pl ~s) system; **tientallig ~** decimal system

stem (stehm) *c* (pl ~men) voice; vote

stemmen (*steh*-mern) *v* vote

stemming[1] (*steh*-ming) *c* mood; atmosphere; spirits

stemming[2] (*steh*-ming) *c* (pl ~en) vote

stempel (*stehm*-perl) *c* (pl ~s) stamp

stemrecht (*stehm*-rehkht) *nt* suffrage

stenen (*staÿ*-nern) *adj* stone

stenograaf (*staÿ*-nōa-*graaf*) *c* (pl -grafen) stenographer

stenografie (staÿ-nōa-graa-*fee*) *c* shorthand

step-in (stehp-*in*) *c* (pl ~s) girdle

ster (stehr) *c* (pl ~ren) star

sterfelijk (*stehr*-fer-lerk) *adj* mortal

steriel (ster-*reel*) *adj* sterile

steriliseren (staÿ-ree-li-*zaÿ*-rern) *v* sterilize

sterk (stehrk) *adj* powerful, strong; **sterke drank** spirits

sterkte (*stehrk*-ter) *c* strength

sterrenkunde (*steh*-rer-kern-der) *c* astronomy

*sterven (*stehr*-vern) *v* die

steun (stürn) *c* assistance, support; relief

steunen (*stǖ*-nern) *v* support

steunkousen (*stǖrn*-kou-sern) *pl* support hose

steurgarnaal (*stürr*-gahr-naal) *c* (pl -nalen) prawn

stevig (*staÿ*-verkh) *adj* solid, firm

stichten (stıkh-tern) v found

stichting (stıkh-tıng) c (pl ~en) foundation

stiefkind (steef-kınt) nt (pl ~eren) stepchild

stiefmoeder (steef-mōō-derr) c (pl ~s) stepmother

stiefvader (stee-faa-derr) c (pl ~s) stepfather

stier (steer) c (pl ~en) bull

stierengevecht (stee-rer-ger-vehkht) nt (pl ~en) bullfight

stijf (stayf) adj stiff

stijfsel (stayf-serl) nt starch

stijgbeugel (staykh-būr-gerl) c (pl ~s) stirrup

*stijgen (stay-gern) v *rise; climb

stijging (stay-gıng) c rise; climb, ascent

stijl (stayl) c (pl ~en) style

*stijven (stay-vern) v starch

stikken (stı-kern) v choke

stikstof (stık-stof) c nitrogen

stil (stıl) adj silent; quiet; still

Stille Oceaan (stı-ler ōā-sāy-aan) Pacific Ocean

stilstaand (stıl-staant) adj stationary

stilte (stıl-ter) c (pl ~s) silence; stillness, quiet

stimuleren (stee-mēw-lāy-rern) v stimulate

*stinken (stıng-kern) v *smell; *stink; **stinkend** smelly

stipt (stıpt) adj punctual

stoel (stōōl) c (pl ~en) chair; seat

stoep (stōōp) c (pl ~en) sidewalk nAm

stoet (stōōt) c (pl ~en) procession

stof¹ (stof) nt dust

stof² (stof) c (pl ~fen) fabric, cloth, material; matter; **stoffen** drapery; **vaste ~** solid

stoffelijk (sto-fer-lerk) adj substantial, material

stoffig (sto-ferkh) adj dusty

stofzuigen (stof-sur^ew^-gern) v hoover; vacuum vAm

stofzuiger (stof-sur^ew^-gerr) c (pl ~s) vacuum cleaner

stok (stokl) c (pl ~ken) stick; cane

stokpaardje (stok-paar-t^y^er) nt (pl ~s) hobby-horse

stola (stōā-laa) c (pl ~'s) stole

stollen (sto-lern) v coagulate

stom (stom) adj mute, dumb

stomerij (stōā-mer-ray) c (pl ~en) dry-cleaner's

stomp (stomp) adj blunt

stompen (stom-pern) v punch

stookolie (stōāk-ōā-lee) c fuel oil

stoom (stōām) c steam

stoomboot (stōām-bōāt) c (pl boten) steamer

stoot (stōāt) c (pl stoten) bump

stop (stop) c (pl ~pen) stopper, cork

stopgaren (stop-khaa-rern) nt darning wool

stoplicht (stop-lıkht) nt (pl ~en) traffic light

stoppen (sto-pern) v stop, halt; *put; darn

stoptrein (stop-trayn) c (pl ~en) stopping train, local train

storen (stōā-rern) v disturb; trouble

storing (stōā-rıng) c (pl ~en) disturbance

storm (storm) c (pl ~en) storm; gale, tempest

stormachtig (storm-ahkh-terkh) adj stormy

stormlamp (storm-lahmp) c (pl ~en) hurricane lamp

stortbui (stort-bur^ew^) c (pl ~en) downpour

storten (stor-tern) v *shed; deposit

storting (stor-tıng) c (pl ~en) remittance, deposit

*stoten (stōā-tern) v bump

stout (stout) *adj* naughty, bad

stoutmoedig (stout-*mōō*-derkh) *adj* bold

straal (straal) *c* (pl stralen) squirt, spout, jet; ray, beam; radius

straalvliegtuig (*straal*-vleekh-tur^{ew}kh) *nt* (pl ~en) turbojet, jet

straat (straat) *c* (pl straten) street; road

straatweg (*straat*-vehkh) *c* (pl ~en) causeway

straf (strahf) *c* (pl ~fen) punishment; penalty

straffen (strah-fern) *v* punish

strafrecht (*strahf*-rehkht) *nt* criminal law

strafschop (*strahf*-skhop) *c* (pl ~pen) penalty kick

strak (strahk) *adj* tight; **strakker maken** tighten

straks (strahks) *adv* in a moment

strand (strahnt) *nt* (pl ~en) beach

streek (strāyk) *c* (pl streken) region; district, country, area; trick

streep (strāyp) *c* (pl strepen) line; stripe

streng (strehng) *adj* strict, harsh; severe

stretcher (*streht*-sherr) *c* (pl ~s) camp-bed; cot *nAm*

streven (*strāy*-vern) *v* aspire

strijd (strayt) *c* fight, combat, battle; struggle, strife, contest

*****strijden** (*stray*-dern) *v* *fight; struggle

strijdkrachten (*strayt*-krahkh-tern) *pl* armed forces

*****strijken** (*stray*-kern) *v* iron; *strike, lower

strijkijzer (*strayk*-ay-zerr) *nt* (pl ~s) iron

strikje (*strik*-^yer) *nt* (pl ~s) bow tie

strikt (strikt) *adj* strict

stripverhaal (*strip*-ferr-haal) *nt* (pl -ha-

len) comics *pl*

stro (strōa) *nt* straw

strodak (*strōa*-dahk) *nt* (pl ~en) thatched roof

stromen (*strōa*-mern) *v* stream, flow

stroming (*strōa*-ming) *c* (pl ~en) current

strook (strōak) *c* (pl stroken) strip

stroom (strōam) *c* (pl stromen) stream; current

stroomafwaarts (strōam-*ahf*-vaarts) *adv* downstream

stroomopwaarts (strōam-*op*-vaarts) *adv* upstream

stroomverdeler (*strōam*-verr-dāy-lerr) *c* distributor

stroomversnelling (*strōam*-verr-sneh-ling) *c* (pl ~en) rapids *pl*

stroop (strōap) *c* syrup

stropen (*strōa*-pern) *v* poach

structuur (strerk-*tēwr*) *c* (pl -turen) structure; fabric, texture

struik (strur^{ew}k) *c* (pl ~en) scrub, bush, shrub

struikelen (*strur^{ew}*-ker-lern) *v* stumble

struisvogel (*strurss*-fōa-gerl) *c* (pl ~s) ostrich

studeerkamer (stēw-*dāyr*-kaa-merr) *c* study

student (stēw-*dehnt*) *c* (pl ~en) student

studente (stēw-*dehn*-ter) *c* (pl ~s) student

studeren (stēw-*dāy*-rern) *v* study

studie (*stēw*-dee) *c* (pl ~s) study

studiebeurs (*stēw*-dee-bürrs) *c* (pl -beurzen) scholarship

stuitend (*stur^{ew}*-ternt) *adj* revolting

stuk¹ (sterk) *adj* broken; ~ *gaan *break down

stuk² (sterk) *nt* (pl ~ken) part, piece; lump, chunk; fragment; stretch

sturen (*stēw*-rern) *v* *send; navigate

stuurboord (*stēwr*-bōart) *nt* starboard

stuurkolom (stēwr-kōā-lom) c steering-column

stuurman (stēwr-mahn) c (pl -lieden, -lui) steersman, helmsman

stuurwiel (stēwr-veel) nt steering-wheel

subsidie (serp-see-dee) c (pl ~s) subsidy

substantie (serp-stahn-see) c (pl ~s) substance

subtiel (serp-teel) adj subtle

succes (serk-sehss) nt (pl ~sen) success

succesvol (serk-sehss-fol) adj successful

suède (sēw-vai-der) nt/c suede

suf (serf) adj dumb

suiker (surew-kerr) c sugar

suikerklontje (surew-kerr-klon-tYer) nt (pl ~s) lump of sugar

suikerzieke (surew-kerr-zee-ker) c (pl ~n) diabetic

suikerziekte (surew-kerr-zeek-ter) c diabetes

suite (svee-ter) c (pl ~s) suite

summier (ser-meer) adj concise

superieur (sēw-per-ree-Yūrr) adj superior

superlatief (sēw-perr-laa-teef) c (pl -tieven) superlative

supermarkt (sēw-perr-mahrkt) c (pl ~en) supermarket

supplement (ser-pler-mehnt) nt (pl ~en) supplement

suppoost (ser-pōast) c (pl ~en) custodian, usher

surfplank (serrf-plahngk) c (pl ~en) surf-board

surveilleren (serr-vay-Yai-rern) v patrol

Swahili (svaa-hee-lee) nt Swahili

symbool (sim-bōal) nt (pl -bolen) symbol

symfonie (sim-fōa-nee) c (pl ~ën) symphony

sympathie (sim-paa-tee) c (pl ~ën) sympathy

sympathiek (sim-paa-teek) adj nice

symptoom (sim-tōam) nt (pl -tomen) symptom

synagoge (see-naa-gōā-ger) c (pl ~n) synagogue

synoniem (see-nōā-neem) nt (pl ~en) synonym

synthetisch (sin-tāy-teess) adj synthetic

Syrië (see-ree-Yer) Syria

Syriër (see-ree-Yerr) c (pl ~s) Syrian

Syrisch (see-reess) adj Syrian

systeem (seess-tāym) nt (pl -temen) system

systematisch (seess-tāy-maa-teess) adj systematic

T

taai (taaee) adj tough

taak (taak) c (pl taken) task ; duty

taal (taal) c (pl talen) language ; speech

taalgids (taal-gits) c (pl ~en) phrase-book

taart (taart) c (pl ~en) cake

tabak (taa-bahk) c tobacco

tabakswinkel (taa-bahks-ving-kerl) c (pl ~s) tobacconist's

tabakszak (taa-bahk-sahk) c (pl ~ken) tobacco pouch

tabel (taa-behl) c (pl ~len) chart, table

tablet (taa-bleht) nt (pl ~ten) tablet

taboe (taa-bōō) nt (pl ~s) taboo

tachtig (tahkh-terkh) num eighty

tactiek (tahk-teek) c (pl ~en) tactics pl

tafel (taa-ferl) c (pl ~s) table

tafellaken (*taa*-fer-laa-kern) *nt* (pl ~s) table-cloth

tafeltennis (*taa*-ferl-teh-nerss) *nt* table tennis, ping-pong

taille (*tah*-Yer) *c* (pl ~s) waist

tak (tahk) *c* (pl ~ken) branch, bough

talenpracticum (*taa*-ler-prahk-tee-kerm) *nt* (pl -tica) language laboratory

talent (taa-*lehnt*) *nt* (pl ~en) faculty, talent

talkpoeder (*tahlk*-pōō-derr) *nt/c* talc powder

talrijk (*tahl*-rayk) *adj* numerous

tam (tahm) *adj* tame

tamelijk (*taa*-mer-lerk) *adv* pretty, fairly, quite, rather

tampon (tahm-*pon*) *c* (pl ~s) tampon

tand (tahnt) *c* (pl ~en) tooth

tandarts (*tahn*-dahrts) *c* (pl ~en) dentist

tandenborstel (*tahn*-der-bors-terl) *c* (pl ~s) toothbrush

tandestoker (*tahn*-der-stōa-kerr) *c* (pl ~s) toothpick

tandpasta (*tahnt*-pahss-taa) *c/nt* (pl ~s) toothpaste

tandpijn (*tahnt*-payn) *c* toothache

tandpoeder (*tahnt*-pōō-derr) *nt/c* toothpowder

tandvlees (*tahnt*-flāyss) *nt* gum

tang (tahng) *c* (pl ~en) tongs *pl*, pliers *pl*

tank (tehngk) *c* (pl ~s) tank

tankschip (*tehnk*-skhip) *nt* (pl -schepen) tanker

tante (*tahn*-ter) *c* (pl ~s) aunt

tapijt (taa-*payt*) *nt* (pl ~en) carpet

tarief (taa-*reef*) *nt* (pl tarieven) rate, tariff; fare

tarwe (*tahr*-ver) *c* wheat

tas (tahss) *c* (pl ~sen) bag

tastbaar (*tahst*-baar) *adj* palpable; tangible

tastzin (*tahst*-sɪn) *c* touch

taxeren (tahk-*sāy*-rern) *v* estimate

taxi (*tahk*-see) *c* (pl ~'s) cab, taxi

taxichauffeur (*tahk*-see-shōa-fūrr) *c* (pl ~s) cab-driver, taxi-driver

taximeter (*tahk*-see-māy-terr) *c* taxi-meter

taxistandplaats (*tahk*-see-stahnt-plaats) *c* (pl ~en) taxi rank; taxi stand *Am*

te (ter) *adv* too

technicus (*tehk*-nee-kerss) *c* (pl -ci) technician

techniek (tehkh-*neek*) *c* (pl ~en) technique

technisch (*tehkh*-neess) *adj* technical

technologie (tehkh-nōa-lōa-*gee*) *c* technology

teder (*tāy*-derr) *adj* delicate, tender

teef (tāyf) *c* (pl teven) bitch

teen (tāyn) *c* (pl tenen) toe

teer (tāyr) *adj* gentle, tender; *c/nt* tar

tegel (*tāy*-gerl) *c* (pl ~s) tile

tegelijk (ter-ger-*layk*) *adv* at the same time; at once

tegelijkertijd (ter-ger-lay-kerr-*tayt*) *adv* simultaneously

tegemoetkomend (ter-ger-*mōōt*-kōa-mernt) *adj* oncoming

tegemoetkoming (ter-ger-*mōōt*-kōa-ming) *c* (pl ~en) concession

tegen (*tāy*-gern) *prep* against

tegendeel (*tāy*-ger-dāyl) *nt* contrary, reverse

tegengesteld (*tāy*-ger-ger-stehlt) *adj* contrary, opposite

*****tegenkomen** (*tāy*-ger-kōa-mern) *v* *come across, *meet; run into

tegenover (tāy-ger-*nōa*-verr) *prep* opposite, facing

tegenslag (*tāy*-ger-slahkh) *c* (pl ~en) misfortune; reverse

*****tegenspreken** (*tāy*-ger-sprāy-kern) *v* contradict

tegenstander (tāȳ-ger-stahn-derr) c (pl ~s) opponent

tegenstelling (tāȳ-ger-steh-lɪng) c (pl ~en) contrast

tegenstrijdig (tāȳ-ger-stray-derkh) adj contradictory

*tegenvallen (tāȳ-ger-vah-lern) v *be disappointing

*tegenwerpen (tāȳ-ger-vehr-pern) v object

tegenwerping (tāȳ-ger-vehr-pɪng) c (pl ~en) objection

tegenwoordig (tāȳ-ger-vōar-derkh) adj present; adv nowadays

tegenwoordigheid (tāȳ-ger-vōar-derkh-hayt) c presence

tegenzin (tāȳ-ger-zɪn) c aversion

tehuis (ter-hur^ewss) nt (pl tehuizen) home; asylum

teint (taint) c complexion

teken (tāȳ-kern) nt (pl ~s, ~en) sign; indication, signal; token

tekenen (tāȳ-ker-nern) v *draw, sketch; sign

tekenfilm (tāȳ-ker-fɪlm) c (pl ~s) cartoon

tekening (tāȳ-ker-nɪng) c (pl ~en) drawing, sketch

tekort (ter-kort) nt (pl ~en) shortage; deficit; ~ *schieten fail

tekortkoming (ter-kort-kōa-mɪng) c (pl ~en) shortcoming

tekst (tehkst) c (pl ~en) text

tel (tehl) c (pl ~len) second

telefoneren (tāȳ-ler-fōa-nāȳ-rern) v phone

telefoniste (tāȳ-ler-fōa-nɪss-ter) c (pl ~n, ~s) operator, telephonist

telefoon (tāȳ-ler-fōan) c (pl ~s) phone, telephone

telefoonboek (tāȳ-ler-fōan-bōōk) nt (pl ~en) telephone directory; telephone book Am

telefooncel (tāȳ-ler-fōan-sehl) c (pl ~len) telephone booth

telefooncentrale (tāȳ-ler-fōan-sehn-traa-ler) c (pl ~s) telephone exchange

telefoongesprek (tāȳ-ler-fōan-ger-sprehk) nt (pl ~ken) telephone call

telefoongids (tāȳ-ler-fōan-gɪts) c (pl ~en) telephone directory; telephone book Am

telefoonhoorn (tāȳ-ler-fōan-hōa-rern) c (pl ~s) receiver

telefoontje (tāȳ-ler-fōan-t^yer) nt (pl ~s) call

telegraferen (tāȳ-ler-graa-fāȳ-rern) v cable, telegraph

telegram (tāȳ-ler-grahm) nt (pl ~men) cable, telegram

telelens (tāȳ-ler-lehns) c (pl -lenzen) telephoto lens

telepathie (tāȳ-lāȳ-paa-tee) c telepathy

teleurstellen (ter-lūrr-steh-lern) v disappoint; *let down

teleurstelling (ter-lūrr-steh-lɪng) c (pl ~en) disappointment

televisie (tāȳ-ler-vee-zee) c television; cabel-~ cable tv; satelliet-~ satellite tv

televisietoestel (tāȳ-ler-vee-zee-tōō-stehl) nt (pl ~len) television set

telex (tāȳ-lehks) c telex

telkens (tehl-kerns) adv again and again

tellen (teh-lern) v count

telwoord (tehl-vōart) nt (pl ~en) numeral

temmen (teh-mern) v tame

tempel (tehm-perl) c (pl ~s) temple

temperatuur (tehm-per-raa-tewr) c (pl -turen) temperature

tempo (tehm-pōa) nt pace

tendens (tehn-dehns) c (pl -denzen) tendency

tenminste (ter-mɪn-ster) adv at least

tennis (teh-nerss) nt tennis

tennisbaan (teh-nerss-baan) c (pl -banen) tennis-court

tennisschoenen (teh-ner-skhoo-nern) pl tennis shoes

tenslotte (tehn-slo-ter) adv at last

tent (tehnt) c (pl ~en) tent

tentdoek (tehn-dook) nt canvas

tentoonstellen (tehn-toan-steh-lern) v exhibit; *show

tentoonstelling (tehn-toan-steh-ling) c (pl ~en) exposition, exhibition; display, show

tenzij (tehn-zay) conj unless

teraardebestelling (tehr-aar-der-ber-steh-ling) c (pl ~en) burial

terecht (ter-rehkht) adj just; adv rightly

terechtstelling (ter-rehkht-steh-ling) c (pl ~en) execution

terloops (tehr-loaps) adj casual

term (tehrm) c (pl ~en) term

termijn (tehr-mayn) c (pl ~en) term

terpentijn (tehr-pern-tayn) c turpentine

terras (teh-rahss) nt (pl ~sen) terrace

terrein (teh-rayn) nt (pl ~en) terrain; grounds

terreur (teh-rurr) c terrorism

terrorisme (teh-ro-riss-mer) nt terrorism

terrorist (teh-roa-rist) c (pl ~en) terrorist

terug (ter-rerkh) adv back

terugbetalen (ter-rerkh-ber-taa-lern) v *repay; reimburse, refund

terugbetaling (terrerkh-ber-taa-ling) c (pl ~en) repayment, refund

***terugbrengen** (ter-rerkh-brehng-ern) v *bring back

***teruggaan** (ter-rer-khaan) v *go back, *get back

teruggang (ter-rer-khahng) c depression, recession

terugkeer (ter-rerkh-kayr) c return

terugkeren (ter-rerkh-kay-rern) v return; turn back

***terugkomen** (ter-rerkh-koa-mern) v return

terugreis (ter-rerkh-rayss) c return journey

***terugroepen** (ter-rerkh-roo-pern) v recall

terugsturen (ter-rerkh-stew-rern) v *send back

***terugtrekken** (ter-rerkh-treh-kern) v *withdraw

***terugvinden** (ter-rerkh-fin-dern) v recover

terugweg (ter-rerkh-vehkh) c way back

***terugzenden** (ter-rerkh-sehn-dern) v *send back

terwijl (terr-vayl) conj whilst, while

terylene (teh-ree-layn) nt terylene

terzijde (tehr-zay-der) adv aside

test (tehst) c (pl ~s) test

testament (tehss-taa-mehnt) nt (pl ~en) will

testen (tehss-tern) v test

tevens (tay-verns) adv also

tevergeefs (ter-verr-gayfs) adv in vain

tevoren (ter-voa-rern) adv before; van ~ in advance

tevreden (ter-vray-dern) adj satisfied, content

tewaterlating (ter-vaa-terr-laa-ting) c launching

***teweegbrengen** (ter-vaykh-brehngern) v effect

tewerkstellen (ter-vehrk-steh-lern) v employ

tewerkstelling (ter-vehrk-steh-ling) c (pl ~en) employment

textiel (tehks-teel) c/nt textile

Thailand (tigh-lahnt) Thailand

Thailander (tigh-lahn-derr) c (pl ~s) Thai

Thailands (tigh-lahnts) adj Thai

thans (tahns) *adv* now

theater (tay-*Yaa*-terr) *nt* (pl ~s) theatre

thee (tay) *c* tea

theedoek (*tay*-dook) *c* (pl ~en) tea-cloth

theekopje (*tay*-kop-*Yay*) *nt* (pl ~s) teacup

theelepel (*tay*-lay-perl) *c* (pl ~s) teaspoon

theepot (*tay*-pot) *c* (pl ~ten) teapot

theeservies (*tay*-sehr-veess) *nt* (pl -viezen) tea-set

thema (*tay*-maa) *nt* (pl ~'s) theme; exercise

theologie (tay-*Yoa*-loa-*gee*) *c* theology

theoretisch (tay-*Yoa*-*ray*-teess) *adj* theoretical

theorie (tay-*Yoa*-*ree*) *c* (pl ~ën) theory

therapie (tay-raa-*pee*) *c* (pl ~ën) therapy

thermometer (*tehr*-moa-may-terr) *c* (pl ~s) thermometer

thermosfles (*tehr*-moss-flehss) *c* (pl ~sen) vacuum flask, thermos flask

thermostaat (tehr-moss-*taat*) *c* (pl -staten) thermostat

thuis (tur^{ew}ss) *adv* home, at home

tien (teen) *num* ten

tiende (*teen*-der) *num* tenth

tiener (*tee*-nerr) *c* (pl ~s) teenager

tijd (tayt) *c* (pl ~en) time; **de laatste ~** lately; **op ~** in time; **vrije ~** spare time, leisure

tijdbesparend (tayt-ber-*spaa*-rernt) *adj* time-saving

tijdelijk (*tay*-der-lerk) *adj* temporary

tijdens (*tay*-derns) *prep* during

tijdgenoot (*tayt*-kher-noat) *c* (pl -noten) contemporary

tijdperk (*tayt*-pehrk) *nt* (pl ~en) period

tijdschrift (*tayt*-skhrift) *nt* (pl ~en) review, periodical, journal

tijger (*tay*-gerr) *c* (pl ~s) tiger

tijm (taym) *c* thyme

tikken (*ti*-kern) *v* type

timmerhout (*ti*-merr-hout) *nt* timber

timmerman (*ti*-merr-mahn) *c* (pl -lieden, -lui) carpenter

tin (tin) *nt* tin, pewter

tiran (tee-*rahn*) *c* (pl ~nen) tyrant

titel (*tee*-terl) *c* (pl ~s) title; heading; degree

toch (tokh) *adv* still; *conj* yet

tocht (tokht) *c* draught

toe (too) *adj* closed

toebehoren (*too*-ber-hoa-rern) *v* belong; *pl* accessories *pl*

toedienen (*too*-dee-nern) *v* administer

toegang (*too*-gahng) *c* admittance, admission, access; entry, entrance; approach

toegankelijk (*too*-*gahng*-ker-lerk) *adj* accessible

***toegeven** (*too*-gay-vern) *v* admit, acknowledge; *give in, indulge

toehoorder (*too*-hoar-derr) *c* (pl ~s) auditor

toekennen (*too*-keh-nern) *v* award

toekomst (*too*-komst) *c* future

toekomstig (too-*kom*-sterkh) *adj* future

toelage (*too*-laa-ger) *c* (pl ~n) allowance, grant

***toelaten** (*too*-laa-tern) *v* admit

toelating (*too*-laa-ting) *c* (pl ~en) admission

toelichten (*too*-likh-tern) *v* elucidate

toelichting (*too*-likh-ting) *c* (pl ~en) explanation

toen (toon) *conj* when; *adv* then

toename (*too*-naa-mer) *c* increase

***toenemen** (*too*-nay-mern) *v* increase; **toenemend** progressive

toenmalig (*toon*-maa-lerkh) *adj* contemporary

toepassen (*too*-pah-sern) *v* apply

toepassing (*tōo*-pah-sɪng) c (pl ~en) application

toereikend (tōo-*ray*-kernt) adj adequate

toerisme (tōo-*rɪss*-mer) nt tourism

toerist (tōo-*rɪst*) c (pl ~en) tourist

toeristenklasse (tōo-*rɪss*-ter-klah-ser) c tourist class

toernooi (toor-*nōā*ᵉᵉ) nt (pl ~en) tournament

toeschouwer (*tōo*-skhou-err) c (pl ~s) spectator

*****toeschrijven aan** (*tōo*-skhray-vern) assign to

*****toeslaan** (*tōo*-slaan) v *strike

toeslag (*tōo*-slahkh) c (pl ~en) surcharge

toespraak (*tōo*-spraak) c (pl -spraken) speech

*****toestaan** (*tōo*-staan) v allow, permit

toestand (*tōo*-stahnt) c (pl ~en) state; condition

toestel (*tōo*-stehl) nt (pl ~len) apparatus, appliance; aircraft; extension

toestemmen (*tōo*-steh-mern) v agree, consent

toestemming (*tōo*-steh-mɪng) c authorization, permission; consent

toetje (*tōo*-tʸer) nt (pl ~s) sweet

toeval (*tōo*-vahl) nt chance; luck

toevallig (tōo-*vah*-lerkh) adj accidental, casual, incidental; adv by chance

toevertrouwen (*tōo*-verr-trou-ern) v commit

toevoegen (*tōo*-vōo-gern) v add

toevoeging (*tōo*-vōo-gɪng) c (pl ~en) addition

toewijden (*tōo*-vay-dern) v dedicate

*****toewijzen** (*tōo*-vay-zern) v allot

toezicht (*tōo*-zɪkht) nt supervision; ~ *houden op supervise

toffee (to-*fāȳ*) c (pl ~s) toffee

toilet (tvah-*leht*) nt (pl ~ten) toilet, lavatory, bathroom; washroom nAm

toiletbenodigdheden (tvah-*leht*-ber-nōā-derkht-hāȳ-dern) pl toiletry

toiletpapier (tvah-*leht*-paa-peer) nt toilet-paper

toilettafel (tvah-*leh*-taa-ferl) c (pl ~s) dressing-table

toilettas (tvah-*leh*-tahss) c (pl ~sen) toilet case

tol (tol) c toll

tolk (tolk) c (pl ~en) interpreter

tolken (*tol*-kern) v interpret

tolweg (*tol*-verkh) c (pl ~en) turnpike nAm

tomaat (tōa-*maat*) c (pl tomaten) tomato

ton (ton) c (pl ~nen) cask, barrel; ton

toneel (tōa-*nāȳl*) nt drama; stage

toneelkijker (tōa-*nāȳl*-kay-kerr) c (pl ~s) binoculars pl

toneelschrijver (tōa-*nāȳl*-skhray-verr) c (pl ~s) dramatist, playwright

toneelspeelster (tōa-*nāȳl*-spāȳl-sterr) c (pl ~s) actress

toneelspelen (tōa-*nāȳl*-spāȳ-lern) v act

toneelspeler (tōa-*nāȳl*-spāȳ-lerr) c (pl ~s) actor; comedian

toneelstuk (tōa-*nāȳl*-sterk) nt (pl ~ken) play

tonen (*tōa*-nern) v *show; display

tong (tong) c (pl ~en) tongue; sole

tonicum (*tōa*-nee-kerm) nt (pl -ca, ~s) tonic

tonijn (tōa-*nayn*) c (pl ~en) tuna

toon (tōan) c (pl tonen) tone; note

toonbank (*tōam*-bahngk) c (pl ~en) counter

toonladder (*tōan*-lah-derr) c (pl ~s) scale

toonzaal (*tōan*-zaal) c (pl -zalen) showroom

toorn (*tōa*-rern) c anger

top (top) c (pl ~pen) peak; top, summit

toppunt (*to*-pernt) *nt* (pl ~en) height; zenith

toren (*tōā*-rern) *c* (pl ~s) tower

tot (tot) *prep* until, to, till; *conj* till; ~ **aan** till; ~ **zover** so far

totaal[1] (tōā-*taal*) *adj* total, overall; utter

totaal[2] (tōā-*taal*) *nt* (pl totalen) total; **in** ~ altogether

totalisator (tōā-taa-lee-*zaa*-tor) *c* (pl ~s) totalizator

totalitair (tōā-taa-lee-*tair*) *adj* totalitarian

totdat (to-*daht*) *conj* till

touw (tou) *nt* (pl ~en) twine, rope, string

toverkunst (*tōā*-verr-kernst) *c* magic

traag (traakh) *adj* slow; slack

traan (traan) *c* (pl tranen) tear

trachten (*trahkh*-tern) *v* try, attempt

tractor (*trahk*-tor) *c* (pl ~en, ~s) tractor

traditie (traa-*dee*-tsee) *c* (pl ~s) tradition

traditioneel (traa-dee-shōā-*nāyl*) *adj* traditional

tragedie (traa-*gāy*-dee) *c* (pl ~s) tragedy

tragisch (*traa*-geess) *adj* tragic

trainen (*trāy*-nern) *v* drill, train

tralie (*traa*-lee) *c* (pl ~s) bar

tram (trehm) *c* (pl ~s) tram; streetcar *nAm*

transactie (trahn-*zahk*-see) *c* (pl ~s) deal, transaction

transatlantisch (trahn-zaht-*lahn*-teess) *adj* transatlantic

transformator (trahns-for-*maa*-tor) *c* (pl ~en, ~s) transformer

transpiratie (trahn-spee-*raa*-tsee) *c* perspiration

transpireren (trahn-spee-*rāy*-rern) *v* perspire

transport (trahn-*sport*) *nt* (pl ~en) transportation

transporteren (trahn-spor-*tāy*-rern) *v* transport

trap (trahp) *c* (pl ~pen) stairs *pl*, staircase; kick

trapleuning (*trahp*-lūr-ning) *c* (pl ~en) banisters *pl*

trappen (*trah*-pern) *v* kick

trechter (*trehkh*-terr) *c* (pl ~s) funnel

trede (*trāy*-der) *c* (pl ~n) step

*****treffen** (*treh*-fern) *v* *hit; *strike

trefpunt (*trehf*-pernt) *nt* (pl ~en) meeting-place

trein (trayn) *c* (pl ~en) train; **doorgaande** ~ through train

trek[1] (trehk) *c* (pl ~ken) trait

trek[2] (trehk) *c* appetite

*****trekken** (*treh*-kern) *v* pull; *draw; extract; hike

trekker (*treh*-kerr) *c* (pl ~s) trigger

trekking (*treh*-king) *c* (pl ~en) draw

treuren (*trūr*-rern) *v* grieve

treurig (*trūr*-rerkh) *adj* sad

treurspel (*trūrr*-spehl) *nt* (pl ~en) drama

tribune (tree-*bēw*-ner) *c* (pl ~s) stand

tricotgoederen (tree-*kōā*-gōō-der-rern) *pl* hosiery

triest (treest) *adj* depressing

trillen (*tri*-lern) *v* tremble; vibrate

triomf (tree-*ᵞomf*) *c* (pl ~en) triumph

triomfantelijk (tree-ᵞom-*fahn*-ter-lerk) *adj* triumphant

troepen (*trōō*-pern) *pl* troops *pl*

trommel (*tro*-merl) *c* (pl ~s) canister; drum

trommelvlies (*tro*-merl-vlees) *nt* (pl -vliezen) ear-drum

trompet (trom-*peht*) *c* (pl ~ten) trumpet

troon (trōān) *c* (pl tronen) throne

troost (trōāst) *c* comfort

troosten (*trōāss*-tern) *v* comfort

troostprijs (*tróast*-prayss) *c* (pl -prijzen) consolation prize

tropen (*tróa*-pern) *pl* tropics *pl*

tropisch (*tróa*-peess) *adj* tropical

trots (trots) *adj* proud; *c* pride

trottoir (tro-*tvaar*) *nt* (pl ~s) pavement; sidewalk *nAm*

trottoirband (tro-*tvaar*-bahnt) *c* (pl ~en) curb

trouw (trou) *adj* true, faithful

trouwen (*trou*-ern) *v* marry

trouwens (*trou*-erns) *adv* besides

trouwring (*trou*-rıng) *c* (pl ~en) wedding-ring

trui (trur^{ew}) *c* (pl ~en) jersey

Tsjech (ts^yehk) *c* (pl ~en) Czech

Tsjechisch (ts^yeh-kheess) *adj* Czech

tube (*tēw*-ber) *c* (pl ~s) tube

tuberculose (tēw-behr-kēw-*lóa*-zer) *c* tuberculosis

tuchtigen (tukh-*ti*-gern) *v* chastise, punish

tuin (tur^{ew}n) *c* (pl ~en) garden

tuinbouw (*tur^{ew}m*-bou) *c* horticulture

tuinman (*tur^{ew}n*-mahn) *c* (pl -lieden, -lui) gardener

tuit (tur^{ew}t) *c* (pl ~en) nozzle

tulp (terlp) *c* (pl ~en) tulip

tumor (*tēw*-mor) *c* (pl ~s) tumour

Tunesië (tēw-*náy*-zee-^yer) Tunisia

Tunesiër (tēw-*náy*-zee-^yerr) *c* (pl ~s) Tunisian

Tunesisch (tēw-*náy*-zeess) *adj* Tunisian

tuniek (tēw-*neek*) *c* (pl ~en) tunic

tunnel (*ter*-nerl) *c* (pl ~s) tunnel

turbine (terr-*bee*-ner) *c* (pl ~s) turbine

Turk (terrk) *c* (pl ~en) Turk

Turkije (terr-*kay*-er) Turkey

Turks (terrks) *adj* Turkish; ~ **bad** Turkish bath

tussen (*ter*-sern) *prep* between; among, amid

tussenbeide *komen (ter-serm-*bay*-der *kóa*-mern) interfere

tussenpersoon (*ter*-ser-pehr-sóan) *c* (pl -sonen) intermediary

tussenpoos (*ter*-ser-póass) *c* (pl -pozen) interval

tussenruimte (*ter*-ser-rur^{ew}m-ter) *c* (pl ~n, ~s) space

tussenschot (*ter*-ser-skhot) *nt* (pl ~ten) partition; diaphragm

tussentijd (*ter*-ser-tayt) *c* interim

twaalf (tvaalf) *num* twelve

twaalfde (*tvaalf*-der) *num* twelfth

twee (tvāy) *num* two

tweede (*tvāy*-der) *num* second

tweedehands (tvāy-der-*hahnts*) *adj* second-hand

tweedelig (tvāy-*dáy*-lerkh) *adj* two-piece

tweeling (*tvāy*-ling) *c* (pl ~en) twins *pl*

tweemaal (*tvāy*-maal) *adv* twice

tweesprong (*tvāy*-sprong) *c* (pl ~en) fork, road fork

tweetalig (tvāy-*taa*-lerkh) *adj* bilingual

twijfel (*tvay*-ferl) *c* (pl ~s) doubt

twijfelachtig (*tvay*-ferl-ahkh-terkh) *adj* doubtful

twijfelen (*tvay*-fer-lern) *v* doubt

twijg (tvaykh) *c* (pl ~en) twig

twintig (*tvın*-terkh) *num* twenty

twintigste (*tvın*-terkh-ster) *num* twentieth

twist (tvıst) *c* (pl ~en) quarrel

twisten (*tvıss*-tern) *v* quarrel, dispute

tyfus (*tee*-ferss) *c* typhoid

type (*tee*-per) *nt* (pl ~n, ~s) type

typen (*tee*-pern) *v* type

typisch (*tee*-peess) *adj* typical

typiste (tee-*pı*-ster) *c* (pl ~s, ~n) typist

U

u (ew) *pron* you

ui (ur^{ew}) *c* (pl ~en) onion

uil (ur^{ew}l) *c* (pl ~en) owl

uit (ur^{ew}t) *prep* from, out of; for; *adv* out

uitademen (ur^{ew}t-aa-der-mern) *v* expire, exhale

uitbarsting (ur^{ew}t-bahr-stern) *c* (pl ~en) outbreak

uitbenen (ur^{ew}t-bāy-nern) *v* bone

***uitblinken** (ur^{ew}t-bling-kern) *v* excel

uitbreiden (ur^{ew}t-bray-dern) *v* extend, enlarge, expand

uitbreiding (ur^{ew}t-bray-dıng) *c* (pl ~en) extension

uitbuiten (ur^{ew}t-bur-tern) *v* exploit

uitbundig (ur^{ew}t-bern-derkh) *adj* exuberant

uitdagen (ur^{ew}-daa-gern) *v* dare, challenge

uitdaging (ur^{ew}-daa-gıng) *c* (pl ~en) challenge

uitdelen (ur^{ew}-dāy-lern) *v* distribute; *deal

***uitdoen** (ur^{ew}-doōn) *v* *put out

uitdrukkelijk (ur^{ew}-drer-ker-lerk) *adj* express, explicit

uitdrukken (-ur^{ew}-drer-kern) *v* express

uitdrukking (ur^{ew}-drer-kıng) *c* (pl ~en) expression; phrase

uiteindelijk (ur^{ew}t-*ayn*-der-lerk) *adj* eventual; *adv* at last

uiten (ur^{ew}-tern) *v* express; utter

uiteraard (ur^{ew}-ter-*raart*) *adv* of course, naturally

uiterlijk (ur^{ew}-terr-lerk) *adj* outward, external, exterior; *nt* outside; look

uiterst (ur^{ew}-terrst) *adj* extreme; utmost, very

uiterste (ur^{ew}-terr-ster) *nt* (pl ~n) extreme

***uitgaan** (ur^{ew}t-khaan) *v* *go out

uitgang (ur^{ew}t-khahng) *c* (pl ~en) way out, exit; issue

uitgangspunt (ur^{ew}t-khahngs-pernt) *nt* (pl ~en) starting-point

uitgave (ur^{ew}t-khaa-ver) *c* (pl ~n) expense, expenditure; edition, issue

uitgebreid (ur^{ew}t-kher-brayt) *adj* comprehensive, extensive

uitgelezen (ur^{ew}t-kher-lāy-zern) *adj* select

uitgestrekt (ur^{ew}t-kher-strehkt) *adj* vast

***uitgeven** (ur^{ew}t-khāy-vern) *v* *spend; publish, issue

uitgever (ur^{ew}t-khāy-verr) *c* (pl ~s) publisher

uitgezonderd (ur^{ew}t-kher-zon-derrt) *prep* except

uitgifte (ur^{ew}t-khıf-ter) *c* (pl ~n) issue

***uitglijden** (ur^{ew}t-khlay-dern) *v* slip

uithoudingsvermogen (ur^{ew}t-hou-dıngs-ferr-mōā-gern) *nt* stamina

uiting (ur^{ew}-tıng) *c* (pl ~en) expression

***uitkiezen** (ur^{ew}t-kee-zern) *v* select

***uitkijken** (ur^{ew}t-kay-kern) *v* watch out, look out; ~ **naar** watch for

zich uitkleden (ur^{ew}t-klāy-dern) undress

***uitkomen** (ur^{ew}t-kōā-mern) *v* *come out; *come true; *be convenient; ~ **op** open on

uitkomst (ur^{ew}t-komst) *c* (pl ~en) issue

uitlaat (ur^{ew}t-laat) *c* (pl -laten) exhaust

uitlaatgassen (ur^{ew}t-laat-khah-sern) *pl* exhaust gases

uitlaatpijp (ur^{ew}t-laat-payp) *c* (pl ~en) exhaust

***uitladen** (ur^{ew}t-laa-dern) *v* unload, discharge

uitleg (*ur^{ew}t*-lehkh) c explanation

uitleggen (*ur^{ew}t*-leh-gern) v explain

uitlenen (*ur^{ew}t*-lay-nern) v *lend

uitleveren (*ur^{ew}t*-lay-ver-rern) v extradite

uitmaken (*ur^{ew}t*-maa-kern) v matter; determine; *put out

uitnodigen (*ur^{ew}t*-nōa-der-gern) v invite; ask

uitnodiging (*ur^{ew}t*-nōa-der-gıng) c (pl ~en) invitation

uitoefenen (*ur^{ew}t*-ōō-fer-nern) v exercise

uitpakken (*ur^{ew}t*-pah-kern) v unpack; unwrap

uitputten (*ur^{ew}t*-per-tern) v exhaust

uitrekenen (*ur^{ew}t*-rāy-ker-nern) v calculate

uitrit (*ur^{ew}t*-rıt) c (pl ~ten) exit

uitroep (*ur^{ew}t*-rōōp) c (pl ~en) exclamation

** **uitroepen** (*ur^{ew}t*-rōō-pern) v exclaim

uitrusten (*ur^{ew}t*-rerss-tern) v rest; equip

uitrusting (*ur^{ew}t*-rerss-tıng) c (pl ~en) equipment; gear, kit, outfit

uitschakelen (*ur^{ew}t*-skhaa-ker-lern) v switch off; disconnect

** **uitscheiden** (*ur^{ew}t*-skhay-dern) v quit

** **uitschelden** (*ur^{ew}t*-skhehl-dern) v call names

uitslag (*ur^{ew}t*-slahkh) c (pl ~en) result; rash

** **uitsluiten** (*ur^{ew}t*-slur^{ew}-tern) v exclude

uitsluitend (*ur^{ew}t*-*slur^{ew}*-ternt) adv solely, exclusively

uitspraak (*ur^{ew}t*-spraak) c (pl -spraken) pronunciation; verdict

uitspreiden (*ur^{ew}t*-spray-dern) v expand

** **uitspreken** (*ur^{ew}t*-sprāy-kern) v pronounce

uitstapje (*ur^{ew}t*-stahp-^yer) nt (pl ~s) trip, excursion

uitstappen (*ur^{ew}t*-stah-pern) v *get off

uitstekend (ur^{ew}t-*stāy*-kernt) adj fine, excellent

uitstel (*ur^{ew}t*-stehl) nt delay; respite

uitstellen (*ur^{ew}t*-steh-lern) v delay, postpone; adjourn

** **uittrekken** (*ur^{ew}t*-treh-kern) v extract

uitverkocht (ur^{ew}t-ferr-kokht) adj sold out

uitverkoop (*ur^{ew}t*-ferr-kōap) c sales

** **uitvinden** (*ur^{ew}t*-fın-dern) v invent

uitvinder (*ur^{ew}t*-fın-derr) c (pl ~s) inventor

uitvinding (*ur^{ew}t*-fın-dıng) c (pl ~en) invention

uitvoer (*ur^{ew}t*-fōōr) c exportation

uitvoerbaar (ur^{ew}t-*fōōr*-baar) adj feasible

uitvoeren (*ur^{ew}t*-fōō-rern) v carry out; implement, perform, execute; export

uitvoerend (*ur^{ew}t*-fōō-rernt) adj executive; **uitvoerende macht** executive

uitvoerig (ur^{ew}t-*fōō*-rerkh) adj detailed

uitwerken (*ur^{ew}t*-vehr-kern) v elaborate

** **uitwijzen** (*ur^{ew}t*-vay-zern) v expel

uitwisselen (*ur^{ew}t*-vi-ser-lern) v exchange

** **uitzenden** (*ur^{ew}t*-sehn-dern) v *broadcast, transmit

uitzending (*ur^{ew}t*-sehn-dıng) c (pl ~en) broadcast, transmission

uitzicht (*ur^{ew}t*-sıkht) nt (pl ~en) view

uitzondering (*ur^{ew}t*-son-der-rıng) c (pl ~en) exception

uitzonderlijk (ur^{ew}t-*son*-derr-lerk) adj exceptional

** **uitzuigen** (*ur^{ew}t*-sur^{ew}-gern) v *bleed

ultraviolet (erl-traa-vee-^yōa-*leht*) adj ultraviolet

unaniem (ēw-naa-*neem*) adj unanimous

unie (ēw-nee) c (pl ~s) union

uniek (ēw-neek) adj unique

uniform¹ (ēw-nee-form) adj uniform

uniform² (ēw-nee-form) nt/c (pl ~en) uniform

universeel (ēw-nee-vehr-zāyl) adj universal

universiteit (ēw-nee-vehr-zee-tayt) c (pl ~en) university

urgent (err-gehnt) adj pressing

urgentie (err-gehn-see) c urgency

urine (ēw-ree-ner) c urine

Uruguay (ōō-rōō-gvigh) Uruguay

Uruguayaan (ōō-rōō-gvah-ᵞaan) c (pl -yanen) Uruguayan

Uruguayaans (ōō-rōō-gvah-ᵞaans) adj Uruguayan

uur (ēwr) nt (pl uren) hour; **om … ~** at … o'clock; **uur-** hourly

uw (ēw°°) pron your

V

vaag (vaakh) adj vague; faint; dim

vaak (vaak) adv often

vaandel (vaan-derl) nt (pl ~s) banner

vaardig (vaar-derkh) adj skilled, skilful

vaardigheid (vaar-derkh-hayt) c (pl -heden) skill; art

vaart (vaart) c speed

vaartuig (vaar-tur°ewkh) nt (pl ~en) vessel

vaarwater (vaar-vaa-terr) nt waterway

vaas (vaass) c (pl vazen) vase

vaatje (vaa-tᵞer) nt (pl ~s) keg

vaatwerk (vaat-vehrk) nt crockery

vacant (vaa-kahnt) adj vacant

vacature (vah-kah-tēw-rer) c (pl ~s) vacancy

vacuüm (vaa-kēw-erm) nt vacuum

vader (vaa-derr) c (pl ~s) father; dad

vaderland (vaa-derr-lahnt) nt native country, fatherland

vagebond (vaa-ger-bont) c (pl ~en) tramp

vak (vahk) nt (pl ~ken) profession, trade; section

vakantie (vaa-kahn-see) c (pl ~s) holiday, vacation; **met ~** on holiday

vakantiekamp (vaa-kahn-see-kahmp) nt (pl ~en) holiday camp

vakantieoord (vaa-kahn-see-ōart) nt (pl ~en) holiday resort

vakbond (vahk-bont) c (pl ~en) trade-union

vakkundig (vah-kern-derkh) adj skilled

vakman (vahk-mahn) c (pl -lieden) expert

val¹ (vahl) c fall

val² (vahl) c (pl ~len) trap

valk (vahlk) c (pl ~en) hawk

vallei (vah-lay) c (pl ~en) valley

*__vallen__ (vah-lern) v *fall; *__laten ~__ drop

vals (vahls) adj false

valuta (vaa-lēw-taa) c (pl ~'s) currency

van (vahn) prep of; from; off; with

vanaf (vah-nahf) prep from, as from

vanavond (vah-naa-vernt) adv tonight

vandaag (vahn-daakh) adv today

*__vangen__ (vah-ngern) v *catch; capture

vangrail (vahng-rāyl) c (pl ~s) crash barrier

vangst (vahngst) c (pl ~en) capture

vanille (vaa-nee-ᵞer) c vanilla

vanmiddag (vah-mɪ-dahkh) adv this afternoon

vanmorgen (vah-mor-gern) adv this morning

vannacht (vah-nahkht) adv tonight

vanwege (vahn-vāy-ger) prep on account of, for, owing to, because of

vanzelfsprekend (vahn-zehlf-sprāy-kernt) adj self-evident

*varen (vaa-rern) v sail, navigate
variëren (vaa-ree-Yāy-rern) v vary
variététheater (vaa-ree-Yāy-tāy-tāy-Yaa-terr) nt (pl ~s) variety theatre; music-hall
variétévoorstelling (vaa-ree-Yāy-tāy-vōar-steh-ling) c (pl ~en) variety show
varken (vahr-kern) nt (pl ~s) pig
varkensleer (vahr-kerss-lāyr) nt pig-skin
varkensvlees (vahr-kerss-flāyss) nt pork
vaseline (vaa-zer-lee-ner) c vaseline
vast (vahst) adj fixed, firm; steady, permanent; adv tight; ~ menu set menu
vastberaden (vahss-ber-raa-dern) adj resolute
vastbesloten (vahss-ber-slōa-tern) adj determined
vasteland (vahss-ter-lahnt) nt mainland; continent
*vasthouden (vahst-hou-dehn) v *hold; zich ~ *hold on
vastmaken (vahst-maa-kern) v fasten; attach
vastomlijnd (vahss-tom-laynt) adj definite
vastspelden (vahst-spehl-dern) v pin
vaststellen (vahst-steh-lern) v establish, determine
vat (vaht) nt (pl ~en) cask, barrel; vessel
*vechten (vehkh-tern) v *fight; combat, battle
vee (vāy) nt cattle pl
veearts (vāy-ahrts) c (pl ~en) veterinary surgeon
veel (vāyl) adj much, many; adv much, far
veelbetekenend (vāyl-ber-tāy-ker-nernt) adj significant
veelomvattend (vāyl-om-vah-ternt)

adj extensive
veelvuldig (vāyl-verl-derkh) adj frequent
veelzijdig (vāyl-zay-derkh) adj all-round
veen (vāyn) nt moor
veer (vāyr) c (pl veren) feather; spring
veerboot (vāyr-bōat) c (pl -boten) ferry-boat
veertien (vāyr-teen) num fourteen; ~ dagen fortnight
veertiende (vāyr-teen-der) num fourteenth
veertig (vāyr-terkh) num forty
vegen (vāy-gern) v *sweep; wipe
vegetariër (vāy-ger-taa-ree-Yerr) c (pl ~s) vegetarian
veilig (vay-lerkh) adj safe; secure
veiligheid (vay-lerkh-hayt) c safety; security
veiligheidsgordel (vay-lerkh-hayts-khor-derl) c (pl ~s) safety-belt; seat-belt
veiligheidsspeld (vay-lerkh-hayt-spehlt) c (pl ~en) safety-pin
veiling (vay-ling) c (pl ~en) auction
vel (vehl) nt (pl ~len) skin
veld (vehlt) nt (pl ~en) field
veldbed (vehlt-beht) nt (pl ~den) camp-bed
veldkijker (vehlt-kay-kerr) c (pl ~s) field glasses
velg (vehlkh) c (pl ~en) rim
Venezolaan (vāy-nāy-zōa-laan) c (pl -lanen) Venezuelan
Venezolaans (vāy-nāy-zōa-laans) adj Venezuelan
Venezuela (vāy-nāy-zēw-vāy-laa) Venezuela
vennoot (ver-nōat) c (pl -noten) associate
vensterbank (vehn-sterr-bahngk) c (pl ~en) window-sill

vent (vehnt) *c* chap, guy

ventiel (vehn-*teel*) *nt* (pl ~en) valve

ventilatie (vehn-tee-*laa*-tsee) *c* (pl ~s) ventilation

ventilator (vehn-ti-*laa*-tor) *c* (pl ~s, ~en) ventilator, fan

ventilatorriem (vehn-tee-*laa*-to-reem) *c* (pl ~en) fan belt

ventileren (vehn-tee-*lay*-rern) *v* ventilate

ver (vehr) *adj* far; remote, far-away, distant

verachten (verr-*ahkh*-tern) *v* scorn, despise

verachting (verr-*ahkh*-ting) *c* scorn, contempt

verademing (verr-*aa*-der-ming) *c* relief

veranda (ver-*rahn*-daa) *c* (pl ~'s) veranda

veranderen (verr-*ahn*-der-rern) *v* change; alter, transform; vary; ~ in turn into

verandering (verr-*ahn*-der-ring) *c* (pl ~en) change; alteration; variation

veranderlijk (verr-*ahn*-derr-lerk) *adj* variable

verantwoordelijk (verr-ahnt-*voar*-der-lerk) *adj* responsible

verantwoordelijkheid (verr-ahnt-*voar*-der-lerk-hayt) *c* (pl -heden) responsibility

verantwoorden (verr-ahnt-*voar*-dern) *v* account for

verband (verr-*bahnt*) *nt* (pl ~en) connection, relation; bandage

verbandkist (verr-*bahnt*-kist) *c* (pl ~en) first-aid kit

verbazen (verr-*baa*-zern) *v* astonish, amaze, surprise; **zich ~** marvel

verbazing (verr-*baa*-zing) *c* astonishment, amazement, surprise

zich verbeelden (verr-*bayl*-dern) fancy, imagine

verbeelding (verr-*bayl*-ding) *c* imagin-

ation

***verbergen** (verr-*behr*-gern) *v* *hide; conceal

verbeteren (verr-*bay*-ter-rern) *v* improve; correct

verbetering (verr-*bay*-ter-ring) *c* (pl ~en) improvement; correction

***verbieden** (verr-*bee*-dern) *v* prohibit, *forbid

***verbinden** (verr-*bin*-dern) *v* link, connect, join; dress; **zich ~** engage

verbinding (verr-*bin*-ding) *c* (pl ~en) link; connection; **zich in ~ stellen met** contact

verbindingsstuk (verr-*bin*-ding-sturk) *nt* adaptor

verblijf (verr-*blayf*) *nt* (pl -blijven) stay

verblijfsvergunning (verr-*blayfs*-ferr-ger-ning) *c* (pl ~en) residence permit

***verblijven** (verr-*blay*-vern) *v* stay

verblinden (verr-*blin*-dern) *v* blind; **verblindend** glaring

verbod (verr-*bot*) *nt* (pl ~en) prohibition

verboden (verr-*boa*-dern) *adj* prohibited; ~ **te parkeren** no parking; ~ **te roken** no smoking; ~ **toegang** no entry, no admittance; ~ **voor voetgangers** no pedestrians

verbond (verr-*bont*) *nt* (pl ~en) union

verbranden (verr-*brahn*-dern) *v* *burn

verbruiken (verr-*brur*ew-kern) *v* use up

verbruiker (verr-*brur*ew-kerr) *c* (pl ~s) consumer

verdacht (verr-*dahkht*) *adj* suspicious

verdachte (verr-*dahkh*-teh) *c* (pl ~n) suspect; accused

verdampen (verr-*dahm*-pern) *v* evaporate

verdedigen (verr-*day*-der-gern) *v* defend

verdediging (verr-*day*-der-ging) *c* defence

verdelen (verr-*day*-lern) *v* divide

***verdenken** (verr-*dehng*-kern) *v* suspect

verdenking (verr-*dehng*-king) *c* (pl ~en) suspicion

verder (*vehr*-derr) *adj* further; *adv* beyond; ~ **dan** beyond

verdienen (verr-*dee*-nern) *v* earn; **make; deserve, merit

verdienste (verr-*deens*-ter) *c* (pl ~n) merit; **verdiensten** *pl* earnings *pl*

verdieping (verr-*dee*-ping) *c* (pl ~en) storey, floor

verdikken (verr-*di*-kern) *v* thicken

verdoving (verr-*doa*-ving) *c* (pl ~en) anaesthesia

verdraaien (verr-*draa*ᵉᵉ-ern) *v* wrench

verdrag (verr-*drahkh*) *nt* (pl ~en) treaty

***verdragen** (verr-*draa*-gern) *v* endure, **bear; sustain

verdriet (verr-*dreet*) *nt* grief, sorrow

verdrietig (verr-*dree*-terkh) *adj* sad

***verdrijven** (verr-*dray*-vern) *v* chase

***verdrinken** (verr-*dring*-kern) *v* drown; **be drowned

verdrukken (verr-*drer*-kern) *v* oppress

verduidelijken (verr-*dur*ᵉʷ-der-ler-kern) *v* clarify

verduistering (verr-*dur*ᵉʷss-ter-rehn) *c* (pl ~en) eclipse

verdunnen (verr-*der*-nern) *v* dilute

verdwaald (verr-*dvaalt*) *adj* lost

***verdwijnen** (verr-*dvay*-nern) *v* vanish, disappear

vereisen (verr-*ay*-sern) *v* demand, require; **vereist** requisite

vereiste (verr-*ayss*-ter) *c* (pl ~n) requirement

Verenigde Staten (verr-*ay*-nerkh-der-*staa*-tern) United States, the States

verenigen (verr-*ay*-ner-gern) *v* join; unite; **verenigd** joint

vereniging (verr-*ay*-ner-ging) *c* (pl ~en) association; union, society, club

verf (vehrf) *c* (pl verven) paint; dye

verfdoos (*vehrf*-doass) *c* (pl -dozen) paint-box

verfrissen (verr-*fri*-sern) *v* refresh

verfrissing (verr-*fri*-sing) *c* (pl ~en) refreshment

vergadering (verr-*gaa*-der-ring) *c* (pl ~en) meeting; assembly

vergeefs (verr-*gayfs*) *adj* vain; *adv* in vain

vergeetachtig (verr-*gayt*-ahkh-terkh) *adj* forgetful

***vergelijken** (vehr-ger-*lay*-kern) *v* compare

vergelijking (vehr-ger-*lay*-king) *c* (pl ~en) comparison

***vergeten** (verr-*gay*-tern) *v* **forget

***vergeven** (verr-*gay*-vern) *v* **forgive

zich vergewissen van (verr-ger-*vi*-sern) ascertain

vergezellen (verr-ger-*zeh*-lern) *v* accompany

vergiet (verr-*geet*) *nt* (pl ~en) strainer

vergif (verr-*gif*) *nt* poison

vergiffenis (verr-*gi*-fer-niss) *c* pardon

vergiftig (verr-*gif*-terkh) *adj* toxic

vergiftigen (verr-*gif*-teh-gern) *v* poison

zich vergissen (verr-*gi*-sern) **be mistaken; err

vergissing (verr-*gi*-sing) *c* (pl ~en) oversight; error, mistake

vergoeden (verr-*goo*-dern) *v* **make good, reimburse; remunerate

vergoeding (verr-*goo*-ding) *c* (pl ~en) remuneration

vergrootglas (verr-*groat*-khlahss) *nt* (pl -glazen) magnifying glass

vergroten (verr-*groa*-tern) *v* enlarge

vergroting (verr-*groa*-ting) *c* (pl ~en) enlargement

verguld (verr-*gerlt*) *adj* gilt

vergunning (verr-*ger*-ning) *c* (pl ~en)

licence, permit, permission; **een ~ verlenen** license

verhaal (verr-*haal*) *nt* (pl -halen) story; tale

verhandeling (verr-*hahn*-der-lıng) *c* (pl ~en) essay

verheugd (verr-*hürkht*) *adj* glad

verhinderen (verr-*hın*-der-rern) *v* prevent

verhogen (verr-*hōa*-gern) *v* raise

verhoging (verr-*hōa*-gıng) *c* (pl ~en) rise, increase

verhoor (verr-*hōar*) *nt* (pl -horen) examination, interrogation

verhouding (verr-*hou*-dıng) *c* (pl ~en) affair

verhuizen (verr-*hur*ᵉʷ-zern) *v* move

verhuizing (verr-*hur*ᵉʷ-zıng) *c* (pl ~en) move

verhuren (verr-*hēw*-rern) *v* *let; lease

verifiëren (vāy-ree-fee-ʸ*āy*-rern) *v* verify

vering (*vāy*-rıng) *c* suspension

verjaardag (verr-ʸ*aar*-dahkh) *c* (pl ~en) birthday; anniversary

*****verjagen** (verr-ʸ*aa*-gern) *v* chase

verkeer (verr-*kāyr*) *nt* traffic

verkeerd (verr-*kāyrt*) *adj* false, wrong

verkeersbureau (verr-*kāyrs*-bēw-rōa) *nt* (pl ~s) tourist office

verkeersopstopping (verr-*kāyrz*-op-sto-pıng) *c* (pl ~en) traffic jam

verkennen (verr-*keh*-nern) *v* explore

*****verkiezen** (verr-*kee*-zern) *v* elect

verkiezing (verr-*kee*-zıng) *c* (pl ~en) election

verklaarbaar (verr-*klaar*-baar) *adj* accountable

verklaren (verr-*klaa*-rern) *v* state, declare; explain

verklaring (verr-*klaa*-rıng) *c* (pl ~en) statement, declaration; explanation

zich verkleden (verr-*klāy*-dern) change

verkleuren (verr-*klūr*-rern) *v* fade; discolour

verknoeien (verr-*knōō*ᵉᵉ-ern) *v* muddle

verkoop (*vehr*-kōap) *c* sale

verkoopbaar (verr-*kōa*-baar) *adj* saleable

verkoopster (verr-*kōap*-sterr) *c* (pl ~s) salesgirl

*****verkopen** (verr-*kōa*-pern) *v* *sell; **in het klein ~** retail

verkoper (verr-*kōa*-perr) *c* (pl ~s) salesman; shop assistant

verkorten (verr-*kor*-tern) *v* shorten

verkoudheid (verr-*kout*-hayt) *c* cold

verkrachten (verr-*krahkh*-tern) *v* rape

verkrijgbaar (verr-*kraykh*-baar) *adj* obtainable, available

*****verkrijgen** (verr-*kray*-gern) *v* obtain

verlagen (verr-*laa*-gern) *v* lower, reduce; *cut

verlammen (verr-*lah*-mern) *v* paralise

verlangen[1] (verr-*lah*-ngern) *v* wish, desire; **~ naar** long for

verlangen[2] (verr-*lah*-ngern) *nt* (pl ~s) wish; longing

verlaten (verr-*laa*-tern) *adj* desert

*****verlaten** (verr-*laa*-tern) *v* *leave; desert

verleden (verr-*lāy*-dern) *adj* previous; *nt* past

verlegen (verr-*lāy*-gern) *adj* shy; embarrassed

verlegenheid (verr-*lāy*-gern-hayt) *c* shyness, timidity; **in ~ *brengen** embarrass

verleiden (verr-*lay*-dern) *v* seduce

verleiding (verr-*lay*-dıng) *c* (pl ~en) temptation

verlenen (verr-*lāy*-nern) *v* grant; extend

verlengen (verr-*leh*-ngern) *v* lengthen; extend; renew

verlenging (verr-*leh*-ngıng) *c* (pl ~en) extension

verlengsnoer (verr-*lehng*-snoor) *nt* (pl ~en) extension cord

verlichten (verr-*likh*-tern) *v* illuminate; relieve

verlichting (verr-*likh*-ting) *c* lighting, illumination; relief

verliefd (verr-*leeft*) *adj* in love

verlies (verr-*leess*) *nt* (pl -liezen) loss

*****verliezen** (verr-*lee*-zern) *v* *lose

verlof (verr-*lof*) *nt* (pl -loven) leave; permission

verloofd (verr-*lōaft*) *adj* engaged

verloofde (verr-*lōaf*-der) *c* (pl ~n) fiancé; fiancée

verlossen (verr-*lo*-sern) *v* deliver; redeem

verlossing (verr-*lo*-sing) *c* (pl ~en) delivery

verloving (verr-*lōa*-ving) *c* (pl ~en) engagement

verlovingsring (verr-*lōa*-vings-ring) *c* (pl ~en) engagement ring

vermaak (verr-*maak*) *nt* entertainment, amusement

vermageren (verr-*maa*-ger-rern) *v* slim

vermakelijk (verr-*maa*-ker-lerk) *adj* entertaining

vermaken (verr-*maa*-kern) *v* entertain, amuse

vermeerderen (verr-*māyr*-der-rern) *v* increase

vermelden (verr-*mehl*-dern) *v* mention

vermelding (verr-*mehl*-ding) *c* (pl ~en) mention

vermenigvuldigen (verr-may-nerkh-*ferl*-der-gern) *v* multiply

vermenigvuldiging (verr-may-nerkh-*ferl*-der-ging) *c* (pl ~en) multiplication

*****vermijden** (verr-*may*-dern) *v* avoid

verminderen (verr-*min*-der-rern) *v* decrease, lessen, reduce

vermindering (verr-*min*-der-ring) *c* (pl ~en) decrease

vermiste (verr-*miss*-ter) *c* (pl ~n) missing person

vermoedelijk (verr-*mōo*-der-lerk) *adj* presumable, probable

vermoeden (verr-*mōo*-dern) *v* suspect

vermoeien (verr-*mōo*ᵉᵉ-ern) *v* tire; **vermoeid** weary, tired

vermogen (verr-*mōa*-gern) *nt* (pl ~s) ability, faculty; capacity

zich vermommen (verr-*mo*-mern) disguise

vermomming (verr-*mo*-ming) *c* (pl ~en) disguise

vermoorden (verr-*mōar*-dern) *v* murder

vernielen (verr-*nee*-lern) *v* wreck, destroy

vernietigen (verr-*nee*-ter-gern) *v* destroy

vernietiging (verr-*nee*-ter-ging) *c* destruction

vernieuwen (verr-*nee*ᵒᵒ-ern) *v* renew

vernis (verr-*niss*) *nt/c* varnish

veronderstellen (verr-on-derr-*steh*-lern) *v* assume, suppose

verontreiniging (verr-ont-*ray*-ner-ging) *c* (pl ~en) pollution

verontschuldigen (verr-ont-*skherl*-der-gern) *v* excuse; **zich ~** apologize

verontschuldiging (verr-ont-*skherl*-der-ging) *c* (pl ~en) apology

verontwaardiging (verr-ont-*vaar*-der-ging) *c* indignation

veroordeelde (verr-*ōar*-dāyl-der) *c* (pl ~n) convict

veroordelen (verr-*ōar*-dāy-lern) *v* sentence

veroordeling (verr-*ōar*-dāy-ling) *c* (pl ~en) conviction

veroorloven (verr-*ōar*-lōa-vern) *v* allow, permit; **zich ~** afford

veroorzaken (verr-*ōar*-zaa-kern) *v* cause

veroveraar (verr-*ōa*-ver-raar) *c* (pl ~s)

conqueror

veroveren (verr-*ōā*-ver-rern) *v* conquer

verovering (verr-*ōā*-ver-ring) *c* (pl ~en) conquest

verpachten (verr-*pahkh*-tern) *v* lease

verpakking (verr-*pah*-king) *c* (pl ~en) packing

verpanden (verr-*pahn*-dern) *v* pawn

verplaatsen (verr-*plaat*-sern) *v* move

verpleegster (verr-*plāykh*-sterr) *c* (pl ~s) nurse

verplegen (verr-*plāy*-gern) *v* nurse

verplicht (verr-*plikht*) *adj* obligatory, compulsory; ~ *zijn om* *be obliged to

verplichten (verr-*plikh*-tern) *v* oblige

verplichting (verr-*plikh*-ting) *c* (pl ~en) engagement

verraad (ver-*raat*) *nt* treason

* **verraden** (ver-*raa*-dern) *v* betray

verrader (ver-*raa*-derr) *c* (pl ~s) traitor

verrassen (ver-*rah*-sern) *v* surprise

verrassing (ver-*rah*-sing) *c* (pl ~en) surprise

verrekijker (veh-rer-*kay*-kerr) *c* (pl ~s) binoculars *pl*

verreweg (veh-rer-*vehkh*) *adv* by far

verrichten (ver-*rikh*-tern) *v* perform

verrukkelijk (ver-*rer*-ker-lerk) *adj* delightful, wonderful

verrukking (ver-*rer*-king) *c* (pl ~en) delight; *in* ~ *brengen* delight

vers¹ (vehrs) *adj* fresh

vers² (vehrs) *nt* (pl verzen) verse

verschaffen (verr-*skhah*-fern) *v* furnish, provide

verscheidene (verr-*skhay*-der-ner) *num* various; several

verscheidenheid (verr-*skhay*-dern-hayt) *c* (pl -heden) variety

verschepen (verr-*skhāy*-pern) *v* ship

* **verschieten** (verr-*skhee*-tern) *v* fade

* **verschijnen** (verr-*skhay*-nern) *v* appear

verschijning (verr-*skhay*-ning) *c* (pl ~en) apparition

verschijnsel (verr-*skhayn*-serl) *nt* (pl ~en, ~s) phenomenon

verschil (verr-*skhil*) *nt* (pl ~len) difference; distinction, contrast

verschillen (verr-*skhi*-lern) *v* differ; vary

verschillend (verr-*skhi*-lernt) *adj* unlike, different; distinct

verschrikkelijk (verr-*skhri*-ker-lerk) *adj* terrible; horrible, frightful, awful

verschuldigd (verr-*skherl*-derkht) *adj* due; ~ *zijn* owe

versie (*vehr*-zee) *c* (pl ~s) version

versiering (verr-*see*-ring) *c* (pl ~en) decoration

versiersel (verr-*seer*-serl) *nt* (pl ~s, ~en) ornament

* **verslaan** (verr-*slaan*) *v* defeat, *beat

verslag (verr-*slahkh*) *nt* (pl ~en) report, account

verslaggever (verr-*slah*-khāy-verr) *c* (pl ~s) reporter

zich * **verslapen** (verr-*slaa*-pern) *oversleep

versleten (verr-*slāy*-tern) *adj* worn-out, worn; threadbare

* **verslijten** (verr-*slay*-tern) *v* wear out

versnellen (verr-*sneh*-lern) *v* accelerate

versnelling (verr-*sneh*-ling) *c* (pl ~en) gear

versnellingsbak (verr-*sneh*-lings-bahk) *c* (pl ~ken) gear-box

versnellingspook (verr-*sneh*-lings-pōā) *c* gear lever

versperren (verr-*speh*-rern) *v* block

verspillen (verr-*spi*-lern) *v* waste

verspilling (verr-*spi*-ling) *c* waste

verspreiden (verr-*spray*-dern) *v* scatter, *shed

* **verstaan** (verr-*staan*) *v* *understand

verstand (verr-*stahnt*) *nt* brain; wits

pl, reason; **gezond** ~ sense

verstandig (verr-*stahn*-derkh) *adj* sensible

verstellen (verr-*steh*-lern) *v* patch

verstijfd (verr-*stayft*) *adj* numb

verstoppen (verr-*sto*-pern) *v* *hide

verstoren (verr-*stoā*-rern) *v* disturb; upset

***verstrijken** (verr-*stray*-kern) *v* expire

verstuiken (verr-*stur*ew-kern) *v* sprain

verstuiking (verr-*stur*ew-kıng) *c* (pl ~en) sprain

verstuiver (verr-*stur*ew-verr) *c* (pl ~s) atomizer

versturen (verr-*stew*-rern) *v* *send off, dispatch

vertalen (verr-*taa*-lern) *v* translate

vertaler (verr-*taa*-lerr) *c* (pl ~s) translator

vertaling (verr-*taa*-lıng) *c* (pl ~en) translation; version

verteerbaar (verr-*tāyr*-baar) *adj* digestible

vertegenwoordigen (verr-*tāy*-ger-*vōār*-der-gern) *v* represent

vertegenwoordiger (verr-*tāy*-ger-*vōār*-der-gerr) *c* (pl ~s) agent

vertegenwoordiging (verr-*tāy*-ger-*vōār*-der-gıng) *c* (pl ~en) representation; agency

vertellen (verr-*ter*-lern) *v* *tell; relate

vertelling (verr-*teh*-lıng) *c* (pl ~en) tale

verteren (verr-*tāy*-rern) *v* digest

verticaal (vehr-tee-*kaal*) *adj* vertical

vertolken (verr-*tol*-kern) *v* interpret

vertonen (verr-*tōā*-nern) *v* exhibit; display

vertragen (verr-*traa*-gern) *v* delay, slow down

vertraging (verr-*traa*-gıng) *c* (pl ~en) delay

vertrek¹ (verr-*trehk*) *nt* departure

vertrek² (verr-*trehk*) *nt* (pl ~ken) room

***vertrekken** (verr-*treh*-kern) *v* *leave; depart, *set out, pull out

vertrektijd (verr-*trehk*-tayt) *c* (pl ~en) time of departure

vertrouwd (verr-*trout*) *adj* familiar

vertrouwelijk (verr-*trou*-er-lerk) *adj* confidential

vertrouwen (verr-*trou*-ern) *nt* confidence, trust, faith; *v* trust; ~ **op** rely on

vervaardigen (verr-*vaar*-der-gern) *v* manufacture

vervaldag (verr-*vahl*-dahkh) *c* expiry

vervallen (verr-*vah*-lern) *adj* expired; due

***vervallen** (verr-*vah*-lern) *v* expire

vervalsen (verr-*vahl*-sern) *v* forge, counterfeit

vervalsing (verr-*vahl*-sıng) *c* (pl ~en) fake

***vervangen** (verr-*vah*-ngern) *v* replace, substitute

vervanging (verr-*vah*-ngıng) *c* substitute

vervelen (verr-*vāy*-lern) *v* bore; bother

vervelend (verr-*vāy*-lernt) *adj* dull, boring, annoying; unpleasant

verven (vehr-vern) *v* paint; dye

vervloeken (verr-*vlōō*-kern) *v* curse

vervoer (verr-*vōōr*) *nt* transport

vervolg (verr-*volkh*) *nt* (pl ~en) sequel

vervolgen (verr-*vol*-gern) *v* continue; pursue

vervolgens (verr-*vol*-gerss) *adv* then

vervuiling (verr-*vur*ew-lıng) *c* pollution

verwaand (verr-*vaant*) *adj* conceited, snooty

verwaarlozen (verr-*vaar*-lōā-zern) *v* neglect

verwaarlozing (verr-*vaar*-lōā-zıng) *c* neglect

verwachten (verr-*vahkh*-tern) *v* expect; anticipate

verwachting (verr-*vahkh*-ting) c (pl ~en) expectation; outlook; **in ~** pregnant

verwant (verr-*vahnt*) adj related

verwante (verr-*vahn*-ter) c (pl ~n) relation

verward (verr-*vahrt*) adj confused

verwarmen (verr-*vahr*-mern) v heat, warm

verwarming (verr-*vahr*-ming) c heating

verwarren (verr-*vah*-rern) v confuse; *mistake

verwarring (verr-*vah*-ring) c confusion; disturbance; **in ~ brengen** embarrass

verwekken (verr-*veh*-kern) v generate

verwelkomen (verr-*vehl*-kōa-mern) v welcome

verwennen (verr-*veh*-nern) v *spoil

***verwerpen** (verr-*vehr*-pern) v turn down, reject

***verwerven** (verr-*vehr*-vern) v acquire

verwezenlijken (verr-*vāȳ*-zer-ler-kern) v realize

verwijden (verr-*vay*-dern) v widen

verwijderen (verr-*vay*-der-rern) v remove

verwijdering (verr-*vay*-der-ring) c removal

verwijt (verr-*vayt*) nt (pl ~en) reproach; blame

***verwijten** (verr-*vay*-tern) v reproach

***verwijzen naar** (verr-*vay*-zern) refer to

verwijzing (verr-*vay*-zing) c (pl ~en) reference

verwonden (verr-*von*-dern) v wound, injure

verwonderen (verr-*von*-der-rern) v amaze

verwondering (verr-*von*-der-ring) c wonder

verwonding (verr-*von*-ding) c (pl ~en) injury

verzachten (verr-*zahkh*-tern) v soften

verzamelaar (verr-*zaa*-mer-laar) c (pl ~s) collector

verzamelen (verr-*zaa*-mer-lern) v gather; collect

verzameling (verr-*zaa*-mer-ling) c (pl ~en) collection

verzekeren (verr-*zāȳ*-ker-rern) v assure; insure

verzekering (verr-*zāȳ*-ker-ring) c (pl ~en) insurance

verzekeringspolis (verr-*zāȳ*-ker-rings-pōa-lerss) c (pl ~sen) insurance policy

***verzenden** (verr-*zehn*-dern) v despatch, dispatch

verzending (verr-*zehn*-ding) c expedition

verzet (verr-*zeht*) nt resistance

zich verzetten (verr-*zeh*-tern) oppose

verzilveren (verr-*zil*-ver-rern) v cash

***verzinnen** (verr-*zi*-nern) v invent

verzinsel (verr-*zin*-serl) nt (pl ~s) fiction

verzoek (verr-*zōōk*) nt (pl ~en) request

***verzoeken** (verr-*zōō*-kern) v request, ask

verzoening (verr-*zōō*-ning) c (pl ~en) reconciliation

verzorgen (verr-*zor*-gern) v look after, *take care of; tend

verzorging (verr-*zor*-ging) c care

verzwikken (verr-*zvi*-kern) v sprain

vest (vehst) nt (pl ~en) cardigan; waistcoat, jacket; vest nAm

vestigen (*vehss*-ter-gern) v establish; **zich ~** settle down

vesting (*vehss*-ting) c (pl ~en) fortress

vet¹ (veht) adj fat; greasy

vet² (veht) nt (pl ~ten) fat; grease

veter (*vāȳ*-terr) c (pl ~s) lace

vettig (*veh*-terkh) *adj* greasy, fatty

vezel (*vāy*-zerl) *c* (pl ~s) fibre

vibratie (vee-*braa*-tsee) *c* (pl ~s) vibration

video camera (*vie*-dee-oo *kaa*-mee-raa) *c* video camera

video cassette (*vie*-dee-oo ka-*seter*) *c* video cassette

video recorder (vie-dee-oo rie-*kor*-derr) *c* video recorder

vier (veer) *num* four

vierde (*veer*-der) *num* fourth

vieren (*vee*-rern) *v* celebrate

viering (*vee*-ring) *c* (pl ~en) celebration

vierkant (*veer*-kahnt) *adj* square; *nt* square

vies (veess) *adj* dirty

vijand (*vay*-ahnt) *c* (pl ~en) enemy

vijandig (vay-*ahn*-derkh) *adj* hostile

vijf (vayf) *num* five

vijfde (*vayf*-der) *num* fifth

vijftien (*vayf*-teen) *num* fifteen

vijftiende (*vayf*-teen-der) *num* fifteenth

vijftig (*vayf*-terkh) *num* fifty

vijg (vaykh) *c* (pl ~en) fig

vijl (vayl) *c* (pl ~en) file

vijver (*vay*-verr) *c* (pl ~s) pond

villa (*vee*-laa) *c* (pl ~'s) villa

vilt (vilt) *nt* felt

*****vinden** (*vin*-dern) *v* *find; *come across; consider

vindingrijk (*vin*-ding-rayk) *adj* inventive

vinger (*vi*-ngerr) *c* (pl ~s) finger

vingerafdruk (*vi*-ngerr-ahf-drerk) *c* (pl ~ken) fingerprint

vingerhoed (*vi*-ngerr-hōōt) *c* (pl ~en) thimble

violet (vee-Yōa-*leht*) *adj* violet

viool (vee-Yōa̅l) *c* (pl violen) violin

viooltje (vee-Yōa̅l-t Yer) *nt* (pl ~s) violet

vis (viss) *c* (pl ~sen) fish

visakte (*viss*-ahk-ter) *c* (pl ~n, ~s) fishing licence

visgraat (*viss*-khraat) *c* (pl -graten) fishbone

vishaak (*viss*-haak) *c* (pl -haken) fishing hook

visie (*vee*-zee) *c* vision

visite (vee-*zee*-ter) *c* (pl ~s) visit; call

visitekaartje (vi-*zee*-ter-kaar-t Yer) *nt* (pl ~s) visiting-card

viskuit (*viss*-kur ew t) *c* roe

vislijn (*viss*-layn) *c* (pl ~en) fishing line

visnet (*viss*-neht) *nt* (pl ~ten) fishing net

vissen (*vi*-sern) *v* fish

visser (*vi*-serr) *c* (pl ~s) fisherman

visserij (vi-ser-*ray*) *c* fishing industry

vistuig (*viss*-tur ew kh) *nt* fishing tackle, fishing gear

visum (*vee*-zerm) *nt* (pl visa) visa

viswinkel (*viss*-ving-kerl) *c* (pl ~s) fish shop

vitamine (vee-taa-*mee*-ner) *c* (pl ~n, ~s) vitamin

vitrine (vee-*tree*-ner) *c* (pl ~s) showcase

vlag (vlahkh) *c* (pl ~gen) flag

vlak (vlahk) *adj* flat; smooth; level, plane

vlakgom (*vlahk*-khom) *c/nt* (pl ~men) rubber

vlakte (*vlahk*-ter) *c* (pl ~n, ~s) plain

vlam (vlahm) *c* (pl ~men) flame

vlees (vlāyss) *nt* meat; flesh

vlek (vlehk) *c* (pl ~ken) stain, spot, blot

vlekkeloos (*vleh*-ker-lōass) *adj* stainless, spotless

vlekken (*vleh*-kern) *v* stain

vlekkenwater (*vleh*-ker-vaa-terr) *nt* stain remover

vleugel (*vlur̄*-gerl) *c* (pl ~s) wing;

grand piano

vlieg (vleekh) c (pl ~en) fly

*vliegen (vlee-gern) v *fly

vliegramp (vleekh-rahmp) c (pl ~en) plane crash

vliegtuig (vleekh-tur^{ew}kh) nt (pl ~en) aircraft, aeroplane, plane; airplane nAm

vliegveld (vleekh-fehlt) nt (pl ~en) airfield

vlijt (vlayt) c diligence

vlijtig (vlay-terkh) adj industrious; diligent

vlinder (vlin-derr) c (pl ~s) butterfly

vlinderdasje (vlin-derr-dah-sher) nt (pl ~s) bow tie

vlinderslag (vlin-derr-slahkh) c butterfly stroke

vloed (vloot) c flood

vloeibaar (vloo^{ee}-baar) adj liquid, fluid

vloeien (vloo^{ee}-ern) v flow; **vloeiend** fluent

vloeipapier (vloo^{ee}-paa-peer) nt blotting paper

vloeistof (vloo^{ee}-stof) c (pl ~fen) fluid

vloek (vlook) c (pl ~en) curse

vloeken (vloo-kern) v curse, *swear

vloer (vloor) c (pl ~en) floor

vloerkleed (vloor-klayt) nt (pl -kleden) carpet

vloot (vloat) c (pl vloten) fleet

vlot (vlot) nt (pl ~ten) raft

vlotter (vlo-terr) c (pl ~s) float

vlucht (vlerkht) c (pl ~en) flight

vluchten (vlerkh-tern) v escape

vlug (vlerkh) adj fast, quick, rapid; adv soon

vocaal (voa-kaal) adj vocal

vocabulaire (voa-kaa-bew-lair) nt vocabulary

vocht (vokht) nt damp

vochtig (vokh-terkh) adj humid, moist; damp, wet

vochtigheid (vokh-terkh-hayt) c humidity, moisture

vod (vot) nt (pl ~den) rag

voeden (voo-dern) v *feed

voedsel (voot-serl) nt food; fare

voedselvergiftiging (voot-serl-verr-gif-ter-ging) c food poisoning

voedzaam (voot-saam) adj nutritious, nourishing

zich voegen bij (voo-gern) join

voelen (voo-lern) v *feel; sense

voeren (voo-rern) v carry

voering (voo-ring) c (pl ~en) lining

voertuig (voor-tur^{ew}kh) nt (pl ~en) vehicle

voet (voot) c (pl ~en) foot; **te ~** on foot, walking

voetbal (voot-bahl) nt soccer

voetbalwedstrijd (voot-bahl-veht-strayt) c (pl ~en) football match

voetganger (voot-khah-ngerr) c (pl ~s) pedestrian

voetpad (voot-paht) nt (pl ~en) footpath

voetpoeder (voot-poo-derr) nt/c foot powder

voetrem (voot-rehm) c foot-brake

vogel (voa-gerl) c (pl ~s) bird

vol (vol) adj full; full up

volbloed (vol-bloot) adj thoroughbred

*volbrengen (vol-breh-ngern) v accomplish

voldaan (vol-daan) adj satisfied

voldoende (vol-doon-der) adj sufficient, enough; ~ *zijn *do, suffice

voldoening (vol-doo-ning) c satisfaction

volgen (vol-gern) v follow; **volgend** subsequent, next, following

volgens (vol-gerns) prep according to

volgorde (vol-gor-der) c order, sequence

*volhouden (vol-hou-dern) v *keep up; insist

volk (volk) *nt* (pl ~en, ~eren) people; nation; folk; **volks-** national; popular; vulgar

volkomen (voal-*koa*-mern) *adj* perfect; *adv* completely

volkorenbrood (vol-*koa*-rerm-broat) *nt* wholemeal bread

volksdans (*volks*-dahns) *c* (pl ~en) folk-dance

volkslied (*volks*-leet) *nt* (pl ~eren) folk song; national anthem

volledig (vo-*lay*-derkh) *adj* complete

volmaakt (vol-*maakt*) *adj* perfect

volmaaktheid (vol-*maakt*-hayt) *c* perfection

volslagen (vol-*slaa*-gern) *adj* total, utter

volt (volt) *c* volt

voltage (vol-*taa*-zher) *c*/*nt* (pl ~s) voltage

voltooien (vol-*toa*ee-ern) *v* complete

volume (voa-*lew*-mer) *nt* (pl ~n, ~s) volume

volwassen (vol-*vah*-sern) *adj* adult; grown-up

volwassene (vol-*vah*-ser-ner) *c* (pl ~n) adult; grown-up

vonk (vongk) *c* (pl ~en) spark

vonnis (*vo*-nerss) *nt* (pl ~sen) verdict, sentence

voogd (voakht) *c* (pl ~en) tutor, guardian

voogdij (voakh-*day*) *c* custody

voor (voar) *prep* before; ahead of, in front of; for; to

vooraanstaand (voar-*aan*-staant) *adj* leading, outstanding

*voorafgaan (voar-*ahf*-khaan) *v* precede

voorai (voa-rahl) *adv* essentially, especially, most of all

voorbarig (voar-*baa*-rerkh) *adj* premature

voorbeeld (voar-*baylt*) *nt* (pl ~en) example, instance

voorbehoedmiddel (voar-ber-*hoot*-mi-derl) *nt* (pl ~en) contraceptive

voorbehoud (voar-ber-*hout*) *nt* qualification

voorbereiden (voar-ber-ray-dern) *v* prepare

voorbereiding (voar-ber-ray-ding) *c* (pl ~en) preparation

voorbij (voar-*bay*) *adj* past, over; *prep* past, beyond

*voorbijgaan (voar-*bay*-gaan) *v* pass

voorbijganger (voar-*bay*-gah-ngerr) *c* (pl ~s) passer-by

voordat (voar-*daht*) *conj* before

voordeel (voar-*dayl*) *nt* (pl -delen) advantage; profit, benefit

voordelig (voar-*day*-lerkh) *adj* advantageous; cheap

zich *voordoen (voar-*doon*) *v* occur

voorgaand (voar-*khaant*) *adj* previous, preceding

voorganger (voar-*gah*-ngerr) *c* (pl ~s) predecessor

voorgerecht (voar-ger-*rehkht*) *nt* (pl ~en) hors-d'œuvre

voorgrond (voar-*gront*) *c* foreground

voorhanden (voar-*hahn*-dern) *adj* available

voorheen (voar-*hayn*) *adv* formerly

voorhoofd (voar-*hoaft*) *nt* (pl ~en) forehead

voorjaar (voar-ʸaar) *nt* springtime, spring

voorkant (voar-*kahnt*) *c* front

voorkeur (voar-*kürr*) *c* preference; **de ~ *geven aan** prefer

voorkomen¹ (voar-*koa*-mern) *nt* look, appearance

*voorkomen² (voar-*koa*-mern) *v* occur, happen

*voorkomen³ (voar-*koa*-mern) *v* prevent; anticipate

voorkomend (voar-*koa*-mernt) *adj* obliging

voorletter (*vōar*-leh-terr) *c* (pl ~s) initial

voorlopig (vōar-*lōa*-perkh) *adj* provisional, temporary; preliminary

voormalig (vōar-*maa*-lerkh) *adj* former

voorman (*vōar*-mahn) *c* (pl ~nen) foreman

voornaam¹ (vōar-*naam*) *adj* distinguished; **voornaamst** *adj* principal, main, leading, chief

voornaam² (*vōar*-naam) *c* (pl -namen) first name, Christian name

voornaamwoord (*vōar*-naam-vōart) *nt* (pl ~en) pronoun

voornamelijk (vōar-*naa*-mer-lerk) *adv* especially

vooroordeel (*vōar*-ōar-dāyl) *nt* (pl -delen) prejudice

vooroorlogs (vōar-*ōar*-lokhs) *adj* pre-war

voorraad (*vōa*-raat) *c* (pl -raden) stock, store, supply; provisions *pl*; **in ~ *hebben** stock

voorrang (*vōa*-rahng) *c* priority; right of way

voorrecht (*vōa*-rehkht) *nt* (pl ~en) privilege

voorruit (*vōa*-rur^ew t) *c* (pl ~en) windscreen; windshield *nAm*

***voorschieten** (*vōar*-skhee-tern) *v* advance

voorschot (*vōar*-skhot) *nt* (pl ~ten) advance

voorschrift (*vōar*-skhrift) *nt* (pl ~en) regulation

***voorschrijven** (*vōar*-skhray-vern) *v* prescribe

voorspellen (vōar-*speh*-lern) *v* predict, forecast

voorspelling (vōar-*speh*-ling) *c* (pl ~en) forecast

voorspoed (*vōar*-spōot) *c* prosperity

voorsprong (*vōar*-sprong) *c* lead

voorstad (*vōar*-staht) *c* (pl -steden) suburb

voorstander (*vōar*-stahn-derr) *c* (pl ~s) advocate

voorstel (*vōar*-stehl) *nt* (pl ~len) proposition, proposal; suggestion

voorstellen (*vōar*-steh-lern) *v* propose, suggest; present, introduce; represent; **zich ~** conceive, fancy, imagine

voorstelling (*vōar*-steh-ling) *c* (pl ~en) show, performance

voortaan (*vōar*-taan) *adv* henceforth

voortduren (*vōar*-dēw-rern) *v* continue; **voortdurend** continuous, continual

***voortgaan** (*vōart*-khaan) *v* continue; proceed

voortreffelijk (vōar-*treh*-fer-lerk) *adj* excellent; exquisite

voorts (vōarts) *adv* moreover

voortzetten (*vōart*-seh-tern) *v* carry on, continue

vooruit (vōa-*rur^ew*t) *adv* ahead, forward; in advance

vooruitbetaald (vōa-*rur^ew*t-ber-taalt) *adj* prepaid

***vooruitgaan** (vōa-*rur^ew*t-khaan) *v* advance

vooruitgang (vōa-*rur^ew*t-khahng) *c* progress, advance

vooruitstrevend (vōa-rur^ew t-*strāy*-vernt) *adj* progressive

vooruitzicht (vōa-*rur^ew*t-sikht) *nt* (pl ~en) prospect

voorvader (*vōar*-vaa-derr) *c* (pl ~s, ~en) ancestor

voorvechter (*vōar*-vehkh-terr) *c* (pl ~s) champion

voorvoegsel (*vōar*-vōokh-serl) *nt* (pl ~s) prefix

voorwaarde (*vōar*-vaar-der) *c* (pl ~n) condition; term

voorwaardelijk (vōar-*vaar*-der-lerk) *adj*

conditional

voorwaarts (*vōar*-vaarts) *adv* onwards, forward

voorwenden (*vōar*-vehn-dern) *v* pretend

voorwendsel (*vōar*-vehnt-serl) *nt* (pl ~s, ~en) pretext, pretence

voorwerp (*vōar*-vehrp) *nt* (pl ~en) object; **gevonden voorwerpen** lost and found

voorzetsel (*vōar*-zeht-serl) *nt* (pl ~s) preposition

voorzichtig (vōar-*zıkh*-terkh) *adj* careful; gentle

voorzichtigheid (vōar-*zıkh*-terkh-hayt) *c* caution

*voorzien (vōar-*zeen*) *v* anticipate; ~ **van** furnish with

voorzitter (*vōar*-zı-terr) *c* (pl ~s) chairman, president

voorzorg (*vōar*-zorkh) *c* (pl ~en) precaution

voorzorgsmaatregel (*vōar*-zorkhs-maat-rāy-gerl) *c* (pl ~en) precaution

vorderen (*vor*-der-rern) *v* *get on; confiscate, claim

vorig (*vōa*-rerkh) *adj* last; past

vork (vork) *c* (pl ~en) fork

vorm (vorm) *c* (pl ~en) shape; form

vormen (*vor*-mern) *v* shape; form

vorming (*vor*-mıng) *c* background

vorst¹ (vorst) *c* (pl ~en) ruler, monarch, sovereign

vorst² (vorst) *c* frost

vos (voss) *c* (pl ~sen) fox

vouw (vou) *c* (pl ~en) fold; crease

*vouwen (*vou*-ern) *v* fold

vraag (vraakh) *c* (pl vragen) question; inquiry, query

vraaggesprek (*vraa*-kher-sprehk) *nt* (pl ~ken) interview

vraagstuk (*vraakh*-sterk) *nt* (pl ~ken) problem, question

vraagteken (*vraakh*-tāy-kern) *nt* (pl ~s) question mark

vracht (vrahkht) *c* (pl ~en) freight, cargo

vrachtwagen (*vrahkht*-vaa-gern) *c* (pl ~s) lorry; truck *nAm*

*vragen (*vraa*-gern) *v* ask; beg; **vragend** interrogative

vrede (*vrāy*-der) *c* peace

vreedzaam (*vrāyt*-saam) *adj* peaceful

vreemd (vrāymt) *adj* strange; odd, queer; foreign

vreemde (*vrāym*-der) *c* (pl ~n) stranger

vreemdeling (*vrāym*-der-lıng) *c* (pl ~en) foreigner; stranger, alien

vrees (vrāyss) *c* dread, fear

vreselijk (*vrāy*-ser-lerk) *adj* terrible; horrible, dreadful, frightful

vreugde (*vrūrkh*-der) *c* (pl ~n) gladness, joy

vrezen (*vrāy*-zern) *v* dread, fear

vriend (vreent) *c* (pl ~en) friend

vriendelijk (*vreen*-der-lerk) *adj* friendly; kind

vriendschap (*vreent*-skhahp) *c* (pl ~pen) friendship

vriendschappelijk (vreent-*skhah*-per-lerk) *adj* friendly

vriespunt (*vreess*-pernt) *nt* freezing-point

*vriezen (*vree*-zern) *v* *freeze

vrij (vray) *adj* free; *adv* pretty, fairly, quite, rather

vrijdag (*vray*-dahkh) *c* Friday

vrijgevig (vray-*gāy*-verkh) *adj* liberal

vrijgezel (vray-ger-*zehl*) *c* (pl ~len) bachelor

vrijheid (*vray*-hayt) *c* (pl -heden) freedom, liberty

vrijkaart (*vray*-kaart) *c* (pl ~en) free ticket

vrijpostig (vray-*poss*-terkh) *adj* bold

vrijspraak (*vray*-spraak) *c* acquittal

vrijstellen (*vray*-steh-lern) *v* exempt;

vrijgesteld exempt

vrijstelling (*vray*-steh-ling) *c* (pl ~en) exemption

vrijwel (*vray*-vehl) *adv* practically

vrijwillig (vray-*vi*-lerkh) *adj* voluntary

vrijwilliger (vray-*vi*-ler-gerr) *c* (pl ~s) volunteer

vroedvrouw (*vroot*-frou) *c* (pl ~en) midwife

vroeg (vrookh) *adj* early

vroeger (*vroo*-gerr) *adj* prior, previous, former; *adv* formerly

vrolijk (*vroa*-lerk) *adj* gay, cheerful, merry, joyful

vrolijkheid (*vroa*-lerk-hayt) *c* gaiety

vroom (vroam) *adj* pious

vrouw (vrou) *c* (pl ~en) woman; wife

vrouwelijk (*vrou*-er-lerk) *adj* female; feminine

vrouwenarts (*vrou*-ern-ahrts) *c* (pl ~en) gynaecologist

vrucht (vrerkht) *c* (pl ~en) fruit

vruchtbaar (*vrerkht*-baar) *adj* fertile

vruchtensap (*vrerkh*-ter-sahp) *nt* (pl ~pen) squash

vuil (vur^ew^l) *adj* filthy, dirty; *nt* dirt

vuilnis (*vur^ew^l*-niss) *nt* garbage

vuilnisbak (*vur^ew^l*-niss-bahk) *c* (pl ~ken) rubbish-bin, dustbin; trash can *Am*

vuist (vur^ew^st) *c* (pl ~en) fist

vuistslag (*vur^ew^st*-slahkh) *c* (pl ~en) punch

vulgair (verl-*gair*) *adj* vulgar

vulkaan (verl-*kaan*) *c* (pl -kanen) volcano

vullen (*ver*-lern) *v* fill

vulling (*ver*-ling) *c* (pl ~en) stuffing, filling; refill

vulpen (*verl*-pehn) *c* (pl ~nen) fountain-pen

vuur (vew^r) *nt* (pl vuren) fire

vuurrood (*vew*-roat) *adj* scarlet, crimson

vuursteen (*vew*r-stayn) *c* (pl -stenen) flint

vuurtoren (*vew*r-toa-rern) *c* (pl ~s) lighthouse

vuurvast (*vew*r-vahst) *adj* fireproof

W

*****waaien** (*vaa^ee^*-ern) *v* *blow

waaier (*vaa^ee^*-err) *c* (pl ~s) fan

waakzaam (*vaak*-saam) *adj* vigilant

waanzin (*vaan*-zin) *c* madness

waanzinnig (vaan-*zi*-nerkh) *adj* mad

waar[1] (vaar) *adj* true; very

waar[2] (vaar) *adv* where; *conj* where; ~ **dan ook** anywhere; ~ **ook** wherever

waarborg (*vaar*-borkh) *c* (pl ~en) guarantee

waard (vaart) *adj* worthy of; ~ *zijn* *be worth

waarde (*vaar*-der) *c* (pl ~n) worth, value

waardeloos (vaar-der-*loass*) *adj* worthless

waarderen (vaar-*day*-rern) *v* appreciate

waardering (vaar-*day*-ring) *c* appreciation

waardevol (*vaar*-der-vol) *adj* valuable

waardig (*vaar*-derkh) *adj* dignified

waarheid (*vaar*-hayt) *c* (pl -heden) truth

waarheidsgetrouw (*vaar*-hayts-kher-trou) *adj* truthful

*****waarnemen** (*vaar*-nay-mern) *v* observe

waarneming (*vaar*-nay-ming) *c* (pl ~en) observation

waarom (vaa-*rom*) *adv* why; what for

waarschijnlijk (vaar-*skhayn*-lerk) *adj* probable, likely; *adv* probably

waarschuwen (*vaar*-skhew^{oo}-ern) *v* warn ; caution ; notify

waarschuwing (*vaar*-skhew^{oo}-ing) *c* (pl ~en) warning

waas (vaass) *nt* haze

wachten (*vahkh*-tern) *v* wait ; ~ **op** await

wachtkamer (*vahkht*-kaa-merr) *c* (pl ~s) waiting-room

wachtlijst (*vahkht*-layst) *c* (pl ~en) waiting-list

wachtwoord (*vahkht*-voart) *nt* (pl ~en) password

waden (*vaa*-dern) *v* wade

wafel (*vaa*-ferl) *c* (pl ~s) waffle, wafer

wagen[1] (*vaa*-gern) *c* (pl ~s) cart

wagen[2] (*vaa*-gern) *v* dare, venture, risk

wagon (vaa-*gon*) *c* (pl ~s) carriage, waggon ; passenger car *Am*

wakker (*vah*-kerr) *adj* awake ; ~ *worden wake up

walgelijk (*vahl*-ger-lerk) *adj* revolting, disgusting

walnoot (*vahl*-noat) *c* (pl -noten) walnut

wals (vahls) *c* (pl ~en) waltz

walvis (*vahl*-viss) *c* (pl ~sen) whale

wand (vahnt) *c* (pl ~en) wall

wandelaar (*vahn*-der-laar) *c* (pl ~s) walker

wandelen (*vahn*-der-lern) *v* stroll, walk

wandeling (*vahn*-der-ling) *c* (pl ~en) stroll, walk

wandelstok (*vahn*-derl-stok) *c* (pl ~ken) walking-stick

wandkleed (*vahnt*-klayt) *nt* (pl -kleden) tapestry

wandluis (*vahnt*-lur^{ew}ss) *c* (pl -luizen) bug

wang (vahng) *c* (pl ~en) cheek

wanhoop (*vahn*-hoap) *c* despair

wanhopen (*vahn*-hoa-pern) *v* despair

wanhopig (vahn-*hoa*-perkh) *adj* desperate

wankel (*vahn*-kerl) *adj* unsteady

wankelen (*vahn*-ker-lern) *v* falter

wanneer (vah-*nayr*) *adv* when ; *conj* when ; ~ **ook** whenever

wanorde (*vahn*-or-der) *c* disorder

want (vahnt) *conj* for

wanten (*vahn*-tern) *pl* mittens *pl*

wantrouwen (*vahn*-trou-ern) *nt* suspicion ; *v* mistrust

wapen (*vaa*-pern) *nt* (pl ~s, ~en) weapon, arm

warboel (*vahr*-bool) *c* muddle, mess

waren (*vaa*-rern) *pl* goods *pl*, wares *pl*

warenhuis (*vaa*-rer-hur^{ew}ss) *nt* (pl -huizen) department store

warm (vahrm) *adj* warm ; hot ; ~ *eten dine

warmte (*vahrm*-ter) *c* warmth ; heat

warmwaterkruik (vahrm-*vaa*-terr-krur^{ew}k) *c* (pl ~en) hot-water bottle

was[1] (vahss) *c* laundry, washing

was[2] (vahss) *c* wax

wasbaar (*vahss*-baar) *adj* washable

wasbekken (*vahss*-beh-kern) *nt* (pl ~s) wash-basin

wasecht (vahss-*ehkht*) *adj* fast-dyed

wasgoed (*vahss*-khoot) *nt* washing

wasmachine (*vahss*-mah-shee-ner) *c* (pl ~s) washing-machine

wasmiddel (*vahss*-mi-derl) *nt* (pl ~en) detergent

waspoeder (*vahss*-poo-derr) *nt* (pl ~s) washing-powder

*wassen (*vah*-sern) *v* wash

wassenbeeldenmuseum (vah-ser-*bayl*-der-mew-zay-^yerm) *nt* (pl ~s, -musea) waxworks *pl*

wasserette (vah-ser-*reh*-ter) *c* (pl ~s) launderette

wasserij (vah-ser-*ray*) *c* (pl ~en) laundry

wastafel (*vahss*-taa-ferl) *c* (pl ~s)

wash-stand

wasverzachter (*vahss*-ferr-zahkh-terr) *c* (pl ~s) water-softener

wat (vaht) *pron* what; ~ **dan ook** whatever; anything

water (*vaa*-terr) *nt* water; **hoog ~** high tide; **laag ~** low tide; **stromend ~** running water; **zoet ~** fresh water

waterdicht (*vaa*-terr-dıkht) *adj* rainproof, waterproof

waterkers (*vaa*-terr-kehrs) *c* watercress

watermeloen (*vaa*-terr-mer-lōōn) *c* (pl ~en) watermelon

waterpas (*vaa*-terr-pahss) *c* (pl ~sen) level

waterpokken (*vaa*-terr-po-kern) *pl* chickenpox

waterpomp (*vaa*-terr-pomp) *c* (pl ~en) water pump

waterski (*vaa*-terr-skee) *c* (pl ~'s) water ski

waterstof (*vaa*-terr-stof) *c* hydrogen

waterstofperoxyde (*vaa*-terr-stof-pehr-ok-see-der) *nt* peroxide

waterval (*vaa*-terr-vahl) *c* (pl ~len) waterfall

waterverf (*vaa*-terr-vehrf) *c* water-colour

watten (*vah*-tern) *pl* cotton-wool

wazig (*vaa*-zerkh) *adj* hazy

we (ver) *pron* we

wedden (*veh*-dern) *v* *bet

weddenschap (*veh*-der-skhahp) *c* (pl ~pen) bet

wederverkoper (*vāy*-derr-verr-kōa-perr) *c* (pl ~s) retailer

wederzijds (vāy-derr-*zayts*) *adj* mutual

wedijveren (*veht*-ay-ver-rern) *v* compete

wedloop (*veht*-lōap) *c* (pl -lopen) race

wedstrijd (*veht*-strayt) *c* (pl ~en) competition, contest; match

weduwe (*vāy*-dew⁰⁰-er) *c* (pl ~n) widow

weduwnaar (*vāy*-dew⁰⁰-naar) *c* (pl ~s) widower

weeën (*vāy*-ern) *pl* labour

weefsel (*vāyf*-serl) *nt* (pl ~s) tissue

weegschaal (*vāykh*-skhaal) *c* (pl -schalen) weighing-machine, scales *pl*

week (vāyk) *c* (pl weken) week

weekdag (*vāyk*-dahkh) *c* (pl ~en) weekday

weekend (*vee*-kehnt) *nt* (pl ~s) weekend

weemoed (*vāy*-mōōt) *c* melancholy

weer¹ (vāyr) *nt* weather

weer² (vāyr) *adv* again

weerbericht (*vāyr*-ber-rıkht) *nt* (pl ~en) weather forecast

*weerhouden (*vāyr*-*hou*-dern) *v* restrain

weerkaatsen (vāyr-*kaat*-sern) *v* reflect

weerkaatsing (vāyr-*kaat*-sıng) *c* reflection

weerklank (*vāyr*-klahngk) *c* echo

weerzinwekkend (*vāyr*-zın-*veh*-kernt) *adj* repulsive, repellent, revolting

wees (vāyss) *c* (pl wezen) orphan

weg¹ (vehkh) *adv* gone, away; lost; off

weg² (vehkh) *c* (pl ~en) way; road; **doodlopende ~** cul-de-sac; **op ~ naar** bound for

*wegen (*vāy*-gern) *v* weigh

wegenkaart (*vāy*-ger-kaart) *c* (pl ~en) road map

wegennet (*vāy*-ger-neht) *nt* (pl ~ten) road system

wegens (*vāy*-gerns) *prep* because of, for

*weggaan (*veh*-khaan) *v* *go away

wegkant (*vehkh*-kahnt) *c* (pl ~en) roadside, wayside

*weglaten (*vehkh*-laa-tern) *v* omit, *leave out

*wegnemen (*vehkh*-nay-mern) *v* *take out, *take away

wegomlegging (*vaykh*-om-leh-ging) *c* (pl ~en) diversion

wegrestaurant (*vehkh*-rehss-tōa-rahnt) *nt* (pl ~s) roadhouse; roadside restaurant

wegwerp- (*vehkh*-vehrp) *adj* disposable

wegwijzer (*vehkh*-vay-zerr) *c* (pl ~s) milepost, signpost

*wegzenden (*vehkh*-sehn-dern) *v* dismiss

wei (vay) *c* (pl ~den) meadow

weigeren (*vay*-ger-rern) *v* refuse; deny

weigering (*vay*-ger-ring) *c* (pl ~en) refusal

weiland (*vay*-lahnt) *nt* (pl ~en) pasture

weinig (*vay*-nerkh) *adj* little; few

wekelijks (*vāy*-kerr-lerks) *adj* weekly

weken (*vāy*-kern) *v* soak

wekken (*veh*-kern) *v* *awake, *wake

wekker (*veh*-kerr) *c* (pl ~s) alarm-clock

weldra (*vehl*-draa) *adv* soon, shortly

welk (vehlk) *pron* which; ~ **ook** whichever

welkom (*vehl*-kom) *adj* welcome; *nt* welcome

wellicht (veh-*likht*) *adv* perhaps

wellust (*veh*-lerst) *c* (pl ~en) lust

welnu! (vehl-*new*) well!

welvaart (*vehl*-vaart) *c* prosperity

welvarend (vehl-*vaa*-rernt) *adj* prosperous

welwillendheid (vehl-*vi*-lernt-hayt) *c* goodwill

welzijn (*vehl*-zayn) *nt* welfare

wending (*vehn*-ding) *c* (pl ~en) turn

wenk (vehngk) *c* (pl ~en) sign

wenkbrauw (*vehngk*-brou) *c* (pl ~en) eyebrow

wenkbrauwstift (*vehngk*-brou-stift) *c* (pl ~en) eye-pencil

wennen (*veh*-nern) *v* accustom

wens (vehns) *c* (pl ~en) wish, desire

wenselijk (*vehn*-ser-lerk) *adj* desirable

wensen (*vehn*-sern) *v* wish, desire; want

wereld (*vāy*-rerlt) *c* (pl ~en) world

wereldberoemd (*vāy*-rerlt-ber-rōomt) *adj* world-famous

wereldbol (*vāy*-rerlt-bol) *c* globe

werelddeel (*vāy*-rerl-dāyl) *nt* (pl -delen) continent

wereldomvattend (*vāy*-rerlt-om-vah-ternt) *adj* global, world-wide

wereldoorlog (*vāy*-rerlt-ōar-lokh) *c* (pl ~en) world war

werk (vehrk) *nt* work; labour; occupation, employment; business; **te ~ *gaan** proceed; ~ **in uitvoering** road up

werkdag (*vehrk*-dahkh) *c* (pl ~en) working day

werkelijk (*vehr*-ker-lerk) *adj* actual, true; substantial, very; *adv* really

werkelijkheid (*vehr*-ker-lerk-hayt) *c* reality

werkeloos (*vehr*-ker-lōass) *adj* unemployed; idle

werkeloosheid (vehr-ker-*lōass*-hayt) *c* unemployment

werken (*vehr*-kern) *v* work; operate

werkgever (*vehrk*-khāy-verr) *c* (pl ~s) employer

werking (*vehr*-king) *c* operation, working; **buiten ~** out of order

werknemer (*vehrk*-nāy-merr) *c* (pl ~s) employee

werkplaats (*vehrk*-plaats) *c* (pl ~en) workshop

werktuig (*vehrk*-tur^{ew}kh) *nt* (pl ~en) tool; utensil, implement

werkvergunning (*vehrk*-ferr-ger-ning) *c* (pl ~en) work permit; labor permit *Am*

werkwoord (*vehrk*-vōart) *nt* (pl ~en) verb

****werpen** (*vehr*-pern) *v* *cast, *throw

wesp (vehsp) *c* (pl ~en) wasp

west (vehst) *c* west

westelijk (*vehss*-ter-lerk) *adj* westerly

westen (*vehss*-tern) *nt* west

westers (*vehss*-terrs) *adj* western

wet (veht) *c* (pl ~ten) law

****weten** (*vāy*-tern) *v* *know

wetenschap (*vāy*-ter-skhahp) *c* (pl ~pen) science

wetenschappelijk (vāy-ter-*skhah*-per-lerk) *adj* scientific

wettelijk (*veh*-ter-lerk) *adj* legal

wettig (*veh*-terkh) *adj* legal, lawful; legitimate

****weven** (*vāy*-vern) *v* *weave

wever (*vāy*-verr) *c* (pl ~s) weaver

wezen¹ (*vāy*-zern) *nt* (pl ~s) creature, being

wezen² (*vāy*-zern) *nt* essence

wezenlijk (*vāy*-zer-lerk) *adj* essential

wie (vee) *pron* who; whom; ~ **dan ook** anybody; ~ **ook** whoever

wieg (veekh) *c* (pl ~en) cradle

wiel (veel) *nt* (pl ~en) wheel

wielrijder (*veel*-ray-derr) *c* (pl ~s) cyclist

wierook (*vee*-rōak) *c* incense

wig (vɪkh) *c* (pl ~gen) wedge

wijd (vayt) *adj* broad, wide

wijden (*vay*-dern) *v* devote

wijk (vayk) *c* (pl ~en) quarter, district

wijn (vayn) *c* (pl ~en) wine

wijngaard (*vayn*-gaart) *c* (pl ~en) vineyard

wijnkaart (*vayng*-kaart) *c* (pl ~en) wine-list

wijnkelder (*vayng*-kehl-derr) *c* (pl ~s) wine-cellar

wijnkelner (*vayng*-kehl-nerr) *c* (pl ~s) wine-waiter

wijnkoper (*vayng*-kōa-perr) *c* (pl ~s) wine-merchant

wijnoogst (*vayn*-ōakhst) *c* (pl ~en) vintage

wijnstok (*vayn*-stok) *c* (pl ~ken) vine

wijs¹ (vayss) *adj* wise

wijs² (vayss) *c* (pl wijzen) tune

wijsbegeerte (*vayss*-ber-gāyr-ter) *c* philosophy

wijsgeer (*vayss*-khāyr) *c* (pl -geren) philosopher

wijsheid (*vayss*-hayt) *c* (pl -heden) wisdom

wijsvinger (*vayss*-fɪ-ngerr) *c* (pl ~s) index finger

wijting (*vay*-tɪng) *c* (pl ~en) whiting

wijze (*vay*-zer) *c* (pl ~n) manner, way

****wijzen** (*vay*-zern) *v* point; direct

wijzigen (*vay*-zer-gern) *v* change, alter, modify

wijziging (*vay*-zer-gɪng) *c* (pl ~en) change, alteration

wil (vɪl) *c* will

wild (vɪlt) *adj* wild; savage, fierce; *nt* game

wildpark (*vɪlt*-pahrk) *nt* (pl ~en) game reserve

willekeurig (vɪ-ler-*kūr*-rerkh) *adj* arbitrary

****willen** (*vɪ*-lern) *v* want; *will

wilskracht (*vɪls*-krahkht) *c* will-power

wimper (*vɪm*-perr) *c* (pl ~s) eyelash

wind (vɪnt) *c* (pl ~en) wind

****winden** (*vɪn*-dern) *v* *wind; twist

winderig (*vɪn*-der-rerkh) *adj* windy, gusty

windmolen (*vɪnt*-mōa-lern) *c* (pl ~s) windmill

windstoot (*vɪnt*-stōat) *c* (pl -stoten) gust

windvlaag (*vɪnt*-flaakh) *c* (pl -vlagen) blow

winkel (*vɪng*-kerl) *c* (pl ~s) store, shop

winkelcentrum (*vɪng*-kerl-sehn-trerm) *nt* (pl -tra) shopping centre

winkelen (*vɪng*-ker-lern) v shop

winkelier (vɪng-ker-*leer*) c (pl ~s) shopkeeper

winnaar (*vɪ*-naar) c (pl ~s) winner

***winnen** (*vɪ*-nern) v *win; gain

winst (vɪnst) c (pl ~en) profit; gain, winnings pl, benefit

winstgevend (vɪnst-*khā̄y*-vernt) adj profitable

winter (*vɪn*-terr) c (pl ~s) winter

wintersport (*vɪn*-terr-sport) c winter sports

wip (vɪp) c (pl ~pen) seesaw

wirwar (*vɪr*-vahr) c muddle

wiskunde (*vɪss*-kern-der) c mathematics

wiskundig (vɪss-*kern*-derkh) adj mathematical

wissel (*vɪ*-serl) c (pl ~s) draft

wisselen (*vɪ*-ser-lern) v change; exchange

wisselgeld (*vɪ*-serl-gehlt) nt change

wisselkantoor (*vɪ*-serl-kahn-tōar) nt (pl -toren) money exchange, exchange office

wisselkoers (*vɪ*-serl-kōōrs) c (pl ~en) exchange rate

wisselstroom (*vɪ*-serl-strōam) c alternating current

wit (vɪt) adj white

wittebroodsweken (*vɪ*-ter-brōats-vāy-kern) pl honeymoon

witvis (*vɪt*-fɪss) c (pl ~sen) whitebait

woede (*vōō*-der) c anger, rage

woeden (*vōō*-dern) v rage

woedend (*vōō*-dernt) adj furious

woensdag (*vōōns*-dahkh) c Wednesday

woest (vōōst) adj wild, fierce; desert

woestijn (vōōss-*tayn*) c (pl ~en) desert

wol (vol) c wool

wolf (volf) c (pl wolven) wolf

wolk (volk) c (pl ~en) cloud

wolkbreuk (*volk*-brūrk) c (pl ~en) cloud-burst

wolkenkrabber (*vol*-ker-krah-berr) c (pl ~s) skyscraper

wollen (*vo*-lern) adj woollen

wond (vont) c (pl ~en) wound

wonder (*von*-derr) nt (pl ~en) wonder, miracle; marvel

wonderbaarlijk (von-derr-*baar*-lerk) adj miraculous

wonen (*vōā*-nern) v live; reside

woning (*vōā*-nɪng) c (pl ~en) house

woonachtig (vōan-*ahkh*-terkh) adj resident

woonboot (*vōan*-bōat) c (pl -boten) houseboat

woonkamer (*vōang*-kaa-merr) c (pl ~s) living-room

woonplaats (*vōam*-plaats) c (pl ~en) domicile, residence

woonwagen (*vōan*-vaa-gern) c (pl ~s) caravan

woord (vōart) nt (pl ~en) word

woordenboek (*vōar*-der-bōōk) nt (pl ~en) dictionary

woordenlijst (*vōar*-der-layst) c (pl ~en) vocabulary

woordenschat (*vōar*-der-skhaht) c vocabulary

woordenwisseling (*vōar*-der-vɪ-ser-lɪng) c (pl ~en) argument

***worden** (*vor*-dern) v *become; *go, *get, *grow

worm (vorm) c (pl ~en) worm

worp (vorp) c (pl ~en) cast

worst (vorst) c (pl ~en) sausage

worstelen (*vor*-ster-lern) v struggle

worsteling (*voar*-ster-lɪng) c (pl ~en) struggle

wortel (*vor*-terl) c (pl ~s, ~en) root; carrot

woud (vout) nt (pl ~en) forest

wraak (vraak) c revenge

wrak (vrahk) nt (pl ~ken) wreck

wreed (vrāyt) *adj* harsh, cruel
*__wrijven__ (*vray*-vern) *v* rub
wrijving (*vray*-vɪng) *c* (pl ~en) friction
wurgen (*verr*-gern) *v* strangle, choke

Z

zaad (zaat) *nt* (pl zaden) seed
zaag (zaakh) *c* (pl zagen) saw
zaagsel (*zaakh*-serl) *nt* sawdust
zaaien (*zaa*ee-ern) *v* *sow
zaak (zaak) *c* (pl zaken) cause; case, matter; business
zaal (zaal) *c* (pl zalen) hall
zacht (zahkht) *adj* soft; gentle, smooth, mild, mellow
zadel (*zaa*-derl) *nt* (pl ~s) saddle
zak (zahk) *c* (pl ~ken) pocket; sack, bag
zakdoek (*zahk*-dōōk) *c* (pl ~en) handkerchief; **papieren ~** tissue
zakelijk (*zaa*-ker-lerk) *adj* business-like
zaken (*zaa*-kern) *pl* business; **voor ~** on business; **~ *doen met** *deal with
zakenman (*zaa*-ker-mahn) *c* (pl -lieden, -lui) businessman
zakenreis (*zaa*-ker-rayss) *c* (pl -reizen) business trip
zakhorloge (*zahk*-hor-lōā-zher) *nt* (pl ~s) pocket-watch
zakkam (*zah*-kahm) *c* (pl ~men) pocket-comb
zakken (*zah*-kern) *v* fail
zaklantaarn (*zahk*-lahn-taa-rern) *c* (pl ~s) torch, flash-light
zakmes (*zahk*-mehss) *nt* (pl ~sen) pocket-knife, penknife
zalf (zahlf) *c* (pl zalven) ointment, salve
zalm (zahlm) *c* (pl ~en) salmon
zand (zahnt) *nt* sand

zanderig (*zahn*-der-rerkh) *adj* sandy
zanger (*zah*-ngerr) *c* (pl ~s) vocalist, singer
zangeres (zah-nger-*rehss*) *c* (pl ~sen) singer
zaterdag (*zaa*-terr-dahkh) *c* Saturday
ze (zer) *pron* she; they
zebra (*zāy*-braa) *c* (pl ~'s) zebra
zebrapad (*zāy*-braa-paht) *nt* (pl ~en) pedestrian crossing; crosswalk *nAm*
zedelijk (*zāy*-der-lerk) *adj* moral
zeden (*zāy*-dern) *pl* morals
zee (zāy) *c* (pl ~ën) sea
zeeëgel (*zāy*-āy-gerl) *c* (pl ~s) sea-urchin
zeef (zāyf) *c* (pl zeven) sieve
zeegezicht (*zāy*-ger-zıkht) *nt* (pl ~en) seascape
zeehaven (*zāy*-haa-vern) *c* (pl ~s) seaport
zeehond (*zāy*-hont) *c* (pl ~en) seal
zeekaart (*zāy*-kaart) *c* (pl ~en) chart
zeekust (*zāy*-kerst) *c* (pl ~en) seacoast
zeeman (*zāy*-mahn) *c* (pl -lieden, -lui) seaman
zeemeermin (*zāy*-māyr-mın) *c* (pl ~nen) mermaid
zeemeeuw (*zāy*-māy∞) *c* (pl ~en) seagull
zeep (zāyp) *c* soap
zeeppoeder (*zāy*-pōō-derr) *nt* soap powder
zeer (zāyr) *adj* sore; *adv* very, quite
zeeschelp (*zāy*-skhehlp) *c* (pl ~en) sea-shell
zeevogel (*zāy*-vōā-gerl) *c* (pl ~s) seabird
zeewater (*zāy*-vaa-terr) *nt* sea-water
zeeziek (*zāy*-zeek) *adj* seasick
zeeziekte (*zāy*-zeek-ter) *c* seasickness
zegel (*zāy*-gerl) *nt* (pl ~s) seal
zegen (*zāy*-gern) *c* blessing
zegenen (*zāy*-ger-nern) *v* bless

zegevieren (záy-ger-vee-rern) v triumph

*zeggen (zeh-gern) v *say; *tell

zeil (zayl) nt (pl ~en) sail

zeilboot (zayl-bōat) c (pl -boten) sailing-boat

zeilclub (zayl-klerp) c (pl ~s) yacht-club

zeilsport (zayl-sport) c yachting

zeker (záy-kerr) adv surely; adj certain, sure; ~ **niet** by no means

zekering (záy-ker-rıng) c (pl ~en) fuse

zelden (zehl-dern) adv seldom, rarely

zeldzaam (zehlt-saam) adj rare; uncommon, infrequent

zelf (zehlf) pron myself; yourself; himself; herself; oneself; ourselves; yourselves; themselves

zelfbediening (zehlf-ber-dee-nıng) c self-service

zelfbedieningsrestaurant (zehlf-ber-dee-nıngs-rehss-tōa-rahnt) nt (pl ~s) self-service restaurant

zelfbestuur (zehlf-ber-stēwr) nt self-government

zelfde (zehlf-der) adj same

zelfmoord (zehlf-mōart) c (pl ~en) suicide

zelfs (zehlfs) adv even

zelfstandig (zehlf-stahn-derkh) adj independent; self-employed; ~ **naamwoord** noun

zelfstrijkend (zehlf-stray-kernt) adj drip-dry, wash and wear

zelfzuchtig (zehlf-serkh-terkh) adj egoistic

*zenden (zehn-dern) v *send

zender (zehn-derr) c (pl ~s) transmitter

zending (zehn-dıng) c (pl ~en) consignment

zenit (záy-nıt) nt zenith

zenuw (zay-néw°°) c (pl ~en) nerve

zenuwachtig (záy-néw°°-ahkh-terkh)

adj nervous

zenuwpijn (záy-néw°°-payn) c (pl ~en) neuralgia

zes (zehss) num six

zesde (zehss-der) num sixth

zestien (zehss-teen) num sixteen

zestiende (zehss-teen-der) num sixteenth

zestig (zehss-terkh) num sixty

zet (zeht) c (pl ~ten) move; push

zetel (záy-terl) c (pl ~s) chair; seat

zetpil (zeht-pıl) c (pl ~len) suppository

zetten (zeh-tern) v place; *lay, *set, *put; **in elkaar** ~ assemble

zeurpiet (zūrr-peet) c (pl ~en) bore

zeven¹ (záy-vern) num seven

zeven² (záy-vern) v strain, sift, sieve

zevende (záy-vern-der) num seventh

zeventien (záy-vern-teen) num seventeen

zeventiende (záy-vern-teen-der) num seventeenth

zeventig (záy-vern-terkh) num seventy

zich (zıkh) pron himself; herself; themselves

zicht (zıkht) nt sight; visibility; **op** ~ on approval

zichtbaar (zıkht-baar) adj visible

ziek (zeek) adj ill, sick

ziekenauto (zee-kern-ōa-tōa) c (pl ~'s) ambulance

ziekenhuis (zee-ker-hur°°ss) nt (pl -huizen) hospital

ziekenzaal (zee-ker-zaal) c (pl -zalen) infirmary

ziekte (zeek-ter) c (pl ~n, ~s) disease; ailment, illness, sickness

ziel (zeel) c (pl ~en) soul

*zien (zeen) v *see; notice; **er uit** ~ look; ***laten** ~ *show

zienswijze (zeens-vay-zer) c (pl ~n) outlook

zigeuner (zee-gūr-nerr) c (pl ~s) gipsy

zijbeuk (*zay*-bürk) *c* (pl ~en) aisle

zijde[1] (*zay*-der) *c* silk

zijde[2] (*zay*-der) *c* (pl ~n) side

zijden (*zay*-dern) *adj* silken

zijlicht (*zay*-lıkht) *nt* sidelight

zijn (zayn) *pron* his

*zijn (zayn) *v* *be

zijrivier (*zay*-ree-veer) *c* (pl ~en) tributary

zijstraat (*zay*-straat) *c* (pl -straten) side-street

zilver (*zıl*-verr) *nt* silver

zilveren (*zıl*-ver-rern) *adj* silver

zilverpapier (*zıl*-verr-paa-peer) *nt* tinfoil

zilversmid (*zıl*-verr-smıt) *c* (pl -smeden) silversmith

zilverwerk (*zıl*-verr-vehrk) *nt* silverware

zin[1] (zın) *c* sense; desire; ~ *hebben in *feel like, fancy

zin[2] (zın) *c* (pl ~nen) sentence

*zingen (*zı*-ngern) *v* *sing

zink (zıngk) *nt* zinc

*zinken (*zıng*-kern) *v* *sink

zinloos (*zın*-lōass) *adj* senseless

zintuig (*zın*-tur^ewkh) *nt* (pl ~en) sense

zitkamer (*zıt*-kaa-merr) *c* (pl ~s) sitting-room

zitplaats (*zıt*-plaats) *c* (pl ~en) seat

*zitten (*zı*-tern) *v* *sit; *gaan ~ *sit down

zitting (*zı*-tıng) *c* (pl ~en) session

zitvlak (*zıt*-flahk) *nt* bottom

zo (zōa) *adv* so, thus; such; **zo'n** such a

zoals (zōa-*ahls*) *conj* like, as; such as

zodat (zōa-*daht*) *conj* so that

zodra (zōa-*draa*) *conj* as soon as

*zoeken (*zōō*-kern) *v* look for; *seek, search; hunt for

zoeker (*zōō*-kerr) *c* (pl ~s) view-finder

zoen (zōōn) *c* (pl ~en) kiss

zoet (zōōt) *adj* sweet; good; ~ maken sweeten

zoetzuur (*zōōt*-sewr) *nt* pickles *pl*

zogen (*zōa*-gern) *v* nurse

zogenaamd (zōa-ger-*naamt*) *adj* so-called

zolder (*zol*-derr) *c* (pl ~s) attic

zomer (*zōa*-merr) *c* (pl ~s) summer

zomertijd (*zōa*-merr-tayt) *c* summer time

zon (zon) *c* (pl ~nen) sun

zondag (*zon*-dahkh) *c* Sunday

zonde (*zon*-der) *c* (pl ~n) sin

zondebok (*zon*-der-bok) *c* (pl ~ken) scapegoat

zonder (*zon*-derr) *prep* without

zonderling (*zon*-derr-lıng) *adj* funny, queer

zone (*zaw*-ner) *c* (pl ~s) zone

zonlicht (*zon*-lıkht) *nt* sunlight

zonnebaden (*zo*-ner-baa-dern) *v* sunbathe

zonnebrand (*zo*-ner-brahnt) *c* sunburn

zonnebrandolie (*zo*-ner-brahnt-ōa-lee) *c* suntan oil

zonnebril (*zo*-ner-brıl) *c* (pl ~len) sunglasses *pl*

zonnescherm (*zo*-ner-skhehrm) *nt* (pl ~en) awning

zonneschijn (*zo*-ner-skhayn) *c* sunshine

zonnesteek (*zo*-ner-stāyk) *c* sunstroke

zonnig (*zo*-nerkh) *adj* sunny

zonsondergang (zons-*on*-derr-gahng) *c* (pl ~en) sunset

zonsopgang (zons-*op*-khahng) *c* (pl ~en) sunrise

zoogdier (*zōakh*-deer) *nt* (pl ~en) mammal

zool (zōal) *c* (pl zolen) sole

zoölogie (zōa-ōa-lōa-*gee*) *c* zoology

zoom (zōam) *c* (pl zomen) hem

zoon (zōan) *c* (pl zonen) son

zorg (zorkh) *c* (pl ~en) concern, worry, care; trouble

zorgen voor (*zor*-gern) look after, *take care of; see to

zorgvuldig (zorkh-*ferl*-derkh) *adj* careful

zorgwekkend (zorkh-*veh*-kernt) *adj* critical

zorgzaam (*zorkh*-saam) *adj* thoughtful

zout (zout) *nt* salt; *adj* salty

zoutvaatje (*zout*-faa-t^yer) *nt* (pl ~s) salt-cellar

zoveel (*zōā*-vāyl) *adv* so much

zowel ... als (*zōā*-veh ... ahls) both ... and

zuid (zur^{ew}t) *c* south

Zuid-Afrika (zur^{ew}t-*aa*-free-kaa) South Africa

zuidelijk (*zur^{ew}*-der-lerk) *adj* southern, southerly

zuiden (*zur^{ew}*-dern) *nt* south

zuidoosten (zur^{ew}t-*ōā*ss-tern) *nt* southeast

zuidpool (*zur^{ew}*t-pōāl) *c* South Pole

zuidwesten (zur^{ew}t-*vehss*-tern) *nt* south-west

zuigeling (*zur^{ew}*-ger-ling) *c* (pl ~en) infant

***zuigen** (*zur^{ew}*-gern) *v* suck

zuiger (*zur^{ew}*-gerr) *c* (pl ~s) piston

zuigerring (*zur^{ew}*-ger-ring) *c* (pl ~en) piston ring

zuigerstang (*zur^{ew}*-gèrr-stahng) *c* (pl ~en) piston-rod

zuil (zur^{ew}l) *c* (pl ~en) column, pillar

zuilengang (*zur^{ew}*-ler-gahng) *c* (pl ~en) arcade

zuinig (*zur^{ew}*-nerkh) *adj* economical, thrifty

zuivelwinkel (*zur^{ew}*-verl-ving-kerl) *c* (pl ~s) dairy

zuiver (*zur^{ew}*-verr) *adj* pure, clean

zulk (zerlk) *adj* such

***zullen** (*zer*-lern) *v* *will, *shall

zus (zerss) *c* (pl ~sen) sister

zuster (*zerss*-terr) *c* (pl ~s) sister; nurse

zuur[1] (zēwr) *adj* sour

zuur[2] (zēwr) *nt* (pl zuren) acid

zuurstof (*zēwr*-stof) *c* oxygen

zwaaien (*zvaa*^{ee}-ern) *v* swing; wave

zwaan (zvaan) *c* (pl zwanen) swan

zwaar (zvaar) *adj* heavy

zwaard (zvaart) *nt* (pl ~en) sword

zwaartekracht (*zvaar*-ter-krahkht) *c* gravity

zwager (*zvaa*-gerr) *c* (pl ~s) brother-in-law

zwak (zvahk) *adj* feeble, weak; faint; dim

zwakheid (*zvahk*-hayt) *c* (pl -heden) weakness

zwaluw (*zvaa*-lēw^{oo}) *c* (pl ~en) swallow

zwanger (*zvah*-ngerr) *adj* pregnant

zwart (zvahrt) *adj* black

Zweden (*zvāy*-dern) Sweden

Zweed (zvāyt) *c* (pl Zweden) Swede

Zweeds (zvāyts) *adj* Swedish

zweefvliegtuig (*zvāy*-fleekh-tur^{ew}kh) *nt* (pl ~en) glider

zweep (zvāyp) *c* (pl zwepen) whip

zweer (zvāyr) *c* (pl zweren) ulcer, sore

zweet (zvāyt) *nt* sweat, perspiration

***zwellen** (*zveh*-lern) *v* *swell

zwelling (*zveh*-ling) *c* (pl ~en) swelling

zwembad (*zvehm*-baht) *nt* (pl ~en) swimming pool

zwembroek (*zvehm*-brōōk) *c* (pl ~en) swimming-trunks, bathing-trunks, bathing-suit

***zwemmen** (*zveh*-mern) *v* *swim

zwemmer (*zveh*-merr) *c* (pl ~s) swimmer

zwempak (*zvehm*-pahk) *nt* (pl ~ken) swim-suit

zwemsport (*zvehm*-sport) *c* swimming

zwendelarij (zvehn-der-laa-*ray*) *c* (pl ~en) swindle

*zweren (*zvāy*-rern) *v* *swear, vow
*zwerven (*zvehr*-vern) *v* roam, wander
zweten (*zvāy*-tern) *v* sweat, perspire
*zwijgen (*zvay*-gern) *v* *be silent, *keep quiet; tot ~ *brengen silence; zwijgend silent

zwijn (zvayn) *nt* (pl ~en) pig
Zwitser (*zvit*-serr) *c* (pl ~s) Swiss
Zwitserland (*zvit*-serr-lahnt) Switzerland
Zwitsers (*zvit*-serrs) *adj* Swiss
zwoegen (*zvoo*-gern) *v* labour

Menu Reader

Food

aalbes redcurrant
aardappel potato
  ~**puree** mashed potatoes
aardbei strawberry
abrikoos apricot
amandel almond
  ~**broodje** a sweet roll with almond-paste filling
ananas pineapple
andijvie endive (US chicory)
  ~**stamppot** mashed potato and endive casserole
anijs aniseed
ansjovis anchovy
appel apple
  ~**beignet** fritter
  ~**bol** dumpling
  ~**flap** puff-pastry containing an apple slice
  ~**gebak** cake
  ~**moes** sauce
Ardense pastei rich pork mixture cooked in a pastry crust, served cold in slices
artisjok artichoke
asperge asparagus
  ~**punt** tip
aubergine aubergine (US eggplant)
augurk gherkin (US pickle)

avondeten dinner, supper
azijn vinegar
baars perch
babi pangang slices of roast suck-(l)ing pig, served with a sweet-and-sour sauce
bami goreng a casserole of noodles, vegetables, diced pork and shrimps
banaan banana
banketletter pastry with an almond-paste filling
basilicum basil
bediening service
belegd broodje roll with a variety of garnishes
belegen kaas pungent-flavoured cheese
biefstuk fillet of beef
  ~**van de haas** small round fillet of beef
bieslook chive
bitterbal small, round breaded meatball served as an appetizer
blinde vink veal bird; thin slice of veal rolled around stuffing
bloedworst black pudding (US blood sausage)
  ~**met appelen** with cooked apples

bloemkool cauliflower

boerenkool met worst kale mixed with mashed potatoes and served with smoked sausage

boerenomelet omelet with diced vegetables and bacon

bokking bloater

boon bean

borrelhapje appetizer

borststuk breast, brisket

bosbes bilberry (US blueberry)

bot 1) flounder 2) bone

boter butter

boterham slice of buttered bread

bouillon broth

braadhaantje spring chicken

braadworst frying sausage

braam blackberry

brasem bream

brood bread

  ~ **maaltijd** bread served with cold meat, eggs, cheese, jam or other garnishes

  ~ **pudding** kind of bread pudding with eggs, cinnamon and rum flavouring

broodje roll

  ~ **halfom** buttered roll with liver and salted beef

  ~ **kaas** buttered roll with cheese

bruine bonen met spek red kidney beans served with bacon

Brussels lof chicory (US endive)

caramelpudding caramel mould

caramelvla caramel custard

champignon mushroom

chocola(de) chocolate

citroen lemon

cordon bleu veal scallop stuffed with ham and cheese

dadel date

dagschotel day's special

dame blanche vanilla ice-cream

with hot chocolate sauce

dille dill

doperwt green pea

dragon tarragon

drie-in-de-pan small, fluffy pancake filled with currants

druif grape

duif pigeon

Duitse biefstuk hamburger steak

Edam, Edammer kaas firm, mild-flavoured yellow cheese, coated with red wax

eend duck

ei egg

eierpannekoek egg pancake

erwt pea

erwtensoep met kluif pea soup with diced, smoked sausages, pork fat, pig's trotter (US feet), parsley, leeks and celery

exclusief not included

fazant pheasant

filet fillet

  ~ **américain** steak tartare

flensje small, thin pancake

foe yong hai omelet with leeks, onions, and shrimps served in a sweet-and-sour sauce

forel trout

framboos raspberry

Friese nagelkaas cheese made from skimmed milk, flavoured with cloves

frikadel meatball

frites, frieten chips (US french fries)

gaar well-done

gans goose

garnaal shrimp, prawn

gebak pastry, cake

gebakken fried

gebonden soep cream soup

gebraden roasted

gedroogde pruim prune

gehakt 1) minced 2) minced meat
~ **bal** meatball
gekookt boiled
gekruid seasoned
gemarineerd marinated
gember ginger
~ **koek** gingerbread
gemengd assorted, mixed
gepaneerd breaded
gepocheerd ei poached egg
geraspt grated
gerecht course, dish
gerookt smoked
geroosterd brood toast
gerst barley
gestoofd braised
gevogelte fowl
gevuld stuffed
gezouten salted
Goudakaas, Goudse kaas a renowned Dutch cheese, similar to *Edam*, large, flat and round; it gains in flavour with maturity
griesmeel semolina
~ **pudding** semolina pudding
griet brill
groente vegetable
Haagse bluf dessert of whipped egg-whites, served with redcurrant sauce
haantje cockerel
haas hare
hachee hash of minced meat, onions and spices
half, halve half
hardgekookt ei hard-boiled egg
haring herring
hart heart
havermoutpap (oatmeal) porridge
hazelnoot hazelnut
heilbot halibut
heldere soep consommé, clear soup
hersenen brains

hete bliksem potatoes, bacon and apples, seasoned with butter, salt and sugar
Hollandse biefstuk loin section of a porterhouse or T-bone steak
Hollandse nieuwe freshly caught, filleted herring
honing honey
houtsnip 1) woodcock 2) cheese sandwich on rye bread
hutspot met klapstuk hotch-potch of mashed potatoes, carrots and onions served with boiled beef
huzarensla salad of potatoes, hard-boiled eggs, cold meat, gherkins, beetroot and mayonnaise
ijs ice, ice-cream
inclusief included
Italiaanse salade mixed salad with tomatoes, olives and tunny fish
jachtschotel a casserole of meat, onions and potatoes, often served with apple sauce
jonge kaas fresh cheese
jus gravy
kaas cheese
~ **balletje** baked cheese ball
kabeljauw cod
kalfslapje, kalfsoester veal cutlet
kalfsrollade roast veal
kalfsvlees veal
kalkoen turkey
kapucijners met spek peas served with fried bacon, boiled potatoes, onions and green salad
karbonade chop, cutlet
karper carp
kastanje chestnut
kaviaar caviar
kerrie curry
kers cherry
kievitsei plover's egg
kip chicken

kippeborst breast of chicken

kippebout leg of chicken

knakworst small frankfurter sausage

knoflook garlic

koek 1) cake 2) gingerbread

koekje biscuit (US cookie)

koffietafel light lunch consisting of bread and butter with a variety of garnishes, served with coffee

kokosnoot coconut

komijnekaas cheese flavoured with cumin seeds

komkommer cucumber

konijn rabbit

koninginnesoep cream of chicken

kool cabbage

~ **schotel met gehakt** casserole of meatballs and cabbage

kotelet chop, cutlet

koud cold

~ **vlees** cold meat (US cold cuts)

krab crab

krabbetje spare rib

krent currant

kroepoek large, deep-fried shrimp wafer

kroket croquette

kruiderij herb, seasoning

kruidnagel clove

kruisbes gooseberry

kwark fresh white cheese

kwartel quail

kweepeer quince

lamsbout leg of lamb

lamsvlees lamb

langoest spiny lobster

Leidse kaas cheese flavoured with cumin seeds

lekkerbekje fried, filleted haddock or plaice

lendestuk sirloin

lever liver

linze lentil

loempia spring roll (US egg roll)

maïskolf corn on the cob

makreel mackerel

mandarijntje tangerine

marsepein marzipan

meikaas a creamy cheese with high fat content

meloen melon

menu van de dag set menu

mossel mussel

mosterd mustard

nagerecht dessert

nasi goreng a casserole of rice, fried onions, meat, chicken, shrimps, vegetables and seasoning, usually topped with a fried egg

nier kidney

~ **broodje** roll filled with kidneys and chopped onions

noot nut

oester oyster

olie oil

~ **bol** fritter with raisins

olijf olive

omelet fines herbes herb omelet

omelet met kippelevertjes chicken liver omelet

omelet nature plain omelet

ongaar underdone (US rare)

ontbijt breakfast

~ **koek** honey cake

~ **spek** bacon, rasher

ossehaas fillet of beef

ossestaart oxtail

oude kaas any mature and strong cheese

paddestoel mushroom

paling eel

~ **in 't groen** braised in white sauce garnished with chopped parsley and other greens

pannekoek pancake

~ **met stroop** pancake served with treacle (US syrup)

pap porridge

paprika green or red (sweet) pepper

patates frites chips (US french fries)

pastei pie, pasty

patrijs partridge

peer pear

pekeltong salt(ed) tongue

pekelvlees slices of salted meat

peper pepper

~ **koek** gingerbread

perzik peach

peterselie parsley

piccalilly pickle

pinda peanut

~ **kaas** peanut butter

pisang goreng fried banana

poffertje fritter served with sugar and butter

pompelmoes grapefruit

portie portion

postelein purslane (edible plant)

prei leek

prinsessenboon French bean (US green bean)

pruim plum

rabarber rhubarb

radijs radish

rauw raw

reebout, reerug venison

reine-claude greengage

rekening bill

ribstuk rib of beef

rijst rice

~ **tafel** an Indonesian preparation composed of some 30 dishes including stewed vegetables, spit-roasted meat and fowl, served with rice, various sauces, fruit, nuts and spices

rivierkreeft crayfish

rode biet beetroot

rode kool red cabbage

roerei scrambled egg

roggebrood rye bread

rolmops Bismarck herring

rolpens fried slices of spiced and pickled minced beef and tripe, topped with an apple slice

rookspek smoked bacon

rookworst smoked sausage

roomboter butter

roomijs ice-cream

rosbief roast beef

rozemarijn rosemary

runderlap beefsteak

rundvlees beef

Russische eieren Russian eggs; hard-boiled egg-halves garnished with mayonnaise, herring, shrimps, capers, anchovies and sometimes caviar; served on lettuce

salade salad

sambal kind of spicy paste consisting mainly of ground pimentos, usually served with *rijsttafel*, *bami* or *nasi goreng*

sardien sardine

saté, sateh skewered pieces of meat covered with a spicy peanut sauce

saucijzebroodje sausage roll

saus sauce, gravy

schaaldier shellfish

schapevlees mutton

scharretong lemon sole

schelvis haddock

schildpadsoep turtle soup

schnitzel cutlet

schol plaice

schuimomelet fluffy dessert omelet

selderij celery

sinaasappel orange

sjaslik skewered chunks of meat, grilled, then braised in a spicy sauce of tomatoes, onions and bacon

sla salad, lettuce

slaboon French bean (US green bean)

slagroom whipped cream

slak snail

sneeuwbal kind of cream puff, sometimes filled with currants and raisins

snijboon sliced French bean

soep soup

~ **van de dag** soup of the day

sorbet water ice (US sherbet)

speculaas spiced almond biscuit

spek bacon

sperzieboon French bean (US green bean)

spiegelei fried egg

spijskaart menu, bill of fare

spinazie spinach

sprits a kind of shortbread

spruitje brussels sprout

stamppot a stew of vegetables and mashed potatoes

steur sturgeon

stokvis stockfish (dried cod)

stroop treacle (US syrup)

suiker sugar

taart cake

tarbot turbot

tartaar steak tartare

~ **speciaal** extra-large portion, of prime quality

tijm thyme

tjap tjoy chop suey; a dish of fried meat and vegetables served with rice

toeristenmenu tourist menu

tomaat tomato

tong 1) tongue 2) sole

tonijn tunny (US tuna)

toost toast

tosti grilled cheese-and-ham sandwich

tournedos thick round fillet cut of prime beef (US rib or rib-eye steak)

truffel truffle

tuinboon broad bean

ui onion

uitsmijter two slices of bread garnished with ham or roast beef and topped with two fried eggs

vanille vanilla

varkenshaas pork tenderloin

varkenslapje pork fillet

varkensvlees pork

venkel fennel

vermicellisoep consommé with thin noodles

vers fresh

vijg fig

vis fish

vla custard

vlaai fruit tart

Vlaamse karbonade small slices of beef and onions braised in broth, with beer sometimes added

vlees meat

voorgerecht starter or first course

vrucht fruit

vruchtensalade fruit salad

wafel wafer

walnoot walnut

warm hot

waterkers watercress

waterzooi chicken poached in white wine and shredded vegetables, cream and egg-yolk

wentelteefje French toast; slice of white bread dipped in egg batter and fried, then sprinkled with cinnamon and sugar

wijnkaart wine list

wijting whiting
wild game
   ~ **zwijn** wild boar
wilde eend wild duck
witlof chicory (US endive)
   ~ **op zijn Brussels** chicory
   rolled in a slice of ham and
   oven-browned with cheese
   sauce

worst sausage
wortel carrot
zachtgekookt ei soft-boiled egg
zalm salmon
zeekreeft lobster
zeevis saltwater fish
zout salt
zuurkool sauerkraut
zwezerik sweetbread

Drinks

advocaat egg liqueur
ananassap pineapple juice
aperitief aperitif
bessenjenever blackcurrant gin
bier beer
bisschopswijn mulled wine
bittertje bitter-tasting aperitif
boerenjongens Dutch brandy with
   raisins
boerenmeisjes Dutch brandy with
   apricots
borrel shot
brandewijn brandy
cassis blackcurrant liqueur
chocolademelk, chocomel(k) chocolate drink
citroenbrandewijn lemon brandy
citroenjenever lemon-flavoured
   gin
citroentje met suiker brandy flavoured with lemon peel, with
   sugar added
cognac brandy, cognac
donker bier porter; dark sweet-
   tasting beer
druivesap grape juice

frisdrank soft drink
gekoeld iced
genever see *jenever*
Geuzelambiek a strong Flemish
   bitter beer brewed from wheat
   and barley
jenever Dutch gin
jonge jenever/klare young Dutch
   gin
karnemelk buttermilk
kersenbrandewijn kirsch; spirit
   distilled from cherries
koffie coffee
   ~ **met melk** with milk
   ~ **met room** with cream
   ~ **met slagroom** with whipped
   cream
   ~ **verkeerd** white coffee; equal
   quantity of coffee and hot milk
   zwarte ~ black
Kriekenlambiek a strong Brussels
   bitter beer flavoured with mo-
   rello cherries
kwast hot or cold lemon squash
licht bier lager; light beer
likeur liqueur

limonade lemonade
melk milk
mineraalwater mineral water
oude jenever/klare Dutch gin aged in wood casks, yellowish in colour and more mature than *jonge jenever*
oranjebitter orange-flavoured bitter
pils general name for beer
sap juice
sinas orangeade
spuitwater soda water
sterkedrank liquor, spirit
tafelwater mineral water

thee tea
 ~ **met citroen** with lemon
 ~ **met suiker en melk** with sugar and milk
trappistenbier malt beer brewed (originally) by Trappist monks
vieux brandy bottled in Holland
vruchtesap fruit juice
warme chocola hot chocolate
wijn wine
 droge ~ dry
 rode ~ red
 witte ~ white
 zoete ~ sweet
wodka vodka

Mini-Grammar

Articles

Dutch nouns are either common gender (originally separate masculine and feminine) or neuter.

1. Definite article (the)

The definite article in Dutch is either **de** or **het**. **De** is used with roughly two thirds of all common-gender singular nouns as well as with all plural nouns, while **het** is mainly used with neuter singular nouns and all diminutives:

de straat the street	**het huis** the house	**het katje** the kitten

2. Indefinite article (a; an)

The indefinite article is **een** for both genders, always unstressed and pronounced like *an* in the English word "another". As in English there is no plural. When it bears accent marks (**één**) it means "one" and is pronounced rather like a in "late", but a pure vowel, not a diphthong.

een man	a man	**een vrouw**	a woman	**een kind**	a child
mannen	men	**vrouwen**	women	**kinderen**	children

Plural

The most common sign of the plural in Dutch is an **-en** ending:

krant	newspaper	**woord**	word	**dag**	day
kranten	newspapers	**woorden**	words	**dagen**	days

a) In nouns with a double vowel, one vowel is dropped when **-en** is added:

uur	hour	**boot**	boat	**jaar**	year
uren	hours	**boten**	boats	**jaren**	years

b) most nouns ending in **-s** or **-f** change this letter into **-z** and **-v** respectively, when **-en** is added:

prijs	the price	**brief**	letter
prijzen	prices	**brieven**	letters

Another common plural ending in Dutch is **-s**. Nouns ending in an unstressed **-el**, **-em**, **-en**, **-aar** as well as **-je** (diminutives) take an **-s** in the plural:

tafel/tafels	table(s)	**winnaar/winnaars**	winner(s)
deken/dekens	blanket(s)	**kwartje/kwartjes**	25-cent piece(s)

Some exceptions:

stad/steden	town(s)	**auto/auto's**	car(s)
ship/schepen	ship(s)	**paraplu/paraplu's**	umbrella(s)
kind/kinderen	child(ren)	**foto/foto's**	photo(s)
ei/eieren	egg(s)	**musicus/musici**	musician(s)

Adjectives

When the adjective stands immediately before the noun, it usually takes the ending **-e**:

de jonge vrouw	the young woman
een prettige reis	a pleasant trip
aardige mensen	nice people

However, no ending is added to the adjective in the following cases:

1) When the adjective follows the noun:

| **De stad is groot.** | The city is big. |
| **De zon is heet.** | The sun is hot. |

2) When the noun is neuter singular and preceded by **een** (a/an), or when the words **elk/ieder** (each), **veel** (much), **zulk** (such) and **geen** (no) precede the adjective:

een wit huis	a white house
elk goed boek	each good book
veel vers fruit	much fresh fruit
zulk mooi weer	such good weather
geen warm water	no hot water

Demonstrative adjectives (this/that):

this	**deze**	(with nouns of common gender)
	dit	(with nouns of neuter gender)
that	**die (daar)**	(with nouns of common gender)
	dat	(with nouns of neuter gender)
these	**deze**	(with all plural nouns)
those	**die (daar)**	(with all plural nouns)

| **Deze stad is groot.** | This city is big. |
| **Dat huis is wit.** | That house is white. |

Personal pronouns

Subject		**Object**	
I	**ik**	me	**mij** or **me**
you	**jij** or **je** (fam.)	you	**jou** or **je** (fam.)
you	**u** (pol.)	you	**u** (pol.)
he	**hij**	him	**hem**
she	**zij** or **ze**	her	**haar**
it	**het**	it	**het**
we	**wij** or **we**	us	**ons**
you	**jullie** (fam.)	you	**jullie** (fam.)
they	**zij** or **ze**	them	**hen**

Possessive adjectives

my	**mijn**
your	**jouw** (fam.)
your	**uw** (pol.)
his	**zijn**
her	**haar**
its	**zijn**
our	**ons** (with singular neuter nouns)
	onze (with singular nouns of common gender and all plurals)
you	**jullie** (fam.)
their	**hun**

Verbs

First a few handy irregular verbs. If you learn only these, or even only the "I" and polite "you" forms of them, you'll have made a useful start.

1) The indispensable verbs **hebben** (to have) and **zijn** (to be) in the present:

I have	**ik heb**	I am	**ik ben**
you have	**jij hebt**	you are	**jij bent**
you have	**u hebt**	you are	**u bent**
he/she/it has	**hij/zij/het heeft**	he/she/it is	**hij/zij/het is**
we have	**wij hebben**	we are	**wij zijn**
you have	**jullie hebben**	you are	**jullie zijn**
they have	**zij hebben**	they are	**zij zijn**

2) Some more useful irregular verbs (in the present):

Infinitive		**willen** (to want)	**kunnen** (can)	**gaan** (to go)	**doen** (to do)	**weten** (to know)
I	**ik**	wil	kan	ga	doe	weet
you	**jij**	wilt	kunt	gaat	doet	weet
you	**u**	wilt	kunt	gaat	doet	weet
he	**hij**	wil	kan	gaat	doet	weet
she	**zij**	wil	kan	gaat	doet	weet
it	**het**	wil	kan	gaat	doet	weet
we	**wij**	willen	kunnen	gaan	doen	weten
you	**jullie**	willen	kunnen	gaan	doen	weten
they	**zij**	willen	kunnen	gaan	doen	weten

3) Infinitive and verb stem:

In Dutch verbs, the infinitive generally ends in **-en: noemen** (to name).

As the verb stem is usually the base for forming tenses, you need to know how to obtain it. The general rule is: the infinitive less **-en**:

infinitive: **noemen**   stem: **noem**

4) Present and past tenses:

First find the stem of the verb (see under 3 above).
Them add the appropriate endings, where applicable, according to the models given below for present and past tenses.

Note: in forming the past tense, the **-de/-den** endings shown in our example are added after most verb stems. However, if the stem ends in **p, t, k, f, s,** or **ch**, add **te/-ten** instead.

Present tense		Past tense	
ik noem	I name	**ik noemde**	I named
jij noemt	you name	**jij noemde**	you named
u noemt	you name	**u noemde**	you named
hij/zij/het noemt	he/she/it names	**hij/zij/het noemde**	he/she/it named
wij noemen	we name	**wij noemden**	we named
jullie noemen	you name	**jullie noemden**	you named
zij noemen	they name	**zij noemden**	they named

5) Past perfect (e.g.: "I have built"):

This tense is generally formed, as in English, by the verb "to have" (**hebben**) (see page 339) + the past participle.

To form the past participle, start with the verb stem, and add **ge-** to the front of it and **-d** or **-t** to the end:

infinitive:	**bouwen** (to build)
verb stem:	**bouw**
past participle:	**gebouwd**

The past participle must be placed *after* the object of the sentence:

Ik heb een huis gebouwd.　　I have built a house.

Note: Verbs prefixed by **be-, er-, her-, ont-** and **ver-** do not take **ge-** in the past participle.

Instead of **hebben,** the verb **zijn** (to be) is used with verbs expressing motion (if the destination is specified or implied) or a change of state:

Wij zijn naar Parijs gevlogen.　　We have flown to Paris.
Hij is rijk geworden.　　He has become rich.

Negatives

To put a verb into the negative, place **niet** (not) after the verb, or after the direct object if there is one:

| **Ik rook.** | I smoke. | **Ik heb de kaartjes.** | I have the tickets. |
| **Ik rook niet.** | I don't smoke. | **Ik heb de kaartjes niet.** | I don't have the tickets. |

Questions

In Dutch, questions are formed by placing the subject after the verb:

| **Hij reist.** | He travels. | **Ik betaal.** | I pay. |
| **Reist hij?** | Does he travel? | **Betaal ik?** | Do I pay? |

Questions are also introduced by the following **interrogative pronouns:**

Wie (who)	Who says so?	**Wie zegt dat?**
	Whose house is that?	**Van wie is dat huis?**
Wat (what)	What does he do?	**Wat doet hij?**
Waar (where)	Where is the hotel!	**Waar is het hotel?**
Hoe (how)	How are you?	**Hoe gaat het met u?**

Irregular verbs

The following list contains the most common strong and irregular verbs. If a
compound verb or a verb with a prefix (*be-, con-, dis-, im-, in-, mis-, om-, on-,
ont-, ver-*, etc.) is not listed, its forms may be found by looking up the basic
verb, e.g. *verbinden* is conjugated as *binden*.

Infinitive	*Past*	*Past participle*	
bakken	bakte	gebakken	*bake*
barsten	barstte	gebarsten	*burst, crack*
bederven	bedierf	bedorven	*spoil*
bedriegen	bedroog	bedrogen	*deceive*
beginnen	begon	begonnen	*begin*
bergen	borg	geborgen	*put*
bevelen	beval	bevolen	*order*
bewegen	bewoog	bewogen	*move*
bezwijken	bezweek	bezweken	*succumb*
bidden	bad	gebeden	*pray*
bieden	bood	geboden	*offer*
bijten	beet	gebeten	*bite*
binden	bond	gebonden	*tie*
blazen	blies	geblazen	*blow*
blijken	bleek	gebleken	*prove to be*
blijven	bleef	gebleven	*remain*
blinken	blonk	geblonken	*shine*
braden	braadde	gebraden	*fry*
breken	brak	gebroken	*break*
brengen	bracht	gebracht	*bring*
buigen	boog	gebogen	*bow*
delven	delfde/dolf	gedolven	*dig up*
denken	dacht	gedacht	*think*
dingen	dong	gedongen	*compete (for)*
doen	deed	gedaan	*do*
dragen	droeg	gedragen	*wear*
drijven	dreef	gedreven	*float*
dringen	drong	gedrongen	*push*
drinken	dronk	gedronken	*drink*
druipen	droop	gedropen	*drip*
duiken	dook	gedoken	*dive*
dwingen	dwong	gedwongen	*force*
eten	at	gegeten	*eat*
fluiten	floot	gefloten	*whistle*
gaan	ging	gegaan	*go*
gelden	gold	gegolden	*be valid*
genezen	genas	genezen	*heal*
genieten	genoot	genoten	*enjoy*
geven	gaf	gegeven	*give*
gieten	goot	gegoten	*pour*
glijden	gleed	gegleden	*slide*
glimmen	glom	geglommen	*shine*
graven	groef	gegraven	*dig*

grijpen	greep	gegrepen	*catch*
hangen	hing	gehangen	*hang*
hebben	had	gehad	*have*
heffen	hief	geheven	*raise*
helpen	hielp	geholpen	*help*
heten	heette	geheten	*be called*
hijsen	hees	gehesen	*hoist*
houden	hield	gehouden	*keep*
jagen	jaagde/joeg	gejaagd	*chase*
kiezen	koos	gekozen	*choose*
kijken	keek	gekeken	*look*
klimmen	klom	geklommen	*climb*
klinken	klonk	geklonken	*sound*
knijpen	kneep	geknepen	*pinch*
komen	kwam	gekomen	*come*
kopen	kocht	gekocht	*buy*
krijgen	kreeg	gekregen	*get*
krimpen	kromp	gekrompen	*shrink*
kruipen	kroop	gekropen	*creep*
kunnen	kon	gekund	*can*
lachen	lachte	gelachen	*laugh*
laden	laadde	geladen	*load*
laten	liet	gelaten	*let*
lezen	las	gelezen	*read*
liegen	loog	gelogen	*tell lies*
liggen	lag	gelegen	*lie*
lijden	leed	geleden	*suffer*
lijken	leek	geleken	*seem*
lopen	liep	gelopen	*walk*
malen	maalde	gemalen	*grind*
meten	mat	gemeten	*measure*
moeten	moest	gemoeten	*must*
mogen	mocht	gemogen/gemoogd	*may*
nemen	nam	genomen	*take*
prijzen	prees	geprezen	*praise*
raden	raadde/ried	geraden	*guess*
rijden	reed	gereden	*ride*
rijgen	reeg	geregen	*thread*
rijzen	rees	gerezen	*rise*
roepen	riep	geroepen	*call*
ruiken	rook	geroken	*smell*
scheiden	scheidde	gescheiden	*separate*
schelden	schold	gescholden	*call names*
schenken	schonk	geschonken	*pour*
scheppen	schiep	geschapen	*create*
scheren	schoor	geschoren	*shave*
schieten	schoot	geschoten	*shoot*
schijnen	scheen	geschenen	*shine, seem to be*
schrijden	schreed	geschreden	*stride*
schrijven	schreef	geschreven	*write*
schrikken	schrok	geschrokken	*be frightened*

schuiven	schoof	geschoven	*shove*
slaan	sloeg	geslagen	*hit*
slapen	sliep	geslapen	*sleep*
slijpen	sleep	geslepen	*sharpen*
slijten	sleet	gesleten	*wear down*
sluipen	sloop	geslopen	*sneak*
sluiten	sloot	gesloten	*close*
smelten	smolt	gesmolten	*melt*
snijden	sneed	gesneden	*cut*
spinnen	spon	gesponnen	*spin*
splijten	spleet	gespleten	*split*
spreken	sprak	gesproken	*speak*
springen	sprong	gesprongen	*jump*
spuiten	spoot	gespoten	*squirt*
staan	stond	gestaan	*stand*
steken	stak	gestoken	*sting*
stelen	stal	gestolen	*steal*
sterven	stierf	gestorven	*die*
stijgen	steeg	gestegen	*rise*
stijven	steef	gesteven	*starch*
stinken	stonk	gestonken	*stink*
stoten	stootte/stiet	gestoten	*push*
strijden	streed	gestreden	*fight*
strijken	streek	gestreken	*iron*
treden	trad	getreden	*tread*
treffen	trof	getroffen	*hit*
trekken	trok	getrokken	*pull*
vallen	viel	gevallen	*fall*
vangen	ving	gevangen	*catch*
varen	voer	gevaren	*sail*
vechten	vocht	gevochten	*fight*
verbergen	verborg	verborgen	*hide*
verdwijnen	verdween	verdwenen	*disappear*
vergeten	vergat	vergeten	*forget*
verliezen	verloor	verloren	*lose*
vermijden	vermeed	vermeden	*avoid*
verslinden	verslond	verslonden	*devour*
vinden	vond	gevonden	*find*
vliegen	vloog	gevlogen	*fly*
voortspruiten	sproot voort	voortgesproten	*result*
vouwen	vouwde	gevouwen	*fold*
vragen	vroeg	gevraagd	*ask*
vriezen	vroor	gevroren	*freeze*
waaien	waaide/woei	gewaaid	*blow*
wassen	waste	gewassen	*wash*
wegen	woog	gewogen	*weigh*
werpen	wierp	geworpen	*throw*
werven	wierf	geworven	*recruit*
weten	wist	geweten	*know*
weven	weefde	geweven	*weave*
wijken	week	geweken	*yield*

wijten	weet	geweten	*impute*
wijzen	wees	gewezen	*show*
willen	wilde/wou	gewild	*want*
winden	wond	gewonden	*wind*
winnen	won	gewonnen	*win*
worden	werd	geworden	*become*
wreken	wreekte	gewroken	*revenge*
wrijven	wreef	gewreven	*rub*
zeggen	zei	gezegd	*say*
zenden	zond	gezonden	*send*
zien	zag	gezien	*see*
zijn	was	geweest	*be*
zingen	zong	gezongen	*sing*
zinken	zonk	gezonken	*sink*
zinnen	zon	gezonnen	*brood*
zitten	zat	gezeten	*sit*
zoeken	zocht	gezocht	*seek*
zuigen	zoog	gezogen	*suck*
zullen	zou	—	*shall, will*
zwellen	zwol	gezwollen	*swell*
zwemmen	zwom	gezwommen	*swim*
1) zweren	zwoer	gezworen	*swear*
2) zweren	zweerde/zwoor	gezworen	*ulcerate*
zwerven	zwierf	gezworven	*wander*
zwijgen	zweeg	gezwegen	*be silent*

Dutch Abbreviations

A°	*anno*	(built) in the year
afd.	*afdeling*	department
alg.	*algemeen*	general
A.N.W.B.	*Algemene Nederlandse Wielrijdersbond*	Dutch Touring Association
a.s.	*aanstaande*	next
a.u.b.	*alstublieft*	please
Bfr.	*Belgische frank*	Belgian franc
b.g.	*begane grond*	ground floor
b.g.g.	*bij geen gehoor*	if no answer
blz.	*bladzijde*	page
B.R.T.	*Belgische Radio en Televisie*	Belgian Broadcasting Company
B.T.W.	*Belasting Toegevoegde Waarde*	VAT, value added tax
b.v.	*bijvoorbeeld*	e.g.
B.V.	*besloten vennootschap*	limited liability company
C.S.	*Centraal Station*	main railway station
ct.	*cent*	1/100 of the guilder
dhr.	*de heer*	Mr.
drs.	*doctorandus*	Master of Arts
d.w.z.	*dat wil zeggen*	i.e.
EEG	*Europese Economische Gemeenschap*	EEC, European Economic Community (Common Market)
E.H.B.O.	*Eerste Hulp bij Ongelukken*	first aid
enz.	*enzovoort*	etc.
excl.	*exclusief*	exclusive, not included
fl/f	*gulden*	guilder
geb.	*geboren*	born
H.K.H.	*Hare Koninklijke Hoogheid*	Her Royal Highness
H.M.	*Hare Majesteit*	His/Her Majesty
hs	*huis*	ground floor
incl.	*inclusief*	inclusive, included
i.p(l).v.	*in plaats van*	in the place of
ir.	*ingenieur*	engineer
jl.	*jongstleden*	last
K.A.C.B.	*Koninklijke Automobiel- club van België*	Royal Automobile Association of Belgium
km/u	*kilometer per uur*	kilometres per hour
K.N.A.C.	*Koninklijke Nederlandse Automobielclub*	Royal Dutch Automobile Association

K.N.M.I.	*Koninklijk Nederlands Meteorologisch Instituut*	Royal Dutch Meteorological Institute
m.a.w.	*met andere woorden*	in other words
Mej.	*mejuffrouw*	Miss
Mevr.	*mevrouw*	Mrs.
Mij.	*maatschappij*	company
Mr.	*meester in de rechten; mijnheer*	barrister, lawyer; Mr.
N.A.V.O.	*Noordatlantische Verdragsorganisatie*	NATO
N.B.T.	*Nederlands Bureau voor Toerisme*	Dutch National Tourist Office
n.Chr.	*na Christus*	A.D.
nl.	*namelijk*	namely
n.m.	*namiddag*	afternoon
N.M.B.S.	*Nationale Maatschappij der Belgische Spoorwegen*	Belgian National Railways
N.P.	*niet parkeren*	no parking
N.S.	*Nederlandse Spoorwegen*	Dutch National Railways
N.V.	*naamloze vennootschap*	Ltd. or Inc.
p.a.	*per adres*	in care of
pk	*paardekracht*	horsepower
r.-k./R.-K.	*rooms-katholiek*	Roman Catholic
t.e.m.	*tot en met*	up to and including
t.o.v.	*ten opzichte van*	with regard to
v.a.	*volgens anderen, vanaf*	from
V.A.B.	*Vlaamse Automobilisten-bond*	Flemish Automobile Association
v.Chr.	*voor Christus*	B.C.
v.m.	*voormiddag*	morning
V.N.	*Verenigde Naties*	UN
V.S.	*Verenigde Staten*	USA
V.T.B.	*Vlaamse Toeristenbond*	Flemish Tourist Association
V.V.V.	*Vereniging voor Vreemdelingenverkeer*	tourist-information office
zgn.	*zogenaamd*	so-called
Z.K.H.	*Zijne Koninklijke Hoogheid*	His Royal Highness
z.o.z.	*zie ommezijde*	pto, please turn over

Numerals

Cardinal numbers		Ordinal numbers	
0	nul	1e	eerste
1	een	2e	tweede
2	twee	3e	derde
3	drie	4e	vierde
4	vier	5e	vijfde
5	vijf	6e	zesde
6	zes	7e	zevende
7	zeven	8e	achtste
8	acht	9e	negende
9	negen	10e	tiende
10	tien	11e	elfde
11	elf	12e	twaalfde
12	twaalf	13e	dertiende
13	dertien	14e	veertiende
14	veertien	15e	vijftiende
15	vijftien	16e	zestiende
16	zestien	17e	zeventiende
17	zeventien	18e	achttiende
18	achttien	19e	negentiende
19	negentien	20e	twintigste
20	twintig	21e	eenentwintigste
21	eenentwintig	22e	tweeëntwintigste
22	tweeëntwintig	23e	drieëntwintigste
23	drieëntwintig	24e	vierentwintigste
24	vierentwintig	25e	vijfentwintigste
30	dertig	26e	zesentwintigste
40	veertig	30e	dertigste
50	vijftig	40e	veertigste
60	zestig	50e	vijftigste
70	zeventig	60e	zestigste
80	tachtig	70e	zeventigste
90	negentig	80e	tachtigste
100	honderd	90e	negentigste
101	honderdeen	100e	honderdste
230	tweehonderddertig	101e	honderdeerste
1000	duizend	230e	tweehonderddertigste
1001	duizendeen	1000e	duizendste
1100	elfhonderd	1001e	duizendeerste
2000	tweeduizend	1100e	elfhonderdste
1 000 000	een miljoen	2000e	tweeduizendste

Time

Although official time in Holland and Belgium is based on the 24-hour clock, the 12-hour system is used in conversation.

To avoid confusion, you can make use of the terms *'s morgens* (morning), and *'s middags* (afternoon) or *'s avonds* (evening).

Ik kom om vier uur 's morgens.	I'll come at 4 a.m.
Ik kom om vier uur 's middags.	I'll come at 4 p.m.
Ik kom om acht uur 's avonds.	I'll come at 8 p.m.

Days of the Week

zondag	Sunday	*donderdag*	Thursday
maandag	Monday	*vrijdag*	Friday
dinsdag	Tuesday	*zaterdag*	Saturday
woensdag	Wednesday		

Aantekeningen

Notes

352

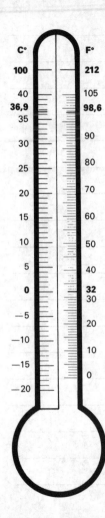

Conversion tables/Omrekentabellen

Meters en voeten
Het middelste cijfer geeft zowel meters als voeten aan, bijvoorbeeld 1 meter = 3,281 voet en 1 voet = 0,30 m.

Metres and feet
The figure in the middle stands for both metres and feet, e.g. 1 metre = 3.281 ft. and 1 foot = 0.30 m.

Meters/Metres		Voeten/Feet
0.30	1	3.281
0.61	2	6.563
0.91	3	9.843
1.22	4	13.124
1.52	5	16.403
1.83	6	19.686
2.13	7	22.967
2.44	8	26.248
2.74	9	29.529
3.05	10	32.810
3.66	12	39.372
4.27	14	45.934
6.10	20	65.620
7.62	25	82.023
15.24	50	164.046
22.86	75	246.069
30.48	100	328.092

Temperatuur
Voor het omrekenen van Celsius in Fahrenheit, moet u het aantal graden Celsius met 1,8 vermenigvuldigen en er dan 32 bij optellen.
Voor het omrekenen van Fahrenheit in Celsius, moet u 32 van het aantal graden Fahrenheit aftrekken en dan delen door 1,8.

Temperature
To convert Centigrade to Fahrenheit, multiply by 1.8 and add 32.
To convert Fahrenheit to Centigrade, subtract 32 from Fahrenheit and divide by 1.8.